YUP'IK ELDERS AT THE ETHNOLOGISCHES MUSEUM BERLIN
Fieldwork Turned on Its Head

Ann Fienup-Riordan

Yup'ik Translations by Marie Meade
German Translations by Sonja Lührmann,
Anja Karlson, and Adelaid Pauls

UNIVERSITY OF WASHINGTON PRESS Seattle & London

in association with

CALISTA ELDERS COUNCIL Bethel, Alaska

For James VanStone, elder among elders

Supported by the National Science Foundation
Association of Village Council Presidents
Calista Elders Council

© 2005 by the University of Washington Press
Printed in China
Designed by Audrey S. Meyer and Ashley Saleeba
12 11 10 09 08 07 06 05   5 4 3 2 1

All rights reserved. No part of this publication may be reproduced or transmitted in any form or by any means, electronic or mechanical, including photocopy, recording, or any information storage or retrieval system, without permission in writing from the publisher.

The paper used in this publication meets the requirements of American National Standard for Information Sciences—Permanence of Paper for Printed Library Materials. ANSI Z39.48-1984. ∞

University of Washington Press
PO Box 50096, Seattle, WA 98145-5096
www.washington.edu/uwpress

Library of Congress Cataloging-in-Publication Data

Fienup-Riordan, Ann.
Yup'ik elders at the Ethnologisches Museum Berlin : fieldwork turned on its head / Ann Fienup-Riordan ; Yup'ik translations by Marie Meade ; German translations by Sonja Lührmann, Anja Karlson, and Adelaid Pauls.
p. cm.
Includes bibliographical references and index.
ISBN 0-295-98464-3 (alk. paper)
1. Yupik Eskimos—Antiquities—Collectors and collecting—Alaska. 2. Yupik Eskimos—Material culture. 3. Jacobsen, Johan Adrian, 1853-1947—Travel—Alaska. 4. Jacobsen, Johan Adrian, 1853-1947—Ethnological collections. 5. Alaska—Discovery and exploration. 6. Ethnological expeditions—Alaska—History. 7. Alaska—Antiquities—Collectors and collecting. 8. Ethnologisches Museum Berlin. I. Title.
E99.E7F48   2005
979.8004'9714—dc22   2004055488

FRONTISPIECE: *Ayaperyaraq (deck stiffener), located below the coaming on the left and right sides of a kayak. IVA5170.*

CONTENTS

FOREWORD BY PETER BOLZ ix

PREFACE Unlikely Partnerships xi

ACKNOWLEDGMENTS xvii

THE GIFT
Johan Adrian Jacobsen Brings Treasures from Alaska 3

THE GIFT-GIVERS
Turn-of-the-Century Yupiit and Their Descendants 39

THE RETURN GIFT
The Yup'ik Delegation 47

FIRST DAY Tools for Ocean Hunting

Seal-hunting Harpoon with Bladder Float 52
Float 54
Walrus-Bladder Water Container 56
Harpoon Used for the Final Kill 58
Seal-hunting Harpoon with Feather Fletching 60
Harpoon for Killing Seals on and around Ice 60
Paddle 60
Gaff 63
Harpoon Points 64
Seal-scratcher 68
Kayak Bow or Keel Protector 69
Cockpit Coaming Stanchion 69
Spear Guards, Connecting Links, and Line Attachers 71
Stone Blades and Points 72

SECOND DAY Bows and Arrows for Hunting and War

Bows 74
Sinew 76
A Child's Bow and a Warrior's Bow 78
Arrows 79

THIRD DAY More Tools for Hunting and Fishing

Throwing Boards   90
Blubber Carrier Shaped Like a Land Otter   94
Bird and Fish Spears   96
Points for Bird or Rabbit Spears   97
Gun or Arrow Support   99
Circle-and-Dot Designs   99
Bullet Mold   99
Primer Box and Gunpowder Container   100
Breastplate for a Backpack   101
Rabbit Snares and Squirrel Snares   102
Two Squirrels   103
Small Fish Trap   105
Ice Dipper   106
Fishing Hook, Line, and Pole   107
Net Floats   109
King-Salmon Net   110
Small-mesh Net   113
Net-making Tools   113
Wooden Fishing Tools   114

FOURTH DAY Wooden and Clay Containers

Tobacco Boxes and Snuff Containers   116
Drum   119
Containers   121
Water Pail and Urine Container   127
Large Food Container   128
Bowl   129
Clay Pot   133

FIFTH DAY Containers of Skin, Gut, and Grass

Things Made of Fish Skin   135
Bag for Dolls   137
Storage and Sewing Bags   138
Loon-skin Bag   143
Woven Things   144

SIXTH DAY Tools for Working on Objects and Materials

Drills   148
Tool for Making Designs   148
Sled-runner Sheathing   149
Hole Punchers   149
Shredders   150
Prying Tool   152
Beaver-tooth Engraving Tools   152
Sharpening Stone   153
Caribou Hoof, Canine Tooth, and Other Raw Materials   154
Wood Splitter or Wedge   154
Hammer   155
Skin Scrapers   155
Women's and Men's Knives   157
Woodworking Tool   159
Stone Blades in Abundance   161

SEVENTH DAY Tools of Daily Life

Grass Mats 164
Lamps and Lamp Wicks 166
Snuff Tobacco 167
Cutting Board 169
Ladles, Spoons, and Dippers 169
Clamshell Spoon 173
Dried Beaver Castors 173
Root Picks 174
Snow Shovel 174
Ax 177
Pestle 177
Fire Starters 179

EIGHTH DAY Personal Adornment and Human Figures

Combs 181
Labrets 183
Women's Labrets 186
Earring Hooks and Earrings 186
Amulets and Human Figures 188

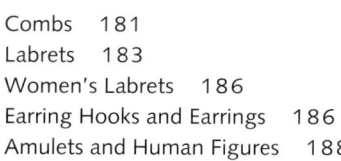

NINTH DAY Women's Sewing Tools and Belts and Men's Hats

Needle Cases 195
Bag Fasteners, Thimbles, and Needles 197
Women's Belts 201
Belt Fasteners 203
Bentwood Hats and Visors 204
Eyeshades 207
Hats and Things for the Fire Bath 208
Feather or Fur Hood 209
Round Fur Caps 210

TENTH DAY Ceremonial Regalia

Necklaces 211
Gloves 213
Dance Headdresses 215
Beaded Dance Hats 217
Armbands 217
Hanging Wooden Figures 219
House Protectors 221
Human Figures 222
Stringed Musical Instrument 223
Shaman Drum and Drum Handles 223

ELEVENTH DAY Dancing with Masks

Masks 228
Mask that Sticks to the Face 229
Legendary Seal Creature 231
Common Loons 234
Ircenrraq Mask 234
Dance Fans 237
Pretend Raven 243
Meadow Jumping Mouse 244

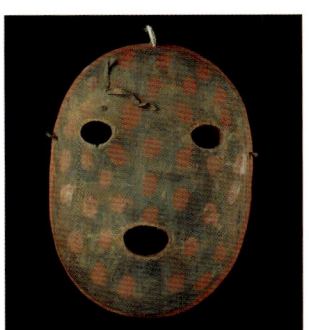
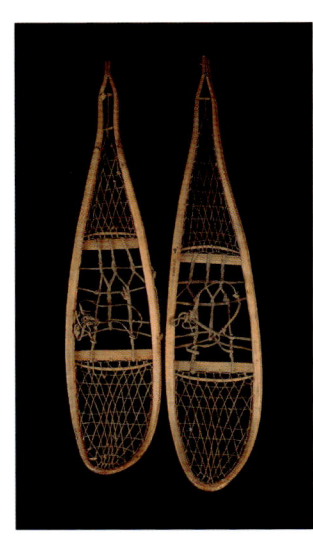

Warriors   245
The Half-faced One   248

TWELFTH DAY Toys and Clothing

Toys and Spinners   250
Turn to Me   250
Darts   250
Balls   251
Story Knives   252
Playing Dolls   254
Model Kayak   261
Model *Qasgi*   261
Bird-skin Parka   264
Ice Skates and Snowshoes   266
Fish-skin Mittens   267
Twined Grass Liners for Skin Boots   267
Waterproof Skin Boots   269

THIRTEENTH DAY Heavenly and Ceremonial Cycles

Circular Calendar   272
Designs of the Sky   272

FOURTEENTH DAY AND RETURN TO ALASKA   279

VISUAL REPATRIATION   280

APPENDIX Additional Masks   291

NOTES   295

GLOSSARY   307

REFERENCES   319

INDEX   325

FOREWORD

WHEN MEMBERS of the Alaskan Yup'ik delegation visited Berlin's Ethnological Museum in September 1997, it was a unique experience, not only for them but for the museum. Never before had a group of Native people come to study one of our collections so intensively. Within a period of three weeks, they looked at and handled nearly two thousand objects, often telling stories about them and demonstrating their use. The eight adults, some over eighty years of age, were probably also the largest group of Arctic people ever to visit Berlin, larger than the Greenland and Labrador Eskimo groups that accompanied Adrian Jacobsen in 1877 and 1880.

Those earlier Eskimo visitors came as members of a *Völkerschau:* exotic peoples from other lands presented to a curious European public. In contrast, the Yup'ik delegation came as researchers, students of a collection from their own culture. From their first day in the museum, the atmosphere was relaxed and trusting. What transpired was a wonderfully reciprocal process: the museum brought forth the many Yup'ik objects it has preserved for more than a century, and the Yup'ik elders, with their wealth of knowledge, brought these objects back to life so that they could tell their own stories and fill in the blank spots on Jacobsen's yellowed, handwritten acquisition cards.

The members of the Yup'ik delegation were representatives of a culture that has survived despite a history of repression and the predictions of nineteenth-century Europe that America's indigenous peoples were an inexorably "vanishing race." This belief fueled Jacobsen's voyage to the Northwest Coast and Alaska to collect remnants of the "original" cultures of these peoples. According to Adolf Bastian, head of Berlin's Royal Ethnological Museum and the founding father of German ethnology, the late nineteenth century was the "twelfth hour" for Native peoples; objects and ideas not collected or recorded then would be lost forever.

The practice of collecting knowledge is deeply rooted in European intellectual traditions. Yet knowledge is not only preserved in books and written documents; it is also embedded in objects of material culture. The difference is that objects do not always speak for themselves but require additional information in order to be interpreted correctly. For Adolf Bastian, objects from nonliterate societies held the same value as the written documents from literate societies because they are the special expression of a unique worldview. In contrast to the wide-spread ideology of cultural evolutionism, which put "primitive" people into the lowest category of humankind, Bastian regarded all people as having equal intellectual potential. Objects created by a society were seen by Bastian as expressions of their collective thinking and therefore manifestations of their *Völkergedanken* (a people's way of thinking), his term for this phenomenon.

But only a comprehensive collection from all parts of the globe would be a secure foundation for future comparative studies in this field. For this reason, Bastian sent out collectors in various directions of the world to gather what they still could get; for him only those objects that were untouched by civilization could tell something about a Native people's original way of thinking. In this way, Bastian and his colleagues in the museum created an archive in which nearly all cultures of the world were represented and in which future generations of scholars will be able to explore the intellectual and material creations of the human race.

Bastian was guided by the spirit of Alexander von Humboldt, the famous Prussian explorer, and not by the spirit of colonialism that dominated the treatment of non-European people at this time. Humboldt was a dedicated antiracist, and he was disgusted by the existence of slavery, examples of which he saw during his travels in the Americas. He opposed the idea of European racial superiority and regarded all humans as equal. With this spirit in mind, Bastian refused to open the Berlin Ethnological Museum for colonial ideologies and activities. He wanted a museum that was dedicated only to science.

Under Bastian's leadership, the American department became the largest in the museum, and even today nearly half of the museum's 500,000 objects come from the American continent, though mostly from South and Central America. By the 1920s, the North American Native collections in Berlin had grown to about 25,000 objects through the acquisition of material either from American dealers or from large American museums in New York, Washington, D.C., or Chicago.

Because of Jacobsen's extraordinary success, the collections of the Arctic and the Northwest Coast were regarded as "complete," and interests turned from these to other regions of America. From the early decades of the twentieth century until the 1990s, the Arctic region fell into neglect, partly from the lack of an Arctic specialist in the museum and partly as a consequence of World War II, which left no space in the newly built museum in Berlin-Dahlem for large-scale exhibitions of the North American collection. In addition to this, a large part of the Alaska collection was confiscated as war booty and only returned in 1992. For all of these reasons, Ann Fienup-Riordan came to Berlin at just the right moment to rediscover these extraordinary objects and bring the "slumbering" Jacobsen collection back to life.

Fienup-Riordan's idea to bring people and objects together within a museum setting proved tremendously fruitful for all. This innovative form of "fieldwork" could become a model for future museum research. The Ethnological Museum is proud to have participated in what amounted to a groundbreaking form of research for a European museum. We deeply thank all of the elders and other participants who were willing to come to Berlin, take part in this project, and make it a success.

Recently, plans have been made to move Berlin's Ethnological Museum to the site of the former palace of the Prussian kings, in the city's center. Public discussion of these plans generated the perennial question: Why does the Ethnological Museum keep so many objects instead of just selecting and keeping the best, most artistic ones?

The Yup'ik delegation, who came all the way from Alaska to Berlin to study the objects of their ancestors, provided the answer to this question: Each single piece that is preserved from the past is a unique document of a culture. This culture may have changed, but it has not disappeared, and each object is a witness of its people's rich heritage. For Native peoples these objects have become symbols of their history and important guideposts for their future.

Everyone interested in Native cultures should be grateful to Adolf Bastian and all those who collected under his guidance and spirit, which foresaw that these objects would be important for future generations. The year 2005 marks the 100th anniversary of Bastian's death. I know he would be pleased to see the rising interest of Native peoples in their cultural heritage. Berlin's Ethnological Museum will make every effort to preserve and make available these objects for future generations who want to learn more about their ancestors' way of life.

Peter Bolz
Curator of North American Ethnology
Ethnologisches Museum Berlin
January 2005

PREFACE Unlikely Partnerships

OUR WORK IN MUSEUMS highlights an unlikely juxtaposition of lives—nineteenth-century German entrepreneurs and scholars; twentieth-century Yup'ik elders and educators; cultural anthropologists and museum professionals. The circumstances that brought us together provide a view into the acquisition and interpretation of one of the world's largest and most impressive collections of Yup'ik material culture.

Our story begins with the life and travels of the Norwegian-born jack-of-all-trades, Johan Adrian Jacobsen. He spent little more than a year in Alaska in the 1880s, and if circumstances had been different, he might have gone elsewhere. Yet his acquisitive efforts collecting ethnographic material "in the last hour" set the stage for an unusual and unprecedented cultural revival more than a century later.

Like Edward Nelson, who collected for the Smithsonian Institution during the same period, Jacobsen arrived in Alaska at a turning point in the history of those he visited. Although epidemic disruption preceded their arrival by fifty years, the region remained largely untouched by the onrush of Euro-American colonial expansion that would eventually alter life throughout the new territory. Close on the heels of their departure, however, missionaries, teachers, miners, and assorted entrepreneurs began active efforts to change the face of life along the Bering Sea coast. The collections that Nelson and Jacobsen acquired in 1878–1881 and 1882–1883, respectively, remain both the first and largest collections of ethnographic objects from the Yukon-Kuskokwim delta anywhere in the world. Gathered within a year of each other, they represent the pinnacles of both American and European collecting of Yup'ik material. Nothing like them has been brought together before or since.

Jacobsen spent the winter following his Alaska sojourn in Berlin cataloging his collection, but his lack of academic training earned him a cool reception among museum professionals. Franz Boas worked at Berlin's Royal Ethnological Museum (Königliches Museum für Völkerkunde, now the Ethnologisches Museum Berlin) and perused Jacobsen's accession records, complaining about inaccuracies and exaggerations.[1] Although the objects that Jacobsen obtained from Yup'ik villages had a place of honor on exhibit in the museum's North American hall, the bulk of his collection rested in obscurity for more than fifty years—half that time in the Royal Museum in the center of Berlin, and since 1921 in the museum's new storage and exhibition space in the leafy suburbs of Dahlem. This quiet existence was not to last.

In 1934, one year after Hitler came to power, the museum was ordered to divide its collections into irreplaceable objects (which would be removed from the museum if Berlin were to come under attack), valuable objects (which would be stored safely in the building), and everything else (which would be left to fate). By 1939, packing was in progress. When bomb attacks started, museum personnel boarded up the windows and stored crates of valuable objects in bunkers and anti-aircraft towers. Soldiers moved most of these crates to the potassium mines of Grasleben in eastern Germany when the military reclaimed the towers. Additional crates, packed under difficult conditions by a group of women students and French prisoners of war, were sent by small freight boat and train to the mines, where they were stored until the war's end. In all, about three thousand crates from the museum, including most of the North American collections, went to Grasleben.[2]

Other crates, including those containing the exhibited North American collection, remained in Dahlem at the museum. In May 1945 the Soviet army occupied Berlin, and until April 1946 they carried away the remaining museum contents to Leningrad. Like the French Impressionist paintings confiscated by the Soviets from Germany after the war and kept in hiding at the Hermitage for more than fifty years, Yup'ik objects (as well as many other things) were taken by train through Poland to Leningrad, where they were unpacked and inventoried. In 1977–1978 these ethnographic collections—altogether 44,561 objects—were sent to the Leipzig Museum for Ethnology (Grassi Museum) in East Germany.

In fall 1946 the British military moved 175,000 objects from all sections of the Ethnologisches Museum Berlin (known

The "Yup'ik delegation" at work in collections. Dietrich Graf, Ethnologisches Museum Berlin.

to English speakers as the Berlin Ethnological Museum)—including those stored in the Grasleben mines—to the castle in Celle in northern Germany. One part-time ethnological curator looked after this enormous collection, and time and neglect began to take their toll. The museum was not notified of the collection's location until 1951, and by 1956 it was returned to Berlin. The American military also had captured some crates, which were returned to Berlin in 1956 and 1958.[3]

Concern and confusion about the fate of the lost Berlin pieces continued long after the war's end. Many believed that the Alaska material had been destroyed.[4] An exhibition of Native American pieces in Leningrad and word-of-mouth reports from Americans who attended a conference of Americanists at the Grassi Museum in 1985 indicated that at least some of the Berlin pieces had survived. Not until the Berlin Wall fell in 1989 was the extent of the collection's survival known.

In May 1990, nine months after the opening of the wall, Berlin museum representatives went to Leipzig, where they found nearly forty-five thousand objects stored in the Grassi Museum. Most were still in the crates that had carried them to Leipzig twelve years before. They had been unpacked and inventoried in Leningrad. The return of collections began in 1990 and lasted until 1993. Between twenty thousand and twenty-five thousand ethnographic objects are still missing, but for the rest, their fifty-year odyssey was at an end.[5]

I first visited the Berlin Ethnological Museum in 1994, looking for material for a Yup'ik mask exhibit. I was stunned to find museum staff industriously unpacking this extraordinary Yup'ik collection, second only to Nelson's in size and scope, yet with accession records still handwritten in old German script. I spent my brief stay in Berlin busily photographing masks.[6] Along with pictures, I brought home a desire to return to Berlin and dig deeper into Jacobsen's treasures.

After the mask exhibit, *Agayuliyararput* (Our Way of Making Prayer), opened in Anchorage in 1996, a team of Yup'ik elders (a term of respect used statewide to refer to older, knowledgeable Alaska Native men and women), community leaders, and I began planning for that return visit, and the National Science Foundation funded our project through a grant to the region's nonprofit corporation, the Association of Village Council Presidents. After a year's preparation, our seven-member "Yup'ik delegation" set out from Anchorage on September 5, 1997.

The group included Marie Meade as translator; Andy Paukan, mayor of St. Marys and our videographer; four elders representing the different areas of the region—Wassilie Berlin from the Kuskokwim, Paul John from Nelson Island, Annie Blue from Bristol Bay, and Catherine Moore from the Yukon; and me as guide. Henry Alikayak from Manokotak and Esther Ilutsik from Dillingham joined us later. We spent three weeks working at the Berlin museum. As with the mask exhibit, what the elders sought was not so much the collection's physical return to Alaska, but the return of the history and pride that it embodied.[7]

The book is divided into three sections: "The Gift," "The Gift-Givers," and "The Return Gift." This heuristic framework was inspired by the seminal work of French anthropologist Marcel Mauss, whose discussion of the role of gift-giving stands as a charter in twentieth-century anthropology. Here I use gift exchange as a metaphor for Yup'ik elders' work in museums to highlight the positive reciprocal relations that characterized their work and to provide an alternative to the often contentious relations between the owners of objects and the Native descendants of their makers.

In his essay "The Gift," Mauss argues that the exchange of gifts in so-called "archaic" societies dominates social and moral relations and that "things given have a soul that compels them to return to their original owner who gave them away."[8] Over the years, scholars have pointed out many ways in which Mauss misconstrued the Maori concept of the *hau,* the spirit of the gift. Yet his original insight into the importance of what he called "the system of total prestations" has proved foundational in our understanding of human social relationships. Among Yup'ik people to this day, giving, receiving, and returning gifts retain extraordinary power and importance in both ritual and everyday contexts.[9] Not only is a person admonished to share one's material wealth but also one's knowledge, which, like fish, must be given away lest it rot one's mind. The knowledge elders share in the following pages constitutes a "return" not only in allowing an essential aspect of the objects Jacobsen collected to come home to Alaska but in providing elders with what they viewed as an empowering opportunity to share what they know, enriching us all in the process.

The introductory section, "The Gift," describes Jacobsen's life and travels in Alaska and the collection that he brought to Berlin. Although an abridged edition of his 1884 travelogue was published in English in 1977,[10] there has been no critical biography of this important yet ambiguous figure. Without a clear understanding of who Jacobsen was and why and how he came to Alaska, the full significance of the collection he amassed and the unintended consequences of his collecting remain obscure. Working to collect the remnants of peoples thought to be on the edge of extinction, Jacobsen likely never imagined what a gift the objects he collected would be to the descendants of their makers.

The second section, "The Gift-Givers," describes the people of southwestern Alaska as they were in Jacobsen's time and as they are today. It also introduces the reader to the Yup'ik men and women who traveled to Germany to work with Jacobsen's collection and the significance of their trip for the process of reclaiming their past. Most descriptions of Alaska collections have been compiled by visiting observers with various levels of observational skill and access to information. Descriptions in this book foreground statements by men and women whose culture the collection represents. The information results from their firsthand experiences of working with similar objects or seeing them in use, making their personal histories as important to understand as Jacobsen's.

The third section, "The Return Gift," consists of fifteen chapters—one for each day of our work in the Berlin Ethnological Museum, and a concluding chapter on the nature of that work. The objects Jacobsen collected are discussed in approximately the order in which we examined them, with the narrative weaving together Jacobsen's descriptions of the objects and the stories they evoked. Information on some object types has been gathered together for clarity and accessibility. For example, although elders looked at bows on both their first and second days in the museum, the reader can find all the information they shared in the second day's discussion. In most cases this is noted with clauses such as "the next week we saw" or "later that day we looked at. . . ." My attempt throughout has been to retain and communicate a sense of the elders' active participation, while also making it possible for readers to locate important information about particular objects.

I could have organized this book entirely by object type, like other books on Arctic material culture. Erasing the narrative frame, however, like other categorical practices that distance people from lived experience, would have real consequences in communicating what we learned in Berlin. Organizing the discussion around the trip, on the other hand, can contribute not only to discussions of Yup'ik material culture, but to considerations of how discussions of material culture in other parts of the world can take place. The challenge has been to present things clearly and to provide a narrative flow that reflects all the respect, excitement, and humor that characterized the elders' interactions with the objects and with each other. In fact, the elders displayed a definite logic both in the information they chose to share and in the way they shared it, working together to educate both Marie and me, whom they found wanting.

The collection is comprehensively examined in this book, combining Jacobsen's accession information (translated from German for the first time) with what the elders said about the pieces and the experiences they shared. These chapters, illustrated both with photographs of the objects and of the elders examining them, highlight the visual power of this magnificent collection. The elders' narrative also embodies the power of the human spirit to use collections of old things and knowledge of the past to create meaning for the future.

Detailed endnotes have been appended to the elders' examination of the collection. Without repeating Jacobsen's unpublished accession records verbatim, these endnotes summarize information on object types of interest to the specialist, including accession numbers (preceded by "IVA"). As described in the first section, "The Gift," Jacobsen's accession records vary greatly in their detail and usefulness. Many contain no more than an object's name and place of origin, referring the reader to a single accession card containing a more detailed description. This book's combination of descriptive text (including the most useful of what both Jacobsen and elders said about the objects) and technical endnotes are an attempt to provide both engaging and comprehensive access to the Jacobsen collection.

Working through the collection, weaving together Jacobsen's information and what the elders had to say, creates a very different book from that written by Edward Nelson a century before, but one that complements Nelson's classic ethnography. For example, Nelson described labrets in naturalist fashion, detailing the size and shape of the dozens of pairs he collected.[11] In contrast, our Yup'ik delegation said little about individual labrets. Paul John, however, told a long story describing the origin of labrets in commemoration of two hunters' encounter with walrus, which appeared to them in human form. References to Nelson's discussion of objects comparable to those Jacobsen collected are given in endnotes throughout the text, allowing the reader to use this book as a companion to Nelson and vice versa. A detailed index also insures that readers interested in particular object types (bows, parkas, masks), materials (grass, gut, sinew), and Yup'ik practices (warfare, the Messenger Feast, seal hunting) know where to go for information.

Though some of the elders speak English, our conversations in collections proceeded uninterrupted in Yup'ik, and I tape-recorded everything we said.[12] Marie prepared full transcriptions and translations of these tapes, producing close to fifteen hundred pages during the next two years. I have tried to mirror Yup'ik narrative style—rich in examples attributed to named orators, with interpretation kept to a minimum. In this way it parallels contemporary elders who instruct the younger generation by giving them accounts of what they have seen and heard from particular persons during their lives. Yup'ik orators expect each listener to interpret what they say differently and to find new meanings in their words—meanings that I might have missed or not understood.

These are Yup'ik voices—individual, not general. The voice of Jacobsen is also present, warts and all. My voice is clear as well, although my authorship has been decentered, and Marie's painstaking translations are quoted at length. I added few comparative comments. My effort has been to let the elders tell their story, intertwined with what Jacobsen had to say. The elders trusted Marie and me to be accurate, be respectful, and listen to and hear their emphasis—recording not just what they said but how they said it. Many recognize that issues of authority are even more important than issues of representation.[13] My presumption in working with these men and women is that they, not I, are the experts.

In quoting the elders I often removed the repetitions characteristic of Yup'ik oratory (but not necessarily written language) and summarized many stories to enable readers to more easily grasp the essential parts of our work together. As I did when I wrote *The Living Tradition of Yup'ik Masks,* each time I quoted an elder, I retained that quote in full, in Yup'ik and English, in a separate document that Marie and I have turned into a bilingual book authored by elders entitled *Ciuliamta Akluit/ Things of Our Ancestors.* The stories they shared were too numerous and rich for a single book, and Yup'ik readers especially will appreciate the opportunity to enjoy the full complexity and eloquence of their descriptions in their own language.

The elders also provided invaluable technical and linguistic information that Jacobsen and Nelson (neither of whom could speak the language) failed to record. For example, when we came upon fish-skin clothing, elders went into great detail describing how fish skin was prepared for use. Their narratives were also rich in Yup'ik vocabulary, including several hundred terms recorded here for the first time in the glossary.

In recent decades we have learned both the selective character of recollections of the past as well as how these recollections both shape and are reshaped by the present. In "speaking their past" in the 1990s, elders chose stories they believed most relevant to contemporary social and political circumstances. Their recitations simultaneously confirmed the value that they placed on the traditions they recalled and the contradictions they saw between the traditional "rules for right living" and "unregulated" modern life. One might account for their words as part of the Yup'ik search for identity, but such a quest did not motivate the specific form their oratory took or precisely what was being said. To understand these things, we need to explore the content of what they shared, not its effects, in the detailed descriptions in the third section, "The Return Gift."[14]

Today anthropology stands at a crossroads, and this book is an attempt to move it in a new direction. Some declare that we really can know nothing, and others say that even if we could learn something, non-Native scholars should not be the ones to tell it. Increasingly, indigenous people worldwide are encouraged to speak for themselves. Anthropologists already are viewed by some as unwanted and unnecessary intermediaries. As Julie Cruikshank says: "The issue of who controls images and representations of First Nations portrayed locally and to the larger world remains at the core of land claims negotiations. . . . Control of narrative representation, like transfers of land, carries material consequences."[15]

Anthropologists increasingly recognize culture as a dynamic process, not a bound object that is internally homogeneous and continuous over time.[16] Yet this rejection of an objectivist, ahistorical concept of culture is occurring just as Native peoples worldwide endorse essentialism as a powerful antidote to the Western definition of their views of the world as "primitive," "simple," and "doomed." A new identity politics has emerged in which concepts of tradition (themselves often derived from popular anthropology of previous decades) are used to create difference and claim special rights. This self-conscious culturalism, in which one's culture is seen as something one possesses, a thing that should be "maintained" and "preserved," is firmly rooted in the wider society.

While acknowledging the limits of anthropological knowledge and the need for indigenous people to represent themselves, many eloquently attest to the critical job anthropology can still perform in cross-cultural understanding. As indigenous people seek to explain themselves in new global contexts, anthropology can help us understand this transnational process of translation. Citing Clifford Geertz, Fred Myers states that anthropology's project is no longer to represent others; rather, "translation is the ethnographic object."[17] In viewing indigenous performances, he says, representation (the process of "culture making") can be seen as a form of social action in its own right. Cruikshank extends the discussion, stating that questions of intercultural translation are central to late-twentieth-century anthropology: "Anthropology has emerged from a decade of self-scrutiny less confident about both objectivist and constructivist claims, but aware that throughout the world boundaries of culture, race, gender, class, and religion are drawn ever more firmly as positions to speak from. . . . Anthropology's project of analyzing how translation occurs across such boundaries has never seemed more important."[18]

Contemporary anthropological theory views the formation and re-formation of ethnic identity and the boundaries between groups as a creative, negotiated process. But this creativity and inventiveness is always culturally constituted in the present and grounded in the past.[19] Yupiit and non-Yupiit speak to each other from culturally specific positions, and anthropology can and should help provide critical perspective on these ongoing conversations, both their origins and destinations. Instead of anthropology seeking to represent others, to describe "the Native point of view" as an end in itself, increasingly the ethnographic project is to help understand how indigenous people present themselves both at home and abroad.

Finally, the book's concluding chapter, "Visual Repatriation," discusses the potential of this kind of "reverse fieldwork" to enrich our understanding of Native American collections all over the world. From the beginning, the Yup'ik reaction to learning about the existence of Yup'ik collections has been gratitude and pride. Andy Paukan stated it well:

I'm thinking that coming to Germany to examine these objects will make it easier for us to explain our culture to our young people and to our children. We will be able to tell them things with no reservations. Our work will make it easier to prepare teaching material about our culture for our younger generations, our children, our grandchildren, to our peers and even our own parents and grandparents. With this work, our roots and culture will come closer to us.

This attitude toward collections as opportunities to affect the future was the primary reason that elders and regional leaders in Alaska supported this project and agreed to travel so far and work so hard. While in Germany, they saw themselves not as sightseers or solitary researchers, but as representatives of the Yup'ik nation. The men and women who traveled to Berlin were the recognized "professors" from their regions and were chosen for both their ability and their willingness to share what they knew. They spoke about the collections not for my benefit or for that of the scholarly community, but to enlighten and empower their descendants. In the process, they have enlightened and empowered us all.

ACKNOWLEDGMENTS

AS MUCH AS ANY PROJECT I have ever undertaken this book is the work of many hands. Funding came from a number of sources. A major four-year research grant from the National Science Foundation, Office of Polar Programs, supported both the elders' work in Berlin and the research and writing that followed. The Rockefeller Foundation and the Alaska Humanities Forum provided additional funds for translation, and the Rasmuson Foundation helped purchase necessary equipment. All grants and support went directly to the Association of Village Council Presidents, and I am indebted to their president, Myron Naneng, and excellent accounting department for guiding me through the technical requirements of such a large project. The staff of the Anchorage Museum of History and Art, especially director Pat Wolf and archivists Diane Brenner, Mina Jacobs, Elaine Williamson, and Janet Klein, provided invaluable nuts-and-bolts support. Finally, the Calista Elders Council and its director, Mark John, gave us the help we needed to bring this enormous project to completion. Both the Rasmuson Foundation and The Rockefeller Foundation also provided invaluable support to the Calista Elders Council in the form of publication grants, without which we could never have produced this color catalog of the Jacobsen collection.

First and foremost, thanks to Wassilie Berlin, Paul John, Annie Blue, Catherine Moore, Henry Alikayak, Andy Paukan, Esther Ilutsik, and Marie Meade, who traveled so far from home and worked so hard to make the original vision of this new way of working in collections a reality. As their comments make clear, they found the trip rewarding and in the end were glad they came. This does not lessen the fact that it took real courage, strength, and dedication to make the journey.

During our stay in Berlin, we were graciously hosted at the Ethnologisches Museum Berlin (Berlin Ethnological Museum) by North American curators Peter Bolz and Hans-Ulrich Sanner, collection managers Horst Wedell and Günter Lüttschwager,

Dance mask from St. Michael. IVA4460.

and conservator Barbara Gesell. Work in the Jacobsen Archives (located in the Museum of Ethnology Hamburg), the repository for Jacobsen's personal papers, was made possible by Corinna Raddatz and Director Wulf Köpke. My Yup'ik colleagues and I remain in their debt, not only for the information shared but the warmth and friendliness of our reception. We are also grateful to Axel and the staff at the nearby Pension Dahlem, who made sure we were comfortable when our day's work was done.

The efforts that went into translating written and oral sources pertaining to Jacobsen's collection were also extraordinary. First and foremost, my associate, Marie Meade, with whom I collaborated on the 1996 Yup'ik mask exhibit, roughly transcribed and translated everything the elders shared during our three weeks in Berlin as they spoke entirely in Yup'ik. She and Anna Jacobson then worked together reviewing all transcripts and preparing final translations. As the following pages make clear, their contributions have been enormous.

At the same time my reading of German archival sources was made possible by the hard work of a number of excellent translators, foremost Sonja Lührmann, who translated a selection of Jacobsen's personal papers and journals both at the Berlin Ethnological Museum and the Museum of Ethnology Hamburg, as well as Hilke Thode-Arora's excellent bibliography of Jacobsen's publications. Anja Karlson, Adelaid Pauls, and Karin Berning had the daunting task of tackling Jacobsen's handwritten accession records, requiring both skill and patience. Adelaid Pauls and Richard Bland also generously translated numerous articles both by and about Jacobsen, all of which contributed immeasurably to my ability to understand the man behind the collection. All of these detailed and valuable translations—elders' transcripts, personal documents, accession records, published articles—have been archived at the Anchorage Museum of History and Art and the Calista Elders Council office in Bethel, Alaska, for future reference. The Calista Elders Council has also published a bilingual companion volume to this book *Ciuliamta Akluit/ Things of Our Ancestors*.

Barry McWayne provided the fine color photographs of the objects Jacobsen collected, assisted in Berlin by conservator Helene Tello, allowing readers a glimpse of this fine collection. I took all of the color action shots of the elders working in collections during our September 1997 visit. The Berlin Ethnological Museum's photographer, Dietrich Graf, also spent time with us during our visit, and the book includes several black-and-white portraits that he made. Historic photographs were provided by Jacobsen's grandson, Johannes Adrian Jacobsen Jr., and both the Berlin Ethnological Museum and the Jacobsen Archives in the Museum für Völkerkunde, Hamburg. Particularly important are the reproductions of the original maps of Jacobsen's travels in Alaska included in his 1884 publication and provided by the Alaska and Polar Regions Department of the University of Alaska Fairbanks. Longtime associates Patrick Jankanish and Matt O'Leary prepared the map of historic and contemporary southwestern Alaska communities.

A book like this does not move from rough draft to finished form without the critical comments and advice of friends, colleagues, and expert reviewers. My friend and teacher, the late Jim VanStone, and my newest colleague, Peter Bolz, gave generously of their time and expertise to read and comment on an earlier version, for which I am very grateful. Jim VanStone was originally invited to travel to Germany with our group, not as an outside expert but as an elder among elders. A bad back prevented him from making the trip, and I especially wanted him to share in the high points of our expedition.

I am also grateful to Igor Krupnik, who invited me to present a preliminary trip report at the Jesup Centenary Conference at the American Museum of Natural History in New York City in November 1997, right after our return. This presentation, and subsequent comments by Julie Cruikshank, Susan Kaplan, and Allen McCartney, were instrumental in encouraging me to structure the book in its present form. Judith Meidinger once again applied her fine editorial skills to smoothing the manuscript's rough edges. And special thanks to Marilyn Trueblood, Audrey Meyer, Naomi Pascal, Pat Soden, Ashley Saleeba, Kerrie Maynes, and the dedicated staff of the University of Washington Press for working so hard to turn the manuscript into the book you hold in your hands.

My Yup'ik associates and I have agreed that we will donate royalties from this book to the Calista Elders Council, to support their work in documenting what Yup'ik elders have to say. Elders shared knowledge with Marie and me not for our benefit alone, but for the benefit of their young people. It is important that this attempt to share what we learned continues to benefit those who come after us.

Last but not least, thanks to my parents, Ken and Beth Fienup; my children, Frances, Jimmy, and Nick; and, as always, my husband, Dick. They make my work both possible and worthwhile.

Inuguaq (toy doll) from between the Kuskokwim and Nushagak Rivers. IVA5317.

THE GIFT

To give something is to give a part of oneself, . . . while to receive something is to receive a part of someone's spiritual essence. To keep this thing is dangerous . . . because it comes morally, physically, and spiritually from a person. Whatever it is . . . it retains a hold over the recipient. The thing given is not inert . . . and strives to bring to its original clan and homeland some equivalent to take its place.

—MARCEL MAUSS, "THE GIFT"

Painted wooden ladles from the Kuskokwim. Paul noted, "They are painted with personal designs done with black pigment." From left to right: IVA3780, IVA4551, IVA4552.

1 Risö, Norway, Jacobsen's birthplace. In the foreground is a hjeld (rack on which fish are dried). Jacobsen Archives, Museum für Völkerkunde, Hamburg.

JOHAN ADRIAN JACOBSEN BRINGS TREASURES FROM ALASKA

JOHAN ADRIAN JACOBSEN was born on October 9, 1853, on the island of Risö near Tromsö, Norway, above the Arctic Circle (fig. 1). The sea was part of his life from earliest childhood "because almost daily we went between our little islands in our boats to hunt and fish. . . . As far back as my memory goes I can remember struggles with the watery elements that my father and his crew had to pass through on their fishing expeditions." Jacobsen's formal schooling was erratic, as communication between the islands and the mainland was difficult. Classroom work was limited to seven-week periods in spring and fall, when he and his siblings were free to attend school. Yet, like his Yup'ik contemporaries growing up half a world away on the coast of the Bering Sea, Jacobsen's early life prepared him for his future work. Describing his childhood in his autobiography, *The White Frontier,* Jacobsen simultaneously positioned himself as an ethnographer of the exotic and someone with an exotic life: To him Alaska seemed very much like home.[1]

Jacobsen's brother, Johan Martin, went to sea at age fifteen, and their father bought an atlas to follow his eldest son's travels. Fascinated, young Adrian acquired both a knowledge of geography and a desire to see the world. When his brother returned eight years later, their father bought a fishing boat, which Martin captained and Adrian sailed on as a cabin boy. Later he traveled with his brother to Spitsbergen for summer fishing and reindeer hunting: "Even though I was very young I took part in the hunt with great enthusiasm and excitement . . . thinking I was luckier than any other person." At sea he encountered seals, walrus, beluga whales, polar bears, and seabirds—all the major species of the Bering Sea coast.[2]

Jacobsen spent summers in Spitsbergen until he was sixteen, when his father allowed him to attend navigation school in Tromsö to earn his captain's certificate. He took his first independent fishing voyage in April 1870, sailing across the banks of Spitsbergen and returning to Norway with a full load. In the fall, Martin, who was then living in Hamburg, Germany, visited Risö. Although Adrian wanted to return with Martin, his father needed him at home, and he went to Spitsbergen for another two summers. Adrian finally traveled to Germany in 1874. Although he found his brother's commercial activities in Hamburg less than exciting, he stayed through the winter and began to learn German. That spring he went to sea again, sailing with a Norwegian captain to Valparaiso, Chile, in early 1875. Jacobsen worked briefly in Chile, first as a helmsman on a Chinese ship, then in a fishing business in partnership with a Dane and a Swede, and finally together with a Finnish dock master on ship repairs. By November he was ready to return to Europe and again boarded a Norwegian ship with lading for Hamburg, reaching Germany by mid-February 1877.

Not long after his return, Jacobsen became acquainted with animal dealer Carl Hagenbeck, a relationship that would shape his life. Hagenbeck, like his father before him, was in the "exhibition business" in Hamburg, initially with animals but more recently with *Völkerschauen* (folk shows or ethnic exhibitions). Hagenbeck was looking for someone to bring several Eskimo families from Greenland to Hamburg for exhibition. He had offered the job to one of Jacobsen's friends, who had told him that such a venture would be impossible. Hearing this, the twenty-three-year-old Jacobsen purportedly called out enthusiastically, "If Hagenbeck wants his Greenlanders, I will get them for him." The next morning he went to Hagenbeck and told him he would bring the Eskimos. "Do you trust yourself to do that?" Hagenbeck asked. Jacobsen's apocryphal response was, "Why not?" to which Hagenbeck (also a man of rapid decision) responded, "You are my man. You shall travel!" The matter was settled.[3]

As Greenland was a colony of Denmark, Jacobsen journeyed first to Copenhagen to get permission to bring Inuit to Europe. There he told the minister of the interior of "Hagenbeck's desire to present an ethnographic exposition so that one would obtain in Germany a concept of the life and work of this unique people." Permission granted (a feat in itself), Jacobsen traveled to the west coast of Greenland at the end of April to try to convince several Inuit to leave home for Germany. A group of six eventually agreed to accompany him, taking along a collection of tools, clothing, kayaks, an umiak, a sled, and dogs to help demonstrate their way of life. Contrast this with the circumstances of the group of Yup'ik elders whom Jacobsen indirectly drew to Europe 120 years later. Whereas Jacobsen lured the Greenlanders with promises of money and a chance to experience the non-Native world,[4] Yup'ik elders came to Germany to reflect on their ancestors' handiwork.

The Eskimo *Völkerschau* was a great success in Hamburg that fall, and in late October Jacobsen traveled with the group to Paris: "Here the Eskimo driving their dogsleds and small skin boats was new and wonderful. Never before had there been such a display of an ethnic culture." The group went on to visit Brussels, Belgium; then in Germany, Cologne on the Rhine, Berlin, Dresden, and back to Hamburg; before returning to Copenhagen in mid-May and arriving home in Hamburg in July. No sooner had the Greenlanders set sail than Jacobsen traveled to Lapland for Hagenbeck to gather both a collection of objects and people to bring to Germany. The peripatetic Jacobsen traveled with this group as well, moving from city to city until Hagenbeck sent him word that he needed him to go to Le Havre, France, to meet three Patagonians arriving on a German steamer.[5]

These initial ventures were so successful that in 1879 Jacobsen and Hagenbeck purchased a ship, the *Eisbär* (polar bear), to undertake collection trips and transport ethnic groups. Jacobsen first sailed to Greenland, landing in Jacobshaven in July 1880. This time, however, the Danish inspector refused exit visas for the Inuit, and Jacobsen set his course first for Cumberland, on Baffin Island, and then on to the Moravian settlement of Hebron on the Labrador coast. Local missionaries opposed his idea, so Jacobsen sailed to northern Labrador, where he succeeded in persuading a family of "pagan natives" to make the journey. By late September the group reached Hamburg, where Hagenbeck announced his new *Völkerschau,* and Jacobsen once again set out touring, first to Berlin, then Prague, Czechoslovakia; Darmstadt and Krefeld, Germany; and Paris.[6]

All went well at first, and letters from Hagenbeck reflect a showman's eye for what would please his European audience: "[Mr. Schoepf, director of Dresden's zoological garden] writes me that on Sunday the seal is to be hunted, skinned, and eaten by the Eskimos; I implore you to leave out the first part of the program, for I do not want the animal to be harpooned in the pond."

Disaster struck in mid-January when all the Inuit contracted smallpox and died. From Hamburg Hagenbeck wrote to Jacobsen, who was also sick, expressing dismay and asking him to stay in Paris until he had fully recovered. Hagenbeck also advised him to burn all the Eskimos' personal belongings and sell the collection: "I do not want it in Hamburg because I don't want to see any more of the Eskimo things. What people pay for it I don't care, just away with it and that means *everything* without exception."

The aftermath of this tragedy was another turning point in Jacobsen's life. Adolf Bastian, director of the ethnological division of Berlin's Royal Museum of Ethnology, wrote to Jacobsen (whom he addressed as "highly esteemed sir") within a week on this very matter, expressing his regret at the Eskimos' death and asking if the museum might purchase "desired objects," including snowshoes from Labrador, a tambourine drum from Greenland, objects from graves, snow goggles, "Gods," "idols," and models. Thus began a relationship that would continue for years and provide the Berlin museum with more than fifteen thousand objects.[7]

"HAGENBECK'S TRAVELER" AND BASTIAN'S ROYAL MUSEUM OF ETHNOLOGY

Adolf Bastian's letter requesting the Eskimo objects for the Royal Museum was not the first interchange between the two men. Bastian had been in touch with Jacobsen six months earlier concerning objects the Eskimos were making for the museum, as had Bastian's assistant, Mr. Bauer. In fact, it was Bauer who wrote to Bastian in March 1881, referring to Jacobsen as "Hagenbeck's traveler" and encouraging Bastian "in the interest of the discipline, to pay him good prices for his things, since this man seems to be destined to be of much service to science in the future." Bastian not only purchased the collection, he set in motion plans to hire the collector.[8]

In later years Jacobsen would come to share Bauer's view that he was destined to serve science. In the closing lines of his undated manuscript "A Sailor's Life," he wrote:

With these shows [of Eskimos in Europe] I ended my voyages to Greenland. They primarily served the purpose of *making money* and had fully satisfied my hopes in that respect. In this sense I had realized my goals. But along with that something more valuable had formed, unnoticeable at first, and becoming more and more apparent to me: a better eye for life, its general striving and being. I had become inwardly more resolved and had matured to a sailor of special essence, who had at his disposal, besides a rich experience, a certain ability and will. Thus equipped I entered the second part of my life . . . mainly devoted to the task to serve my part of *science.* I was only up to this task after fulfilling the former ones.[9]

Jacobsen and Bastian united radically different backgrounds and personalities in pursuit of their common purpose. Jacobsen was the immigrant son of a Norwegian sea captain, a man of action without formal education whose command of German left much to be desired. Bastian, on the other hand, was a trained physician who had circled the globe as a ship's surgeon, widely read and well educated, and master of a dozen languages. He was the first German scholar to hold a position in anthropology and in years to come would establish himself as among the discipline's founding fathers. Beginning his tenure as chief of ethnology at the Royal Museum in 1876, five years after German unification, he used the nation's burgeoning desire for colonial expansion to encourage support for his museum. Germans, he argued, needed knowledge of the world's peoples if Germany was to take its rightful place in foreign trade and diplomacy.[10]

The 1880s were a period of rapid expansion of museums

in both the United States and Europe, and Bastian and his contemporaries saw themselves as "gathering the quickly disappearing documents for the future writing of the 'Book of Mankind.'" This was the height of "salvage anthropology"—the view that so-called primitive cultures worldwide were on the verge of extinction. Museums and their supporters believed that they were fighting the clock, gathering collections "in the last hour." In a letter seeking support for Jacobsen's collecting efforts, Bastian wrote: "Unfortunately, every year is precious, because the natural peoples, who we most need to look to for ethnological collections, will not wait, *they are vanishing so rapidly on all sides under our very eyes that every year, every month almost can bring irreplaceable losses if we remain idle.* . . . Ethnology must no longer wait. . . . It must itself send out travelers to the few points where such can still be got, to save what is left." Jacobsen was one such traveler. It was up to Bastian to find funds to underwrite the venture.[11]

THE FORMATION OF THE SUPPORT COMMITTEE AND JACOBSEN'S DEPARTURE FOR NORTH AMERICA

The Prussian parliament had generously provided for the young science of ethnology, appropriating funds for the construction of a new museum "for the honor of German science." One of Bastian's greatest achievements was the building of a separate museum of ethnology, Königliches Museum für Völkerkunde (Royal Museum of Ethnology), completed in 1886. The museum was built in a grand style, designed to showcase the kaiser's international reach, and opened in Berlin's center. How to acquire comprehensive collections remained a problem. Bastian quickly realized that donations would be an inadequate means of achieving his hoped-for ends of building an ethnological archive for future generations. Comprehensive collections required systematic collecting expeditions, the cost of which the Prussian state grant to the museum could not cover.[12]

Ambitious for the advancement of German ethnology, Bastian could have accomplished nothing without the backing of a small, influential group of German businessmen and philanthropists. Like Bastian, these men were fired with pride in the fatherland. Moreover, several were amateur ethnologists, both willing and able to dedicate their considerable resources to the service of science. This combination of chauvinistic pride and capitalistic affluence was not unique to the German upper class, and the 1880s was a veritable golden age for museums both in Europe and the United States.[13]

Within months of the death of the Labrador Inuit, Bastian wrote to a wealthy Prussian, August von Le Coq, describing both his potential opportunity and dilemma. He noted that "the animal trader Hagenbeck . . . has developed a pool of experienced collectors," among whom the most skilled was Jacobsen. As a result of the failure of the Labrador venture, Hagenbeck had given up plans to send Jacobsen there again. Jacobsen came to see Bastian, asking if he could be of use in Berlin. Bastian had cherished hopes of expanding the Royal

2 Johan Adrian Jacobsen in 1881, age twenty-seven, shortly before his collecting trip to North America for Berlin's Royal Ethnological Museum. Ethnologisches Museum Berlin.

Museum's collection with material from the northern North American coast (even then recognized as a "crossroads of continents") since his visit to Oregon the previous year. He wrote: "If the museum were funded as required by the . . . urgent needs of ethnology, then I would not hesitate one moment to rent his ship immediately for 2–3 years and then tell him the route he will have to follow. The costs . . . will amount to 15,000–20,000 Mark per year, . . . the collections which could be gained . . . could represent ten times this value or far more in the scientific sense." A similar plea, penned during the same period, concludes, "The history of ethnology would enshrine in grateful memory the names of these noble patrons and friends who selflessly helped it in times of need."[14]

Bastian's requests were not in vain. By early March he wrote Jacobsen that he had a potential sponsor in Le Coq, who would visit Jacobsen in person in Hamburg. Bastian advised the young man to discuss everything "with this benefactor of ethnology," especially the business aspects of the plan. Following the meeting, Le Coq wrote Bastian: "He seems to be still young, and I hope that . . . he will turn out to be the competent useful man you take him for." Le Coq also spoke with Hagenbeck concerning the rental of the ship and some discussion followed as to whether or not, in exchange for a low rental fee, Hagenbeck should be granted some use of the ship as long as his "private goals" did not conflict with Bastian's.[15]

Le Coq estimated that a consortium of ten interested parties would be enough to fund the venture, and he advised Bastian to consult the "shrewd banker" Emil Hecker on the details. Hecker responded enthusiastically, asking Bastian for twenty copies of his proposal to circulate among acquaintances who might be both willing and able to give 5,000 Mark to the purposes of science. Although personal gain was not the object of the expedition, Le Coq discussed with Hecker both the risks of the trip, the possibility of really valuable objects being brought back, and the necessity of being able to depend on the government purchasing the collection. Both men agreed that Bastian must give detailed instructions to Jacobsen to insure that he did not bring back "worthless" objects already present in museums.[16]

By the end of July 1881, the Hülfscomite für Vermehrung der Ethnologischen Sammlungen der Königlichen Museen (Committee to Support the Expansion of the Ethnological Collections of the Royal Museums) had been formed and included, along with Le Coq and Hecker, a distinguished group of Berlin notables: Isidor Richter, Gerson von Bleichröder (Chancellor Otto von Bismarck's banker), M. L. Goldberger, Valentin Weisbach, Wilhelm Maurer, and Johann Baptist Dotti. According to its founding charter, the Support Committee would consult with the administration of the Royal Museum and send out travelers to countries designated by the museum to make ethnographic collections, which would then be sold to the museum. The sum paid would be used to fully or partially reimburse the donors, but any remaining profits would be used to finance new expeditions. Each member gave a minimum of 3,000 Mark, and out of the initial capital of 32,000 Mark the Support Committee provided Bastian with a preliminary amount of 16,000 Mark. Finally, the Support Committee asked Bastian to engage Jacobsen, their first choice for leading an expedition.[17]

The original plan had been for Jacobsen to sail the *Eisbär* on an extended voyage to South America, Polynesia, British Columbia, the west coast of Alaska, and northern Asia. This route reflected a comprehensive collecting plan, motivated by both the importance of northern tribes to fill gaps in the Royal Museum's collections and the urgent need, given the rapid "disintegration of primitive originalities." By mid-July, however, Bastian had given up the idea for an independent boat charter and ordered Jacobsen to go at once to British Columbia and start collecting. What had changed, and why the sudden hurry? Bastian had discovered that the Bremen Geographical Society was planning to mount an expedition to Alaska and Siberia by the brothers Arthur and Aurel Krause, and he was determined that his man "precede the Bremish venture." Receiving word of his engagement, the ever-active Jacobsen was equally anxious to be off, noting that "the floor is burning under my feet from long idleness." He sailed from Hamburg less than a week later, on July 31, 1881.[18]

JACOBSEN ON THE NORTHWEST COAST: 1881

Arriving in New York on the ship *Australia*, Jacobsen traveled by rail to San Francisco, then north to Victoria, British Columbia (fig. 3). From there he visited the "Charlottes" (Queen Charlotte Islands) and Fort (Prince) Rupert before returning to Victoria.[19] After ten days spent packing and shipping "my constantly increasing collections," he left for the north and west coasts of Vancouver Island, where he traveled for two months. Both trips were marked by quick traveling and rapid collecting. Letters of introduction preceded him wherever he went, opening doors and soliciting needed guidance and advice. Jacobsen wrote to Bastian that "all persons . . . received me in the best possible manner." Bastian was also careful to follow Jacobsen's visits with letters of thanks for donations to the museum as well as acknowledgment in scholarly publications.[20]

Jacobsen approached the coast with high expectations, seeking pieces from "the good old days." He purchased most objects directly from the Natives, but occasional pieces and a great quantity of additional information came from longtime non-Native residents, including William Charles of the Hudson's Bay Company, Alexander Mackenzie of Masset, and a Mr. Blankenship at Fort Rupert. Jacobsen's first letters reported good hunting but high prices: "The curiosity sellers here are tremendously dear with their stuff, but I have seen some quite pretty things among them." High prices often put things out of reach, and Jacobsen repeatedly labeled the Haida entrepreneurs the "local Jews." At Skidgate Inlet he wrote: "The objects I wanted to purchase were very expensive, and the people offered them at such exorbitant prices that only an antiques collector would be able to buy them." America, he noted, was the most expensive country he had ever traveled in, and he wished (not for the last time) that he had "our ship" so that he might visit coastal islands and "load it with curiosities."[21] He apologized both for omitting to collect important items as well as for the inevitable purchase of duplicates, noting "one cannot collect in order when one has little time." The "vacuum cleaner" approach to collecting was never more honestly described: "It sometimes happens that I see a piece which I must have—I buy it—then in the next village I see a better object of the same sort and buy that—and so I get many duplicates—often I forget that I already have one."[22]

Writing to Bastian in early fall, Jacobsen noted that his trip to the islands was ill timed—the salmon were running and everybody was on the coast fishing. Nothing was available at these fish camps, as people left their most beautiful things at home. Traveling conditions also were difficult, and Jacobsen did not think highly of his Native companions. He blamed a capsized canoe on the "good-for-nothing" Indians and complained that he never met "more insolent people." Jacobsen later lamented the Natives' constant begging and stealing of his trade goods. If he failed to appreciate his hosts' personal qualities, he recognized their skillful workmanship and referred to the Northwest Coast natives as "nations of artists, for there is nothing they use that is not skillfully decorated with meaningful designs." Jacobsen's 1884 published account of his trip (as well as Erna Gunther's 1977 abridged translation) downplays these racist impressions rooted in nineteenth-century European views of non-European, non-Aryan others. Even these more public documents have an undercurrent of racism, as when Jacobsen notes that the addition of a Dane to his party "increased our white contingent against the redskins."[23]

Despite high prices, Jacobsen purchased much fine material, including an enormous Haida totem pole from the village of Masset in the Queen Charlotte Islands. The arrival of the missionaries at Masset had worked in Jacobsen's favor: "The fact that Captain Jim had been converted to Christianity and had adopted many ways of the white man accounts for his readiness to sell the pole." Early Christianization and Europeanization in other places led to disappointment: "I was very anxious to see Port Simpson, the largest village of the Tsimshian, and never in my life was I more disappointed than when I first saw this place. Instead of stately totem poles, . . . I saw nothing but modern European-type houses. . . . So Port Simpson was the first Indian village in which I bought nothing because there was nothing to obtain." He would repeat this complaint as he traveled south from Victoria the next spring: "The trip . . . was not very productive, because these Indians have been Christians for a long time—and as everywhere, where the Indians have been Christianized, there are few curios to be found." Yet on Hope Island north of Vancouver he had trouble getting things for the opposite reason: "Here the old Indian ways continued unchanged and consequently the people were not inclined to sell me their dance masks and rattles."[24]

After visiting the Queen Charlottes, Jacobsen traveled to the west coast of Vancouver Island, returning to Victoria in January 1882. The trip was difficult, although objects were less expensive off the normal trade routes. The season's bad weather had brought economic distress, which in turn depressed prices and enabled him to buy some things cheaper than would have been possible in the summer: "The West-Coast Vancouverians are the biggest savages which I have seen so far and are very hardy. They go almost naked at big dances and celebrations. . . . I have often had it that I bought one object 3–5 times—in which they took it back again the next moment—especially when it was something coming from their forefathers—just things I wanted most." Although Jacobsen purchased most of what he acquired, at Alert Bay he wandered through graveyards, seeking human remains. Near Koskimo he took a skull from a graveyard "for scientific study," and not for the last time.[25]

Jacobsen continued to move quickly and spread a wide net. He was well aware of the inflationary effects of his ambitious itinerary: "Here I must defend their demands, since . . . through the speed I required I made myself and everyone very uncomfortable because of my burning desire as a collector." Jacobsen's various accounts reflect an underlying bravado and pride in his colonial exploits. When his Native traveling companions lamented his risky travel decisions in dangerous winds and

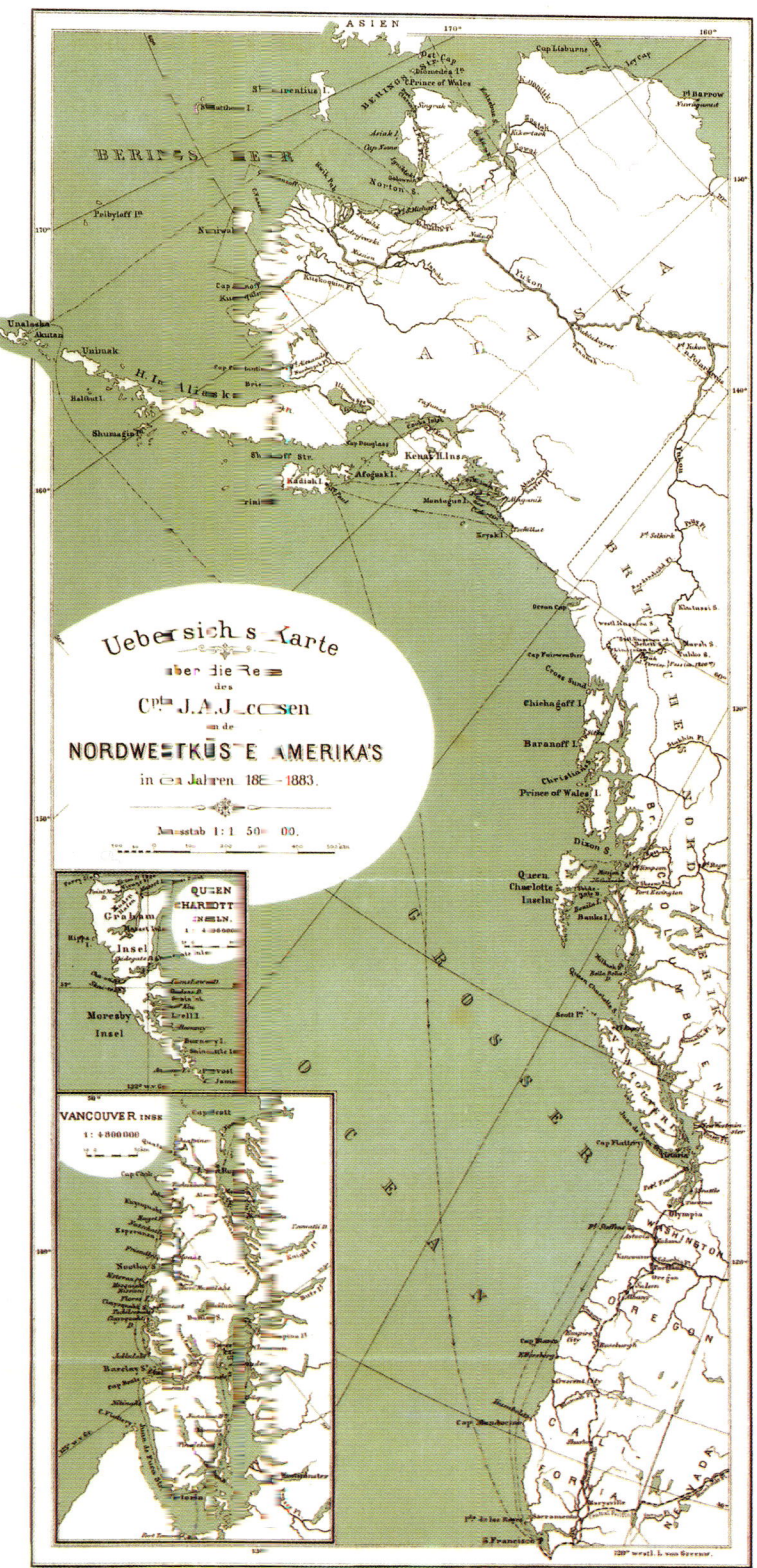

3 Map of Jacobsen's trip to the Northwest Coast of North America, included in his original 1884 publication. Alaska and Polar Regions Department, University of Alaska Fairbanks.

waters on the west coast of Vancouver Island, he remarked, "They were right, sir, [but] they had not the slightest interest in the Berlin Museum, which was the cause of this dangerous trip."[26]

In January 1882, Jacobsen wrote to Bastian requesting more

money and anxiously asking him to trust that he was buying really valuable things, though nothing had arrived in Berlin yet. From the beginning he felt the conflict between infinite wants and limited means. In September he had written Hagenbeck: "And the things—yes there are masterworks among them—one could spend a fortune to get all the things—I would like to buy everything—now I often have to look into the wallet since money has little value here—and the Indians are damned clever at trading, they are the local Jews—and what is worse they do not want to sell their things at least not so that other Indians see it—and I have now got a big sack and pack everything inside . . . that partly helps."[27]

Jacobsen collected according to Bastian's priorities, which he adopted as his own throughout his work in the North. Masks and other religious emblems were particularly desirable, as were "idols and Gods" of the local population. "Carvings of bone, wood, and shell" were also a strong preference and well represented in Jacobsen's North American collection, reflecting the nineteenth-century desire for evidence of ancient civilizations. Jacobsen judged the "Bella Bella" (Kwakiutl), Tsimshian, Haida, and Tlingit "tribes with a great past, but now . . . on the verge of extinction." Because these peoples were viewed as having one foot still in the Stone Age, recent productions of a "traditional" character were also acceptable, and Jacobsen even commissioned special pieces when he was unable to buy a particular item.[28]

Collecting clan property along the Northwest Coast constantly challenged Jacobsen's patience, and he continually compared the difficulties he was having with the relative ease of purchasing objects in Greenland and Lapland. On the Northwest Coast, however, "the Indians do not want to sell me any more since they had an argument after I left in the fall, because it is forbidden among them to sell their sacred objects. . . . When they see money again the trading spirit overcomes them."[29]

Despite these difficulties, Jacobsen's hurried visits up and down the coast were remarkably successful. Writing to Hagenbeck, he enthused: "I have things which people who have lived among the Indians for 20 years have not seen—particularly among dancing things, e.g. masks and rattles. When these guys start dancing with them—then it looks fine, the house is lit in the middle with a big fire—then all kinds of figures dance around it—ravens, eagles, owls, fish, devils, all kinds of human faces—in short there is probably not a single carnival where you can see more dramatic figures than in the Indian dances."[30]

By January 1882, the first shipment had arrived in Berlin, and Bastian was well satisfied. Others agreed, calling Jacobsen's collection "first rate," and Hagenbeck would later marvel at "the tremendous energy you must have deployed to acquire such a huge collection." Yet even before Jacobsen began to gain confidence in his collecting along the Northwest Coast, correspondence with both Bastian and Hagenbeck was exploring where he should go next. Jacobsen's letters offer a fascinating glimpse of how the decision to go to Alaska was made. Bastian and Jacobsen had seriously considered other alternatives.[31]

In December 1881, Bastian wrote to Jacobsen suggesting that he spend the rest of the winter in Sonora and Colorado or, if he felt there was enough to occupy him, continue on the Northwest Coast. In spring Bastian wanted Jacobsen to consult with the chief of the Hudson's Bay Company on a plan for "traversing the north all the way to Canada, via Fort Edmonton, Fort Garry, and Fort York." Jacobsen, however, had already heard glowing reports of the Alaska coast, "the Eldorado for a collector." Moreover, he believed that travel in the interior of British Columbia and northern Canada would require expensive Indian guides, whereas in Alaska he hoped to be able to travel with Alaska Commercial Company agents. Most important was the famed availability of artifacts in Alaska. People acquainted with the territory had told him that *Curiositäten* were abundant there and cheaper than anywhere else.[32] Jacobsen wrote Bastian: "Now to the most important issue of the travels, namely, what I can bring back. From the entire interior maybe five or six objects (such as moccasins, bows, leggins, maybe a buckskin dress, and tomahawks). From Alaska, though, I can bring back a hundred different things, and now more hunting after curiosities is going on in Alaska than elsewhere, just because there was still something to be got there until now, whereas in a few years it will be there as everywhere."[33]

By the end of January 1882, Jacobsen and Bastian had tentatively agreed on a four-month trip to Alaska. Jacobsen was to set out from San Francisco early enough in the season to allow him to return to Sitka by October. Jacobsen soon realized this plan was unrealistic and in a letter to Bastian noted that everyone agreed that it was impossible to collect in Alaska without spending the winter. He wrote that at the moment "there is a young man [Edward Nelson] from the Smithsonian [in Bristol Bay] and both the brothers Krause from Bremen are at Chilkoot. . . . I heard of them already in Victoria and had hoped to reach the Yukon from San Francisco this spring and from there to collect everything to the south before these gentlemen came up so far north." It would take until July to reach the Yukon, and there would be no way to get back before winter since the boat would stay there only a few days. Jacobsen wanted to stay and travel upriver to make the long trip worthwhile. He asked Bastian to telegraph instructions whether to go to the interior United States and on to Canada or to southern or northern Alaska: "It is a big decision and I don't dare decide by myself."[34]

Not knowing where to go, Jacobsen was also up in the air about whom he would be working for. At the same time that he exchanged letters with Bastian and the Support Committee, he kept Hagenbeck apprised of his progress. Responding to Jacobsen's glowing descriptions of the dramatic objects and people along the coast, Hagenbeck wrote in early December 1881: "I have already read today's letter [of November 3] from you 3 times and will read it several times more until I have enough of it because from this morning I have been thinking of nothing else but of the Indians you think you can bring." A month later, Hagenbeck wrote again, mentioning the Koskimo

8 THE GIFT

natives whom he hoped Jacobsen could employ for a new *Völkerschau:* "If you bring those Indians (where the women have the long heads and are painted and have sticks in nose and lips) then I am certain that we will make a great profit." Hagenbeck immediately contacted the Support Committee concerning this plan, and Richter wrote to Jacobsen on their behalf that the committee had agreed, in part "because this will also advance the interests of anthropology and ethnology." By the end of January 1882, plans were in place for Jacobsen to work for Hagenbeck once again, beginning March 1.[35]

As the death of the Labrador Inuit freed Jacobsen to collect for the Royal Museum, death once again upset plans for a Northwest Coast "ethnic exhibition." Jacobsen had written Hagenbeck in November, congratulating him on the success of his current Patagonian show, adding that "there remains only one wish—that they all stay alive." His wish did not come true. On March 17, 1882, Jacobsen received a telegram from Hagenbeck: "Engage nothing—particulars later." A letter followed the same day: "During the past three weeks five of my good poor Patagonians died, partly of pneumonia. . . . You know that I am a philanthropist and you can imagine how this misfortune has affected me so that I firmly resolved never again to arrange people's exhibits." Hagenbeck immediately sent home the five survivors and wrote to Bastian to arrange for Jacobsen to continue his work for the museum.[36]

Bastian replied that Jacobsen should head north that summer "to visit, if possible, the islands of Bering Strait (perhaps with a whaler), since this will give you the opportunity to meet the tribes of America and Asia in their trading relations." As along the Northwest Coast, Jacobsen was instructed to collect "carvings, masks, harpoons, labrets, idols, etc." Bastian reviewed the different parts of coastal Alaska that Jacobsen might visit, concluding that "these conditions might have changed in the meantime, and once you are there you will best learn for yourself exactly how to proceed."[37] Although his plan was to collect in Alaska, it was still far from settled that he would visit the Yup'ik homeland.

Jacobsen wrote at the end of April that he had received Bastian's letter instructing him to go north. By then the steam whalers had already left, and he had to wait for a sailing ship in June. Trading vessels would leave San Francisco before the June whalers, but he had decided to wait for the whalers, as they would give him an opportunity to go to the Diomedes and from there to Kotzebue Sound and down along the coast to the Kuskokwim. A month later, he reported that his reception at the whaling company had been less than friendly, as they considered taking passengers more trouble for them than it was worth. As the whalers refused to guarantee that they would pick him up on the Diomedes in the fall, "I have decided to accompany some gold miners from Arizona who have rented a schooner here to go to the Yukon between June 8 and 12. . . . I will live in St. Michael and from there start my operations going southward." Like voyagers on the starship *Enterprise,* Jacobsen's ambition was to go where no one else had gone before.[38]

Again Jacobsen regretted not having his own ship, which would have allowed him to visit "every little village." Ironically, if he had had his own vessel, the shallow seas of the Bering Sea coast and the shifting channels of the Yukon and Kuskokwim Rivers would have forced him to forgo collecting in Yup'ik communities. Jacobsen definitely did not take a direct path to southwestern Alaska, and the itinerary that allowed him to amass the finest collection of Yup'ik artifacts in the world was the product of months of disappointments, negotiations, and expediencies.

In early June 1882, Jacobsen finally settled on overwintering in Alaska, since the prospecting party he was going with had a little steamer built that would take them up the Yukon River. He thanked Bastian for the $2,500 he had received for his travels: "Whether that will be enough for two years all depends—how much luck I have in finding good opportunities for trips, how much I buy—and what prices are like there." He regretted that he would not be able to receive news from Europe during his travels. He would be without an address for more than a year.[39]

NORTH TO ALASKA: 1882

On June 13, 1882, Jacobsen boarded the schooner *Tiurnen* and sailed out of San Francisco Bay. The first stop was Unalaska, where he met *New York Herald* correspondent Henry D. Woolfe, who asked to accompany him north. "I believe he will go along to St. Michael,' Jacobsen wrote Bastian, "and will have enough trotting around between the Eskimo villages, especially in winter." He was not disappointed, and their partnership lasted for several thousand miles.[40]

The *Tiurner* arrived at St. Michael on July 30, and Jacobsen began collecting as soon as he disembarked (fig. 4). The Alaska Commercial Company agent, Henry Neumann, gave him a small chest full of items for the museum, and he was able to purchase various articles from a group of King Islanders, who arrived by skin boat to trade. He wrote Bastian: "Things are *inexpensive* here, and I arrange it so that the Indians and Eskimos are paid high prices for items for Europe. . . . I am sending a biscuit box with artifacts to San Francisco with the captain with whom I came up. . . . The collection from this place takes small space because most items are bone or stone (also skins). However, one needs 'boxes' for the masks from the upper Yukon River, especially the special shaman masks." He noted happily that people seemed willing to sell these masks, as most were burned after use and remade annually.[41]

Notwithstanding its auspicious beginning, Jacobsen wrote Bastian that he was not the first collector in the region: "Unfortunately a certain Nielsor [sic] of the Smithsonian Institute was here [1878–1881]; he made through the Yukon, Norton Sound to Sledge Island, the entire coast to the Kuskokwim River. He made a nice collection and not so costly, and now the best and inexpensive items are found at the Smithsonian."[42] Regret that "Mr. Nielson" (Edward Nelson) got all the good stuff peppers Jacobsen's letters and journal entries throughout his travels in

4 St. Michael, Alaska, Jacobsen's base camp during his year in Alaska. Hamburg Archives

Alaska. Fortunately, he was mistaken, and enough remained to provide the Royal Museum with an encyclopedic collection of Yup'ik material culture. Moreover, although Jacobsen's Alaska collection is somewhat smaller than Nelson's, the overall quality of the artifacts is excellent. Jacobsen may have been second in time, but thanks to Bastian and the Support Committee, he had much more money to spend—$2,500, compared to less than $1,000 given to Nelson by the Smithsonian.[43]

One happy offshoot of Nelson's departure was that he left behind Petka, an experienced Creole interpreter of Russian and Yup'ik descent. Jacobsen hired him for what he thought to be high wages, "but the man was trustworthy and familiar with the region" and thus worth his fee. Other major contributors to his success were the Germans, Finns, Swedes, Scotsmen, as well as fellow countrymen whom he encountered in his travels, most either traders or agents of the Alaska Commercial Company. The Bering Sea coast had a small but truly international non-Native population at the turn of the century. Many of the principals of the Alaska Commercial Company in San Francisco were Germans, and Jacobsen had the support of a network of Scandinavian and German businessmen throughout the Pacific Northwest.[44]

"I REVEL IN ARTIFACTS"

Jacobsen made four major journeys during his year on the Bering Sea coast, roughly one in each cardinal direction. The first began within a week of his arrival (fig. 5), when he, Woolfe, and Petka accompanied the prospecting party up the Yukon River: "I went with the mining company to the mouth of the Tanana River where the miners pass the winter—a stretch of 900 English miles. From there I went downriver in the skin boat (baidarka) to Anvik, where the native Ingalik are so poor in items of earlier days that I could not collect anything, but from Anvik to [St. Michael], I made a good collection, especially stone and bone items, also masks. I also bought the items at a low price, so that the entire trip up and down will cost only about $200."[45]

The party moved slowly upriver. Stopping roughly every six hours to cut wood for fuel, they averaged 20 to 25 miles a day. They passed numerous small villages, camps, and Alaska Commercial Company posts at Kotlik, Andreafski, Russian Mission, and Nulato. Trade goods at these outposts included cotton drill, powder, lead, percussion caps, tobacco, matches, knives, and beads. Jacobsen did little trading on his way upriver. His journal does not note a purchase until he "bought some curios" at Russian Mission, including stone axes, spear points, and bone carvings. He did, however, tell people in the villages where they landed that he would return on his way downriver and buy the artifacts they assembled, thus giving them time to create the ethnographic collection he desired.[46]

Above Russian Mission the party entered Ingalik territory, and Jacobsen noted a change in vegetation with conifer forests crowding the banks. There was "little to buy since the Indians here have nothing and are like all Indians shameless in their demands." As they continued upriver, Jacobsen recorded one particularly unusual encounter: "An Indian, probably a shaman, came to the river bank and made all kinds of shaman's signs, first he crossed himself . . . and I did likewise which increased his fright. It is either a madman or one who has never seen a steamer and thought we were monsters. The Indians we have with us interpret his gestures as if he wanted to send our steamer to the ground, saying that the last act is the same as the shamans use to bewitch somebody."[47]

On August 27 they arrived at Nuklukayet, "happy that the towing job was over." Returning downriver, there was still nothing to be had among the Indians: "All their [non-European] possessions are 1 birch canoe, 1 wooden table, and a birch-bark basket." Although his Ingalik collection was limited in variety, in the end it totaled approximately two hundred pieces: "Among them were bows and arrows and an iron lance with a strong wooden shaft, as well as modern hunting gear.... The Ingalik, like the Kwikpakmiut [people of the Yukon], have special eating dishes for both men and women.... [O]ne finds many birch-bark vessels as well as wooden water buckets and dippers." Jacobsen also noted their fine birch-bark canoes, and he bought two models.[48]

Arriving in Koserowski, the last of the Ingalik villages, Jacobsen not only bought several items, he also helped himself to a grave box and the wrapped body of a woman wearing a cap of glass beads. Although his published account minimizes his impropriety ("The young Indian who was with us did not raise any objection to our taking these pieces"), his actions would have serious consequences during his year in Alaska.[49]

Jacobsen often encountered graves and grave goods during his travels. Down river at Ekojelt-Pileramiut, he noted that people did not wish to sell him anything from their burial sites: "On many Eskimo graves there were carved figures of the deceased, heavily decorated with beads, especially the female figures.... On the boxes were also masks of animals and spirits. It was distressing that these pieces could not be bought." Farther down the Yukon, however, just above Andreafski, Jacobsen did collect a grave monument on which had been carved a hunting scene with a bear pierced by an arrow (fig. 6): "The grave was evidently a cenotaph, since there were no human remains, and I took it to be a memorial to someone killed by a bear. Since this monument would be admired by many more people in the newly completed Royal Museum of Ethnology in Berlin than here on the banks of the Yukon, and since it was made to be seen, I took it with me."[50]

Along with purchasing artifacts and examining graves, Jacobsen occasionally explored archaeological sites, including an abandoned site near the village of Ka-krome, consisting of

5 Map of Jacobsen's travels on the lower Yukon, included in his original 1884 publication. Alaska and Polar Regions Department, University of Alaska Fairbanks.

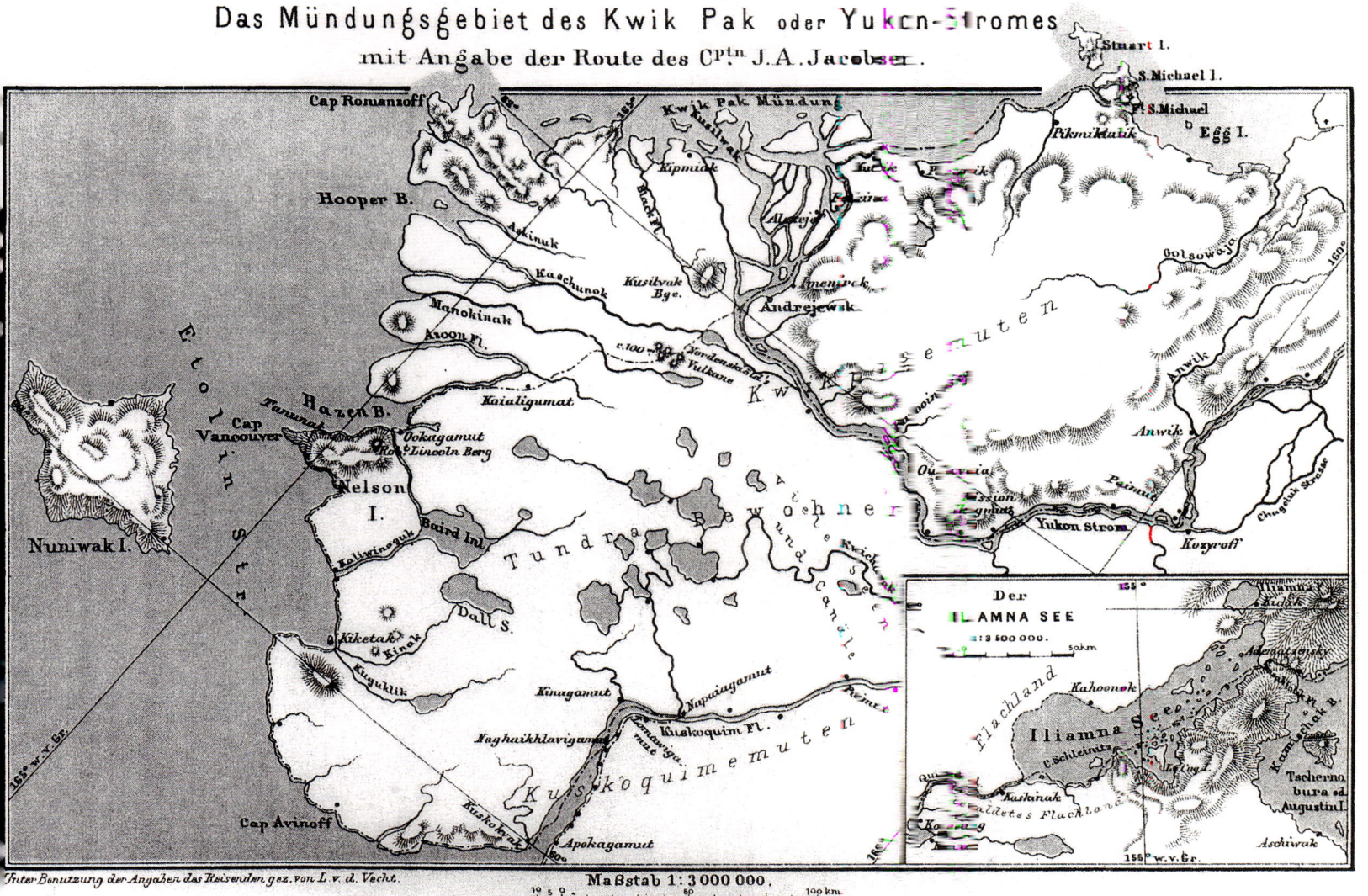

hundreds of house pits along a four-mile stretch of riverbank. He also spent a day climbing the stone outcrop just below Nunalcanahuk, said to have been the bone-littered nest of an enormous legendary bird: "Went there and found that it was a fable about the nest, not any bones."⁵¹

Jacobsen traveled quickly downriver: "The next morning we started early and came to the village of Ka-krome, where my purchases took an hour . . . and I went on." Jacobsen later noted that longer visits in the villages were not profitable, "as the Eskimos take these only as occasions for the most shameless begging." He collected both real and "fake" artifacts (made by carving knives of soft stone and boiling them in oil to make them look old): "Came to the village Dakkitkjaremut where I bought very many things, among them several good stone axes (3 fake ones). Everything quite cheap. Left at 12 noon, reached Ankasagemut (Rasboinsky in Russian), bought here as well a lot of stone things, snow goggles, etc." From here his "lucky period of collecting" began: "For in the villages of the lower Yukon there was much more to be found. I especially bought stone knives and axes."⁵²

Writing to Bastian on his return to St. Michael, Jacobsen enthused over this first trip among the "Stone Age Eskimos": "I have found various fragments of mammoth. . . . The natives of the coast live more in the Stone Age in that they use stone lance tips. I have many stone axes, knives, arrows and lance tips, skin cleaners, etc. of stone. In short, I revel in artifacts." At trip's end, along the coast to Pastolik, shallow water prevented approaching the village to make purchases, but "a message from us brought out six kayaks and I bought stone axes, lance points, and so forth."⁵³

Jacobsen's successes, however, came at a price. Although absent from his letters to Bastian and muted in his published accounts, Jacobsen's journal constantly referred to the harsh traveling conditions he endured, including lice ("you get so full of them it is a pity among these people"), the plague of mosquitoes ("Against their relentless pursuit . . . there is no defense. . . . No philosophy protects against mosquitoes!"), cold and rain, uncomfortable living quarters, sleepless nights due to noise and crowded conditions, and "unreliable Indians." A low point occurred one rainy day just after the party left Pastolik. Petka assured Jacobsen that there were places to camp farther along, but this proved untrue. The party nearly capsized as they tried to come ashore: "I was glad that we had saved our lives. I gave my Indian what he deserved because he knew the coast and still gave such irresponsible advice."⁵⁴

Returning to St. Michael on September 18, 1882, after a journey of more than 1,800 miles, Jacobsen wrote letters to Bastian in German and to family and friends in Norwegian. He devoted most of his time to his collection, which he found in deplorable condition: "Although the pieces were made in the Alaskan climate, they were not expected to go through two shipwrecks when . . . I could not give them the conservator's care they deserved." Jacobsen and Petka unpacked, dried and cleaned, labeled, and finally repacked each item. Although unable to provide proper names for Ingalik objects, Petka helped label the Yup'ik collection. The consistency in names Jacobsen recorded for animal face masks, such as "pretend seagull," "pretend walrus," and "pretend king salmon," point to a single source of information—Petka.⁵⁵

Waiting for freeze-up, Jacobsen found himself with time on his hands: "I was faced with perhaps several weeks of waiting which is the most difficult situation for someone accustomed to action." He took part in several hunting trips around St. Michael and finally left by skin boat for Golovnin Bay with a load of goods that the local trader Mr. Lorenz was sending north (fig. 7). The weather was stormy and cold, however, and Norton Sound quickly froze over, forcing Jacobsen to continue his journey by dogsled. From Golovnin Bay Jacobsen headed west at the end of November with a Native from that area: "We followed not the seacoast, but went over Golovnin Bay. . . . After six days of difficult work, we reached Kawiarsak [Qawiaraq]. From there I set out for Port Clarence and farther west to Singrak, where we met open water Dec 7."⁵⁶

Initially, Jacobsen did not get as many "curios" as he had hoped, as again "Mr. Nielson" had proceeded him. But his trip was not entirely in vain: "I collected many bone carvings and

6 *Bear figure. Jacobsen wrote: "Memorial for a hunter who lost his life on a hunt. At least that is assumed (one found traces of a fight between a bear and a man), and the monument was erected on the spot . . . where he had left his boat. There is a figure of a carved wooden bear; the bear's mouth is painted red; an imitation arrow is crudely carved out of wood; this arrow penetrated the bear's chest, exiting on its back. There is also a bow tied to the bear. The entire image stands on a post three to four feet of the ground. The bear's belly shows traces of being wedged onto the post." IVA4200.*

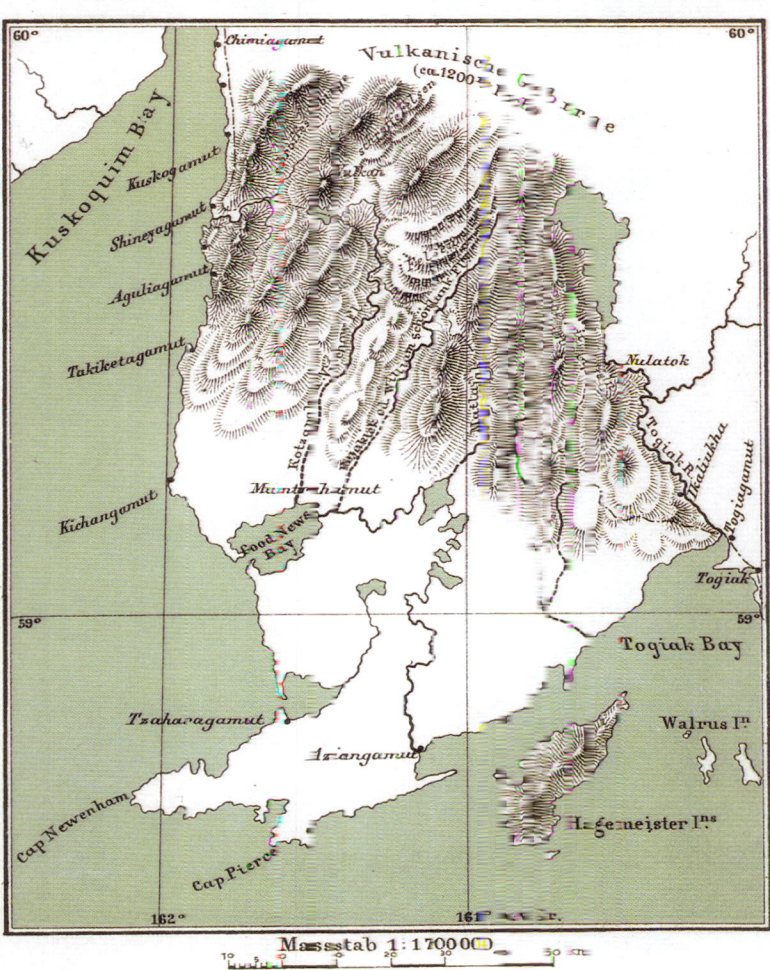

7 Maps of Jacobsen's travels north and south of St. Michael, Alaska and Polar Regions Department, University of Alaska Fairbanks

next pendants of greenstone, which the Eskimo regard as a precious stone." On December 12 he turned back toward Golovnin Bay, having added several hundred pieces to his collection.⁵⁷

Jacobsen's letters to Bastian concentrated on detailed itineraries, plans for coming trips, and information on his progress gathering objects. His journals (also written in German), however, contain a wealth of ethnographic detail, much of which he later expanded in published accounts. On October 31, for example, he described the first of many healing ceremonies he observed: "At night a shaman made much art. Eisick's [Isaac's] son had been sick and a wooden God-idol was put in his sack the previous spring. Meanwhile no ax could be used [until] after the shaman had carried out his sorcery (with sighing and shouting . . . and some shaman tricks) the use of axes was permitted again to great joy."

On November 22 he attended a major ceremonial event—a Feast for the Dead:

Left in the morning . . . for "Ingniktok" where the festival [for a deceased person] was being held. . . . I have to admit that I was surprised when I entered the "Kasschim" [*qasgi*],* or crawled inside through the underground passage. There were three rows—or parquet, balcony, and gallery—the last filled with young Eskimos and eskimettes naked and half naked. . . . The dancers sat on finery for the dance. . . . The men were dressed . . . with gloves which went up to the shoulder and hung with the beaks of sea birds. . . . There were about 150 people in the house and there was a terrible smell because the house was small and so many people packed together like herrings in a vat. . . . Before touching the food or drink you let some of it [fall] while saying the name of the deceased.

Jacobsen noted that the hosts gave gifts in groups of twenty, including small caribou bags, handkerchiefs, large *kanleika* (hooded gut-skin parka), and boots. A month later he attended another major component of the winter ceremonial cycle—the Bladder Festival: "In the 'Casigit' [*qasgi*] at night the women were given gifts, because tomorrow morning the sea bladders will be buried into the sea, the gifts were given from the hole in the ground."⁵⁸

Unlike his contemporary, Edward Nelson, a trained naturalist who removed himself from the events he witnessed in his published accounts, Jacobsen remained very much present in

*Native names recorded by Jacobsen have been capitalized and placed in quotation marks, as they appear in Jacobsen's original records. Italicized words are in the standard Yup'ik orthography (see Jacobson 1984). Note that Yup'ik nouns ending in *q* are singular, *t* plural, and *k* dual.

his descriptions. The travelogue he published on his return to Berlin never was considered "science" in the same way as Nelson's third-person ethnographic observations.[59] Like the modern field-worker, Nelson was informed by scholarly training, while Jacobsen remained "Bastian's traveler," a division of labor that twentieth-century ethnology would eschew. Putting himself into his narrative like the best postmodern ethnographer, Jacobsen was both behind and ahead of his time.

If Jacobsen's public accounts betray his personal views of the people and places he encountered, his private journals were even more revealing. Living more intimately with the local population than he had during his trip with the prospectors up the Yukon, he used his journal to vent myriad frustrations and complaints. He was generally disdainful of the speed at which he was able to move: "We went from Qunikok to the village farther down at the mouth of the river about 3 miles, where we stopped according to savage ways, because if you travel with them and depend on them you are forced to take in every little village." His mood had not improved the next day: "Haven't slept a wink during the night—the dogs howled like demons—the children cry, the people smell because the house was cramped, in short it has been a pure Eskimo night—and we hurried to get away in the morning." Later he noted that "the begging for tobacco is almost unbearable in this region." Stealing was also a problem: "Traded with the people today, but I had to stop soon because they were so insolent in their demands and what they had was not of value—in the end they started to steal from me." He concluded: "Unfortunate is the man who travels in this country, everything he has with him must be shared with these people while if you want only the smallest thing from them, the first question is what do you pay for it."[60]

Jacobsen characteristically presented himself as a hearty adventurer, often the first white man to travel through the region. He emphasized the rigors of his upbringing and how they had prepared him for the task at hand: "I can guarantee that seal fat . . . tastes very good, for I ate this in my home during childhood." His journal often references the future traveler, as though Jacobsen intended this raw document as guidebook as well as for scientific consumption. Returning from Kotzebue Sound, he wrote, "I would advise every traveler to bring iron neckband and chains, then to fasten the dogs every night." His published accounts also continually named features of the landscape in true explorer fashion, including Bastian Lake and Geyser on Seward Peninsula, Hagenbeck River ("but the Eskimo call it Unalitschok"), Richter Lake, and Le Coq Island. None of these dedications appear in Jacobsen's private journals, and they may have been added later at his German editor's or others' suggestions.[61]

Jacobsen's Iñupiaq hosts received him with a mixture of awe and aggression: "They handled me as if I were a wonderful animal . . . [and] were so excited about my visit that they raised hell all night. . . . The next day, 6 December, I was invited by the inhabitants of Singrak to the 'Kassigit' [qasgi] for a ceremonial welcome." Jacobsen found this treatment as a "curiosity" irritating: "I began trading with the people, but without much success, and was quite annoyed at their begging and aggressive behavior, which included examining me physically. . . . As I was already very much annoyed by their behavior I paid no attention to the taboo and mended my torn clothing against their protests."[62] Conversely he relied on his strong personality as protection from what he viewed as "fraud" on their part: "The natives, who believe that might makes right, take every opportunity to outdo a weaker white man. I often found that my energetic personality was my only protection from both the Eskimo and the Indians. . . . If one can once support such a statement with a powerful physique one can establish a reputation and protection from fraud."[63]

Along with his blatant disregard for taboos on work and travel that interfered with his plans, Jacobsen's lack of sympathy often translated into his unwillingness to heed Iñupiaq rules of hospitality. His journal makes clear events that are left unexplained in his "polite," published descriptions of his own impolitic behavior. For example, when approaching Shaktolik, Jacobsen declined small gifts that required return gifts of greater value. His published account then notes that "for some reason" residents did not want his party to approach their village: "The people in this region are very superstitious, and as I found out later they believed our presence might be harmful to two sick children." His journal entry for October 20, however, was more direct: "We were met by the inhabitants who brought us a little piece of ice and a piece of wood and also gifts. But I refused the gifts as I know from experience that they are only given to get back ten times as much. That made them angry, and when I went ahead they told me that there were many sick people in the village and small houses so that I camped a mile from the village."[64]

Jacobsen's journal entries only rarely recount the personal costs of his year abroad. On December 24, 1882, he wrote, "It is a sad Christmas Eve and I hope to spend the next one in a better way—perhaps among my friends and relatives—there is nothing but trouble and deceit." Although Jacobsen commented often on both physical difficulties and "unreliable" Natives, he barely mentioned missing the companionship of home. He concentrated instead on projecting the image of a man of action, busy in the present, which, whether frustrating or satisfying, fully engaged his attention.[65]

By December 26, Jacobsen had returned to Norton Sound, where the weather remained miserable far into January 1883. Nevertheless, on January 13 he and Woolfe set out on their third expedition—a thirty-eight-day trip to Kotzebue Sound with five sleds and thirty dogs. The trip began poorly: "Our provisions are exhausted and we now quarrel among the people." Their guide, Isaac, turned back, and they carried on with four sleds. The weather continued to deteriorate. Farther north, they encountered a starving population and bought only a few "curios" at high prices: "Progress is slow on our trip everything is against us . . . I would advise everyone not to come here because the people are pure scoundrels." On February 3, Jacobsen wrote: "It seems that my trip has been entirely in vain, . . . everything I heard about the many curios supposed to be here is only a lie—there is nothing among this indolent and lazy population, *not* even fish although the river swarms with fish, they are really too lazy and I am annoyed that I came, because all the hardships and deprivations are in vain." Things got worse the next day when he arrived at Kajatolik: "Bought a greenstone pipe—and a clear transparent 'Totak' [*tuutaq*, "labret"]—paid for both objects a monstrous price for local circumstances—unfortunately I discovered in daylight that the 'Totak' seems to come from a colored bottle from a polar voyager of old times—and got terribly mad—to be cheated like that. Only one thing is certain—that this 'Toutak' [also *tuutaq*, "labret"] and pipe have acquired a great celebrity, for I heard about it from other people. . . . It is hard to endure just a few days . . . and I cannot advise every traveler enough against coming here . . . because you need to have a donkey's patience to deal with these people."[66]

On February 5, another trade went sour. In his published account, Jacobsen presents himself as the hero of the day who, wearing a revolver and large knife, routed a disgruntled Native. Once again, Jacobsen's private journal gives a very different version: "The house was full of begging Eskimos right from morning, Woolfe had bought a pair of boots yesterday—today the Eskimo came back with the things—and explained he did not want to have them and as Woolfe refused him the exchange—so he threw the things right in his face. We (Woolfe) had to exchange it because we are up against at least 30 persons here—and since it is only trifles—so we keep peace . . . you cannot rely on the Eskimos here it is disagreeable."[67]

The next day, however, another group arrived with fur and "curios," and both Woolfe and Jacobsen had good trading, selling almost all the things they had brought. They headed home in stormy weather and nearly drowned their first night out when caught in a storm surge. Luckily a Native companion discovered the rising tide, and "there followed just a chaos with everybody trying to save [themselves] and never have I seen the Eskimos work better. In a quarter of an hour everything was on the sleds and the dogs hitched."[68]

Throughout his tenure in Alaska, Jacobsen remained preoccupied with the acquisition of nephrite (jade), or "greenstone," a material that was a topic of heated debate in late nineteenth-century anthropology. On December 1, he noted a rare greenstone amulet like others he had seen and wished to buy but which so far no one would sell. On January 25, 1883, he "bought first specimen of greenstone 'Toutak.' It was very expensive, because only a few pieces are left here on the coast. I paid for it according to local prices, about $15 (1 piece drill and 20 plaits tobacco)." Jacobsen would later write Bastian from St. Michael, "I got only a few artifacts here; the most significant were three greenstone lip ornaments, one almost 3 inches long, a greenstone pipe and all kinds of bone items, small greenstone knives for wood carving and also half-rounded knives used for fish and skins. Finally, I bought in St. Michael, a rare greenstone dagger, the only specimen now here. I paid a high price for it—it cost me $25 but it is the only one of its kind and so I bought it. Farther North, there are many specimens like it, and much cheaper."[69]

If his acquisition of nephrite was the high point of his trip, his grave-robbing along the Yukon marked the low. On February 20, 1883, Jacobsen wrote in his journal that on his return "Isack told me that the Ingalik had come close to Unalakleet with many men . . . to kill me and that they had threatened to find me even if they had to go to St. Michael. It is also said that they stopped one of the Company traders thinking it was me—the guys seem to be crazy, so much trouble for a skull." Two days later he wrote, "We are 8 sleds and about 25 men in case the Ingalik await us near Unalakleet we can almost put up a battle." Arriving in Unalakleet on February 24, "one hour later 7 sleds came here from Nulato. They were from AC Company Mr. Waldron . . . who told me that when the Ingalik could lay their hands on me then it would cost my life . . . I will send back the head so that the matter is settled."

This was the last reference to the "Lead" incident that Jacobsen made in his private journal, but he wrote Bastian a long account a month later describing how during the previous summer he had collected a mummy and three skulls, one from Tanana and two from the Lower Yukon. Later Jacobsen's Native guides broadcast the incident, and Jacobsen was threatened. He complained that everyone, including Nelson who visited the area had taken skulls, but that now "the entire blame falls on me." Worse yet, Mr. Scheffelin, one of Jacobsen's traveling companions during his Yukon trip, had agreed to pay the Natives $100 in restitution. Jacobsen considered this a mistake, as it encouraged others to seek compensation "for every one will come and say he is related to him who lost the head."

Jacobsen wrote Bastian that he had determined to return the heads, but Mr. Lorenz advised against it. Instead, Lorenz invited the Indians into his home at St. Michael and read to them from an illustrated medical book, telling them that since they demanded medicines from the Europeans, the Europeans needed skulls to study and determine which medicines would be useful. Jacobsen concluded

This explanation seemed to make an impression; unfortunately, there now came the report of Scheffelin's thoughtless act, which spoiled everything. I am sorry that this has happened, my only fault . . . is that I took the heads when I had Indians in the boat; however, those Indians lived so far down river that I was sure no report would reach there, even if they talked about it. You may perhaps hear the story in another light, but the story on my word of honor, is no more or less than what I have reported here.

Even if Bastian never heard the story in another light, Jacobsen certainly told it differently. His published journal describes Lorenz's "ethnological lecture" as having had good results and satisfying the Ingalik but makes no reference to Scheffelin's payment. Fifty years later, in the chapter of his memoirs entitled "Hostile Indians," Jacobsen transformed himself from the apologetic but blameless collector to the brave defender of the fort. The later rendition had the Ingalik on the "war-path" destroying whole villages their "battle fires" visible in the night.

15 JACOBSEN BRINGS TREASURES FROM ALASKA

He included the same colorful account in notes for a public talk, "Travels in Alaska," accompanied by photographs of coastal graves and Native skulls collected in the name of science. No further incident is known following Lorenz's lecture with the medical book. Bastian expressed his regret that Jacobsen had "come to [his] unpleasant position through the said combination of momentous coincidences" and hoped that the incident would pass without further consequences: "Anthropological collections are always a tricky matter, as lies in the nature of the thing, and for that reason I always try to avoid direct orders, because . . . the matter is best left to the discretion of the traveler in each case, and to the circumstances, as they turn out to be at each location."[70]

Back in St. Michael, Jacobsen turned his attention to packing and shipping his collection. He wrote to Bastian: "I am sending you from here, 6 large chests with artifacts and mammoth bones; 1 chest, which will get there in mid or end of August; a small chest with heads and mummies. In the mammoth bone chest is an Ingalik coffin which belongs with the mummy. The coffin is painted with hunting scenes; this will help when the chest is reassembled in Berlin. The small chest with the most valuable things: the 'Toutak,' pipes, greenstone knives, neck pendants, etc. I am sending separately with a sailboat. The things are all fine workmanship, similar to Mexican things often seen in museums." He closed with hopes that the things he had sent from British Columbia had arrived as well as a request that the Royal Museum guarantee a $100 payment to the Alaska Commercial Company agents in exchange for sending the museum things from Nunivak Island, Sledge Island, and King Island—places where Jacobsen did not go: "I hope you agree with me in this, for I have given orders to H[enry] Neumann here through a Swede who travels to Nunivak every summer to collect such things and through the inhabitants of King Island who come down here every summer."[71]

HEADING SOUTH: 1883

Jacobsen had used St. Michael as his base camp during his first six months in Alaska, traveling in three directions: "To the east I traveled 900 English miles, west to the Bering Sea, and north to Kotzebue Sound, and on these three journeys I collected about 700 ethnographic objects." It only remained for him to travel south toward the Kuskokwim and Nushagak Rivers and on to Cook Inlet and Kodiak Island, where he could board a vessel for home. Before setting out, he had all his clothing washed and repaired. He also wrote letters and reports and gave directions for Lorenz to send his collection to Europe on the first ship that spring.[72]

Jacobsen left St. Michael on March 18, 1883, heading down the coast to Kotlik and up the north mouth of the Yukon River as far as Andreafski (fig. 8). There he hired guides to take him across the tundra to the coast and south toward Nelson Island. The weather was initially miserable, with mixed rain and snow, and it took him twelve days to reach Andreafski. He found traveling among the Yupiit (plural of Yup'ik) easier, noting "the people here are better than the Eskimo living in the north." Writing from Nushagak two months later, he expanded on this comparison: "The Innuit tribes living from Kwik-pak [the Yukon] to Kodiak are dirty and peaceful while the Eskimos living from Cape Prince of Wales Peninsula and farther north are an energetic and war-like tribe and I never thought I'd meet an Eskimo tribe with so much courage, those are also much more cleanly and are great travelers." Jacobsen's published accounts reiterate his impression of "filthy coastal people" living in "houses half full of dirt and water." This negative presentation reflects the season in which he traveled. When he noted people living in "miserable huts that in the spring are so damp inside they appear more like a swamp than a dwelling," he was experiencing breakup at its worst. This was the season when most coastal residents abandoned their sod homes in favor of tents at spring camp to await the summer fishing season.[73]

His first stop south of St. Michael was Pastolik. There he bought a number of pieces, including dance masks, although traveling by sled limited what he could carry. Just as Jacobsen left some things that were entered in his private journal unsaid in his published accounts, cryptic journal entries often translated into long descriptive passages in his book. For example, on March 22, 1883, he noted simply "Stay in Kotlik." He would later give a detailed account of this pleasant interlude visiting the Alaska Commercial Company station manager, Mr. Kamkoff, including a refreshing steam bath and participation in a dart game that he had learned in Golovnin Bay and saw again here on the lower Yukon (see "Twelfth Day: Toys and Clothing"). He was able to increase his store of objects as well as information: "Even though I had been here twice before . . . I had made no purchases, but now I found a few pieces. My collection had increased on the way from Fort Saint Michael, so I packed it and asked Mr. Kamkoff to ship it to Fort Saint Michael for further transport in the spring. . . . My host was very familiar with the regions into which I was going and gave me long descriptions of the customs of the people, but all this unfortunately was in Russian."[74]

Ascending the Yukon as far as Andreafski, Jacobsen turned south: "The tundra was flat as a lake, and only the big reaching-in mountain Ingeritla [Ingril'er] on the Koslewak [Kusilvak] could be seen. . . . We had taken along a young man here as guide because it is so difficult to find our way on the tundra, it looks just like a sea. You see no straw or anything reminiscent of land." Continuing southwest across this flat expanse, they arrived at Ingril'er, which Jacobsen was surprised to find was a group of five extinct crater volcanoes: "I climbed the lowest—about 100–150 feet high." His journal notes the craters' local name, "Poppsulik" (*pupsulek,* "crab"), but in his published account, he renamed them for "the most famous Arctic explorer of our century, the Nordenskjold group."[75]

Traveling south to Kajaluigemuitten (Kayalivik), Jacobsen again noted the difficulty he had in finding a guide: "After I had threatened the people with shooting . . . I got a young man." He continued to Jukkak, a trader's abandoned residence, where "all inhabitants . . . are terribly dirty and in clothing also not

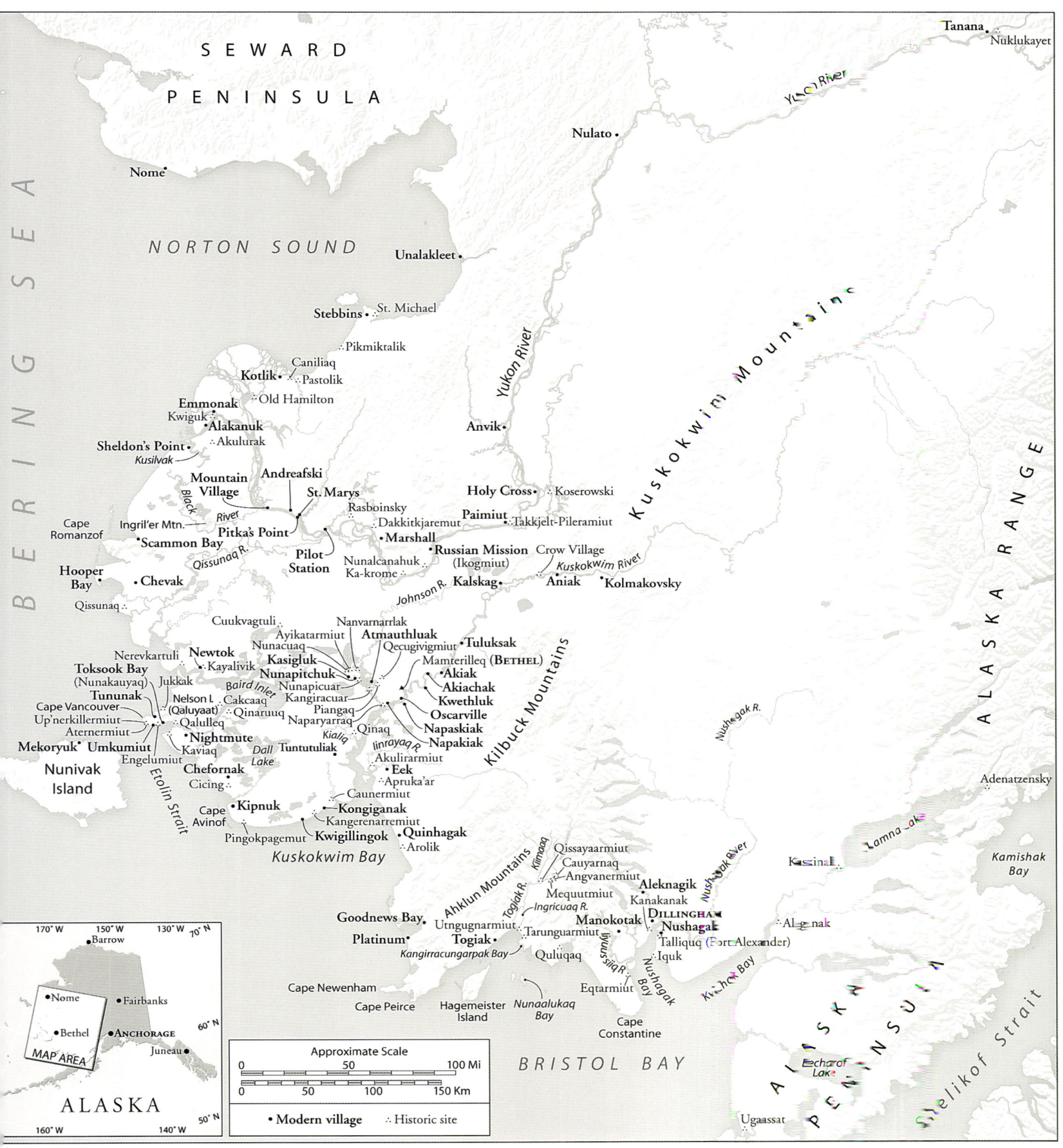

8 Map of the Yukon-Kuskokwim delta region, 2006. Patrick Jankanish.

half as cleanly and nice as the Malemut of the north, but are of a better character." He reached Nelson Island the next day, where unfortunately trading was not what he had hoped: "Most of the people died during the winter, and as there was so much disease among the natives, there have been no festivals here and so no masks can be had." He did, however, see grave monments in Tununak, which he interpreted as evidence of a "highly developed society": "I saw different wooden figures inlaid with bone, the arms of walrus teeth, these monuments were for people who had lost their lives during the hunt (in the water, on the mountains in a snowstorm)."[76]

Crossing to Umkumiut on Nelson Island's south side, he did some trading: "There are 2 'Kassegim' [qasgit] and many people here.... I immediately started exchanging tobacco, needles, etc. for curios but the inhabitants did not have anything besides individual bone things, but were all mad and wanted to trade. Tobacco in particular seems to be a good article here." To his chagrin, however, "Nielson has taken the best things."[77]

From Nelson Island, Jacobsen traveled quickly south along the coast, as the snow was melting fast. Suffering from snow-blindness in spite of colored glasses and wooden snow goggles, he continued collecting as he went. At the village of Pingokpagemut, he noted both the women's unusual jewelry and the people's character: "The women here are decorated with beads very much from their hair around the neck, and the lower lip has 3 holes through which beads are hanging, and under the nose up to 6 big blue beads among some girls. They do not tatoo the chin, as the Malemut, but when they have a line then it is away from the mouth and downward, all very dirty and dressed in rags, but otherwise good hearted, a little given to stealing, and seem very simple minded." Jacobsen also was "a little given to stealing." Reaching Kangerenarremiut on April 12, 1883, he noted that it had the largest qasgi he had seen and elaborate graves: "There were many things such as lances, hats, guns, articles of clothing, etc. We stole a woman's belt here without the Eskimos present seeing it."[78]

By the middle of April, Jacobsen had left the Bering Sea coast and was heading up the "funnel-shaped spreading mouth of the Kuskokwim." Again he had trouble finding his way and forcibly got help, though published accounts report merely that they "engaged a guide": "Came across the village [just below Bethel] where luckily we found a family. At first no one wanted to come along as guide but when I threatened to tie one of the women to the sled an Indian [sic] came."[79]

On April 15 Jacobsen arrived at Mamterilleq, the Alaska Commercial Company post near present-day Bethel. Once again he sorted and labeled what he had collected on his way down the coast, packing everything to send to San Francisco on the first ship. He wrote in his journal that he had gotten few artifacts along the Kuskokwim as "Nielson has been here also." Again he regretted not having his own ship so that he might visit Nunivak. Travel by sled also limited what he could carry away. The trip had been hard. He observed: "My eyes are very bad—and I am half dead from the hardships that I have suffered in the past 14 days. Truly you need patience and an iron energy to travel in such a way in such a country, but if you have said A you also have to say B." This proverb, meaning you have to finish what you start, was a guiding motto for Jacobsen throughout his journey.[80]

Starting off again downriver, Jacobsen traveled with the conceit that he was the first Euro-American to do so, although in fact a number of Russian missionaries, explorers, and traders had preceded him: "The only circumstance that made me hesitate to take this route was that this area had never been crossed by a white traveler; but this urged me to continue rather than restraining me." Heading down the coast, Jacobsen turned up the Arolik River, following the winter trail over the mountains to Togiak. He found the crossing over high peaks and valleys exhilarating after the delta lowland's seemingly endless expanse. During this final stretch, he was more complimentary of his Native traveling companions than he had been in months: "My Indians [sic] and the guide are the best and most energetic I have had in this country and I will reward them accordingly. Without such people I surely would not have got [through] under these difficult conditions."[81]

In Togiak he congratulated himself on "using the Arctic winter . . . from the first snowflake to the last for expeditions by sled" for fully six months, from October 23 through April 24. Three days later he continued by boat, passing rock outcrops and named points said to represent people frozen in stone (see page 193). At Togiak he had to leave his dogs behind. Many had been with him throughout his months in Alaska, and he wrote in his journal: "I was sorry in spite of everything . . . because they have served me faithfully and they were all standing on shore as if they wanted to say farewell." As he headed down the coast, his feeling for the local population was not so positive: "The people here are terribly stupid and it is almost impossible to deal with them."[82]

On May 1, 1883, Jacobsen finally arrived at Fort Alexander, headquarters of the Alaska Commercial Company on the Nushagak River, "where I want to rest awhile." Rest might mean a break from traveling but not from collecting. His luck, however, had turned. He wrote Bastian: "I am afraid that the more I come south, the more is the influence of civilization on the population, the fewer are the curios or things suitable for a museum; it's already very little here and will probably be less on Cook Inlet." The corrupting effects of civilization were not the only things Jacobsen blamed for poor trading:

Along the Nushagak, the people make bone work, but since all has been ordered before, the stranger gets none of it. There is here a Signal Station whose observer [Charles L. McKay] has plundered, as all do here, the local area for the Smitzonia. He has in his collection very nice things. The Eskimos are now angry that they sold him their stone axes and knives. I have promised them higher prices if they will only bring me things, but it is now too late. That's what happens to me: Almost everywhere, Smitzonia has always the upper hand.[83]

Jacobsen again sorted and packed his collections for shipment back to Germany: "I send from here 3 boxes (small) curios and a parcel containing spear, lances, bows, arrows, etc., under Mr. Richter's address." Some artifacts were packed in biscuit boxes, a marked contrast to the specially designed crates used to move Yup'ik masks back to the Bering Sea coast for exhibit a century later. Writing to Bastian, Jacobsen was aware of the weaknesses of his collection. He specifically asked that Bastian write the Alaska Commercial Company in San Francisco and ask them to authorize their agents to collect objects for the museum that he had not been able to get "especially clothing from different regions, and things from Nunivak where Karel Pettersen [Charles Petersen] the trader from Andreafski goes every summer." Jacobsen considered the garments he saw unacceptable for a museum collection: "[It] is hardly to be obtained in one piece, for all go about with torn clothing." Had he stayed longer in one place, he might have been able to commission women to sew new clothing. As it was, Jacobsen sent few Yup'ik garments, torn or whole, to the Royal Museum.[84]

LEAVING SOUTHWESTERN ALASKA FOR HOME: 1883

Jacobsen continually made and modified his plans as he went along. He initially decided to cross to the other side of the Alaska Peninsula, traveling from Bristol Bay by boat upriver to Lake Iliamna, following the ninety-mile lake, then over to Cook Inlet. He waited at Fort Alexander for two weeks for the ice to go out of the lake, finally setting out on May 19, 1883. Ten days later the party reached the village of Kaskinak, whose inhabitants had moved to the Kuskokwim for the summer: "Here were several graves with the same painted walls as on the Kuskokwim with caps and belts embroidered with beads. We took everything along, that is my men took it. I kept an old belt decorated with reindeer teeth." Continuing down Lake Iliamna, the party arrived at Adenatzensky a week later. The Russian trader there told him that he had missed the annual trading ship from Kodiak by three days and that he would have to go overland to Cook Inlet to find passage home. Before leaving, Jacobsen had a steam bath: "Afterwards I saw myself in the mirror for the first time since God knows when and was astonished to see my face so old and unkempt did I look."[85]

By June 5 Jacobsen reached Cook Inlet, traveling by *baidarki* (skin boat) to Tyonek, collecting as he went: "I bought several curios but nothing special—of antiquities there is nothing here, some bead embroideries, articles of clothing, hunting implements, etc., everything is expensive and they only take money [not trade articles as previously]. The cheap time is over." From Tyonek he crossed Cook Inlet to Fort Kenai, where he had expected to find letters with instructions from Berlin: "Think of my disappointment when I arrived without finding the expected reports." From Kenai, Jacobsen headed down the coast to Ninilchik. Not only did prices continue high, but traveling became increasingly expensive. When his men slept through an outgoing tide, Jacobsen wrote with exasperation: "That is what the damned guys here are like. They demand high pay and do nothing. I could have bashed their heads in for rage."[86]

Jacobsen continued south to Fort Alexander, crossing Kachemak Bay to Seldovia. While he waited for passage to Kodiak, he occupied himself with a week's excavation at the deserted settlement of Soonroodna, probably in China Foot Bay, where during one day five men dug down three feet "without finding anything of significance." He also visited cave burials looking for masks and other valuables, but collapsed cave openings prevented entry. Prior to his departure for Kodiak on July 7, he wrote in his journal "Of all Alaska the peninsula of Kenai as well as all of Cook Inlet is the most miserable I have ever come across in my life—the population insolent in their demands and altogether a miserable country."[87]

Jacobsen had hoped to go to San Francisco from Kodiak, but contrary to what traders had told him, no ship was due until September. Sitting still was not an option for this man of action, and he made brief trips to both Prince William Sound and the Copper River region. In Prince William Sound, he once again visited graves: "I made very good additions to the collection, among other things, 6 mummies . . . and a number of skulls." Traveling on to the Copper River, he "made purchases, but the people had only little." Traveling south to Alaganik, he encountered the same high prices he had on the Northwest Coast the year before: "[I] started to buy curios but the natives demanded such insolent prices that I had to give up soon—it is exactly the same here as what you find among the Tlingsian and Haida."[88]

Jacobsen finally returned to Kodiak on August 18 and ten days later boarded a ship for San Francisco. He jotted down his last journal entry on September 22, heading into San Francisco Bay. A letter from Bastian awaited him, asking Jacobsen to make a quick collecting trip to Arizona and visit the Yuma, Mohave, Yaqui, and Navajo. Bastian was less than optimistic, however, as these tribes were "roaming in scarcity" and probably did not own many things. He believed that richer prospects could be expected in the lands of the Zuni, Hopi, and Pueblo, where Jacobsen should especially direct his attention to "idols and other carvings, to masks and costumes (which however are kept secret, but should be accessible to a traveler of your experience), to clay vessels with decorations, small ornaments and tools (only of native manufacture of course) even if poorly represented."[89]

Jacobsen wrote Bastian from San Francisco that he had no great hopes for collecting much among the Zuni and Apaches, "but I will do my best, for among people so tyrannically treated by whites, one must stay a while before one can collect things." After several very disappointing weeks traveling in the Southwest, during which he gathered about 100 objects, he wrote from St. Louis, Missouri, that he had been told that the Apaches "own nothing that is not given them by the government" and that, being ill and having only $200 left for collecting, he had decided not to visit the Pueblos but to return to Europe.[90]

Jacobsen did, however, ask permission to visit the Smithsonian in Washington, D.C., "for it would be too much use for me could I take some notes there, in these surely very rich collections." On October 27, he wrote in his journal "Reached Washington. Changed my dress and went to the Schmittsonian Institute." He spent the whole day at the museum, making the acquaintance of Director Spencer F. Baird (Bastian's American counterpart) and a Professor Raus, who "showed me all the sights and there are lots of them in the Schmitzonia because it is the most complete collection of American curios in existence." The next day he had a long visit with the Alaska collector William H. Dall. The following day he saw skeletal material at the Naval Medical Museum, then went back to the Smithsonian to take notes on its collections. The fourth and final day of his visit he was invited to give a short report on his travels in America and "said farewell to all in the Schmitzonia Institute." Jacobsen set sail from New York within a week, arriving in Hamburg November 19, 1883, and Berlin four days later.[91]

UNPACKING THE COLLECTION IN BERLIN: "YOU HAVE MADE YOURSELF IMMORTAL"

In early August 1883, just as Jacobsen set sail for Kodiak, Bastian wrote the manager of the Alaska Commercial Company in Sitka, asking for word of "our traveler." Those in Berlin had not heard from him since his return from the Yukon the previous September. Less than a month later, both Bastian and Richter were relieved to receive telegrams, followed by letters. Hagenbeck wrote from Hamburg that just recently he had said to his wife that he wondered "whether my good Jacobsen is still alive." He also sent word of the museum's enthusiastic response as Jacobsen's Northwest Coast collections began to arrive: "In Berlin Prof. Bastian thinks of Jacobsen that he is the best *man* for the job one could find and how happy they are with your things you *can* see from the fact that they have already published a wonderful (artistic?) book with illustrations of your things. In one word my good Jacobsen you have made yourself immortal."[92]

Bastian sent Jacobsen a more formal greeting, saying that he was looking forward to the opportunity to welcome him in person and thanking him "for the important services rendered to ethnology with such admirable perseverance and such a correct understanding of our tasks, during the years of your exhausting voyages, with the richest success." No sooner had Jacobsen arrived in Hamburg than he received a telegram from Bastian, inviting him to a meeting in Berlin. A month later, in the name of the Support Committee, Richter invited Jacobsen to a formal banquet in his honor to be held on December 21, 1883—a solstice feast paralleling Bladder Festivals then under way in Yup'ik communities back in Alaska. At the banquet, it was announced that he would receive a "premium" of 1,500 Mark both "in honor of services rendered to science" and as partial compensation for the financial loss he had sustained during his absence. This was in addition to his salary of 200 Mark per month, totalling 6,000 Mark for two and one-half years of travel, not a large sum by contemporary standards.[93]

Both Bastian and the Support Committee had good reason to be pleased. The collection, which had begun arriving in January 1882, was spectacular, containing hundreds of items never seen until then in Europe. Even before Jacobsen's return, the Support Committee had underwritten a lavish publication, *America's Northwest Coast. The Latest Results of Ethnological Travels. From the Collections of the Royal Museums in Berlin*, containing color lithographs of a selection of the finest pieces of Jacobsen's Northwest Coast collection and an introduction by Bastian. In his report to the Royal Museum's general administration, Bastian reiterated "the magnificent success" of Jacobsen's trip:

From one of the ethnologically most important parts of the globe for which so far scientific studies had to do without the foundation of actual material, we now own a representation so comprehensive and rich as from hardly any other, and the significance of the same must be considered even higher since rescue was achieved at the last moment, for even though the tribes of the American Northwest Coast with their physically more hardy nature also resist the threatening doom better than weaker natural peoples [*Naturvölker*], their psychic originalities are still, as is confirmed more irrefutably by every bit of news currently coming in, in a process of the most rapid disintegration and disappearance.

Bastian finally noted that the achievements of both his "traveler" and the Support Committee were being praised by the discipline.[94]

However pleased he was with the quality and quantity of objects, Bastian was not blind to Jacobsen's shortcomings. As he worked on documents accompanying the Northwest Coast material before Jacobsen's return, he noted the collector's "passing attention" to "legends and customs." Bastian hoped that Jacobsen would add more information when he returned, grist for the scientific mill. Even so, he felt fortunate that Jacobsen's "rescue operation" had been in time. Over the next ten years, the Support Committee would send out many expeditions under Bastian's direction, filling the shelves of the Royal Museum during a decade of collecting not surpassed before or since. Bastian was convinced that they had intervened "to do the right thing at the right time." He wrote: "Surveying in the rooms of the museum the halls and closets which have been filled with collections by the travelers sent out by the committee, then it seems to be a kind of conquest of the world, because almost all parts of our globe are represented in documents which have since become unobtainable, fallen prey to an inevitable doom." In 1898 a less-fortunate collector for the Royal Museum would write: "I myself unfortunately did not come . . . in Bastian's famous twelfth hour, but towards 4:30 in the morning, when it was an uncertain twilight, neither day nor night, in one word the most unpleasant, most desolate hour."[95]

Jacobsen spent the winter back in Berlin unpacking and cataloging his collection. One immediate result was a special exhibit in the rooms of the old stock exchange on Museum Island. The Berlin Anthropological Society arranged a private viewing on March 19, 1884, "to visit the most wonderful and significant ethnological collection which has ever been brought together by one collector in one region of our globe." The formal announcement noted that the big hall contained 4,000 objects from Alaska while the other 3,000 artifacts were "still swimming at sea." Scholars and donors were invited to view bone and stone items related directly to their own prehistory.

While Ingalik objects were seen as tainted "by the influence of the white traders . . . the Eskimo things belong to the full fledged Stone Age . . . which could be considered as a kind of mirror image of a previous development of our own [European] prehistoric time." Professor Rudolf Virchow, the article noted, had already pointed out that "a peculiarly shaped [Eskimo] scraper resembles one found in a [prehistoric] Swiss pole house." The elaborate Yup'ik masks Jacobsen had collected were not even mentioned, as they were not considered comparable evidence of antiquity.[96]

Many who had followed Jacobsen's journey through his letters, which were printed as news items in Adrian Woldt's scientific newsletters, flocked to the exhibition. It received rave reviews. Following the Berlin Anthropological Society's private showing, Crown Prince Friedrich and the Prussian minister of culture attended a gala opening, during which Jacobsen and Bastian conducted these luminaries on an exhibit tour. Nine months later, the king approved 25,000 Mark for the Royal Museum's acquisition of the remainder of the collection.[97]

Along with objects of bone and stone, the exhibition also included seventy-four pieces of nephrite (jade) that Jacobsen had collected with such enthusiasm, well aware of the anthropological interest they would generate. This interest in nephrite came from the fact that, although it was known to exist in raw form only in Turkestan, East Asia, Siberia, and New Zealand, its use was much more widespread, notably in European Neolithic sites. The distribution of nephrite tools was an important question in diffusionist ethnology of the time. Scholars had elaborated the theory that it had been brought to Europe by "Aryan" migrations from Asia. Other scholars disputed this theory, saying that there were probably other sources of nephrite not yet known to geologists. Until 1883, only objects made of jadeite (a jadelike stone, but not true jade) had been found in the Americas (from Mexico, South and Central America, and most recently Alaska). Thus, the nephrite objects Jacobsen brought home caused quite a stir in anthropological circles, and both he and Bastian received a number of scholarly queries: Had Jacobsen actually seen raw nephrite in situ, were these places venerated by the Natives, were jade objects plentiful, and might they be exported to Asia or Mexico? The geologist Andreas Arzruni (who had published several articles on stone axes and on nephrite in different areas of the world) asked Bastian to supply a splinter of the presumed nephrite for analysis, and Jacobsen himself published a description of his finds in the popular journal *Globus*.[98]

THE TRAVELER'S BOOK: "TREASURES OF MEMORY"

Along with work unpacking his collection and preparing it for exhibition, Jacobsen spent his first months back from Alaska working on transforming his journal into a travel book. Bastian spearheaded this project, and no sooner had Jacobsen returned to European soil than Bastian began to look for a publisher for his traveler's accounts. He first wrote to Hermann Costenoble of Jena: "It is Capt. Jacobsen, who sent out . . . [to the Royal Museum, enriched the same with incomparable valuable collections, but at the same time brings back a wealth of observations from hardly known . . . regions of the far North, some of which he was the first European to traverse. The characteristics of the local tribes . . . intertwined with the personal adventures . . . I wanted to notify you first, because the book seems to fall into the class of those that you requested several times: popular and attractive, though on a scientifically valuable foundation." In correspondence on Jacobsen's behalf, Bastian depicted his protégé's memories as fleeting and in as much need of salvage as the primitive cultures he had been sent out to document:

To the luck and skill with which they were made is added an extraordinary observational talent, and our traveler, as I could see from our conversations, is full of a wealth of the most precious treasures of memory, as valuable for science (totally new in part), as they are attractive and exciting for the listener, because they deal with the wondrous habits of all kinds of tribes whose names are hardly known so far, and adventurous experiences on top of that, on a daring voyage at sea and on shore, high up into the far North, up to the outermost of the Eskimo tribes hardly ever visited by Europeans. You can imagine that it is my strong wish to see the personal experiences of the traveler fixed, that is to say printed in a book, and that before it is too late, because the restless guest wants to leave again already and there will scarcely be a few months' time.[99]

Publisher Max Spohr of Leipzig wrote to Jacobsen that he had read in the newspaper of his intention to produce an account of his travels. Spohr promised to produce "a beautiful edition, worthy of the high value of the work." He and Bastian were in communication, and by early March 1884 a contract was signed. Spohr requested that they specify the illustrations so that work on woodcuts could start at once. Both Bastian and Jacobsen wanted to publish the book as soon as possible, and Spohr said it could be done. Spohr did not even have the complete manuscript in hand before he began moving it through the publication process. Bastian apologized for this irregularity, noting that this was "because Jacobsen, who is not inclined to sit still, only consented to becoming a writer after prolonged persuasion, and also because he, as a Norwegian needs to have the assistance of a writer to bring everything into the right form. This writer has fortunately been found."[100]

The writer Bastian referred to was Adrian Woldt, a scientific journalist and member of the Berlin Anthropological Society. He and Jacobsen worked together to transform Jacobsen's rough journal account into a polished presentation. In mid-January 1884, Jacobsen wrote to his fiancée Hedwig Klopfer (fig. 9), that in the mornings at the museum he sorted his collections, and from 3 until 8 P.M. or later he and Woldt worked on his travelogue: "I do it less for my profit but to make my name as a traveler better known."[101]

Although Jacobsen and Woldt appear to have collaborated amicably, Jacobsen was not entirely happy with the arrange-

9 Hedwig Klopfer as a young woman. Johannes Adrian Jacobsen Jr.

ment. He complained to Hedwig: "My writer is a capable man in his trade and I have known him for years, but an unpleasant character—and I have to give him half the income." Jacobsen wished, not for the last time, that Hedwig (a native German) already was his wife so that she could be his writer and they could put the money into their own pockets. The original agreement called for Jacobsen and Woldt to split the publisher's fee of 1,400 Mark. By February 27, Woldt's share had increased to 1,000 Mark, and in the end Jacobsen got only 250 Mark. Although Woldt hoped to collaborate with Jacobsen on future writing projects, his high fee was certainly one reason the two never worked together again.[102]

A comparison between Jacobsen's unpublished Alaska journals and Woldt's published version shows that Woldt may have been worth his fee. Probably it was Woldt who edited out most of Jacobsen's complaints and in their place added many complimentary flourishes, including naming more lakes, rivers, and volcanoes after Bastian and individual members of the Support Committee. Otherwise, the published account reads remarkably close to the unpublished journal. Jacobsen gave Woldt his journals to work from, and it is likely that the two went through them together page by page so that Jacobsen could expand upon particular events. Thus, he had an opportunity soon after his return to retell the high points of his trip while they were still fresh in his mind. A greater gap exists between Woldt's account and romanticized versions that Jacobsen published years later, especially *The White Frontier,* than between Woldt's account and the original unpublished journals.

Jacobsen kept busy working with Woldt for much of March 1884. He wrote to Hedwig that he would not be able to visit her as promised because the publisher wanted him to meet with the cartographer, and Woldt needed him to stay in Berlin to finish the manuscript by the end of the month. Woldt also consulted Bastian on prepublication publicity: "[T]o [honor] Jacobsen more now I would like to offer [excerpts] to some political newspapers. . . . For instance for the *Nationalzeitung* I am thinking of 'Among the Cannibals of Vancouver.'"[103]

The book, titled *Captain Jacobsen's Journey to the Northwest Coast of America, 1881–1883,* came out in July 1884 after numerous small delays. Although it got good reviews, it did not sell well, and even Spohr, who was in this line of publishing "more out of personal interest than for profit," was not optimistic that he would recover his costs. Woldt believed that the book's high price (15 Mark) and its "bad promotion" by Hagenbeck's colleague, Fritz von Schirp, in *Berliner Nachrichten,* which was read in scientific circles "with a mere shrug," were responsible for its lackluster sales. Here Woldt touched on the fine line Jacobsen walked all his life between popular culture and science. He warned Jacobsen: "Our scientific circles have very tender ears for such things. When Hagenbeck lets Schirp write a leaflet for him that doesn't concern you, and no one will take Mr. Hagenbeck for a scholar anyway; but you have to preserve your reputation as scientific traveler for the future." Woldt concluded that Hagenbeck's business would also run better "if he used a bit more science in it." Ironically Spohr later noted that one reason for poor sales was the book's overly academic title, which he found "not at all thrilling." Perhaps the book's best praise came from friends back in Alaska. Henry Neumann wrote Jacobsen from St. Michael that he found his description of Alaska very truthful.[104]

JACOBSEN'S ACCESSION RECORDS: FACT AND FICTION

Woldt assembled Jacobsen's most important observations about the people and places he had seen during his two and one-half years traveling in North America into a published account, which Erna Gunther published in English in abridged form in 1977 (fig. 10). Information on the objects he collected, however, had a different trajectory. If Woldt's editing helped to gain Jacobsen immortality in the world of letters, Jacobsen's creative use of language in the thousands of pages of accession records he compiled to accompany his collection have gained him a different kind of notoriety among would-be translators and museum professionals.[105] While traveling, Jacobsen kept lists of objects collected, including where he had obtained them, sometimes adding Native names. He occasionally identified a particular village but more often gave general geographic locations, such as "Kwikpagemuit" or "Kuigpakmutten" for Kuigpagmiut (people of the Yukon River, from Kuigpak, literally, "Big River"). He also affixed cardboard tags to each object, on which he wrote some basic information. During the winter of 1884, he used these lists and tags as the basis for close to seven thousand individual records for the objects he brought home. Jacobsen fell short of writing an accession card for every object, and an unidentified staff member later finished the task based on Jacobsen's tags and lists. Although both the original lists and handwritten records remain, most tags referred to while writing the accession cards have since been destroyed.[106]

Jacobsen presumably collected most of his information during his travels, some from Native informants and some from non-Native travelers and traders. Although the journals themselves contain little specific information on objects, Jacobsen often refers to detailed conversations, as when the Alaska Commercial Company agent, Mr. Karnkoff, gave him "long descriptions of the customs of the people," albeit in Russian.[107]

Some entries were short and easy to translate. For example, the object numbered IVA7259 is simply identified as a wooden snuff box. Other objects were given detailed descriptions, such as IVA5230, a Nushagak harpoon, which merited a long paragraph. Some accession information is clearly secondhand, gathered after the fact. For example, a letter from Alexander Mackenzie acknowledges receipt of Jacobsen's inquiry about the meaning of the "heraldic pole" he had collected the year before. Mackenzie had spoken to the person from whom Jacobsen had made the purchase and was able to send Jacobsen its name, history, and an explanation of its emblems. Such long-distance fieldwork was nothing to be ashamed of in the late nineteenth century, when collections often were increased in the same fashion.[108]

Although Jacobsen's methods were not by definition suspect, their results were inconsistent. Jacobsen's contemporary, the young ethnologist Franz Boas was perhaps his greatest critic. Both used the same interpreter, George Hunt, during their work on the Northwest Coast, and Boas later used many of the objects Jacobsen collected in 1881 and 1882 to illustrate his 1895 article "The Social Organization and Secret Societies of the Kwakiutl Indians." Boas complained, however, that Jacobsen's data were unreliable and in an 1887 article refuted a number of explanations Jacobsen gave for his Northwest Coast material, supplying "correct" interpretation of the animals depicted and associated myths. Jacobsen took Boas's attack head on and in an 1891 article on Northwest Coast secret societies pointed out that, although his descriptions were in conflict with Boas's reports, "I believe full accountability for what I say can be accepted, since I know a great deal from my own observations and I have learned much from my brother Filip," then living and working in British Columbia.[109]

It would be easy, based on long-term fieldwork and information obtained from living elders, to point out the numerous errors and inconsistencies in Jacobsen's accession records for Yup'ik objects. Instead, the body of this book attempts to search out and highlight the original information found there. While Jacobsen was certainly no Boas or Nelson, he included much that is useful. Many masks, for example, are accompanied by long, rambling accounts that, while not entirely accurate, make clear how complex their original stories were.

The amount of information contained in the accession records is both a blessing and a curse. Much is "original" in more than one sense. Previously unknown and never before published, it has both linguistic and ethnographic value, but it also is original in form, displaying creative spellings and unique grammatical constructions that have frustrated more than one translator. Jacobsen spoke the low-German Hamburg dialect that he had learned when he worked for his brother, and he wrote accordingly. It was not until much later in life that he mastered German script.

10   This picture makes clear who the two persons on the cover of Erna Gunther's 1977 translation of Jacobsen's 1884 publication really are: on the left Jacobsen, on the right his friend Adolf Schoepf, the director of the Dresden zoo. In this reversed photo, the original studio portrait made in Dresden has been altered and shows Jacobsen on the right and Schoepf on the left, with a photo of Henry D. Woolfe, Jacobsen's traveling companion, pasted over it. The photo may have been altered for use as a model for a woodcut to be published in Jacobsen's book to show Jacobsen and Wolfe traveling together. Hamburg Archives.

Throughout his museum career, Jacobsen received mixed messages concerning his command of German. As early as 1881, even before the Support Committee decided to send him to collect in Alaska, he was assured that his limited German was not a problem. Bastian's assistant, Mr. Bauer, wrote Jacobsen that he had forwarded his letter on to the director: "You should not be ashamed of your grammar in front of him, after all you are a foreigner, and writing in German is *very difficult* for all foreigners."[110] Yet Jacobsen's concern that his rough German keep him from being taken seriously was not unfounded. His letters and journals often displayed a fascinatingly original use of language, as if he recognized no boundaries between German and his native Norwegian. Sometimes it is difficult to tell which language he was using. In naming people and places, his orthography was consistently inconsistent, even within the same paragraph, and his punctuation was minimal. This grammatical creativity was not restricted to personal papers. Jacobsen displayed the same style in the thousands of accession records he penned for the museum. He had his good and bad days: Some records are clear, while others are impossible to understand, let alone translate.[111]

Jacobsen recognized his failings and remained sensitive about his command of German throughout his life. In 1883 the director of Dresden's Museum of Anthropology and Ethnology, A. B. Meyer, wrote with a question on nephrite. He began his letter in German, then switched to English because, he noted, Jacobsen seemed to be more fluent in that language. Jacobsen took great pains to respond in perfect German. Unfortunately, the dozens of accession records Jacobsen penned daily during the winter of 1884 do not reflect comparable attention to detail.[112]

CHOOSING A COMPANION FOR LIFE: "MY DARLING ADRIAN"

When Jacobsen returned to Berlin in November 1883, Bastian and Hagenbeck were not the only ones glad to see him. Jacobsen had left a sweetheart in Dresden, twenty-year-old Hedwig Klopfer. A native of Werdau, near Zwickau, Hedwig and her mother moved to Dresden after her father's death. Jacobsen's sister-in-law, Henny, would later admonish him: "You should not torture the poor girl for nothing. There really aren't that many selfless people here on earth who like us just for our own sakes; unfortunately we often come to this realization too late, and we should not let ourselves be taken in by a shiny outside, and take *no colorful pebble* for a *jewel*. You see, I for my side, when it comes to preaching morals, am just as hopeless as you when it comes to flirting! Well, in the end it might be a birth defect in you and you can't help it."[113]

The "birth defect" that Henny referred to was Jacobsen's recurrent womanizing. Letters scattered throughout his personal archive attest to his philandering ways. For example, several months after his arrival in Alaska, his friend Henry Neumann wrote from St. Michael, asking how he liked the "Eskimettes" as he traveled north: "Have they a pretty young one? . . . Anikan, Masha, Palisha, Akulina, and a whole regiment of other beauties are sending their regards." Later he teased: "The womenfolk are always asking me when you are coming back." On his way home from Alaska, Jacobsen found himself the object of a schoolgirl's crush, and he received a letter addressed to "my dear darling Adrian" from Maria Langrehr, the fourteen-year-old daughter of the German family who hosted him while he was in San Francisco.[114]

Back in Germany, Jacobsen rekindled his relationship with Hedwig, whom he had courted but broken with before his departure, and they were engaged in early December 1883. The day after leaving for Berlin, he wrote to her in Dresden: "It still seems like a dream to me, this morning I asked myself if it is really true, that we belong to each other, I had got used to the thought that I should die an old bachelor—in fact I have always doubted that I was at all capable of making a woman happy, especially since I am condemned to lead a true nomad's life." The letter continues with a note of disappointment uncharacteristic of both Jacobsen's Alaska journals and less personal correspondence. He points out that his letters cannot be like those a young man writes to his bride, "when everything is full of light—when the whole spirit is full of optimism and hope—it is rather that of a man who goes toward the future with knowledge—and as you know—where there is knowledge, illusions are chased away. How I would love to trade with youth once more, and would let experience go. Perhaps then my life would not become such a series of shipwrecks as it has been. Now you shall become the saving plank that will guide me across all stormy waters, but do you [know] how much the wreck is ruined, to which you have entrusted yourself as pilot, and the consequences which will come from this?"[115]

To what disappointments did Jacobsen allude, so recently returned from such a successful expedition? In public he appeared more gallant schooner than wreck. True, he had been warmly received in Berlin, but at age thirty, his future line of work remained unclear. He knew already that his work in the museum would probably be brief and the best he could hope for was to be sent on another collecting trip. Although he had proved himself a capable "man of action," his immigrant standing and social class put definite limits on his rise in the museum world, Bastian's encouraging words not withstanding. More serious still were his "rough speech" and lack of formal education. The fieldwork of educated men such as Boas and Nelson was informed by their scholarship, whereas Jacobsen remained "Bastian's traveler," always acting under instructions.

Another sore point was the fact that the two and one-half years he had spent traveling for the Royal Museum had been a financial loss. Jacobsen considered the 1,500 Mark the Support Committee had given him as a percentage of the profit "a ridiculous sum," although his employers probably thought it more than generous for the immigrant son of a Norwegian fisherman. He later wrote Hedwig: "I am almost sorry to have collected all these beautiful things [for these Berliners] because one must starve in the process." Hedwig tried to bolster his confidence: "My dear sheep you write you will have to continue for some more years to lead a nomad's life now, if you have the earnest wish . . . why shouldn't it be possible to find something better for you . . . than the wild traveling life, see perhaps Mr. Hagenbeck will be able to be your angel. . . . Should you go on another voyage then at least take better care not to go to all that trouble for nothing but to get a good profit from it."[116]

Hedwig also advised Jacobsen on a more personal matter, encouraging him to be faithful: "If you my darling had many vices, so for my sake and for your own, make yourself strong, and seek to chase away the evil thoughts, think of the future . . . you won't stay young forever, in old age you would repent it all the more. . . . The thought not to see you here for Christmas, that you may perhaps have a good time with another young girl, is painful to me, well maybe you will be true to your word since you wanted to remain *true* and love *truly* from now on." Jacobsen assured her that he would not look at other girls since he had the most beautiful for himself, but added: "Write me soon. . . . You know that I am a child of the moment and what is nearest to me makes the strongest impression."[117]

A touching exchange occurred just before Christmas, when Hedwig sent Jacobsen thanks for the gift of a pin: "It's just that you shouldn't have bought me a pin, there's that superstition that all piercing objects pierce love apart, now imagine my worry if that should happen." Jacobsen protested: "You say that it shouldn't have been a pin because the pin destroys love. That cannot be, since the pin is made especially to reunite divided parts, to fit together what was torn . . . so, you see . . . a pin should precisely be a good omen for love." Ironically, Jacobsen's objection parallels his published complaints about the "foolish superstitions" and taboos of the Yupiit, who likewise admonished against the use of sharp objects in some contexts lest the soul's path to the land of the dead be cut or obscured. In another exchange that contemporary Yupiit would have found familiar, Jacobsen asked Hedwig to help him to follow the right path in his future work: "I know this is asking for much but much is needed, and because I think that you are capable of it all so I have chosen you as companion for life."[118]

TO SIBERIA IN 1884: "PRINCE OF COLLECTORS"

Adrian and Hedwig's correspondence is laced with plans for the future. Even before his solstice fete with the Support Committee, he wrote that Hagenbeck had visited him in Berlin and that he had decided to return to Alaska with his own money: "Who risks nothing, gains nothing. This time I will risk everything, if I win we can get married by next winter and if I lose I will shoot a bullet through my head." Plans remained unsettled, however, and he intended to ask the Support Committee how much they would be willing to pay him per year as "their traveler." Just after Christmas, it was decided that he would work at the museum until late March 1884, then with Hagenbeck's assistance return to Alaska to put together another ethnic exhibition. Hagenbeck had found that he could hire four or five Eskimos with labrets for six months for $1,500 to $2,000 per month, and Jacobsen hoped to make good money. It was even possible that he might stay, and he asked Hedwig how she would like to live in America.[119]

During the months of uncertainty immediately following Jacobsen's return, Hagenbeck and Bastian vied for his allegiance. Hagenbeck advised caution in dealing with the museum: "Just don't say any more than necessary since you will not get much gratitude, those good people do not know such a thing. More when I talk to you, just don't tell Woldt too much." He wrote that he could understand that the Support Committee did not want to let Jacobsen go, but under the circumstances no one could blame Jacobsen if he left them, as "everyone is closest to himself" (a proverb meaning you have to take care of your own interests first). Bastian, on his side, worked to keep Jacobsen in Berlin. Not only did he find a publisher and writer for his travel book, he spoke repeatedly to the Support Committee on Jacobsen's behalf. In a mid-February letter to the committee, for example, he related the matter of Jacobsen's financial losses during his absence, saying that they were obliged to help him out, and asked the committee's support to "keep him in Berlin."[120]

Jacobsen's friend and traveling companion, Henry D. Wolfe, also stayed in touch, telling of the articles he had written about their trip and hoping that Hagenbeck would pay for the two of them to return to Alaska and "go for mammoth bones." He wrote again from Point Hope in July encouraging Jacobsen to return as "there are quantities of curios to be bought here."[121]

As for Jacobsen, if he could not land a steady job at the museum (which his lack of academic training made unlikely) he, too, preferred the life of a collector to other career options. In March he wrote Hedwig that he had been asked to head a company being formed for herring fishing off Iceland. He refused, however, "because it suits me better to be Indian and Eskimo catcher than some herring catcher." Still planning to return to Alaska, he invited his younger brother, Johan Filip, to move from Hamburg (where he was living with their brother Johan Martin) to Berlin to help unpack the collection and so begin to learn how to handle artifacts, as he wanted to take him on his next trip. Jacobsen's plans, however, remained unsettled. The Alaska Commercial Company sent word that prices were up, making trading more expensive, and if he got to St. Michael he risked having to spend the winter. To make matters worse, in early April he and Hagenbeck met with Bastian, who stubbornly refused to let Jacobsen go before the end of the month.[122]

On April 18, 1884, Jacobsen unpacked the last box at the museum. He wrote Hedwig that the book manuscript was at page 400, illustrations almost complete, and that he planned to visit the cartographer to check place names. As promised, Bastian (who had already heard of Jacobsen's engagement to Hedwig) spoke to the committee about Jacobsen's future. He regretted that the museum had no funds to hire travelers but must wait until after the move to the new building when the state might give them more money. He wrote Jacobsen that the committee was willing to send him on another trip with a higher salary. In two years Jacobsen might be able to get a permanent position at the museum and have a more quiet life, but the salary would be no more than 3,000 Mark a year. Although not part of the Royal Museum's scientific staff, the conservator, Eduard Krause, was paid 2,900 Mark annually and was of much more use to the museum than Jacobsen could be as a nontraveler since Krause wrote scholarly articles and reports. Jacobsen concluded that it would be best to continue as a traveler for the time being, and if the museum could offer him a proper salary in two years' time he would take it, enabling him and Hedwig to settle down.[123]

In early May the Support Committee sent Bastian formal notice of the successful conclusion of their first expedition and plans for their second. After purchase of Jacobsen's collections by the museum, a profit of slightly less than 3,000 Mark remained. The committee gave this "as extra payment to Captain Jacobsen, who has only received a very small compensation for his manifold efforts." At the same time, they approved the plan to send him on a second, yearlong expedition to Siberia, the Amur region, and Sakhalin with estimated costs of between 15,000 and 18,000 Mark. Jacobsen wrote Hedwig that his salary was to be 6,000 Mark, "which is pretty nice for a man with such insignificant schooling." This expedition delayed but did not cancel his work for Hagenbeck gathering Natives for a *Völkerschau*. Fillip left Germany that summer for British Columbia, where he immediately started buying things to accompany an exhibition of the so-called "Longheads" of Quatsino Inlet (Kwakiutl with artificially deformed craniums). Jacobsen planned to meet Fillip in Victoria the next spring at the conclusion of his work for the museum.[124]

Jacobsen's Siberian trip began well. He left Berlin at the end of May 1884, and six weeks later wrote Hedwig a teasing letter while aboard a steamer on Lake Baikal:

I found yesterday on my return a letter from Prof. Bastian in which he flatters me prettily by calling me the prince of all collectors, and plans to send me on my return on an expedition to the South Sea and says among other things that even if I should enter into the port of marriage, it would not hinder the trip since on such a trip— I could take my wife along.

Are you coming? It would be very educational for you . . . then you will have opportunity to walk under palm trees, to bathe every morning together with sharks in the green sea, . . . but bananas and fried pheasant you like to eat? Well we will see, since a lot of water may run on the beach before it comes to that.

He concluded: "My big [totem] pole which I brought from America was the first piece in the New Museum—a good omen isn't it?"[125]

By October Jacobsen congratulated himself on already reaching Sakhalin, collecting as he went. Bastian had advised him to focus on things preserved "in primitive originality." Altai objects, for example, were not so interesting to the museum since they were strongly influenced by the well-known styles of surrounding peoples. Krause wrote to Jacobsen that initially Bastian was not satisfied with the shipments from Siberia, as they included too many pieces of clothing and too few articles relating to religion. Krause, however, drew his director's attention to the extraordinary embroidery, and finally Bastian began to appreciate it: "Your last shipments from the Goldis and Gilyaks are quite excellent again, quite 'Jacobsen.' How do you manage to get the folks to part with all their idols? When I go down the great row of the latter I am always amazed that they have not killed you yet, you kidnapper en gros of saints. Well, bravo! As you well know, the things connected with the soul-life of peoples arouse the most interest."[126]

As during his year in Alaska, Jacobsen was less effective in recording "pagan customs" than in obtaining associated artifacts. He wrote Bastian from Kazan:

I could not get much information concerning evident remains of religious customs. The same is true here that I said in my last letter, . . . the people are intimidated, but I met some enlightened ones who were willing to give me a demonstration of the hocus-pocus of divine worship as it was customary among their forefathers. But since the whole act is said to consist of no more than bowing, etc., about which enough has been written already, I declined as I had to hurry to get on.[127]

Traveling for the Royal Museum again, Jacobsen exuded self-confidence. He admonished Hedwig to continue to study English so that she might help him become a famous man. He also privately stated his preference to continue working for the Royal Museum: "You see in principle I like the position at the museum better than with Hagenbeck, one gets a lot of honor during the trip and is linked to far less worry, because once the collections are packed into a box I have little to worry about— but with the people the worries just start the day one has hired them."

Over the next twelve months, Jacobsen traveled overland from Germany to the Far East, gathering an enormous quantity of objects on the way. He first collected from the Finns living along the Volga, crossed the Kirgiz Steppe, visited the Altai Kalmucks, then turned to the still-pagan Buryats on the upper Lena River, finally reaching the Amur River region. He traveled downriver by steamer and rented boat, collecting among the Goldi. From the mouth of the Amur, he traveled to Sakhalin for the winter. Returning to mainland Asia, he traveled through Korea, finally making a side trip to Japan, where he bought Hedwig "ethnographic objects to turn our parlor into a museum." He liked the Far East but found it expensive: "All is so entirely different here from Europe."[128]

Although Jacobsen obtained many fine pieces, he judged this collection trip one of his most difficult. From Biysk, Russia, he wrote Bastian that even deep in the mountains "people do not sell any of their religious paraphernalia—when the governor wanted a shaman's coat it had to be taken with the help of the military." Concerning collecting in Siberia, he noted: "In later years when the people are less superstitious it will be possible to make a nice collection here, as it is now we have to take everything almost by force and pay dearly at that, it's a stubborn people." Work on Sakhalin was also hard and expensive, yielding relatively little. In the winter he saw the Sakhalin Ainu, whom he judged "nothing original any more."[129]

BRINGING BELLA COOLA TO EUROPE: 1885

In May 1885, Jacobsen left Japan to join his brother Fillip, who had been making collections in British Columbia in preparation for Hagenbeck's planned *Völkerschau*. The pair arrived in Victoria in early June and initially tried to hire a group of Kwakiutl "Longheads." But the Indians changed their minds and fled while the brothers were away on Vancouver Island making collections to accompany the show. They were able to replace them with nine Bella Coola men in Victoria.[130]

Hagenbeck told Jacobsen to let him know as soon as he had hired the Indians and to send descriptions of their repertoire so that he could look for venues. Hagenbeck was no neophyte in the business of "people shows," and he expected success: "As you know I had in these last 8 years something like 900 foreign peoples here with me in Europe and all were sent back promptly and richly rewarded and many of these people are wealthy now and lead a carefree life and the people you are to engage now I will also look after in just the same way."[131]

Jacobsen and his troupe arrived in Hamburg on August 15, 1885, and set out immediately on tour from town to town. As it turned out, Hagenbeck actually had booked few venues, and plans were made and remade as they went along. As part of the show, the troupe demonstrated "original dances" of the Bella Coola. Over time, however, these performances were expanded, both to meet audience expectations and to reduce boredom among troupe members. Costumes and repertoire were also varied to incorporate the eclectic mix of Bella Coola, Tsimshian, and Tlingit material that the brothers had collected.[132]

Although the year passed without major disaster, it also passed without marked success. In October Jacobsen complained to Bastian that the show was a financial failure. Apparently the Bella Coola did not look like the stereotypic "red Indians," and more than one newspaper accused the show of being a sham. To the public, the sacred dances were almost completely incomprehensible. Audiences were also disappointed that the troupe consisted of only men (the typical *Völkerschau* displayed family groups). Not unlike his complaints that "Nielsen" had spoiled his chances in Alaska, Jacobsen's correspondence continually complained about poor attendance and a cool reception by European audiences. Toward the end of the trip, the Bella Coola themselves were also the objects of his dissatisfaction. He wrote: "Today is the last day with the people and I am not sorry for it, because it is a miserable business, and never will be anything else. The people also now make no more effort, they don't want to work anymore." The novelty also had worn off for the Bella Coola, and they were ready to go home.[133] One bright spot during the year was Jacobsen's marriage to Hedwig on November 21, 1885, in Dresden, where Jacobsen had an address in the zoological garden, after which he continued on tour with the Bella Coola.

In contrast to the general public, the scholarly reaction to this "ethnic exhibition" was enthusiastic. Opening performances in Berlin included lectures by renowned German physical anthropologist Rudolf Virchow, Adolf Bastian, and another eminent Northwest Coast traveler, Aurel Krause. Bastian's young assistant, Franz Boas, was also in the audience. Boas worked with the Bella Coola while they were in Berlin, also worked in Jacobsen's collection at the museum, and later traveled to British Columbia to carry out additional studies. Jacobsen's work with Northwest Coast people and material turned out to be a critical foil against which Boas, a founding father of twentieth-century American anthropology, would later measure his success.[134]

CROSSROADS: TO INDONESIA IN 1887

Jacobsen kept in touch with Bastian during his year traveling with the Bella Coola. Correspondence included negotiations regarding the sale of the collection that the brothers had made to accompany their show as well as inquiries about prospects for future trips. A June 1885 letter reminded Bastian that he had said that there might be a position at the museum during the move to the new building. The Bella Coola would be leaving the following month, and Jacobsen would be out of a job again:

Wouldn't it be possible to arrange for a position for me with a yearly fixed salary in the Ethnological Museum? I would gladly undertake a journey again later if I had hope of getting a fixed position. As you know esteemed Professor I have gotten quite familiar with ethnology and I would almost find it wrong if I had to give it up altogether, I am so to speak at the crossroads of life where it is time to choose something specific and only two things remain to me either emigrate to America, or try to get into a business here. With ethnographic exhibitions, which I counted on with such certainty last year nothing is to be done at the moment because competition is too great and public interest too small.

This was neither the first nor the last time Jacobsen pressed Bastian to give him a "fixed position," and Bastian's response was invariable: No job today, but ask again tomorrow. In this case, Bastian regretted that the position of worker during the move was already occupied but thought that something might open up in summer or fall. In closing he advised Jacobsen to have a catalog printed of the Northwest Coast collection that he had gathered to accompany the Bella Coola exhibition to send to museums in America and Russia.[135]

Following this exchange, Jacobsen wrote Hedwig that since neither Hagenbeck nor the museum could offer him work, he would accept her brother's offer to go into the straw-hat business with him in Dresden. He remarked that the by-then-pregnant Hedwig seemed to have as little enthusiasm for the project as he did, but they needed to settle on something. Bastian offered part-time museum work a month later, but it was too late—Hedwig was already in Dresden making arrangements for their move, and Jacobsen conceded that he would have to learn a lot about making straw hats.[136]

On July 21, 1886, the Bella Coola set sail for home accompanied by Fillip, who would remain in British Columbia as a fur trader, becoming in future years a collector in his own right. Less than a week later, Hedwig had a baby boy, whom they named Harald. By fall the straw-hat business was launched, financed in part by Jacobsen's loan of 7,800 Mark to Hedwig's brother, Emil Hugo Klopfer, to be paid back when he sold his business. Although Jacobsen apparently made some attempt to establish himself in Dresden, his career as a hat maker was short lived. On November 5, 1886, he wrote to Bastian that he was once again in search of employment, complaining that his brother-in-law was "totally different than the people I am used to" and that "I am too little of a businessman to be of much use." Bemoaning the fact that his earlier luck had left him, he pleaded for work, including traveling if necessary.[137]

Bastian again responded that the museum had no position for Jacobsen at the moment, but he thought he might be able to find funds to send him to a part of the world from which the museum lacked objects. He cautioned that funds would be limited and that Jacobsen would be able to go on only short trips from a base and would have to find other ways of making money to support himself. Ideas for profitable enterprises were never lacking in Jacobsen's fertile imagination. If his occupations over the years were diverse and eclectic, the possibilities he contemplated were even more so. Usually he was considering two or three ideas at a time. Just before he took up the hat business, he was in correspondence with a Mr. Nielson and others developing a zoological garden. Following the straw-hat fiasco, he wrote to Mr. Frank of the Alaska Commercial Company about a possible position, but nothing was available. Hagenbeck wrote to him in March 1887, applauding Jacobsen's idea of going to Japan with a trained elephant and promising to support him if things went well. Several years later, animal trader J. Menges wrote that he thought Jacobsen's idea of a whaling station on Sakhalin would be profitable if he could find investors: "In Germany people are afraid to start something like that . . . [but] in England or in the United States you would be most likely to find the money."[138]

In the end, Jacobsen accepted Bastian's offer to go on a collecting trip to the "Indian Archipelago" (Indonesia) with ornithologist H. Kuhn, who was familiar with local languages. Jacobsen wrote Hedwig from Berlin that he would leave by the end of September 1887, and that, although separation would be hard, they must accept it. He feared that they would lose all the money they had loaned her brother. Meanwhile, the infamous Fritz von Schirp had written in several papers that Jacobsen was going to India "to open up the land for trade," and Bastian was furious.[139]

On September 5, 1887, Hedwig telegramed her husband that their second son, Paul, had arrived. Jacobsen wrote back immediately, expressing joy mixed with regret that he could not leave Berlin as he was in the middle of negotiations with Richter concerning his expedition. Hedwig's next letter spoke of her loneliness and fear for the future. As yet no one knew of the baby's birth, only her sister and brother-in-law came to see her, and she felt like a girl who had borne an illegitimate child.[140]

Jacobsen and Kuhn departed from Hamburg on October 1, 1887. Jacobsen wrote to Hedwig often during their passage to Singapore, where they arrived November 11. His first reaction was that he might stay and start a tobacco plantation on Sumatra, and he told Hedwig that he was sure she would like it there. He had no confidence that he would be able to find a position in Germany, nor did he believe he would get a position at the museum. He suffered from the separation a great deal, and he saw from her letters that she suffered, too.[141]

From Singapore the pair traveled by way of Surabaya to Macassar, where they purchased a Native boat and continued their journey. Jacobsen hated the tropical heat. To make matters worse, he contracted malaria and could not go on to the Philippines. He later wrote: "When I fell ill during the 2nd year here I did not feel so much the physical decrepitude, but more the depression laying itself on my soul from the view of the lush green of the tropical flora covered in dust by the dry monsoon. I closed my eyes and felt refreshed by the memories of my native Polar Sea with its cold, healthy, pure air. At that time my preference for the North was definitely decided, and it has also been my outward fate to visit the South no more." This third and final expedition ended Jacobsen's collecting activities for the Royal Museum, and he returned to Germany in October 1888, having assembled more than one-fifth of their collections.[142]

WORK IN MUSEUMS: "UNGRATEFUL MEN OF SCIENCE"

Bastian wrote to Jacobsen in November 1888 following his return, saying that he would notify him when the work of putting up the new museum's Asian exhibit had progressed far enough for him to help with the Indonesian material. As always, Bastian stated that they might temporarily hire Jacobsen while continuing to seek a permanent position for him in Berlin. Bastian also encouraged Jacobsen to publish material from his travels. During the next five years, Jacobsen published close to two dozen articles in both popular and scientific journals, hoping that these scholarly pursuits would help him on his way to permanent employment.[143]

In March 1889, Jacobsen started work on the Indonesian exhibit at the Royal Museum but at the disappointing salary of only 100 Mark a month. He had been told, however, that a job might open for him at the new Museum für Deutsche Volkstrachten und Erzeugnisse des Hausgewerbes (Museum of German Folk Costume and Products of Domestic Crafts), scheduled to open within the year pending government funding. Jacobsen's letters to Hedwig give a window into the politics and perennial lack of funds that pervade museums to this day. Less than two weeks into the job, he wrote:

Today the museum budget is to be debated in a commission—and B.[astian] was beside himself because it was said that they would cut down on all his posts—he drove like a madman about town and looked for Wirchow [sic]—since he didn't find him he quarreled first with Dr Voss—and later with Krause—In short everybody avoided him. Now I am curious what they will approve. I have only seen him 2 times since I came here it is best like this until this storm is over. With the new [costume] museum there seems to be progress, the painter Klingelhöfer from Marburg is here with 110 No. old German costumes which the gentlemen want to buy. Of course it will still be many months until one will know—or until possibly the government will take charge of the matter.[144]

At the end of April 1889, Jacobsen wrote that the new museum was due to open in the fall and that Virchow had indeed offered him a position as curator at 2,400 Mark a year. By June the family was settled in Berlin.[145] That summer he accompanied a collector on a trip through Tyrol and Switzerland and in October visited Sweden. Ominously, when Hagenbeck's friend Menges congratulated Jacobsen on his new job, Menges warned: "[I]f it is not absolutely necessary, I would not agree to undertake such travels as the one to Siberia, unless the conditions are totally brilliant. Otherwise nothing comes out of it that is worth the trouble, and you never get any thanks for it, because there surely is no more ungrateful lot, and I may add, more presumptuous and in some respects even more ignorant lot than the 'men of science.'"[146] In fact, the satisfaction of a permanent post lasted little more than a year. By October 1890, lack of funds forced Virchow to cut Jacobsen's position. Discouraged and unemployed, the young father furiously addressed a broad mix of journal editors and animal trainers about work possibilities.

By spring 1891, the ever-resilient Jacobsen appeared to be on his feet again, directing an ethnographic exhibition in Cologne, probably in connection with the sale of his Northwest Coast collection. The exhibition, "Länder- und Völkerkunde" (Geography and Ethnology), was held at the Kaisergarten and included pieces from his personal collection, supplemented by material from Hagenbeck and his brother-in-law, Johann Friedrich Gustav Umlauff, a Hamburg dealer specializing in ethnographic objects. The exhibition met with enough success that Umlauff proposed a comparable exhibit in Berlin. Jacobsen agreed, but this second show did not enjoy the same success. The editor of *Das Ausland* congratulated Jacobsen but noted that the show was more popular with the experts: "The big public will have more enjoyment with Buffalo Bill." Ironically, where Jacobsen sought to make a living attracting the public to an exhibition, he attracted experts. When he tried to make money writing articles for the experts, success again eluded him.[147]

Jacobsen's last bid for a permanent museum position was in Norway in 1893. He proposed to Mr. Bull of the new National Ethnografiske Forening (National Ethnographic Association) in Bergen that he be hired for three years to collect for the future museum. For him to do so, however, he sought the association's promise of a permanent position, as a return to Norway would force him to give up all his museum connections in Germany. He also claimed that the Royal Museum wanted him for another collecting trip and was planning to hire him at a salary of 6,000 Mark and a share in the profits. Thus, he wanted assurance of a good salary in Norway to be able to make the move.[148]

The Bergen museum was unable to offer a permanent post, but in May the committee asked Jacobsen to come for a year, hoping to raise interest among potential donors. He spent the summer collecting in Norway, and by September 1892 he was on his way to Bergen, where he hoped to stay. Hedwig went to live with Jacobsen's family in Risö and her husband advised her to learn Norwegian. In Bergen, however, Jacobsen found a cool reception and (once again) a museum unable to raise the hoped-for funds. The result was that Jacobsen was hired through the middle of February 1893. In January he exhibited the things he had collected so far in an effort to interest more contributors, without success.[149]

SCHOLARLY ASPIRATIONS

Jacobsen's brief tenure in Bergen was his last serious attempt to gain a permanent museum position, a dream he had chased for close to a decade. Since returning from Alaska, he had aspired to scientific as well as popular recognition. Encouraged by Bastian and hoping that scholarly publication would help him toward the museum job he so dearly wanted, Jacobsen wrote for both semiscientific and popular journals. His first was the trip report he presented at the 1883 meeting of the Society of Anthropology, Ethnology, and Prehistory, which appeared in the society's journal, *Zeitschrift für Ethnologie* (*Journal for Ethnology*).[150]

Beginning in 1887, teacher Otto Genest wrote a series of five articles following Jacobsen's account of his Siberian trip for the popular journal *Globus*. Adrian Wolct had asked to edit the Siberian material but for more pay than before, and he wrote Jacobsen that he should think of the benefit it would bring to his reputation. Jacobsen chose Genest instead, and Genes traveled between Halle and Berlin during summer and fall 1887 to work on the manuscript. The pair approached Max Spohr in Leipzig, but he had sold his business due to health problems. Other than the *Globus* articles, they were unable to find a publisher for a book comparable to Wolct's 1884 account, and Jacobsen's description of his Siberian travels never made it into print.[151]

Jacobsen was most prolific between 1889 and 1894. He produced two more articles for *Zeitschrift für Ethnologie* on Northwest Coast secret societies and a dozen articles for the scholarly journal *Das Ausland*, published by Karl von den Steinen, another collector funded by the Support Committee. Five more articles came out in *Globus* during the same period, including a nine-part series on Jacobsen's trip to Southeast Asia with Kuhn. Both *Das Ausland* and *Globus* were periodicals intended for broad audiences. They covered a range of topics, including geography, ethnography, archaeology, and botany in "foreign" countries other than Germany. Jacobsen's descriptive articles ran the gamut, including Bella Coola legends, bore amulets, Eskimo pictographic writing, seal hunting in the Bering Sea, and the cutting-edge, nineteenth-century topic of nephrite tools in America and Siberia. In 1890 he even published an article on German folk costumes, based on his work at the Museum of German Folk Costume. In 1891 *Das Ausland* published perhaps his richest contribution—the three-part article "Life and Ways of the Eskimos"—in which he presented himself as pure ethnologist. The article is a rich source of information both on artifacts and social customs, much of which is also contained in his 1884 travel book.[152]

Most articles reflect Bastian's interests and influence, as well as Jacobsen's experience. Bastian, widely traveled and even more widely read, brought a broad comparative perspective to his work. He considered Jacobsen's largely descriptive accounts as "raw data" rather than science. He was interested in recording Jacobsen's observations and personal experiences, whether or not this would translate into advancement for his traveler.

In his early efforts to gain renown, Jacobsen's limited command of written German forced him to rely on writers such as Woldt and Genest. Beginning in 1889, however, he authored his own articles, which were edited for grammar and style by Hedwig and others. Von den Steinen of *Das Ausland* encouraged Jacobsen to submit articles and assured him that his language skills were no impediment: "As for the German, don't worry about it; it is in fact necessary to edit the articles stylistically, but it is self-evident that this will happen with the closest possible attachment to your style and that the contents will remain untouched."[153]

In most cases, the content of these articles seems to be Jacobsen's. One telling exception is his description of Eskimo pictographic writing. In the original manuscript, Jacobsen simply wrote that pictographic writing to preserve one's deeds for future generations was widespread in North America. The editor added information on the origin of writing from pictographs with references to Egypt, Assur, and the Aztecs. The "active editing" that Jacobsen's academic writing required highlights the fact that his problems were more than grammatical. His lack of formal education limited the degree to which he could engage in scholarly debate and the comparative perspective this required. Although his experiences were broad, he never managed to overcome this shortcoming. After 1894, Jacobsen gave up academic pretensions and the publication of scholarly articles.[154]

LIFE AND WORK OUTSIDE THE MUSEUM

Jacobsen's life swung between two worlds, science and entertainment. When it became apparent that the museum job in Norway was not working out, he was quick to accept Hagenbeck's offer to travel to Chicago for the World's Columbian Exposition in early 1893. Hedwig (trained by Mrs. Umlauff) accompanied him as an assistant, while their two sons remained with relatives in Dresden. Among the midway amusements, the Jacobsens set up shop in Hagenbeck's Zoological Arena and World's Museum, exhibiting, among other things, the unsold portion of the Bella Coola collection. Wedged between animal displays and ethnic exhibitions, they were back in show business. A printed price list advertised 670 pieces from British Columbia at $4,500—by far the largest and most expensive collection Hagenbeck had to offer, including masks, tools, secret society paraphernalia, baskets and boxes, and models of totem poles and boats. Chicago's Field Museum acquired most of this collection, while the remaining 1,000 objects that Adrian and Fillip had collected for their Bella Coola show were spread between a half dozen European museums.[155]

After their return to Germany in late 1893, Jacobsen entertained various employment possibilities with museums but was intrigued by suggestions that he go into the hotel business. Hagenbeck advised against it, especially in Berlin, but to no avail. Jacobsen leased the Hotel Bauer on Unter den Linden. His friend, Menges, the animal trainer, told him to become a

11 Jacobsen, Hedwig, and son Paul with the cooks for the main restaurant at the zoo in Stellingen, 1908 or 1909. Hamburg Archives.

member of the German Colonial Association to increase business through acquaintance with officials traveling to Berlin. Whether or not Jacobsen did so is unclear, but he tried another method with unhappy results. In spring 1895, he was fined 242 Mark for having a *Schankwirtschaft* (public house selling alcohol) without a license or paying taxes.[156]

Jacobsen's court sentence was the least of his troubles in 1895. In mid-July the again-pregnant Hedwig had discovered his secret correspondence with "the adulteress B" and wrote him a furious letter. She said that she had become suspicious because he had been avoiding her lately and continued: "May Heaven forgive you what you have done to me! . . . Never return here again; I cannot live with you anymore, because a father for my children you never were, love and interest you had neither for them nor for me." With God's help, she said that she hoped that their third child would be born "without the father's presence, who with his false thoughts just wishes the little worm as far from himself as possible. You should have married a comedian and not a simple good girl, who does not fit a character like you." Hedwig planned to rely on her brother-in-law, for whom she was working, for support: "Consider yourself a free man, as far as I'm concerned you are; be happy, enjoy the days. All of your things here can be sent to you; . . . I don't want anything as a memento. I told all to my brother-in-law. . . . Don't write to me; I am not accepting any letters. Farewell."[157]

Hedwig's incriminating letter recorded what must have been a low point in their marriage and has no parallel in Jacobsen's personal archives. If there were others, Jacobsen did not keep them. Perhaps he was willing to rely on the discretion of future researchers, or perhaps he did not see it as something to be hidden. The letter's preservation says as much about late nineteenth-century views of adultery in general as it does about Adrian and Hedwig's relationship in particular. It is the single example of marital distress in a lifetime's correspondence.

That the couple made up is clear from later letters, which were remarkable only in their scarcity during the next several years. Sometime during 1895, Jacobsen gave up the hotel business. From November on, he gave as his address W. Engert's Zoological Garden in Dresden, where he was managing a restaurant. He attempted to publish articles on his Indonesian voyage during this period, but both French and Scandinavian journals turned him down. Personal correspondence was written in a mix of German and Norwegian. The family continued to grow. An 1898 New Year's card from Jacobsen's sister-in-law, Henny, sent greetings to the Jacobsens and their four sons—Harald, Paul, two-year-old Hjalmar, and one-year-old Wilhelm.[158]

Jacobsen's mother died in November 1900, and his father wrote asking for Fillip's address in British Columbia. Jacobsen's archive contains many letters between parents and child. Although Jacobsen traveled the world, his journeys rarely took him back to his boyhood home. His father, whom he once described as "one of the noblest and best men who ever our sinful earth did see," complained that he would not get to see his sons before he died and, in fact, he rarely did see them.[159]

Although the Jacobsens intended the move to Dresden as permanent, their old friend Hagenbeck had one more offer up his sleeve. At the turn of the century, he established Stellingen Animal Park in Hamburg. He proposed that Jacobsen take over management of the large restaurant there, and in 1907 Jacobsen accepted, moving the whole family to Hamburg (fig. 11). This time they prospered. Their sons grew up in a world where it made sense to ask (as Wilhelm did) whether the polar bear had eaten the shark in the zoological garden that was their backyard. Jacobsen kept a hand in Hagenbeck's traveling-show ventures, and in 1910 he went to South Dakota to bring back a group of Oglala-Sioux for a *Völkerschau*. The Sioux were more popular with the German public than the Bella Coola, as they looked the part of authentic "red" Indians. Once again, Jacobsen and Hagenbeck turned a profit catering to the European fascination with America's first peoples.[160]

World War I brought hardship and disruption to the Jacobsen family (fig. 12). All four sons served in the army. Both Willy and Paul were wounded, and Paul remained a prisoner of war in England from 1914. Jacobsen later asked the government to post at least one of his sons closer to home, but his request was denied. Happily, all returned home safely after the war.[161]

Adrian and Hedwig were still in Stellingen in October 1920 when the park closed, as many animals had either died or been sold. Although they had thought of returning to Dresden, they decided to remain where they were, but the seventy-year-old Jacobsen could not sit still for long. In 1922 he traveled with a film company to Norway, and in the summers of 1923 and 1924 he led hunting trips to Spitsbergen and Novaia Zemlia for wealthy German merchants and nobility. In 1925 he tried to drum up more business with a slide lecture, "German Hunting and Research Trips to the Northern Polar Sea," which stressed how interesting, potentially profitable, and comparatively inexpensive such ventures were. He also gave illustrated talks on Alaska, possibly for a fee. His lecture manuscripts, one in German and one in Norwegian, were a mix of historical facts and personal experiences, as when he showed a photograph of the Nome gold fields, claiming that "during my travels 5 years before I slept on gold without suspecting it." In 1926 he traveled to Norway to hire Lapps for yet another *Völkerschau*, the last of his career (fig. 13).[162]

After retiring from the restaurant business, Jacobsen made proposals to collect for The Field Museum in Chicago and the American Museum of Natural History in New York, but both turned him down. Once again he set his mind to publishing accounts of his travels. This time, however, he eschewed the scientific journals he had courted in his youth and sought more popular venues. In summer 1914 he had been unsuccessful in finding a publisher for his manuscript, "Mit Wagen, Boot und Schlitten durch Sibirien und Ostasien" (By Wagon, Boat and Sled through Siberia and East Asia), edited by Hans Lorenz Lorenzen. He was, however, able to publish "Unter den Alaska-Eskimos: Erlebnisse und Forschungen" (Among the Alaska Eskimos: Experiences and Investigations) in 1924–1925. The

12   The Jacobsen family at the Hamburg Zoo, 1913. From left to right: Hjalmar, Harald, Hedwig, Adrian, Paul, and Wilhelm. Johannes Adrian Jacobsen Jr.

13   The elderly Jacobsen explaining a newly planned hunting trip to the Polar Sea to a group of friends, 1926. Hamburg Archives.

material was not new but, rather, a reprint of the Alaska chapters in his 1884 book with minor additions and deletions. It opens with his arrival at St. Michael and closes as he bids goodbye to his dogs in Togiak, saying that parting from them was harder than parting from some people.[163]

Jacobsen's final portrait of his life's adventures was published in 1931 as *The White Frontier: Adventures of an Old Sailor all around the Arctic Circle,* intended for a popular audience. Perhaps the most interesting chapters are the first three, in which he described his hardy upbringing in Norway as preparation for the life he would lead. He devoted an entire chapter to his sled dogs and another to the legendary man-eating bird, whose nest he explored on his trip down the Yukon River in fall 1882. Chapter 16, "Hostile Indians," is the dramatic retelling of his confrontation with the Ingalik over his theft of several skulls. Fifty years after the fact, this incident (like many others) was much exaggerated, resembling a wild-west encounter with Indians circling the fort. The book included a brief biography by Albrecht Janssen as postscript. How much editing Janssen undertook on *White Frontier* is unclear. In 1939 Janssen wrote publishers on Jacobsen's behalf, suggesting publication of yet another account of his travels in British Columbia and Alaska as well as the unpublished "World of Polar Animals," but nothing came of either project.[164]

Having lost his savings to inflation following World War I, Jacobsen had good reason to keep active with exhibitions and popular publications into old age. He succeeded in getting a modest monthly government pension of 80 Mark from 1926 through 1935, based in part on his contributions to state museums over the years. The Jacobsens continued living in Stellingen, still occasionally receiving mail at Hagenbeck's zoo. A 1927 newspaper clipping identifies "Father Jacobsen" as one of the zoo's personnel.[165]

Hedwig died in Stellingen in 1937, and Adrian remained there until his house was destroyed by bombs in 1943. Fortunately his papers had been donated to the German-Nordic Society's archive in Hamburg-Altona ten years earlier. After World War II, the Nordic Archive was dissolved and the Jacobsen material given to Hamburg's ethnological museum.

Having lost everything in the bombing, Jacobsen moved to Norway to live with relatives. His last letter, written in Norwegian to his daughter-in-law, Hedwig Jacobsen, bid farewell to his family and to the world. He died on January 18, 1947, at age ninety-three, and his ashes were later buried at Stellingen in the family grave beside Hedwig. In 1964 a small street in Hamburg-Stellingen was named Jacobsenweg in his honor. Even after his death, Hamburg newspapers reported on him, usually in connection with Hagenbeck, an indication that he was not forgotten in the town where he finally found his home and where most of his descendants live today.[166]

A PLACE IN HISTORY

Jacobsen left a remarkable legacy, particularly from the dozen years he collected for the Royal Museum. He carried out three major expeditions—to North America in 1881–1883, to Siberia and East Asia in 1884–1885, and to Indonesia in 1887–1888—bringing more than twelve thousand objects into collections. He enriched not only the Royal Museum, but museums all over the world that either traded for or purchased the many duplicate items he brought home (fig. 14).[167]

Not only did Jacobsen fill storage rooms to overflowing, by the early 1890s he had dozens of publications to his name, more than enough to gain many contemporary scholars university tenure. He also had influential friends, Adolf Bastian first and foremost. Museum archives contain dozens of letters Bastian wrote on Jacobsen's behalf, both for help while he was in the field and support on his return. Scholars also sought him out, including Smithsonian director Spencer F. Baird and Danish ethnologist Hinrich Rink, who continued a correspondence through the early 1890s. Following his trip to Alaska, Jacobsen acquired considerable personal renown, and Bastian received letter after letter from would-be travelers eager to accompany "the Captain" (a title Jacobsen cultivated but may never have earned).[168]

Even though Jacobsen was both well known and sought after, his immigrant standing and lack of formal academic training meant that he could visit the museum world yet never take up permanent residence. Bastian, who considered Jacobsen a useful "traveler" but never a fellow scientist, always encouraged him that something might come through. It certainly served Bastian's interests to do so. In his letter to Jacobsen regarding the asking price of his Bella Coola collection, he asked Jacobsen to think of their past and future work together and not ask too much. That "future work together" was never specified, and when it failed to materialize, it proved correct Menges's warning about untrustworthy "men of science."[169]

Jacobsen appears to have been a charming man, often with several women writing to him at once. He was a man of business with big plans such as traveling with a trained elephant or establishing a whaling station. His restaurant at Stellingen Park was probably his most successful venture, but he lost his savings following the first world war and spent his final decades promoting himself to make ends meet. Although his government pension was some compensation, Jacobsen always felt that the museum had underpaid him. Bastian, on the other hand, probably felt he was giving the young man a fair wage, considering his training and social position.

Indeed, Jacobsen was a man of his time. While he was discriminated against as the immigrant son of a Norwegian fisherman, he shared racist leanings with many of his generation. Yet these personal biases do not negate the effect of his actions. Jacobsen's work in Alaska and elsewhere gave him a place in history. His collecting expedition through the Yup'ik heartland represents the last major effort of its kind in southwestern Alaska.

As we have seen, Jacobsen took a circuitous route to Alaska. Had things been otherwise, including means of transport and available funds, he might easily have gone elsewhere. Ironically, the fact that it was remote and inhospitable were parts in its favor. Collectors had already picked over more accessible places, and the objects that remained were expensive. In Alaska Jacobsen hoped to find abundant "curiosities" at reasonable rates. He was not disappointed. Along with his nemesis Edward Nelson, he gathered unparalleled collections.

Although Jacobsen was the instrument, the major instigators of his expedition were the Royal Museum and its dynamic director, bent on salvaging the remnants of primitive peoples before they were swept away in the onrush of civilization. This nineteenth-century view of the world underlay Bastian's sense of mission, and he in turn sought out a "man of action" to execute his plan. Yet all Bastian's passionate desire to collect before it was too late and all Jacobsen's energy would have come to nothing had it not been for the Support Committee's philanthropic backing, made possible by a happy combination of national pride and capitalistic resources.[170]

The combination of Bastian's vision and the Support Committee's financial backing sent Jacobsen traveling through Yup'ik country at lightning speed. Often he did not even overnight in the communities where he did his collecting. Although the Support Committee later sent scholars into the field to do more systematic collecting in other parts of the world, none were sent to Alaska.

We are fortunate that Jacobsen concentrated his efforts "from the first to last snowflake," when people had gathered into winter villages, rather than scattered over the landscape in hundreds of small seasonal camps. Jacobsen was also lucky in the Yup'ik attitude toward the objects he desired. He had some trouble collecting sacred and clan property in more traditional

Northwest Coast communities, where these objects were still invested with meaning and their owners were reluctant to part with them. Among the Yupiit, however, Jacobsen was able to buy extraordinary masks and ceremonial paraphernalia, not because they no longer had meaning but because of the Yup'ik requirement that these spiritually charged pieces be discarded after use and newly made every year. He had more difficulty getting nephrite amulets and "idols," although he was not above walking off with grave goods when Natives refused to sell. Though Jacobsen stole some material, he paid for most of what he collected. Douglas Cole points out that the collecting process was a "normal" trading relationship. It was also a grossly unequal colonial relationship with all the cards stacked on Jacobsen's side. The bottom line is that today Yup'ik patrimony remains in German hands.[171]

When Yup'ik elders visited Berlin and saw the things Jacobsen had collected, their reaction was gratitude and pride. The elders valued the objects because they allowed them to recall and share stories and their relation to particular contemporary situations. The museum staff had feared that the elders would see their fine collection and want to reclaim it, but this was not the case. Instead, elders left no richer in material wealth but with their mental suitcases filled to overflowing with new stories and experiences. They had repossessed what was truly valuable, and the museum could keep the rest.

Jacobsen certainly provided the Royal Museum an unparalleled collection, but the information he gathered left much to be desired. His grab-and-run technique was in sharp contrast to that of the consummate field-worker, Boas, who waited days before making purchases and recorded detailed information about the objects he collected. Boas later used Jacobsen's collection as a point of departure, searching out the meanings Jacobsen had left invisible. Boas wrote Bastian in 1893 on stationery of the World's Columbian Exposition that he had shown a "carefully selected party of Indians from Vancouver Island ... photographs and drawings from Jacobsen's collection, and it turned out that the people know the history of each piece in the most exact manner." He asked Bastian to send him photographs of all the objects Jacobsen had collected from the Kwakiutl, including household items and tools. In return he would provide detailed explanations gathered from the Natives.[172]

Bastian sent Boas the requested drawings, giving Kwakiutl elders access to Jacobsen's collections in the best way he could. One hundred years later, the Berlin Ethnological Museum gave Yup'ik elders not only pictures of things Jacobsen had collected from their homeland, but an opportunity to explore and explain them in person. What follows is their return gift.

14 Exhibition case in the old Berlin Ethnological Museum in 1926 showing Jacobsen's Yup'ik and Iñupiaq material. Note the large painted drum, as well as the pair of tuunraq masks on either side of the Kuskokwim swan mask. A tiny ivory dance-house model is also visible in the lower right and wooden and ivory dolls in the lower left. Ethnologisches Museum Berlin.

THE GIFT-GIVERS

This is the instruction down in our village during the spring. When one goes to the ocean and brings back a sea mammal, his wife divides all of it up. When she is done, she calls all her neighbors, and she gives it all out. That is how those coastal people are. Food and everything that could be divided is given to those one thinks about. They say that it will be replaced by more.

—FRANK ANDREW, KWIGILLINGOK

Jacobsen reported that half-faced masks such as this were used by women during "memorial festivals" to impersonate the spirit of the dead and report from their world. Annie Blue models the mask on p. 249. IVA4386.

Group of wooden and ivory iqmiutaat (tobacco boxes). IVA4644, IVA4640, IVA4641, IVA4666, IVA4648, IVA4657.

TURN-OF-THE-CENTURY YUPIIT AND THEIR DESCENDANTS

JACOBSEN DESCRIBED the people he encountered during his travels in southwestern Alaska, both in his trip report and a series of articles on the "Life and Ways of the Eskimos."[1] His experiences in Greenland, Labrador, and the Northwest Coast gave him a comparative perspective. He recognized the linguistic continuity of Inuit peoples all across the Arctic, noting that a Greenlander could communicate with an Iñupiaq speaker from northern Alaska. The Yupiit (from *yuk,* "person," plus *pik,* "real or genuine," literally, "real people") are members of this larger family of Inuit cultures, extending from Prince William Sound on the Pacific coast of Alaska to both sides of Bering Strait and from there thousands of miles north and east along Canada's Arctic coast and into Labrador and Greenland. Within that extended family, however, they are members of the Yup'ik-speaking, not Inuit/Iñupiaq-speaking, branch.

A BOUNTIFUL HOMELAND

The lowland delta through which Jacobsen traveled is as much water as land. Looking down from a high point on the Yukon River, he aptly described how "the small waterways and lakes lay on the land like a net."[2] Southwestern Alaska's coastal landscape consists of a broad, marshy plain resulting from thousands of years of silting action by the Yukon, Kuskokwim, and Nushagak Rivers. The sea is shallow, the land flat, and fall storms can push the tide inland as much as thirty miles. Low volcanic domes on Nelson and Nunivak Islands and outcroppings of metamorphic rock in the vicinity of Cape Romanzof provide the only relief. Weather can be harsh, ranging from -80 degrees F in winter to +90 degrees F on a windless July day. Precipitation averages no more than twenty inches a year, including fifty inches of snow. Even during the darkest midwinter months, the sun rises above the horizon for at least five hours a day.

Jacobsen's comparative perspective also allowed him to see what many Euro-American observers of the North missed—the richness of the subarctic tundra environment, which, although treeless along the coast, nourishes an array of flora and fauna. Referring to all Alaska, he wrote: "According to the Eskimo beliefs, they reside in the true Eldorado for their immense area is traversed by countless small rivers which are the richest in fish in our entire globe. Also, the land is relatively rich in wild animals. The ocean is populated by millions of sea animals of all kinds which fall to the skillful hunter."[2]

Indeed, the Alaska coast presents a rich field, and within Alaska the Yukon, Kuskokwim, and Nushagak River deltas are by far the richest. Each spring millions of migratory birds, including five species of geese, sandhill cranes, whistling swans, and a variety of ducks and seabirds, such as pintails, oldsquaws, and king eiders, fly north to nest in the ample wetlands. Each summer five species of salmon—king (chinook), red (sockeye), coho (silver), pink (humpback), and chum (dog)—surge up the rivers and streams to spawn. Numerous other fish species populate the coastal waters of the Bering Sea, including herring, halibut, flounder, tomcod, and smelt, while the tundra lakes and streams are rich in freshwater species, such as whitefish, northern pike, burbot, trout, whitefish, blackfish, and the tiny sticklebacks or needlefish. Sea mammals can be taken along the coast from early spring into the late fall, including walrus, beluga whales, and the all-important seals, which supply both meat and oil for food and skins for clothing. During fall and winter, men hunt and trap smaller land animals such as hare, fox, muskrat, and mink as well as larger ones including moose, caribou, and bear.

Breakup releases an ample drift of logs downriver every spring, so the Yupiit—though living beyond the reach of the dense forests of the interior—were well supplied with wood, which they used to build their homes, boats, tools, and elaborate ceremonial accouterments. Throughout spring and summer, edible greens were also abundant, including those of marsh marigolds and wild celery, as well as the roots and shoots of wild parsnips. From late August through September, men, women, and children fanned out over the tundra in search of salmonberries, blueberries, crowberries, and cranberries. This wealth of fish, birds, plants, and animals provided a rich

39

resource base in the past, and harvesting this bounty continues to be an important focus of activity today.

Building on their natural wealth, the Yupiit had developed a complex cultural tradition prior to the arrival of the first Euro-Americans in the early 1800s. The abundance of fish and wildlife along the Bering Sea coast allowed for a more settled life than that enjoyed by Inuit peoples in other parts of the Arctic. Like the northern Inuit, the coastal Yupiit were nomadic, yet their rich environment allowed them to remain within a relatively fixed range. Each of at least a dozen regional groups demarcated a largely self-sufficient area, within which people moved freely throughout the year in their quest for food. At the time Jacobsen arrived, Yup'ik territory extended upriver to the vicinity of Paimiut on the Yukon River and Crow Village on the Kuskokwim, at which point they came into contact with Athapascan people.

Interregional relations were not always amicable. Intermittent skirmishes between regional groups regularly interrupted delta life prior to the arrival of the Russians in the early 1800s. Ironically, death itself brought this killing to an end when a dramatic population decline resulted from the diseases that accompanied contact with Euro-Americans. Although few Russians settled in southwestern Alaska, the larger Russian trade network to the south introduced smallpox into the region, devastating the Native population. Entire villages disappeared, and as many as 60 percent of the original Yup'ik population—estimated to be approximately fifteen thousand—was dead by June 1838.[4]

The effects of the smallpox epidemic of 1838–1839, combined with subsequent epidemics of influenza in 1852–1853 and 1861, produced a decline and a shift in the population and undercut interregional social distinctions. Although the introduction of communicable diseases damaged traditional social groups and patterns of intergroup relations before Jacobsen's arrival, it left largely intact the routines of daily life. Small bands of extended family groups continued to move over the landscape, seeking the animals they needed to support life and gathering in winter villages for an elaborate annual ceremonial round.

TURN-OF-THE-CENTURY VILLAGE LIFE

The Yup'ik people were left largely to their own devices into the early decades of the twentieth century. When the elders who traveled to Berlin were young, their families, scattered in dozens of seasonal camps and winter villages, followed the seasonal round of their forebears. Travel was still by skin boat, both the single-person kayak and the larger *angyaq*.

The bilateral extended family, numbering up to thirty persons, was the basic social unit. Spanning two to four generations, including parents, offspring, and parents' parents, the group might also encompass parents' siblings or their children. An overlapping network of family ties joined people in a single community.

Extended family groups lived together most of the year but normally not in family compounds. Rather, winter villages were divided residentially between a communal men's house or houses (*qasgi*) and smaller sod houses (*enet*) occupied by women and young children. Married couples or groups of hunters often moved to outlying camps for fishing and trapping during the spring and fall. Families gathered when temperatures dropped below freezing and sometimes during the spring seal-hunting and summer fishing seasons. Winter villages like those Jacobsen visited ranged in size from a single extended family to a few hundred people.

All men and all boys older than five ate their meals and slept in the *qasgi*, the social and ceremonial center of village life. Jacobsen noted correctly that every large village had one or more "festival houses, called 'Kassigit' or 'Kassagim' used for ceremonies, councils, as residences, and as bathhouses." A man's wife or daughters brought him his meals in the *qasgi*. It was also the location of the ubiquitous "fire bath," which Jacobsen described in a way that debunked another common misconception: "It is the general belief that the Eskimos are among the dirtiest people on earth but their cleanliness is very real." He continued:

When the Eskimo have a bath, the window covering as well as part of the floor are removed, a big fire is lit in the hollow. The bather sits on the remaining boards as close to the fire as possible, takes off his coat, as well as his shoes, and covers his head with a seabird skin cap. The women who serve bring to each bather a respirator of braided grass equipped with a wooden peg which is to be held by the teeth and closing tightly the mouth and nostrils, to be used when the whole house is filled with smoke. Grass picked and dried during the summer and called "Kreuti" [*perriutet*] serves as towels. A bowl filled with snow and urine provides the soap. It is believed that with the urine, the cleansing can be completed sooner, and as the snow melts, the solution becomes more liquid. Through the resulting heat from the fire, the body perspires and the moisture is wiped off. Also curious is a type of modesty which uses a six-inch-long thread. The naked Eskimo, in consideration of the serving women, ties the praeputium (penis) together with the string so that only the glands are visible.[5]

Jacobsen's collection contains most of these objects—bird-skin hat, respirator, bowl, even grass towel—but not the thread (see Figure 9.32).

Each man's place in the *qasgi* reflected his social position, and the men's house framed a number of internal distinctions, including those between young and old, married and unmarried, and host and guest. The social structure of the *qasgi* mirrored that of the natural world. The Yupiit believed that sea mammals lived in huge underwater *qasgit* (plural), where they ranged themselves around a central fire pit in ranked fashion. From these underwater homes, they viewed their treatment by people and, based on what they observed, chose whether to give themselves to human hunters.

The hunters who gave the most thought and care toward the animals they sought were richly rewarded, both socially and materially. The *nukalpiaq,* or good provider, was a man of considerable importance in village life. Not only did he contribute wood for the communal sweat bath and oil to keep the lamps lighted, he also figured prominently in midwinter ceremonial distributions, during which local extended families vied with one another to see who could give the most.

The elders who traveled to Berlin in 1997 had as youths listened in the *qasgi* to their fathers and grandfathers discuss the hunt and talk about the rules for living. This tradition of oral recitation continues, but the elders' generation was the last to be raised within the *qasgi.* Young men received essential education as they listened to and observed the older men at work. Elders encouraged them to try their hand at carving and fixing tools like those Jacobsen collected. They also admonished young men and women to perform helpful acts while keeping their minds filled with thoughts of the animals on whose goodwill their lives depended. People believed that thoughtful actions cleared a path for the animals they would someday hunt.

Into the early decades of the 1900s, the Yupiit gathered after freeze-up in winter villages, where they enjoyed a varied and elaborate ceremonial season. Each ceremony emphasized a different aspect of the relationships among humans, animals, and the spirit world. The Bladder Festival (*Nakaciuryaraq,* literally, "way of doing something with bladders"), along with related ceremonies, ensured the rebirth and return of the animals in the coming harvest season. During the annual Feast for the Dead (*Merr'aq,* from *meq,* "water," which the thirsty dead desire), people elaborately fed and clothed living namesakes to provide for and honor the souls of their departed relatives. Jacobsen attended several such feasts, at which he received many valuable objects as gifts.[6] The Great Feast for the Dead (*Elriq*) served the same function within human society as the Bladder Festival within animal society, expressing and ensuring continuity between the living and the dead. The intravillage *Petugtaq* (literally, "something tied on") and the intervillage Messenger Feast (*Kevgiryaraq,* named for the two messengers—*kevgak*—sent to invite the guest village) played on, exaggerated, and reversed normal social relationships between husband and wife and between host and guest. The Messenger Feast also served important social functions, including display of status, social control, and redistribution of wealth. At the same time, it provided a clear statement to the *yuit* (persons) of the animals that the hunters were once again ready to receive them. Finally, the *angalkuq* (shaman) directed masked dances during *Agayuyaraq* (literally, "way of dancing with masks"), also called *Itruka'ar* in some areas, dramatically re-creating past encounters with spirits to elicit their participation in the future. Together these ceremonies embodied a cyclical view of the universe whereby right action in the past and present reproduced abundance in the future.

CHANGES WITHIN AND WITHOUT

Jacobsen made the general statement that the people he encountered on the Bering Sea coast were both the least known and most numerous and had experienced the least non-Native influence of any Eskimo group.[7] In fact, the Yupiit remain both the most populous Alaska Natives and among the most traditional Native Americans. Significant Euro-American settlement did not occur in southwestern Alaska until the end of the nineteenth century. Though rich in the natural resources necessary to support a scattered and seasonally nomadic population, the Bering Sea coast is notoriously lacking in the commercially valuable resources—gold, sea otters, bowhead whales—that first attracted non-Native entrepreneurs to other parts of Alaska. Because of its geographical isolation and dearth of commercial resources, the Yukon-Kuskokwim delta was virtually ignored by outsiders during the years prior to Jacobsen's visit. Russian traders and Orthodox priests migrated inland along the delta's major rivers beginning in the 1830s and contemporary Yupiit still refer to white people as *kass'aq* or *kass'at,* from Russian *kazák,* which becomes "cossack" in English.[8] But the people living along the Bering Sea coast between the Yukon and Kuskokwim Rivers did not experience extended contact until nearly a century later.

The arrival of missionaries dramatically altered village life. First came Russian Orthodox priests in 1845 to work out of Ikogmiut (Russian Mission) on the Yukon River. Orthodox hegemony was challenged in 1885 by the establishment of a Moravian mission at Bethel on the Kuskokwim River and three years later by the founding of a Catholic mission on Nelson Island, which moved to Akulurak at the mouth of the Yukon a year later. These two missions, which would soon dominate the region, made a much more sustained bid to convert the "baptized heathen" to whom the Russian Orthodox laid claim. Moreover, both made concerted efforts to alter the Yup'ik way of life, especially along the Yukon and Kuskokwim Rivers near their mission stations. Our group of elders reflected the efforts of these missions and included members of all three religious denominations active in the region to this day—Catholic, Moravian, and Russian Orthodox.

The year 1900 constituted a major demographic marker in the region. The influenza epidemic that arrived that year with the annual supply vessels halved the Native population in just three months. Although coastal communities were not as severely affected, many winter villages on the Yukon and Kuskokwim were abandoned. A sharp increase in the region's white population matched the decline of the Native population, the Nome gold rush having spawned a concerted effort to locate mineral deposits along the upper Yukon and middle Kuskokwim and a lucrative commercial salmon fishery beginning to take hold in Bristol Bay.

The Yup'ik people supplied fish and cordwood to miners and steamship captains and participated in an expanding fur market, which brought substantial changes to their domestic economy. By the 1920s, when the elders who traveled to Berlin were children, valued trade goods—including flour, tea, tobacco, sugar, cloth, homegrown vegetables, and the rare piece of penny candy—could be had at trading posts in Bethel, Dillingham, Tununak, and St. Michael. Both mission and Bureau of Indian Affairs (BIA) schools had been established in a dozen central locations, and Akiak boasted the region's first hospital, with eleven beds.

Much had changed in southwestern Alaska by statehood in 1959, but much remained the same. The continuities between past and present were as significant as the innovations. Most people continued to speak the Central Yup'ik language, enjoyed a rich oral tradition, participated in large ritual distributions, and focused their lives on extended family relations that were bound to the harvesting of fish and wildlife. They never converted to gardening or reindeer herding, regardless of sustained missionary and federal encouragement to do so. The coastal population had declined dramatically, but its geographical isolation and commercial insignificance had inhibited change. The seasonal cycle of activities remained much the same as that of their ancestors.

YUPIIT ENTER THE MODERN WORLD

Village life changed considerably during the second half of the twentieth century. Following earlier epidemics, improved health care and the decline of infant mortality allowed population to surpass its aboriginal number. Today, more than thirty thousand Yupiit live in southwestern Alaska, scattered among seventy small communities of one hundred fifty to eight hundred inhabitants each, as well as the large regional centers of Bethel and Dillingham. Villages each have both an elementary and a secondary school, city government or traditional council, health clinic, church or churches, airstrip, electricity, and, increasingly, running water and flush toilets. The residential separation of men and women has been abandoned in favor of single-family dwellings. Children divide their time between household chores, hunting and harvesting activities, attending school, and playing video games and basketball in high school gymnasiums like their counterparts in the Lower 48, rather than listening for hours to elders' stories and oral instruction.

During the decade after statehood, Alaska Natives generally were viewed as extremely disadvantaged and the Yupiit of the Yukon-Kuskokwim delta region as one of the most impoverished groups among them. Relative to other parts of rural Alaska, the availability of Western material goods was minimal, modern housing nonexistent, and educational levels low; in addition, tuberculosis—as destructive as earlier influenza and smallpox epidemics—ran rampant. The Great Society dispatched scores of "VISTAs" (Volunteers in Service to America) to the region as soldiers in President Johnson's War on Poverty.

Events in the 1970s launched a new era throughout rural Alaska. Passage of the Alaska Native Claims Settlement Act (ANCSA) in 1971 transformed land tenure in the state and is the major determinant of land status in Alaska today. It extinguished aboriginal land claims statewide, giving in return fee-simple title to forty-four million acres of land and nearly one billion dollars to twelve regional and one nonresident for-profit corporations as well as more than two hundred village corporations. These organizations administer the land and money received under ANCSA. Among these, the Calista Corporation and Bristol Bay Native Corporation were established to manage the corporate resources of southwestern Alaska.

In 1976 the "Molly Hootch decision" (*Hootch v. Alaska State Operated Schools,* named for a Yup'ik student who sued the state for the right to be educated in her home village) mandated sweeping educational reform. Local high schools sprang up in all the communities in the region, which had previously sent their children to boarding schools in Bethel, St. Marys Catholic Mission, or BIA schools outside the region and in some cases outside the state.

ANCSA cleared the way for construction of the Trans-Alaska Pipeline, and the state's share of the oil profits gushed into public works projects and social programs. Supported by ANCSA village corporation activity and state services, the communities of southwestern Alaska experienced steady growth during the 1970s and 1980s. Villages burgeoned in both population and modern facilities, and employment income and cash transfers of other kinds provided some support for local subsistence harvesting activity.

The regional economy shifted radically as the delta's population coalesced at permanent sites. Along with the continued importance of subsistence harvesting activities, the most significant feature of village economy in southwestern Alaska today is its dependence on government. Commercial fishing and trapping, craft sales, and local service industries provide only a small portion of the total local income. As much as 90 percent flows through the village economies from the public sector, including both wages and salaries and various state and federal transfer payments.

Men and women in contemporary communities participate in the economy as clerks, welfare recipients, commercial fishermen, and bureaucrats but also partially support themselves through subsistence hunting and fishing. Integration into the larger economy is marginal, and domestic activities focus on extraction and consumption rather than investment and production. The combination of wage employment and the harvest of local resources for both commercial and subsistence use dominates. Dependence on public sources of income limits economic diversity. In this mixed economy, both transfer payments from government agencies as well as wages are used to pay for the snowmobiles, skiffs, motors, ammunition, and fuel required by modern harvesting. A man needs money now to hunt and fish, and his success at the "traditional" tasks of harvesting animals is directly tied to his ability to harvest cash. As the market economy of southwestern Alaska continues marginal, hunting and fishing are activities that many find difficult to afford.

High rates of alcoholism, child abuse, sexual assault, suicide, violent crime, and mental health problems plague the region. Infant mortality has dramatically declined during the last twenty years, but the suicide rate has increased from 5.5 to 55.5 per 100,000 people during the same period—five times the national toll. Alcohol is a contributing factor in nearly all cases.[9]

As public moneys declined in the 1990s, residents struggled to find solutions to village problems and ways to continue to live in their traditional homeland. Many Yupiit still see themselves living in a highly structured relationship with the resources of their environment, not merely surviving off them. Although Central Yup'ik is declining in Yukon and Nushagak River communities, it continues as the primary language for most people living in coastal and tundra villages. Public housing programs have dictated the construction of single-family housing, yet elaborate patterns of interhousehold sharing, adoption, and hunting partnerships continue to nourish extended family relationships. People remain strongly committed to traditional harvesting activities and continue to share products of the hunt.

The passage of ANCSA and, more recently, heightened awareness of domestic problems have created a diffuse yet important cultural reformation in much of southwestern Alaska. Consciousness-raising has concentrated contemporary Yup'ik efforts on maintaining control of land, resources, and local affairs; improving residents' health and sense of well-being; and adhering to cultural and linguistic traditions. Signs of this reformation abound—in the Yupiit Nation sovereignty movement, debate over subsistence rights, revival of intra- and intervillage dance festivals, hosting of elders' conferences, increased awareness of and concern for the preservation and use of Yup'ik language and oral traditions, and trips like ours to far-flung museums to document and share traditional knowledge.

Articulation of issues of Native cultural identity and political control indicates a growing awareness of the value of being a Yup'ik person in the modern world. Men and women—like those who traveled to Berlin—increasingly dedicate their energies to communicate the Yup'ik view of the world to the younger generation. Their efforts reflect the desire of many Yup'ik people to gain recognition of their unique past, parts of which they hope to carry into the future.

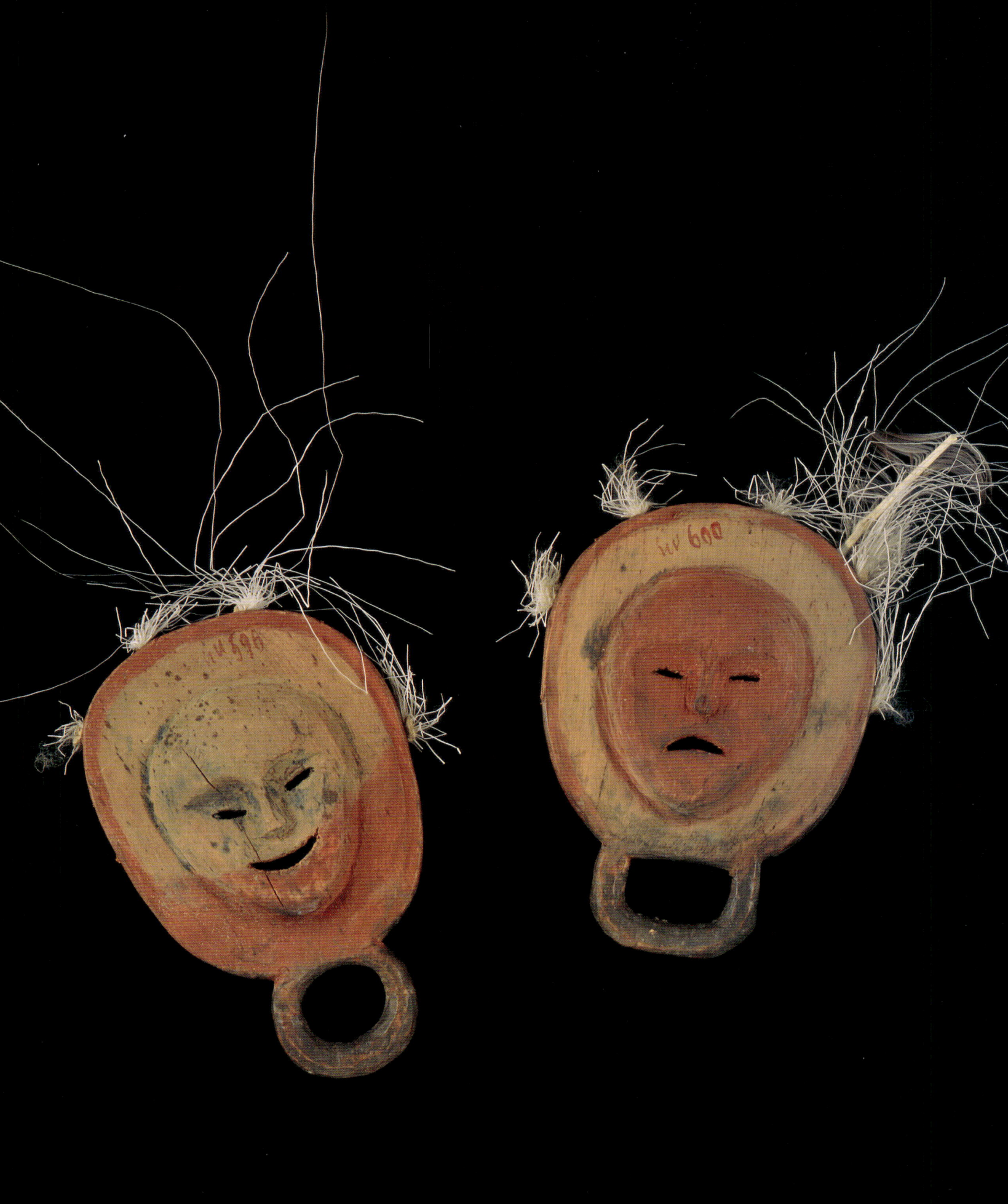

THE RETURN GIFT

"Give as much as you receive and all is for the best."

—MAORI PROVERB, QUOTED BY MARCEL MAUSS, "THE GIFT"

Pair of women's dance fans from between Cape Vancouver and the Kuskokwim, originally rimmed with caribou hair and feathers. As was often the case, the fans are opposites, one with a woman's downturned mouth and the other the smiling face of a man. IVA5199a, b.

The "Yup'ik delegation" to Berlin. From left to right: Catherine Moore, Wassilie Berlin, Paul John, Annie Blue, Marie Meade, Andy Paukan, and Ann Riordan. Dietrich Graf, Ethnologisches Museum Berlin.

THE YUP'IK DELEGATION

THE "YUP'IK DELEGATION" that set out from Anchorage on September 5, 1997, included four elders representing the different parts of the region—Wassilie Berlin from the Kuskokwim, Paul John from Nelson Island, Annie Blue from Bristol Bay, and Catherine Moore from the Yukon. They were accompanied by translator Marie Meade, community leader Andy Paukan, and me. The elders came to share their knowledge with each other and, through Marie's translations and Andy's video recordings, with Yup'ik and non-Yup'ik people worldwide.

Recognized as knowledgeable experts in their home communities, each was both willing and able to share their expertise. The eloquent commentary they provided, speaking only in Yup'ik and following Yup'ik protocols,[1] is testimony to that knowledge. Moreover, what they said about the *ak'allat* (old things) directly reflects each speaker's personal history.

Eighty-one-year-old Wassilie Berlin—Uqsungiar in Yup'ik—was our eldest group member. He was born at the mouth of the Kuskokwim River. By his fifth birthday, however, his mother, Nunurta, died, and, because he was one of many sons, his father, Paiyaq, decided to send him to the Moravian Children's Home. While Wassilie was waiting to be taken upriver to the orphanage, a relative took him in, and he still remembers his disappointment at not being able to go to the home and learn English.

Although close to his father and brothers, Wassilie stayed with different families in the Akula (tundra) area. Life was hard and his possessions few. Looking at arrows Jacobsen had collected, Wassilie spoke of how touched he had been when a visiting stranger gave him one of his own well-made arrows. He also modestly described his surprise when the drummers invited him to join them at a Messenger Feast, as he did not think he deserved the honor. He noticed a young woman named Alice at the same feast and thought to himself that someday he would like to marry her. After an arranged marriage failed, he fulfilled that wish, and he and Alice (until her death in 2003) and some of their eight children and numerous grandchildren live in Kasigluk, where his sons continue to hunt and fish in the same area Wassilie roamed in his younger years.

Annie Blue—Cungauyar in Yup'ik—was also born in 1916 at the village of Qissayaarmiut on the Togiak River to Ertnakok Ivan and Martha Tsihegak. The only girl among many brothers, she was treasured and well provided for as she grew up. She still remembers how her mother sat by her side during the period of seclusion that followed her first menstruation.

When I was young, my teacher was an old woman, my grandmother, named Apurin. As I was growing up, she talked to me, and her words were pointing directly into my future. . . . I also tried to do as my parents said. I had many male siblings, but today they are all gone. My older brother and younger brothers didn't live a long life since they didn't live according to our parents' guidance. I remember when our mentors talked to us children, my brothers would run out of the house slamming the door behind them. But that old woman . . . used to say that when people lived according to their own will they usually didn't live long enough to smell the tail-end of life, *alam iqua narqerraarluku*.

Back when I was growing up, I realized my parents were in the Russian Orthodox faith. . . . When we lived inside the river, there were no white people and no teachers. That was why the other children and I didn't go to school. . . . I'm always regretful about it; my father wanted to bring my late younger sibling and me down to the mouth of Togiak River where there was a school, but my mother didn't want him to because she didn't want to worry about us. Sometimes I'm sorry that I can't communicate with white people and wish I could talk to them in English.

Though isolated, Annie's upriver home had occasional non-Native visitors.

When I first became aware up at the mouth of Kiimaaq River, . . . there was a *kass'aq* in the house with us . . . named Butch Smit. He always brought my dear father with him when he looked for gold. I remember my dear aunt, Butch's wife, packing me around on her back outside. She really adored me and always had me sleep by her. Butch Smit was the first white man I saw. There was another white man they called Guy . . . who was also a gold seeker at the mouth of the Kiimaaq. . . .

After I got older, I started seeing other white people. I'd see Makneq [the Reverend Drebert, the Moravian missionary who baptized her] when he came by dog team. . . .

When my late husband and I went over to Talliquq [Fort Alexander] to get married, I went up to see my aunt and I was very bashful because there were many people watching. When my aunt took me down to the boat and we met people on the way, she said, "I'm bringing this poor girl down because she is so bashful of the people around. . . . Togiak girls are very shy because they don't look into young men's eyes."

In 1942 Annie's family moved to Togiak on the coast, where many people gathered around the new Moravian mission and school. There was no dancing in Togiak, but Annie still remembers the dances she observed when she was young. She later stayed in a tuberculosis sanatorium in Tacoma, Washington, for two years. She married Billy Blue in the early 1930s, and together they had six children. Like her siblings, all of her children but one daughter, Martha, have died, many suddenly under tragic circumstances. She has many grandchildren, however, and nearly two dozen great-grandchildren. She is also active in village life, serving as a church elder, village council member, and judge in the local tribal court. Today's young people make her happy by calling her "Mom." "When they do that," she says, "it seems like my ground gets elevated."

Catherine Moore, whose Yup'ik name is Akiuk, was born in 1920 in a fish camp near Bethel to Cungaiyaq and Umalik Andrews, both of whom died when she was young. She was adopted by a couple from Tununak: "I remember when Cuk'uq came and got me and took me down to the boat. Then we went to Tununak, and it was there that I gained more awareness." But her adoptive father, Kaltauk, also died, and her adoptive mother, Anoktak, remarried a man with children of his own. Unlike Annie, Catherine experienced the hardships of an orphan, rejected and excluded from many experiences. She described how she once tried to prepare a sealskin poke: "I kept tearing the skin. They didn't let me try anymore since I couldn't learn, but they just let me do the seal's face. . . . Since I wasn't allowed to work on a seal, I tried to help by taking the fat and putting it into bowls." This statement is typical. Although lacking the support of a large family when she was young, Catherine was tenacious; throughout the years, she did the best she could and succeeded in living a satisfying life.

The only non-Natives Catherine saw when she was young were the Jesuit priests who visited Nelson Island. When she was fourteen, she was sent north to Akulurak at the mouth of the Yukon to attend the mission school, where she gained a good command of English, something no other elder in our group possessed. Catherine stayed at the mission until 1942 when she married Willie Moore and moved with him to Kwiguk, then later to Emmonak. There she and her husband raised ten children, nine of whom live in Emmonak to this day. Reflecting on her life, she concluded: "It wasn't fun at all being an orphan and wishing you had what other girls with fathers and mothers had and were wearing. When I talked about my childhood, some of my friends would say, 'You are no longer longing for things. God granted you many sons, and you always have food.'"

Paul John was born on the Bering Sea coast below Nelson Island in 1929, the much-loved only surviving child of Anna Angayiq and John Kungurkaq of Chefornak. They named him Aquqsak, but after the death of his older brother, Kangrilnguq, his father gave him that name as well. Although Paul had no formal education and limited English, his energy and intelligence earned him the respect of his peers. In 1953 he married Martina Usugan of Nightmute, and they continued to lead a migratory life, moving between seasonal camps such as Umkumiut, Kaviaq, and Qinaruuq until settling down in Nightmute so that their children could attend school. All nine graduated from high school and four from college, three with master's degrees. In the 1960s, Paul was among the first Nelson Islanders to work as a commercial fisherman in Bristol Bay, and he was instrumental in making it possible for other Nelson Islanders to follow his example.

Describing his youth, Paul noted:

I'm still quite young, but the place where I grew up remained in its original form for years because Western ways weren't introduced to us for a long time. I was seven years old when I saw a priest for the first time . . . and they started baptizing people and conducting marriages. . . . Before seeing *kass'at,* our people living their old ways were recognized as *makugtalriit* [literally, "those who live through hardship, hard work, endurance"]. . . . I had already gotten married and had children when the first school was built in my village. . . . I've been able to talk about our ancestral ways because I observed and experienced it and heard it being talked about by those around me as I was growing up.

Indeed, Paul listened well and today is recognized not only as an expert orator, but as a leader among his people. He is the traditional chief of both the village of Toksook Bay (which he helped to found in 1964 to avoid the annual move between the winter village of Nightmute and spring camp at Umkumiut) and the Association of Village Council Presidents. He is also a board member of numerous regional organizations, including the Yukon Kuskokwim Health Corporation and the Calista Elders Council, and has testified before numerous commissions both nationally and internationally on behalf of Yup'ik people. The year before our trip to Berlin, the Alaska Federation of Natives named him "Elder of the Year" for his work in strengthening and increasing understanding of Yup'ik traditional knowledge. He and Martina are both leading members of the Toksook Bay dance group, and both are committed to seeing the best of the Yup'ik past carried into the future.[2]

Andy Paukan, one of our two "elders-in-training," was born in Akulurak in 1939 and raised in the village of St. Marys on the Yukon River. His father, Jimmy Paukan, was a strong mentor. Following our trip to Berlin, Andy told me, "It was through my dad that I became a Yup'ik person. He is the person I can't forget. And Paul John, too, is carrying it on." Andy has been a leader in his own right. Until a tragic accident in January 2004, he was a bilingual teacher in the village school, mayor of St. Marys, and a driving force behind the St. Marys dance group. In 1992 he won the Alaska Federation of Natives' "Educator of the Year" award for his outstanding work, including work in museums. In 1989 he was actively involved in bringing artifacts from Sitka's Sheldon Jackson Museum to a four-day exhibit in Mountain Village, for which the Association of Village Council Presidents honored him as Citizen of the Year. He took a backseat while in Germany, much more a listener than a speaker, but we could never have made the trip to Berlin without his constant support and participation.

Our language expert, Marie Meade (Arnaq, or "woman"), was born to Elena and Nick O. Nick (Wassilie's youngest brother) in 1947 and was raised in the tundra village of Nunapitchuk. Her father's father, Paiyaq, came from the Akulmiut region where Marie grew up, while her father's mother came from near Qinaq on the lower Kuskokwim. Her mother's father came from around Kayalivik north of Nelson Island and his wife from the Qissunaq region. Like Andy and Catherine, Marie is bilingual, educated in Nunapitchuk and Bethel.

Marie has worked as a Yup'ik language specialist for more than thirty years. She worked with Irene Reed and others on the state's earliest bilingual education material in the early 1970s. She also wrote a number of children's books and was involved in helping to design curriculum for bilingual programs. In the 1980s, she collaborated with Japanese linguist Osahito Miyaoka on a review of Central Yup'ik grammar. At the same time, she worked as a translator on a massive project to document historic sites, sponsored by the Bureau of Indian Affairs ANCSA Office. From 1993 through 1996, Marie and I worked together on the *Agayuliyararput* Yup'ik mask exhibit and the accompanying bilingual catalog. Since then we have continued our collaboration with this work. At present she also teaches Yup'ik at the University of Alaska Anchorage. Marie is a leading member of the Yup'ik community in Anchorage, a proud grandmother, and a good friend.

During our last week in Berlin, Esther Ilutsik (Arnaq) of Dillingham and Henry Alikayak (Qilu) of Manokotak joined us from the Bristol Bay region. Henry was born in Quluqaq (Kulukak) in 1929, the second of Alexie and Betusia Alikayak's fifteen children. He moved to Manokotak in 1946, married Julia Martin, and had eight children. He has worked as both a commercial and subsistence fisherman all his life and, like Paul John, is active in many village and regional organizations. Also like Paul, he is widely respected for both his intelligence and his willingness to share what he knows.

Esther, our youngest group member, was born to George and Lena Ilutsik at Kanakanak and raised in the village of Aleknagik in the 1960s. Her father was originally from Quluqaq and her mother from Old Togiak. Esther received a bachelor's degree in elementary education and her master's in education administration from the University of Alaska Fairbanks in 1990. That year she began work with Yup'ik elders, inquiring about traditional knowledge as a founding member of the Ciulistet Research Group, which has since inspired educators throughout the state to create similar programs. Esther is presently working as a research associate with the Bristol Bay Campus of the University of Alaska in Dillingham, continuing to both document and share traditional knowledge. When I asked Esther to describe her life and work, she concluded: "I am fascinated with the knowledge that Yup'ik elders continue to share It amazes me how much oral information has not been shared with a couple of generations and that elders have waited patiently to share the information that they possess. It all speaks of the incredible respect and patience that they possess."

DEPARTURE: SEPTEMBER 1997

Our trip to Berlin was fraught with potential complications. Most of the elders spoke no English, two were in their eighties, and none had ever gone so far from home. The two eldest, Annie and Wassilie, were particularly hesitant. Annie told us later, "When we were getting ready to travel from Alaska, I was apprehensive about our trip . . . but my only daughter really wanted me to go. . . . She'd tell me that if I went, everything would be fine . . . and that she would always pray for me." Wassilie also worried about the trip. Paul and Catherine, however, had traveled to New York City to visit the National Museum of the American Indian the previous spring and were less reluctant to travel.

Our biggest challenge turned out to be leaving the United States. We began the process of applying for passports months before departure. All the elders had problems documenting their existence. Wassilie's birth and baptismal certificates had burned in a fire, Paul's had official names in both Yup'ik and English, and Catherine had conflicting dates of birth. Officials were leery of issuing them documents necessary for foreign travel, but in the end Paul and Catherine received temporary passports just days before our scheduled departure.

Our group gathered in Anchorage two days early, as potential bad weather in their home villages made it risky to wait until the day before to fly into town. From the airport they scattered throughout the city, staying with children, grandchildren, and friends. The next day we met at the bank to change money, and everyone was given a pocket camera to record the high points of the trip. Paul and I went shopping for a suitcase with wheels, which he packed with dried fish, seal oil, tea bags, sugar, and salt.

Our plane took off early the next morning, and Paul and Wassilie spent much of the twenty-four-hour flight glued to the windows. Flying east, we saw sunrise the next morning over the Atlantic, and the immense distance we were traveling became real.

ARRIVAL IN BERLIN

Customs nodded us through, fish and all, and in Berlin we took a cab to Unter den Eichen and the hotel Pension Dahlem—a three-story brick building with no elevator, steep stairs, and a back garden filled with apple trees, which we were quick to harvest. This comfortable, working-class establishment catered to construction tradesmen in Berlin during the week and German tourists and student soccer teams on weekends. We were given three big rooms at the back of the building on the third floor. By leaving our doors open, we could create the sense of a house with adjoining rooms.

Our first meal in Berlin, at a corner restaurant, included five orders of grilled salmon. The next morning we enjoyed an enormous breakfast of cheeses, meats, rolls, and coffee in the hotel's sunny dining room. In the evenings that followed, we alternated between dining out and dining in. Although guests were not normally permitted to cook, the hotel owner let us use a huge pot, in which he boiled eggs for breakfast, to cook soups, which Marie and I would carry upstairs and serve on the table in her and Annie's room.

The next day was Sunday. We rested in the morning, then took the train to the River Havel, where we rode a boat past huge houses and elegant gardens through the canals to the lake, Wannsee. Annie was impressed by the lakeside plants and berry bushes, and everyone wanted to stop and gather the fruit. All were interested in the men fishing and the *qugyuk* (whistling swan) swimming on the lake. After a day in the open air and a dinner of dried fish in our hotel, we spent fifty dollars in change calling home, marveling that back in Alaska everyone was just waking up while it was about time for us to go to sleep. The long-distance talking made everybody happy, and we sat around the tiny hotel entryway for more than an hour singing and talking before going to bed. Our work in the museum would begin the next day.

FIRST DAY Tools for Ocean Hunting

GETTING STARTED

We arrived at the Berlin museum's back door at 8 A.M., full of anticipation. The caretaker for North American collections, Horst Wedell, escorted us up to the third-floor storage area. He spoke no English and we spoke no German, so we smiled and nodded and waited for curator Peter Bolz in the wide, sunlit hallway at the top of the stairwell. At one end a door opened into the storage area, and at the other was the entrance to the museum's exhibit space. In between was a large room banked with windows opening into a courtyard below, letting light flood in on the floor-to-ceiling painting of scantily clad hunters in the Amazonian rain forest. Eight Formica-topped tables had been drawn together, two abreast, to provide our work space for the next three weeks.

Peter arrived soon after and showed us into the storage area where the Yup'ik artifacts were kept. Everyone walked quietly past South American feather headdresses and Kwakiutl carvings. The air was still and warm, smelling of camphor, old wood, and leather. The far southwest corner was devoted to the "Arktis" (Arctic), including collections from Greenland, Canada, and Alaska (fig. 1.1). No one touched anything, and we said little as Peter pointed out Yup'ik masks on a far wall and the accouterments of daily life stored in well-organized drawers and shelves behind glass doors. After peering into closed cases, we gathered in an aisle to sing *Tarvarnauramken*, an old Yup'ik dance song describing the traditional act of purifying oneself with the smoke of *tarvaq* (wild celery) (fig. 1.2). Both Catherine and Marie had brought their dance fans, and they gracefully went through the motions while the rest of us sang:

Tarvarnauramken
May I purify your body

Ellugarnauramken
May I brush off defects from your body

Pikaniraniartuten
So you may have renewed strength

After the purification song, we walked back to the sunny hallway to begin our work. Peter asked us what we would like to see first. Having passed an impressive cabinet holding har-

1.1 *Wassilie Berlin, Paul John, and Annie Blue standing in front of the "Arktis" section in the Berlin Ethnological Museum. Dietrich Graf, Ethnologisches Museum Berlin.*

1.2 *Our group gathered in prayer before beginning work in collections.*

poons and spears from every part of the Arctic, we decided to begin with those from our area. This was a good choice, as it was the first case in the first row of Arctic artifacts, and for the remainder of our stay we worked systematically down one aisle and up the next until we had seen all two thousand Yup'ik things. Peter later told us that although representatives from other indigenous groups had come for two- to three-day visits to the museum, ours was the first group to work through an entire collection.

As the elders made themselves comfortable around the tables in the sunny workroom outside the collection area, Peter brought me a slim stack of paper—the original accession records, stored for more than a century with the objects they described. I quickly thumbed through, pulling out the fifteen cards designating Yup'ik things—most marked either "Kwigpagmiut," "Kuskokwagmiut," Nushagak River, or Nunivak Island—and handed them to Herr Wedell, who went back into collections to retrieve the harpoons. This would be our method for the rest of the stay. Herr Wedell would give me the records, I would draw out the ones identified as Yup'ik, and he would pull them from collections, load them onto rolling carts, and wheel them out for us to examine. What began as formal requests relaxed as the days went by, but our method stayed the same.

As we waited for Herr Wedell to bring the first pieces, we gathered around the tables. The women all wore *qasperet* (cotton dresses), and Paul and Andy wore the short cotton parkas that they used for dancing. Wassilie had also dressed carefully, and everything he wore was clean and new, including his sneakers and a cap with the "Akula Fox" logo of Kasigluk High School. When all were seated, Marie put a tape in the recorder and began to record, giving the date and listing all our names and where we were from. She then turned to Annie and asked in Yup'ik, "Do you want to begin in your usual manner?" Annie stood and prayed to God in her language:

Almighty Father, Master of the Universe, who gives guidance to all, we are here now according to your plan. You lead us on unforeseen paths in goodness. As children we were totally unaware of the many places we would travel to in our lives. We give thanks to you for bestowing life upon us up to this time. . .

Father, you know me very well. I have faced the threat of being removed from this world, but when I became aware of this I beseeched you for help. I understand now that my life was spared . . . because of the work we are doing now. Thank you so much. . . .

We ask that you help us to do our work through you. Grant us wisdom in our endeavors. . . . Through Jesus our Savior lead us in Your Goodness. Amen.

Aklegaq / Seal-hunting Harpoon with Bladder Float

The first piece we examined was a Nushagak harpoon, with line, socket piece, and barbed point (fig. 1.3, fig 1.4).[1] Marie handed it to Wassilie, the eldest present, saying that although he was from the tundra area, he might know what it was. Wassilie identified it as a seal-hunting harpoon but noted that it was missing its *egun* (throwing board). He also named the *imgun* (coiled sealskin line) attached to the *kukgar* (barbed harpoon point): "These weapons were used for sea mammals. Hunters used them when seals popped up in the water near them. They would stalk the animal and continue to spear it as it popped in and out of the water."

Wassilie continued, describing the *yualu qip'aq* (twisted sinew twine) used to attach the harpoon head and the little *qerruinaq* (harpoon float): "It's probably a bladder. It was used to

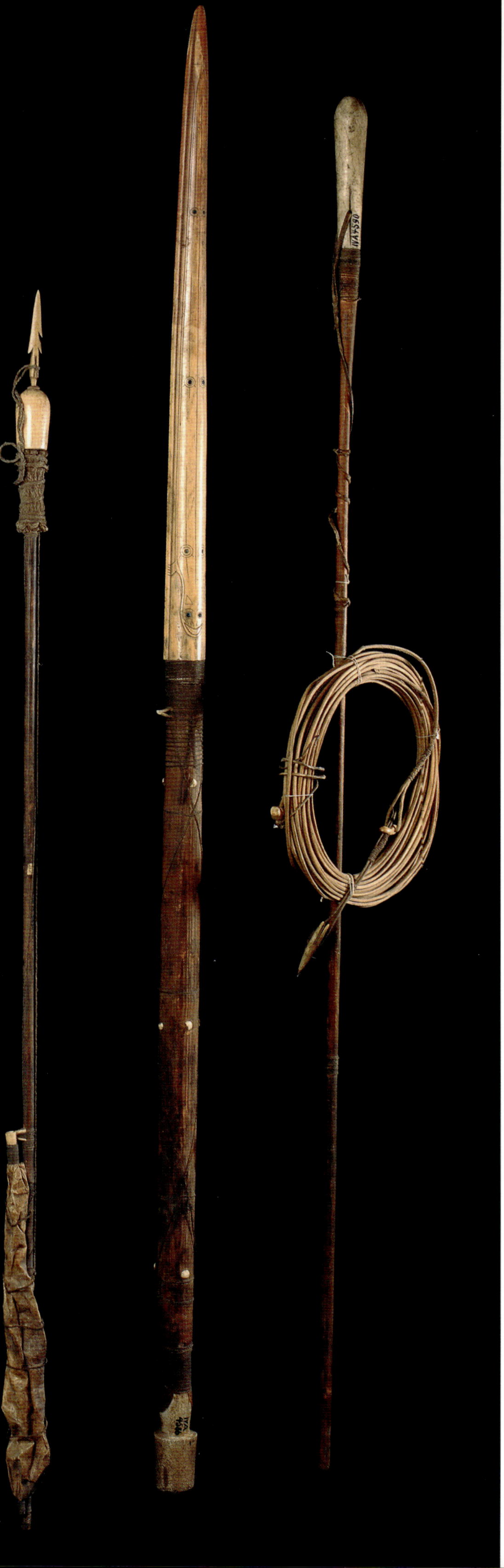

1.4   Nushagak seal-hunting harpoon socket piece and barbed point set into a cushioning wood plug to absorb the impact. Jacobsen wrote: "Seal harpoon such as is mainly used in this area on open water. The hunter takes along one or two small bow harpoons and a bow on his kayak. Upon spotting a seal emerging from the waves, the hunter shoots an arrow at the animal from a great distance. If he strikes the seal, it is usually the case that other hunters in kayaks form a ring around the wounded animal. As soon as the animal surfaces again, this harpoon is thrown against the animal to kill it. Sometimes only this harpoon is used, provided the animal is close. The line connecting the harpoon with the shaft is made of sinew. The harpoon is made of reindeer antler. Once the hunt is over, the harpoon and harpoon line are put aside just as it is stored now. The harpoon is always thrown with a throwing board." IVA5230.

1.3   Harpoons; one (far left) with a bladder float used to slow the wounded animal, the middle one used on walrus and beluga for the final kill, and the last with a walrus-skin line used to kill seals sleeping on ice. IVA5230, IVA4586, IVA4590.

1.5   Harpoon socket piece and barbed point from the Yukon River mouth, carved in the shape of a toothy predator to enhance the hunter's success when hunting smaller sea mammals in open water with drag and float gear. Barbed points such as these catch beneath the animal's blubber and hide. Each has a line hole in its butt end and is thrown with a female-socketed harpoon shaft. As such points can easily tear out, they are released from the hunter's direct control and set loose attached to inflated sealskins or bladder floats, which tire the animal. IVA4576

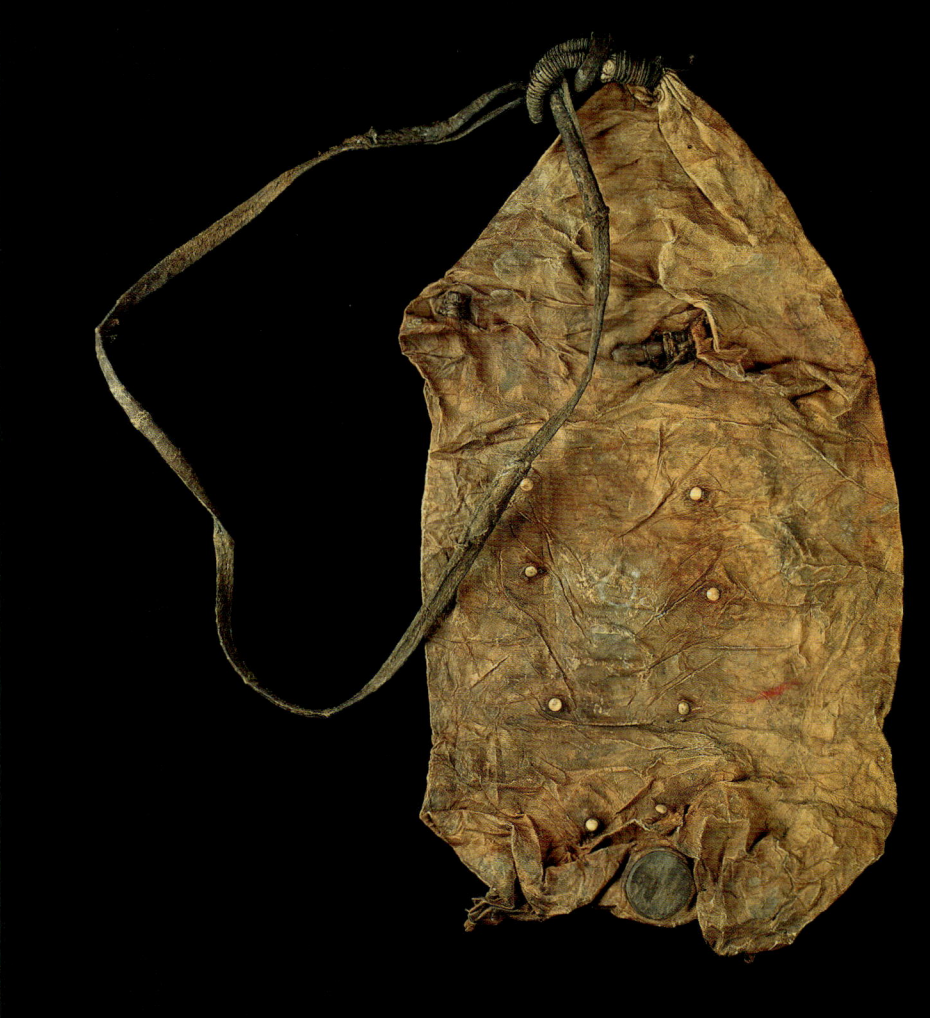

keep the weapon visible. When the animal was hit and this was inflated, it would slow it down." Paul added his observations, noting that in the coastal area this weapon was known as an *aklegaq*, named for its walrus-bladder *(aklegaa)* float: "This was used to hit the seal first when it was hunted. This walrus bladder was inflated before the weapon was thrust. . . . It was used like a buoy and kept the animal visible once it was struck."

Paul also noted that the sinew twine (called *piirraq* or *piirrayagaq* in the coastal area and *qip'aq* on the tundra) was woven with three strands, like braided hair: "On the mainland they used caribou *uliutet* [backbone muscles split to make sinew]. The coastal people always tried to use the *uliutet* of beluga whales. They also used the muscles of a kind of bird." Catherine then spoke for the first time, distinguishing between the upper and lower layers of muscles used to make sinew: "There are two layers of muscles on the animal's back. The top layers were called *uliutet*. The underlayer, the muscle inside the meat, was called *eglu*. The muscles in the meat were long. Both layers of muscles could be called *yualuq* [sinew]. . . . Caribou and beluga both have *uliutet*, and down inside the meat are the *eglut*."

Later we looked at five small ivory nozzles (fig. 1.6), three from the Kuskokwim and two from Nushagak, used to inflate bladder floats.[2] At first Wassilie was mystified, and Andy teased, "Our ancestors forgot to patent these gas hose connectors!" Paul held it to his lips, saying: "This is a device used to inflate [the float for] an *aklegaq*. . . . It's a *qerrurcuun* [float nozzle]

1.6 Ivory nozzle used to inflate a harpoon float. IVA2846.

1.7 Looking at this float, Paul remarked, "When I was young, my late parents provided me with a poke like this made out of a hair seal. I'd keep the inflated seal poke on top of the qamigautek [kayak sled], which was placed behind me on the kayak. The coiled line was placed in front of the kayak opening on the right side with the float at its end." Note the plugs used to close the seal's nipple and genital hole. IVA5392.

used to inflate *qerruinat* [harpoon floats]. . . . A float was usually made out of a whole hair-seal skin. Those should be placed in that category." Wassilie added: "It was attached to something securely, and the grooves helped it to stay in place."

Qerruinaq / Float

Having spoken about the floats attached to sealing harpoons, all were interested when Herr Wedell brought a Kuskokwim float (fig. 1.7) out of collections.[3] Paul spoke first:

This was an implement that hunters always took with them when they hunted in the ocean . . . called *qerruinaq*. People were instructed to grab the *qerruinaq* when their kayaks overturned accidentally. . . . It was processed to remove its hair. Perhaps people from the Aleutian Islands used it as a float. . . . It's not a hair seal or a spotted seal. By looking at its nipples, I'm thinking that it's a sea otter.

Wassilie agreed with Paul that the float came from outside his area: "From what I heard, long ago people from the Kuskokwim went far away to trade with people. The ancestors were very resourceful." Paul continued:

A leather rope that they called a *qavyak* is attached to this piece. It was made from a walrus skin that was scraped and made thinner before it was cut into a rope. A *qerruinaq* was tied to the end of that *usaaq* [line].

Paul then took the float and demonstrated how it could be thrown from the kayak:

After the hunter threw the harpoon at a seal, he'd push the *qerruinaq* into the water. This *qerruinaq* would let one know where the animal was, and it would also exhaust it as it tried to escape. This aided us tremendously when we harpooned animals.

Also, there is a limit to how much air you put in when inflating it. As you inflate it, you push down to judge the amount of air in it. You know when it has sufficient air because the front appendages become level with the highest point on the inflated seal poke . . . as you apply pressure between the front appendages. . . . If this part is partially submerged, it provides a drag against the struggle of the seal. This is the reason they limited how much air was put inside. . . . If the *qerruinaq* had too much air inside, it would surface and skip along on the water when the seal started to pull, trying to escape.

Wassilie said that he had heard the same thing. Then Catherine spoke about another lifesaving property of the walrus-skin line:

Looking at the skin rope attached to this *qerruinaq*, I'm reminded of my past because I observed walrus skins being scraped. I used to see coiled lines of rope like this hanging in food shecs.

One time when Ap'ayagaq [a *tuqluun*, or variation on a kinship term; literally, "little grandfather"] was making rope, I asked, "Why do you always make rope like this?" He replied that they stored it because it wasn't used only for hunting equipment, but during famine it could be cooked and used as food. He also said that since they couldn't throw it out, they saved it for the time of privation.

Wassilie spoke last, recalling more uses of walrus-skin line:

Qavya [skin rope] was very useful when I was little. When I first became aware of my surroundings, my family had an *angyapiaq*, a large frame boat covered with bearded-seal skins. The skins were lashed onto the frame with these ropes. Since people did not have nails, the skin covering was stretched to fit the boat frame, then lashed onto the frame using rope, which was put through the set holes, starting from the front to the back and all the way around. People living in the coastal areas always had a supply of *qavya*. They used it to barter with the inland people. The coastal people came in their kayaks to trade with people living in fish camps along the Kuskokwim in the summer. People from the coastal areas always wanted skins for parkas.

Before the *qerruinaq* could be inflated, all holes in the skin had to be plugged. Later during our stay we looked at thirteen *unguquutat* (plugs) (fig. 1.8).[4] Adding detail on a particularly well-made plug, Jacobsen wrote: "This device is put into the

1.8 Ivory float inflation nozzle and plugs used to close holes in sealskins, also possibly used as amulets. Jacobsen wrote that the larger plugs were used to close female genital holes or nipples, while the smaller ones closed spear and harpoon holes. Clockwise from upper left: IVA4521, IVA3241, IVA4960, IVA7220.

leather edges of the hole with the help of strong seal straps, which are gathered and tied and therefore make the hole airtight. When decorated with faces, these also serve as amulets or protectors for the sack."[5] None of the elders recognized Jacobsen's designations for the plugs, "Totapit" or "Totapak," which is not surprising, as Jacobsen translated it on one record as "lip peg" (*tuutaq*, "labret"), perhaps confusing the name of the plug with the name for the tiny bead labrets that decorated some of the faces. The men did, however, recognize the plugs and their use but said that they could not share what they knew with us women lest it make us uncomfortable during intercourse with our husbands. Catherine said that we didn't mind not knowing.

We also examined two circular faces with chin tattoos and downturned mouths, denoting a "pretend woman" (*arnaruaq*), from Cape Vancouver that Jacobsen said were kept in the house as good-luck amulets.[6] He noted that they had the same form and side indentations as plugs used to close the holes in the seal's skin to prevent the seal from losing too much blood and sinking. He added correctly that the downturned mouth, slanted eyes, and broad nose typically represented a female seal, making their use to plug sealskins all the more suggestive.

Finally, Paul and Wassilie noted that similar plugs were used to close bearded-seal stomachs filled with seal oil to take on hunting trips. Paul viewed two carved wooden faces from Cape Vancouver, one walrus and one human, as plugs for holes of all kinds.[7]

Qeciqutaq / Walrus-Bladder Water Container

Earlier we had examined a faded Nushagak remnant[8] that Catherine instantly identified as a "Yup'ik thermos":

Here's a walrus bladder from long ago. I used to see these because I grew up in Tununak. Those who prepared them never let us touch them when they worked on them. They prepared them very well. It was used as a water container when one was out on the ocean. Its mouth was made to be sturdy. . . . When we were ready to bring them down, they'd tell us to be very careful and not to drop them on the ground.

When men were getting ready to hunt at sea, they would ask us to fill these from the rushing streams even though we were very young. Since we girls were always helpful, I really enjoyed filling these with water and bringing them down to the kayaks. . . . Since I wasn't so big, the walrus-bladder water bag was very heavy when I carried it. These water bags had plugs. The men kept the water containers in twined grass bags as they traveled on the ocean.

The "plugs" Catherine referred to did not surface until the following week, when we looked at six ivory and wooden funnels (fig. 1.9, fig. 1.10) from all over the region,[9] which Jacobsen wrote were used to fill "seal bladder" water containers taken on hunting trips. Paul described their use in more detail: "These ivory pieces were where water went into this *qeciqutaq*. Walrus and bearded-seal bladders were used as water bottles. When the bladder had been processed and dried, a piece of ivory was fixed as a spout, with a wooden piece to cover the hole attached to the side with a string. Once the wood was stuffed into the hole, water couldn't leak from the bladder water holder."

We also had a chance to look at a Nushagak water container (fig. 1.12)[10] in fine condition. Everyone had something to say, not only about the container but about the care it had been given. Although Jacobsen wrote that it was a seal bladder, Paul

1.9 Ivory funnel used to fill bladder water containers. IVA5400.

1.10 Wassilie pretending to sip from the ivory funnel of a bladder water container. IVA5400.

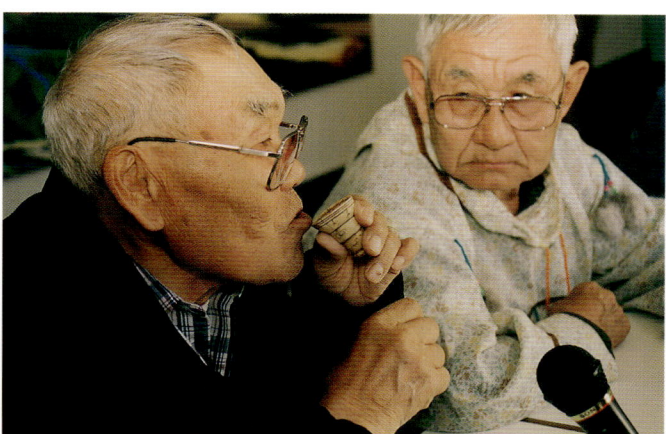

1.11 A painted bladder ("Neggasuk Agligakrak") from Golovnin Bay that Jacobsen reported to be a seal bladder like those displayed during the Bladder Festival. This would be rare indeed, as bladders were returned to the sea after the festival. Paul was unequivocal in his interpretation: "This looks like a water container . . . used to carry water by hunters before water jugs were introduced." IVA3061.

1.12 Wassilie remarked that the tiny ivory cup attached to the end of his Nushagak bladder water container "was such a perfect device for drinking that it was impossible to spill any water from it." IVA 5370

and Wassilie identified it as a walrus bladder filled with water and carried in the kayak by hunters. Wassilie added: "This *tuluq* [ivory piece] is called the *pasvaagun* [plug or stopper] for the *qeciqutaq*. It's so perfect it looks like it was made in a factory. And this part is a little cup for the water. After it was filled one would drink, then close the *qeciqutaq* again." Paul noted that the pieces at the spouts were called *pasvaagutet:* "This wasn't the only place they were used. When they prepared to fill hair seals or *useqnaaraat* [two-year-old spotted seals] with seal oil, they used a stopper at the spout of the seal poke, and it was also a *pasvaagun*."

Andy asked why the century-old container wasn't dry and brittle, and Catherine noted that things that have been in salt water don't get brittle and hard. Wassilie mentioned that there were many uses for these water containers: "The berry pickers . . . filled them with berries and carried them on their backs inside twined-grass backpacks. It was always neat and clean when berries were carried on backs in containers like these." Catherine continued:

When I watched my stepmother filling a beluga stomach with berries, I was amazed at how much it could hold. . . . After she had rested for a while with the load of berries on her back, I'd have to pull as hard as I could to help her stand up again. . . . When we got home, she'd transfer the berries into an *imarnin* [seal-gut parka]. She'd close the hood hole and the sleeve holes and fill the *imarnin* from the bottom. . . . Then she'd put the *imarnin* full of berries in a twined-grass basket and close it tightly so water wouldn't enter. She'd wade out into the water pulling the berry basket tied to a piece of driftwood, . . . then push the basket down into the water, with the piece of driftwood visible on the bank. . . . Then during freeze-up one day, she asked me to go with her while she fetched the berry basket. She'd pull up the *imarnin* filled with berries inside a basket twined from *qayikvayak* [wheat grass, *Agropyron* sp.]. When she opened up the gut parka back home, we'd find the berries

1.13 Harpoon used for the final kill, decorated with a toothy grin and blue-bead eyes. The harpoon has a collared socket piece and is used with a fixed foreshaft. The lance at the opposite end is made from a split length of walrus tusk. IVA4586.

1.14 Paul lancing an imaginary walrus under the table. IVA4586.

1.15 Paul demonstrating how to thrust the large Nunivak harpoon.

still in the same condition they were when they were put in the water. That was how they stored their salmonberries back in those days.

When they gathered blackberries, they'd temporarily store them in twined baskets. . . . They never stored blackberries in water. They'd leave them out on the tundra and keep filling the basket until full, . . . then get them when it frosted and store them in the root cellar.

Aangruyak / Harpoon Used for the Final Kill

Next we examined another Nushagak harpoon shaft.[11] Paul used it as an excuse to describe the *aangruyak* (harpoon used for the final kill):

I mentioned that a weapon called an *aangruyak* was used for the final kill when hunting bigger animals. . . . When a hunter thrust this weapon at an animal, the point, its *aangruyak*, went inside the animal and was detached from the tip. Once the point was lodged inside the animal and they continued to hit it with the *aangruyak*, the animal would weaken and die.

Later that morning we looked at three more weapons that Paul and Wassilie identified as *aangruyiit*. All were gifts to Jacobsen from the Andreafski trader Charles Petersen, who had collected them during annual trips to Nunivak Island. They were heavier than the other harpoons, and Wassilie noted that they were used on big animals that were hard to kill, including walrus and beluga. Each had a heavy socket piece with a detachable point on one end and a long ivory lance tip on the other, one of which (fig. 1.13)[12] was decorated with an animal figure with blue beads as eyes. Taking the weapon in his hands, Paul thrust it at an imaginary walrus under the table (fig. 1.14, fig. 1.15) and said:

This was also a hunting tool from Nunivak. Its tip was used to hit an animal. The other end could have been used to kill it once it was hit. It probably was used to chip the ice when they were hunting. . . . It had *qirussit* [designs] . . . that look like *mengkuk* [men's labrets (dual)]. The first people from Nunivak I saw had *mengkuk* on their chins . . . reminding people of walrus. Men with *mengkuut* thought they looked like walrus with tusks.

We would return to this point in days to come.

1.16 Seal-hunting harpoon with flight-stabilizing feathers but no float, meant to be used with a throwing board. Paul recalled that hunters with a good sense of measurement were able to hit seals by aiming and harpooning at the spot just ahead of the ripples made by the seal swimming close to the water's surface. IVA4575.

1.17 Two toggling harpoons, for killing seals on and around ice floes. Jacobsen reported that the triangular socket piece was unique to the people of southwestern Alaska and was carved from walrus ivory, its weight carefully measured with the buoyancy of the wooden shaft so that only the uppermost point rose above the water. The weight was essential so that the harpoon could reach the seal and penetrate its skin. The openings in the socket piece were to prevent it from bending. IVA171a, b.

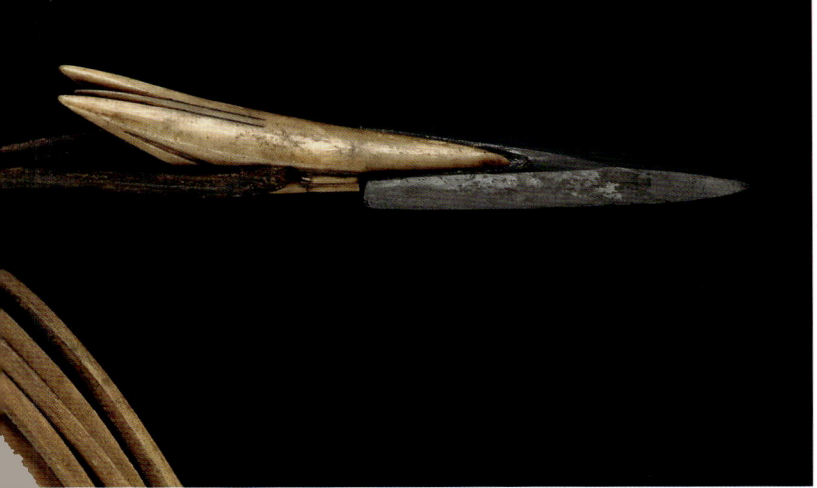

1.18 Toggling harpoon point attached to the coiled line of the toggling harpoon in figure 1.3. The point is forced deep into its target on the end of a slender foreshaft. When the line tightens, the spur at the point's base twists it sideways, toggling it firmly beneath the animal's blubber and holding the animal fast. IVA4590.

Nagiiquyaq wall'u Nanerpak / Seal-hunting Harpoon with Feather Fletching

The next harpoon (fig. 1.16) from the Kuskokwim was different from either we had so far examined.[13] It had two sets of flight-stablizing feathers (which Jacobsen noted was rare) to keep it straight, but no float. Meant to be used with a throwing board at considerable distance, when it struck the animal the harpoon point freed itself from the shaft which the animal dragged behind. Wassilie spoke without hesitation:

Kuskokwim people called this a *nagiiquyaq* . . . with two sets of *nakrutet* [fletching, flight-stabilizing feathers]. My late father and others called these feathers *agayiinraat* [cormorant feather attachments]. . . . Our ancestors cherished them. Mainlanders acquired such feathers only by trading . . . with things the coastal people needed. Back in those days, people always tried to help each other.

Paul added that the piece had the same name on Nelson Island but was called a *nanerpak* in the Yukon area. He also noted that Nelson Islanders called the cord attached to the spearhead *usaaq*, while farther south it was called *kinguliraq*, and that the feathers were from the tails of cormorants, a powerful sea-hunting bird. Wassilie added with feeling, "I have tail feathers like these at my home. I'm not going to use them, but I've carefully put them away and kept them with me."

When we looked at a smaller shaft head for a *nagiiquyaq*,[14] Paul commented: "Because this was made for a boy, it's smaller than the adult size. Obviously, a boy that was cherished by a father or a grandfather had his first kayak, and this little *nagiiquyaq* was made for him for training purposes."

Asaaquq / Toggling Harpoon for Killing Seals on and around Ice

We examined two light toggling harpoons (fig. 1.17) used from the mouth of the Yukon as far south as Cape Avinoff.[15] Wassilie immediately pointed out how the ivory socket pieces were bent in from age and that one was decorated with the face of a small seal. Paul added: "These two weapons—one side of each point was straight and smooth. These weapons were called *asaaquk* [dual]. Hunters used them when they went after seals sitting on ice. When they approached a sleeping seal on the ice, . . . they'd try to thrust the weapon with this smooth side down; it would slide on the snow toward the animal and the point would hit it and get lodged."

When we looked at a complete seal-hunting harpoon (fig. 1.18) from Nelson Island,[16] Wassilie noted its *imgutaq* (coiled line), then gave Paul the microphone to comment:

As I said earlier, it was a weapon that was used to try to kill seals sleeping on ice or bobbing up and down in the water. Its *usaaq* [line] has a *cavek* [toggling harpoon point] attached to it. Since this looks like an old one, this ivory piece had an *umi* [stone point] made of *ulukaq* [slate or other stone formerly used as a blade on women's knives and spear points]. . . . It has no feather *nakrutet*, or *culut*. It was thrown at a target with a *nuqaq* [throwing board], but its *nuqaq* is not here.

The next day, when presented with an ivory socket piece for an *asaaquq*,[17] Paul added detail:

This *asaaquq* was used with an *usaaq* attachment. The *usaaq* was neatly coiled [on the kayak bow] on the *acaluq* [kayak float board]. Measuring the distance with his arms and estimating the length of the line, [the hunter] thrust the weapon with this kind of a tip toward a target. . . . *Asaaqut* were weapons that were used to harpoon seals that were farther away from the hunter. . . . And they attached a float to the weapon, too, which was kept on the back of the kayak and tied to the end of the *usaaq*. When the hunter hit the target, he'd push the float into the water. The hunter would try to kill the seal, following the float the animal was dragging.

Two more harpoons from the Yukon received a brief inspection.[18] Catherine thought the first looked like an ice pick, but Wassilie corrected her, noting that it was a hunting tool. The second had the remains of *urasqaq* (white clay paint) on its shaft, and Jacobsen wrote that all hunting equipment (kayaks, paddles, hats, and harpoon shafts) was painted white so that the boats and their passengers were less visible among the ice floes. Wassilie noted a rock that added weight to the weapon, and Andy remarked on the dried blood around the connection between the spearhead and shaft: "I thought our ancestors didn't have any glue. Why does that look like it was glued in place?"

Anguarun / Paddle

A wooden paddle (fig. 1.19) from the Yukon was the next piece presented.[19] Wassilie began: "The blade of this *anguarun* [single-bladed paddle] was made differently than ours [on the Kuskokwim]. . . . [It] was quite inflated. I used to make paddles with thin blades. . . . We called the handle grip *kangkupaguaq* . . . and attached it to the top end so that it wouldn't come off easily." Paul (fig. 1.20) commented on its black-painted designs:

1.19 Single-bladed paddles, including thin-bladed paddle painted with white clay from Togiak, larger-bladed paddle characteristic of the Yukon with red and black designs, and plain wooden paddle. Wassilie remarked that the thin blade of the Togiak paddle prevented the wind pushing it when one was paddling. Paul added, "If the blade was wide, as you lifted it up in the wind it would be pushed back, making it difficult for you to move it to the other side of the kayak." From left to right: IVA4589, IVA5597, IVA4345.

1.20 Paul paddling through collections. Dietrich Graf, Ethnologisches Museum Berlin.

I'm curious about the designs on [this piece]. According to Yukon people, these four designs going up and down were called *alngat* [decorations, marks]. We called them *qaralit*. Whoever owned this paddle obviously decorated it with designs that belonged to his family, a design that was passed down from generation to generation. If the owner lost it, someone would find it and know the owner by looking at the design.

Paul closed with another remark on terminology, noting that the word for handle or grip on Nelson Island was *qaquaq*, not *kangkupaguaq* as on the Kuskokwim.

Wassilie and Paul then discussed a Nushagak paddle.[20] First Wassilie observed that its blade was longer than the first one, though the paddle itself was shorter: "It's because we come from different lands and waters." He then said that the handles of the two paddles were the same: "Like the ones I used to see, its grip is not made of wood. Some paddles had handles made of antler. Here you could see the hole where a *teggera'ar* [hardwood] nail was inserted." Paul also found the handle worth comment: "[S]ince men sometimes paddled a long time out on the ocean in the wind, the oceangoing paddles were made like this with handles that weren't exactly round. If they paddled day and night out there, or even several days, this prevented their palms from wrinkling and peeling."

Next was a paddle collected on the lower Yukon.[21] Both men carefully examined its blade. Wassilie spoke first: "Since this came from the Yukon, it resembles the one we looked at. And the *quaguut* [central ridges] on the blade helped to keep it from turning, since this was obviously used in strong current. And its hand grip was not made separately and attached but was made as part of the handle. We are aware that the current on the Yukon River is different from that on the Kuskokwim." Paul added that in the coastal area, the ridge on the paddle was called *qengartaq*, not *quaguk*: "The paddles used on the ocean had deeper *qengartat* . . . that prevented the paddle blades from breaking. And paddles that had *qaquat* [grips] like this were called *qaquaqnginaq*. The grip is all one piece with the paddle handle."

1.21 Wooden gaff with caribou-antler hook, a tool that ocean hunters could not do without. The gaff could be used as a walking stick, to pull hard-to-reach items out from inside a kayak, and to retrieve a kayak that floated away. IVA5243.

1.22 Paul demonstrating the use of the all-important *negcik* (gaff). Dietrich Graf, Ethnologisches Museum Berlin.

1.23 Paul commented: "This small hook was used by women when harvesting food to hook and pull edible plants like buttercups from lakes and ponds." IVA4344.

1.24 Paul demonstrating the lifesaving capacity of a negcik (gaff), which could be used to hook under the chin of a hunter who had fallen in the ocean out of reach of his companion. IVA3013.

Another single-bladed paddle from Togiak had a long, narrow blade with shallower ridges, painted with *urasqaq* (white clay) and *avisgaq* (black pigment).[22] Wassilie noted that *uqviinraq* (willow root) had been tied around the middle of the handle, perhaps to repair damage. Paul explained the willow root as an inherited family design, possibly added for identification.

Negcik / Gaff

After studying paddles, we turned to a simple boat hook (fig. 1.21) from Fort Alexander with a caribou-antler hook on one end and a point on the other.[23] This was an essential tool for men traveling and hunting on ice, and Paul (fig. 1.22) spoke at once and at length, describing practices he had personally experienced:

The length of this is just right . . . and it resembles the ones I saw in my village. This is a piece hunters never left behind when they hunted with kayaks during the springtime. This is called a *negcikcuar* [small gaff].

When a person was walking around on ice by his kayak, he was advised to hold his *negcikcuar* if he wasn't holding a *negcigpak* [large gaff]. . . .

They also used the *negcikcuar* to push carcasses deep inside the front or the back of the kayak . . . where the arm couldn't reach. And when they came back from hunting, they'd use the *negcikcuar* to reach in and pull out carcasses from deep inside the kayak.

If a hunter came back using the *negcikcuar* as a walking stick, it was understood that he had caught a bearded seal that was down at the shore, waiting to be picked up by his family. But if a hunter walked up pulling his kayak sled, they'd know right away that he hadn't caught a bearded seal. Since he was pulling a sled, they understood that it was loaded with the hair seal he had caught. When food was not readily available, as soon as a hunter killed a hair seal he would immediately load it up in his little kayak sled and hurriedly take it home.

It was something hunters would not do without . . . and had more than one use. . . . Since they used its hook to pull things, they called it *negcikcuar*, but the long gaff they always kept on the front surface of their kayaks was called *negcik*.

Marie then presented a Kuskokwim gaff,[24] and her uncle Wassilie commented on the fine workmanship: "Like the first one, this was used by our ancestors as a *negcikcuar*. This hook is decorated quite well. And the handle has *kumgat* [incised designs] from top to bottom. Since it could be used as an *ayaruq* [walking stick], the side of the handle has designs as an added feature."

Paul concluded by describing the lifesaving uses to which a *negcikcuar* might be put: "If a hunter's kayak floated away on an ice floe, he'd throw the *negcikcuar* on his back and bite the end of the line, then swim toward his kayak . . . and when he reached the ice floe, he'd use it to climb on the ice and retrieve his kayak."

When we looked at another small hook (fig. 1.23) from the Yukon,[25] Wassilie identified it at once as a woman's tool: "The end of this is a hook, but there's nothing at the tip of the pole. It has a design all the way down like the Kuskokwim piece we were looking at. . . . It looks like a piece that was used by women . . . to hook and retrieve things that were hard to reach."

A week later we looked at a group of bone hooks, originally attached to wooden shafts. Jacobsen noted that the largest was incised to prevent it from becoming crooked with age. Paul identified it without hesitation (fig. 1.24), adding new information:

This is a *negcik* [gaff or boat hook], an instrument men always carried when they traveled in kayaks out on the ocean. Men were told to use this on ice, even though it looked safe to walk on. These always had wooden handles. A man always used this to lean on when he got into his kayak, and he also used it as support when he came out of his kayak. . . .

If one of two hunting partners fell into a crack in the ice and the partner couldn't reach him with his hand, he was told to hook him below the chin with his gaff to pull him up. Though he's pricked in the skin with the point, it was this implement that could rescue him.

Three smaller bone hooks were equally recognizable.[26] Jacobsen reported that holes in the bone served to fasten the hook with leather strips to the handle. The craftsman had no saw, so would bore a row of holes in the direction he wished to separate the bone and then easily break the piece off. Paul continued describing the gaff's use:

These three were also used in kayaks. This is a *negcikcuar* [small gaff]. The handles on these were usually a little shorter than arm's length. Men made these using their own bodies as measurement. They always had a sharp point at the bottom tip . . . used to chip off the edge of the ice. And when they caught big seals and the ice edge was too high to easily pull up the catch, they used this implement to level off the side where they were going to pull up the animal.

Paul identified the two smallest hooks from St. Michael and the Yukon[27] as belonging to short-handled gaffs used for retrieving nets or harpoon gear, or as boat hooks:

Men also carried implements like these they called *tallirpacuaraat* [small, short-handled gaffs; literally, "small, big arms"] in their kayaks. They were little ivory gaffs with short handles. They could stuff them inside the front of of their kayaks. Their handles weren't thick. And when [a hunter] couldn't grab something deep inside his kayak, he'd pull out his *tallirpacuar* and use it as a hook to take it.

Wassilie examined two more hooks from the lower Yukon,[28] judging them to be from the top end of an *ayaruq* (walking stick) used to retrieve things one could not reach by hand, including fish traps or nets from the water and blubber from the inside of the kayak. He interpreted the last two "hooks" that Jacobsen excavated near St. Michael and the lower Yukon[29] as parts of the kayak around which the *tapraq* (skin line) was wound: "They were placed on each side near the *ceturyaq* [kayak front area]. I saw kayaks with these in different lengths. . . . The taller one was filled with a longer skin line. And one on the other side was shorter."

Wassilie's final comment reflected on the way Paul and he were working together: "Since some people here are confused about these things, Paul and I, the elders present, are trying to explain things to them as a team. This kind of teamwork was called *asguristeksaraq* [from *asgur-*, "going against"] by our ancestors."

Cavget, Kukgarpiit-llu / Harpoon Points

We followed our discussion of the all-important *negcik* with consideration of a collection of much smaller objects. I selected a box containing some sixty harpoon points of various kinds, originating from the Seward Peninsula south to Cook Inlet.[30] This box exemplified both the strengths and weaknesses of the museum's organization of Jacobsen's collection. Without translated accession records, Yup'ik objects were inseparable from Iñupiaq ones. At the same time, the wide-ranging sample gave elders the opportunity to make comparative statements that the presentation of single objects from their particular areas never could.

Paul first picked up and described a toggling harpoon point with ivory base and thin metal blade (fig. 1.25): "They called these *cavget* [from *caveg-*, "to work"] because they usually turned sideways once they penetrated the animal's flesh. When this entered the target, the pressure would allow the tip to turn,

1.25 Metal-bladed *cavgek* (toggling harpoon points), which turned when they penetrated the animal's flesh, used mostly in winter hunting on the ice for large seals and for beluga in summer. The spurred bases may represent the tucked wings of the hunter who appeared to the seal in bird form. IVA3703, IVA6685.

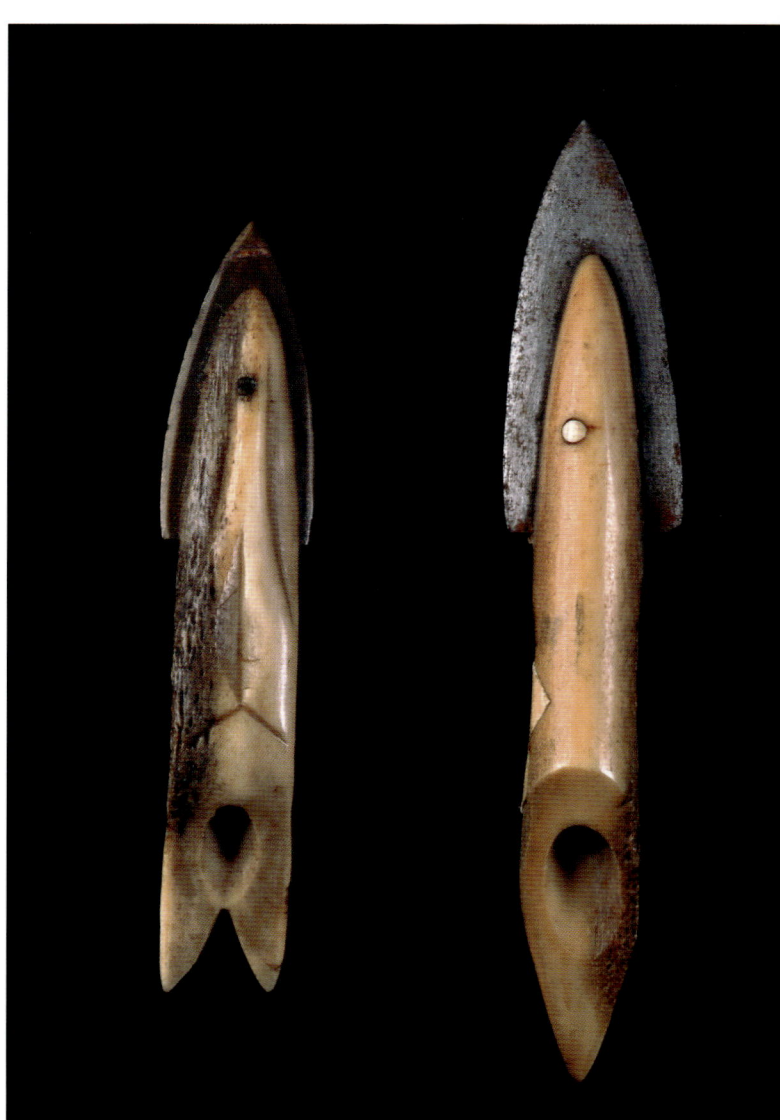

making it difficult to come out as the animal pulled forward."

Wassilie followed with a story evoked by the sight of this hunting tool. It was no simple descriptive impulse. Like his explanation of Paul and his working relationship, the tale centered on the relationship between two hungry men from different areas working together to accomplish a common goal. And, as in all the information that they shared that day, Wassilie and Paul worked together to tell the story. Wassilie began:

Back in those days, I heard a story about two men. I'm sure they had this kind of weapon. The story is told about two men who, during a period of famine and bad weather, went out in search of the reflection of open water in the ocean, seen in the sky as a dark blue line [*qiugaarculleq*]. A man who was looking for the reflection of open water encountered an enemy warrior. . . . As one of the men harpooned an animal with a *cavek* like this, the other man slowly stood up nearby.

Andy and Paul discussed where the men came from and determined that one was from Naparyaar (Hooper Bay), while the other was from Caniliaq at the mouth of the Yukon River. Paul then took up where Wassilie left off:

Yes, when the man from Naparyaar was preparing to leave, he had packed some split wood because he knew that the reflection was difficult to see during the day. At night before he went to bed, he erected a stick near where he slept, set another stick beyond it, and set yet another beyond the second one [to create a sight line toward the reflection of open water that he could see in the dusk]. He did this because he knew it would already be daylight when he began traveling the next day.

When he got up at daylight and the reflection of open water in the sky had already disappeared, he used the sticks to guide him as he traveled. . . . Before he left he had sold his old skin boat for ten slices of dried fish. He took five pieces with him when he went out, as well as five blackfish. He left the rest behind for his family.

As he came down to the open water, when he caught a *metrar* [common eider]—our northern neighbors call it *angiikvak*—he grabbed it first by its head when retrieving it with his kayak. Then after he pulled it out of the water, he took it by its feet and lifted it, putting its mouth above his own. He first drank the saliva of the bird rather than eating any of the food he had brought. The saliva was like fresh food eaten after a time of privation.

Then he looked around and saw a bearded seal sitting on the ice at the edge of the open water. He began to move forward, hunting it. When he was close enough to strike the seal, he started to lift his harpoon, and the other man appeared on the other side with a harpoon in his hand ready to strike. Both men were ready to strike the seal at the same time.

Then the man from Naparyaar held back his harpoon. He didn't want to strike before the other man. Then after the other man harpooned the animal, he thrust his own *asaaquq* [toggling harpoon], and they both hit the animal.

He ran toward the seal. Then the man from the north told him to go behind him. After they killed the seal, since they were both weakened from privation, they helped each other pull the *usaak* [lines] that were attached to their harpoon tips embedded in the seal. In that way, they pulled the seal up to the ice.

The man from Naparyaar suggested that they have a bit to eat before working on the seal. After the man from the north was silent for a while, he told him that he was completely out of food.

After they got their kayaks together and he took his small provisions out, the northern man said, "Amazingly, there's still food available." Then he tipped his head to look into the back of his kayak and said, "When I suffered from hunger pains and I looked at that thing in there and remembered what it used to eat, I felt better." When the man from Naparyaar looked inside the back of the kayak, he saw a bleached dog's skull. . . .

Since the man from Naparyaar was stronger, he started giving the man from the north small amounts of food at a time to strengthen him. . . . When he got stronger, they split the seal in half, and when they were ready to part, the man from the north told the man from Naparyaar to come and visit him in the summer. He told him that he would hang a wolverine skin on a post next to his home in the village.

The following summer [the man from Naparyaar] went to [the man from the north's] village. When he was ready to go back to Naparyaar, he told his host to come and visit him, too. He told [his host] that he would erect an *unrapigaq* [small, thin log] with its root side up next to his house. That was how they told the story about those two men.

1.26 Kukgaracuar (small barbed harpoon points) used on harpoons with feathered shafts that were thrown with a throwing board when hunting smaller sea mammals in open water with drag and float gear. IVA6342, IVA6341, IVA6339.

After Paul spoke, we continued looking at the points. This time, however, we did not consider them one by one. Instead, Marie and Andy took all twenty-two *kukgaracuaraat* (small barbed harpoon points), both Yup'ik and Iñupiaq,[31] out of the box and placed them together (fig. 1.26). Most were made of either caribou antler or walrus ivory. When the sorting was complete, Paul noted: "They were used on *nagiiquyat* and *nanerpiit* [seal-hunting harpoons used with spear throwers]." Jacobsen's records for individual points confirmed what the elders said—that these harpoons were thrown with a throwing board when hunting seals in open water: "Often the seal has to be struck several times with the throwing harpoon before it is killed. The seal gradually tires and can be killed with a spear."

Andy and Marie then arranged a group of six larger points, several of walrus ivory and the rest of caribou bone (fig. 1.27).[32] Paul and Wassilie identified them as *kukgarpiit* (large barbed harpoon points) used on *tegutet* (large harpoons used without a throwing board). Whereas Paul and Wassilie recognized *kukgarpiit* as a distinct type of harpoon head, for Jacobsen, *kukgarpiit* and *kukgaracuaraat* were large and small versions of the same thing.

Wassilie reminded us that points with "steps" like these were always called *kukgar*. Paul explained:

Each "step" on spear points like these has a name. If a spear point like this was shot at an animal and only the first step went in, the hunter would say that his weapon had gotten in as far as its *cirliqsuutii* [from *cirliqe-*, "to have a hard time"]. This first step at the tip was called *cirliqsuun* [literally, "thing that makes one suffer"].

If it went in as far as the second step, it was said that it had gone in as far as *cirliqsuutem qullia* [one above the thing that makes one suffer] . . . or *cirliqsuutem kangiqliik* [two closer to the *kangia* (top end) of the *cirliqsuun*]. And if it went all the way in, it was said that *ngelliarrluni* [it had gotten in to the end]. The *kukgarpiit* "steps" had names like that.

Paul and Wassilie identified the next five barbed points as *neqsuutet*, or points used on fish spears (fig. 1.28).[33] Jacobsen identified most as "bone points for seal and salmon harpoons" from the Yukon and Norton Sound. One he called a "peculiar harpoon . . . intended for sea animals with fur skin, since the barbs are very small and could hardly hold a fish."[34]

We then returned to the mixed group of Yup'ik and Iñupiaq *cavget*[35] that had been separated from the other points. Marie had noted earlier that some of the *umit* (points) were missing and that one point was schist while another was jade. Wassilie picked up one with a copper blade, saying that this was a hard metal. Paul stated again: "They were points that were used on *tegutet* [large harpoons without throwing boards], but since

1.27 *Kukgarpiik* (large barbed harpoon points) used on harpoons without a throwing board. IVA5402, IVA4792.

1.28 *Neqsuutet* (barbed points used on fish spears). IVA3940, IVA3947.

1.29   Five harpoon heads. From left to right: neqsuun (fish-spear point), kukgarpak (large barbed harpoon point), another barbed fish-spear point, cavek (toggling harpoon point), and kukgar-cuar (small harpoon point). IVA3947, IVA5402, IVA6341, IVA3703, IVA3919.

1.30   Large cavek (toggling harpoon point) used in ocean hunting, with a wooden sheath to protect the blade from becoming dull or piercing the kayak skin. IVA4624.

they turned when they penetrated into flesh, we called them *cavget*. And when this sinew line got pulled back, this allowed the point to turn, lodge tightly inside, and not easily come out of the animal." Jacobsen noted that these toggling harpoon points were used mostly in winter hunting on the ice for large seals and for beluga in summer. Like the other harpoon heads, they were made of either caribou antler or walrus ivory. Andy and Marie put the points back in the box, careful to group them according to their Yup'ik designations.

We returned to harpoon points later in the week (fig. 1.29). Jacobsen collected hundreds of pieces of stone and bone in his efforts to document this presumably "Stone Age" civilization, including two schist harpoon points from the Yukon mouth.[36] Everyone was fascinated by these fragments, as they all had been born into a world in which iron already dominated. Paul remembered seeing stone tools in his youth south of Nelson Island, but they were gone before he was old enough to use them.

At first Marie, Annie, and Catherine took them to be *cingilegiit* (arrow points). Wassilie spoke: "These are called *umik* [stone points]. I've heard that these were the kind of arrow points they used during warfare. This would easily penetrate a person's body." Paul referred back to the *asaaquq* (toggling harpoon) we had already looked at: "These *umit* were used

67   FIRST DAY TOOLS FOR OCEAN HUNTING

1.31 Harpoon heads for sea-mammal hunting. Paul explained: "The wooden stretcher kept the twine from getting wrinkled when it dried. They would detach the stretcher before they placed the tip in the harpoon. And when they removed the wet tip from the harpoon, they placed the harpoon head in its stretcher until the line dried." IVA5248, IVA4626.

on animals, too. Earlier we saw a *cavek* [toggling harpoon point] with a point that looked like this. They were the *umit* of *cavget*."

We also examined a covered *cavek* (fig. 1.30) from the Kuskokwim.[37] Jacobsen recorded that the perforated iron blade was attached to an ivory harpoon head with sinew to prevent it getting lost. The harpoon line and air bag would have been attached to the leather thong at the base of the harpoon head. Wassilie began: "This blade, evidently, was made after metal was introduced. When this point was thrust at a target and yanked, the point would turn inside the flesh, hooking it tightly to the animal. At one time this had a shaft attached to it. The attached twine is still very dry, and the end is gone now."

Paul continued:

This was used in ocean hunting. The twine attached to the harpoon point was called *tukarta*. This little case was called *qisran*. It's a covering for the blade that's attached to this *cavek*. This *tugrutii* [shaft] probably had an attachment that was called *itercaraq*. This *cavek* was used on a harpoon and its shaft is very long. This may have been used by our ancestors to hunt belugas. My late great-grandparent from Apruka'ar probably owned it.

Everyone laughed.

Finally we looked at four smaller, covered *cavget*, one each from the Yukon, Kuskokwim, Cape Vancouver (Nelson Island), and Fort Alexander.[38] The Nelson Island harpoon head (fig. 1.31) was the most complete, made of caribou antler with a schist tip. Jacobsen wrote that this kind of harpoon was mainly used for sealing in open water after the seal had been wounded.

Examining another Nushagak covered point (also shown in fig. 1.31)[39] with schist tip, wooden sheath, and detachable wooden stretcher to dry the harpoon line, Paul described how the hunter would remove the stretcher and ready the *cavek* for use:

This *cavek* was used by attaching it to a *tegun* [large harpoon without throwing board]. The *nillaraun* [wooden stretcher for the harpoon line] is still attached to the shaft because you can take it on and off easily. Since harpoon shafts were made to easily detach, if they were getting ready to use this on a *tegun*, they'd remove this [stretcher] first, and . . . tie the end of the line to the harpoon head and then to the end of the *tegun*. . . . Then when the harpoon was put away after use, the string was put back here, and this helped to keep the string stretched in place. The *qisran* [wooden sheath] was removed, and the *cavek* was placed on the *tegun*.

These points were the first of many we would see in the Berlin museum. Andy picked one up when Paul was done, examined it carefully, then used it to break the plastic wrapping on a video tape so he could continue recording.

Aiggatet wall'u Cetugyugun / Seal-scratcher

We briefly considered an *aiggatet* (seal-scratcher) from the Yukon area (fig. 1.32), called *cetugyugun* (literally, "device for scratching") on the coast.[40] In some areas, hunters used these when stalking seals sleeping on ice to imitate the sound of a seal working at its breathing hole, thus reassuring their prey. Paul took it in hand and commented: "This *cetugyugun* was used by people out there [northern people]. When a hunter spotted a seal and it went under water, he'd use this to try and trick the seal into coming closer to him. During this time now, a hunter will use his paddle to scratch the ice, and while he does that a seal will come back up in the water . . . because they are curious about the sound." Paul then playfully raised the scratcher to his head and described a new use for an old tool (fig. 1.33), singing in English, "This is the way we comb our hair." Everyone laughed.

1.34 Paul describing how bow and keel protectors prevented the kayak bottom from tearing when its nose hit ice or rocks. IVA3649, IVA3650.

Cen'gaq / Kayak Bow or Keel Protector

Paul immediately identified two pieces of bone (fig. 1.34) from the Yukon[41]:

They called each piece a *cen'gaq* [bow or keel protector]. . . . When there were no nails, these were used as fasteners by poking a hole in the kayak. These are shorter than the ones used at home. The ones I saw didn't have sides like this, though, except at the side where it was attached. My kayaks had those pieces. The *cen'gat* prevented the front bottom part of the kayak from tearing when the nose hit ice or rocks.

Wassilie's explanation of another small bone piece from the Yukon[42] corresponded exactly with Jacobsen, who had written that it was a decoration for a chest and, if larger, could have been used as protection for a kayak keel: "Since I spotted these holes for nailing it down, I'm thinking this was a *cen'gaq* . . . that was attached to the bottom back part of a kayak . . . to keep the needle ice from rubbing against the kayak cover."

Ayaperyaraq / Cockpit Coaming Stanchion

Next we turned to a wooden image from the coast near Cape Vancouver, which Jacobsen had difficulty identifying (fig. 1.35). He labeled it a "Thunnerasut, the one having the form of an almighty spirit," and wrote:

A masklike amulet? kept in the house as a good-luck charm and blessing. Possibly the spirit of a deceased person is staying in this form. Judging by the four holes, four posts had been inserted, [just] as in No. 5182 [mask illustrated in Fienup-Riordan 1996, 222]; this usually points to the lampposts that were found standing in front of the great houses and lit during big festivals. . . . The masklike amulet in the middle has a face resembling that of a sun mask.

1.32 Wooden seal-scratcher with four seal claws attached to simulate a seal flipper. IVA4232.

1.33 Paul using the seal-scratcher and singing "This is the way we comb our hair."

1.35 Ayaperyaraq (deck stiffener), located below the coaming on the left and right sides of a kayak, on which one braces one's hands when getting in and out. Jacobsen reported that such carvings might also be used as amulets. Nelson collected similar paired smiling-male and frowning-female images that the hunter lashed inside his kayak's coaming to spiritually "balance" his craft. IVA5170.

1.36 The reverse side of the deck stiffener with downturned mouth. IVA5169.

1.37 Annie's downturned mouth matching the "woman's face" carved on a kayak deck stiffener. IVA5169.

1.38 Bone and ivory "spear holders" carved in the shape of various sea mammals attached to the kayak's gunwales to prevent harpoons and lances from falling overboard as the hunter approached his quarry. Jacobsen wrote: "These devices are pulled through the leather straps running across the kayak so that they stand with their points in the upright position." From left to right: IVA4873, IVA4540, IVA4877.

Later we looked at a similar "amulet" from Cape Vancouver (fig. 1.36), also designated a "Thunnerasut." Although each image may have been kept in the house as an *iinruq* (amulet), originally each was one of a pair of deck stiffeners placed below the coaming on the left and right sides of a kayak to provide the boat and its owner with both the physical and spiritual balance necessary to succeed during the hunt. Wassilie identified it correctly:

It's an *ayaperyaraq* [cockpit coaming stanchion, the central deck stiffener on which one braces one's hands when getting in and out].... There were two *ayaperyarak,* one on each side of the coaming. Some have eyes carved into them, and some were painted with red ocher....

They prevented the person from falling while getting in and out of the kayak. All kayaks had *ayaperyarat* on them. This has a woman's face with a downturned mouth carved on it. Perhaps the other side would have a man's face carved on it.

Holding the board aloft, Annie matched its "woman's face" for the camera (fig. 1.37).[43]

Several other figures were briefly identified as *iinrut.* The first was a wooden hunting amulet from Cape Vancouver in the shape of a white whale.[44] A substance taken from a bird skin had been wound around it. Jacobsen reported that every hunter had such an amulet, which came in a variety of shapes. He had found it nearly impossible to obtain one, as they were always taken in the kayak and on the hunt. Noting the whale figure's sinew attachment, Marie remarked that *iinrut* were sometimes hung above or near their owner's sleeping area: "The *iinruq* helped the person stand firmly against harm and evil."[45]

Akagyailkutet, Aklicarat, Kepirtat-llu / Spear Guards, Connecting Links, and Line Attachers

Later in the week, we looked at two shelves containing a mixture of small ivory attachments. Without a second look, Paul separated them into three groups. The first was a group of spear guards with flattened bases and curved, upturned points, from every part of the region (fig. 1.38, fig. 1.39).[45] Many were finely carved in the shape of animal heads or tails. Paul gave this account:

Akagyailkutet [spear guards, used to prevent weapons from falling overboard while the kayak hunter approached his quarry, from *akag-,* "to roll"] were tied to kayaks with skin rope and detached only when the rope was untied. Once the skin ropes were attached, these were not taken on and off but kept there all the time. If the hunter was right-handed, his spear, either *nanerpak* or *tegun,* would always be placed on the right side of his kayak.

Earlier we saw some skin line. Men carried these on their kayaks when they hunted out on the ocean. All of these don't look exactly alike, but they were all used the same way.

Having dispatched one type of ivory accouterment, Paul turned to the next, described by Jacobsen simply as "buckles or connecting links on harpoon lines" (fig. 1.40), all from the Kuskokwim.[47] According to Jacobsen: "The harpoon is usually fastened on a short leather strap six to eight inches long (doubled) and then fastened to the harpoon with this apparatus. This manner of fastening is best seen on No. 4590 [fig. 1.3 above] and 4592." Paul elaborated:

These are the *algarcarai* [their keepers], located at the end of the line where the point attaches to it. These anchored the line so that the point would not detach from the rope when the seal is pulling and struggling to get away, dragging the line. There at the end of the *usaaq,* as you wind the line, you thread the line through this and wind it on the other side, then continue winding. Then wind whatever is left over securely so it won't break off. If they secured the *tukarta* [twine] of the *kukgarpak* [large barbed harpoon point] or *cavek* [toggling harpoon point], it would be hard to loosen quickly, preventing it from coming off....

You thread the point through here, then you will see a pair of ropes that are folded and threaded together, then you pull it so it will be more secure. Then after it is threaded where the folded and threaded point line is, this is where they are placed, and then it goes underneath the line and is threaded again. These two are the *aklicarak,* the joints that are used to attach the *cavek.*

These look exactly like the ones that were used back home. . . . You can make out the place where the line was attached. After putting the *cavek* at the end of the line, the line is threaded through here. And since this is inserted from below, it can hold the *tukarta* securely. These others obviously were used exactly like this one.

Finally Paul commented on a half dozen harpoon line attachers (see also fig. 1.40),[48] each of which was fastened to the end of the harpoon line to serve as a handle or hand grip and keep the line from slipping through the hand:

These are attached to the end of this *usaaq*. And they are called *kepirtat* [line attachers, from *kepe-*, "to cut off"]. If a hunter on land throws his spear and hits his target, this *usaaq* will unwind as it goes forward. This is where the hunter holds and pulls once the line is all out when it is being pulled by the catch.

They always used *qerruinat* [harpoon floats] to retrieve their catch. When the hunter was preparing to use the float, he'd thread the end of the *usaaq*, which had a loop at the end, and wrap it around and secure it to the bottom appendages. Since the float was secured to the line in this fashion, the struggling seal would not be able to loosen the float, even though there were no knots to secure it.

When he was done, Paul grouped the ivory pieces for storage as he had described them. The next morning I found them mixed according to their original confusion, but the distinctions we had recorded could always be used to regroup them.

Ulukat, Umit-Ilu / Stone Blades and Points

It was getting late, but we looked at a box of stone points before we quit for the day. Like Jacobsen, everyone was impressed by their age. Whereas Jacobsen had taken stone tools as evidence of the "primitive" state of their makers, the elders marveled at the skill their ancestors must have had to master their environment with stone tools. Holding a harpoon point, Wassilie

1.39 A pair of spear guards carved in the shape of a beluga. IVA4878, IVA4879.

1.40 An ivory harpoon-line attacher fastened to the end of the harpoon line to keep the line from slipping through the hand, along with four connecting links for harpoon lines. Clockwise from the top: IVA4825, IVA4697, IVA4701, IVA4698, IVA4814.

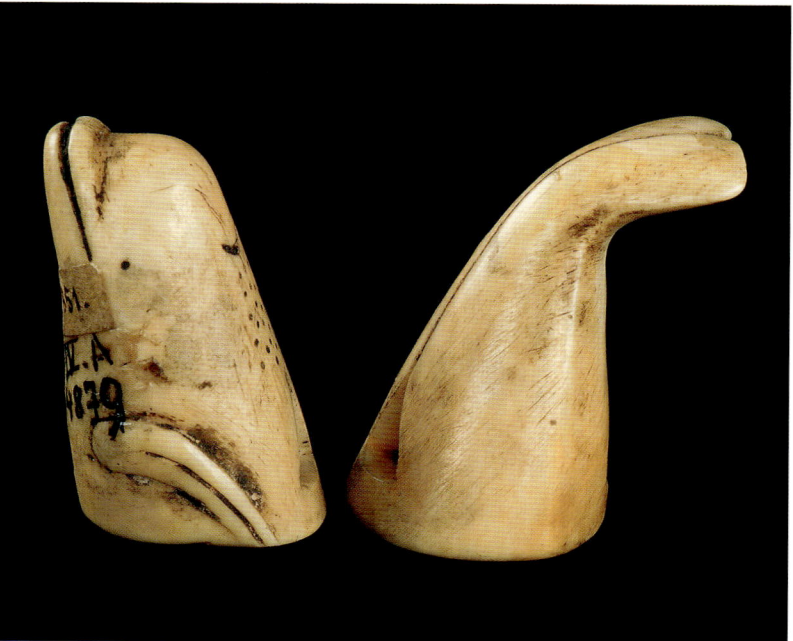

recalled the continued use of stone tools in contrast to the dangers associated with metal in some contexts.

Back in those days, people strictly observed *eyagyarat* [traditional abstinence practices associated with pregnancy, birth, miscarriage, puberty, and death]. They also used *ulukaq* [slate or other stone used as a blade] to cut people's hair instead of using a metal tool. . . . *Ulukaq* was safe to use on people who were observing *eyagyarat*. A woman who was observing *eyagyarat* also could use *ulukaq* . . . to cut food for cooking.

One time our late Angayuqacuar was observing *eyagyarat* because he was a *yuungcaraq* [patient, one being ministered to by a shaman]. During that time, our mother always braided his hair. We were told not to cut his hair with modern cutting tools. Though a man, his long hair was always in braids . . . as long as he was observing *eyagyarat*.

And then the time finally came to cut his hair; my parents truly believed the fact that he was a *yuungcaraq*. They placed a wooden board under his hair, and they used an *ulukaq* to cut his hair.

Paul (fig. 1.41) noted that the stone points had two names: "These are very old objects here that our ancestors used. Some are called *kapuutet* [needles or spear points],[49] and others are called *umit* [stone points, points of *cavget*].[50] These are the names of the stone hunting tools our ancestors used." Wassilie concluded: "Back when people used stone implements for

1.41 While examining stone blades, one long point caught Paul's attention: "This looks like a piece they called *everquun* [tool for prying or unraveling] back in my home. When they prepared to remove the skin covering from kayaks, first the stitching was moistened, then they'd use this kind of tool to pull the thread out. The old kayak or boat skin would then be replaced. The stitches around the rim opening of a kayak were called *pall'illrit*. And when they pulled the thread on top from the opening to the tail of the kayak, they'd say they were undoing the *ikavsianra*." IVA5136.

hunting, these were what they used. They made and shaped these by using other stones." It was no wonder another stone point mystified the group, as Jacobsen had collected it north of the Copper River.[51]

The last piece we looked at was a well-worn stone lance point from St. Michael that Jacobsen said had been used for hunting beluga.[52] Paul suggested another use: "Perhaps this was an *iinruq* [amulet] . . . probably kept in a little bag and worn as a necklace by someone. They were made from *ulukat*. They made their *uluaq* and *umit* from the stone." "I think these are very, very old," said Marie. Her uncle agreed: "These were made before people began to improve in their work. They are well made, from many years ago."

SECOND DAY Bows and Arrows for Hunting and War

Urluvret / Bows

We returned to the museum the next morning rested and eager to continue, as we knew better what to expect. We immediately set to work on the varied group of bows Jacobsen had collected and the museum now stored in a case alongside the harpoons. The first (fig. 2.1), from the middle Yukon, was used for hunting large land animals.[1] As with most men's items, Wassilie began:

This is an old bow with *cagnirqun* [cross lashing holding the sinew backing onto the body of the bow; literally, "device for tightening," from *cagni-*, "to be tight, taut"]. But apparently the parts that went with the *cagnirqun* have. . . . fallen off. You can see that it had been broken.

I used to see these, and some of the people living around Kuskokwim Bay had bows with *cagnirqun* like this. This bow has no bowstring. When they were going to set the bowstring, they'd dip the bow in water and let it sit there for a while, then they'd pull it out and put their knee here to hold it down, then set the bowstring. Some had very strong arms when they did this. . . .

They used these to hunt animals, including caribou. And I used to see men hunting on the ocean. When a seal came up, they would dip the bow in water a few times before stringing their bows.

The second bow was also from the Yukon.[2] Wassilie continued:

This bow . . . is complete, with everything on it. . . . Its *cagnirqun* was made of sinew, as you can see. It's a little different from the ones I saw in the past. The *qelun* [bowstring] is made of sinew . . . woven from strands of *uliutet*. And the *urcik* [two loops at the end of the bowstring] were attached like one I saw before.

If the bowstring wasn't tight enough, they'd take it off and twist

2.1 Bows of varied sizes from the Yukon. The wrapped sinew cross lashing strengthened the bows and prevented them from breaking when taut. Paul noted, "At home when bows had cross lashing, they called them *cukangegcautait* [those that travel at a steady, fast pace] because they helped the arrows go faster and farther." From top to bottom: IVA4356, IVA4359, IVA4360.

2.2 Wassilie demonstrating how a man's bow should measure from the tip of one index finger to the other. IVA4588.

it more before setting it again. Then they'd pull the string to see if it was tight enough.

They made bows out of wood called *quarnat* [larch]. That kind of thin-grained wood is hard. In the spring, our late father made bows for us when we needed one.

The third bow was from the Kuskokwim,[3] and Wassilie was even more enthusiastic: "Here's another bow. Its cross lashing apparently rotted and fell off. This is decorated with the designs we had on our bows called *kumgaq*, a design of the Kuskokwim people." He then stood and demonstrated how bows were made to fit a particular person (fig. 2.2). With arms outstretched, the bow should measure from the tip of one index finger to the other: "If this bow was going to be mine, the maker would measure it like this. . . . I used a bow for quite a long time hunting muskrats."

The fourth bow was from the Yukon.[4] Wassilie spoke: "This bow is different from the Kuskokwim kind. It has a design at the place where you hold it. The sides of the bow have no design and are very smooth. As I look at it, I'd say it was made for a young man. The bow was made with no added features . . . in recent times. The bowstring was made from factory-made string. Our bows had this kind of string, too."

Herr Wedell brought two more bows for us to examine, one from Nushagak (fig. 2.3, fig. 2.4) and one from the middle Yukon (fig. 2.5, fig 2.6).[5] The Yukon bow resembled the one we had already seen, but it was larger and had more elaborate designs. Wassilie began at once to talk about it: "This bow is nice and wide . . . and decorated with pictures of caribou, which were caught with weapons like these. These weapons were used to kill muskrats and birds and in hunting different kinds of animals, . . . including dangerous animals such as bears."

Andy pointed at the bow's designs, noting that they depicted the animals it had been used to hunt. Wassilie continued:

Yes, the animals that this weapon typically captured are visible as designs on this bow. Apparently hunters were able to capture big animals, too, back in those days. I used to hear such hunting stories, including the story about a man from the Yukon who killed a bear. . . .

As the man and his grandson were going along, the hunter said, "Oh my! Look at the rabbit back there." Then he took his bow and shot an arrow at it. Immediately after he shot, they heard a loud rustling sound from the direction the arrow had gone. The arrow was released with such force that when it struck the bear's chest, it catapulted the animal backward and impaled it against the tree. The story about the man who shot and left a bear hanging from a tree after saying that he had spotted a rabbit was a story that was told again and again throughout the area. But I've heard some people say, "The animal probably wasn't exactly hanging, but perhaps the upper part of its body was elevated a little."

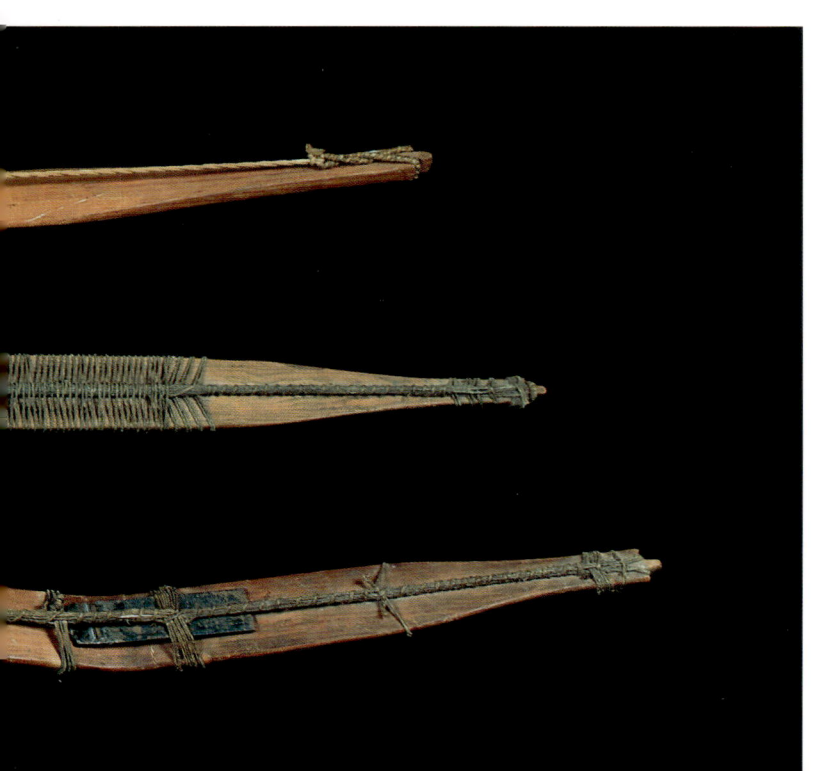

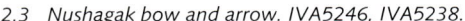

2.3   Nushagak bow and arrow. IVA5246, IVA5238.

Reportedly, that man made his bows by hardening the wood of young trees. That kind of wood was very difficult to break. Gosh, that man surely had strength using his bow and arrow at that time.

Andy asked if this was the kind of bow used in the past to wage war, and Wassilie said that it was. Paul continued talking about the significance of the bow's designs:

By looking at the animal designs on the bow, animals that were normally hunted for food, it's easy to understand that it was used as a request to *Ellam Yua* [the Person of the Universe] for sustenance. Since the ancestors were firm in their determination, they were able to acquire even big animals with these weapons.... These were the animals the ancestors sought with a strong mind. And *Ellam Yua* granted them the things they asked for.

Yualuq / Sinew

After examining bows, Wassilie and Paul repeated their named parts: *qelun* (bowstring), *cagnirqun* (cross lashing), and the two notched ends called *qeluyarak* (the way the *qelun* is pulled) on the coast and *teruk* on the Kuskokwim. They then spoke about the sinew out of which both the bowstring and cross lashing were made. Wassilie noted that both were made from an animal's *uliutet* (the top layer of backbone muscles split to make sinew) and that both caribou and beluga had two layers of *uliutet* on their back against the meat. Paul remarked that when he was little, they were always eager to get beluga sinew, which could be as long as a grown man: "When kayak-making time arrived, they'd begin hunting belugas for their sinew." He said that people also welcomed the chance to get sinew when they found a beached dead whale, as beluga, bowhead, and humpback whales all produced long, thick sinew.

Continuing to examine the bow, Marie observed that the bowstring was not straight. Paul explained that when the bowstring was twisted and became shorter, it tightened the bow. Marie noted that it seemed as if the large Yukon bow[6] required long strands of sinew, and Paul concurred. Catherine then described how sinew was made: "As a person wove sinew strands to make thread, she'd add more to each strand to make it longer.... When two strands were woven, the thread was called *qip'aq*. And when three strands were woven, it was called *piirraq*."[7]

After closely examining the bow, all agreed that its bowstring was made with *piirrayagaat* (three-stranded, twisted sinew twine). Paul noted that *qip'aq* was used to sew clothing, while *piirrayagaq* thread was used to sew boat and kayak covers. *Ikavsiarutkanek* was what they called the completed thread. Catherine continued:

They made thread like this after shredding sinew into many strands, and a strand of sinew wasn't just picked up and used for sewing. After sinew was dampened, it was cut up into long strips of equal thickness. The strands were a little thick if they were going to be woven into *piirrayagaq* thread ... [and] thinner if they were going to be *qip'aq* threads. The women I observed when I was little did that....

They used a special tool made of walrus tusk called *talun* to shred sinew into strips.... When a sinew was cut up, first ... it was twisted and secured. The end of the strand that would be added to as you wove the thread was thinner. The strands were all equally thick. As I cut up sinew, they told me to cut the strand into even thicknesses.

We don't know what kind of animal that completed sinew like this came from. But long pieces like this, well, the *uliutet* of belugas and whales were thick. They have a lot of sinew because they have two *uliutet* on each side. The caribou have *uliutet,* also. Now, down deeper, below the *uliutet,* the sinew was referred to as *eglupik* [genuine sinew]. The *eglupiit* were thicker and didn't resemble the *uliutet.*

Annie commented for the first time:

Yes, they've just talked about them accurately. And when my late grandmother sewed kayak coverings, she used her foot to pull the thread. When she prepared thread for kayak cover sewing, she made *piirrayagaq* thread....

When I was little, the *uliutet* sinew from caribou were the only threads used for sewing skin and durable items. Woven sinew like this was the only strong thread that was available.

The *qip'aq* thread was used for sewing boot soles. But when they made thread to use on objects such as these [bows], they wove

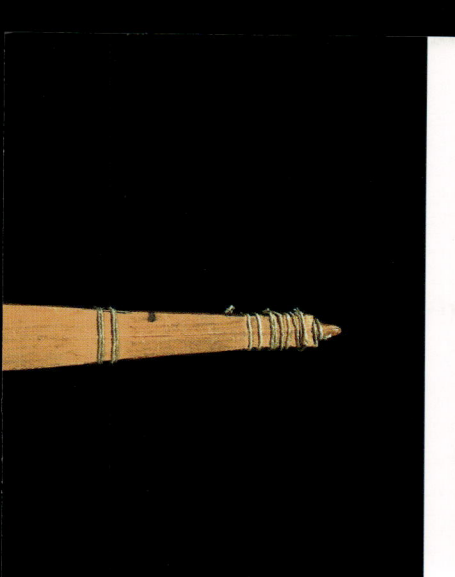

2.4 Sinew binding on a Nushagak bow. IVA5246.

2.5 Sinew cross lashing and painted designs on an elaborate bow from the middle Yukon. IVA6976.

2.6 Notched end of the same bow from the middle Yukon. IVA6976.

the strands like these. They used another tool to stretch out the sinew. When they were processed correctly, they were very good.

Paul commented that women knew exactly the thread length required for certain items: "When my late grandmother prepared thread for kayak making, she stretched out her arms to measure the length of the thread as she wove, and when the thread reached a certain measurement, she'd stop.... The threads to be used on certain parts of the kayak were at different lengths." Wassilie had a similar experience:

I used to watch women sewing kayak coverings, too. When they made thread for kayak stitching, the threads were about an arm's length or a little more. The end of the thread where the needle would be going was woven thin. They worked very neatly and carefully when they made sewing threads....

She just mentioned how the stitches were made. There was a particular animal-part tool they used when they sewed; you know the land otters have little penis bones. They tied the thread around that little bone and pulled it to tighten the stitches....

Then when they were done with what they were sewing together, like a kayak, . . . they pulled one side first and then the other. Then the skin was fitted on to the kayak frame. The regular stitches were finished on the inside. That was how they covered boat frames, too.

Paul added the names of those who sewed the different parts of the kayak skin covering according to the area they were sewing:

Ciulilriit [those making the front] were women sewing the front part of the kayak. *Kingulilriit* [those making the back] were ones who were sewing the stern. And *caugarnilria* [the one turning it?] also sewed a part. . . . And *pupsirluki* [pinching it?] was also a word they used. . . . Then when the stitching on the outside was done, they'd sew the inside with regular stitches and call it *ilulirluki* [doing the inner surface?].

And sometimes while women were weaving sinew for thread, they'd say that they were making thread for the inside part of the kayak: *ilulitkiurniluteng.* Or, if they were making sinew thread to be used on the outside of the covering, they'd say *amiutekiurniluteng.* They had different words they used to describe their work in kayak making.

Annie responded: "Yes. When the *ikavsiaq* stitches [cross-stitches, from *ikani-*, "across there"] were done on the seam, the seam was stitched again with a different thread and needle, and that stitching was called *qall'iluku* [topstitching, from *qalli-*, "to be on top"]. The thickness of the thread was different. The thickness of the thread was measured again for this stitching, which was sewn from either the front or the back to the hole of the kayak." Paul concluded: "When you observed women sewing, *ikavsialriit,* after they pierced the needle on the seam they tried to pull the thread evenly toward themselves and again on the other side. The needle was always pushed in this direction [toward the person's body]. The skins on the sides were pulled tightly together . . . and aligned with the *amuvik* [kayak stem] on top."[8]

Wassilie reiterated the importance of keeping the seams aligned with the frame when covering a kayak:

When they were ready to sew the top of the kayak, they stitched it on the inside almost to the mouth. It was important to keep the seams and the ends even. When the top part was sewn, the small holes kept the seams from moving. And when that part was sewn, the skin around the mouth wasn't pulled too tightly. They usually inserted another pointed piece joining the two pieces near the mouth. And when the sewing was done, a person went inside the kayak and pulled the first stitching that was placed inside at the beginning of the process.

A Child's Bow and a Warrior's Bow

We turned next to a small child's bow from King Island.[9] Although it was not from our area, everyone had something to say about it. Catherine noted that they made small bows like this for both boys and girls: "Though we were all girls in our family, they made bows for us, too. We usually shared a bow. We used them to practice on little birds. The bow line of this wasn't made from woven tree bark lining. I think this is a strip of animal skin. This bow looks like the one I used back when I was little." Wassilie continued: "When we were little boys, [men] made bows for us, and we used them to train ourselves, . . . to practice on little birds. As we got older, they used the distance between our outstretched arms as measurements when they made our bows." Paul noted that even little bows like this one provided food and clothing that sustained people's lives: "When a little boy caught a little bird for the first time, the boy's grandfather or father honored his successful hunt and gave away food and clothing to members of the other village during the yearly dance festival, the Messenger Feast. A little bow like this provided members of the whole village with food and clothing."

Last we considered a bow collected from the Aglurmiut living in the vicinity of Bristol Bay.[10] Marie asked Annie to talk about it, which she did reluctantly: "These men could talk about this first. . . . These were probably used by Aglurmiut during warfare. The bow was the only hunting tool used by people, and was cared for with respect. The owner never left it lying around but always put it up somewhere. A woman was not allowed to step over it, either."

Wassilie was impressed by the bow's unusual design and briefly described the history of bow-and-arrow warfare in which the bow might have played a part:

When I started traveling over to Bristol Bay, when the older folks told stories, I heard them referring to the people living below Iquk as Aglurmiut. . . .

It was said that when the Kuskokwim warriors got stronger, they came over the mountains and slowly came down the Nushagak River, killing everyone. They wiped out the people living on that river, moving down toward the mouth. *Iggluteng* [falling down] was the word describing what they did. Then the people living in the lower part of the river began moving out toward the mouth as far as Iquk . . . [and] were referred to as Aglurmiut. They were the survivors who remained when the first white people arrived in the area. . . . Some of the Kuskokwim warriors went down the Kuskokwim and traveled over down below, and the two forces met on the Nushagak River. That was how the Kuskokwim warriors fought to wipe out the whole population of Bristol Bay.

Paul said that although he had not heard many stories from the Nushagak area, he had heard this and believed Wassilie: "The history of warfare among our ancestors is true. That is why people have relatives living far away, because some people never returned to their home after waging war. People found their relatives, even though they were living far apart."[11]

Annie had been listening to the men, and when Paul was done she spoke at length, telling the story of the mischievous Qilagtaq, a man who always used a bow:

The grandfather of this certain family living at Togiak was a proficient hunter. . . . Though guns had been introduced, he always used bows to hunt. It was said the first guns were very powerful. They were called *itukellriit* [muzzle-loading guns].

Qilagtaq always used bows while hunting because he wasn't satisfied with the first gun. He lived several generations back . . . [and] wasn't from the ancient times. . . . He didn't use [guns] because sometimes the animals would escape. . . .

Then on one hunting occasion he shot a caribou with his bow and arrow but missed it, and the caribou became angry and chased him. As he was running, he ran between two trees growing close together, thinking that the caribou wouldn't be able to run through. As he ran, he looked back and saw that the angry caribou had plowed over the two trees like they were blades of grass. . . .

Then he climbed up a leaning tree—my, how brave he was. When the caribou came upon the tree, it circled the tree several times, then kicked the bottom of it with its hooves, cracking it in the middle. As the tree cracked . . . while the caribou was looking up at him, he aimed and shot it with his arrow.

As soon as the arrow struck, the caribou fell backward. It was said that he emphasized that part when he told the story.

Annie went on, describing Qilagtaq's youthful exploits at length—including swimming in his mother's *qaliluk* (caribou parka), so ruining her cherished possession, and giving away a large bowl of *akutaq* without asking. Qilagtaq himself told people about his misdeeds before he died, warning them not to repeat what he had done but to live according to the old teachings.

Everyone listened to Annie with enjoyment, as these were stories they had not heard. Finally she circled back around to the bow and the design Qilagtaq created to commemorate his encounter with the angry caribou:

Qilagtaq was quite a character. . . . He had asked one of his grandsons to take good care of his bow and arrows after he died. He also made a wooden bowl for my older brother just before he died. Inside down at the bottom of the bowl, he etched a caribou with an arrow stuck in its armpit. And next to the caribou design, he also etched a figure of a standing man. The same design was usually used on drumheads. And there was one drumhead with a drawing of Qilagtaq up in a tree with a caribou looking up at him. He etched that one incident of his life on the bases of bowls. His earlier descendants continued using the same designs, but his present descendants no longer do so.

Pitegcautet / **Arrows**

When we returned from lunch, we found two dozen arrows laid on the table, ready for us to examine. We were excited because, although we had already looked at bows and arrow points, these were our first arrows. Picking up a bird arrow (fig. 2.7) from Nushagak[12] with three feathers at the end and three serrated prongs made of caribou antler and turned inward against each other, Wassilie began:

Arrows are placed in front of us in different sizes. These were used to hunt waterfowl and muskrats back in those days. When they shoot ivory-pointed arrows at quick-moving animals, the point lodges firmly in the flesh so that it wouldn't fall out when the animal tries to escape. Then one would pick up the arrow with the

2.7 *Nushagak bird arrow with three serrated prongs whose inner surfaces have rows of back-slanting barbs. The multiple points both provide a wider striking range and catch the feet and wings of several birds in flight. IVA7177.*

animal attached and hit it on the head. When it became dizzy, one would remove the arrow, then pull its heart until it made a certain sound. Then you'd know that it was dead. That was how they killed muskrats.

Wassilie then named the parts of the arrow: the *nakrutet* (flight-stabilizing feathers), the *agayiinraat* (cormorant feathers used as fletching), and the *tapengyaarayaagaq* (sinew binding) at the *teru* (butt end, notch) to keep it from breaking. He then described how arrows were made:

This is a *pitegcaun* [arrow]. In the spring before the birds arrived, they would make arrows by first splitting an *unarciaq* [prepared piece of straight-grained wood] into strips. After they roughly whittled the strips of wood, they steamed them in a fire bath. Then after steaming them several times, they took them outside and smoothed them by shaving them with a crooked knife. We called these *pingayupegcetaat* [three-pronged arrows, from *pingayun*, "three"]. These points look like they were made from bone, not from ivory. When they were done making the arrow shafts, they'd grab a handful of wood chips and run the shaft through, smoothing it out.

Examining the arrow more closely, Andy asked Wassilie to explain why small "steps" had been cut into the feathering. Wassilie answered that this was to help them hold their shape and to keep them afloat.

Paul continued describing how *pingayupegcetaat* were used to hunt animals, birds, and fish.

Our ancestors used these for hunting whatever they could acquire. They also used them to hunt molting birds in the summer. When they hunted birds and animals that dive in the water, they would shoot them even though they surfaced far away.

And some hunters used them to shoot birds that were flying close to the ground. Sometimes they hit birds with these, though they were flying high. And if this three-pronged arrow hits a flying

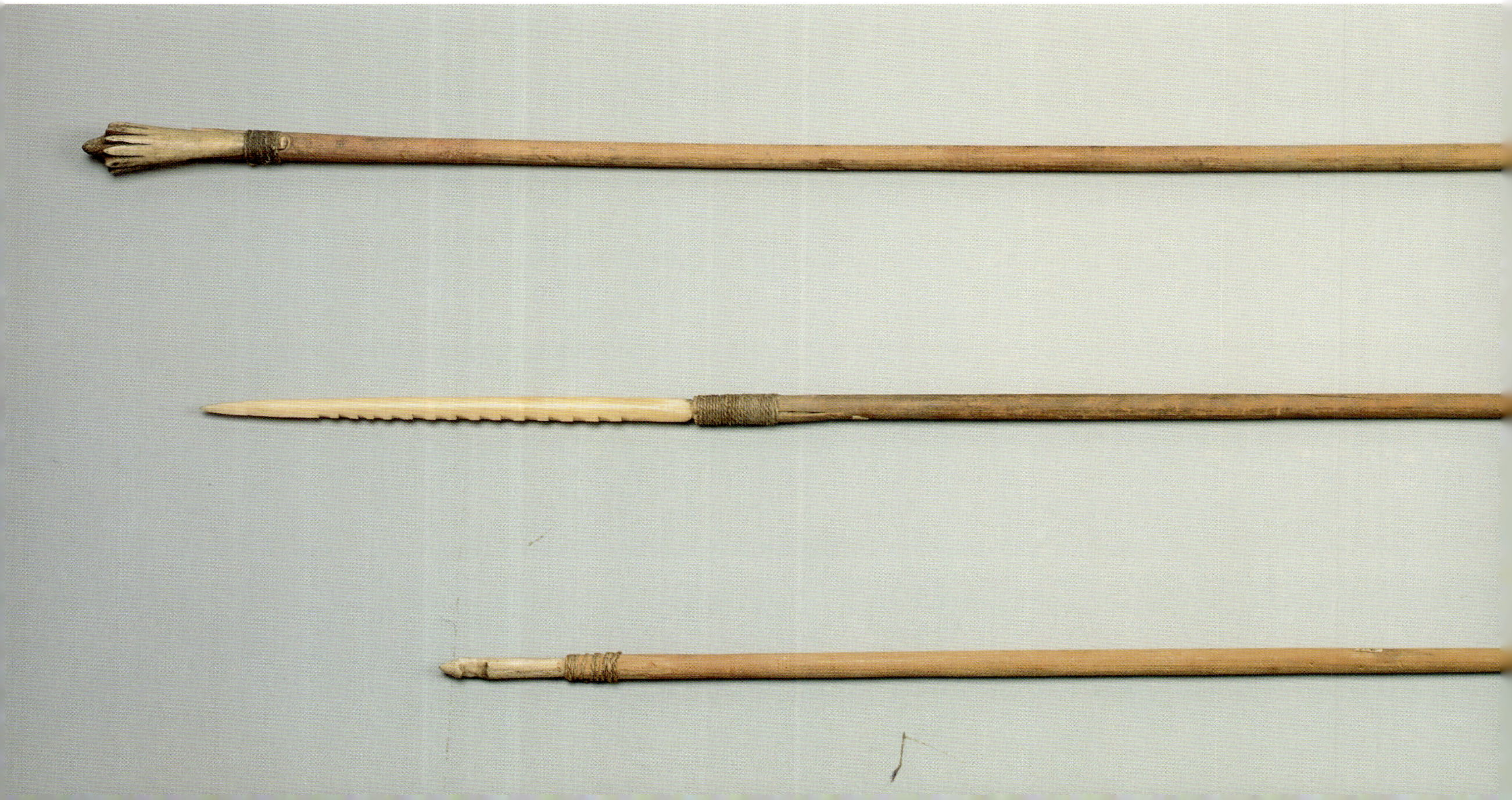

2.8 Paul demonstrating how a man would extend his arm to check the length of an arrow. The shaft should extend from under his arm to the tip of his middle finger.

2.9 From top to bottom: Akitnaq (blunt-tipped bird-hunting arrow), arrow with barbed point used for hunting and for war, and young boy's "thrust arrow." IVA4321, IVA4322, IVA5222.

bird on its wing, it would snap it and make the bird fall. . . .

When they could see them, they used arrows to capture fish swimming in shallow water.

Paul also commented that a person used his arm as a measurement for the length of his arrows (fig. 2.8): "Since the arm was extended when the bow was drawn, one wanted one's arrow long enough so that it wouldn't lose its support when the bow was fully drawn. . . . You'd use the length of your extended arm or a little longer as a measurement when you made your arrows and never shorter than your arm. Body measurements were always used when they made tools for themselves."

Wassilie agreed, recalling that when he was young, the men used his arm as a measurement when making him arrows. He remembered using such arrows to hunt molting geese before he had his first gun, concluding, "These hunting tools were used up until my generation. They aren't visible within the lives of those living today."

The conversation then returned to bow-and-arrow warfare, and former war leaders such as Urluverpak and Apanuugpak were briefly discussed. Warfare, they recalled, ended relatively recently (the early 1800s). Annie remembered her great-grandmother mentioning meeting a woman covered with scars on her face and body where she had been bound with spruce roots while a captive. She had been treated cruelly, but her tormentors had suffered the consequences: "She told her that her captor would bind her and sometimes put her in the entryway for people to step on. Some people avoided stepping on her when they entered, but some, even women, would step right in her face when they entered or left the house. She told her that those who stepped on her were *yuunguilriit* [arrogant?]. She said that the people who hadn't stepped on her were doing well and still alive. You see, that *qaneryaraq* [saying] is the truth."

Next we considered two blunt-tipped bird-hunting arrows

from the Yukon, called *akitnat*, with shafts painted with red ocher and caribou-antler tips.[13] Wassilie noted that the swan quill fletching was called *qugyinraat* (from *qugyuk,* "whistling swan") and was often painted with a design between the stabilizer and notch. Paul talked about how this type of arrow was used for hunting little birds, such as *ayungnaaraat* (knots) or *augtuaraat* (red phalaropes)[14] and *imaqcaaraat* (northern phalaropes), during the spring thaw because they glided over land when shot, echoing Jacobsen's comment that blunt-tipped arrows were used in bird hunting because they did not break when hitting against stones and trees. Paul also mentioned the *caniryiik* (dual form of *caniryak*), the two extra points sometimes placed on the shaft near the main tip of this type of arrow and elongated so as to impale its target: "Sometimes when the main point goes right by the target, this piece that's out sideways will hit and kill it."

Jacobsen identified the next arrow we looked at as a small Nushagak "thrust arrow" used by young boys, particularly for bird hunting in the summer (fig. 2.9).[15] Wassilie agreed: "This arrow was made for a boy. Its shaft is painted with red ocher. I recognize these three painted designs along the bottom part of the fletching. They always painted designs close together here with red ocher. And the area below the feathers is painted as always with red ocher, beginning from the binding to the notch This arrow's fletching was made with feathers placed on the two sides of the notched end of the shaft. This arrow is as long as the arrows we had when we were boys. The point is made from bone and has only one jag projecting on one side of the tip because it's made for a child."

Wassilie then commented that *pitegcautet* (arrows) were always called *qerrut* during warfare. He wanted to wait until evening to tell the long story of why this name was used, but Marie insisted. His story, which everyone was hearing for the first time, told how the ancestors of the people of Napaskiak went out to meet their enemy, accompanied by a boy named Putukuilnguq. When they came to the mouth of the Kuskokwim, they met two enemy warriors, who fled down into the ocean. Putukuilnguq followed them, while his companions, including his father, stayed behind. Although the companions began to worry, the father was confident his son could take care of himself. Sure enough, soon they noticed a kayak approaching from down below, and they recognized Putukuilnguq, who returned carrying a warrior's head inside his kayak. After this encounter, the men headed home:

As they continued, they avoided being detected by their enemy and eventually reached the mouth of the Kuskokwim and traveled back upriver. The Kuskokwim people fought with people who were living in the area extending from the east side of the mouth of the Kuskokwim down to Bristol Bay.

They paddled fleeing from their enemy . . . using double-bladed paddles at the time. As they fled, the father of Putukuilnguq fell behind. The others would look back and see him coming behind them. Then one of them said, "Oh, dear! Putukuilnguq, your poor father is going to be captured by the enemy." But Putukuilnguq

2.10 Set of five arrows from the Yukon. From top to bottom: umilek (arrow with a stone point), pingayupegcetaaq (three-pronged arrow), akitnaq (blunt-tipped bird-hunting arrow), akulmiqurcetaaq (two-pronged bird arrow), and urugnaq (arrow with a barbed ivory point). IVA6974c, a, b, e, f.

kept going straight ahead, paddling very fast. Presently, one of them said again, "Oh dear, Putukuilnguq, your poor father is going to be captured by the enemy." Then finally the young man, who had gone with the warriors for the first time, said, "Let it be. He's drawing the enemy's fire, and they're wasting their *qerrut* [arrows]." After he said that, they continued to go at the same speed.

Oh my, as Putukuilnguq's father began to catch up with the others, oh my! [chuckle]. He had helped them escape the enemy and had prevented them catching up.

When the enemy stopped following them, they landed on the shore. . . . When they went up, they saw that Putukuilnguq's father was wearing a belt. When he came out of his kayak, he removed his belt and started to brush down his body. As he brushed his body, there was a clattering sound from the enemies' arrow points. Evidently he had something that prevented arrow points from penetrating his body. The arrow points that the enemy had shot had just fallen inside his garment. And when he stood up, the arrow points started to drop down to the ground with a clatter.

Wassilie remarked that there were many stories about the warrior Putukuilnguq. He briefly mentioned one more, recalling the *aklegaq* (seal-hunting harpoon) we had seen the day before:

82   THE RETURN GIFT

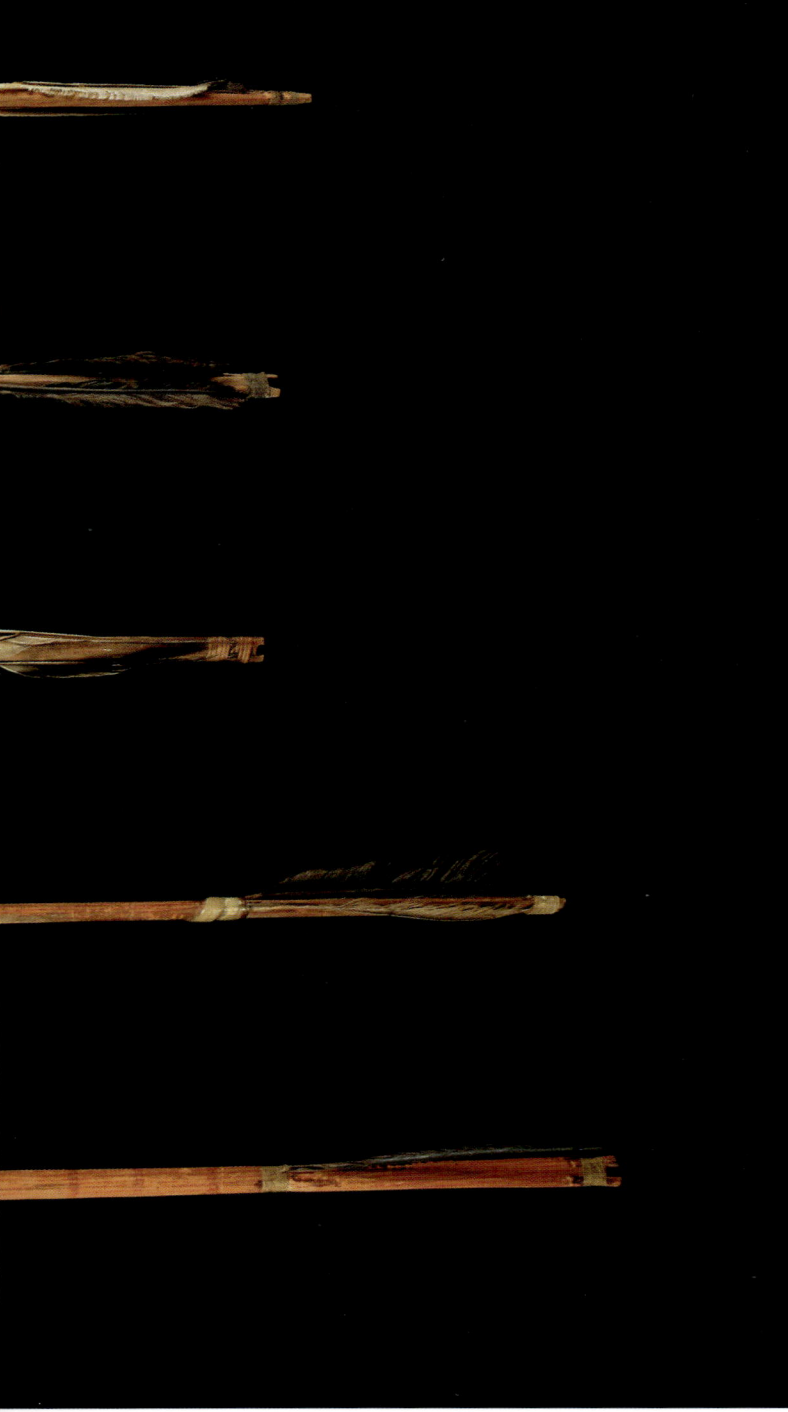

arrow was made in the recent times, and red ocher paint is still on it. It's tied with factory-made string and not sinew thread. Its *nakrutet* look like they were from a real bird. The end of the *nakrutet* has been pushed inside the wood. Its fletching is made of geese feathers.

Finally we looked at a set of five arrows (fig. 2.10) from the Yukon, including one each of three of the arrow types we had already discussed—*pingayupegcetaaq*,[17] *akitnaq*,[18] and *akulmiqurcetaaq*—as well as two arrows we had not encountered—*urugnaq*, an arrow with barbed ivory points, and *umilek,* an arrow with an *umi* (stone point).[19] Paul commented: "By looking at the points, these two have different names. An ivory point that looks like this is called *urugnaq*. And this has an *umi*. . . . They were used to hunt larger animals. They were probably used on humans back in those days." Jacobsen reported the same thing—that the barbed arrow Paul designated *urugnaq* was used for caribou and larger land animals.

Herr Wedell now brought us a dozen large arrows, which the elders divided into two groups based on point size rather than where they came from. The first consisted of arrows (fig. 2.11, fig 2.12) from the Yukon and Nushagak used when hunting seals from a kayak, when the animals were too far to be hit with a regular spear.[20] The arrows were shot from a bow at the emerging seal. Bigger harpoons were used when the seal had tired, and it was finally dispatched with a lance. Paul spoke first:

All of these are called *pitegcautet* [arrows], but these have *kingulirat* [lines, from *kingu-*, "back part, area behind"] at the tip. These arrows are called *kinguliralget*. When the arrow struck the animal, the point would penetrate the skin, and the *kinguliraq* would prevent the arrow from falling off and keep it attached to the animal. All of these are called *kinguliralget pitegcautet*.

The second group of eight arrows from the Kuskokwim and Nushagak Rivers were also used for seal hunting in open water.[21] Jacobsen called them "Pititsirak" or "Piktsautit," which he translated as "arrow," while Wassilie viewed them as *pitegcirat* (large arrows or spears). Wassilie continued:

They are in different sizes. One arrow is very heavy. This *pitegciraq* was obviously owned by a big, strong person with a very tight bow. Its [ivory] arrow point resembles the point of a *nagiiquyacuar* [small seal-hunting spear]. All of these are the same. Their points are real *kukgarapiayagaat.* In the Kuskokwim, the arrows' *nakrutet* [flight-stabilizing feathers] are called *agayiinraat* if they were made from cormorant feathers. In some areas, the *nakrutet* are also called *culut.*

Later in the week, Wassilie's attention was attracted by an ivory socket piece (fig. 2.13) from Nushagak made to hold a point like a *pitegciraq*.[22] Marie then asked Wassilie if he had used tools like these, and he answered by recalling an act of generosity.

When I was a young boy, I didn't live with my family. When children became orphans, they usually were raised by a second fam-

While going home after warring with the enemy, Putukuilnguq, now a great hunter and provider, would grab his *aklegaq* at the beginning of the bluffs below the Unguquutaq [place where the cliffs are interrupted] above Napakiak and throw it, aiming toward the cliffs. His spear would fly with great speed through the sky and land with a loud impact, so loud that its echo was heard by people in Napaskiak. At that time, the people were watchful at all times. The people in Napaskiak would hear the echo and know that their warriors were coming home. . . . Let's end the story here.

We examined a Yukon arrow with two points made of caribou antler, attached so that one barbed hook pointed in each direction.[16] According to Jacobsen, it was used for hunting seabirds. Wassilie was the first to comment:

This arrow is called *akulmiqurcetaaq*. It was used on birds. This

ily. When I was with the second family, I used to make my own bow and arrows when I was able to.

Then one summer we were at a fish camp at the mouth of Apruka'ar. One morning I went out and noticed a kayak turned on its side to make a shelter for someone who had arrived in the night. A visitor from Quinhagak had arrived when we were asleep.

Then in the morning I hunted little birds with my bow and arrow. Later on the visitor gave me his arrow. When I examined it, it had a different kind of arrow point. I realized that it was a *pitegciraq*. The other arrow he gave me had a metal arrow point called *meq'ercetaaq* [arrow point that detaches in the flesh, from *meqe-*, "to shed"]. Since he felt sorry for me, he had given me his own arrows. In his view, I probably looked like a poor orphan boy with no provider. I was very grateful at that time.

Marie continued to probe, asking them to talk a little more about warriors. Wassilie demurred, saying that these ivory-pointed arrows were never used in warfare but only those with stone points called *umit* that were able to cause serious puncture wounds on the skin. Paul, however, took up the request and briefly recalled an apocryphal episode in the life of the famous warrior Apanuugpak who, like the father of the warrior Putukuilnguq, had the ability to withstand enemy arrows.

My home has always been called Qaluyaat [Nelson Island]. I've heard that Apanuugpak was raised in Engelumiut on the Qaluyaat. . . . It was said that there was a *qanitaq* [dumping place, midden] on that old site.

It was said that when Apanuugpak got ready to go to war, he used to put mussel shells on his chest inside his *imarnin* [seal-gut rain parka] and put a belt around his waist. They say when the enemy shot arrows at him, the arrows hung from his *imarnin,* unable to penetrate his body. After the enemy was shooting at him, one of his men said, "Though arrows are landing on you, why don't they penetrate your body?" He answered, "You've seen the dumping place of Engelumiut. When arrows land on me, they are actually landing on the *qanitaq* of Engelumiut." With the two mussel shells he had put inside his *imarnin,* his willpower had created a thick layer of shells on his body, making it impossible for an arrow to penetrate.

Paul then recounted the beginning of bow-and-arrow warfare. He noted that in mainland villages, warfare was said to have begun when violence escalated following the accidental blinding of a boy by his playmate in a game of darts. Along the coast, however, warfare arose when a man who had married into a village returned home and lied to his people. According to the story, the man always made paddles with points on their ends. When he went hunting, sometimes his partners failed to return. The man drowned his partners by piercing their kayaks with his paddle to claim their catch. One man, however, escaped this fate by plugging the hole

2.11 *Three large arrows and a seal-hunting harpoon. From top to bottom: pitegciraq (lance or spear), kinguliraq (arrow with attached line), pitegciraq, and asaaquq (small sealing spear with barked point). IVA5240, IVA5238, IVA4578, IVA4576.*

2.12 The fletching of a pitegciraq (large arrow), called agayiinraat if made from cormorant feathers. IVA5240.

2.13 Ivory socket piece carved in the shape of a ferocious predator, with an opening between the teeth filled with wood in which a point could be inserted like the points on pitegcarat. The fine workmanship on this simple hunting tool reminded Wassilie of the powerful amulets that shamans provided their clients in the past. IVA5404.

with a piece of seal fat and returning to the village. When the villagers learned what had happened, they didn't do anything at first. Later, when the man asked for help stretching the skin over his new kayak frame, one of the older men said, "*Kitaki* [well then]. Those young boys he hasn't killed yet, come forward." The first group of boys put the skin covering on as it was normally done, but the second group applied more pressure to the frame, breaking it to pieces. As the last group of boys continued to flatten the kayak, the man went out of the *qasgi*, got his things, and left the village. Returning to his home, he lied to his relatives, telling them that the other village was getting ready to attack them. They believed him and sent their warriors forward to fight. Paul concluded, "I've heard that was the beginning of warfare on the coast."

Later we looked at a second group of seven arrows from Nushagak, brought to Berlin in 1834 aboard the Prussian trade ship *Princess Louise* (fig. 2.14). Although they were not part of Jacobsen's collection, the elders were anxious to see them, as they were among the museum's earliest collections and their oldest Yup'ik pieces. Two had ivory points and *kingulirat* (lines) attached near the front.[23] Wassilie began:

These were probably used for hunting marine mammals. When the arrow was shot, the point came off and its line unwound as the point propelled straight through the air without straying. These

2.14 Nushagak arrows brought to Berlin in 1834 aboard the Princess Louise. The top two arrows have caribou-antler points (the first with a schist tip), and the bottom three ivory points have lines attached. Paul and Wassilie identified the last as a seal-hunting weapon. From top to bottom: IVA138d, IVA138f, IVA138b, IVA138g, IVA138.

arrows are both complete with *culut* [flight stabilizers] made from quill vanes taken from waterfowl. They attached three evenly spaced quill vanes as stabilizers to the other end so that the arrow would go in a straight line when shot, rather than spinning through the air as some arrows do.

Paul noted that when a seal was too far to hit with a *nanerpak* or a *nagiiquyaq*, they used arrows that had *kingulirat* like these to try to hit them. If they were far, the arrows were shot with bows to try to disable them: "For that reason they made large, barbed points such as these on arrows with lines."

The next two arrows had caribou-antler points, one with a schist tip.[24] Again, Wassilie spoke first:

One of them has an *umi* [stone point] made so that it would detach when it pierced an animal's flesh. It has a kind of point that was called *ekillugnarqellria* [one that could cause bad injury to the flesh]. These arrows have identical designs on them and their undersides were painted with red ocher. And on top below the stabilizers there is a design painted with *qesuuraq* [blue paint], and both arrows have blue designs. They are from earlier times.

Paul reiterated that arrows like these with *umi* points were used on large game. Like the arrow Wassilie had received from the Quinhagak visitor, each had a *meq'ercetaaq* (detachable point):

When a person shot an arrow like this at a large animal such as a caribou, the point would detach in its flesh, penetrate deep into its flesh, and kill it. Compared to today, our ancestors lived difficult lives and worked hard to survive. They made their own hunting tools, and though they lived far apart, some of their tools were almost alike with minute differences.

From ancient times *Ellam Yua*, whom we call God today, always provided our ancestors with sound minds so that they could survive. The lifeways given to our ancestors by *Ellam Yua* have been passed to us today, but today we utilize the tools and lifeways that the white people have introduced to us.

Paul and Wassilie identified the next piece as a small sealing harpoon, like those we had already examined.[25] Wassilie added detail about the function of the weapon's sinew binding, called *atanrautaq*: "Here, close to the end, it has sinew binding. The line continues to go down and is attached to the part down there.... Even if this piece broke in half, the twine would help keep the bottom part from sinking. And the part would not fall off. The seal would continue to swim, pulling the broken pieces."

The remaining pieces were quickly scanned. Wassilie identified one as a *nanerpak* (seal-hunting harpoon), and Paul said that the other was the handle for a spear used with a throwing board.[26]

We returned to a group of five arrows with large, barbed ivory points that Jacobsen had collected on the Yukon[27] and described as having been used for hunting and war. Neither Wassilie nor Paul had seen arrows like them, but they had heard of them. Wassilie noted that these, too, had *meq'ercetaaq* points, that is, points that came off when the arrow struck its quarry. He said that such arrows were called *atauciqerrnat*. Paul added that arrows with barbed ivory points were called *cingigturat* in his area, but were also known as *urugnat*. He continued: "I've heard stories about certain individuals who used *pitegcirarpiit* [arrows with big points] to kill animals that were difficult to catch. Perhaps these arrows with huge points were the *pitegcirarpiit* they referred to in the stories.... But people I saw didn't own arrows that were elaborately done like these.... And since metal had been introduced already, metal points were made more because they were easier to work with."

Wassilie recalled the use of arrows with metal points: "I've heard that when an arrow was shot at an animal, it went all the way in and the only part you could see was the *nakrutet*. The arrow would go all the way through a caribou. They killed caribou by shooting them once. They also used these arrows on dangerous animals like bears. That's the way I understand these arrows that were made after metal was introduced."

Paul followed with a short story about a person who used a metal-tipped arrow to kill a caribou.

One day a man came to a village where he had an *iluraq* [male cross-cousin] who was recognized as a good caribou hunter. At his arrival, the *iluraq* brought him dried caribou ribs for his meal in the *qasgi* and a bowl filled with seal oil. After handing food to his guest, his host said, "During your hunting years, I wonder what kind of animal that you've killed made you the proudest to be a hunter?" Though he was a good hunter, his *iluraq* replied, "Ah. In terms of hunting, I don't have anything to brag about. I suppose you're the one who has such egotism for bringing up the question." Then his *iluraq* pointed his nose farther up in the air and said, "When I hit a male caribou with my arrow and it falls to the ground and kicks its feet several times, that's the moment I feel like a genuine *nukalpiaq* [great hunter and provider]."

Everyone laughed, and Wassilie added, "Some hunters teased each other like that. The word to describe that kind of teasing was *piltaaqaulluteng*." Paul continued:

The visitor was a skilled hunter of both land and sea animals. After his *iluraq* described what made him feel like a genuine *nukalpiaq*, the visitor said, "Aa. Whenever I hit a male caribou and I see it falling to the ground and kicking, my mind doesn't get influenced one way or the other. I keep my feet grounded as I watch it fall." Applying more force to his words, the *iluraq* asked, "Then what kind of animal makes you proudest when you kill it?" The visitor said, "Well, when I'm hunting way out on the ocean and the shoreline has disappeared behind me and a seal I hit with my spear begins pulling my kayak sideways and I'm all alone, that's the time I feel like a genuine *nukalpiaq*." Then the *iluraq* said, "I guess I would feel the same way if I did that, too." Again the visitor said, "Instead of guessing, you should check out every hunting endeavor to experience them firsthand."

After Paul's story, our systematic examination of the collection briefly came to a halt. Andy picked up an arrow and looked down its shaft, taking its measure (fig. 2.15). Herr Wedell brought us one of the large, sinew-backed bows we had looked at earlier, and Wassilie took it in hand along with an arrow to show us how they were used (fig. 2.16). Crouching low, he held the bow perpendicular to his body, moving slowly forward toward imagined prey. Turning toward us, he explained how the bowstring was drawn tight.

I've heard that when hunters owned bows with tight strings that were hard to pull, they would gather rocks to put weight on themselves before putting their strings on. The extra weight from the rocks stabilized them when they put the string to the bow. When

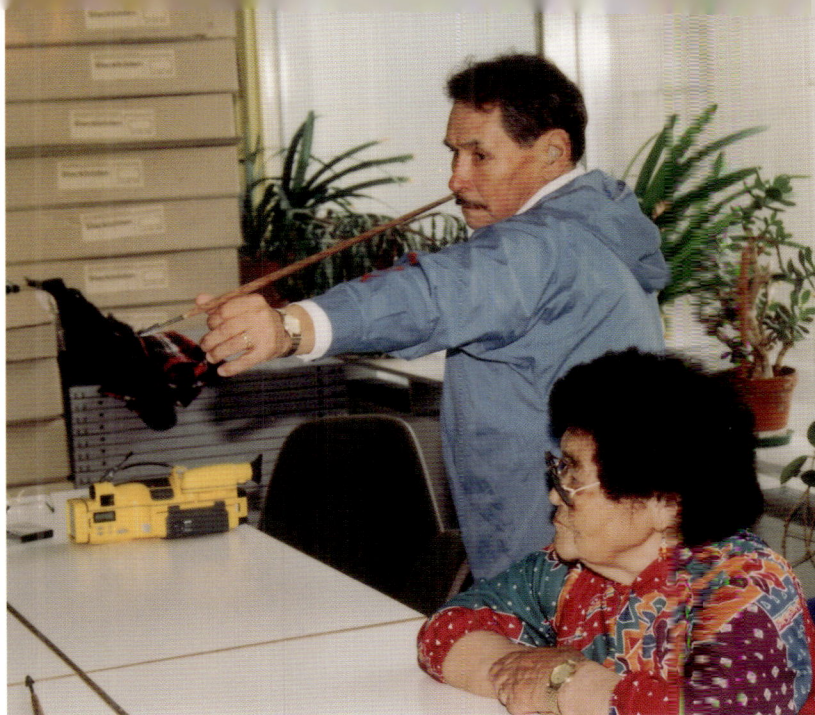

2.15 *Andy judging the straightness of an arrow shaft.*

they spotted caribou in the distance, that was how they'd string their bows.

When the bow was not in use, the other end of the string was released . . . and attached close to the end where they had taken it off. When the wood part of the bow was stiff, it was difficult to bend enough so that the string could reach the part where the released string was reattached. . . .

These sinews have immense strength. If the string wasn't tight enough, they'd remove it and shorten the loop . . . making the string just right.

Finally we returned to four slate-bladed arrows from the Yukon with red and black designs.[28] Paul acknowledged that these *umilget* (arrows with *umit* [stone points]) were like those we had already examined: "Perhaps these were made after the time of warfare, but arrow points like these were made to kill either animals or humans because they were able to cause great injury on impact. They aren't so different from the arrows we saw before, but these points were surely made for bigger targets." Returning to an anecdotal frame, he briefly mentioned another well-known episode in the adventures of the warrior Apanuugpak, highlighting the fearlessness of his young companion.

When enemy warriors surrounded Apanuugpak and his cousin Pangalgalria over in Iiyuussiiq near Eqtarmiut, . . . their nephew would say, "Someone is throwing these things away that are so hard to make." He'd grab them from the water and put them in his kayak. His uncles discovered that he was collecting *qisratet* [arrow-point covers]. Goodness! The lad wasn't worried at all, since he was optimistic about going home later on.

Marie then asked her uncle to sing the *anqaraun* (warrior song) composed by Apanuugpak, telling about the time he

2.16 Wassilie demonstrating the use of a bow and arrow. Dietrich Graf, Ethnologisches Museum Berlin.

cried as he anticipated his ultimate death when he lost his kayak. Wassilie sang the chorus, followed by two verses.

> Aa-aa-a ang'a-aa
> Ii-ii-I iya-aa
> Agi-ii-I iya-aa
> Ii-ii-I iya-aa
>
> Someone sing for that one down there
>
> Yii-ii-rri-ii
>
> Somewhere I
> I'm crying
> Iiyuussiiq River
> As I was about to swim across it
> Someone sing for that one down there
>
> Yii-ii-rri-ii
>
> Somewhere I
> I was thrilled
> One with a big caribou parka
> As I was about to meet him
> Someone sing for that one down there
>
> Yii-ii-rri-ii

Wassilie commented that Kuskokwim and Nelson Island people sang this and other warrior songs when they performed *ingulautet* (slow, old-style songs) in the late summer or early fall. Those in Bristol Bay, he added, sang it a little differently, and Annie sang the version she had heard as a child (fig. 2.17): "If that's you, I will give you an arrow point you could have, one you could use to kill the warriors with." Paul then told another part of the story of which the song was a part.

It was said that Apanuugpak, Pangalgalria, and the nephew were tracking Iruvertuq, who had his kayak loaded with caribou meat. They caught up with him, and instead of capturing him, they allowed him to keep moving forward, . . . knowing that he couldn't elude them. As they continued on, Iruvertuq would turn around and say, "If you're going to get me, do it now before you get caught in a snare set by Eqtarmiut." Then Iruvertuq, with a kayak loaded with caribou meat, suddenly started to make an effort to escape. When the other three chased him, suddenly there was a village. They had inadvertently allowed Iruvertuq to reach Eqtarmiut as they followed him.

When the village got alerted . . . the three warriors were suddenly surrounded by the enemy with no way to escape. Apanuugpak in his panic was gulping down salt water. It was during this time that their nephew was gathering *qisratet* in the water, saying, "Those people who act randomly keep throwing away these things that are hard to come by." He kept picking them up and putting them into his kayak. When Apanuugpak was gulping down salt water, his cousin Pangalgalria asked, "Why are you drinking this salty water? Look at our nephew. He sure isn't worried. Every time he sees a *qisran* float by his kayak, he takes it and throws it into his kayak." Then Apanuugpak regained his composure and said, "Okay. Cover my back as I look for a way out."

As soon as he said that, they looked toward the village and saw Eyarralek talking and waiting next to the *qasgi*. . . . He knew that he was a mighty warrior.

As Apanuugpak was zigzagging across looking for an escape route, the two were following behind him as planned. As Eyarralek was near a group of young warriors, one of the warriors yelled out. Then Apanuugpak suddenly turned to the smallest warrior in the group and yelled and paddled his kayak really fast as the two followed him. As the frightened young warriors rushed to make way for them, one of them crashed into Eyarralek's kayak, capsizing it. As the escaping warriors swiftly paddled by, one of them used his *nagiiquyaq* with crane-feather stabilizers to stab Eyarralek as he emerged from underwater.

2.17 *Annie moved to sing a song about warfare by the arrows she was examining.*

After the Eqtarmiut warriors brought their fallen warrior up to their village they were resentful, knowing that the enemy had killed their leader with a weapon that they all regarded as inferior. The spear point was made from *cirunqatak* [old antler], and it had crane-feather stabilizers. It was hard for them to accept his death by such an inferior weapon.

The elders enjoyed listening to each other as much as Marie and I enjoyed listening to them. When Paul finished, Wassilie picked up where he left off, describing Apanuugpak and his companions' escape from the Eqtarmiut warriors and their safe return up the Kuskokwim. One story led to another, and Wassilie recalled another close call by Apanuugpak when he was caught in enemy territory at sunset. It was after that frightening experience, Wassilie said, that he composed another *anqaraun*. Once again, Wassilie and Annie sang different versions of the song.

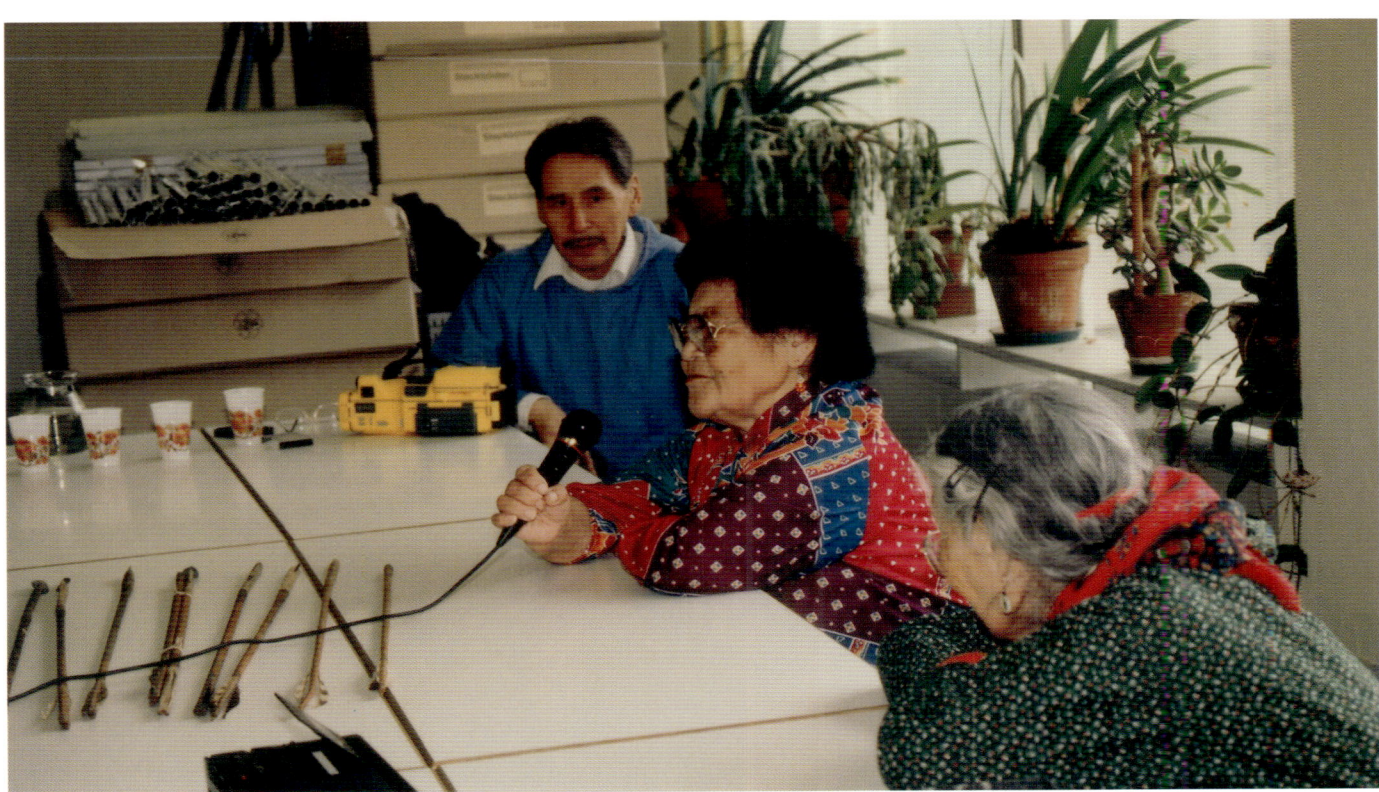

THIRD DAY More Tools for Hunting and Fishing

Nuqat wall' Egutet / Throwing Boards: "Our Ancestors Used Them Like Guns"

Our third day began with the careful scrutiny of a dozen throwing boards (also known as spear throwers) from different areas. Like the arrows we had already examined, their use had been discussed when we viewed seal and bird spears the day before. Wassilie picked up a board from the Kuskokwim, and Paul took one from the coast. Annie took one collected from the warlike Aglurmiut of the Nushagak region and used it as a gun to "shoot" the men across the table.

The boards were of different sizes with a variety of grips (fig. 3.1).[1] On the upper end of each was a bone insert, often equipped with an *aklicaraq* (small peg) that fit into the end of the throwing harpoon. Wassilie explained that a hunter would dip his throwing board in water, and the damp *aklicaraq*, fit tightly into the end of the spear, helped it stay in place.

Wassilie and Paul carefully examined throwing boards from the Yukon, Kuskokwim, and Nushagak areas (fig. 3.2). Wassilie noted the *kumgaq* (incised design) on both sides of one Kuskokwim board. Taking it up, he spoke briefly: "They used these pieces to throw *nagiiquyat* [seal-hunting weapons] and *nuusaarpiit* [three-pronged fish or bird spears]. . . . The end of this throwing board is quite thick. They would turn this over and hit their catch with it."

Paul referred to throwing boards as *nuqat*, while Wassilie called them *egutet*. Both men spoke about why some things had different names in different areas. Wassilie began:

Down where we live, there are many people named Nuqarrluk [literally, "old *nuqaq*"]. And these were called *egutet* because of that. The people from Tuntutuliak *qul'arenqegtut* [avoid using names of the deceased]. . . .

Say that a person named Nuqarrluk died. People in that village preferred not to call these *nuqat* by his name. Respecting the parents of the deceased, they started calling it an *egun*. Though they were aware that their names were *nuqat*, they called them *egutet*.

Paul continued:

Since people's names derive from everything around us, *qul'aryaraq* [giving objects different names out of respect for the dead] was the reason some things have different names in certain areas. In my village this [arm] is called *talliq*. But in a village where there are people named Tallilek, it is called *agaran*. . . . We call this [thumb]

3.1 Throwing boards with different grips. Most had two bone pegs to provide the fingers with a better grip, others had only notches for the fingers, while some from the lower Yukon had pegs as well as a hole through the board to insert the index finger. From top to bottom: IVA4307, IVA4306, IVA4593.

kumluq because in our village there's no Kumluq or Kumurpak. But in villages where people have names deriving from *kumluq*, they call the thumb *ayaun*.

Wassilie commented that this particular throwing board fit him perfectly, and Andy pointed out that a man's board measured from his elbow to the end of his forefinger (fig. 3.3). Paul showed that in his area the length of the *nuqaq* was determined by taking the handle in his left hand, then bending his right elbow and resting it on the top of his fist. A *nuqaq* of the proper length should come to the top of his curled thumb. He continued, comparing *nuqat* to guns:

They used *nuqat* like these on bigger seals out on the ocean. They also used them on birds. People back in those days used them as their guns.

They said that different *nuqat* had varied results when used. Some were considered to be *uyaqsunaqluteng*, which meant that when used for casting a spear, they would hit with accuracy and precision. If the hunter possessed such a *nuqaq*, they would say that it was excellent.

Having been born after the introduction of guns and having heard about *nuqat*, I realize that guns with straight, smooth barrels also shoot with accuracy and precision. Comparing the characteristics of the *nuqat* and some guns today, I came to the conclusion that the accuracy of the *nuqat* was due to the straight, rounded groove that ran from where it was held to its end. . . . If one holds the *nuqaq* like this [fig. 3.4], aiming it at the prey, the spear would fly straight to the target. Even though the handle is well made, if this [groove] is not straight, the spear thrust from it would miss the prey and just land beside it.

Nuqat were also used with *asaaqut* [toggling harpoons], which we described a little yesterday. If the line attached to the *asaaquq* was long enough, the hunter would throw it at a target, even though it was quite far. As a hunter throws the *asaaquq*, its line looks like the hunter's entrails unraveling through the air when one views the scene out of the corner of one's eye. That was what they said about it.

Nuqat were very important weapons in those days. They were used on sea mammals and on prey that was both far and near. The spear used with the *nuqaq* worked like a bullet . . . used for a gun. Our ancestors used the *nuqaq* like a gun.

Paul then added a story about a *nuqaq*. He told how long ago, when hunters used *nagiiquyat* and *asaaqut* to hunt seals, a boy and his brother-in-law (a *narussuli*, "skilled harpooner") went to the ocean to hunt. The ocean ice began to pile up, making hunting difficult, and days passed without any luck. The boy's mother began to worry, realizing that the two were their primary providers. When her husband got ready to go

3.2 Spear and throwing board, which increases the power and speed of the spear by effectively lengthening the arm. At the end of the board is a small ivory peg into which the shaft fits to stabilize the spear before launching. IVA6368a, b.

3.3 Wassilie showing how a man's throwing board should measure from his elbow to the end of his forefinger. For larger harpoons, a longer throwing board would be used, measuring the length of a man's forearm to his forefinger, plus his three middle fingers placed crosswise against the board.

3.4 Wassilie demonstrating use of a throwing board to launch a nuusaarpak (bird spear). First he stubbed the upper end of the harpoon shaft against the piece of bone on the groove at the end of the throwing board. Then he held the board with his right hand so that his fingers came to rest between the bone pegs. The harpoon rested on his little and ring fingers, pressed tightly against the board, while his middle finger and thumb met above the shaft, pressing onto the rest of the fingers, thus grabbing the board tight. Dietrich Graf, Ethnologisches Museum Berlin.

down to the ocean, she packed most of the family's dwindling food supply in a bag and gave it to her husband, instructing him to give it to the two hunters after taking a little for himself. When the father arrived, however, he did not give them the food.

The son-in-law had brought several *usaat* (skin lines), and he gave one to the boy and told him to go to his father and offer to trade it for food for their supper. The boy did as he was told, but the father refused, saying of his son-in-law, "He should have offered me his *egun* rather than his *usaaq*." When the boy returned to his brother-in-law and told him what his father had said, the man took up his *nuqaq* and pretended to throw his spear, saying, "I'm not offering him my *egun*. We'll hunt for food tomorrow."

The next morning the water had begun rising and the ice had moved back, creating a lake. As the men looked, they saw a bearded seal coming up through the water, making its mating call. The son-in-law tied his two lines together, took his *egun*, and lifted his *asaaquq*. When the seal surfaced, he thrust his weapon, and, as the line unraveled behind the *asaaquq*, it looked as if his entrails were flying out from his abdomen. The *asaaquq* landed in the seal's spine, making the hunter's words from the night before come true.

After cutting up the meat and sharing it with the other

hunters, the son-in-law sent the boy back to the village, holding his gaff upright, *uurcaryaraq* (alerting the people that a bearded seal had been caught) and asking them to bring a sled to haul home the catch. His mother welcomed him, asking if they had received the food she had sent the day before. When her son told her that her husband had kept it for himself, she was very angry but told her son to let his father be. When her husband returned, however, she scolded him fiercely, mentioning every aspect of his bad character. Paul concluded: "It was said that her husband died of shame and deep sorrow at that time." Annie commented, "His wife got him with her mouth," and Paul agreed: "His wife had good reason to berate him. I don't think anyone treats his son like that. This object has allowed me to tell the story."

Wassilie followed immediately with another story:

One day men were going after a seal at the mouth of Kialiq. Our family was not wealthy because our mother was ill and couldn't do much work.

Early in the morning people spotted a seal. When we heard people going "*quaq, quaq*" outside our tent, our dear father said, "A seal has surfaced and been spotted!" Then we all ran out of the tent. The weather was calm. The other hunters had swiftly gotten their kayaks ready to go. Our dear old father ran down to his kayak and pulled out his *nagiiquyaq* [seal-hunting weapon] and attached its point, getting it ready. He attached points for two spears, getting them ready for the hunt.

Then, shortly, the seal they'd spotted surfaced for air. When it came up, one of the hunters shot it with his *pitegciraq* [lance] and hit it. . . . The seal dove in the water and was gone for a while before resurfacing farther away. Then I saw my dear late father dipping his *egun* in the water on the side of his kayak. . . . Then he took his *nagiiquyaq* and set it, straightened up in his kayak, then lifted the weapon and cast it. As I watched the *nagiiquyaq* going through the air in an arc, I noticed it was quivering. . . . As it was coming down toward the seal, the seal dove into the water. The weapon hit the water and started going down, then stopped just before the water reached its feather stabilizers. After it stopped, it continued going down into the water and disappeared. Then the man who had struck the seal first with an arrow yelled, "Got it!" The *nagiiquyaq* went into the water and didn't come back up.

Then, as we looked, the *nagiiquyaq* popped up in the water. Evidently its line had broken, and the point was still stuck in the seal. The kayaks continued following the injured seal and disappeared behind the bend. After being gone for a while, they came back. The other boys and I were standing on the shore, expectantly.

We used to call our dear father Paiyaq. The kayaks were coming back, gliding right on top of the water. When our dear father came around the bend, his kayak was obviously loaded. One of the people standing on the shore with us said, "Little Paiyaq has evidently bagged it."

After they carried the seal up on land, they looked for Paiyaq's *kukgar* [barbed harpoon point attached to the *nagiiquyaq*] but couldn't find it. And the man who was the first to hit the seal with his *pitegciraq* examined his little spear point, saying that if his spear point was chipped and they didn't find Paiyaq's spear point, he would claim the dead seal. They continued to examine the carcass, and when they parted its flippers, they discovered that the *nagiiquyaq* had struck there. As the animal dove down, the spear point had hit it there. Once they found it, my dear father began to cut up the seal.

Paul followed with the tale of another hunt in which claiming the catch was at issue. He explained that in the past, when spear points were made of ivory and when hunters tried to decide who should claim the catch, they would examine the hunter's spear point, and if it was chipped, they would let him have the catch. Sometimes hunters had difficulty determining who should claim it:

Once, while the men were debating, one of them who had shot his harpoon at the seal went over to his kayak and appeared to be looking for something. Then, upon hearing one hunter wondering out loud who should claim it, he returned, saying, "Oh my. My spear point has a chip on it." Then one of the men said, "Perhaps this carcass belongs to you." While he was talking, one of the hunters saw a little piece of something white stuck on his beard.

They all looked and saw that it was a little chip from a spear point. When they placed the chip on the *nagiiquyaq* to see if it matched, sure enough it did. They then reasoned that when the man went over to his kayak, he had broken off a piece from the tip of his spear point, and it landed on his beard when he spat it out.

Everyone laughed, and Wassilie exclaimed, "He really wanted to claim the catch!"

Marie asked if they had used *nuqat* like these, and both men said they had. Wassilie added, "Remember what I said yesterday. All of these objects we are looking at were things we used and we are the last generation that used them." Annie admitted her ignorance, stating that when she first saw the *nuqaq*, she thought it was a toy gun and didn't realize it was a hunting tool: "I grew up as a river dweller far inland. Hunters didn't use this kind of equipment up there. . . . I wish all the boys back home would hear what these two men have been talking about."

Catherine, on the other hand, was familiar with throwing boards, as they are used on the Yukon today by women and children as well as men:

When I moved to the Yukon, the men were still using *nuqat*. Even children had their own *nuqat*. Men owned *nanerpiit* and *nuqat*. Whenever someone made my grandchildren brand-new *nuqat* and *nanerpiit*, they would come running into my house beaming with gratitude. At the present time, men back home are still using them. . . .

My late husband would hand me his *nanerpak* and *nuqaq*, telling me to shoot what we were pursuing. I just couldn't see myself using a *nanerpak* with a *nuqaq*.

One time we were hunting seals down on the ocean. . . . As I turned, I looked right into the watching eyes of the seal floating right next to our boat. Since I wasn't sure how to react, I speared the seal as hard as I could on its vertebra. It splashed me as I fell on my seat. I killed my first bearded seal! After that, hunting became enjoyable for me.

Marie expressed her surprise that women used *nuqat*. Paul noted that it was rare in his area, but not unknown:

I've heard a story about a woman who had several brothers. The woman had her own kayak. Since she was skilled in men's work, she was deemed their equal. When she hunted with her brothers, she often would be the one to kill the prey they were pursuing.

Then one day one of her brothers hid her *nuqaq*. They got tired of her taking the seals away from them. When a seal was spotted, she and her brothers quickly readied their equipment for the hunt, but her *nuqaq* was missing!

As she looked, her brothers were already down in the water going after the seal. When she couldn't find her *nuqaq* right away, she quickly looked for a curved bone taken from a spotted seal's front appendage. Since she cooked and discarded bones for them, she knew that the spotted seal's flipper bone is more curved than that of other seals. When she found an *aklanquq* [front flipper bone], she joined her brothers and used it as a *nuqaq* to kill the seal before her brothers did.

Annie had heard a similar story and retold it with gusto, concluding, "She used the *kucuquk* [pelvic bone] as an *egun* to snatch the seal away from her brothers."

Before we closed our discussion of throwing boards, Andy asked Paul and Wassilie to clarify the distribution of the catch. Paul began:

Earlier I thought about *pitaryaraq* [the process of distributing seal to a group of hunters after a hunt]. When a group of hunters went after a bearded seal, the hunter who struck the animal first, either with an arrow or a spear, would officially claim the catch. And he would determine how the catch was distributed to others, referred to as *nengiit* [portions or shares of a catch].

And if a second hunter struck the seal with his weapon, they'd say that he had *aqsataraa* [the stomach part, from *aqsak*, "stomach"]. The second man received *qat'gagyui* [from *qat'gaq*, "chest"], the ribs and intestines of the seal.

And if a third man struck the seal with his weapon they'd say that he had *kuyagtaraa* [from *kuyak*, "hip"], and he received the meat from the lower part of the animal. At home, that's the total number of hunters who have the right to claim portions of the meat on a single successful hunt. The other hunters would then receive some meat with a little bit of liver and oil. The first three hunters kept the skin, intestine, and bottom portion.

Wassilie noted that in his area, the hunter to receive the ribs was referred to as *irnerrlugtalria* (the one with *irnerrluk* [seal gut]). Paul continued: "The first hunter received the skin, oil, and *keggatai* [top back?]. The second hunter received the chest and intestines, and the third hunter received the bottom portion referred to as *kuyai*."

Wassilie then stated that on the lower Kuskokwim, after a hunter caught a seal and brought it up on land they opened it up, and the hunter might say *uqurtayagarceciyugyaaquq* (that he would like to offer oil with his catch, from *uqiqur*, "to distribute *uquq* [seal blubber]"):

After the *uquq* was removed from the belly and the back, he'd ask all the little boys to come forward and he gave them each a piece of blubber. Then the boys ran home to give the oil to their mothers. Later that day, the parents of the boys who had taken oil began to bring choice food to the gathering. They'd bring tea, and some brought tobacco. That was a custom that people observed sometimes with a seal that was caught. When a seal was caught, a hunter directed this custom to gather families in friendship and love.[2]

Uqisaqsuun / Blubber Carrier
Shaped Like a Land Otter

Our next object was a wooden *uqisaqsuun* (blubber carrier) like those used in the ritual distribution Wassilie had just described (fig. 3.5).[3] The device, so important in the processing of sea mammals, had been carved in the shape of a land otter with a deep red gash down its back. According to Jacobsen, seal blubber was pulled onto the thin wooden form and carried door-to-door for distribution after a kill. No one commented further on the object's function. Rather, its shape inspired Annie (fig. 3.6) to give a long, sometimes emotional account of the creature *paalraayak*, named in Nelson's *The Eskimo about Bering Strait* ([1899] 1983) but until now a mystery.

They have mentioned *paalraayak*. And recently, I think it was the year before last, somebody mentioned that there was such a creature in the area behind Assigyugpak. It was said that *paalraayiit* were able to move around underground. . . .

One spring a couple was hunting ground squirrels in the mountains around Assigyugpak. In the past, people were told never to go in the area behind Assigyugpak. Since the younger generations don't pay attention to the old teachings, they have begun to travel in that once-restricted area. . . .

One day when the couple went to that area behind their camp, they saw an animal that resembled a land otter. They said that *paalraayiit* resemble land otters.

After looking at this carving, I'd very much like to tell you this story.

As they observed the animal that resembled a land otter, they noticed that when it moved, it would burrow into the ground and come back up again. As the couple continued, the sled they were pulling started to sink into the ground. Normally the ground in the spring is still frozen hard. As the couple walked, their feet would sink into the ground, and when a person came, the whole process stopped and they were on top of the ground. They found themselves near their camp, . . . and they saw the creature that resembled a land otter disappear into the ground.

It was said that *paalraayiit* picked on *caagnitellriit* [people restricted from certain activities due to death, first menses, childbirth, or miscarriage]. *Paalraayiit* resided in the mountains. There are many mountains in our area, as you know. Since there were many mountains, the *caagnitellriit* were restricted from roaming in them. . . .

It was said that when *paalraayiit* saw a person, they swam all

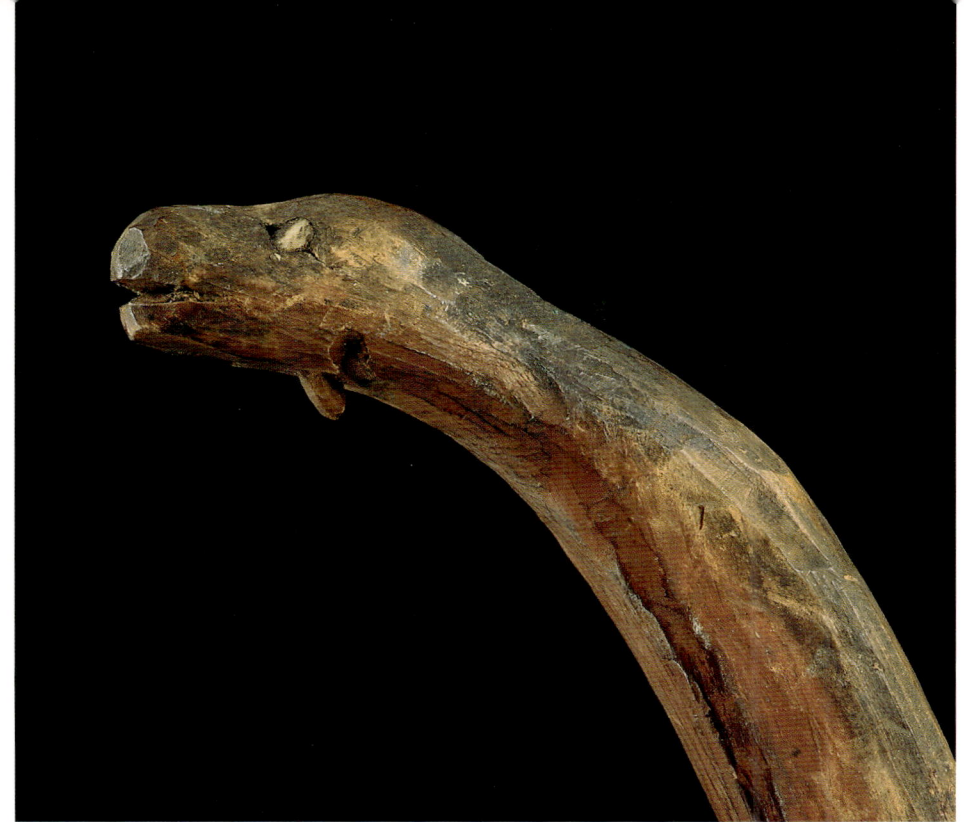

3.5 *Uqisaqsuun* (blubber carrier) carved in the shape of a land otter IVA5353.

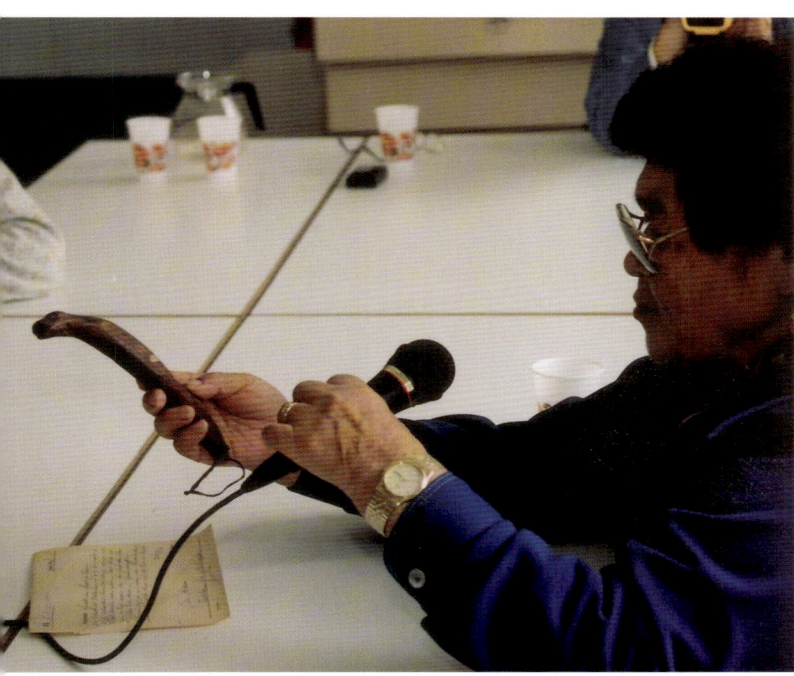

3.6 "After looking at this carving, I'd very much like to tell you this story," Annie said, launching into a detailed account of the creature *paalraayak* sometimes encountered in the mountains near her home. IVA5353.

over one's body and would begin tossing up and down in front of one's nose.

When it came to that stage, a person died. *Paalraayiit* turned into *amikuut* [extraordinary underground creatures, changeable and difficult to capture] after a period of time. When I was a girl, people talked about seeing their tracks. They'd say that they saw unusual tracks up on the lowlands made by *amikuk*.

Annie's account meant different things to those assembled in Berlin. For me it was exciting to hear her solve a long-standing scholarly riddle. But Annie's motive for telling this story was not academic. As she made plain in her telling, in the past there were rules that guided a young person's actions, which we ignore at our peril. She wants the younger generation to hear her sto-

ries and gain awareness of their history so that they can avoid very real dangers in the world today.

Mention of *paalraayiit* brought to mind other dangers that *caagnitellriit* (restricted ones) might experience. Annie described how the impurities associated with birth, death, and menstruation made both men and women vulnerable to the *ircenrraat*, extraordinary persons also sometimes encountered in the wilderness. She told the story of her father's hunting partner, whose wife had just started menstruating. When he went to check his traps, his companions told him that if he caught an animal not to touch it and that they would kill it for him. But later, when the man heard a fox trying to escape his trap and no one was around, he killed it and went to rejoin his companions. As he was going, he heard voices saying that someone had spotted the ripples of an animal in the water. Then someone yelled, "There! Hit it hard!" When he lowered his body to his knees, he heard someone say, "Oh dear! It just dove into the water!" The hunter realized that the *ircenrraat* were hunting him like a sea mammal, and to escape he threw himself on the ground and stayed very still until they gave up the hunt. Wassilie said that he recognized all that she said, as he had experienced the same thing. Once he had heard the sound of *ircenrraat*, but as his companions approached, the sound faded away.

Finally Annie spoke briefly about the restrictions she experienced after her own first menstruation. She was allowed to drink only once in the morning and once at night, lest her

body rot. And she could never drink stooping down, as it was believed that the water's vapor could cause blindness later in life. Nor could she eat salmonberries lest she develop a deadly stomach disease. Wassilie concurred, "If a person went against the restrictions, the *ircenrraat* would make that person suffer."

Nuusaarpiit / **Bird and Fish Spears**

On the first day, we had looked at a bird spear (fig. 3.7) from the lower Yukon, originally used with a throwing board.[4] Wassilie marveled at the three ivory barbs mounted halfway up the shaft. Paul explained their function: "Back when birds flew closer to the ground, a hunter threw this spear at a low-flying bird, and if the first point didn't hit the target, the second point could hit the wing, bringing down the bird. This spear was used on flying birds."

Looking at another bird spear from the Iliamna district (also shown in fig. 3.7),[5] Wassilie recalled the tool's many uses: "Evidently, the points to the piece were once flared. But since walrus ivory tends to bend with age, you can see that these have become crooked. These were spears that we always called *nuusaarpiit*. They were used to kill many kinds of animals, including birds . . . and small fish that were swimming on the surface of the water."

Later we looked at three serrated points of single-tipped *nuusaarpiit* from the Yukon.[6] Paul spoke:

These were used for hunting by our ancestors. And sometimes right after freeze-up they'd make holes in the ice and wait for the fish to come, *igvarcetaarturluteng* [from *igvar-*, "to come into view"] as they called it. And when a fish came, they'd strike it with this kind of tool to capture it. They'd catch different kinds of fish that were swimming under the ice in this fashion. The way our ancestors tried to stay alive was incredibly difficult.

Annie picked up one point from the Yukon,[7] using it as an opportunity to talk about the treatment of fish as well as their means of capture:

My dear father had *nuusaarpiit* with jagged metal points . . . like this that were very good for capturing animals. In the fall he brought home lots of spawning fish we hung to dry.

When he brought the fish home, we'd cut off their *amait* [head cartilage] and eat them raw. We also ate their heads raw. We'd hang the fish that were caught by the *nuusaarpak* to dry, and we called them *tamuanat*. When dried, we'd dip them in seal oil and eat them. Our mother put the fish away before it was too dry. She'd also dig a hole in the ground and drop their bones in. People didn't just leave fish bones out in the open anywhere.

Nowadays, it's terrible. . . . There's decaying fish along the river that were discarded by white people who were trying to [sport] fish. They usually let the fish go after they capture it. I'm mentioning this because I want to say it now.

3.7 Nuusaarpiit (spears used with throwing boards to hunt birds and fish), one with three prongs at the tip and the other with prongs halfway up the shaft. From left to right: IVA6368, IVA4350.

One last group consisted of seven barbed *neqsuutet* (fish spear points) from the Yukon River and Norton Sound.⁸ Jacobsen wrote that all were used for fishing, especially for salmon: "Such harpoons are particularly used for harpooning fish from the baskets or barricades erected all over the mouths of rivers in summer." One from the Yukon was made to be fastened to a pole and used to spear pike that had been lured by decoys.⁹ Most points were rounded at the bottom, so that they could be stuck into wooden shafts, and had a hole on the lower end to take the harpoon line.

Handling the points, Wassilie added what he knew: "These *neqsuutet* were called *cetugnat* [implements to go after fish swimming close to the water's surface]. They were made out of caribou antlers. King salmon and dog salmon were caught with these." Paul added that, like seals, when fish swim close to the surface you can see the ripples of their movement in the water: "When people hunted them with these, they'd throw the weapon into the ripples to try and hit them. . . . They called it *qavlunarluteng* [making a wake on the water's surface by swimming just below]."

Nuiret / Points for Bird or Rabbit Spears

The *nuusaarpiit* were followed by a simple caribou-antler point (fig. 3.8) from the Yukon.¹⁰ Wassilie identified it right away as a *nuiq* (spear point for a bird or rabbit spear, also called a *nuiq*). Paul spoke with conviction: "This would surely be a spear point for a bird or rabbit spear. They were used to spear birds and rabbits. When they speared those little creatures with this weapon, they'd say *nuiqerluku* [spearing it]." Wassilie added, "They were spears that were used on rabbits when they drove them, *unguluki*. I've heard of a saying, *Nuuyaarraanka neqarraanka* [my little spears, my little foods]."

The modest object evoked abundant recollections. Marie turned to her uncle and asked, "Do you know a story about it?" Wassilie immediately began to tell a tale of betrayal and revenge in which a sharp-pointed cutting knife played a pivotal part. It was the story of the powerful shaman Ircaqurrluk, who had lived in the distant past. Five brothers, all *nukalpiat* (great hunters), had a sister whom they dearly loved. She became sick, and the brothers asked Ircaqurrluk to cure her, promising to pay him well. Ircaqurrluk didn't respond, however, until the brothers promised the old man that if he cured their sister he could take her as his wife. He saved the young girl and married her, but one day he couldn't find her. While taking a fire bath, however, he turned to a bucket filled with water. Reflected in its surface was the Yukon River, and in it he saw a man paddling downriver toward his village. As he approached, Ircaqurrluk's wife came down to the riverbank to fetch water. Then the young man loaded her into his kayak and continued downriver.

Ircaqurrluk recognized the one who had taken his wife, and he traveled to the young man's village. He arrived in the evening and went to the porch of the *qasgi*, where he waited for the women to bring food for their men. When his wife came in, he told her to come back out to the porch after giving her husband food. They then left the village but soon realized that they were being followed. As they continued he allowed his wife, who he could see was pregnant by the other man, to walk in front of him. Periodically he pushed her forward with his *ayaruq* (walking stick), to which a *nuussiq* (cutting knife) was attached. When those following got closer, he pushed his wife to the ground and quickly slashed her stomach open. He then continued to his own village, leaving his dead wife behind.

The next day Ircaqurrluk took a fire bath, and when he was finished, he took his knife and walked up to the oldest brother and said, "Take this now and kill me. This is the weapon that was used on your younger sister." But the four oldest brothers just stood there, knowing that the old man was a powerful *angalkuq* and that they would all suffer the consequences. Although the youngest brother started to reach for the knife several times, the others pulled him back. Since they refused to take the knife, Ircaqurrluk cut it into five identical pieces and gave one to each brother, telling them they could use them as blades for their *mellgaraat* (crooked knives). Wassilie continued to the story's end:

So time passed and the young woman's brothers didn't do anything to the old man. Sometime later, the brothers prepared to honor their deceased sister. They observed *Elriyaraq* [ceremony honoring the spirits of the dead]. . . .

When they began their feast, they offered clothing to the individuals who carried their sister's name. When they pulled out a bag

3.8 Caribou antler *nuiq* (spear point for a bird or rabbit spear). IVA3949.

filled with things, the eldest brother called Ircaqurrluk to come forward. . . . The eldest brother pulled a pair of beautiful women's boots made from caribou leggings out of the bag. Then he said to him, "Well then, put these boots on."

Oh my, Ircaqurrluk flashed a big smile and put the boots on. Then the brother pulled out an undergarment and presented it to him to put on. The boots and the undergarment were made of skin that was very soft. When the undergarment was presented to him, he smiled and put it on. The garment was made for a woman.

Then the brother pulled a beautiful woman's parka from the bag. When the parka was presented, Ircaqurrluk smiled broadly and put it on. Then the brother told him to go back to his place. They displayed their grief and viewed him as the bearer of their sister's spirit and clothed him. During *Elriyaraq*, the families offered clothing from head to toe to individuals whom they viewed as bearers of the spirits of their deceased relatives. . . . And the parents offered clothing to children who were the same age as the child they had lost.

Ircaqurrluk went back to his place. When he sat down he became warm and soporific, so he laid back and fell asleep. He went into a long, deep sleep. He woke up and realized that his body had gotten very stiff. The brothers had dampened his new garments to make them feel very soft and velvety before they were presented

3.9 *Irunguaq (rifle support) with caribou-antler forks to hold up the gun's barrel, which Jacobsen said the Russian traders introduced at the same time they brought guns to the area in the 1820s. IVA4210.*

3.10 *Wassilie kneeling to demonstrate the use of an irunguaq (arrow or rifle support). Dietrich Graf, Ethnologisches Museum Berlin.*

to him. And while he slept his new garments had stiffened as they dried, so he couldn't move his body. Then Ircaqurrluk got choked up with tears. He began to cry. And as a result, he died. That was the way the young woman's brothers killed him.

This story is like a *quliraq* [traditional tale], because during the time the events took place, people weren't like today's humans. It happened in the ancient times. I'll end the story here.

Irunguaq / Gun or Arrow Support

We next looked at two wooden gun-crotch supports (fig. 3.9, fig. 3.10) from the Yukon.[11] Catherine had seen men on the Yukon using similar supports made out of metal. Paul also recognized them based on stories he had heard: "Warriors lying close to the ground would use an *irunguaq* [literally, "pretend *iruq* (leg)"] like this for their bow when they crawled toward their enemy . . . and when they hunted animals." Andy, however, found the tool puzzling, and it confirmed his view that Jacobsen had collected many items that were used before Andy had been born.

Kassugaliiret / Circle-and-Dot Designs

Neither Paul nor Wassilie recognized the next four objects—two shaft straighteners, a semicircular device (fig. 3.11) from Cape Vancouver like those attached to the forklike rifle support, and the head of a bullet starter, used to force the bullet into the barrel.[12] They took them as opportunities to comment on their ancestors' fine handiwork. Paul remarked, "Though they didn't have perfect tools to work with, our ancestors always decorated their things to look beautiful."

Wassilie then pointed out the circle-and-dot motif and explained how they were made: "A small *kassugaliilissuun* [literally, "device for going around"] was used to make the circle-within-a-circle design. The designs were called *kassugaliiret* [circle-and-dot designs, from *kassug-*, "to go around, to encompass"]. A *cet'rautaq* [mark] was also made in the middle. These *kassugaliiret* were painted with *avisgaq* [black pigment] for sure."

Marie asked if the circle-and-dot designs might also be called *iinguat* (literally, "pretend eyes"), and Paul said they could. Wassilie continued explaining how it was made: "First, a hole was made in the middle. Placing one side of the tool in the hole, you'd begin twirling the end of the other side around and around until a circle was made with a dot in the middle. *Kassugaliiret* was the name given to the design because of the circles around the dot."

Puulissuun wall' Imiteq / Bullet Mold

Next I brought forward three bullet molds from the Yukon, one made entirely of soapstone and the other two (fig. 3.12) of stone inserted in wood.[13] Each was made so that it could be flipped open like a pocket watch. Wassilie immediately recognized them:

I've heard that the first guns had wide barrels. And since they were loaded from the front, [people] made ammunition for them. Finished ammunition made in a *puulissuun* [device for making *puulit* (bullets)] was spherical in shape. This could have been used to make ammunition for those they referred to as *imarpalget* [muzzle-loading guns, from *imarkaq*, "lead"].

In those days they formed ammunition using these bullet molds made of stone. They also made blocks out of wood for the bullet molds. Then they made a hinge in the front end of the wooden block, held together with a wooden pin. This part has a hole going right through it for pouring lead. The device they used to drill holes in these was called a *qiivuusaaq* [drill]. This hinge was made with an *iqukeggun* [engraving tool].

These two pieces are held squarely together. These leather thongs were used to hold the two pieces tightly. The heat from the melted lead was intense. Some used calfskin for this part . . . so one would not touch it. Gosh, our ancestors were clever. This was made this way to avoid getting burned.

Paul continued:

Since people back home call *puulit* [bullets] *imat,* they called these

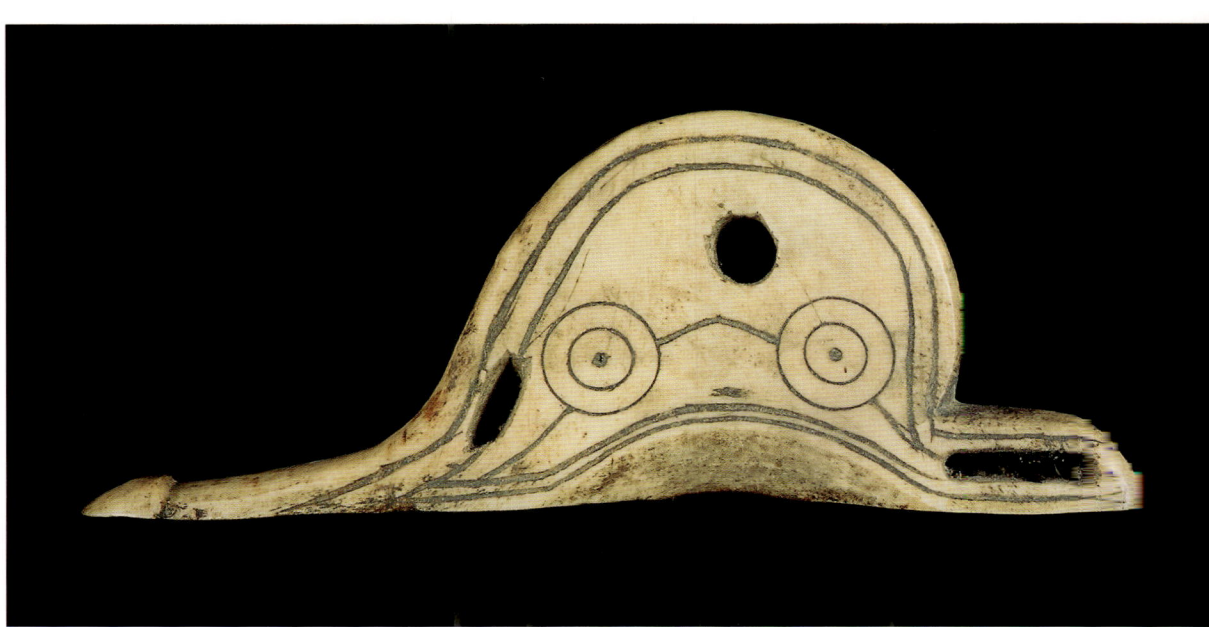

3.11 Carved ivory attachment to the forklike rifle support, one of many objects displaying delicate ring ornamentation known as kassugaliiret (circle-and-dot designs). Paul commented, "People who lived in the distant past appreciated objects with decorations. Affirming their love for detail, they created things they needed with designs like these." IVA4959.

imitet [bullet molds]. These are devices to make bullets after melting lead. Have you not seen lead being melted? When it's melted, it becomes liquid like water and very easy to pour. You'd fill this little part to the brim with melted *imarkaq*. After you closed it for a while and opened it, you'd find a round, hardened pellet. It quickly turned into a *puuli*.

Kenivik, Puyurkarvik-llu / **Primer Box and Gunpowder Container**

Later in the week, we looked at other tools related to nineteenth-century firearms. The first was a primer box from the Kuskokwim (fig. 3.13).[14] As it was from his area, Wassilie spoke first:

This ivory is nicely decorated. . . . The side is covered with *kassugaliiret* [circle-and-dot designs] and some designs that look like little mountains. I'm suspecting this was used as a *nutegcuun* [device for shooting] for *kaapcelaat* [caps, bullets] used on the first [precision] guns. The pieces that were placed at the base of the barrel below the ear . . . were kept dry in bags. Those parts that were

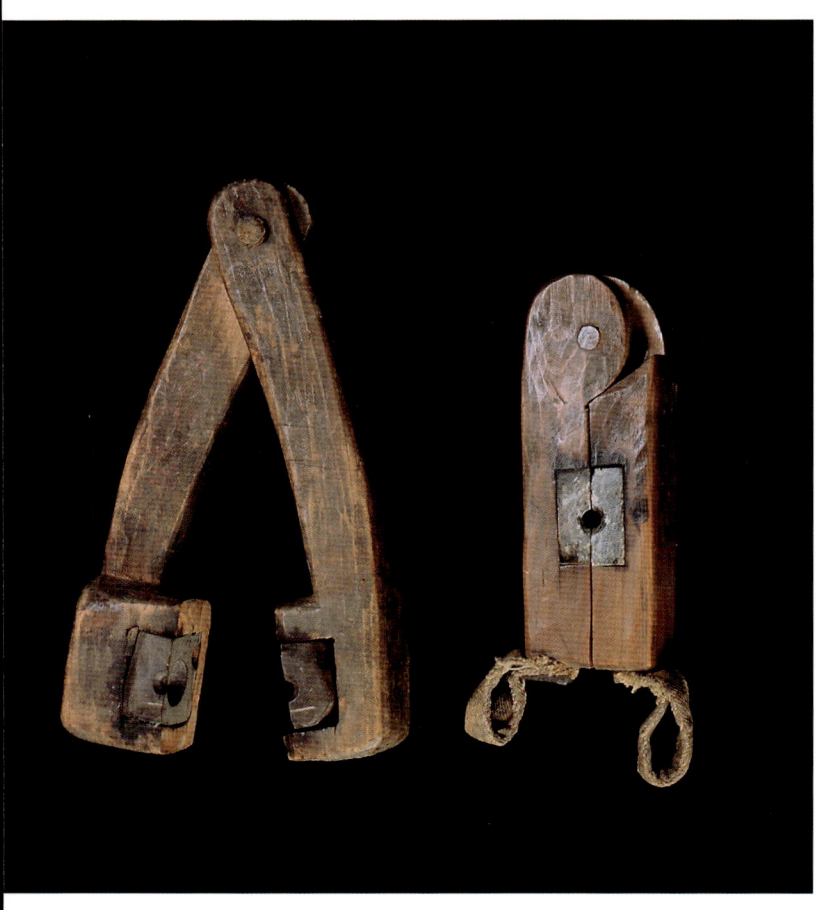

3.12 Wooden bullet molds lined with roughly fitted ground-stone chambers into which hot lead was poured to create the pellets used as ammunition in front-loading rifles. IVA4121, IVA4122.

3.13 Walrus-ivory *kenivik* (primer box), with tight-fitting wooden base and lid and a wooden *puyurkarvik* (gunpowder container), accompanied by a tiny ivory *puyurkirissuun* (powder measure) shaped into a cormorant head and used to measure out a single charge of powder. IVA4656, IVA4654, IVA3752.

3.14 Wassilie pouring imaginary powder from the walrus-shaped container into an ivory powder measure: "If a gun was loaded from the mouth, they would remove the container's cover and fill it up until it got full. It was then poured into the mouth of the gun."

inserted in that part of the gun were also called *canegngalnguut* or *kaapcelaat*.

Paul said that on Nelson Island, they called it a *kenivik* (primer box): "The *kenret* [flame, matches] for guns were kept dry in tight containers like these. When the fire exploded from the impact of the trigger, it would help the bullet to travel out of the gun."

Wassilie then picked up a wooden powder horn from the Kuskokwim[15]: "This is a *puyurkarvik* [gunpowder container, from *puyurkaq*, "gunpowder"] shaped like a walrus." He noted that several smaller ivory and bone containers[16] were for day trips: "The hunter will fill it a little bit and drop it into his *ugalguutaq* [little storage container] if he wasn't going very far to hunt."

Jacobsen had also collected seven small powder measures from the coast and along the Kuskokwim, made from both ivory and antler.[17] Several were carved in the shape of birds' heads, which Jacobsen identified as seagulls but may be cormorants, known for their hunting skills. Holding the powder horn in one hand and a bird-shaped measure in the other, Wassilie poured imaginary powder, loaded an imaginary gun, and prepared to shoot (fig. 3.14).

Later we would see another small powder measure,[18] which Paul admired:

Back in the days when guns were loaded through the front barrel, this was used for gunpowder. The size of this piece is just right. The amount of gunpowder that was put in the gun was measured exactly. You didn't want to put in too much or too little when you were ready to shoot at a target. This *puyurkirissuun* [powder measure] also was used to pour out the powder. The gun was held upright, and the powder was poured in through the barrel when it was loaded.

101 THIRD DAY MORE TOOLS FOR HUNTING AND FISHING

Tassiitaq / Breastplate for a Backpack

We had fun with the next piece, a wooden carrying yoke (fig. 3.15) from Fort Alexander.[19] Annie stood, holding it across her chest:

I haven't seen a *tassiitaq* in a very long time. Oh, it's so good to see one again. My dear father always had these in his possession. This was how they used them. They'd fill their pack, then attach it to a *tassiitaq*, and then use it to backpack things. The *tassiitaq* prevented one from getting a sore ribcage. I don't see these anymore. Now people use the kinds that cause pain around the underarms.... In Kuiggluk, people gathered berries... using an *amrayak* [backpack].... When a person carried a loaded *amrayak* on her back, you'd see her swaying from side to side. This is an excellent pack carrier, the best device for carrying heavy loads on one's back.

Wassilie examined two more wooden yokes from the Yukon,[20] which Jacobsen said were used by hunters and their wives to carry a dead animal by tying it with a pair of legs at each end of the yoke so that its belly touched the carrier's back

People never did without these. My dear father also had a *tassiitaq* like this. Since caribou roamed on lands away from waterways, men trekked far inland searching for them. Down where we lived, I used to see many high hills in one area. On one of the hills, there is a man-made high place specifically built up as a lookout for caribou. They had a type of pack made out of heavy-duty woven grass with evenly spaced holes woven into its upper edge.... They were made so that the holes would match the spacing of the knobs built onto the *tassiitaq*.

Holding the first yoke up to his chest, Wassilie added with a straight face: "When she tried it on her chest, it looked

3.15 Annie modeling a wooden *tassiitaq* (breastplate for a backpack) like those she had seen when she was young. IVA4554.

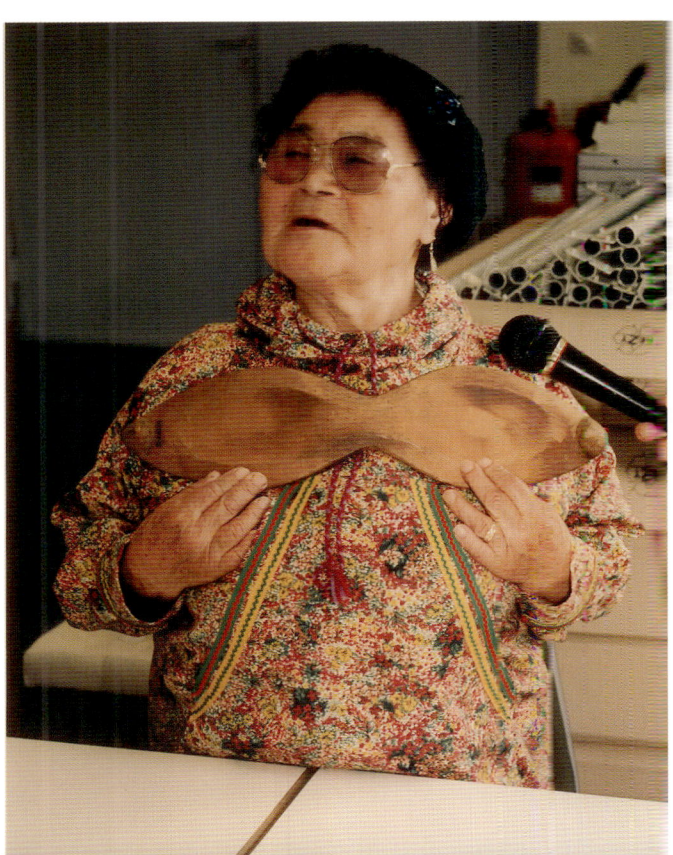

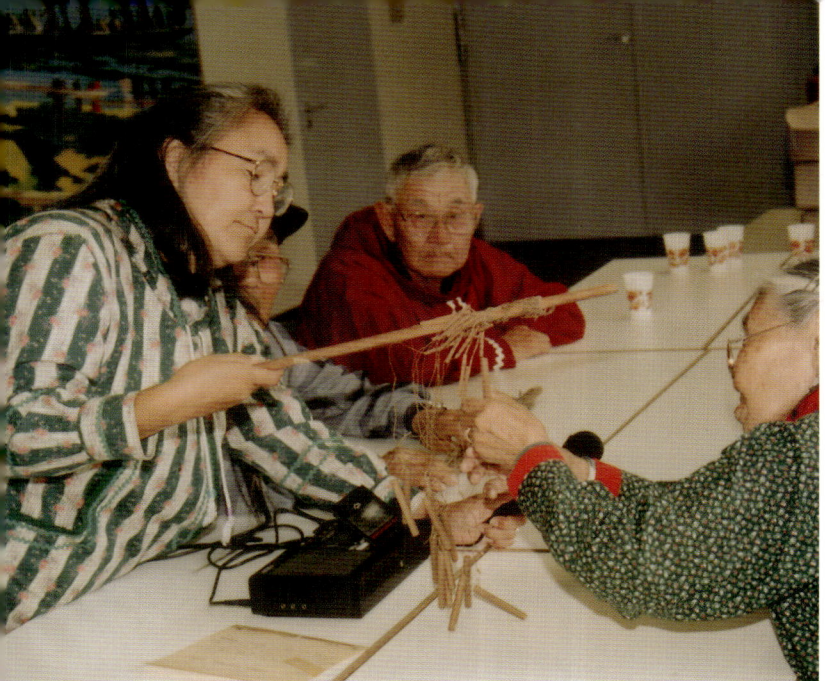

perfect for her. Perhaps the one who used it placed it perfectly above her breasts like that." Everyone chuckled, and Wassilie explained: "Sometimes I use humor to make you laugh, especially when you become sleepy and start dozing off."

Negat Makikcat-llu / Rabbit Snares and Squirrel Snares

As our mirth subsided, we took up a single rabbit snare that Jacobsen had collected from the Yukon (fig. 3.16).[21] The sinew mesh had been stretched over a broken piece of snowshoe so that it would retain its shape. Wassilie immediately recognized the contraption: "These snares have loops at their ends attached to a wood piece. These might be called *meluurutet* [wooden snare attachments]. It has an *urciq* [loop] attachment to it . . . at the end of the snare where the *ipuutet* [wooden snare attachments] are attached. . . . At home, wooden snare attachments were strengthened by weaving wing-feather quills onto them so that tundra hares would not break or cut the line. I'm sure that these snares were used on tundra hares and snowshoe hares."

Paul did not recognize the device, and Catherine noted that these were not used in the coastal area: "But when I came to the Yukon, they had snares. Since ptarmigan are weaker than rabbits, they made snares for them out of twine. The rabbit snares were made from metal wire." Wassilie, however, found the snare evocative:

Our first summer fish camp was located on wooded land with a smooth area behind it. One day our late brother said he was going into the woods to set snares. He said that he saw rabbit trails back there. Then he left. The next day I went with him when he checked his snares. I saw many rabbit trails as we were going up. I looked and saw a rabbit hanging above the ground ahead of us. My late brother had set a *negapiaq* [snare that springs into the air when it catches something]. The snare was tied to a young willow tree, and he had made a groove where it was tied so the snare would not slip off the wood. . . . Since the tree was attached by its roots, he had put a piece of wood near the root area as a trigger. When the trigger was touched lightly, that wood was ready to fall to the side. When the wood fell, the branch sprang up, pulling the rabbit by its neck, choking it to death as the snare tightened.

Annie was as quick to recognize the next pieces—*makikcat* (spring snares for ground squirrels) (fig. 3.17) from the Kuskokwim[22]—as Wassilie had been to recognize the rabbit snares.

These are definitely *makikcat*. This part is *akmagartaa* [willow-bark lashing?] . . . tied tight. You get a stick for this [lashing], and then you plant the stick's other end in the ground outside the squirrel's den. Then you place the lashing flush with the entrance of the den. Then you attach this sinew to the bottom through its inside. Then cover the sides of the den with soil. . . . When the squirrel walks through, the stick would spring upward to the outside of the den, snaring the squirrel and choking it to death. When you set one *makikcat* on several dens, you'd catch all of them at once.

They made them out of vanes split from bird-wing quills. There

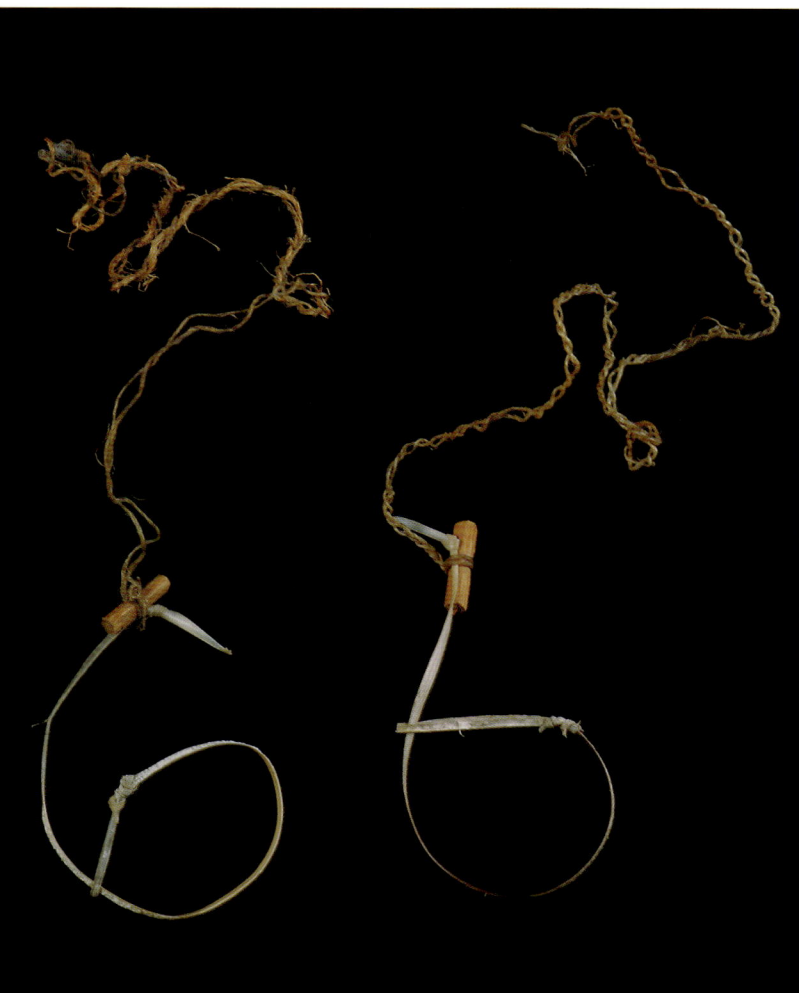

3.16 *Wooden snare attachments for negat (rabbit snares). IVA4224.*

3.17 *Makikcat (spring snares for ground squirrels). IVA4997.*

3.18, 3.19, 3.20 Annie using her fingers to demonstrate how a squirrel would approach a snare, put its head through the hole, and become trapped in the snare loop. IVA5426.

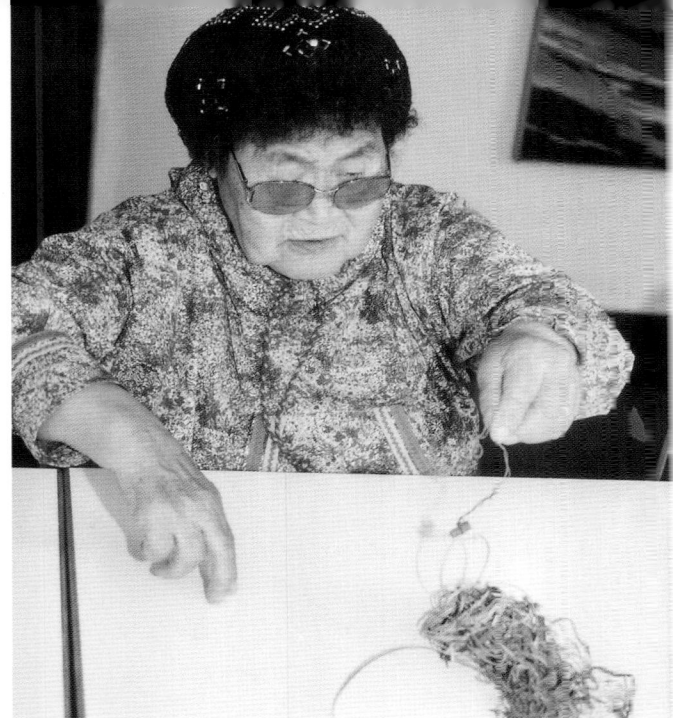

are some feathers that were considered to hold together well when woven. I think they are raven quill vanes. It is said that there is a place up the Togiak River where people gathered raven-wing quills. They use very lightweight, rough rocks to split the quill vanes.

These are definitely *makikcat* because they have an *utngugartaq* [trigger string].... When the squirrel walked through the trap and pushed the trigger string, the stick would spring up, snaring the squirrel at the neck, thus killing it. I have used these, too. When metal leg-hold traps were few, my mother always used these.... Oh my! I wish that these were mine.

People using *makikcat* would catch many bundles [forty-five pelts each] for squirrel parkas in one season. And more than once my mother caught several bundles for squirrel parkas in one season. These are very nice *makikcat*. Where in the world did they get them? Give these to me. [laughter] . . .

There's another kind of squirrel snare, *puukaqercetaat* [touch and spring snares, trigger snares]. A stick is planted in the ground with the top end bent over the narrow trail of a squirrel. After measuring the height of the squirrel's appendages, the trigger for this snare was set at that level. When the squirrel touched the trigger, then you've caught your squirrel. Another piece of wood was added to the trap, so the squirrel couldn't chew the line and break it and get away.

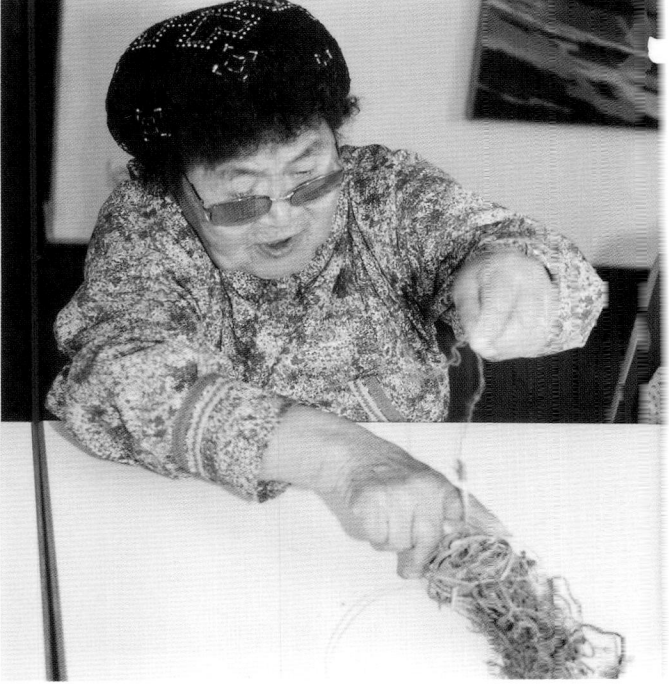

Later we looked at a Nushagak squirrel snare,[23] which Annie also described in detail (fig. 3.18, fig. 3.19, fig. 3.20), noting that after checking the trap, it would be reset, catching squirrels again and again. She also pointed out that its *niss'ut* [quill attachments] were made from seagull wing feathers, but that those made from raven wing feathers were considered better: "Raven feathers were tougher and stronger and lasted longer. When wing feathers were fixed to use in *makikcat,* they'd loosen them, split them, and file them with a *keggalrun* [literally, "device to rub or smooth out"] to smooth the edges." Finally she commented that squirrels would spoil in warm weather if the traps were not checked right away and that when many squirrel holes are in an area, they were called *ngel'ulluut.*

Qanganaak / Two Squirrels

Later in the week two arctic-ground-squirrel skins (fig. 3.21) from the Nushagak River enriched our understanding of snares and their use. Jacobsen wrote that they were intended as material for a girl's cap, but noticing their bead adornments, Annie told a different story:

When I was a girl, in the summer these squirrels were made into dolls with clothing. This squirrel doll has earrings, necklace, bracelet, and *cigvik* [nose septum decoration].... This is a very nice squirrel doll. It looks like it's a squirrel that would come out of its den and begin defecating. When we looked for squirrel dens in the springtime, the squirrels standing in front of their dens looked very

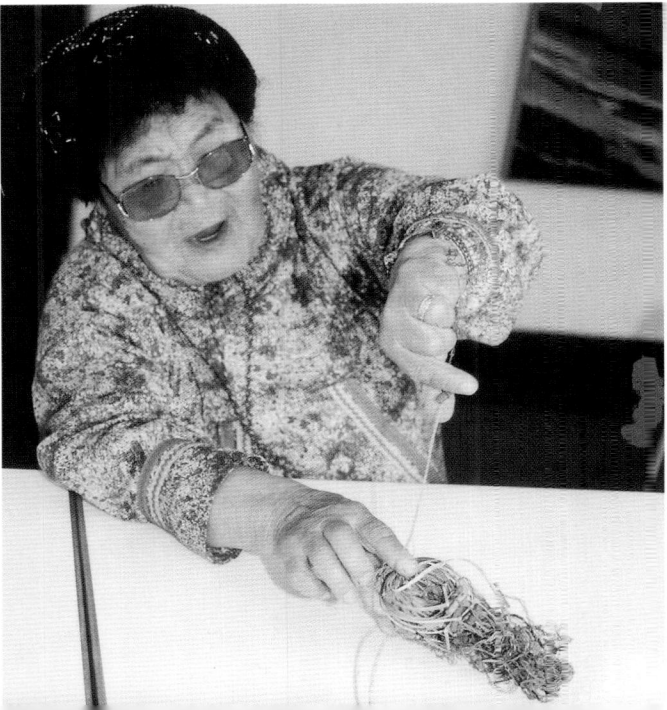

dark and obvious on the snow from a distance. When we saw a little black speck in the snow, we'd begin walking toward it. As we approached, it would stand up and turn and slowly go into its den. When we came to its den, we'd shovel the snow a bit around the hole and set the squirrel trap. And when the squirrel came out of its hole again, it got trapped. Hunters loved catching squirrels in the spring.

We also see squirrels like that when we pick berries in the fall. . . . When they run around going after each other, they are a beautiful sight. Squirrels get fat in the fall. We usually hang them to dry. Dried and boiled squirrel is a delicious meal.

Up inside Togiak River in the mighty mountains, there used to be many squirrels. When I was younger, we hunted for squirrels up in that area. We had a big family, but . . . our mother made parkas for all of us, sewing all night long under a night lamp. When she sewed all night, she called it *atakuliluni*. We were clothed from head to toe. People in those days were skillful with their hands.

Sometimes she'd finish many parkas before the Messenger Feast. . . .

A man's parka was made with sixty squirrel pelts, and a woman's parka takes a little over fifty pelts. I used to sell squirrel pelts until recently.

Holding a squirrel doll in each hand, Annie (fig. 3.22) told us a story:

One day a squirrel came out of its den. When she came out, she looked around and saw that the snow had melted enough to reveal ground in many spots around her den. She said, "Oh my, I apparently am coming out of my den quite late this spring. And obviously the other squirrels came out already. While I'm standing here, I wish my *ilungapak* [female cross-cousin of a female] would come." Then, shortly after she mentioned that, her *ilungapak*, the ptarmigan, suddenly flew down from the sky and landed next to the den, calling, "*Qangqiirriiriirii* [Squirrelrelrelrell]. Well, my *ilungapak*, you've finally come out." And she added, "Gosh, it's so good to see you. Instead of standing here, let's do a dance contest." Then the squirrel said, "Okay, you dance first." Then the ptarmigan started to dance, singing:

> Joining
> Hunting
> On the mountain
> Joining
> Hunting
> On the mountain
> I am looking
> Out to the edge of the sky
> From this mountain

When ptarmigan stopped dancing, she said, "Oh, my back is hurting! You should not have asked me to dance first. Now, would you please dance." When the ptarmigan sat down, squirrel said, "Okay, let me dance."

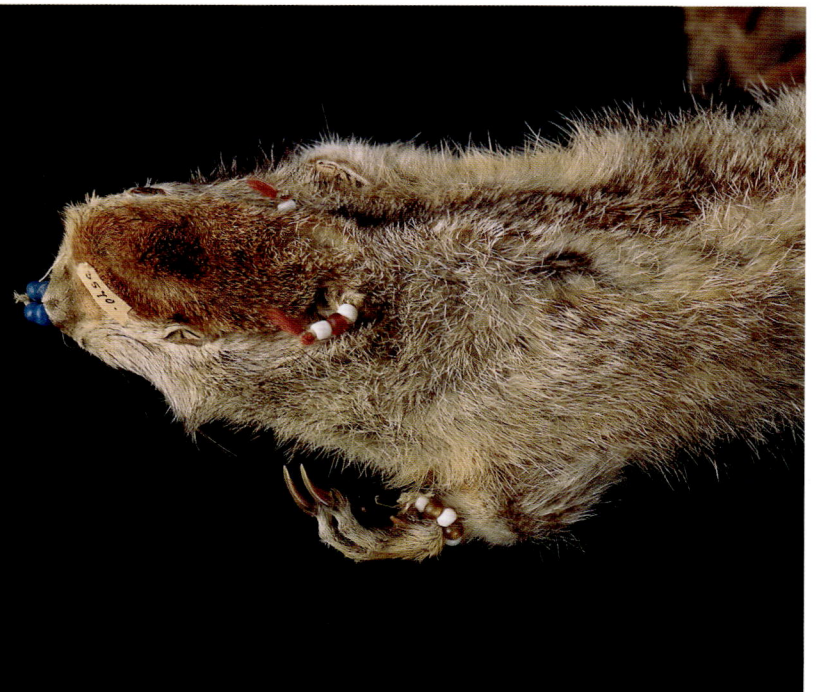

3.21 Annie said that the bead ornaments on this squirrel skin indicated that it was used as a doll. IVA5477, IVA5485.

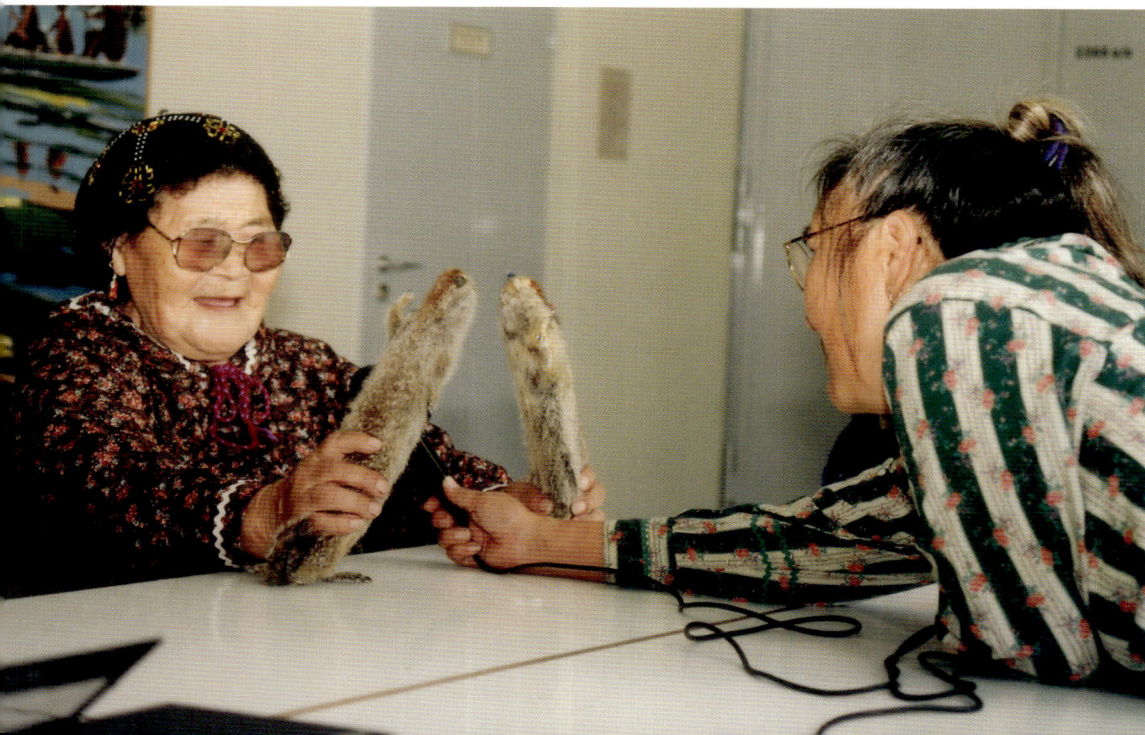

3.22 Annie using the squirrel-skin dolls to tell a lively story about squirrel and ptarmigan.

Aa-aa-aa
Imaa-aa-aa
Yii-I-rri-imaa-aa-aa

On the mountain's ?sayangaani
May I do the ingula *[woman's slow, old-style dance]*

Imaa-aa-aa
Yii-I-rri-imaa-aa-aa

When the squirrel stopped dancing, she said, "Ouch! My back is hurting, too. When I got trapped in the *makikcat,* my back got injured when I tried to release myself, and now it hurts every time I do something." When ptarmigan didn't respond, squirrel looked and discovered that she had died with a smile on her face. Then squirrel got disgusted and jabbed the dead ptarmigan on her nose with her middle finger and said, "Oh my! How contemptuous, and here she was the one who wanted to dance first." After that the squirrel ate her *ilungapak* ptarmigan for many days.

Answering a query by Catherine, Annie confirmed that the squirrel had sung an *ingulaun* (old-style song), telling the story of another squirrel who refused to be trapped by a messy woman:

But when it came to a trap that was neatly set, it went in and got trapped. And when . . . the owner of the trap arrived, it tried to turn around, and when the trapper smiled, it smiled back at him. It responded, even though it was dead. The trapper took the squirrel home and skinned it and cooked it. When it got cooked, it called the person and said, "I'm done, remove me from the fire." Then the person dished the cooked squirrel into a bowl and ate it.

Annie closed with a traditional story ending: "*Tuaten tua-i pitaluni kingunermikun ayagtuq nak'riluni* [As I end the story here, may it continue on its path straight and smooth]."

Noting that there were no squirrels where he lived, Paul asked if what he had heard was true—that one should not sleep on the ground when squirrels were beginning to come out of their dens. Annie said that ever since she was little, people always placed willow branches beneath their bedding as protection lest a squirrel emerge while they slept.

Taluyacuar / Small Fish Trap

Next we examined a small fish trap (fig. 3.23) from the Yukon.[24] At first I took it for a model or toy, but Paul agreed with Jacobsen that this was a real tool. Catherine also recognized the little trap as an important implement in a coastal landscape dominated by sloughs and streams:

This trap looks exactly like the trap I had when we lived around Nightmute. I think we were staying at Cakcaaq at the time. In front of our place there was a little river where blackfish and needlefish were running heavily. There were several bags on the shore.

Then I told my late sister that we should make fish traps for ourselves since I knew how to weave grass. After we gathered wheat grass, I started weaving. But I couldn't make the *iluliraq* [funnel]. We tried to set the trap when it was done, but the fish would escape

3.23 *Taluyacuar* (small fish trap) from the Yukon, a long cage with inverted conical opening, set in places where stream channels concentrate the movement of fish. Paul noted, "This is an old, old *taluyacuar*. Knowing that food was not readily available to them, people in the past used this crudely made fish trap . . . to catch a few blackfish or some other fish on a little rushing stream or someplace fish were coming through." IVA7251.

after they entered because it didn't have a funnel. Then our Ap'ayagaq made a funnel for it. We set the trap back and checked it now and then, but they didn't let us eat the fish that were caught. We kept a grass basket on the shore by our trap for our fish . . . When the river started to freeze, we pulled out our trap and our basket was filled with fish . . . that were offered during *Elriq* [the Great Feast for the Dead].

105 THIRD DAY MORE TOOLS FOR HUNTING AND FISHING

Although Annie had seen wire blackfish traps, she was amazed by this trap since she had never before seen traps made of wood. Wooden fish traps are still used along the coast and on the Yukon, and Catherine could describe the trap's construction: "These *cigyiit* [slats] were made from *unarciat* [straight-grained pieces of wood]. The *amaaret* [strapping around the slats] was made from willow roots." Later Wassilie talked about the *unarciat* and the tools used to work them.

Unarciat were used to make *taluyarpiit* [large fish traps] . . . used to catch whitefish, burbot, and pike, too. . . . The smaller *ekiarqitet* [wood splitters] were used on *unarciat* that were prepared to be used for blackfish traps. And a *kaugtuutacuar* [small hammer] was used for the *unarciat*. . . . I have many different kinds of *unarci-iyurcuutet* [tools to work on wood] up there with me. That was how *unarciat* were used . . . to make blackfish traps and mink traps . . . called *taluyaruat*. When I had ten traps, I used to think I had a lot with me back in those days. When chicken wire arrived, I started using up to sixty traps in one season.

Wassilie then described checking his traps, twenty in one day, and how his sons and grandsons hunt in the area around Kasigluk to this day.

Qenuirun wall' Imairitek / Ice Dipper

We took a break to stretch and drink water. Peter gave us each a paper cup, which we kept and used during the rest of our stay. Far from being annoyed by this frugality, the elders admired our German hosts' careful shepherding of resources.

Now we looked at three dippers (fig. 3.24) from the Yukon and one made of caribou antler with braided sealskin strips from Nelson Island.[25] Jacobsen wrote that these were used to bail pieces of ice out of the hole when checking or setting nets or fish traps or when getting water. Wassilie remarked: "Long ago we called these *qenuirutek* [ice dippers (dual)]. . . . I, too,

3.24 Ice dipper from the Yukon, which Jacobsen wrote was used to clear the hole of ice when checking or setting nets or fish traps or when getting water. The dipper's webbing is made from split roots. Detail below. IVA4341.

3.25 Bone sinker with attached hooks, used for catching whitefish, trout, and pike. IVA3884.

used these all the time when I set my blackfish trap. . . . This looks like the one I have at home, but they are made of bone. . . . They always carried these when they checked their blackfish traps. When the trap was filled with blackfish, this was used to scoop out the fish to lighten the trap first."

Paul added the coastal name for dipper—*imairitek*—and Wassilie repeated a guiding principle of our investigations: "These have many names. We Yupiit have numerous names to describe something." He then added even more detailed terminology, transforming the simple dipper into an object lesson in the technical vocabulary that was a part of every person's repertoire in the past: "The bottom part of the scoop is the part we called *nulukek*. Since they were made long ago, the twine was made from split roots. The bottom mesh we called *kuvyakuiner*. We'd say that the *nulukek* had *kuvyakuiner* mesh on it. Even though this *qenuirun* is old, the *nulukek* is still in good condition."

We then looked at a Kuskokwim dipper,[26] and Wassilie recalled: "It looks like the *pertaq* [bentwood rim] was made from driftwood. . . . When they took fire baths, they bent the driftwood like this rim." Finally, Marie held up a broken dipper rim made of caribou antler[27] that Jacobsen had found at a Yukon "archaeological site." Wassilie not only knew what it was but how it had been acquired: "You could see the holes where the twine was threaded to create the *nuluq*. Here's where they meet. This piece was evidently picked up from the ground somewhere."

Manaqutaq / Fishing Hook, Line, and Pole

The afternoon, rich with stories and songs, had gone by quickly. With new energy the group considered various kinds of fishing equipment. Jacobsen had collected dozens of caribou-antler and walrus-ivory fishing hooks with iron and bone barbs, used for catching whitefish, trout, and pike.[28] Several pike lures had old nails as points and caribou-sinew line. Some had bits of red wool to attract the fish, while others had white and blue glass beads. Jacobsen commented on one bone Kuskokwim fish lure and hook[29] used during spring breakup: "I have seen on one day up to fifty trout (the so-called "Sulanchpak") being caught. At those places where the ice remains, they drill holes and fish with a short spear."

When we looked at the fishing gear, the women were the first to respond. Annie held a *kis'un* (sinker) with two hooks attached (fig. 3.25)[30] and called out cheerfully, "I'm catching a fish!" Catherine picked up a similar set from the Yukon[31] and spoke at length, recalling the hours she had spent out on the nearshore ice, holding a six-foot line jigging for fish:

I see this as the kind used on *iqalluat* [arctic cod]. When I first became aware over in Tununak, in the fall and spring people continually hooked for fish even though the fish got skinny in that season. When I first moved to the Yukon area, people didn't hook for fish at all.

Then one time when my late husband and I were out on the ocean, . . . I noticed *iqalluat* swimming in the water. We were at

3.26   Bone fish decoys used for pike fishing in the Yukon area. Jacobsen noted that they were usually attached to a rod and moved back and forth on the water's surface, attracting pike and other big fish, which were speared with either spears or bone harpoons. IVA3870.

3.27   Bird-shaped *pugtaqutat* (net floats), used on drift nets for salmon. Good hunters themselves, birds helped the net do the same. IVA4075, IVA4078, IVA4247.

the mouth of the Yukon River. My late husband said, "I didn't know there were *iqalluat* around here." Time went by and I never saw people hooking for fish.

Then in the fall, one day Thomas Luke's sister's son came in with a bowl in his hand. . . . I opened the container and found *iqalluat* inside. I was so happy. Then her husband made me an ivory fishing hook. Over in Tununak we always used ivory hooks. Then during that fall season we were the only ones who went out to hook fish.

Today many people hook for fish in the Yukon since they have learned about it. . . . Once in a great while we'd catch a *qusuuq* [smelt] and people would rejoice. They used them for bait. . . . Real *kis'utet* [sinkers] were used on our hooks. This has a bone sinker. They always had two places to put the bait. . . . When the water had strong current, we used sinkers on the hooks.

After the hooks, we turned to a dozen ivory and bone fish decoys used for pike fishing in the Yukon area (fig. 3.26).[32] Jacobsen gave three different terms for the decoys: "Nerallenlok," "Suukquak" (*suguaq*, literally, "pretend person"), and "Menakutak" (*manaqutaq*, "fishing hook, line, and pole"). Although they recognized them as tools for fishing, none in our group had used comparable lures. They were, however, interested in the material out of which they were made. Wassilie pointed out the thick nail holes and said that it looked like the piece was made from an old dogsled or kayak sled runner. Paul agreed: "Our minds are one toward these pieces." Both also mentioned the possibility that the figures could have been used as *iinrut* (amulets) to protect their owners from harm. This was a recurring reaction to the ivory and bone figures that Jacobsen had brought home.

Pugtaqutat Lugluqussaat-llu / Net Floats

Jacobsen had also collected a group of bird-shaped "net swimmers" (fig. 3.27) from the lower Yukon,[33] all of which he designated "Poktareutitt," noting that they were used on drift nets for salmon and that "the shape was chosen to better grab the same." These *pugtaqutat* (gill-net floats) excited considerable interest. Wassilie was again the first to comment:

These lifelike waterfowl figures are being displayed on the table. Their sides and surfaces are decorated and painted. Looking at it perked up my memory, and turning it upside down I see a hole where a line can be strung. In the past people had small-mesh gill nets, and when they set them they would attach a waterfowl-figure float at the end of smaller floats. The float looked like a bird floating in the water at the end of the net. . . . Our dear father's gill net had a *qaqatak* [red-throated loon] figure at its end. The gill nets caught not only fish but waterfowl, because the waterfowl were attracted to the floats.

Marie handed Wassilie another wooden float from the lower Yukon,[34] carved to look like interlocking ovals. He continued, with Paul nodding in agreement:

This also has a hole where a line can be strung. Since this was made to look like it was inflated, I thought of a *lugluqussaaq* [net float].

3.28 Yukon "net swimmer" carved in human form. Annie asked if it was an *iinruq*, as spirits usually had crooked eyes and big mouths, echoing Jacobsen's comment that the figure was some kind of "protecting spirit." Wassilie said, "It's a float, and here's the hole for stringing. This float evidently was owned by an important man, someone higher class than me." IVA4074.

Long ago the gill nets were drifted along the river, and if the net did not catch fish, they adjusted the line attached to the net and to the float by extending them to the depth in the river where the fish may be swimming. If the gill net catches fish at a certain depth, then the person adjusts the rest of the line to that depth. A float made that possible. This can easily float in the water because it is made out of *mimernaq* [root portion of a driftwood tree trunk].

Another Yukon "net swimmer" (fig. 3.28) had been carved in human form. Wassilie confirmed that another dozen simple wooden floats functioned just like the others.[35] He added that on the Kuskokwim, they used inflated loon throats to make floats, as the throats are both thick and sturdy.

109 **THIRD DAY** MORE TOOLS FOR HUNTING AND FISHING

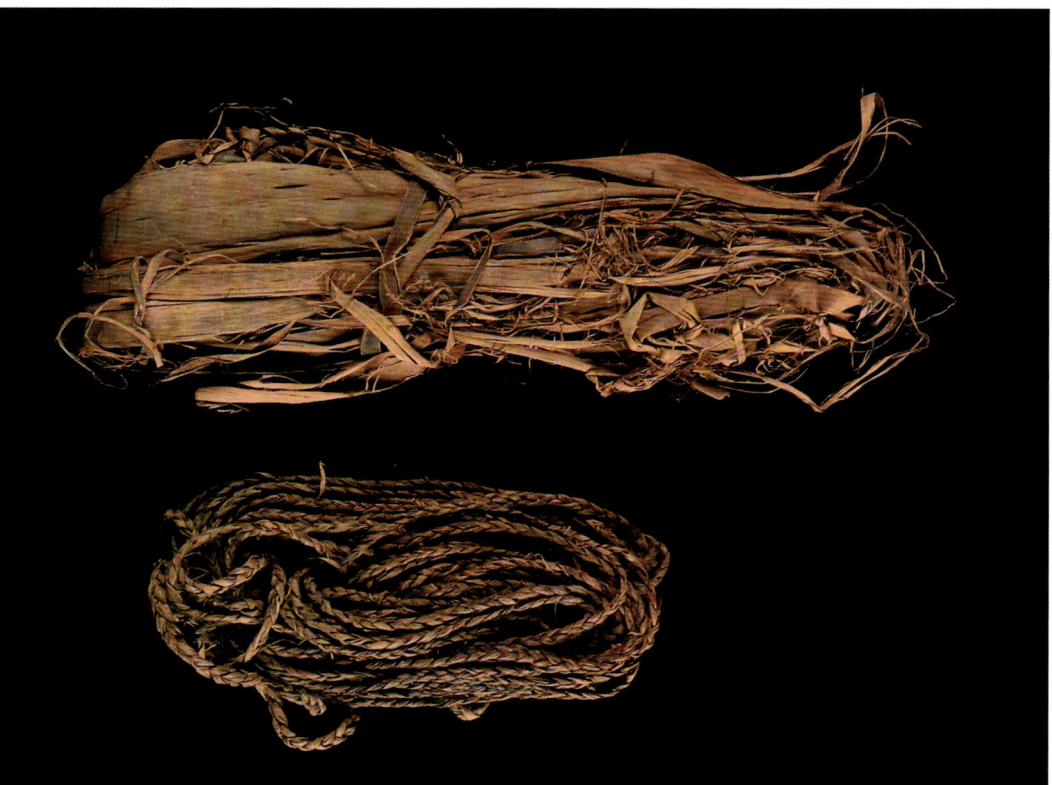

3.29 Wassilie, Marie, and Paul examining a king-salmon net made from *piirraq* (braided willow-bark line). Dietrich Graf, Ethnologisches Museum Berlin.

3.30 A large bundle of willow bark and a smaller bundle of braided willow-bark line. Paul commented, "When commercially made items were rare, . . . they used these ropes made from the inner lining of young willow shoots in their fishnets or as ropes to bind things." Annie exclaimed, "They sure put a lot of labor into their work." IVA4293, IVA5094.

Taryaqvagcuun wall' Allegpak / King-Salmon Net

Our third day ended with examination of an expertly crafted king-salmon drift net (fig. 3.29) from the Yukon,[36] known as either *taryaqvagcuun* (from *taryaqvak*, "king salmon") or *allegpak*. Wassilie examined the mesh with his fingers and said:

Back then, they made large-mesh gill nets out of *allek* [inner fibrous layer of young willow bark, from *alleg-*, "to tear"]. *Allget* are the thin layers on *enrilnguut* [young willow shoots] that lie right under the tree bark. Some people used sinew twine to make gill nets, too. A few strands of *yualuq* [sinew] were entwined to make twine. When they made gill nets, they made their depth shallow. . . .

Sometimes a fisherman might catch a total of twenty king salmon in a season. People considered such a man to have caught plenty.

This is a *taryaqvagcuun* [king-salmon gill net] . . . made from *allek*. During the early spring, the bark was peeled off young willow trees, then the outer layer of bark was removed. What was left was the *allek,* which was then dried . . . and split into strands with a *talun* [shredder, fiber splitter]. These strands were then intertwined into a more stable twine. Back in those days, people were quite ingenious. . . .

When *allek* dried, it turned red like this. This is its natural color. I've seen *allek* back in those days. This wasn't dyed.

Later in the week, we examined a bundle of willow bark from the lower Yukon, along with two bundles of willow-bark line (fig. 3.30).[37] Wassilie spoke with authority:

Our ancestors in the Kuskokwim area worked on *allget* all the time, . . . which they made into nets called *allegpiit*.

Back in those days, they carried the nets in their kayaks all the time. Then in the spring, a hunter would spot an arctic loon as he was hunting. And as soon as he spotted the loon, he'd set the end of his net at the narrow part of the river . . . and begin going toward the loon as fast as he could in the kayak. Once the loon dove into the water, he'd herd it toward the net. When the loon got caught, the hunter took it and killed it. Loons were prized catches. Loon skins were used for parkas. The loon's throat was also used as a float on king salmon nets.

Marie asked if the net would have had floats on a float line and sinkers on its lead line, and Wassilie said yes, adding, "Perhaps we'll see the bone sinkers later on." The next morning we did examine several dozen *kis'utet* (net sinkers, labeled "Kittet," "Kitett," or "Kitet" by Jacobsen) from the Yukon, used on salmon drift nets. Paul and Wassilie divided them according to the material from which they were made—stone, caribou antler, or mammoth bone (fig. 3.31).[38] In every case, their assessment agreed with Jacobsen's recorded information.

Paul had been listening quietly and, as we returned the net to its place in storage, took the opportunity to tell the story of a king salmon who appeared in human form.

King salmon transformed themselves into human beings and kept a person as their guest in their village. He did not realize they were king salmon since he had fainted when his kayak turned over in the water. When he regained consciousness, he found himself lying on a beautiful sandy beach and his kayak was on shore nearby. When he gained consciousness, he went in his kayak along the shore. When he came to the mouth of a river, he noticed signs of human habitation. So he went upriver, and as he went along he saw a village. As he approached, a couple just arriving from a hunting trip greeted him. They took him to their home as their guest and provided him with food for as long as he stayed with them.

Then one day the host family said it was time to go upriver. They prepared to go by getting their provisions ready and some water. As the couple went upriver, he followed them. As they were approaching a village, he saw men fishing with gill nets. Their nets were set at various levels. Some nets were up in the air with only the bottom part touching the water, and other nets were halfway in the water.

Then he noticed a net that was set properly with just the floats visible above the water. A man was sitting still at the end of the net. The husband turned to him and told him that the salmon had always come to that particular fisherman year after year. He said they came to him yearly because they were taken care of so carefully and no part of them was strewn on the ground for people to walk on. He also said that he always kept them in a good place once they were ready to be put away. And they always put their bones away so people wouldn't step on them. They always came to that fisherman with a net set appropriately in the water.

Then the couple said, "*Kitaki* [Well then], before you go up to the level of the human world, look at us. After you watch us, you can go up to the world of the humans. Examine us closely, for you think we are human beings like you." Then the husband sitting back-to-back with his wife in a kayak began to paddle toward the fisherman's net. As soon as their kayak touched the net, the couple he had stayed with suddenly disappeared and two king salmon began to splash in the water. It was at that moment that he found himself at home and began living with his people again.

That's the only story I know concerning fish.

3.31 Net sinkers made (from top to bottom) of mammoth bone, caribou antler, and stone. Paul was familiar with mammoth-bone sinkers, saying, "This is part of a tusk of an animal called a *quugiinraq* (mastodon) that looked like a big elephant that was around long ago." IVA4079, IVA6991, IVA4092.

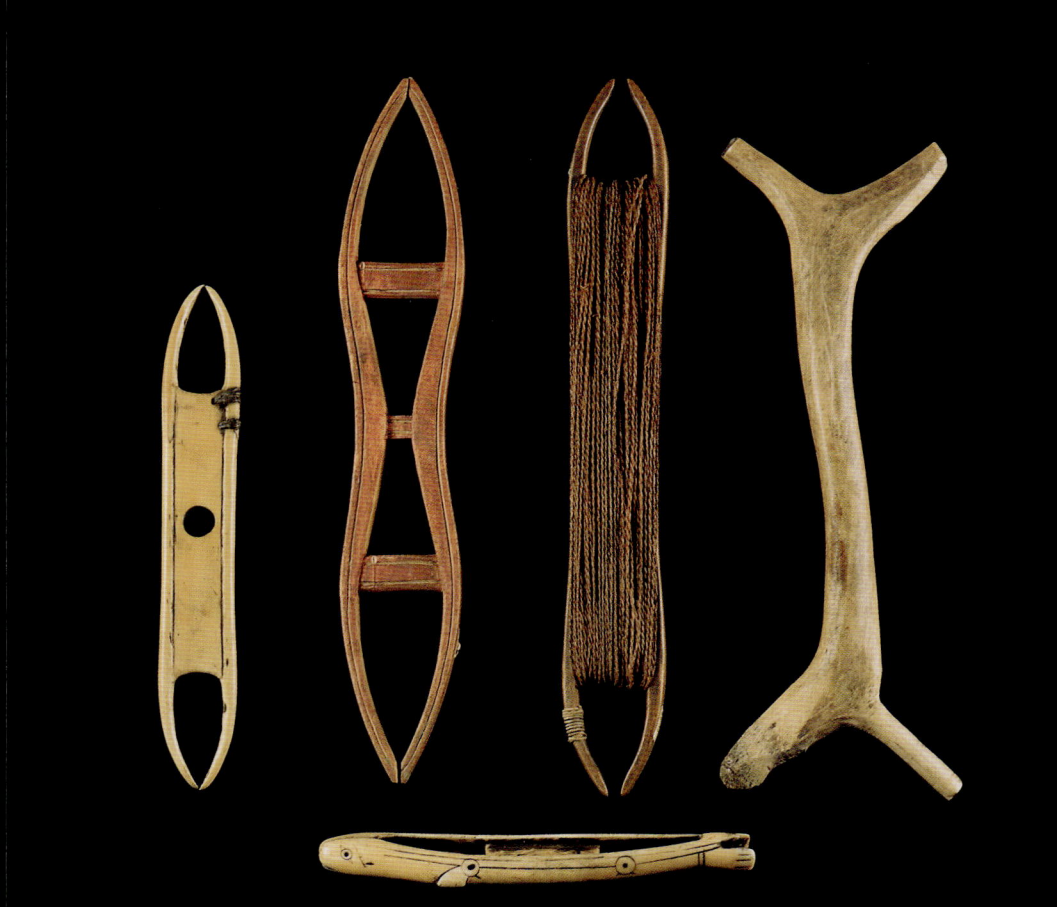

3.32 Kuvyacuar (small-mesh net) used to catch both whitefish and salmon. Both the mesh as well as the net's qemiq (sinker and float line) were made of allek (inner layer of willow bark). Although the net might not be deep, Wassilie pointed out that when wet, it lengthened and its mesh size increased. IVA4286.

3.33 Net-making shuttles in a variety of sizes. The shuttle on the far left has a mend on its side, and the smallest shuttle is seal-shaped. From left to right: IVA4673, IVA3716, IVA3717, IVA4181, IVA4674 (bottom).

3.34 Net gauges for different-size nets. From top to bottom: IVA4102, IVA4094, IVA7248.

Kuvyacuar / Small-mesh Net

Jacobsen had also collected two smaller nets (fig. 3.32) from the Yukon,[39] which were used to catch both whitefish and smaller salmon. Wassilie said that the *kuvyacuar* (small-mesh gill net) was fifteen *yagneq* (the length of one's arms fully extended), which was considered long. Simple wooden floats and caribou-antler sinkers were attached, and Wassilie noted that the small floats all had fish-scale designs on them and were tied with willow roots. He continued, describing how nets were strung:

At the time when manufactured cord was first introduced, the gill nets were made from unraveled cords. Floats were made from *mimernaq* [driftwood tree-trunk root] and sinkers from small pieces of bone. Then the top meshes of the gill net were first folded mesh by mesh, and the float line was strung through it. Then you post a piece of wood into the ground and attach the end of the float line to it. If I was putting the floats on this net, I would count the mesh, then divide the mesh into groups, and then put the floats evenly on the line according to the number of groups of mesh. Then I repeat the same process as I did with the float line when I do the sinker line. The sinkers were put on the sinker line exactly the same way the floats were put on top. That was how they made nets and their sinkers and floats.

When another elder and I first worked with the students in the school, we made a fishnet . . . of several fathoms. I suggested to my partner that we finish the net as it was done long ago. I made the floats out of *mimernaq*. The other elder made the sinkers out of moose antlers. Then we attached the floats and sinkers exactly the way it was done in the past. When we were done we stretched it out, and it was beautiful.

Net-making Tools

Later in our stay, we examined a group of different-size ivory and wood net-making shuttles for knotting fishnets and storing thread, including ten *qilagcuutet* (netting shuttles, from *qilag-*, "to knit or make net") from the Yukon[40] and seven *imruyutaat* from the Kuskokwim and Nushagak.[41] Although most were empty, several were filled with either sinew or bark line. All were plain except for three ivory shuttles carved as seals (fig. 3.33). Paul summed up their use:

These were implements used in making tools to harvest food . . . called *imruyutaat* back home. When they wove twine to make fishnets, they prepared long twine for making nets. And when they got ready to make a net, they would fill an *imruyutaq* like this with enough twine before they started making the net. And since fish come in different sizes, the *imruyutaat* came in different sizes.

Wassilie added confirmation:

These were filled with prepared twine for making nets and such. This is filled with long, continuous prepared twine. I'd say that this thin braided thread was used to make a dip net. And those little *imruyutaat* were filled with enough twine to make nets to catch little fish. Perhaps this *imruyutaq* was used to begin the bottom part of a dip net used to catch needlefish. And this little ivory piece . . . was an *imruyutaq* for very thin twine. . . .

This twine looks like *allek* [inner lining of willow bark] and not sinew because *allget* were a red color. But this one is filled with sinew.

We also examined an inconspicuous awl from the lower Yukon[42] that Jacobsen said was used to fasten the harpoon head on the shaft of a seal harpoon. Paul identified it as a net-making tool: "This looks like the tool that they used in dip-net making. Its hole here is a little small, but it's the same tool. They'd wind the thread around several times first, then they'd pull it through the hole when they made needlefish or herring dip nets. They were also called *qilagcuutet*."

The same box that held the shuttles also held a dozen net gauges from border villages on the middle Yukon (fig. 3.34).[43] Andy and Marie laid them on the table from smallest to largest. The gauges were made from a variety of materials, including

3.35 Measuring between his knuckle and the base of his thumb, Paul said, "This size gauge was used to make nets to catch small fish, including whitefish."

3.36 Examining a larger mesh gauge, Paul commented, "If I check to see if this [gauge] was the standard size for king-salmon nets, I'd use this body part [from tip of middle finger to middle of palm] as a measurement. . . . And these were used to make whitefish and pike fishnets."

3.37 Paul continued, "You'd begin measuring here [end of palm] to the tip of the [middle] finger . . . to make nets to catch seals and beluga whales. The nets were useless on walrus because they tend to break through. . . . But beluga whales, bearded seals, spotted seals, young bearded seals, and hair seals couldn't escape once they were tangled in the net."

caribou antler, whale and mammoth bone, and walrus ivory. Paul shared his knowledge, including how people used their body parts as measurements in their work (fig. 3.35, fig. 3.36, fig. 3.37):

Back home they call them *negaqeggutet* [net gauges, from *negaq*, "single mesh of a net"] or *qilakeggutet* [from *qilag-*, "to knit or make net"). They are tools for making nets of different mesh. Each gauge is a different length and determines the mesh size of a net, and the mesh size determines what type of fish it would catch. . . .

When the twine is wound once on the gauge, it gives the mesh of the net for catching specific-size fish. The person who used this bound it here and adjusted the other end to increase the mesh as he was making the net.

Wooden Fishing Tools

Two more fishing tools remained to examine. A slim board from the Yukon used to process king-salmon heads for drying[44] reminded Wassilie of his checkered past:

King-salmon eyes are very delicious dried. . . . As boys, when adults weren't looking, we'd look inside smokehouses and snatch the eyes off hanging salmon heads . . . and be naughty and pop them in our mouths.

When they dried king salmon, they'd pop the eyes out, and they'd hang from a little segment from the inside. They were easy to pull off when dried. . . .

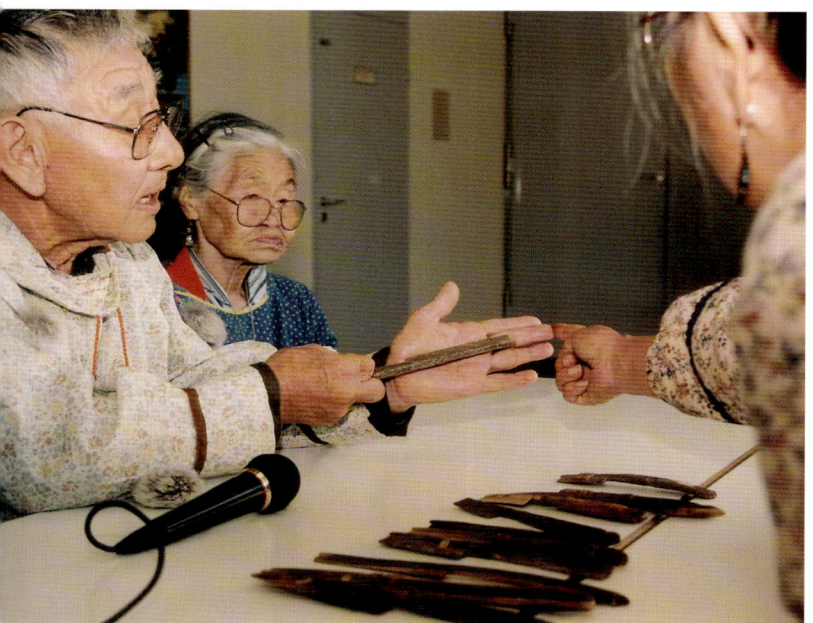

This was a board used to process king-salmon heads for drying. When salmon heads were dried, they called them *qamiqurrluut*. We still dry king-salmon heads today. We eat dried and smoked heads cooked in water, and they are a delicious supplement in the winter.

What looked like a billy club to me turned out to be another well-known fishing tool—a fish striker from the Yukon,[45] which Jacobsen said every fisherman carried in his kayak to kill fish, especially king salmon. Wassilie told Paul that he should speak about it, but Paul deferred to the group's senior member, and Wassilie began: "This is a *kaugtuutaq* [from *kaugtur-*, "to strike with an object"]. It resembles the ones they used in the tundra area to kill bigger fish caught in large fish traps. . . . The thin willow root is used to make the handle slip-proof." Paul elaborated:

Back home we called it *qenngitaq* because the *qennguq* [cartilage] in the fish head is where we hit salmon. . . . Whenever we checked our large fish traps for burbot, we would kill them first, so they would freeze in a straight form, before we stored them side by side in a *tuvqertat* [set of twenty]. If someone mentioned *tuvqertat,* we'd know there were twenty frozen loche fish in that set. . . . At times, after one of the men checked his fish trap . . . if we heard that he had made five *tuvqertat,* we'd immediately know that he had caught one hundred burbot.

Paul concluded graciously, "Since we have different words, we help each other in our descriptions."

Before we went home for the night, Wassilie added one more well-known Kuskokwim tale, recalling the small *taluyaq* (fish trap) we had seen earlier in the day. Like Paul's story, it presented as nonhuman persons the animals that people relied on. Although fishing and hunting technology in southwestern Alaska has been transformed since Jacobsen's day, a uniquely Yup'ik view of how animals respond to these tools remains.

A blackfish was swimming upriver. As it swam with its eyes closed, it would suddenly enter a fish trap, but before it did it would open its eyes. As it swam upriver, it would sing.

As the blackfish swam closer to shore and looked, it saw a woman walking out from a house. Her belt was carelessly tied around her waist, and the strings were flying around in front of her as she walked. The woman looked very untidy and dirty. Her hair was tangled and standing up and not even combed at all. She came out holding a bowl and started to walk toward a dog that was tied. The dog pulled its chain and jumped up and down as she came. As soon as the woman leaned toward the dog, he quickly slurped down the food, splashing broth and bone fragments all over. Then the blackfish said, "*Aullu* [Watch out!] The couple back there will not be pleasant hosts if I visit them. She'll certainly be careless with my bones." Then he continued on upriver, avoiding the blackfish trap that was set in the water below the couple's place.

As he went, he closed his eyes and sang, "Way over there our fish traps are set. I brush my belly against it. I brush my kidneys against it. Some caribou have no teeth." When he opened his eyes again, he saw a beautiful fish trap . . . neatly set in the water. After he thought of going into the trap, he said, "*Ataki* [Well then!], let me check out the owners back there first." He came to the shore and looked and saw a house and noticed that the area around it was clean and tidy. A dog was sitting tied to a pole near the house. While he looked, a woman came out of the house with a belt neatly tied around her waist and her hair evenly braided. She held a bowl in her hands. When the dog saw her come out, he jumped up and started to pull his chain toward her. As she walked up to the dog and told him to behave, he immediately stopped. Then the woman emptied the bowl into the dog's dish. When the dog began to lap carelessly and the woman told him to eat neatly, he immediately listened and began to eat without making a mess. The blackfish said, "I'll go ahead and enter the fish trap down there since this couple will take good care of me. And I can see that the dog back there will eat my bones without making a mess."

That's the story about the blackfish.

FOURTH DAY Wooden and Clay Containers

We returned to the museum Thursday morning, rested and ready to see what surprises Herr Jacobsen had in store. Breakfast had been lively, with Annie and Wassilie continuing to elucidate the lives of extraordinary creatures such as *ircenrraat, amikuut,* and *paalraayiit.* Instead of growing tired as the week wore on, every day we were more adjusted to the time change and more comfortable in the museum.

Iqmiutaat Meluskarviit-llu /
Tobacco Boxes and Snuff Containers

We began the day examining a group of finely carved tobacco boxes,[1] which excited interest and appreciation. Everyone took one in hand, opening lids, extracting imaginary quids of tobacco and ash, and pretending to place them in the mouth. Holding a wooden box (Fig. 4.1) from the Kuskokwim, Wassilie was the first to comment.

People back in those days thought highly of tobacco. They cherished it. Here's an *iqmiutaq* [tobacco box, from *iqmik*, "chewing tobacco"] carved in the shape of a walrus. You see, my dear father was a very skilled craftsman. . . . When his eldest son began chewing tobacco, he made a tobacco box like this but narrower. It was in the shape of a walrus that opened like this, and it had an ivory decoration like this, too. He put little beads for eyes. On the cover there was a little seal handle. My brother would take the head of the little seal to open his box to take some tobacco. He had a nice tobacco box, and sometimes when he wasn't looking, girls would grab it and hide it. Since my older brother was just a boy, he'd cry when he discovered it was gone. . . .

It was painted with red ocher and *avisgaq* [black paint]. This tobacco box is very old. When he opened his tobacco box, it would make this popping sound.

Annie could not contain herself: "These pieces are so fascinating!" (fig. 4.2)

Marie held out two oval ivory boxes (fig. 4.3) from the Kuskokwim with wooden bases and covers.[2] Both were decorated with *kassugaliiret* (circle-dot designs), and she asked her uncle which groups used designs like these. Wassilie answered, "This design was used by people in different areas and not restricted to one area. When *kassugaliiret* were painted with

4.1 Wooden tobacco box carved in the shape of a walrus. IVA4657.

4.4 Tobacco box decorated with ivory inlay. IVA4641.

4.2 Commenting on this tobacco box carved in the shape of three interlocking walrus, Paul enthused: "I'm sure that this was made by a walrus-eating person. Back in those days people really cherished tobacco. They finely crafted their tobacco boxes, too. The middle of these three walrus figures was used to open the box's cover. Gosh, this tobacco box is so nice. I wish I could take it home and have it as my tobacco box." IVA4648.

4.3 Ivory tobacco box with circle-and-dot designs. IVA4666.

black paint on finished ivory, the paint never rubbed off. This design is used on story knives, too." Wassilie picked up another round tobacco box (fig. 4.4) decorated with *qilkirtat* (ivory inlay) like that found on finely made bowls and boxes. Paul continued:

He already talked about these two in his dialect. This tobacco box is decorated with little *ellanguat* [circle-and-dot designs, literally, "pretend or model universes"]. It is also inlaid with lines going outward. People inlaid their own family designs, but these *ellanguaq* designs are used by everyone . . . on things they make. People had their own implements to inlay designs. The *ellanguaq* design is inlaid on these pieces that were made by various people. The sides on this have little inlaid designs with the ends curled up. They made the inlaid designs out of ivory, which made them look very nice. A mushroom figure is carved on the cover of this tobacco box. This is where one took it and lifted it to open it. I bet its content was tasty.

Wassilie confirmed that *ellanguat* designs might also be referred to as *iinguat* (pretend eyes), adding, "It was said they were *ellanguat* one inside the other" (fig. 4.5).

Wassilie then turned to a large, circular baleen container with wooden bottom and lid from the Kuskokwim.[3] He identified it as a *meluskarvik* (container for snuff tobacco) and graphically described its use:

There used to be *meluskaq* [snuff] in here, but its *meluurun* [straw or tube for taking snuff] is gone. It's also decorated with ivory inlay. My late dear father began using *meluskaq* as an adult. In the morning when he first got up, he'd take his *meluskarvik* and tap it a few times, holding it as if it was a precious thing. Then he'd open it, take the tube and snort in one nostril, then in the other. After each snort he would blink a few times, but he never sneezed. After that he would put the snuff box away. I think they stopped sneezing after they'd been using it for some time. He'd say that he was adjusting his vision in the morning.

4.5 Examining a larger tobacco box carved to resemble the ukingucuk (tote hole) at the bow of a kayak, Wassilie commented: "This was made to hold a lot of tobacco. It has an incised design and ivory inlay. I'd say this tobacco box was made by someone older for himself. But a tobacco box that is finely decorated was probably made for a younger person." IVA4640.

4.6 The last box we examined also drew Paul's admiration: "This tobacco box is finely decorated with pieces of ivory. The cover was shaped like a face. Using their creative imagination, our poor ancestors, gosh, . . . looking at their creations from long before the white people came into our world, their craftsmanship is noteworthy." IVA4644.

Paul was deeply moved by his ancestors' handiwork (fig. 4.6): "*Aling* [Oh my!], the work of our people was incredibly fine, and yet the tools they had to work with were crude. When they made holes, a drill was used to create it. The process was difficult and time consuming."

Annie took up a tobacco box and opened it with a quick *pek* sound, which Paul commented sounded like a distant gunshot. Marie then asked if she had seen *curmiit,* or bags to keep tobacco leaves moist, when she was young. Annie explained:

Both my parents used tobacco. Many used tobacco in those days. When a person ran out of tobacco, he'd trade from others who still had some. It was said that people were always running out of tobacco and tea. When people ran out of tea . . . they'd start using plant leaves as a substitute for tea without complaint. They also used *ayuq* [Labrador tea, *Ledum* sp.].

My parents used to add *pelu* [ash] to tobacco and chew it. After taking it out of their mouth, they would roll it in their palm into a little ball and then put it into their tobacco box. They couldn't go without it. My mother used arctic loon skins for *curmiit,* with a string tied to the end of the bird skin.

Paul then asked to say a little about bird-skin tobacco bags:

Our ancestors used bird skins for *curmiit* by turning the bird skin inside out. That way the tobacco flavor would saturate the feathers on the inside. When one ran out of tobacco, one pulled off the saturated feathers and chewed them. I saw people doing that. . . .

Truly, my birthplace was affected by Western ways much later. I grew up when *yuuyaraq* [the Yup'ik way of life] was in its pure form.

Paul was not the only one moved to speak about his past. First Annie, then Wassilie and Catherine, spoke of how few white people they saw along the Togiak and Kuskokwim Rivers and on Nelson Island when they were young. Catherine continued:

When I was growing up, people cherished tobacco and tea. When Nemqerralriq's father was tending a store in Nerevkartuli, he sold tobacco that . . . looked like woven grass. They kept the tobacco in loon-skin bags. First they would roll the leaf tobacco and put it in the bag, then roll the bag and secure it with the string.

One time my stepmother gave me a bag and told me to gather some plants for her tobacco ash. . . . Then I went to the tundra and picked *pellukutat* [coltsfoot leaves, *Petasites frigidus*], but my bag couldn't get full. . . . Poor, when she burned the bundle to make *araq* [ash], the result was just a small amount.

When they ran out of tobacco, they scraped the wood saturated with tobacco from the inside of the box and chewed it. This wood tastes very much like tobacco.

I used to chew tobacco stems when I was little . . . and swallow the juice. When my stepmother found out, she said, "You poor dear one, some young man will pay you tobacco and get you pregnant. When you get addicted to tobacco, you'll do anything to get it. . . ." Since I couldn't talk back, I thought to myself, "I definitely will not do that." As soon as she told me that, I got scared and stopped chewing.

Catherine concluded, "I'm remembering my past since you've been talking about these tobacco boxes."[4]

Marie had one more question for her uncle: "Do you know the song about chewing tobacco?" Wassilie began to sing, mentioning that the song was composed in Nunapitchuk by Aurralria for the ceremony known as *Itruka'ar*.

Yaayiiyaangaa-a-a

Would you give me a little water

Yaayiiyaangaa-a-a

Would you give me a little tobacco

Yaayiiyaangaa-aar
Yaa aarangaa yayiyiirriyaa
Yayiyiirrii-ii

My spiritual being
Would you give me a little tobacco
From the tobacco pouch
Back there
I will award you
A four-legged animal running back there

Yaayiiyaangaa-aar
Yaa araangaa yayiyiirriyaa
Yayiyiirrii-ii

My spiritual being
Would you give me a little water
From the water bucket
Down there
I will award you
A seal sitting on ice down there

Yaayiiyaangaa-aar
Yaa araangaa yayiyiirriyaa
Yayiyiirri-ii

Wassilie and Annie closed with a "fun song." First Wassilie sang:

How I long to have tobacco
Except I do not have any
I am craving for tobacco
Yet I do not have any

Although I want tobacco
I too do not have any
Hey
Hey you over there
Would you please share your tobacco with me

Ragaga agaguata
Ragaga agaguata
Their grand
and illustrious grandfather

Annie followed:

I want to chew tobacco stem
I want to sniff the scent of tobacco
Since my mind is firm and resolute to chew
Oh how I yearn to have tobacco
My sweet friend and cousin
Who wants to sniff tobacco
I want to chew tobacco stem
I want to sniff the scent of tobacco
My sweet friend and cousin
Who wants to sniff tobacco

Cauyaq / Drum: Container for Our Way of Life

We took a break after the vivid recollections the tobacco containers had evoked. The museum staff had been drawn out of their offices by the singing. Now they joined us around the tables as one of them brought out an ivory dance-house model (fig. 4.7) that Jacobsen commissioned in 1883 from a Nushagak craftsman who had made similar models for other traders and museum collectors. A. C. Company representative Mr. Clarke sent it to Berlin in 1884, which might explain why it was not inventoried with the rest of Jacobsen's collection and has no accession number.

The model was disassembled, and at first the group sat quietly, picking up individual ivory figurines for a closer look. The dance house, especially its tiny ivory *cauyaq* (drum), evoked volumes. Paul began: "This piece falls under the meaning of *agayuliyararput* [our way of making prayer]. When [dancing] was used by our ancestors, they were hoping to receive things they asked for. It was used as prayer to ask for everything that enhanced life and well-being. It resembles the title of our gathering here: *Agayuliyararput*."

Andy, who rarely spoke in collections, continued with feeling:

Beginning from the time of our ancestors, this drum has been with us. A Yup'ik person who is all the way inside the drum frame has a full understanding of Yup'ik heritage and culture. Since the arrival of the outside world, people have begun to move out from inside of the drum. And people who came out have begun to forget their heritage. As they go farther and farther away from the drum, their understanding of Yup'ik culture has gotten smaller and smaller. If a Yup'ik person wants to be true to his own identity and return to the drum, he will begin to understand the Yup'ik way of life. If he is outside the drum, he'll have a difficult time understanding it, because those who are outside tend to have misconceptions about their own heritage. But if a person is inside the drum, he will be able to comprehend what it means to be a Yup'ik person.

Wassilie affirmed what Andy had said:

He just said it accurately. When people were summoned to gather around the drum, they came leaving all negative feelings behind. There'd be nothing but good feelings between people coming together from different communities. This *cauyaq* was used to gather people in dance celebration, to maintain harmony and to strengthen family ties. And the guests who came to the dance festival were given the best foods prepared for the event. The way I understand it, the drum can be talked about in many ways.

Paul then took the microphone for the second time (fig. 4.8), adding to Andy's description of the drum as container for the Yup'ik way of life.

4.7 Jacobsen clearly described this dance-house model, although several figures were lost during World War II: Two dancers are man and wife. However, the man has a lip ornament which is not found in that area today; likewise the woman showed a tattoo on the chin, also rarely seen today. Also the woman wears a nose ornament which I have not seen except on mummies in the Prince William Sound area. "To the right and left of the dancers one observes a sitting drummer—such as is similar in all areas around here. In addition, next to each of the two drum beaters, we saw two men supplied with rattles or dance ornaments similar to the ones we obtained in Bristol Bay [IVA6370, also shown in Figure 12.17] which apparently are generally used in dances there. The third figure to the left of the entrance seems to raise the lamps by means of a cord. . . . The man next to him and the one opposite hold their hands high. Next to them is an observer and also two Eskimos. Along the wall opposite the entrance there sit five persons as observers, as well as the dancers." The scene is said to be a true copy of dances which are held in the winter by the people of Nushagak." Ethnologisches Museum Berlin.

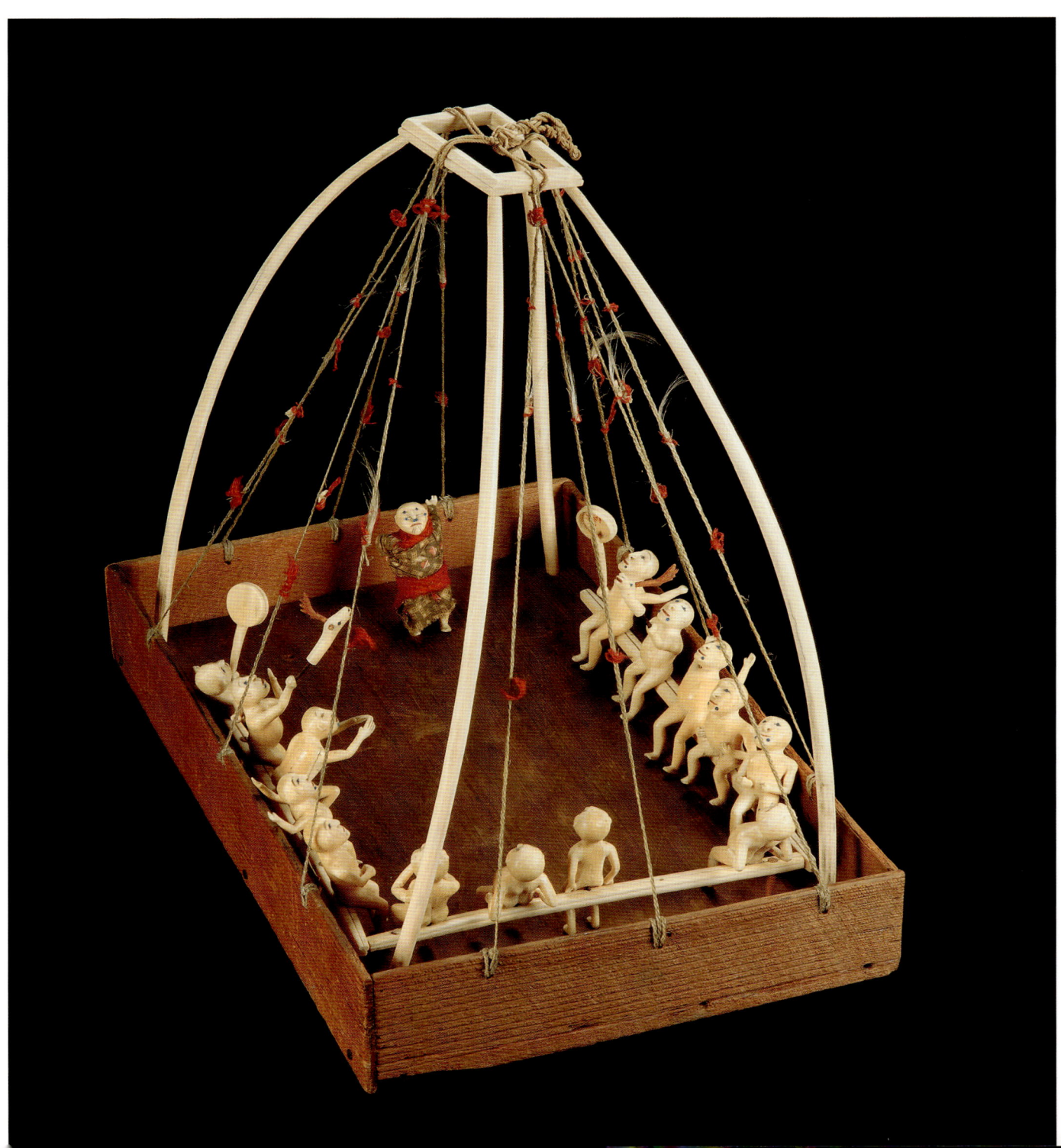

4.8 Paul holding the tiny dance-house drum and describing it as the container for the Yup'ik way of life.

Let me add a little more regarding this drum. Since this drum has always been ours, we've continually stayed inside it. From generation to generation, our ancestors have helped us survive as Yupiit using this drum. And since our people always stayed inside the drum, when they gathered around it, they were in full accord.

Some people look down on the *cauyaq* because of their religious convictions. Some don't want to be around it or feel uncomfortable when people talk about it.... And yet they want to be recognized as Yupiit. But when God created humans and the universe, he made us Yupiit like we were inside the drum already and were to use it in everything we do.

When people tried to acquire the things they needed, they used the drum to try and get them. They created masks that depicted fish and animals from the land and the ocean and other living things, and drummed and danced with them to honor their spirits, and prayed to acquire them.

And when someone was sick, this drum was used when the *angalkuq* worked to heal a patient.

We who are called Yupiit have truly been inside the drum from ancient times. But now since we are outside of the drum, our young people are confused about their path. They continually hear people talking about the importance of knowing one's culture, but when they go to school, the education is from the Western point of view. Though the schools want to teach children about their Yup'ik heritage, their focus is unclear....

If the younger generations begin to understand their heritage through this work, they can begin to move toward the inside of this drum. Those who understand the drum will begin to move inside it.

Catherine enthusiastically supported Paul's recommendation: "Truly, the Yup'ik way of life is inside this. It's a good way. Let the custom of dance return because it doesn't ... encourage bad behavior." Paul continued, bringing the message home and giving our work in the museum new meaning:

This trip that we have made to do this work is not ... insignificant.

The information we are providing regarding these objects is not pointless. The knowledge we are providing must be given to our younger generation, ... who will move toward understanding their history and gain pride in their own Yup'ik identity.

One time an elder talked about this drum in my presence. He said the drum was the voice of God and the drumstick was the tongue. He said that when the drum was struck with the drumstick, we hear the voice of God in many words. That's another meaning behind this drum. The sound of the drum brings out the song with precision and clarity. Using this drum, our Creator spoke to us and said, "You are the Yupiit." That's how the drum is used. I believe in that. Since God can't talk to us in person, the drum is used as an avenue to show us the way.

Earlier we had examined boxes to hold tobacco, a valued item. The drum, too, was seen as a container for what was most valuable in the Yup'ik way of life.

Qemaggviit / Containers

We now turned to a large wooden, teardrop-shaped chest from the Yukon,[5] similar in shape to a small tobacco box.[6] Wassilie recognized it immediately as a *qungasvik* (storage container) for tools and other important items, with a finely carved *kumgaq* (incised design) around its top edge. Paul directed his comments to the driftwood from which it was made:

Since our ancestors weren't surrounded by an abundance of material things, they certainly were destined to use this driftwood to sustain their lives. And driftwood was the strongest and most durable item they possessed. We have already looked at many items that were made with driftwood. From the time of our ancestors, driftwood was used in creating all the tools they used for survival.

Annie was also impressed by the carefully made container. She mentioned that in the past, when people possessed few things, they always used bags and containers to protect them. Both she and Paul recalled smaller storage bags made of skin or cloth, called *ugalguutet*, such as those filled with bullets that men might carry on their shoulders.

Next we examined eight large wooden containers from the Yukon, including five made to hold fishing hooks and gear, two boxes for things like jewelry or sewing equipment, and one fish-shaped needle case.[7] The elders agreed that these were all containers to store things. Wassilie commented, "Containers they made had different designs on them and were figures of different animals and fish. I used to see a few of them around." He said that the first front-loading guns had bullets called *kaapcelaat*, which were also kept dry in containers like these, adding that the bullets had lines on top resembling grass roots, and for that reason were called *canegngalnguut* (from *canek*, "grass").

One container (fig. 4.9) was in the shape of a fish decorated with hair, and Jacobsen wrote that it was used to store bone needles. Like other animal-shaped objects in the collection, it reminded Wassilie of *iinrut* (amulets): "*Angalkut* doctored people back in those days. The person they doctored, the *yuung-*

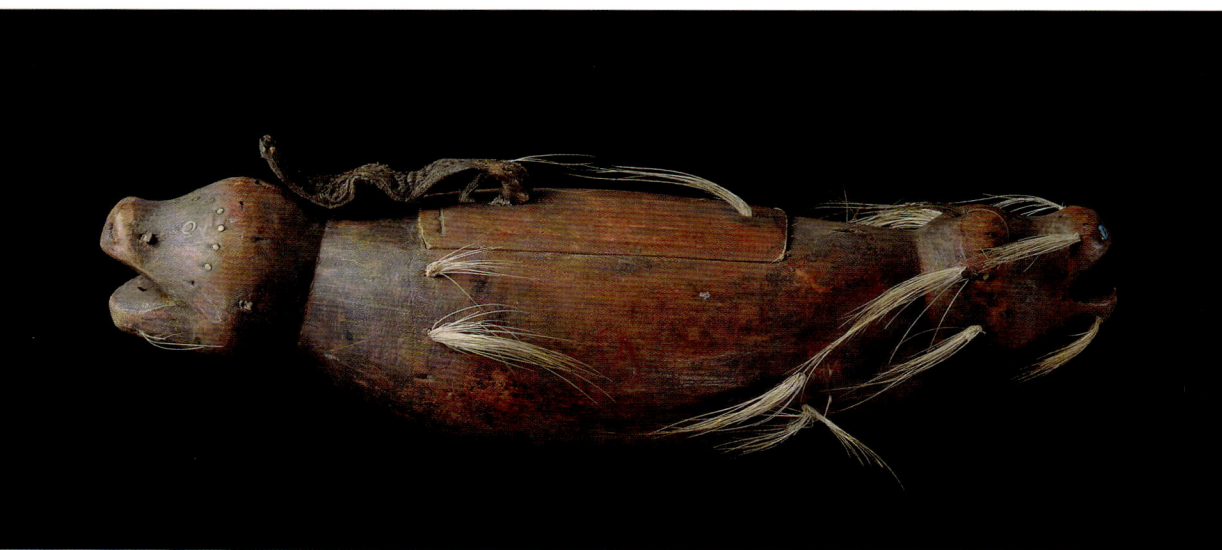

4.9 Fish-shaped container for bone needles, which Wassilie interpreted as an *iinruq* (amulet). IVA3675.

4.10 Fishhook box shaped as a double seal, trimmed with tufts of hair and with beads for eyes and nostrils. The choice of a sea-mammal shape to house fishing tools both recalled and reversed the hook shaped like a land otter used to carry seal blubber (see figure 3.5). IVA3661.

caraq, was given an *iinruq* that would help that person stay healthy. The person kept the *iinruq* in a safe place. This piece has a big mouth, and it has tufts of hair on the top surface. It sure looks like an *iinruq*. It's a figure of a fish with a big mouth."

The most evocative container was a fishhook box (fig. 4.10) in the shape of a double seal. As with the previous carving, Wassilie interpreted this "functional" piece as an *iinruq* charged with healing power:

Our late dear brother was a *yuungcaraq*. His *iinruq* was a little figure of a *tuullek* [common loon] nicely made like this. It was always wrapped in a piece of seal gut. . . . The loon figure was his *napatii* [literally, "support, something that helps one stay alive"]. . . .

Some were kept hanging and others put away in a safe place. The *iinruq* was carved into a figure that resembled the person's *napatii*. Since my brother's *napatii* was a common loon, his *iinruq* was a figure that resembled it . . . and our parents never ate the bird.

Andy exclaimed, "This is the first time I've understood that custom."

Annie (fig. 4.11) asked to see the figure:

I've suddenly remembered something by seeing this. Over in Togiak, this kind of fish once existed . . . that people rarely saw.

Behind the old village of Mequutmiut, there's a lake where you could see the bottom when it's calm and sunny. When the fish came up to the water's surface and allowed a person to see it, it was an incredible experience.

The fish, which was bigger than a kayak, would come up to be seen when a village member was to die soon. It would come up and expose itself to the warmth of the sun. The fish was horrifying, with a huge mouth, but I have never heard of it killing anyone.

Below the [Togiak cannery], there's a lake behind the point they called Kangirracungarpak. The same kind of fish is supposed to reside in that lake, and a *caagnitellria* is not allowed to go into the water. If such a person goes into the water, the monster fish will come up to the surface.

One spring a group of people [from Tarunguarmiut] went out egg hunting. This happened in the recent times, after the time of *qulirat* [legends]. . . . On a little island in the lake, many kinds of birds nested in the spring. The group waded down to the little island in the morning. . . . When they had collected enough eggs, they started to go back to the land.

When the last girl began to go into the water, one of the people in front looked back and noticed water bubbles coming up from the bottom. The young girl had just started to wade into the water to follow the others back to land. The others yelled for her to go

4.11 This seal-shaped box reminded Annie of the amlliq (monster fish) sometimes encountered in her area: "When I saw this piece, I suddenly remembered that fish." IVA3661.

faster, but she didn't listen. Water was coming up, and as it started to reach her waist, she yelled, "*Ala-i* [Oh my!], there's a fish coming up in the water!" The group on land yelled at her, "Jump over it! Jump over it!" They cautioned her not to go around it, . . . but she quickly swerved around it toward the eastern side. Then she suddenly disappeared, and the eggs she held began to float in the water because the little birds had already formed inside. And as soon as she disappeared, the water returned to its original level. They didn't see her again.

4.12 Large wood container encircled with a bone ring displaying circle-and-dot designs. Top and side view. IVA4964.

Annie then told of two similar encounters in the same lake, adding weight to her account. In the first, when another *caagnitellria* was wading back from egg hunting, his companion grabbed him and pulled him to safety. In the second case, a man and his nephew were crossing when they noticed the water rising. The man asked his nephew if his family was doing okay, and the nephew answered that his older sister had died less than a year before:

Then they saw the monster fish right in front of them with spots that were as big as kayak holes. Then Ell'allaller grabbed his nephew and jumped over it, even though the boy pulled back in fear. It was said that . . . if someone who wanted to stay alive stepped over it, it automatically returned to the bottom. . . .

After that, Ell'allaller became energetic and could run fast. Whenever he wanted to jump over something, he learned how, even though it was far. The fish of that lake was called *amlliq* [monster fish, from *amllir-*, "to step over"].[8] The lake is located behind Kangirracungarpak Point. There are many lakes along the ocean down there.

When I saw this piece, I suddenly remembered that fish.

4.13 Fish-shaped box from the Kuskokwim with large glass-bead eyes. The fish's back forms the lid. According to Jacobsen, it was used to store fishhooks. IVA4638.

We now turned to a large, round wood container, also from the Yukon (fig. 4.12). The lid combined a smiling face (usually thought to signify a man) with women's adornments. As on the smaller boxes, Jacobsen wrote that it was for a man's fishing gear, but gave its Yup'ik name as "Ekwiutat" (*iqmiutak,* "tobacco box"). Wassilie gave his considered opinion: "I can't say exactly how these were used, but I'd say this one was a man's container. He probably kept his tools in here." Annie disagreed: "This didn't belong to a man. It belonged to a woman. There's a woman's figure with *cigviit* [nose beads] on its cover. When women had nose beads, I bet it was not easy to blow their noses. These are probably her *caqiqsiik* [side labrets]. Perhaps these two were used to decorate her hair. . . . But the container is cracked. This woven part was used to mend the crack."

Paul joked that the jar was Apanuugpak's homebrew pot, which inspired Annie to tell a story she had heard from a Kuskokwim man named Saggaali. She used the wooden jar as her prop in an unusual object lesson.

I heard him once tell a story about the introduction of alcohol. . . . He said there was a man in a village who was an *angalkuq,* and people in that community would go against him at times. One day he decided to leave the village when it became evident that he was not welcome there.

One day . . . a young man suddenly appeared . . . dressed up with nice clothing and a necktie. The young man asked, "What are you doing out here?" The man replied, "Since I've been here, I haven't been happy. I'm here because the members of my village turned against me." Then the young man said, "Don't be sad. I'm going to make something that will bring you joy." Then he got a container and got busy making something, and when he finished, he wrapped the container with binding. He told him, "Keep on eye on this." He stayed there and checked on the container now and then. He had no appetite and didn't want to eat when the young man offered him food.

Soon the container began to bulge. The young man told him that the contents were starting to bubble and that he would give him some when it was done. Then one day the young man disappeared from the house. . . . He didn't even see him go out through the door. . . . But after he slept and woke up early the next morning, he found the young man sitting in the room. Then he said,

"You've been depressed a long time. If you drink this, you'll forget your worries." Then he gave him a ladleful to drink. After he drank, he started to feel light and cheerful. He began to drink and got happier and happier. Then finally he fell asleep. When he woke up, the young man was gone again.

As he drank again from the container, the young man came in and said, "*Kitaki* [Well then!], when you go home, teach your enemies how to make this." The man went back down to his village with the container. Then after he made the brew, he invited one of the village members and gave him some to drink. Soon the village members started to like him. That was how alcohol was introduced in that area.

Wassilie commented that all the containers spread before us displayed the designs of their individual owners: "Their designs weren't randomly applied but had meaning. I'm sure they put their own designs on them. They've been showing us objects that are very old. Many of these objects have designs from ocean beings."

We continued with our examination, looking at a fish-shaped Kuskokwim box (fig. 4.13) with large blue glass-bead eyes, which Wassilie identified as *pipigaat* (Russian trade beads, literally, "real or genuine things"). Paul spoke at length:

By looking at the ornaments used for eyes on this model, I'm reminded of a story I've heard. Though this is not a model of a killer whale, let me tell the story anyway.

Long ago, at the end of Qaluyaat [the mountains on Nelson Island] below Aternermiut, there were killer whales fighting a humpback whale. People in Aternermiut watched from the shore as they fought. In those days, when killer whales fought humpback whales and killed them, they usually shared their catch with people who witnessed the battle. While the whales fought, people on the shore put offerings into the water, asking the killer whales to share their catch with them. Then one of the people came forward with a single bead in his hand to appeal to the killer whales to kindly share their kill with him. After he made the request, he dropped the bead into the water.

Then right after the killer whales killed the humpback whale, people on the shore saw a young killer whale's dorsal fin ripping through the water, heading slowly toward them. And just before it reached the shore, it slowly emerged from the water and reached up and removed its hood, revealing a young man's face behind it. There were gray hairs beginning to grow in his whiskers. He lifted his arm, and in his hand was the bead that was thrown into the ocean as an offering. And he said, "Apangkuggaq wants me to tell you that he's going to give you the humpback whale he caught, for he is very grateful for the bead you offered him. He said you should retrieve the whale as soon as we leave." Then after he said that, he pulled his hood down and turned and swam toward the ocean as a killer whale. As soon as it reached the others and they all started to swim out into the ocean, people on shore went down and pulled the enormous animal up to land. The fresh meat of the humpback whale that was acquired with a single bead was quickly distributed to every family in the village.

Paul continued, describing how killer whales shared *nengiit* (portions of their catch) with humans:

If people happened to see killer whales fighting another animal in the ocean, they were told to stop and find a safe place on the shore to watch and offer prayers for food and sustenance. It was understood that killer whales were generous with their kill and shared it with others.

They offered people . . . pieces of *mangtak* [beluga skin] with oil that looked like they had been cut into perfect squares with an *uluaq* [woman's knife]. When the killer whales left after they killed the bowhead whale, the pieces floated in the water where the animals fought. The killer whales shared their kill with people who witnessed the fight. When our ancestors received a portion of a kill, they called it their *nengiq* [portion, share].

And when someone came with a group of hunters, even though he wasn't recognized as a skilled hunter, it was understood that he was coming to receive a portion of a kill. *Nengirrassaagartuq* [going to receive a share of the catch] was the word for the person who just came along for that purpose.

Catherine told about the time when she was playing with a group of children on the shore at Up'nerkillermiut, a spring camp on Nelson Island, and saw the dorsal fins of killer whales just offshore. The boys began to throw things at them. A man came down and told them that the animals looked like they were getting ready to come and eat them, and Catherine was genuinely scared.

Paul examined the red-ocher designs on a box's inside cover:

Designs like these . . . revealed the maker's aspirations. The designs weren't randomly applied but were expressions of people's desires to receive what they needed. . . . The designs on objects they used daily were like continuous prayers so that they could be granted food to survive. . . . As they did their daily activities, using objects they created, they were constantly engaged in prayer to God.

Wassilie related the designs to inherited family designs: "When they applied designs on things they made, they didn't do it casually. Designs were family crests and were passed down from generation to generation . . . over many years."

4.14 The blue beads and carved faces on this wooden box from Cape Prince of Wales prompted Wassilie to mention the side labrets his late sister had worn. IVA3039.

4.15 Wooden gear box with a seal body and human head. Looking at it reminded Paul of "that which it was not"—the powerful woman of the sea, Qupurruyuli. IVA3677.

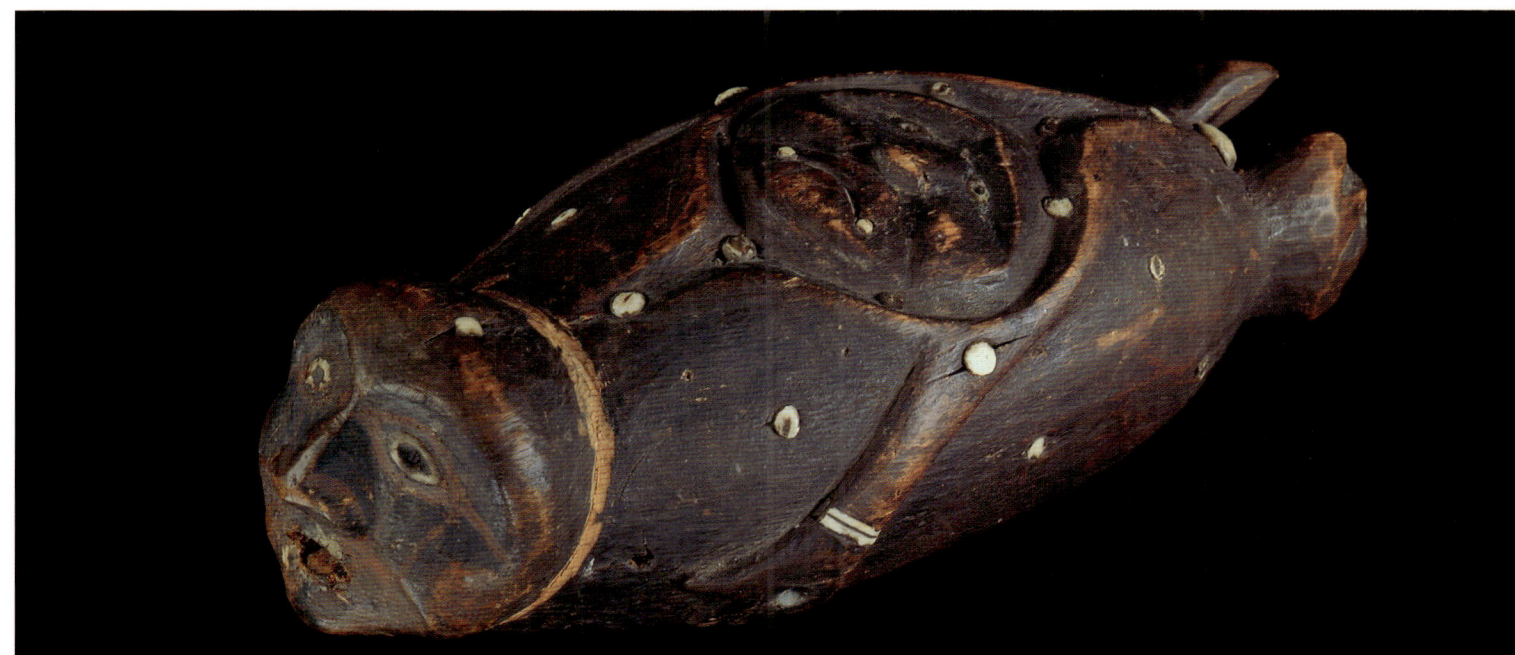

4.16 *Qaltaq (pail) from the Yukon. IVA3902.*

4.17 *Catherine describing a large bent-wood mertarcuun (water bucket, literally, "device to carry water"). IVA4254.*

While Paul had been listening to the others, he had continued to examine an elaborately carved gear box (fig. 4.15) shaped with a seal body and a human head.⁹ He noted the face on the creature's back, with tusklike teeth in each corner of its mouth and arms emerging from each side of the human face. Then he began to tell a story:

This figure doesn't represent *Qupurruyuli*, but let me mention it since it suddenly came to mind. I've mentioned that our ancestors created designs that had meaning.

Qupurruyuli evidently worked in miraculous ways for the person who owned it as a power source. As you know, ice can be very heavy even when it's floating in the ocean waters. And when ice is in the water, it's very difficult to push apart.

The person who owned *Qupurruyuli* as a power source helped his traveling companions go through an ice jam. As he was getting ready to go through the ice, he told his companions not to bump into his kayak's tail as they followed him from behind. . . . And as he continued to paddle forward, the ice began to float to the sides, making a pathway for his kayak while the others followed from behind.

When his companions got curious, they looked and saw a pair of human hands in front of his kayak visible from down below. And since the hands were extended out like this, the ice in front was moving to the sides, making a pathway for the kayak to glide through. A person's long hair could also be seen on the surface of the water in front, with the rest of her hair disappearing into the water beneath. And when they looked down from their kayaks, they saw the rest of her hair in the water down below. Since his *Qupurruyuli* was a woman, her hair was very, very long. They all continued to move forward.

Then just before they reached the open water, the person behind the leader accidentally bumped into the tail of his kayak. Suddenly the ice jammed up around them. But since they were not far from the open water, they pushed their kayaks through the ice the rest of the way.

Since this figure reminded me of that story, I've just recounted it. The man who had *Qupurruyuli* as a power source was able to summon her when he was in trouble in the ocean . . . to help not only himself, but also his traveling companions.

All had listened attentively as Paul spoke. Annie nodded in

appreciation when he was done, saying, "I am hearing this for the first time."

Qaltaq Qurrun-llu / Water Pail and Urine Container

We turned now to a double pail (fig. 4.16) from the Yukon, exciting both Catherine's and Annie's interest.[10] At first Catherine mistook it for *qasrulget* (things made of *qasruq* [birch bark]). Annie had never seen a double pail like this, but she had seen *tumnacuaraat* (small oval wooden bowls with handles): "When I first became aware, I used to see an old woman who always kept a *tumnacuar* filled with water by her side. The little bucket was always covered, but when she was about to do something, she'd take a little sip."

We next looked at a group of bentwood containers. The largest was a red-painted water pail from the Yukon (fig. 4.17).[11] Catherine said that these pieces were rare and only their owners could use them:

When I moved to the Yukon, I saw one person who had a bucket like this. She didn't allow her children to use it. She was the only one who used it. Perhaps the buckets' makers made them with a purpose for the owner. Avegyaq's mother didn't allow us to touch her bucket at all. She'd always take it when she picked berries, and she'd fill it by herself, even though she had many daughters to help her. When she filled her bucket, she'd go home. These buckets contain a lot of berries.

Annie also recognized the piece, and she began to describe the bucket, called a *tuqmik*, owned by her aunt Unanuum. This reminded her of her aunt's wooden *arulamirun* (long-handled ladle, literally, "device to move things around"), used to stir food in a cooking pot. Paul helped to explain the latter, but before doing so asked to say something about our work: "The work of the Yupiit is not identical. Since people in certain areas made things in their own style, we shouldn't say that a certain object we're looking at wasn't complete, but we should try and explain how these things were used by our people." Andy agreed and urged the group to speak only about the objects that we were looking at: "If you talk about things that aren't here, people who are trying to understand those will get confused." Marie disagreed, saying that Annie's description of what she had seen was also important information. Although we never directly confronted the issue again, the discussion remained a reference point in our work together.

Continuing his examination, Wassilie identified the piece as a *mertarcuun* (water bucket):

There used to be a water bucket down on the floor all the time in our house. People always kept water in their homes. The dipper for it is not here, but perhaps it will show up later on. The handle of this water bucket is just perfect. Since my parents had wooden bowls when I first became aware, I'm only mentioning what I saw and not adding other information.

People always decorated things they made. The area around it has a *kumgaq*. This is a *pertaq* [bentwood rim] with the joint on the side. The *allungak* [container bottom] is a separate piece of wood attached to the bottom. When it was used for water, it was very tight at the bottom and didn't leak, but now that it's old, the bottom seam has started to open. (fig. 4.18, fig. 4.19)

We turned to a plain bucket (fig. 4.20) from the Yukon, which Jacobsen also said the Ingalik had made and traded downriver.[12] Yet Yupiit had made similar utensils in the past, and both Paul and Wassilie could describe their construction. Catherine wondered out loud how they made them so smooth, and Paul replied that they rubbed the wood with a *keggalrun* (literally, "device to rub or smooth out") made of "dried ocean foam" (probably pumice, found on the beaches of Nelson Island). He added that it was made of *unarciaq* (straight-grained wood): "There are different kinds of wood, and some are hard and able to bend while others are difficult to bend and break easily. Wood-carvers can look at a piece of wood and begin making it into something if it can bend and not break."

Annie talked about how wood was bent:

When I first became aware, I saw my father bending wood, making things including snowshoes. First he would boil some water on the stove. When the water boiled, he'd drop the wood in the water . . . and keep checking to see how it was doing. Then, when he took the wood out of the water, he'd shape the wood into either *tangluk* [snowshoes] or *pupsugcetaat* [snowshoes with pointed fronts]. This wood probably was shaped in that kind of procedure.

4.18 *Wooden bucket from the Yukon with black designs on a red background, and a smiling face painted in black on the inside bottom. Jacobsen wrote that the black circles painted on the sides represented drums, the symbol of a festival, and that these kinds of wooden containers were mostly made by the Ingalik and used as trade items along the entire river. IVA4245.*

4.19 Catherine admired the bucket's craftsmanship, and Annie remarked, "This was finely made, and the designs are very nice. There's a finely finished human face on the inside with a cute *kakeggluguayaat* [nose septum decoration(?) from *kakeggluk*, "snot"]." IVA4245.

They've said that wood dipped in hot water was easier to bend and shape. The stitches here come from spruce roots.

Wassilie added detail on the bowl-making process: "These were only made in the *qasgi*. A man who was making one like this would dip the wood in hot water when men were taking a fire bath and begin bending the wood in the process. There's a slit around its *allungak* [bottom part] for it to easily slip into place. It's tightly fit into the bottom so water wouldn't leak out."

Considering the same small bucket, Catherine mentioned another use: "Back in those days I also saw little urine containers for children. This is bigger than the ones I saw. Mothers began potty training their babies from the time they were infants. I think that's what this is." Although Jacobsen described another slightly larger wooden container as an eating bowl,[13] Paul viewed it as a *qurrun* (urine container): "If I were you, and it was back in that time, I'd say that I'd like to have it for a urine bucket if I was too old to go outside to pee. . . . I figured it was a urine bucket that was used by an old man or an old woman who got too weak to go outside."

Wassilie echoed Paul's interpretation of the two containers: "My *iluraq* [cousin] here said this was a man's urine bucket. And here's a little *pertayagaq* [small bent thing] that was made for a woman. When I first became aware, our mother had her own urine bucket. After she delivered a child, she'd lift her dress a little and push the bucket in between her legs to use it."

Alvik wall' Ilutuliar / Large Food Container

An enormous wooden food bowl[14] from the Yukon followed the smaller wooden boxes and bowls (see also fig. 4.20). Annie spoke up: "This is about the size of a bowl for making *akutaq*, but it looks tall. Part of it had cracked and was mended. . . . And here are some holes where a line was pierced through. Perhaps my *uicungaq* [teasing cousin] can say more about it." Wassilie responded enthusiastically, "We certainly can talk about it!" Paul continued:

At home we called this an *alvik*. This container had many uses. The family food processor took this and went out to the storage shed to fill it with food and came back into the house with the family meal. *Ciqluaqluni* [from *ciqlugaq*, "partially underground food cache"] was the word they used when she did that. When she came back in with this filled with assorted foods, she would fill the individual dishes of family members.

This container was also used when they made *akutaq*. It was used for food preparation and serving.

Wassilie continued with personal remembrances:

We call this *ilutuliar* [large container, from *ilutu-*, "to be deep"]. My parents had a bowl like this. This was used for making *akutaq*. My mother's *akutaq* bowl was exactly like this, deep enough so that oil couldn't splash out. They cooled the oil by whipping it. . . . Women used this container daily.

Then he finished a story he had begun earlier in which a clever woman saved her husband's life with the help of her *ilutuliar*.

In the story I told, the wife of the eldest brother of the *nukalpikcat* [great hunters] got ready to make *akutaq*. While she sat down with the bowl to begin whipping the oil, she saw the reflection of the skylight up above on the oil inside the bowl. As she looked at the reflection, she noticed someone up there removing the window brace and pulling back the frame to peek inside the house. She immediately recognized that it was the face of a warrior. Instead of telling her husband, she started to whip the oil to make *akutaq*.

The clever wife continued making her *akutaq*. After she had let the *akutaq* set, she told her husband to stay in the house and enjoy the *akutaq*, as he would not have an opportunity to eat it again. That evening she went out to look around and realized they were surrounded by enemy warriors, making it impossible for her husband to escape. She stayed outside doing things. Before she went in, she took her husband's snowshoes by the house and raised her voice, saying, "Oh my, foxes or other little animals might chew their *nulut* [webbing]." Once inside, she dressed her husband in her parka, gave him the snowshoes to hide underneath, and told him to take the water bucket and go down to the waterhole, pretending to get water. Bending his knees to appear like a female, he approached the hole, where he quickly removed his wife's parka and started running. His successful escape is commemorated on parka designs to this day:

As he ran with his snowshoes, he bounded forward very swiftly, running from side to side. Whenever he looked back, some of the *akutaq* he had eaten would come up his throat, spew out of his mouth, and land on the back of his shoulder. With every movement of the head, he kept spitting some *akutaq* onto his shoulders, creating white patches on both sides. He was quick to elude the arrows coming from the enemy. . . .

When the warriors were out fighting, they always used *pupsugcetaat* [pointed snowshoes, from *pupsug-*, "to pinch"]. As the enemy warriors ran after him with their weapons, whenever the front end of their *pupsugcetaat* landed on the *iqalluguat* [snowdrifts in the lee of an object], they would fall down. . . . So he continued to run away, running from side to side as his shoulders turned white. He ran from the enemy toward the place where his younger brothers were staying. He evaded the enemy warriors and arrived in Ayikatarmiut safely. . . .

When women make fancy parkas, they always put white fur strips of a caribou fawn on the garment's shoulders. The designs were called *miryaruak* [literally, "two representing vomit," from *miryaq*, "vomit"].

Left alone, the wife knew the warriors would soon return. So she pulled out another container filled with processed fish eggs, took some in her hand, and rubbed her whole body, including the area between her legs. When the warriors returned, she exclaimed, "Oh no! I'm too repulsive to touch." One of the warriors reached in to check the area between her legs but

4.20 *Group of bentwood containers in different sizes. From top to bottom: IVA4254, IVA4246, IVA4253, IVA3671, IVA4249.*

pulled his hand back saying, "Oh my, she certainly is too rotten to touch!" Although everyone in the room was familiar with this story, they nodded appreciation for Wassilie's dramatic retelling in which, with the help of her food containers, a wise woman saved her family.

Qantaq / Bowl

Our next item was an oval wooden bowl (fig. 4.21).[15] Annie was the first to speak. Once again, her comments took the form of a story:

Bowls like this with a *qaglak* [upper part] were never used when food was offered to the dead. It was believed that when the deceased were offered food in bowls like these, the bottoms usually fell off, losing all the contents.

4.21 Bowl with a qaglak (upper part) and allungak (detachable bottom). Annie remarked, "Bowls like this with a qaglak were never used when food was offered to the dead. It was believed that when the deceased were offered food in bowls like these, the bottoms usually fell off, losing all the contents." IVA4246.

4.22 Seal oil container from the Yukon. IVA4251.

Since my uncle, the late Cukanraralria, was evidently mischievous, even though he was warned, he left the village during the time of Qaariitaaq [ceremony prior to the Bladder Festival, during which the dead visit the living]. It was on the day they observed Elciryaraq [ceremony in which all men receive bowls filled with food in the qasgi] . . . when people abstained from doing certain activities before sunset. . . . Once he was outside the village, he hid and stayed down on the side of a trail. He wanted to see if the elders were telling the truth. While he left the village, he wondered how the deceased would look when they came by.

Then, as he sat, he started to hear voices. People who were approaching sounded happy. When they came into view, they were going along holding gifts they had received. Some were holding bowls filled with *akutaq* topped with pieces of seal ribs. They were people who had died, and they were exactly the way they looked when they were alive, and my uncle recognized them.

During that fall, a couple in the village had lost their only child, a girl. Everyone in the village knew that her parents were very stingy. When their daughter died, they didn't even do a feast for her in their house. And yet her father was a *tuvraq* [dependable hunter]. . . .

As my uncle sat and watched people passing by, he heard someone burst out crying from behind the group. Then shortly the person appeared, and it was that couple's daughter. She was holding a little bucket from her elbow. Whenever she cried out, the lower part of the bucket dropped on the ground while the upper part and the handle remained on her arm. And as she walked by and the lower part dropped, he looked and saw a fermented fish head. She evidently got frightened and released the lower part whenever the fish head opened its mouth.

Then one of her traveling companions said, "How shameful and heartbreaking to see her in this condition while her father, a skillful hunter, brings home all kinds of animals from the sea and land. And her mother is so selfish! I wish they could see their poor daughter trying to bring home food for herself." This event showed the mother's lack of respect for her deceased daughter. Right in front of him, she picked up the bottom part of the bucket, reattached it to the rest of the frame, and continued on with the rest.

My uncle cautioned everyone not to use bowls or containers with two-part frames when they gave food to the namesakes of the deceased. He said that the bottom parts of the containers usually detached and fell off as the person carried the food back to the home of the dead. . . . They would get heavy and difficult to carry.

By the time he got back to his village, he realized that it was morning. When he went into his mother's house, . . . she said, "Ii-i-i [Yes]. I can see that you were out there watching those people who just went home from here. So, what did they look like? You smell of mold and decay. Go out and roll on the ground where the dogs are tied." He went out and rolled on the ground in the dog kennel. After he came back in his mother said, "Perhaps you have something to tell?" He told her that he did have something to say. Then he took his mother to the couple's house. He told them what he saw. The husband . . . said that he had urged his wife to participate in the event, but she had not listened.

Then later, during either the Bladder Festival or *Curukaq* [Exchange Feast], . . . that couple got very busy. They brought bundles of mink pelts and young caribou skin for parkas into the *qasgi*. There's truth in everything.

After that, someone . . . saw the spirit of their deceased daughter in the village . . . wearing beautiful clothing from head to toe, and her hair was nicely combed and pulled back. She was very happy and told that person to tell her parents that they must continue to take part in community events and celebrations. . . . She said that during celebrations, they do come unseen and join the living.

When I saw this little bowl with a *qaglak*, I suddenly remembered that story. . . . I'm saying this so people will know that even though our deceased relatives are with us, we can't see them and aren't aware that they are present. That is the truth.

Paul and Wassilie spoke briefly when Annie was done. Both agreed that it was a woman's bowl like those they had seen their mothers and grandmothers using. Wassilie said that in the tundra area, a bowl like this with a detachable *allungak* (bottom) would be called a *qaglayaaq* (one with a *qaglak* [upper part]). Paul noted that we had not yet seen any men's bowls. The next object we looked at was a small seal-oil container (fig. 4.22) from the Yukon. Although Jacobsen had labeled it "Angutsinerak Kantag" or *angucinraq qantaq* (man's bowl) it also had a detachable bottom. Catherine took it up and spoke at length:

I saw many bowls like these in those days. Mine was an *aluuyacuar* [little wooden bowl]. People cherished their bowls in those days. When we were done with our meal, we always cleaned our bowls. We would lick all the food inside it. Down by the entryway, there were big *qulqitet* [raised platforms or shelves] . . . made so we couldn't reach things on them. Cuk'ayaq's mother took good care of us. When we finished our meals, she'd say, "Make sure you lick your bowl clean." Then she'd take our bowls and place them face down on the shelf. When food was served, they'd always know where our bowls were.

Then one day I brought a meal to the *qasgi* for the first time in my life. It seemed like I was holding a huge *qantaq* with a huge seal rib inside it. The rib was cooked rare with blood oozing out of it. I used to be afraid of the *qasgi* down in Up'nerkillermiut. As you entered the main room in the *qasgi*, you'd go down into the *amiik* [entranceway]. . . . And when I came to the other end, I placed the bowl on the floor up there and began trying to come up through the *pugyaraq* [hole at the end of the tunnel entrance where a person comes up]. On the sides of the *pugyaraq* were two big walrus tusks to hold as you came up. When I entered the *qasgi* that time, I was very frightened.

Annie also had something to say:

This bowl is a good one. It's a cute little bowl. I wish I could eat half-dried fish with it, but such food is not available here.

My brother had a bowl like this . . . with a caribou design. A caribou figure was on many things, including drums. My mother cherished his bowl. My father also had a big bowl decorated like this.

Back in those days, women cared for men's bowls with utmost respect. A man's bowl was never left out in the open but was always put away neatly on a shelf. And when a woman picked up a man's bowl, she was not allowed to take it with her palms down. If a woman picked up a man's bowl like that, it was said that the man's future catch was being covered. And it was important to always keep it clean.

Men's clothing and materials, including their tools and the implements they used for eating, were cared for with respect. It was also important to take care of male babies' urine and not carelessly discard it anywhere. It was said that boys were born with their *cirla* [substance with the power to harm]. And when they got bigger, they would lose their *cirla* and become vulnerable. However, a baby girl was more protected at birth, and in her later years her *cirla* become evident. Later when she started to menstruate, she would be considered overpowering and formidable.

Today it's quite saddening to see what's going on. I don't think men's possessions are kept in their appropriate places anymore. There's so much disorder and confusion in our lives today. And some don't even follow the *eyagyarat* [abstinence practices] anymore.

When a woman continues to mishandle her husband's bowl, he will quickly lose his ability to hunt successfully. And if a mother is careless with her baby boy's urine, her husband will also become unsuccessful in his hunts. That was why such *inerquutet* [prohibitions] were known and passed down . . . and should still be known today.

Annie followed this advice with a story about a successful hunter whose wife, tired of processing his enormous catch, tried to affect his hunting skills. She added things to his food, such as her menstrual blood and her little boy's urine, but his success remained undiminished. Her husband's ability was finally affected when she started feeding him the *ucuilleq* (front lateral fin, from *ucuk*, "genitalia") below a fish's *qurrsaraq* (pee hole). From that experience, people learned that part of the fish could affect a man's hunting skills. Annie said that she still remembered these things because, unlike her siblings who had left the house when her grandmother talked, she had been afraid to go out: "If I had gotten agitated and run out like the rest, I would have been ignorant and not able to share some of her teachings now." Annie concluded, "During this time, a person who keeps the elders' words and does not lose them will do well in life."

Catherine affirmed what Annie had said, adding that she had seen it with her own eyes. She described her poor stepmother on Nelson Island, who took such good care of her husband's possessions that they were rich with food. The eldest sister, however, moved into a home of her own, where she let everything fall on the floor and be stepped on. Catherine vividly recalled the filthy surroundings, including seal pokes under the bed oozing with oil. As a result, the man lost his ability to catch animals, and he died soon after at his fall camp. She concluded, "It's the truth. A woman must care for a man's clothing and things, especially his eating utensils."

Wassilie expressed his appreciation for what they had said: "Our women companions touch upon some of our *qanruyutet* [teachings] as they speak. It's really good to hear some of the familiar words." He then added what he remembered:

This cute bowl made for a child is constructed like a *tumnaq* [large oval wooden bowl] with a *qaglak* [upper part].

When I first became aware, we all had our own wooden bowls for meals. They were finely made bowls painted with red ocher and black paint. This bowl with a design that looks like a little human figure is also painted like that.

We had different designs on our bowls. Both of my older brothers' bowls had caribou designs down on the inside bottom with a black dot in the middle of the figure . . . representing a hole in the body. The figures resembled the caribou seen by an ancient hunter. The old hunter had shot it right through the hole with his arrow, . . . and the figure turned into a caribou. The bowls were well made, with a *kumgaq* [incised design] along the outer edge.

A shallow man's bowl from the Kuskokwim, decorated with a black-painted caribou and two human figures (fig. 4.23), later reminded Wassilie of the design used on his older brother's bowls. He and his younger brother also had bowls with designs: "My bowl had the design of a mink and a land otter, and my younger brother's bowl had a land otter. Our dear father always made those designs on our bowls.... There were four boys in my family. My family owned bowls made out of wood and a few metal bowls. The first metal bowls had fancy designs on them. This child's bowl is so nice, and anyone would love to have it."

Like Catherine and Annie, Wassilie recalled the storage shelf across the back wall of the sod house, on which bowls were stored face down:

Below the shelf, there was another plank to keep other things. And after our dear father checked his traps, our mother placed all of the minks he caught in a row facing the floor on the plank below the shelf. And once in a while when he caught otters, we'd see them there, too. And when she placed the minks there, she'd put bits of food in their mouths. It was her way of welcoming them into our home. That's what people did over there. We've been adding bits of stories like these in our work here....

And when the minks were lying under the shelf, my parents didn't use [metal] bladed tools inside the house. That was an *inerquun* that was taught to our people. They believed that if we handled bladed tools while the minks were resting under the shelf, half our face would get paralyzed in later years.... They were also very careful not to bump their noses on the shelf when they handled the mink ... or hit the noses of land otters on the floor.

Paul reiterated that this was a boy's, not a girl's, bowl. He concluded our discussion of bowls with a mild remonstrance: "Earlier my *nuliacungaq* [female cross-cousin of a male, literally, "sweet little wife"] said she'd like to use it. During our ancestors' time, a woman couldn't use this kind of bowl at all. Women totally respected the rules. Only a boy was allowed to use this bowl."

The next day we examined a large bowl from the Yukon, which Jacobsen also designated an "Angutsinerak Kantag" or *angucinraq qantaq* (man's bowl) that women were not allowed to use.[16] Wassilie spoke first, noting that it was a man's eating bowl called a *nerun*. He pointed out that the bowl was decorated with *kumgaq* all the way around both top and bottom as well as ivory pieces called *qilkirtat*. Wassilie mentioned that the man's bowl was bigger than a normal dish, and Paul elaborated: "The woman usually filled the bowl with food that would last several days on a hunting trip. It was because food wasn't readily available out in the wilderness. They also think about the possibility of bad weather." Annie added that if one hunter met another out on the ocean, they would bring out their bowls and share with one another. She concluded, "Since some women were wise, they'd fill up the bowls with enough food to last for several days."

We turned to another wooden seal-oil bowl from the Yukon with owl figures carved on each end (fig. 4.24). In this case, the

4.23 The black-painted caribou and human figures on this man's bowl reminded Wassilie of the designs painted on his older brother's bowl: "It was said that a hunter would see a caribou with a hole in the middle.... The figure in the front of the caribou is holding an ax and below is an adze. And the figure on this side has an irunguaq [gun support] with a gun on it. If a hunter saw a caribou with a hole in the middle, he was told to shoot the arrow through the hole. The arrow would go through the hole and fly forward as the animal turned into a complete caribou with a hole. This caribou design gave hunters a chance to be more successful in hunting." IVA5130.

4.24 Wooden seal-oil bowl from the Yukon with owl figures carved on each end. IVA4252.

bowl's use drew no comment, and discussion concentrated on *iggiayulit* (great horned owls). Paul mentioned that *iggiayulit* were said to be able to talk, and he recalled that someone he knew heard one saying, "Qutuk is dead" just before his uncle Qutuk actually died. He then asked that the recorder be turned off for a while, and he spoke more about owls and their special powers both to see into and predict the future.

When we began to record again, Catherine told about a boy who had destroyed an owl's nest, killing its young. In retribution, the men of the village perished in the fire bath. Still today, she said, people say that great horned owls are very dangerous. Annie added that when she was young, her mother always warned them not to mock owls, which were abundant in the wooded areas of the Togiak River valley, by imitating their calls. She then told of two men who had camped along the river. Hearing an *iggiayuli* calling, one stood up and mimicked it, singing "*Igg'iggiggiiggii.* Your coat-*ggiiggii*." Shortly after that, owls began to sing emphatically, and the men fled to safety downriver. Annie concluded that *iggiayulit* were truly dangerous birds, and Wassilie agreed, adding that he had heard that there were two kinds of *iggiayulit,* one of which could speak Yup'ik. He then told of an owl that haunted the people of Qinaq, landing near the *qasgi* skylight and frightening its occupants by speaking like a person.

Our last wooden container was another double bowl from the Yukon.[17] Although he had never seen anything like it, Paul conjectured that the bowls were filled with two kinds of food, joking, "If they belonged to children, perhaps they belonged to twins." Wassilie continued:

These two wooden bowls have actual *qaglak* [upper parts], and they look so cute. They'd be good bowls even for an adult. . . . In my observation long ago, when a woman brought a bowl of food to a man in the *qasgi,* he enjoyed sharing his meal with another man. When you observed them enjoying their meal together, it was a beautiful sight. Perhaps a woman filled these two bowls with two kinds of food when she brought food to the *qasgi*.

Marie asked if they might be *qurrulluut* (urine buckets), and Wassilie said no. Catherine noted that they probably didn't bring them into the museum because they smelled like old urine, and Wassilie agreed, adding that they were easy to spot.

All these stories from several pounds of old wood!

Qikuq Egan / Clay Pot

The day was drawing to an end, but our group was still lively, energized by the interesting objects and their many stories. We turned to five clay pots from the middle Yukon, roughly made and hardened in open fires (fig. 4.25).[18] Jacobsen wrote that women made pottery by hand rather than on a wheel: "One takes a flat round stone, covered with animal skin so as to form a handle, and this stone is pressed against the inside of the pot; from the outside, a skin-covered pounder taps against the wall and smooths it." We would later see one of these stone tools (also shown in fig. 4.25),[19] which Wassilie recognized right away as a *manigcissuun* (device for smoothing): "This was used to smooth out and form the shape of the pot before the clay got firm. They also fixed braided string for handles on their upper parts."

Annie, who in her youth had seen clay pots being made, startled everyone with her vivid recollections: "I'm quite amazed looking at this clay object. I've seen things made of *qiku* [clay]. People sometimes find clay objects like this when they dig over in Togiak. Clay is easy to break. When they mixed the clay to make something, they added livers of certain animals, perhaps bird livers. They also added other things. I've heard that dog excrement mixed into clay could thicken it and make it hard and difficult to break."

Ending the day's work, Marie asked Wassilie to talk about the clay cooking pot belonging to his mother that he had mentioned earlier:

When I was a little boy, my parents had a huge clay cooking pot. My dear father talked one time about how the clay pot was made. He said that when they made clay pots, they'd first burn some grass, then mix the ashes into clay with seal oil. He told me that was how they were made.

My parents also had a clay lamp. In the back of the room there was a lamppost. It was wood sticking in the floor with a burl on the top of the stick . . . flattened where the lamp would sit. The *kumarun* [dried-moss lamp wick] was used to light it. A supply of *kumarutet* [wicks] was always hanging on the wall. I became aware after Coleman lanterns were introduced, but the seal oil lamp was used when it ran out of gas. They'd weave a couple strands of *kumarun* and light it up. . . .

There were handles on the rim of the clay pot, and the rim was a little wider and folded out. When the pot was washed, the inside looked very clean and smooth. Sometimes our dear father would turn to our mother and say, "*Kitaki* [Well then], cook something for us that won't taste like bogus food." Then she'd take the clay pot (this was when people cooked in the porch), putting it on the edge of the fire pit with part of the pot sitting on a brace, which was a little bit higher; she'd cook by feeding the fire with wood through the front. Finally after a long time the pot would begin to boil, and once it boiled, it boiled forever. Food cooked in clay pots was a delicacy. . . . The clay pot was very heavy; so was the seal-oil lamp.

Wassilie wondered out loud what had become of that old pot. He thought that it probably fell into the river with their old house when the bank eroded. He was grateful to see these clay objects once again.

4.25 Group of clay pots from the middle Yukon, including a stone tool used to smooth the clay. Jacobsen wrote that the largest was for cooking, while the smaller ones were for seal oil. Both clay pots and wooden containers were important trade items for the Yupiit and Ingalik of the middle Yukon, who exchanged them with coastal people for seal oil and other coastal products. Off the record, Wassilie joked that the cup-size pot with a woven-grass cover to protect it from breaking might have been the warrior Apanuugpak's coffee cup. From right to left: IVA4479, IVA4487, IVA4475, IVA4180, IVA4485.

FIFTH DAY Containers of Skin, Gut, and Grass

Iqertiit / Things Made of Fish Skin

We began Friday morning with three large fish-skin bags, all from the middle Yukon.[1] Jacobsen had collected relatively few sewn items, focusing instead on carvings attesting to ancient "Stone Age" adaptations. After we had spent most of the week focused on wooden tools and boxes, the finely stitched fish skin set off an avalanche of information.

Holding up the smallest but best preserved of the three (fig. 5.1), Wassilie began: "This *iqertak* [thing made of fish skin] . . . was called *kellarvik*. This *kellarvik* made of dog-salmon skins was used as a bag. It's adorned with *kelurqut* [special stitching with caribou throat hair and sinew on thin strips of dyed skin or dried bird-foot leather, from *keluk*, "stitch"]."

Both Paul and Annie noted that such bags were also called *kellarvik* in their homes, and Annie continued:

We call this material *iqertak* [fish skin]. These little black strips are called *it'galqinrat* [from *it'gaq*, "foot"], which are used as a base for *kelurqut*. And this red strip, which is always stitched next to it, is a design that is also stitched on the *qalit* [front and back plates on a woman's fancy parka] and the *qemirrlugutet* [smaller plates below the *qalit*, from *qemirrluk*, "spine"]. As women, we always had materials like these for sewing back in those days. And we always owned bags like these. If someone asked, "Do you have something?" I'd reply, "Oh my, I do have some. It's in my *kellarvik*."

People always had dried fish skin like this. Men wore fish-skin boots in cold weather. Fish-skin material is very tight and durable. It was also made into gloves and mittens. I've watched women processing fish skin like this as well as fish skin for boots they called *amiriit* [waterproof fish-skin boots]. The *amirak* soles were made

5.1 Bag made of dog-salmon skins and decorated with kelurqut (special stitching with caribou throat hair and sinew on thin strips of dyed skin or dried bird-foot leather). IVA4294.

of thick spawning-chum-salmon skins, which were tough and didn't fall apart when men used the boots for hunting. But when the boots were damp, the tie strings weren't bound around the ankles and top too tightly. And because fish-skin boots could get sodden and soft quite fast, they were careful not to put them near fire or in the hot sun.

Wassilie briefly described the preparation of fish skins:

When they prepared fish skins for sewing, they first soaked them in aged urine. After they were soaked, the inner sides were scraped very clean . . . and the skins strung on a cord, hung outside, and freeze-dried in cold winter air. Once they were dried, they used a special tool to remove the scales. As they scraped, the dried scales came off with a crackling sound. That was the way my mother prepared fish skins to make boots and other things for our family.

After the scales were removed, the skins were flattened and stored in a dry place. These fish-skin bags are for storing and keeping things dry.

Paul added what he knew, including the many uses to which fish skin could be put:

Today people dry fish with the skin. When the skin of a dried and smoked fish was going to be processed for sewing, people carefully tore off the meat and ate it. Fish skin was made into many things. The coastal people traded with inland people to get fish skin to make *arilluut* [fish-skin mittens] for their seal hunters to use when paddling in wet weather. The *alliit* [mitten palms] were made with hair-seal skin or spotted-seal skin. When I started to go out, even in the winter, my parents always made me bring my fish-skin mittens. But they'd tell me not to get them wet. When these were lined with something, they were very warm. . . .

I watched my late grandmother carefully scrape all the meat from the skin, and when it was totally clean, she would drop the skin into the *qurrulluk* [urine bucket] to wash. Then she'd wash the skins by hand, and when she was done, she would string the skins on a line and hang them out in the cold to dry, *qerrecqertelluki*. Fish skin that was freeze-dried was difficult to crack or break.

Wassilie added that they kept fish skins in urine for one or two days and cleaned off all the excess oil before they dried them. Processing fish skin was time consuming:

The inside part of the skin had excess material they called *kelipacuut* [from *kelig-*, "to scrape"]. Some men scraped the insides. I do remember a big man named Cacirkaq who did this. "I keep feeling hunger pains today. Please hand that *iqertak* to me," he said, and his wife handed him a fish skin along with her cutting board. He placed the board in front of him and took his *kelipacuutaq* [scraper] and began to scrape the inside skin. He'd push the scraper down on the skin and lift his scraper into his mouth and suck the excess meat and oil, slurping noisily. That process was called *kelipacugluku*. This was always done to a fish skin before it was washed in urine.

Annie added the related *inerquun*: "*Kelipacuk* was available, but they didn't allow us young people to eat it. They told us that if we ate too much *kelipacuk*, our future husbands would not be good hunters. Following that advice, I didn't eat *kelipacuk* when I was little. Boys were not allowed to eat

5.2 Salmon-skin bag from the Yukon decorated with pieces of blackfish skin, attached with regular stitches. IVA217.

it either. If a boy consumed it, he wouldn't be a good hunter. *Tangrriu* [You see]."

Annie's comment evoked a lengthy discussion of other animal parts that young people were prohibited from eating. For example, Paul's grandmother told him he could not eat fish hearts lest his heart pound too fast when he hunted animals, and he suspected it was because these parts were so delicious. Conversely, he was encouraged to eat the part of the seal's stomach called either *mamcat* (from *mamcarte-*, "to be flat") or *elavurcautet* (from *elave-*, "to come down close to the ground"), so that he would appear flattened and therefore less visible when he went after animals. Annie said the same was true in her area: "My mother would tell my brothers that if they started hunting and an animal saw them, they'd look like the ground they were standing on. And since I loved to pick berries, I started eating them along with my brothers, hoping I'd do that too."

The two remaining salmon-skin bags (fig. 5.2) we examined excited the same interest,[2] and Paul had to hold the microphone for Annie as she moved her arms in enthusiastic explanation. The bags were decorated with strips that Jacobsen said were blackfish skins. Annie could not identify them but was sure that they were not the skin of *it'galqinrat* (swan's feet), a common decorative device that we would see later on. She could see that the stitches were made from the inside with regular stitches, *mingqepiarturluni* (from *mingqe-*, "to sew"), not cross-stitching (*ikavsiaquvet*, from *ikani*, "across there"), which was used in kayak making. "I wish I had a needle!" she exclaimed in frustration.

Paul described how *ikavsiaq* stitches were made:

Since the skin you are sewing is wet, your hands keep slipping off as you hold it. As you do the *ikavsiaq* stitching, you'd put a little piece of wood by the edge to keep it from slipping off, trying to keep the seams even. And if you pull the thread through the other side, you'd try to keep the line even. And, again, you'd pierce your needle evenly through the seam on the other side. When you are done, if you'd like, you'd sew it again on top with stitches, *mingqeviarluku*.

Annie commented that this topstitching was called *qall'iluku* (from *qalli-*, "to be on the top, surface"). Paul continued talking about the use of dyed seal intestines for decorative sewing:

In my home, they made long ones like this. *Cungagarciut* [from *cungag-*, "to be greenish in color"] was the name for the process of soaking seal intestines in alder-bark water. The bark "cut into" the seal intestine. Once the intestine was treated like that, it was called *cungagartaq*, even though it didn't look green. It was used to decorate objects like these. I'd say this is dyed seal intestine.

Catherine noted that dyed seal intestines were also used on the lower Yukon: "They'd measure and cut the same length and place it on the seam. The extra part was called *asuirutii*. It was to keep the seams from breaking. I watched people dying these with blackberry and blueberry juice. An intestine like this would have blueberry or blackberry color, too." She added that the side of the fish skin where the scales had been was dark and was not painted, whereas the inside was light in color and was often decorated. She then made everyone laugh with a story about her husband when he was a young boy. Once his mother made him a new pair of fish-skin boots with fish-skin soles, which he wore out to play. He used them to go sliding, but after a while noticed that his boot sole had torn apart. Then he sat down and took his boot off and started eating it. When he was done eating, he went home. Because he was barefoot, his mother scolded him.

Wassilie added information on *cungagaq* (alder-bark dye):

We in the tundra area used *cungagaq* on many finished items. When men were done mending their dip nets, they went out and gathered small [alder] trees and bushes. When they came home, they'd whittle the bark off the bushes and cook them in water until the water got warm. They'd put the finished dip net in the water and leave it there for a period of time . . . and then pull it out and hang it to dry. When the net dried, it would have the dark, murky color of the tundra water. *Cungagaq* came from the bark of *cuukvaguaq* [alder] and *auguqsulit* [red alder]. *Auguqsulit* bark color is darker red. They prepared *auguqsulit* bark when they wanted sharper color. *Cungagaq* was applied on *ivrucit* [waterproof skin boots] to help keep them from shrinking.

Sugarviutaq / Bag for Dolls

Our next pieces were two small fish-skin bags (fig. 5.3).[3] Annie handled one enthusiastically, recognizing its *kelurqut* stitches:

Since those people living in the Kuskokwim area were historically called *munalriit* [dexterous, those with skillful hands], the stitches on this bag are very fine and minuscule. This bag looks like a *sugarviutaq* [bag for dolls, from *sugaq*, "doll"]. I had a *sugarviutaq*, but it was made of woven *taperrnat* [grass] with a swallow sewn onto the base of the bag on the inside . . . to give me strength to travel far and near and for wealth. It was believed that swallows could give a person wealth and possessions. . . . People in those days . . . strove for excellence in their work. These *kelurqut* were surely made with *tengayut* [caribou throat hairs]. They said that *tengayut* never got dirty.

Wassilie also recognized the small container:

When our mother made *amiriit* [fish-skin boots], she saved all the leftover parts and kept them in a fish-skin bag like this. I suddenly remembered that.

After a long winter, spring arrived and days got longer and longer. Then one day (it was probably when our winter food supply was getting low), our dear father turned to his spouse and said, "Gee, how about cooking some fish-skin scraps." As soon as he said that, she'd go out and come back in with a fish-skin bag. She'd open it and take out the fish-skin scraps she had saved. Then she would boil some water in a pot . . . and drop the pieces in. After she left them in the boiling water for a few minutes, she'd dish a few into our individual *qantat* [bowls] and we would eat skin scraps, *qecigpagturluta* [from *qecik*, "skin, leather, hide"]. The scraps were kept in an *iqertak* [thing made of fish skin] like this.

5.3 The decorative border of this small storage bag caught everyone's eyes. Marie asked about the designs, and Wassilie said, "They represent bird feet." Paul teasingly offered another explanation: "They were put here because they thought of our trip to this place. . . . Here's the jet trail, and this is the jet!" IVA7071.

Qungasviit Kakiviit-llu / Storage and Sewing Bags

We now considered a dozen smaller bags made of a variety of materials. Wassilie identified the first salmon-skin bag as either a *kakivik* (sewing bag) or a *curmak* (tobacco pouch), lined with bird skin to make it airtight.[4] Paul immediately recognized the second,[5] made of caribou-foot skin and lined with seal throat, as a sewing bag from the middle Yukon: "The thread and thimble were kept in here. And evidently this was made after *llumarraq* [cloth] was introduced. The needles were pierced through this piece, called *kakisvik* [from *kakite-*, "to pierce a needle into and back out the same side"]. Sewing bags always hung near the person who owned them."

Annie also recognized the piece, including the red material (*kaviragtaq*, from *kavirliq*, "red") from which it was made. She was especially impressed with the fine craftsmanship: "These stitches remind me of sewing-machine stitches. . . . This piece reveals the elegant workmanship of our ancestors and is being documented here so our history is not lost. As reported, only the finest seamstresses made tiny *kelurqut* like this."

Annie then took up a small sewing sack from the Nushagak area, lined with cloth and decorated with bits of yarn.[6] Both she and Paul agreed that the small *qungasvik* was made of squirrel-belly hide, called *kepcetaat* (dyed skins). We next examined a small storage bag from the Yukon, which Paul identified as an *ugalguun* (storage container).[7] He and Wassilie both agreed with Jacobsen that the bag was made with a combi-

nation of *it'galqinrat* (swan feet) and *iglak* (freeze-dried throat) skins. Wassilie noted that the freeze-dried throat skins of both seals and larger land animals were soft like this, and that Akulmiut (tundra people) usually acquired them through trade with coastal people.

We now turned in earnest to seven moose- or caribou-foot-skin *kakiviit* (sewing bags) from the middle and lower Yukon, one from the Kuskokwim, and one walrus-throat skin bag from the Aglurmiut of Bristol Bay.[8] Turning it in her hands, Annie admired the well-made Kuskokwim bag (fig. 5.4, fig. 5.5). Similar to the other bags, it was made of caribou-foot skin, tanned on one side and embroidered with strips of porcupine quills and walrus-throat skin. Other bags included decorative work in bleached seal throat and blackfish skin, and each had a closing thong and ivory or bone bag fastener. Finishing her examination, Annie spoke at length:

The back has little white beads. And its edge is decorated with *kepcetaat* [dyed leather pieces] . . . and bits of yarn. And these tiny *kelurqut* stitches look like they were made with a sewing machine. Actually, sewing-machine stitches are bigger, but these stitches are so tiny [they are] barely visible to the naked eye. And here's some

5.4 Kakivik ("sewing bag") from the Kuskokwim with the ivory bag fastener that would have held the rolled bag shut, as well as an ivory needle case, thimble, and needle like those the bag might have contained. IVA5416 (bag); from left to right: IVA3657, IVA5006, IVA4642a, IVA3777, IVA5345.

5.5 Detail of the Kuskokwim sewing bag, made of caribou-foot skin, tanned on one side and embroidered with strips of porcupine quills and walrus-throat skin. Catherine noted how beautifully it was made with incredibly small stitches. When she was young, she had longed to own one like this, but when she asked, her stepmother told her that she wasn't old enough. IVA5416.

5.6 Seal-gut bag from the Alaska Peninsula. Catherine noted that the two dark pieces on the sides had been sewn with red material between the seams to accent them, adding: "My stepmother told me many times, 'When you see someone sewing or making something, watch very carefully what they are doing. You'll learn by observing others.' I did as told and watched others when they sewed." IVA6988.

nicely stitched small *kassugaliiret* [circle-within-a-circle designs]. Its *kakisvik* [place where needles are kept] is this white material. . . . And these are caribou ear skins. . . . This strip up and down . . . is probably caribou skin, too. . . . And this ivory piece is called *iqugmiutaq* [bag fastener, from *iquk*, "end"] . . . and is covered with *kassugaliiret*. When you roll this *kakivik* . . . you'd fix this string so it wouldn't become loose.

This is the bottom part of these animal skins. It was cut into fringes. Its *tungunqucuk* [added strip of dark skin, from *tungu-*, "to be black"] could be mink or some other animal. . . . And the part around it is a piece of *pukirraq* [white fur from a caribou fawn]. It's been finely stitched into the body, and this *kepcetaaq* has been neatly stitched, too. . . . These sewing bags are so beautifully finished!

Paul added vocabulary from his area: "My *nuliacungaq* here used a different word from the way we say it. The part she called *kakisvik*, we call *kakinqun* back home. And we call these fringes *kelevyat* [from *kelve-*, "to cut skin into strips"]. In our dialect, we'd say this is *kelvumaurluni* [cut into fringes]. Today people say *kepurluki* [cutting them into strips, from *kepe-*, "to cut or sever"]." The bag fastener also had a different name—*kakinquka'ar* (from *kakin*, "pin, fastening peg").

Next we looked at a large, rectangular seal-gut bag (fig. 5.6) from the Alaska Peninsula,[9] and again Annie commented on its construction and design:

Since we've been working here, I've been seeing some things beautifully crafted like this. . . . It is actually done with a pattern they called *tevtara'araat* [from *tevte-*, "to drape over something"]. . . .

Its *kakiyutək* [fasteners] are fixed with *tevtara'ar* stitching. This piece of seal intestine was sewn in very nicely. And these dyed leather pieces were stitched on with a different-colored piece in the middle. This looks like it's factory made, but actually it was made by a Yup'ik person. . . . The inside is stitched with cross-stitching. . . . And in the middle there's a wider piece of seal intestine stitched in. We called this *qerrangellri* [something raised up, from *qerratarte-*, "to rise or lift up"]. Between these strips of dyed skin which we normally called *kepcetaat*, there's another strip of dyed leather stitched in.

And this *turgunqucuk* [added strip of dark skin] . . . is bird skin. This is the first time I've ever seen bird-skin *tungunqucuk*. It's probably cormorant skin. This is very good. . . .

These stitches are called *engigcequmauraliit* [those that lie on it? from *engig-*, "to lie on it"].

Another Yukon sewing kit (fig. 5.7) drew everyone's admiration.[10] Annie said that it was made with *qatviat* (freeze-dried leather), a caribou-skin back, and cloth, with *mingqepiarumalriit* (regular stitches) on the edge. Wassilie noted that the bag was decorated with *pipigaat* (Russian trade beads) and had the canine teeth of mink as *aqevlequtat* (dangling ornaments, from *aqevla-*, "to hang down"). The teeth reminded Annie of belts decorated with caribou teeth that she had seen women wearing when she was young—one belt in particular that was sold to the trader "Uaski" (Frank Waskey): "When the *kass'aq* bought the belt, she lost it." The decorative teeth also stirred Wassilie's memories: "When we first became aware, everyone wore belts. I had a sealskin belt with teeth hanging from it. Its *aqevlequtat* were evenly placed down the belt. My mother made me a belt like these. My older brothers never wore belts that had mink teeth *aqevlequtat*. . . . When I started hunting, it seemed like mink were always there for me to hunt."

Annie identified a seal-gut bag from the lower Yukon as an *ugalguun* (little storage container).[11] She noted that it was nicely made but old and worn. The conversation then turned to the preparation of seal intestines. Annie told Paul that she used a scraper to separate the inner and outer layers. Paul added that when the gut was fresh, its *taiq* (inner layer) was hard to remove: "But if you let the intestine sit for a while, it's easier to take it off. Once the *taiq* comes off, it's edible. One could cook it and eat it." Marie clarified the process: "When the outer layer of the intestine is removed, you'd say *tairniluku*. And once the *taiq* was removed, you'd call it *qiaq*. It's very delicious."

Annie said that her mother used to scrape the intestines of bears (which were even stronger than seal intestines) after letting them age. Wassilie had also observed people cleaning seal intestines and, like both Paul and Annie, recalled that soups made from their contents were a delicacy. Paul added that if a hunter bit the intestine as soon as the seal was caught, it was easier to remove the *qiaq* later on, as the seal was still aware and responsive after death: "Even though seals aren't alive, they are still aware and can feel. When the animal is butchered right after it is killed, its meat is still quivering." Referring to the

5.7 Yukon sewing kit, decorated with the canine teeth of mink. IVA4503.

well-known tale of the boy who lived for a year with the seals in their underwater world, Paul added, "The person who was taken away by the seals said that when his body was being cut into pieces, he sensed it as a tickling feeling."[12]

We turned now to an assortment of small bags (fig. 5.8), including a fish-skin bag from the Kuskokwim, a caribou-bladder bag from Nushagak, a Nushagak gut-skin bag, and a bag from the Yukon made from salmon skin, blackfish skin, and bleached seal throat.[13] The small containers shared a variety of names, including *kalngak, issraka'ar, qemaggvik,* and *kellarvik*. The bladder bag reminded Annie of the *ircaqinraq* (from *ircaquq*, "heart") made from a caribou bladder that she had when she was young. Paul concluded, "Though we can't tell exactly

5.8 Paul and Annie examining an assortment of small bags, including one made from the skin of an unborn seal. IVA5488.

5.9 Noting the strips of dyed skin and fringed sides on this squirrel-skin bag, Annie expressed her gratitude for what she was experiencing: "Gosh, people sure were skillful sewers in those days. I'm so thankful to see their work. Though I had heard about many of these, this work has helped me to understand more." IVA5515.

which animal they came from, it's okay to say what they were made for. It's okay to call these *ugalguutet* [small storage containers made from skin or cloth]."

Our next container was a bag made from the light-colored skin of an unborn seal, with an opening in the neck.[14] Paul commented at length:

This is a baby seal that was still inside the mother. These were made into travel bags for men . . . for ocean hunting. . . . Skin bags like these were called *arr'inat*. In kayak traveling, it was good to have them because . . . though the bottom might get a little wet, the contents were always dry.

This fur is called its *ul'utvak* [newborn skin]. They still have this on when they first come out. . . . But if a hunter caught a baby seal that had lost its fur like this, he'd say he caught a *carriqaq* [from *carrir-*, "to clean or clear off"]. . . . When the baby fur comes off, its permanent fur is already there.

The real seals, such as *issurit* [spotted seals], *makliit* [bearded seals], *nayit* [ringed seals], all have *ul'utvak* babies.

Hunters were warned not to go after newborn walrus, as their mothers were dangerous. Paul said men were especially grateful when they caught a walrus with a baby still inside, as baby walrus skins were made into line for spears that was very strong. He then described the special way in which seals and walrus were skinned to produce the valuable line:

Leather lines were also made from bearded-seal skins. Even in the summer, when a hunter caught his first bearded seal or walrus, they'd cut up the skin *kepelmurluku* [cutting into sections all the way around instead of opening it in the stomach] and give it away. The sections of a hunter's first catch cut all the way around were greatly cherished by everyone. The recipients would be happy and would fix the skin into lines.

Our next piece was a *qungasvik* made from a squirrel pelt trimmed with walrus throat skin, collected between the Kuskokwim and Nushagak Rivers.[15] Annie spoke without hesitation:

As I look at this *qanganaq* [squirrel], I'm recalling a mighty animal I used to hunt. . . . It's decorated and made into a little container. And down below, its little legs and tail have been split into fringes. The bottom borders of parkas were decorated with little squirrel legs and tails topped with a *tungunqucuk* [strip of dark skin]. On the upper Togiak River, people always wore squirrel parkas. This squirrel was very beautiful when it was new. It looks like it was a spring squirrel, but it has turned red because it's so old. . . . This is a big squirrel.

Gosh, people were so innovative back in those days. The upper Nushagak used to have an abundance of squirrels. Hunters caught enough squirrels for several parkas. . . .

This is a nice piece, and its little hands were fixed with little *nunurayagaak* [top parts where tassels could be attached, perhaps from *nunur-*, "to pinch"], with little *kepcetaat* [decorative leather pieces] included. Its little hands are still attached.

Annie now commented briefly on another smaller squirrel-skin bag (fig. 5.9) from the same area, richly decorated with a variety of skins.[16] Wassilie confirmed Annie's account, summing up our morning's work: "These squirrels were fixed as *qungasviit* [bags]. . . . Since she's from a place with lots of squirrels, she's been talking about them. Most of the things we've seen today have been women's work. We've been seeing mostly bags."

Commenting on the last small sewing bag collected south of Nelson Island,[17] Wassilie once again downplayed the distinction between men's and women's tools: "These *kakiviit* were used in hunting and traveling. Travelers always brought *kakivii* with them. I thought of bringing my own very old *kakivik* with me on this trip . . . to show them to you, but I decided not to. Everything is in my old *kakivik*, including my thimble. I always brought them with me when I went hunting as a boy. We were told not to go hunting without our *kakivik*."

Tuullek Qemaggvik / **Loon-skin Bag**

Annie deferred comment on our next item, an unusual loon-skin container (fig. 5.10) from the Yukon, saying, "These men will explain it properly."[18] Paul noted that he had seen several old men with loon-skin *maqissuutet*, or fire-bath hats, to protect their heads from the heat. This loon skin, however, had been fixed into a bag. Wassilie agreed:

I'm viewing this like my *iluraq* [cross-cousin]. The bag's rim once had a string to close it. Gosh, the workmanship on these objects is quite amazing to see. . . . If this was a *maqissuun* [fire-bath hat], it would have a *qaglak* [rim] around here. This is not a *maqissuun* but a *yaqulegpak* [arctic loon] or *tuullek* [common loon]. When people composed songs, this was the bird they aspired to illustrate in their compositions.

5.10   Loon-skin bag from the Yukon. IVA4284.

5.11 Bird-foot-leather bag that Jacobsen received as a present from Charles Petersen at Andreafski and regarded as a special showpiece. IVA5388.

Now, this common loon was not easy for hunters to catch back in those days. Not too far back in time, I heard a song about a common loon composed by an *angalkuq* to mock another *angalkuq*.

Elluralria sang this song in my presence at a gathering in Nunacuaq. This song was composed solely to be sung and danced during *Itruka'ar*. The song was quite entertaining. In the song, Elluralria portrayed his strength and ability.

Jacobsen had received the next small, bird-foot-leather bag (fig. 5.11) as a present from Charles Petersen at Andreafski on the Yukon.[19] Annie examined its parts and materials:

This piece is actually a *qungasvik* [storage bag]. Since it's probably not from the olden days, it has cloth lining. The bottom part is *qagtaq* [U-shaped]. A piece of wolverine is at the bottom, and this piece is painted with red ocher. And this piece is *nerun* [dried esophagus, from *nere-*, "to eat"]. This bag is very beautifully done. And here you can see the tiny beads sewn into it.

144 THE RETURN GIFT

It's also adorned with little *uminguat* [V-shaped] designs. . . .

This piece below is probably *it'galqinraq* [swan-foot leather]. *Kelurqut* [special stitching with caribou throat hair and sinew] were usually stitched on to swan-foot leather. We called these white leather pieces *nerutet*. And here at the rim are some fur pieces used as decoration. This piece of leather is decorated with square black pieces. These aren't beads. They are *it'galqinrat*. And there's another red piece of decoration here. It also has a string to close it after putting something inside. It's a little bag like the *ugalguun* we looked at earlier. This is the neck or *painguyii* [string to close it], . . . to make it look nice. But it has no *tungunqucuk*. People back then finished their work very nicely. This is all I'll say about this. I'm falling in love with this bag.

Tupigat / Woven Things

After a break, we returned to our examination of containers, including a variety of grass bags and baskets. We began with a large multiuse grass bag (fig. 5.12, fig. 5.13) from the tundra area, with willow strips braided into it for decoration.[20] Catherine was first to speak:

Here's a big *issran* [twined grass bag]. Bags like these took a long time to make. First the *taperrnat* [coarse seashore grasses] were dried. They picked the grass with the roots and laid them on rocks. When the grass dried and turned white, the roots were removed. If the grass wasn't completely dried, it tended to break when twined. A weaver will begin at the base, using one blade as thread. When the base is done, you'd begin coming up, twining the side of the bag. Here at the end you'd add more grass to make it wider. . . .

When you begin to twine around the second time, you'd cut those two that were added. You'd keep twining the bottom part . . . in a regular pattern, *tupipiggluni* [genuine twined stitches (fig. 5.14)]. And the top part is woven in a pattern called *mallegtat* [from *malleg-*, "to be close together"]. It was twined straight up without adding more grass to increase the width. . . . They also decorated them with dyed material. This looks like it was dyed with blackberries. This is a very nice bag.

Annie was also impressed, commenting on the patience it took to make such a large bag. In the past she had seen people twining grass all the time, including grass bedding, kayak mats, bags, and baskets: "When I was little, I was surrounded by twiners."

Annie and Catherine spoke about the many things stored in these grass containers, including pelts, provisions, and personal possessions. Even Wassilie was moved to comment: "This is a *qemaggvik* [container for something precious]. When the son of a couple got married, a bag like this would be brought out filled with garments for the new bride. New garments made for a son's future wife were kept hidden in bags like these."

Next we examined a large grass bag from Nushagak, with looser weave and larger stitches.[21] Catherine described its construction: "The beginning part is . . . twined tightly with a regular pattern. When we begin, we knit it three times before we add more. Then either on the fourth or third knot, we'd begin adding to make the sides. The other side is done the same way.

5.12 Multiuse grass bag from the tundra area with willow strips braided into it for decoration. The top part is twined straight up without adding more grass to increase the width, in a pattern called mallegtat. IVA4255.

5.13 Detail of the mallegtat ("closely twined stitches") on the large grass bag. IVA4255.

5.14 Bottom of the twined grass bag, twined in a regular pattern, tupipiggluni ("genuine twined stitches"). IVA4255.

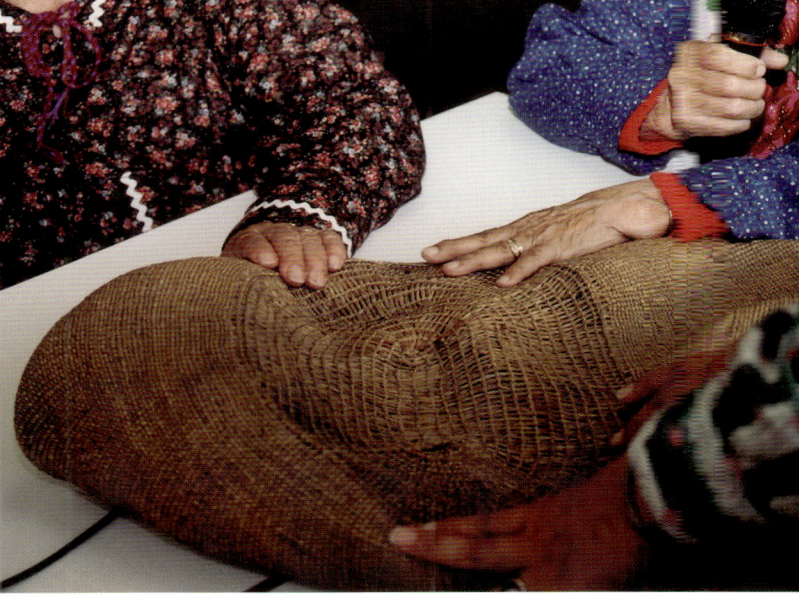

These bags are faster to weave." Wassilie added, "These open-weave grass bags were called *ukilqaaraat* [from *ukineq*, "hole"] because you can see through them." Catherine also remembered the bag's many uses: "I saw bags like these for traveling. We filled them with berries and greens and carried them on our backs. When we picked berries, we'd line the bag with pieces of an old seal-gut garment before we filled it with berries. Bigger bags were also used when we gathered firewood. I don't think they lined the bags when they filled them with things such as mussels, clams, and sea anemones."[22]

We turned to a group of three grass bags from the Yukon and one from the Kuskokwim (fig. 5.15).[23] Catherine commented on how they had been made: "These *tupigat* [twined things] weren't started from the bottoms.... These are made of dried *iitaat* [tall cotton grass]. Over in our area, we call these *qecugat* [from *qecug-*, "to pull out"]. This is a *kalngak* [storage bag] ... used for blackfish."

Holding the two short pieces of grass extending from the base of the Kuskokwim bag, Paul brought the container to life (fig. 5.16):

5.15 Grass bags from the Yukon and Kuskokwim. Although Jacobsen said they were used only in houses and on journeys to protect pottery, Annie remembered similar bags used to store blackberries in water. IVA4260, IVA4276, IVA4391, IVA4468.

5.16 Paul describing the two grass "legs" extending from the base of a grass bag, which enabled it to walk into a sled when its owner asked it to do so. IVA4468.

This bag is made out of cotton grass, but some made bags out of *qayikvayiit* [wheat grass] or *can'get* [grass in general] to store fish in to keep them frozen. . . . In my home, we called them *naparcilluut* [rigid, upright grass baskets] or *kuusqutet*. . . . The *naparcilluut* I saw had two pieces of grass sticking out of the bottom. They'd say these were the legs for the *naparcilluk*. There's a story about a young man who always arrived in the village with a big bag like this in his sled. When people saw him arrive, they'd say, "Gosh, you're such a strong person." Since the young man was an *angalkuq*, he'd reply that whenever he got to a bag with two things like this, he'd say to it, "Well then, get into my sled." The *naparcilluk* would use these two pieces of grass as legs and walk and get into his sled. That was why bags for frozen fish were made like this.

146 THE RETURN GIFT

We turned now to a long, slender grass bag from the Yukon, which Jacobsen said women used for storing sewing items.[24] Our men disagreed. Paul spoke first: "Back home I might mention a wood splitter called a *qupun* and say, 'Would you hand me my wood splitter inside my little bag.' This bag is called *equgcuutnguarraq* [from *equg-*, "wood"]. The tools for splitting wood were called *equgcuutet*." Wassilie agreed: "We called wood splitters *ekiarqitet*. . . . The *kaugtuutacuar* [small club, from *kaugtur-*, "to pound"] would also fit in. I think he and I are pretty close to the accurate description. It's a man's *qemaggvik*."[25]

Our last grass objects were a group of seven baskets from the Yukon, Kuskokwim, and Nushagak regions (fig. 5.17).[26] The baskets were in various sizes and shapes (both round and square) with small necks and not much decoration; several had leather bases. Paul recognized them right away: "These are *aguumaat* [storage baskets] in different sizes. It's obvious that these came from different villages." Annie noted that in her area, they were known as *qungasviit*. Jacobsen reported that the baskets were used to store sewing utensils, but Paul mentioned a wider variety of uses. Turning to Annie, he teased, "My tobacco pouch, my keys, and my money, I'd say I'm putting them in my *aguumaq*."

5.17 Aguumat (grass storage baskets) from throughout the region. Clockwise from the top: IVA4489, IVA5521, IVA7266, IVA4233, IVA4234, IVA4229, IVA4230.

SIXTH DAY Tools for Working on Objects and Materials

Ukicissuutet wall' Kaputat / **Drills**

In his quest for evidence of Stone Age civilizations, Jacobsen had brought hundreds of small and large ivory, bone, and stone objects home to Berlin. Although visually undramatic, each had a story to tell, and our group carefully considered even the smallest fragment. On Monday morning, Paul accurately identified a broken drill shaft from the lower Yukon as the handle of a man's tool.[1] Describing its use, he enriched Wassilie's explanation of the circular designs found on so many Yup'ik things: "It probably had a tip that was used to make *kassugaliiret* [circle-and-dot designs], as mentioned by my friend here. Back home we'd call the tool *ellangualissuun* [device to make *ellanguaq*, literally, "likeness of the universe"]."

We turned to five wooden drills from the Yukon[2] made to be used with a mouthpiece and turned with a leather thong. Jacobsen noted that two might also be twirled with the hands and were used like awls in sewing clothing.[3] Wassilie identified them as *ukicissuutet* (drills, from *uki-*, "to get a hole"), and Paul said that Nelson Islanders called them *kaputat* (pokers, from *kape-*, "to pierce or poke in"):

A person would call this his *kaputacuar* [small *kaputaq*], and some called it *kaputalqaar*. They used these tools to make the black dot designs we saw earlier on ivory story knives. They also used them to make holes on other things. In the past days, we saw some wooden and ivory items with holes on them. This particular tool can easily be recognized as one that was used to drill holes on skin or leather. And you could see the hole where its mouthpiece was inserted.

Wassilie and Paul examined two more drills, one made of wood with a stone point from the Togiak River and a nephrite drill in a horn handle from Cape Vancouver, both of which could have been used with mouthpieces in the past.[4] Wassilie thought they might be drills but deferred to Paul, who recognized them as a variety of engraving tool:

There were many uses for this. We have already seen things where something had been inserted into a hole in wood. This tool was called *iqukeggun* [engraving tool]. It was used to make a hole or depression on something where another part was going to be inserted. The point looks like this because it could be used to make holes on wood. It could also be used to make a long incision on something to make the line design we've seen on things such as wooden bowls.

Cet'raarcuun / **Tool for Making Designs**

Wassilie identified a small iron needle with a wooden handle (fig. 6.1) as a *cet'raarcuun*, or tool for making designs on ivory: "We're looking at these decorated ivory pieces. This tool was used for etching and making lines on objects. . . . This is a *cet'raarcuun*, a tool to make designs on ivory." While Wassilie spoke, Marie balanced the point on the back of her hand, showing how it could be held and thrown from different positions in a game she had played when she was young.

Wassilie gave a detailed explanation of a bone bowl-making tool (fig. 6.2) from the lower Yukon, which Jacobsen designated "Kantag-Kan-Sisiun-atlugnaitnun-Altug-naitnun" (from *qantaq*, "bowl," and *allungaitnun*, "on their *allungat* [bottom parts]"):

The bowls with a separate *qaglak* [upper part] always had an *allungak* [bottom part]. The part of the rim where the bottom would be attached was filed smoothly all the way around. When it was done, the bottom part was fixed and attached to the rim. Once it was snapped into place, it was permanently attached . . . and they'd apply "glue" around so it wouldn't leak. I think this tool was used to waterproof the bowl. The edge at this end was fixed for that purpose. And the other end was used to make a little depression to put a little piece of bone as decoration . . . called *qilkirtat* [inlay]. This was used on different-size bowls, including little ones.

The next day we would see a box containing more than a dozen pieces of ivory and stone inlay,[5] which Wassilie immediately recognized as *qilkirtat*, used to decorate the thick sidewalls of large wooden eating bowls, which Jacobsen said were traded to

Figure 6.1 Wood-handled iron needle for making designs on ivory. The needle is resting on the accession card Jacobsen wrote for it, which includes a drawing of the object. IVA7254.

Figure 6.2 Wassilie demonstrating the use of a bone bowl-making tool from the lower Yukon. IVA4179.

people of the coast for sealskins and oil. Jacobsen acquired the pieces from Norton Sound, but they originated from the Yukon.

Pirlaat / **Sled-runner Sheathing**

Next we looked at a group of bone and antler pieces with drilled holes from King Island.[6] Although the pieces were not from our area, Paul and Wassilie identified them as fragments of *pirlaat* (sled-runner sheathing), out of which tools were often made. Paul noted that the pieces looked as though they had also been in the ground and described the origins of "subsistence digging" in coastal villages for objects for sale and trade: "During the time the first white people arrived in my area, and seeing the new arrivals' interest in acquiring artifacts, people started to dig in old sites to find things. This sled-runner fragment appears to have been in the ground for some time before it was picked. . . . During the time people dug, searching for old things, it was found by someone in the ground." Wassilie agreed: "He was right on the dot describing them. I'd say that they were pieces found by someone digging for artifacts."

The next week we looked briefly at a half dozen larger pieces of sled-runner sheathing made of caribou antler and whale bone from the Yukon, with holes for the wooden nails used to fasten them to the runners.[7] Jacobsen wrote that one could hardly drive a sled with unsheathed runners, as the snow would adhere to them, and that when driving in deep cold, one had to turn the sled over and moisten the runners with snow melted in the mouth to make them very smooth.

Putulirissuutet / **Hole Punchers**

Then we considered several Kuskokwim and Nushagak pieces that Jacobsen identified as spearheads, each with a stone tip, bone forepiece, and wooden handle.[8] Paul, however, suggested another use:

Though these appear to be hunting tools, I don't view them as such. I'd say they were used to *puturcuutnguluki* [make a hole through or drill it]. Before metal was introduced, these were used to make holes in things they were working on that needed them. These had stone points . . . and were used to make holes on skins and such.

Wassilie concluded, "They made little holes on the skins to hang them to dry. *Putulirissuutet* was what we called it."

Talutet / Shredders

Following was a box of *talutet* (shredders) (fig. 6.3, fig. 6.4), collected between Cape Vancouver and the mouth of the Kuskokwim, like those used to prepare grass.[9] They came mixed with Iñupiaq tools, and the elders accurately picked out the

Figure 6.3 Awls for making holes as well as for shredding animal muscle to make thread. IVA4794, IVA4796, IVA4799.

Figure 6.4 Paul described the design of a shredder handle, consisting of a pair of seals whose upper bodies lie together: "Back in those days, people decorated everything they made. These ivory parts were decorated with etched lines . . . going along until you come to kassugaliiret [circle-within-a-circle designs]. And at the top end, there's a carving of a tail." IVA4794.

Figure 6.5 We looked briefly at this linked handle from Cape Vancouver, carved like a moving fish tail from a single piece of ivory. Paul remarked: "Since our ancestors were innovative, this handle was beautifully crafted by someone for this talun [shredder]. It's decorated with these cet'raar [etched designs] and these ellanguat [circle-and-dot designs]. . . . This was obviously the handle of an apparatus used to shred bowhead, beluga, and caribou muscles into sinew thread." IVA4821.

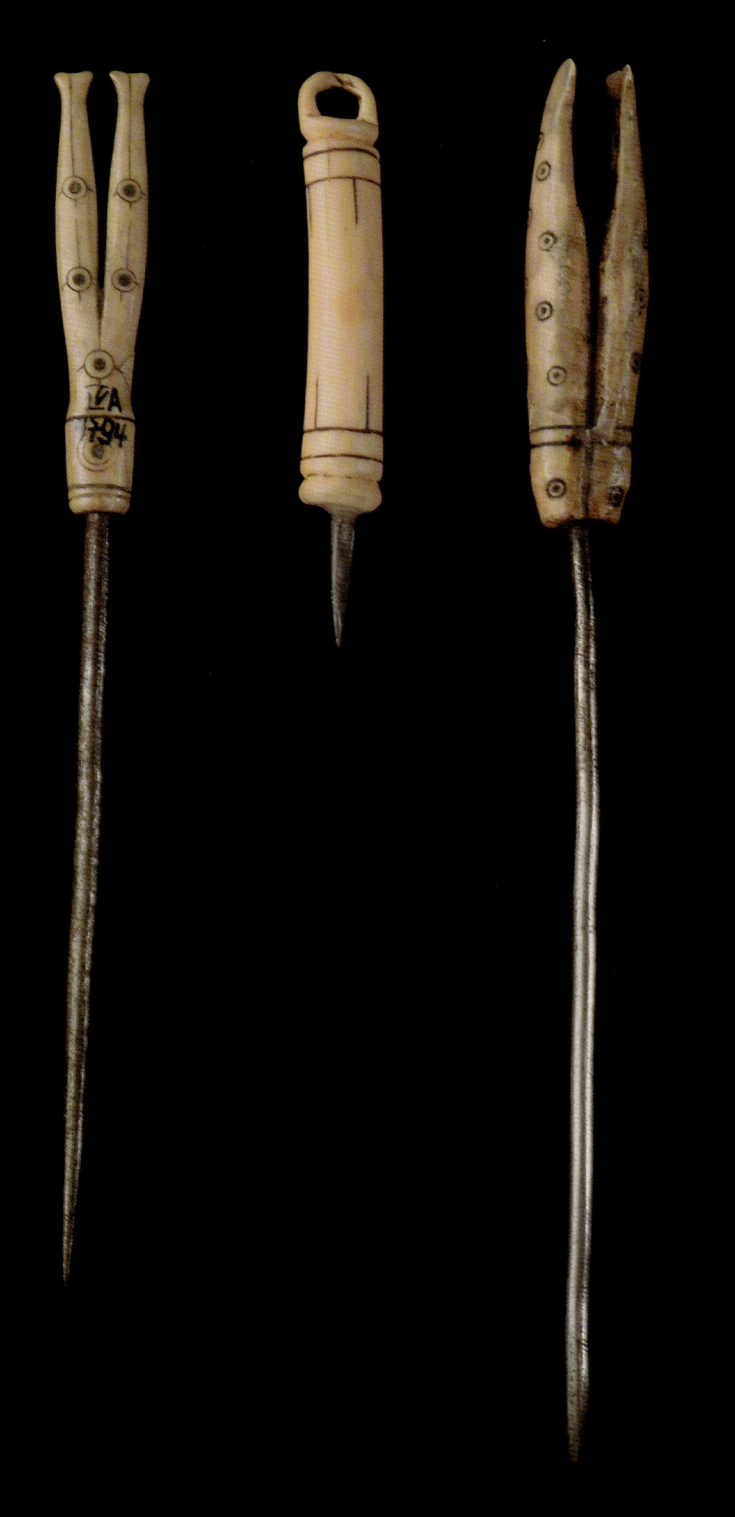
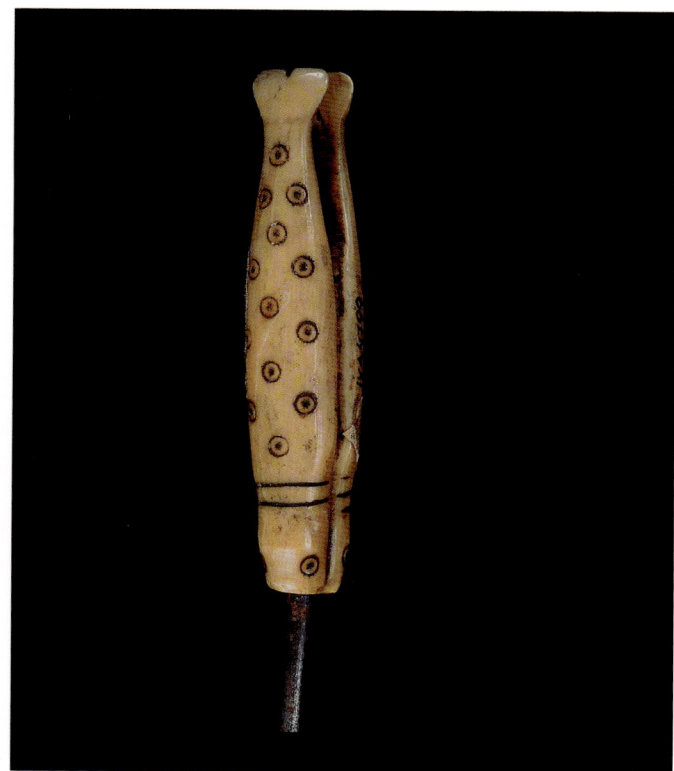

6.6 Wooden shredders with ivory teeth from the lower Yukon, which Jacobsen said were used to remove loose hair and debris from fur as well as to clean grass. IVA3729, IVA3759, IVA7261, IVA4193.

6.7 Wassilie and Paul discussing a caribou-antler prying tool. IVA2783.

ones from their area before I had time to do so using accession records. Jacobsen had identified them all as awls and borers that men used for woodworking and women for making dresses and boots, and he said that their metal points were often heated for better penetration. Wassilie recognized them as *kaputet* (drills) but deferred to Paul for a fuller explanation:

Since the sides are dull though the tip has been fixed into a sharp point, I'm thinking, . . . we've heard that they prepared thread from caribou *uliutet* [top layer of backbone muscles] or beluga and whale *uliutet*. I'd say it was used as a *talun* [shredder] for making thread from animal muscles. Some people called it *qunavun,* and some called it *talun*. And it was used to shred grass when they made *perriutet* [wiping sponges].

Later we examined the linked handle of an awl (fig. 6.5), along with fifteen comblike wooden shredders with ivory or bone teeth (fig. 6.6) from the lower Yukon.[10] Jacobsen noted that these were used to remove loose hair and debris from fur as well as to clean grass. Wassilie returned to an explanation of the single-toothed awls: "These are *talutet* . . . used to shred *yualut* [ligament, muscles]. . . . After the *uliutet* were dampened, these were used to split them into even strings." Catherine then related her experience learning to shred muscles

151 SIXTH DAY TOOLS FOR WORKING ON OBJECTS

6.8 Jacobsen commented that he found beaver-tooth engraving tools like these in almost every house he visited and that men took them along on trips. IVA3710, IVA5396, IVA3707, IVA3708.

for sinew. Her stepmother had given her *eglu* (underlayer of backbone muscles) to prepare. Wanting to play outside with the other children, she quickly split them into strands of different thicknesses with knots on the ends. When her stepmother saw what she had done, she scolded her, saying that if the strings were used in sewing, they would tend to break at the spot where they got thick.[11]

Everquun / **Prying Tool**

We looked at one more tool from Norton Sound (fig. 6.7),[12] about which Jacobsen recorded little but both Wassilie and Paul had something to say. Wassilie began:

This piece is made of caribou antler. It would be called an *everquun*, but it's quite small. . . . The *everquutet* were bigger in the tundra area. They were used to pry at fish.

My late parents always used this kind of *everquun* on bigger food items. In the winter, sometimes they would bring in a container of frozen blackfish and leave it near the drafty doorway. Then . . . they used this tool to pry out fish for our meal. . . . Perhaps it was also used in boat-making. When they covered the kayak frames, they would use it to pull the edge as they stitched it. My friend here has more views on these.

Paul continued:

He called the piece *everquun*, exactly the same word we use at home. This tool was also used in kayak and boat repair. When a hole was patched, it was used to pull from the edge of the skin before poking the needle through. And when they worked on kayaks and the old threads were going to be used again, they didn't cut them but used this kind of tool to pull out the old thread from the *kagaluq* [kayak stern] and the rest of the kayak. And it was used to pull out the binding on objects that had sewn parts.

It was also used to unravel the skin binding on snowshoes if the thread was going to be used again. The tools they called *everquutet* were used to unravel skin thread and bindings on things. There were many uses for this. That's all.

Iqukeggutet / **Beaver-tooth Engraving Tools**

We now turned to a group of wood chisels, each made from a beaver's incisor tooth set in a wooden handle (fig. 6.8, fig. 6.9).[13] Wassilie recognized them right away: "These were used as *iqukeggutet* [engraving tools]. This kind of tool was used in sled making, in snowshoe construction, and on other smaller objects. It was also used as an engraving tool to make designs on bowls and wooden objects."

Wassilie then picked up a single tooth[14] and, holding it firmly in one hand, used it as a whetstone to sharpen his pocket knife: "My father's brother sharpened his crooked knife on a

152 THE RETURN GIFT

6.9 Paul gripped a beaver-tooth tool in his right hand, blade down, and drew it toward his chest in a carving motion: "This tool called *iqukeggun* had many uses. . . . They used it when they hollowed out wood where the joints would be attached in making frames. This tool was used in all woodworking jobs, such as kayak-frame building, canoe building, boat building, snowshoe making, and sled making. These all have *paluqtaat keggutait* [beaver incisor teeth]."

beaver tooth like this. . . . He'd run his blade on the back side of the tooth. He'd first sharpen his *mellgar* or knife on a sharpening stone, then he would use a beaver's incisor tooth to hone its edge. The rough edge created by the stone would be smoothed out when you rubbed it against a beaver tooth. . . . They replaced the teeth with new ones when they wore out."

Ellin / Sharpening Stone

Next we turned to a group of whetstones used by both men and women. Holding one from Cape Vancouver, Paul opened his pocketknife to test its efficacy (fig. 6.10). Jacobsen called all the stones "Slinn," but Paul introduced a more complicated vocabulary, noting that people made whetstones out of different kinds of rocks (fig. 6.11).[15] One stone from the lower Yukon was an *uqu'urniq* (from *uquq*, "oil") and made the best kind of sharpening stone. Two more, also from the lower Yukon, were *teggalqupiaq* (real stone, from *teggalquq*, "stone"). A still larger hard black stone from the lower Yukon was used by women both to smooth leather and to sharpen their *uluat*, and it had its own name: "Though this is a sharpening stone, this side was used for something else. . . . This stone is called *arviiq*. They call the people of Platinum Arviirmiut because there is a lot of this stone there. These three stones all have different names."

Annie added what she knew: "It was a tool that belonged to women, and when we misplaced it we'd begin scolding people around us. This kind of stone sharpened *uluat* very well. I have an *arviiq* sharpening stone I got from Platinum. A person from Platinum once told me that there was an older and more weather-beaten kind of *arviiq*, which is even better than the one I owned." Wassilie also had something to say:

6.10 Paul sharpening his pocketknife on a whetstone from Cape Vancouver: "These are actually sharpening stones. At home they call it *ellin*. If I use this bigger one, I take it and apply saliva to the blade . . . before it is sharpened. If not, the blade will not become too sharp. You'd do this to sharpen the blade on one side, and you'd turn it and sharpen the other side. It was used to sharpen women's knives and regular carving knives." IVA4910.

6.11 Whetstones made from different rocks have different names. The two smallest stones are called *teggalqupiaq*, the large dark stone on the far right is called *arviiq*, and the light stone in the middle is an *uqu'urniq*. These names are descriptive of the rocks' properties—color, hardness, shape—and do not correspond one-on-one with Western scientific classifications such as quartz, slate, or agillite. Clockwise from the upper left: IVA4910, IVA4117, IVA3439, IVA3463. IVA3469.

"One time after my wife went to Togiak, she came back with a stone that resembled this. [Annie's] spouse . . . sent me a sharpening stone. I was quite happy about it, and I'm still keeping it at home. . . . It's a very good stone to sharpen blades."

Later, Paul added another use to which whetstones might be put. In times of sickness, it might be rubbed over a house or person's body to prevent disease from entering.

When they heard about a death, they would let their *angalkut* do what they called *qaniqussuaq* to make themselves stronger . . . so that the sickness would not be able to enter their home. . . .

When they heard that someone died, or if they heard that a number of people were sick in the village next to them, the older women [would say], "Grandchild, go out and rub the outside of our house [with a whetstone]!"

When he goes out, he will pretend to rub the side of the house, coming back in when he had gone around it completely. That was to prevent the sickness from coming into their house. . . . They pretended the sickness was going through the area they were living in.

Cetumquq, Tuluryaaq-llu / **Caribou Hoof, Canine Tooth, and Other Raw Materials**

Jacobsen had collected two animal body parts that past Yupiit had used as tools. The first was a scraper from the lower Yukon.[16] Paul recognized it as a caribou-hoof nail, called *cetumquq*, used as a *keligcuun* (scraper) for bird skins. "I wish I could use it to scrape loon or eider duck skins," he added, pretending to scrape and slurp the contents into his mouth. The second was another small antler prong from St. Michael that Paul said was used as an *everquun* (prying tool).[17] Paul also examined two teeth from the Kuskokwim, which hunters collected for use as ornaments on belts and other ceremonial regalia.[18] He identified one as a walrus tooth and the other as the *tuluryaaq* (canine tooth) of a large animal.

Other raw materials included two pieces of *ulukaq* (slate) from Fort Alexander,[19] like that used to make *umit* (stone points) or blades for *uluat* and adzes, and a piece of nephrite from Unalakleet.[20] Paul examined the nephrite, suggesting that it was like the bead the hunter offered the killer whales in the story told on the fourth day. Catherine remembered seeing similar stones on the beach at Up'nerkillermiut on Nelson Island: "Nowadays when I see diamond jewelry, I always remember the piece I saw once out on the ocean shore. . . . We tried to take it home, but it was very heavy. The one we saw looked exactly like this. It was magnificent. When the sunlight hit it, it truly looked like it was on fire. We mentioned it when we went home, but they didn't do anything about it."

Aivagun, Eqgucuun, Ekiarqin, wall' Qupurrun / **Wood Splitter or Wedge**

We moved on to a box containing eleven caribou-antler wedges (fig. 6.12) from the Yukon and one of petrified walrus ivory.[21] Paul began, again explaining both their names and use:

6.12 Describing this caribou-antler wedge, Wassilie said, "Personally, I can't do without wedges. I have assorted kinds at home. Some are very old. I always keep the one that was once owned by Aalikaar in a safe place. I showed it to his eldest son one time. Aalikaar gave me away when I got married to my first wife. His family always treated me like I was one of them." IVA4025.

Though these are different sizes, they're all one thing. But the name is different in each area. In my home this has two names—*aivagun* and *equgcuun*. I've heard other people call it *ekiarqin* . . . and in some areas *qupurrun*.

This was a tool they couldn't do without to craft wood into hunting tools. When wood was split into pieces for making fish traps and such, this was the tool they always used.

And when someone went out in a kayak, he'd always bring this tool along in case he ran into driftwood he could use for making things. He'd always be prepared to use this tool to split wood in the backcountry.

Paul then handed the microphone to his *iluraq*, and Wassilie replied, "He just talked about these exactly the way they were used. But he didn't say, 'I, too, have one like this at home.'" Paul said that he did have one like it, and everyone laughed.

Paul then asked to add a little, noting that since we had been looking at objects, we had not yet seen a tool made for a left-handed person. By looking at the shape of the point and how the handle was rounded, Paul thought that this tool was, indeed, used by a lefty.[22]

Kaugtuutaq / **Hammer**

Next we examined a huge wooden mallet (fig. 6.13) from the Yukon, with knots at both ends serving as head and handle. Wassilie began:

These are *aavangtak* [tree burls]. This is a heavy, hard larch burl.[23] It is finished as a *kaugtuutaq* [hammer or club, from *kaugtur-*, "to strike with an object"] and used by people to prepare *unarciat* [pieces of straight-grained wood] that are easy to split.... You'd use this to pound on an *ekiarqin* [wedge].

Wassilie then described how in the past, men in the *qasgi* would "argue over the moons," that is, disagree over the name of the month to come. The names were different in different areas, reflecting the different timing of tundra and coastal harvesting activities. Paul jumped into the act, and together they gave a vivid demonstration, arguing back and forth, Wassilie insisting that the new moon was *Tengmiirviguaq* (March, literally, "month when birds pretend to come") while Paul declared it *Tengevqapiar* (April, "month when birds come"). Wassilie concluded: "As the argument heightened, one of them would grab his little *kaugtuutaq* and throw it at the other man. They'd continue to argue, throwing the tool back and forth. Both men would insist on being right when there were no calenders to prove who was correct. That's how things were in the past when I was small."

Burls were not the only naturally occurring hammers. Later that morning, we examined three caribou-antler hammers from the Yukon, each head made of an antler root and a prong for the handle.[24] Each handle had a hole for a loop so it could be hung in the house or on a boat or sled during trips. Jacobsen noted that these hammers were used in the construction of skin boats and to pound nails made of seal teeth, bone, and antler. Everyone took them in hand and hammered imaginary nails into the table. Wassilie briefly described what he remembered: "Perhaps they are all *kaugtuutat*.... I've seen sleds made with this in the past. A piece of *teggera'ar* [hardwood, from *tegge-*, "to be hard or firm"] was first cut, and then you would pound it in like you were crushing it... to secure it. These were used like that in those days."

Calugcissuutet, Urumerutet, Ellumerrutet-llu / **Skin Scrapers**

After lunch we said goodbye to Father René Astruc, a French Jesuit priest who had retired to France after forty years' work in Alaska and had joined us for the weekend. Returning to our sunny workroom, we found an overwhelming number of slate-bladed wooden scrapers spread across the tables, two dozen from the lower Yukon labeled "Kjalugotit" or *calugcissuutet* and ten more from the Kuskokwim and Nushagak regions labeled "Plomeron" (*ellumerrun*) (fig. 6.14, fig. 6.15).[25] Most had stone blades fastened to handles with leather thongs, although the blade of one Yukon scraper was horn.[26] Handles on the Nushagak scrapers were generally longer.[27] Jacobsen wrote that women used such scrapers to prepare all kinds of skins. The pelt was placed between the knees and the scraper held in the hand and scraped along the raw side until all fat was removed. The pelt was often sprinkled with finely ground stone to provide a better grip, and the blade (which wore out and had to be changed often) was fastened with either a sealskin thong or roots.

Undaunted, Andy and Marie lined the scrapers up across the table, and our experts set to work. Annie spoke first:

I do know these are *ellumerrutet,* but they are very old. At first I thought the binding was made of twine you buy in the stores, but I see that it's split leather.... The tools they depended on are quite dull now, but our ancestors were self-reliant. The one who watched over them guided them, allowing them to survive. It seems like these blades couldn't sever anything.

These were used as scrapers when they tanned skins for sewing.... When George Kuku from Quinhagak gave me a tool like this, I was very grateful. I still have it at home. When I was getting ready to leave, I told my family not to let anyone borrow it while I was gone.

Although Catherine had never seen stone-bladed scrapers, like Annie she had metal-bladed ones at home for use on all kinds of land-animal skins except rabbit. Paul spoke briefly about the tanning process:

Back when they worked on caribou skin for parkas, they'd use the tool to press and scrape the skin, and as they did this, you'd hear a crackling sound. This process was called *ayimlluku* [rendering it

6.13a *Paul/Wassilie demonstrating how to split wood using a caribou-antler wedge and wooden mallet. IVA4263, IVA4025.*

6.14 The Yukon scraper on the far left has a horn blade, while the others are schist. The Nushagak scraper on the far right has a long, oarlike handle, a specialty of that area. From right to left: IVA3399, IVA5444, IVA5442, IVA5443.

6.15 Wassilie demonstrating the use of a skin scraper. IVA5442.

pliant, from *ayimte-*, "to break or sever"]. They would say that they had made a parka out of *ayimtat* [skins that had been rendered pliant]. And when someone wore the parka, the skin would be easy to bend in the area where it had been rendered pliant. . . .

Since my wife is always sewing, . . . she always uses her tool like this on skins. Back home we have two names for the tool: *urumerun* and *calugcissuun*.

Catherine described rubbing sourdough on skins to help "break" them before using a scraper to tan the hide. She also remembered the crackling sound the scraper made: "It was fun to hear. . . . As we worked on the skin, it instantly got soft."

Because skins were tanned by men as well as women, Paul spoke from personal experience: "If the skin wasn't smooth, they'd press and push with this tool to stretch the skin and smooth out the edges." Wassilie also remembered the tanning process:

When men in the *qasgi* got ready to tan skin . . . first they'd dampen the skin and fold it and put it away. And when it was ready, they'd use a scraper like this and begin scraping off the excess membrane. These bigger scrapers were used on caribou skins for parkas.

Most of the time I saw men scraping bigger animal skins.

A scraper with this kind of blade was used to render the skin pliable. Afterward it was rubbed with oil and then you'd use your hands to work on the skin to soften it, . . . stretching the skin to make it bigger. I used to watch people working on skins like that for parkas. . . .

They'd use scrapers to tan skin, like wolverines, which were used as tassels on parkas and boots. Wolf skin can also be tanned and scraped. But wolf skin that was going to be used for parka ruffs wasn't softened too much.

One last skin scraper from Fort Alexander had a long iron blade and wide wooden handle meant to be held in both hands.[28] Everyone recognized it as an implement for stretching and scraping skins. Annie spoke first: "I, too, had a *tuluruaq* [from *tuluq*, "ivory," literally, "likeness of ivory"], which I cherished." Catherine knew the tool by another name: "I used to see curved wooden pieces like this, and they called them *assipek*. One time someone gave me an inflated hair seal. I tried to stretch and scrape it, but since I didn't have an *assipek*, the skin kept tearing. It seems like skins are not easy to tan and stretch these days, perhaps because urine isn't used for tanning." Paul also recognized the tool, noting that his wife had two such tools, one bigger than the other. Catherine concluded our discussion of skin-scraping in the past with a revealing comment about its future.

I prepare skins to make boots for my grandchildren, but my sons don't wear boots anymore. One day I turned to my eldest son and said, "You poor ones, you quickly marry someone instead of looking for a person who can sew. I can't make boots for all of my grandchildren because there are too many. When I'm gone, I wonder what is going to happen to you all?" Then my son responded by saying something that I didn't expect to hear from him. He said, "White people do make shoes and boots."

Uluat, Caviggaat-llu / Women's and Men's Knives

After the scrapers, we looked at an abundance of slate-bladed *uluat*, or women's knives, used to skin animals and cut fish (fig. 6.16).[29] The curved knives were of different sizes, and each had a wooden handle into which an arc-shaped blade was either wedged or attached with roots drawn around the handle through a hole in the blade. Taking a large *uluaq* in her hands and pretending to cut fish, Annie began:

These *uluat* were not made in recent times. How impressive these are. I'd say this one was used on king salmon. . . . They used to work with these, even though they are merely stones. . . .

I wonder how they placed these wooden handles so securely so they wouldn't come off. These little ones were used for making boot soles and cutting out patterns. The bigger ones were used on bigger tasks.

Catherine then spoke about the *uluat* she used, reinforcing what Annie had said: "These were not in use when I was little. But . . . I'd say a big one was used on king salmon. I use my big *uluaq* when I work on seals and my smaller *uluaq* on smaller animals. The smallest kinds I use to cut out patterns." She then told of her experience the year before, when she had unsuccessfully tried sewing a boot sole. Then she heard the voice of her late son in her head, advising her to use the *uluaq* he had made for her. She did so, and this time the sewing went smoothly.

Paul was the last to speak, explaining how men as well as women used these tools:

Uluat are considered women's tools, but some men use them when they work on seals. As I view these *uluat*, I think I'd like this one here, which isn't too curved at the bottom, . . . to remove the oil from seals and for butchering meat.

When I go out to the ocean hunting seal, I usually bring a woman's knife besides my own. I find when I use these *uluat*, I work faster on seals. Then when I went moose hunting, I took that *uluaq*, thinking it would work well for land animals. I discovered that *uluat* did not work well on land animals. It took a long time to cut up a land animal with an *uluaq*.

I'm not praising myself, but many times I've used a woman's knife when I cook since I always try to help my spouse.

At the end of the day, we would see three metal-bladed *uluat* with beautifully decorated ivory handles, but these "modern" tools drew no comment.[30]

6.16 Hafted semilunar uluat (women's knives) in a variety of sizes, one with a hole in the handle for a firmer grip. IVA4687, IVA5283, IVA6275.

6.17 Slate-bladed knife from Cape Vancouver used for skinning seals. IVA4680.

6.18 Two cutting knives, each with a slate blade lashed to a wooden handle with willow-root binding. IVA3514, IVA3505.

Now we looked at a single small, slate-bladed *qapiarcuun* (seal-skinning knife) (fig. 6.17).³¹ Annie began:

It's so good to see this little seal-skinning blade . . . looking so nice. Once my mother had my younger sister and me skin seals for seal pokes. I skinned a young hair seal, and my younger sister worked on a nicer-looking seal. . . . Then my younger sister said, "I wonder what it is that I keep hitting with my blade in there?" I looked and saw her blade going in and out through the skin. . . .

Then when the skin came off, she sewed the holes tight enough that it didn't leak air when it was inflated. She kept rubbing something that looked like blood. She left it out to dry and watched it very carefully. Some seal pokes tend to leak air once inflated. But if it had been cleaned properly, it never leaked. They usually put more air in them periodically. . . . Once we moved closer to the ocean, we began working on seals like that. I didn't know how to work on seals, but I learned by watching others when we moved down to the coast.

I haven't skinned a seal for a poke like this for many years. But I've been removing the skin with the blubber on, by first slitting the skin on the abdomen and then carefully removing all the blubber from the skin. And since sealskin is easier to work on when it's cleaned right away, I would wash it before I nailed it to a board, stretching it at the same time for drying.

Although Catherine had grown up on the coast, her adoptive mother had not let her, a poor orphan, learn on her valued skins. As a much-loved only child, Paul had received instruction in *qapiaryaraq*, the process of skinning a seal starting from the head and pulling the skin back over the body rather than splitting the skin:

I've skinned seals the way these two have mentioned. There was a proper way to begin working on an *useqnaar* [two-year-old spotted seal] or *nayiq* [adult hair seal]. I was taught that you'd begin by slitting at the corner of the mouth, then start skinning it going around, working toward the ears and not missing them. That was the traditional way to begin skinning a seal. After skinning, when you get

158 THE RETURN GIFT

6.19 Paul holding a caviggaq (cutting knife) and demonstrating how to scrape fat from a skin.

this far, you take a tool like this [qapiarcuun] and begin skinning from the inside, always securing and pulling from [the side]. When you do that, you will not make accidental holes on the skin.

We examined four men's knives from the lower Yukon (fig. 6.18).[32] Paul took up one *caviggaq* (cutting knife) and showed us how it was held to scrape the tasty fat from a skin (fig. 6.19) or to prepare a skin for drying:

There are many uses for this kind of implement. Back in those days, they dried animal skins. . . . They'd use these to make holes evenly all around the edge of the sealskin, and then pegs were attached to these holes. . . . Then the skin is stretched as the pegs are secured in the ground. The skin is slightly elevated from the ground.

These were also used to make holes to secure the skin to a skinboat frame. They'd pull the skin over the top of the frame, then they would string a thong through the hole and tie it to the wood piece that was built into the inside of the frame for that purpose. Our ancestors' way of life . . . was amazing and difficult. . . .

You can see that . . . this *uluaq* was owned by a person called *qel'ketalria* [one who treasures and takes good care of possessions so they last for a long time]. . . .

These were also used to kill enemies when people waged war.[33] If two people were going after the same enemy, one would hide the knife under his armpit, and the other might hide it inside his boot or under his belt. The two who were pursuing an enemy *nukalpiaq* would carefully plan ahead. . . . As they approached the enemy, they would wait in ambush as planned. They didn't need to use words because they knew exactly what the other was going to do.

We briefly considered a sharp-pointed knife from the Yukon used to bleed a person.[34] Paul said simply, "This is a little *kaputaq* [poker, from *kape-*, "to pierce or poke in"]. . . . They used them on painful parts of the body . . . and also to open up boils." We also looked at five caribou-antler handles for *mellgaraat* (crooked knives) from the Yukon,[35] one of which (fig. 6.20) had a blade cover called a *kegginailitaq*.

Wassilie immediately recognized one last plain bone knife from the Kuskokwim, with roots wound round its handle for

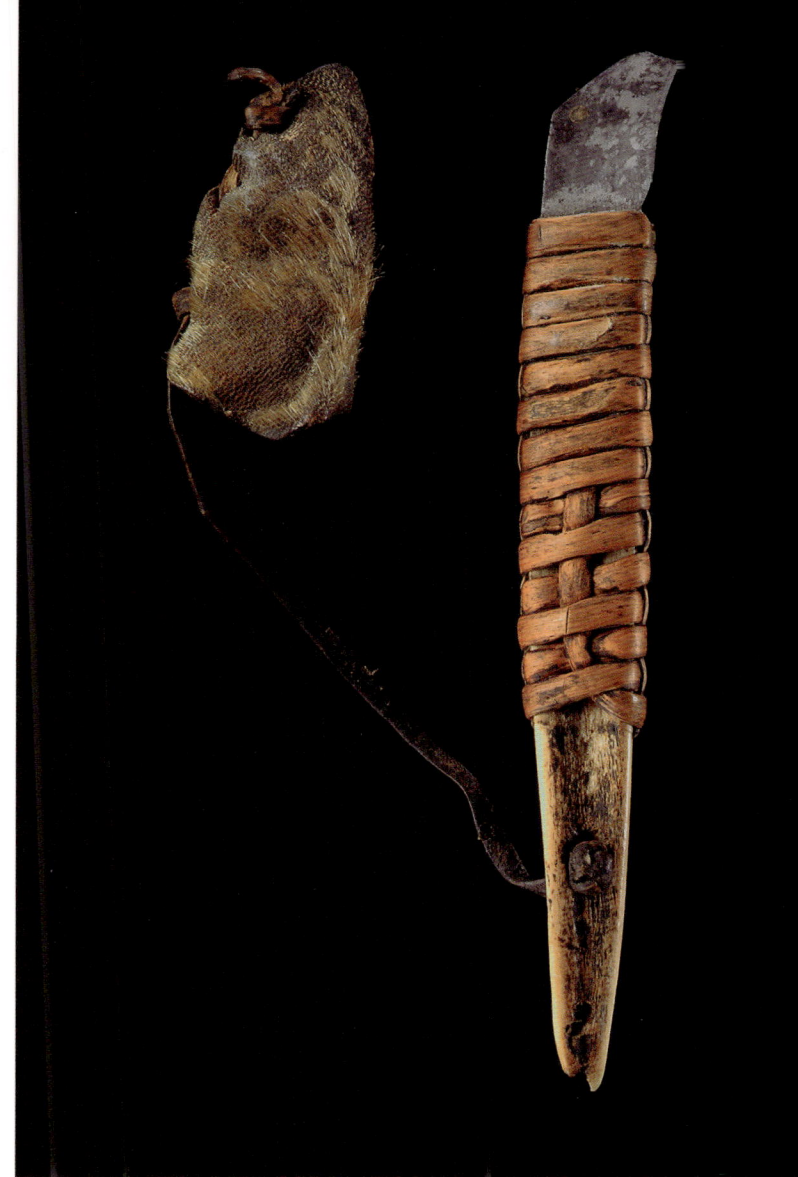

6.20 Mellgar (crooked knife) from the Yukon, complete with blade cover. Jacobsen reiterated that the blades of mellgar—formerly of stone, now iron—were evidence of the recent advance from Stone Age to Iron Age: "With the Eskimo, where the Stone Age was still present, the iron knife is still half in the shaft just like the stone knives were fastened." IVA4158.

a better grip.[36] He took it in his right hand and demonstrated its use (fig. 6.21): "This is a *keliutaq* [scraper, from *kelig-*, "to scrape"]. It was used on loons and common scoters. You'd place a fresh loon skin with the feathers inside on a cutting board and scrape it like this. After scraping like this, you'd pop the juice and oil into your mouth like this and slurp it up. People sure enjoyed bird-skin juice and oil. We'd also use it as oil when we ate dried meat and fish." Everyone laughed as Wassilie finished his imaginary meal.

Kakinqun / **Woodworking Tool**

We now turned to a lance-shaped knife (fig. 6.22) from the Yukon, with raven's-foot designs on its caribou-antler handle. Jacobsen wrote that this and similar tools were used to loosen

6.21 Wassilie gripping a scraper and describing its use to scrape the tasty juice and oil from fresh loon skins. IVA5016.

6.22 Kakinqun (woodworking tool) used to loosen and split birch bark and wood. IVA4004a, b.

6.23 Describing these woodworking tools, Paul stated: "These pieces were used for piercing and drilling . . . wooden objects they were working on. . . . You know, wooden objects usually have designs sketched on them. And some bowls have slits all the way around the edge. This was used for sketching designs on things, and the other end was used as a drill to pierce holes and such." IVA3017, IVA5349, IVA4179.

and split birch bark for making a variety of utensils.[37] Wassilie recognized it:

In the earliest times when metal was scarce, a tiny piece of metal might be protruding out of your pinched thumb and index fingers. . . . This *kakinqun* [woodworking tool, from *kakite-*, "to prick or pierce"] was used for . . . splitting *unarciaq* [straight-grained wood] . . . into *cigyiit* [split strips of spruce wood], and this was used to smooth out the edges.

This piece has a blade like a *mellgar* [crooked knife]. . . . My goodness! People back in those days were incredibly hard-working and persevering. They created tools that worked quite well for their tasks.

Wassilie then elaborated on the kinds of wood such tools were used to work:

We've seen wood with the top part quite curved and the bottom part described as an *unarciaq* . . . with no branches anymore. That kind is called *tegg'eraq* [hardwood]. A person would cut a long part of the tree and take it home, hoping to make a bow out of it. Some of that wood was used for making sleds. They are spruce trees . . . and are called *unarciat*. *Unarciat* were also made into bowls. The *allungak* [bottom] part of the bowl was made from *mimernat* [tree stumps]. Strips of wood were also cut to use as strapping on the trap. The very strong, thin strip was called *nemiarun*.

People made things using the bottom part of spruce trees. If this was a tree, I'd cut it at the base, *qamiqunaq*. This part was used to make bentwood bowls and buckets.

160 THE RETURN GIFT

Another horn-handled *kakinqun* with a tiny metal blade from the Yukon caught their eyes.[38] Paul said, "Since we are living with metal all around us, we both think that piece of metal is small. However, back in that time, a tiny piece of metal like that produced implements that helped people to acquire the food they needed to survive." Holding the knife in front of his face, Wassilie added, "Men also used it to clean bones when they ate." Paul teased, "I have no 'bone-cleaning' implement, and you have one. And after you clean your bone with your tool, you'll turn to me and say, 'I've won.'" Everyone laughed.

Paul was unfamiliar with the next piece, from Fort Alexander,[39] which Jacobsen said was used to press feather quills into arrows, but Wassilie recognized it: "I'd say that this little bone piece was used for making arrows. It's a little *kakinqun*." Jacobsen had described a similar "Kakkineron" (fig. 6.23) from Fort Alexander, also used to make impressions in the arrow's end where the feathers could be placed.[40] This time Paul recognized it immediately as a *kakinqun* and described additional uses, including incising designs and piercing holes.

Stone Blades in Abundance

Viewing the stone-bladed tools stood us in good stead when Herr Wedell brought out six heavy boxes, each filled with dozens of stone blades (fig. 6.24). Providing an eloquent overview, Paul said simply: "All of these were called *caviggaq* [man's knife], *uluaq* [woman's knife], and *nuussiq* [cutting knife]. . . . Blades like this were used in carving caribou, walrus, and bearded seals. They worked very well for them in those days. Viewing the tools our ancestors used, I can't stop thinking what incredible people they were." Wassilie added, "These were shaped by using other stones. How amazing people were who lived in those days. This is the first time some of us are seeing pieces like these." Paul concluded: "These things in the box are all different. Some are blades of *urumerutet* [skin scrapers]. And some are blades of *cikuliurutet* [ice chisels]. And some are *keputet* [adze blades]. Some are broken. . . . They resemble the ones we have already looked at."[41]

An ax blade from Cape Vancouver attracted Paul's particular attention[42]: "Someone shaped this stone into a very fine chisel used for chopping through ice as they continued to harvest food in the winter. A tool like this was traditionally called *cikuliurun* by some and *tugeq* by some. . . . It's easy to see that these pickaxes were used where walrus tusks weren't available and blades were made out of stone."

Two more boxes held *caviggaq, mellgar,* and *uluaq* blades.[43] Jacobsen noted that the blades were originally fastened to wooden shafts and used for woodwork like the knives we had just examined. They had lain undisturbed so long in their box that when Wassilie lifted them out, each left a white shadow on the exposed surface. A fifth box included many broken blades, and on several one could see where their "cheeks" had been struck off to convert them into scrapers "in modern times"—that is, after the introduction of iron.[44] We went through this box at record speed, as its contents resembled things we had already seen. Paul looked bemused as he watched me busily writing down numbers, struggling to keep up. He joked that when he first met me, I was a *nasaurluq* (young girl), but now I was getting to be an old woman.

Our next box was no lighter, containing 101 slate blades, 83 of which Jacobsen described as "fish and skin knives" from the Yukon, some new and others broken and crudely finished.[45] Most were old stone knives made into scrapers and schist and greenstone *uluat* for cutting fish and skins. None had handles, although some had holes where a handle was originally attached. Jacobsen noted that fish scales could still be seen on one *uluaq* blade(fig. 6.25), and that another was made to be used by a young girl to practice cutting up fish and doll clothing.[46] Jacobsen wrote that stone fish knives were still in use because of the

6.24 Boxes filled with stone blades in a variety of sizes and shapes.

6.25 Fish scales can still be seen on this uluaq blade, showing that it was bought while still in use. IVA3479.

6.26 Impressed by this large slate knife blade, Wassilie said: "The piece of thong on its handle was used to tie it to a man's belt, then the knife was inserted under the belt. Men always wore belts in those days, and they kept their knives under their belts when they hunted. The knife is used to butcher big game like caribou. It's a big double-edged knife." IVA4320.

belief that if an iron knife were used, the animals would leave the coast.

Catherine and Annie bent over the box. Taking a large stone blade in her hand, Annie spoke with feeling: "We women always have these by our side in our work. . . . Women back in those days used these nice *uluat* . . . to cut fish and meat for drying . . . and for skinning seals. These smaller ones were used to cut up patterns in sewing and such. How fascinating these are to look at . . . because of the fine workmanship."

Wassilie was especially intrigued by a large slate knife blade (fig. 6.26) strung on a leather thong: "This object was used mostly by men for butchering big animals." Turning the conversation from practical use to historical significance, Paul noted simply, "This knife, evidently, was the double-bladed knife mentioned in a story." Standing, holding the blade in one hand and the microphone in the other, Annie (fig. 6.27) took up Paul's challenge, telling a story similar to that evoked by the *nuiret* (see Day 3), in which a jealous husband kills his faithless wife:

I heard about this knife when the late Apurin told a story . . . about a married couple who resided on the outskirts of a village. The couple had a small son.

I'll tell the story now as I've heard it. I don't like to waste your time, and that's why I don't talk for very long.

The husband had an *ayaruq* [walking stick] he always used when he hunted. A huge double-edged blade was attached to the end of his *ayaruq*. When he was returning to the village from his hunt, the tip of his staff would glisten in the sunlight. The sight would be quite intimidating and scary. Whenever he hunted caribou, he always took his staff with him.

One day when he was out hunting in the morning, a *nukalpiaq* came into the couple's house. The young *nukalpiaq* was so handsome that it was difficult to look away from him.

I want to know this. Who are these people you can't take your eyes off when you look at them?

Paul interjected, "Those who have beautiful faces," to which Catherine smiled and added, "Cute like you." Everyone laughed, and Annie continued:

When the handsome young man came in, he told her that he just happened to run across the house as he was passing by and decided to come in. The woman welcomed him and offered him some food, but he declined. The woman thought her visitor was very handsome and liked him.

6.27 Annie holding a slate knife as she told the story of a jealous husband who killed his unfaithful wife.

When her husband left, the woman had filled his bowl with food, getting it ready for his arrival. Back in those days, women took good care of their spouses. . . .

When the young man asked the woman about how long her husband usually stayed out, she said, "He'll come home just when night is falling. He usually stays out late trying to catch something to bring home." The young man stayed with her. Then, just when it got dark, she heard her husband arriving outside. When he came in, she handed him his bowl filled with food. Her husband noticed that his wife was acting a little strange and couldn't sit still. He said, "What's wrong? You seem to be preoccupied with something." Some people are quite perceptive about things. She told him that she was just fine. Their little son was sleeping on the bedding on the side.

When her husband started to eat and wasn't paying attention anymore, she touched her son gently and woke him up. She picked him up and pulled out her breast to feed him, and every time he started to suckle, she'd pinch him on the buttocks to make him cry. Every time he started to cry, she would try to let him feed again. Then her husband said, "It seems like he's in pain. Did he injure himself somehow?" His wife responded by saying, "I don't know why he keeps crying like he's in pain. I should take him outside while you are eating, for he might disturb your meal." While men ate, their spouses always tried to create a quiet atmosphere for them. She took their son outside. While her husband continued to eat inside, he'd hear the child crying every so often out there.

As soon as they went out, the woman left the child standing on the path and quickly ran down to the river. As she ran down, she could hear sounds coming from the river. The young man had her sit back-to-back with him in his kayak and paddled downriver. While the husband ate, he would hear the child cry after being quiet for a moment. When he finished his food, he went outside to check what was going on. He found the child standing looking down toward the river where his father usually landed his kayak when he returned from hunting. He asked him and said, "Where is your mother?" As soon as he asked, the child pointed to the river. And every time he repeated the question, he would point in the same direction. He took him, and they both went down to check the shore but didn't see anything. They went back up and into the house.

The days following her departure, her husband became distressed. The young man took the woman to another village and married her. She became pregnant and delivered a boy. The young man and the woman raised the child. Then later on the woman began to worry about her other husband and the child they had had together. She began to wish to see her first husband out in the wilderness, but her new family didn't allow her to wander off by herself because they cherished her. Evidently, her second husband always told his family not to let her go out by herself.

The man who had a staff with a double-edged blade on its point was a very fast runner.

Then one day she said, "Oh my! I wish I could go out and fetch food for our evening meal." She left the village, packing her child on her back. She left and kept going until she came to a big hill. She climbed to the top, sat down and began to scan the horizon. As she looked, she noticed something moving in the east. It looked like a bird, but as she looked closer, she realized that it was a person. As the person moved, something glistened as the sunlight hit it. When the person got closer, she recognized him by the staff he was holding. Then she stood up holding her baby so he could see them there. Just beyond where she was standing was a small pile of bluish rocks.

While she stood, he started coming toward them. His staff had a double-edged blade attached to it. When he came closer, she recognized him. As he approached, he obviously had thoughts running through his mind about what she had done. His wife smiled at him, but he didn't smile back. Instead he stopped and sat down a few yards away. He said, "How did you wander off so far from home?" Then she replied, "It wasn't I who wandered off; a man abducted me." He said, "So, is he the father of that child you are holding?" She said that she had gotten pregnant by the man and had had his child.

Then he started to ask her questions. "When you left, you must have gone willingly." She said, "I didn't want to leave, but he forced me to go down and took me away in his kayak." Then her husband bolted toward her and said, "If you didn't want to go, you would have screamed." He grabbed the child by the legs and threw it against the rocks . . . and it immediately died. When he started to reach for her, she cried, "I love you. I love you. I like you." Then he grabbed his wife by her braided hair and pulled her violently. He yanked her along, and as he dragged her body on the ground, he slashed her abdomen open and severed her head with the double-edged blade of his staff. He killed his wife.

I must have fallen asleep when the story reached that point.

We needed to rest as well and closed for the day, reflecting on how powerful these tools had been in their ancestors' hands.

SEVENTH DAY Tools of Daily Life

Tupigat / **Grass Mats**

The next morning we turned our attention from stone blades and tools to some of the objects of everyday life that they had been used to produce. Three large sleeping mats from the Yukon were spread before us when we approached our work tables (fig. 7.1, fig. 7.2).[1] Catherine began, introducing us to the terminology of grass:

This is a *tupigaq* [twined thing, grass mat, from *tupig-*, "to weave or to twine"]. Grass wasn't cut and then twined immediately. When grass was cut, they spread it out to dry and kept it from getting wet. As soon as the grass turned pale, they stored it in the storage shed. They did this with all the grass that was picked. When they gathered *kelugkat* [coarse grass for twining mats], they tried to get the tall ones and not their *angucaluit* [male counterparts, from *angun*, "man"]. The grass used to twine this mat is not *kelugkat* but *iitaq* [tall cotton grass].

The mats were put on the bottom of fish-holding bins, and they were also used to cover the fish in the bins.

Examining the mats, Annie noted that one was made by a left-handed person, while another was made by someone who was right-handed.[2] Catherine said that *nasqiriluteng* (from *nasquq*, "head") was the word they used when they were about to begin twining mats. Paul added what he knew:

Although I'm a man, since people used a lot of twined grass items when I was little, I'd say this twined thing we're looking at is a mat for bedding. This side of the mat is frayed, since it was always on the outer side of the bed. The side that was always on the back of the bed is not frayed. . . . Twined grass mats all begin with the same basic pattern. But since this is a sleeping mat, it is finely twined with smaller mesh they called *mallegtat*.

Paul said that the third mat, with fringes on both ends, resembled the *ikaraliitet* (kayak mats) he used when he was young.[3] Wassilie noted that kayak mats may have been different along the coast, but the mats he had used were not like these, and he thought these were sleeping mats. In the end, the sleeping mat elicited from Paul a good description of that which it was not:

My kayak mats were twined finely with smaller mesh. And the sides weren't frayed like this. My kayak mat wasn't too wide. The kayaks used down on the coast were deeper than the inland kayaks. The kayak mats were twined tightly, and the ends and sides were twined securely so grass wouldn't come off easily. When mats were placed in kayaks, they were laid out like this [fig. 7.3]. This mat might fit in the bottom of the kayak, but it's quite long for a conventional-size kayak. . . .

They harvested a lot of grass. Since it was the women's responsibility, they were told to harvest grass before it became too cold in the fall and the grass was covered with snow. They were told to get the grass before *Ellam Yua* [the Person of the Universe] covered the ground with its huge hands. In the fall, the elders would say to the women, "You young girls go out and begin harvesting some grass. Gather some *taperrnat* [coarse seashore grass] and *kelugkat* before *Ellam Yua* covers them with its huge hands. . . ."

Caranglluk [debris, dust, grass] was used by poor dear old human beings, as they say. That was why they were told to gather the grass before *Ellam Yua* covered it with its huge hands.

Paul also explained how grass was used to line walls during *qasgi* construction:

Before the sod was put on the roof, the women were asked to make grass mats to place between the roof planks and the sod covering. After the *qaniit* [wooden roofing planks] were placed on the frame, the prepared grasses called *qerqulluut* or *eviutet* [from *evek*, "grass"] were placed [over the wood] before the sod was put on the *qasgi* frame. . . .

Grass was also used as a *kangciraq* [tarpaulin]. Loosely twined grass was used as a lining on the inside walls of the houses. Little wooden pegs tacked the *kangciraq* on the wall, keeping it from falling.

Speaking of the many uses of grass reminded Paul of the tale of Apanuugpak's companion, who escaped detection by hiding in an old pit near the village and covering himself with

7.1 Large grass mat from the Yukon. Jacobsen wrote that all had been twined by women for use in houses as sleeping mats and often taken on journeys: "The sod house has sleeping places on three walls separated by a beam from the rest of the floor. The bedding consists mostly of reindeer skins. On the earth floor the mat or hay is placed as padding. During the day it is rolled up and serves as a seat for people." IVA4266.

7.2 The carefully finished edge of a tupigaq (grass mat). IVA4266.

grass. Wassilie also had a personal memory, which he recounted with feeling. When Wassilie was young, he once attended a memorial giveaway in Nunapitchuk, where the sister of the deceased had made many kayak mats to give to young boys in memory of her younger brother: "Sitting in the *qasgi*, I was not expecting to be included as a recipient of such a gift. . . . The couple was down in the middle arranging the gifts for dis-

a grass. It also did not enjoy the time when it was a willow tree. It mentioned that it was exhausting to be pressed down by a layer of snow all winter long.

Kenurrat, Kumarutet-llu / Lamps and Lamp Wicks

After a short break, we looked at an unassuming lump of dried moss torn into strips to be used as lamp wicks on the lower Yukon.[4] Wassilie began: "When people used the original clay lamps, these *kumarutet* were dried and always kept handy. They'd take one strand and use it as a lamp wick until it all burns." Annie also remembered *kumarutet*: "When I was a

7.3 Wassilie demonstrating how a grass mat would be folded when placed inside a kayak.

7.4 Kenurrak (clay lamps) from the Yukon, one holding moss, which served as a wick. The lamps are decorated with lines and pressed-in ring ornaments, and Jacobsen wrote that as many as twenty lamps would be used in the qasgi on meter-high posts to provide light during dance festivals. IVA4474, IVA4478.

tribution. Then after whispering to each other, the wife said, 'Is Uqsungiar here?' I was very surprised! I went down to receive the kayak mat. When she gave it to me, she said, 'I'm giving you this as a gift since you always helped my late brother.'"

Paul closed with a brief reference to grass in oral tradition, recalling the story of the discontented grass plant that Edward Nelson (1899, 505–10) recorded one hundred years before:

During the time of *qulirat* [legends], a human form was developing, going from one form to another, having different guises. As a prelude to developing into a human form, it tried all the plants on earth as guises. When it was a grass, it was not satisfied because too many people harvested it in the autumn. It did not enjoy being

little girl, I would see lighted lamps when I went to some homes. People used oil lamps. In the *qasgi*, too, I'd see lamps all around the room."

Catherine continued with feeling: "It's so nice to see this one. In the fall, people gathered *kumarutet* in bunches. After they were picked, they'd dry them outside in the sun." She then spoke at length about the processing of *urut*, another tundra moss (*Sphagnam* sp.), which was mixed with seal oil, allowed to age, then mixed with blackberries to make a kind of *akutaq* known as *puya*. Paul remarked that *kumarun* grew on dry ground, while *urut* grew in wet areas.

Wassilie added that *urut* were used not only to make *akutaq*:

166   THE RETURN GIFT

"When a container developed a hole, they'd use rancid [urut] plants to repair the hole to seal it." Paul then described using a rancid mixture of moss and seal oil to caulk dried boat-cover seams:

They didn't mention another use of puya. When something is left unused, it usually dries and cracks. The stitches on kayak-skin covers usually loosen from being out in the elements. When stitches became loose, they applied puya to them to waterproof the seams. They would chew puya and use it as caulking on the seams of the kayak bottom. Moss left in seal oil would become rancid. A rancid moss mixture like that was called puya. They also used the aged mixture to make akutaq they called puya. Seal oil normally doesn't get rancid right away. Urut was left out soaked in seal oil to age.

Later that afternoon, we examined a group of clay kenurrat (lamps) from the middle Yukon (fig. 7.4) and one from Nushagak like those Wassilie had mentioned.[5] Wassilie added what he remembered:

The bigger and wider lamps were used in the qasgi. The wooden burl at the upper end of the nanilraq [lamp stand] was slightly hollowed out to hold the lamp. The lamp stands were put near opposite walls of the qasgi . . . with another nanilraq against the back wall. Lamps with a large capacity for oil looked like these. They had kumarutet [wicks] like the ones we saw earlier.

Women placed these little lamps in front of them when they sewed . . . in the evening. A nepiaq [family dwelling] also had a nanilraq against the back wall for bigger lamps with a large capacity for oil. I used to see our clay lamp that looked like this. When our lantern ran out of gasoline, we used our lamp, which was equipped with everything, including a nanilraq. I have been anticipating seeing the things our ancestors used, some of which I have seen in my time, too, and now I'm seeing them.

Catherine vividly recalled the first time she experienced the light of a kerosene lamp, which her grandfather had received as a gift during a Messenger Feast. Paul saw seal-oil lamps during only one winter before kerosene lamps replaced them:

The lamps that I saw used wicks. My grandmother or her daughters would flick off the ash from the wick, and the flame would burn brighter. Kaullriqerluku [removing the ash from the wick] was what they said. The lamp wicks they used were called kumarulluut. People always had a supply of them. When picking the plant, they'd dry it. After they saturated the dried kumarulluut with oil, they used them as fire starters when they lit up their stoves.

Sometimes my grandmother turned to her family and said, "Keep an eye on the lamp wick. When the lower part of the wick becomes visible and is out of the oil, it will burn faster." As the oil got lower, they'd tilt the lamp more to its side. . . . If they saw the lower part of the wick above the oil, she would say, "Add more oil before the wick burns out." When the lamp was lit, it was always tilted to one side.

The lamp reminded Annie of Kumcek, a stingy woman who never let her lamp burn brightly, even though she was rich in oil provided by her five sons. Catherine remembered having her face painted with lamp soot when she was a child prior to the house-to-house visiting that took place during Qaariitaaq every fall:

In Newtok when we were getting ready to participate in Qaariitaaq, . . . before we visited the houses, we gathered in the qasgi to have our faces painted. When I entered the qasgi, I saw four lamps lit in all the corners of the nacitet [split-wood flooring]. It was bright in there. Then someone turned to me and said, "Sit here under the naniq [lamp] so I can paint your face." I laid down under the light as he painted my face. When our faces were painted, we went out.

Meluskaq / Snuff Tobacco

Tobacco was traded into southwestern Alaska from the late 1700s and was a valued commodity, more often chewed and sniffed than smoked. Both Annie and Wassilie had observed the preparation and use of meluskaq (snuff tobacco, from melug-, "to suck in"), and they greeted the tools of the trade—gathered from all over the region and stored on a variety of shelves in the collection—with recognition (fig. 7.5). These included two mortars from the Yukon in which to pound the tobacco, an ivory pestle from Cape Vancouver, three sieves—one from the Kuskokwim, made of caribou antler and decorated with circle designs with a perforated seal-gut bottom, and two from the Yukon—and one tiny bone pipe from the Yukon for inhaling the tobacco mixture.[6]

Taking the mortar, Annie began:

Since I used to see people snort snuff, I recognized this right away as a miilissuun [mortar]. This was filled with tobacco mixed with something. . . . We haven't seen a passiissuun [pestle, from passi-, "to crush"]. The old woman I watched making snuff tobacco carefully processed the tobacco. . . . After she put some finely processed tobacco into her meluskautek [open container from which one could sniff meluskaq], she would take a tube that she had made by cutting off the ends of a bird's ituraq [leg bone], place it in one of her nostrils like this, snort, and cough. . . .

That old lady couldn't go without her meluskautek; she always had to have it in her possession. When the urge to snort snuff came to her, she'd sit on top of a mound, take her snuff box out, and snort and cough out at the end. The poor old woman's nose was always stuffed. Then she would put the cover back on her snuff box. Using snuff did not look so wonderful; sometimes it seemed like a gush of water would flow out of her eyes. Also when she coughed, I would expect to see her cough up snuff along with some mucus.

Wassilie gave another vivid demonstration:

This is a device for making snuff. First the stems are removed from the leaf tobacco, then the leaf is cut into fine strips, after which the prepared tobacco is put along with some araq [punk or willow ash] into the device for grinding. The consistency would be checked while grinding the tobacco, and each time ash would be added as needed. . . . The ground tobacco is then transferred to a kataagun [strainer or sieve]. I'd say the bottom was made of seal intestine.

7.5 Accouterments necessary for making meluskaq (snuff tobacco), including a mortar and ivory pestle to grind the shredded tobacco, a perforated gut-skin sieve to strain the powder, and a bone snuff tube for snorting the mixture into one's nostril. IVA3706, IVA4996, IVA3668, IVA3689, IVA4169.

7.6 Annie pretending to snuff tobacco.

This wood has a line etched on it, and the rim has been fixed so the membrane could be tied around it. . . .

When the mixture turns into fine powder, it is poured into a container and covered. Perhaps this piece once had a cover. *Meluskaq* was taken in the morning. When I watched them, they'd put the end of the *melugcuun* or *meluurun* [tube for taking *meluskaq*] in the nostril and sniff. After they snorted snuff, they would start coughing. They usually snorted snuff twice in each nostril. Then they would close and open their eyes for a moment after they snorted snuff. Our dear late father used to take it in the morning. I used to watch him closely. The mortar and pestle he had for making *meluskaq* were made of wood, and he had a little sifter that was an old baking-powder can. . . . They made little holes in the bottom using a nail.

He'd pour the mixture into the can strainer and sift the powder down into a final container, where it was kept covered. His supply of *meluskaq* lasted for quite a long time. He'd take it in the morning and say that he was adjusting his vision. Some people took it in the evening, too, including old women. They always took some with them when they went out traveling. When people who used *meluskaq* talked, their nostrils were always plugged. That was how they took tobacco.

Smiling, Wassilie invited Annie to partake: "Let her take some *meluskaq*." Accepting the challenge, Annie announced: "I'm going to take some!" With two sniffs and a cough (fig. 7.6), she was done.

Ayallaq / **Cutting Board**

Still smiling, we turned to a pair of cutting boards (fig. 7.7) from the Yukon,[7] which caused Annie to take stock of all our work:

We've been seeing many objects as we worked the last few days. Our men have explained the use of many men's tools since they know what they are. We've also looked at many women's things. This object is called *ayallaq* [cutting board]. . . . Its edges are finely decorated. Both the board's top and bottom and the design on the middle are painted with red ocher.

This is a piece we women use. My mother tanned muskrats using a board like this. It's not easy to work on something without a board like this. We use one to cut fish and such items. Gosh, these beautifully made things are so nice. . . . A woman without an *ayallaq* was viewed as an undesirable mate for a *nukalpiaq*. A woman was not a desired mate if she wasn't an ideal woman, possessing everything she was expected to own.

Catherine added her remembrances:

Back then I also saw cutting boards. I saw a person using a large *ayallaq* made of wood while removing blubber from a seal . . . in a matter of minutes. . . .

Since I started working on sole material for skin boots, I realized that it was not easy to scrape the shaped edges of the sole material on a rough surface. You have to use an *ayallaq* when you prepare the sole material. . . . Men also never do without *ayallat* when they cut meat for cooking.

7.7 Wassilie noted the differences between this cutting board and another plainer one: "That [plain] *ayallaq* looks like it was used for meals every day. . . . This one was used by women when they worked on fancy sewing. It looks spotless and clean." IVA4552.

Paul concluded by mentioning a *qanruyun* taught to young people in reference to cutting boards: "Boys were strictly restricted from getting on *ayallat*. If we sat on them, we would invariably be caught in large waves on the ocean, . . . which would come from behind and cause us to drift away. As boys, we were cautioned about that." Once again, old wood had given the past new life.

Ladles, Spoons, and Dippers

The afternoon was growing late, but we still had time to examine several dozen spoons and ladles stored in a single box. First were four painted wooden ladles (fig. 7.8, fig. 7.9) from the Kuskokwim.[8] Paul introduced the many names these were known by in different areas:

7.8 Painted wooden ladles from the Kuskokwim. Paul noted, "They are painted with personal designs done with black pigment." From left to right: IVA3780, IVA4551, IVA4552.

7.9 A hand painted in black on the ladle pictured here, on the far right. IVA4552.

Nunivak people called these bigger ones *qassuutat* and the smaller ones *qassuuciat*. . . . We [Nelson Islanders] called these *angassacuaraat* [small ladles], and some called them *ipuutet* [ladles]. . . . These little ones were called *qassuuciat*. Nowadays, since the commercially made ones are used, they call them *luuskaat* [spoons, from Russian, "lózhka"]. The original spoons were sometimes called *qassuuciarraq* or *yuurqaarcuun*.

Wassilie noted that four smaller caribou-antler spoons and three wooden ones[9] from the Kuskokwim and Bristol Bay were used for eating *yuurqaaq* (broth or plain soup) (fig. 7.10). He also immediately recognized the special use of two more caribou-antler spoons[10] that Jacobsen had received as a gift from Mr. Clark at Fort Alexander and described as made specially for eating berries at festivals:

Back home, fall time is when the *kavirlit* [cranberries] become ripe. Then if one of their relatives caught whitefish with roe, they would crush the roe, mix in cranberries, and whip up the mixture like whipped cream. When it was done, they'd eat it right away. The mixture was called *qerpertaq*. These spoons with longer handles were used to eat *qerpertaq* back then.

Always precise, Paul added the Nelson Island word for cranberries—*tumaglit*—"because my descendants, grandchildren, and my future grandchildren may not understand the word you were using." He also commented on the spoons' shape: "The spoons they used for taking broth were called *qaaluuciat* or *qalussnguarraat* by some people back in those days. Nowadays, words are changing. We are beginning to use one dialect. This resembles soup spoons from Korea. Yupiit and Koreans made a similar implement even though they were far apart."

We now turned to six bentwood dippers or *qaluuritet*, four from the Yukon, and two from the Kuskokwim and Nushagak (fig. 7.11).[11] Jacobsen wrote that they were used by women for

7.10 Commenting on these caribou-antler and painted wooden spoons, Wassilie noted: "We used these when we ate broth. We'd say, 'Cayuryugpaa [I want broth, from qayuq, broth].' As we do today, people back in those days added fish eggs to soup broth. Broth soups with whitefish eggs were the best. They also added anlleret [cotton-grass roots], which mice had stored in their sheds. Since they were sweet-tasting roots, they added a very nice flavor to soups." IVA4775, IVA4780, IVA7228.

7.11 Bentwood dippers from the Yukon. Paul recalled: "People were told to always use these kinds of dippers when they drank water. Young boys, in particular, were told not to drink by bending over into the bucket. When the one [in the story] who was taken away by the seal bladders saw men kayaking out in the ocean, some that he saw had upside-down buckets covering their heads and faces. His host turned to him and said, 'Perhaps you would not use a dipper when you drink water. Should you bend down into the water bucket to quench your thirst, you will end up like the man we just saw paddling with a bucket over his head. However, if you always use a dipper when you drink water, you will not be like him.'" IVA3694, IVA3691.

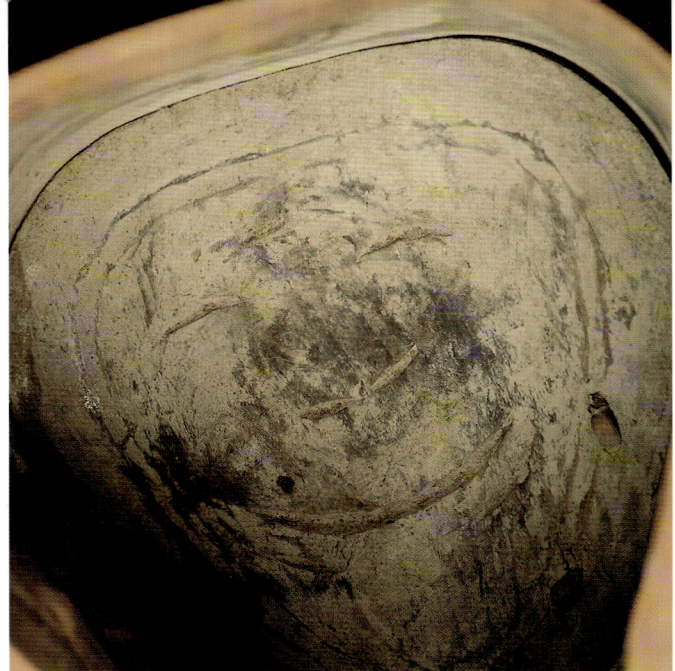

7.12 Faces were often painted inside bentwood dippers, perhaps recalling the use of water containers to see into the future. IVA3694.

getting water, by men to bail boats, and by everyone in the house for drinking water; the larger dipper (with a face painted inside; fig. 7.12)[12] had even been used as a urine bucket: "Strange as it might sound, the Eskimos had chamber pots, yet these did not have a distinct form; most often it was an old water bucket or dipper (like this one)." Although Jacobsen assumed that travelers might then mistake the chamber pot for a drinking container, this is unlikely, as its smell and placement in the house would have made its use clear.

Marie arranged the dippers from largest to smallest, and Wassilie began:

When I first became aware, we had bentwood dippers like these. I'd say that this medium-size one wasn't used when traveling in the wilderness but was used when they fetched water from ice holes. . . .

And this little one [see fig. 7.11] was also made with a little *allungak* [bottom part]. It's a cute bentwood dipper with an incised design on it. A person drank with it out in the wilderness.

Discreetly picking up where Wassilie left off, Paul added detail on both the function and social constraints of the dippers' use:

As I listened to you talking about these, no additional information need be added. But since this one is not too big, people probably used it to drink with either in the *qasgi* or at home. It was also used as a dipper when fetching water from an ice hole.

Back in those days, boys weren't allowed to drink a lot of water, *akunriuresqevkenaki* [controlling one's consumption], as they say. When a boy asked for water, they'd tell him to wait, saying that the taste of food was still in his mouth. And again, when someone asked for water, an elder said, "Would you spit a little." If his spit was not frothy, the elder said, "You still haven't gotten thirsty." But if his spit was frothy, the elder said, "Now you are thirsty. Drink some water." The amount of water taken was also monitored. If a boy drank a lot of water, it could cause his body to become sluggish and weak. At work, his body would tend to get unsteady and lethargic. That was the reason young men were kept from drinking too much water.

When parents raised their children with devotion, although they had dippers like these, they used bird-wing feathers to give the children water. They'd have the child open its mouth and let the water drip down from the quill that had been dipped in water. When the water stopped dripping, they'd use their hands to squeeze out the last bit of water into the child's open mouth. They called giving water that way *miitaa* [from *mer-*, "water, to drink"]. When children weren't allowed to drink a lot of water as they were growing up, their bodies would be quite limber and robust when they grew up. Their flesh would be tough, their bodies would be healthy, and they would be agile and strong.

Paul's comments jogged Wassilie's memory: "The inside bottom of these wooden *mer'utet* [dippers] usually had little faces drawn on them. The big urine buckets had designs of their own." Marie said that she had heard that some people were able to see visions in dippers like these. Wassilie told of one such man:

When a person named Qacungatarli . . . was a boy, someone asked him to bring her some water—perhaps it was his grandmother who wanted water. As he was about to fill the dipper from the water bucket, he saw the face of an old man in the water. The old face was very wrinkled, and his head was covered with white hair. When he backed away without filling the dipper, his grandmother said, "*Waqaa* [What's wrong?]?" He told her that he saw an unpleasant-looking face in the water. Then his grandmother said, "Bring me some water. The face you saw was . . . your own reflection. Though you go through dangerous situations in life, you will not die young. You will live to be an old man." That incident confirmed his power, allowing him to openly ridicule others, *qacuqluki*. Therefore, others began calling him Qacungatarli [One Who Mocks]. His real name was Uyamigaaq. He was a *yuungcaraq* [one given life by an *angalkuq*].

Marie asked Wassilie to explain the meaning of *qacurqiyaraq*, and he replied: "It was when *angalkut* ridiculed each other through their songs. When his grandmother told him that he was going to live to be an old man, . . . he learned to be fearless and mock his fellows. He also was able to survive the dangerous situations he encountered throughout his life."

Paul said that such shaman songs were called *qacurqissuutet* and that other *angalkut* used them as well to ridicule each other. He then described another person who used a water container to see into the future.

Let me tell a story about water buckets, too. A person who looked into the bucket told this story in my presence. They were a family in Tununak. During the time when white people were beginning to appear in our region, his father traveled to St. Michael to buy things from the store there. He was gone for a long time. The man named Aluskaq [a Tununak trader in the 1880s] traveled with him. The man's mother got worried because he was gone far too long.

She was an *angalkuq*, so after performing a certain rite, she told the father's eldest son, "Go over to the bucket and look inside." When he looked in, he saw a boat anchored in a river. He was able to recognize the people in the boat, including his father. He told his grandmother that he could see a boat in a river down there. His grandmother said, "Aa-a. Then they are okay." She performed a certain rite that allowed her grandson to see the travelers on the surface of the water in the bucket.

Paul's conclusion extended the story's implications to the present: "It is true that God created us with ways for our people to survive. There were gifted people among us, with capabilities to help us whenever we were unable to solve problems by ordinary means. If we had continued our ways, there still would be individuals working with such extraordinary gifts among us."

Uiluuyaaq / Clamshell Spoon

Along with carved spoons and ladles, Jacobsen had brought home two unassuming clamshells from the Nushagak region.[13] Annie described how *uiluuyaat* (clamshell spoons, from *uiluq*, "clam, clamshell") were used to scoop oil from cooking pots.

The woman I've called Arnangiltaaq had one like this. When we were living up the Togiak River, since sea mammals were scarce up there, whenever she processed fat from other animals, she would simmer the animal in a pot on a low fire. . . .

And my mother always removed fat from *cavirrutnat* [whitefish]. They used the oil on things, including skins when they tanned them. From the entrails of *anerrlugaat* [saltwater trout], she'd remove the gall from their little livers first and cook them and save the oil for use. Arnangiltaaq would use this kind of ladle to scoop out the oil from the pot. Then she'd separate the livers from the rest and make *akutaq*, mixing it with blackberries. My mother, too, made *akutaq*, using fermented fish eggs and oil. . . . Young Yup'ik people of today regard that kind of food as repulsive.

And they gathered all the discarded bones from *tepet* [aged salmon heads] and cooked them to save the oil. The oil from cooked bone discards didn't have any smell. Nowadays people don't fix that kind of food anymore.

Annie remembered clams as a delicacy, both raw and cooked. Catherine, too, had gathered clams on Nelson Island when she was young, although she had never seen a shell as thick as this. Clams were rarer on the lower Yukon, but she said that because clams were a nomadic animal, they were sometimes found in creeks and sloughs there as well. Even the tundra dweller, Wassilie found the shells familiar: "In my village, people used clamshells. Men also used them as spoons when they ate broth."

Aluqatkat / Dried Beaver Castors

A small, black, stonelike object, mislabeled a harpoon tip, was deceptively ordinary and uninteresting.[14] Wassilie picked it up and smelled it, saying:

Back in those days, people always had *aluqatkat* [dried beaver scent glands or castors]. This is just a piece of one. When people had dry throats, they took a little bite of *aluqatkaq* and chewed it, swallowing the saliva. *Aluqatkat* were used as a remedy. We get *aluqatkat* from male beavers. Back in those days, we used to see many of them hanging to dry in homes, but nowadays, though there are more beavers around, few people dry them for medicinal purposes. . . .

Aluqatkat and stones were used by *angalkut* as weapons against evil and danger. They also used the castor to have power over something such as land that is eroding. They performed a ritual directed at the land, which included pretending to ignite the castors. . . . Also, some of them would anchor the erosion with a little piece of stone set at the edge of the eroding area. When they did this ritual, the erosion would diminish.

Paul followed with a story of the protective power of dried beaver castors:

At home I've only heard about this *aluqatkaq* in a *quliraq*. While a grandmother and her grandchild were residing alone in the backcountry, the grandchild came home one day and excitedly said, "There's a person coming toward our place." Grandmother reached over and pulled out *aluqatkak* [pair of castors] and said, "The person coming might have evil intentions. Go out and anoint our house all around with these." As directed, he went out and anointed their house before the stranger arrived. When he was done, he went in. As they waited, they heard the crackling of the snow as the person arrived at their place and said, "I thought I saw a person walking around this place as I was approaching. I thought this was a house when I saw it from a distance. But I see that it's just a beaver house." When the grandmother allowed the grandchild to anoint their house with this kind, it had transformed into a beaver house. Then after the stranger marveled out loud about the transformation, he continued on his way.

Catherine described the power of *aluqatkaq* to protect riverbanks during spring breakup on the Yukon:

My husband's brother's wife's grandmother used castors, taking them very seriously. The first time I saw her using it was in the spring, when the water was high. . . . She was sitting on the shore chewing something. . . . As we stood watching her, she took the stuff out of her mouth and tossed it into the water along the shore. . . . She said she was trying to stop the flood. She also told her grandchild . . . to pay attention to what she had done. She said that the water's current was extremely strong, and if broken ice got jammed up during breakup, people in that area would be in dire straits. She said the *aluqatkat* could avert this situation.

Annie spoke briefly on the use of beaver castors, called *ic'ukcat* in the Togiak area, as a medicine for people suffering from sore throat as well as something to rub on bodily aches: "When Arnangiltaaq used it, she'd first rub it on the affected area, and then she would blow out through her mouth, saying that the affliction should go to someone else who had the strength to overcome it."

Catherine mentioned the recent increase in the beaver population throughout southwestern Alaska and associated problems, including water pollution and damming of streams.

7.13 *Ciklaq (root pick) used to dig for roots and tubers in the frozen tundra. IVA4183.*

Beavers are powerful animals, however, and difficult to control. She told of a man who destroyed a beaver dam in a river where he set a whitefish net. When he went to check the net the next day, it was ruined. Catherine concluded, "The beavers were not pleased about their broken dam and retaliated."

Ciklat / Root Picks

We now turned to two wooden diggers (fig. 7.13) from the Yukon.[15] Paul deftly demonstrated their use, noting that they were used to chop or shatter something. On Nelson Island they were called *ciklauraat*, while in other places they were *ciklat* (root picks, from *ciklaur-*, "to chop or hack loose"). Catherine added vivid description:

We used these on frozen ground in the spring and fall. People still use them on the Yukon. They are *ciklat* used to dig for *qerqat* ["Eskimo potatoes," *Hedysarum alpinum*]. When I first moved to the Yukon, I was ignorant of the way they did things there. After you loosen a small area of topsoil with a *ciklaq* and pull it up, you'll see a white root with what looks like tentacles. That was what they called *qerqaq*. They are very delicious to eat.

Qanikciurun wall' Pekutaq / Snow Shovel

Paul was even more animated in his active interpretation of a large wooden shovel (fig. 7.14, fig. 7.15) from the Yukon.[16] Standing and holding it in both hands, he spoke at length, bringing to life the rules for living that guided him when he was young.

In our dialect we call this *qanikciurun* [snow shovel, from *qanikcaq*, "snow on the ground"], and other speakers call it *pekutaq*. Before Western-style shovels were introduced, these were very important and constantly used in the winter.

People were told never to leave the shovel behind when they

174 THE RETURN GIFT

traveled using sleds, even in good weather. If the weather changes for the worst, the shovel would be there to make a snow shelter. A shovel like this was a very important tool to keep on hand in the wintertime.

Paul then described the shovel's role in the rigorous training process known as *cilkiayaraq* when an individual went through harsh daily training, hoping to become a good provider and better person. Then he told the story of Qanagaarniarun, a man who underwent a long period of grueling training using a shovel like this:

The men were in the *qasgi,* including . . . Qanagaarniarun. He was married to the daughter of a *nukalpiaq* in the village. They sent a messenger over to his mother-in-law's house, asking for a piece of wood from the roof of her house for fuel for the fire bath. They made the request sound like it was coming from her son-in-law. . . . After the mother-in-law was silent for a moment, she said, "Aa, I've never thought of using the wood from my roof to make a fire bath. Tell him to trade roof wood for himself from those who have them." When the messenger told him the message . . . he realized that his mother-in-law didn't think highly of him as a provider. So he said to his wife, "I'm going to leave you because I feel that I'm taking the place of a *nukalpiaq* who can provide for you in a fashion to which you are accustomed." His wife didn't want him to leave. . . .

He then started *cilkiayaraq* and began training, enduring physical hardship and foregoing sleep. For three years he continuously worked toward his goal, even though he didn't see any results, and on the fourth year he started to see some change when his future catch began to surface from beneath. . . . When he shoveled the snow from the porch floors and his shovel slipped on something, he'd touch it and feel the backbone of a bearded seal on the floor.

7.14 Wooden shovel. Paul pointed out five slits near the handle's base: "In the past, people had their ownership marks on their things. This shovel definitely was owned by a particular person. . . . It is marked with five engraved lines, which that individual used to mark his possessions. If he lost it or if it was stolen, he'd be able to recognize it as his own by this design." IVA4342.

7.15 Wassilie using the wooden shovel to clear a path through imaginary snow.

7.16 Wooden ax with a mastodon-tusk blade secured by *qavyak* (walrus-skin line). Jacobsen wrote that this kind of ax was used in the *qasgi* to cut wood, especially in cases of illness or death when iron tools were proscribed. IVA5256.

7.17 Paul wielding the wooden ax to chop imaginary wood.

And sometimes when he shoveled, his shovel would hit something that turned out to be the tip of a caribou antler sticking up through the floor. Toward the end of his training, the animals he would soon be catching started to reveal themselves to him in that fashion. . . . He began to feel the animal forms while he was shoveling snow from the porch. . . .

And when people began to witness his successful hunts and started to call him a *nukalpiaq*, his mother-in-law wanted to recognize him as her son-in-law again. She wanted him to come home to provide for his child. The man had worked hard and, just like today, turned into a millionaire and a good businessman.

Marie suggested that *cilkiayaraq* was like going to four years of college, and Paul agreed:

He graduated by using this shovel. A shovel was not the only instrument to be used in *cilkiayaraq*. Individuals going through this training would also clean the earthen floors of houses with their hands and carry the debris in their parka skirts to discard outside. We also put our arms inside our parkas and rubbed our bodies with our grimy hands to increase our immunity to sickness. And since the people who participated in this training believed in it, they were healthy throughout most of their lives.

There is a saying that when disease entered a person who tended to be idle, it usually felt welcomed. . . . But when it came to a person who was physically active, it didn't stay long. It would say, "It's not comfortable staying here with this active person." Sickness would stay briefly and leave. . . .

But when sickness was welcomed by a person, it stayed with the host quite comfortably, saying, "This person sure is nice to stay with. I think I'll be with him." These exact lines were said when people were advised about sickness and health.

Although people in the past didn't call God by the same name, they gave their young people guidance in the direction of goodness and truth. . . . The kind of teaching they did about good and evil was no different from the teachings of the churches today. And though they weren't aware of the Ten Commandments, their teachings corresponded to them.

Annie asked if Qanagaarniarun went back to his wife, and Paul said no. Wassilie then stood and demonstrated how Qanagaarniarun had slept during his training—by sitting and placing a stick in the ground right below his forehead, so that when he fell forward in exhaustion the stick would wake him up. He then continued the story as he remembered it:

When he became a *nukalpiaq*, his father-in-law came to him and said, "You should go back to your wife and child and provide for them." He answered, "When they begin asking for fire-bath wood, you'll probably tell me to trade myself for wood for some roof. . . ."

Evidently, when snow got deep all around and wood became scarce, they used to begin trading for wood for the fire bath . . . and to heat homes, too.

Paul explained *cayugtuucaraq* (process of acquiring firewood for a fire bath, from *cayuq-*, "to pull something"):

Cayugtuucaraq was a practice the people used to acquire wood that they needed by requesting it or trading for it with little things. . . .

A person would enter the *qasgi* holding a piece of firewood. . . . As I understood it, he'd give the piece to his cousin and not his uncle or his own brother. He'd come in and place the firewood on his cousin's lap. Because his cousin understood the system, he would think, "My cousin here wants me to get a piece of firewood for the fire bath." He would immediately go out and come back in, holding a piece of wood, placing it on another cousin he felt comfortable with.

That process would continue until there was enough wood for a fire bath. That was how *cayugtuucaraq* worked. That was what they did to take fire baths in the winter.

We had spent a half-hour with a wooden shovel and came away with a fuller understanding of the unique practices and view of the world that guided its use. Once again, I was confronted with the *alerquutet* (prescriptions) and *inerquutet* (prohibitions) organized around real objects and activities.

Ciklaq / **Ax**

After looking at the shovel, we examined a heavy, well-worn wooden ax (fig. 7.16) from the Nushagak region.[17] First Paul (fig. 7.17), then Wassilie, Annie, and Andy hefted the enormous tool, chopping imaginary wood. Paul summed up his feelings:

This looks like the ax I saw in New York [when he was a guest at the National Museum of the American Indian]. . . . Since it was the first time I saw one like it in my life, I kept returning to it. . . . I was intrigued by it and thought of how a piece like this was created and used by the people way before white people arrived in our area. . . .

This old piece shows us that our ways go back to ancient times. . . . It appears to have been used a lot by the owner long ago. I really don't want to see our ways lost by our descendants. Our work here today is an effort to help our young understand our history. . . .

Today, since our lives are in much turmoil, we are living in the midst of problems. If our young people began to learn about Yup'ik culture, . . . they might ask this question, "How did our ancestors survive generation after generation before the white people arrived?" Perhaps if they begin to look at pictures and written explanations of these objects, they might change their destructive lifestyles and begin to appreciate who they are. I've just mentioned what I've been thinking about as we were looking at these objects.

There was no more eloquent statement of the significance of our work.

Passin / **Pestle**

We turned to a pestle (fig. 7.18, fig. 7.19) from the mouth of the Kuskokwim.[18] Annie took it in her hands and stood to speak: "This is a *passin* [pestle, from *passite-*, "to press by putting pressure"]. It was made and decorated very nicely. At home there's a person who inherited a tool like this, and it hangs on her wall, but it's not adorned like this. My aunt had a *passin*

7.18 Passin (pestle) carved from a walrus tusk with an eagle-head handle and decorated with circle-and-dot designs. Paul recalled: "Since we ate needlefish, I used to watch my grandmother use this kind. She'd come in with a wooden bowl and begin crushing the needlefish inside the bowl using a passin, making sure all the fish were crushed. When the fish were crushed, the little spikes would come off. She'd also use it to crush fish liver she was getting ready for akutaq . . . and to fix things other than fish. This was a tool used by women for many tasks." IVA5427.

7.19 The pestle's eagle-head handle. IVA5427.

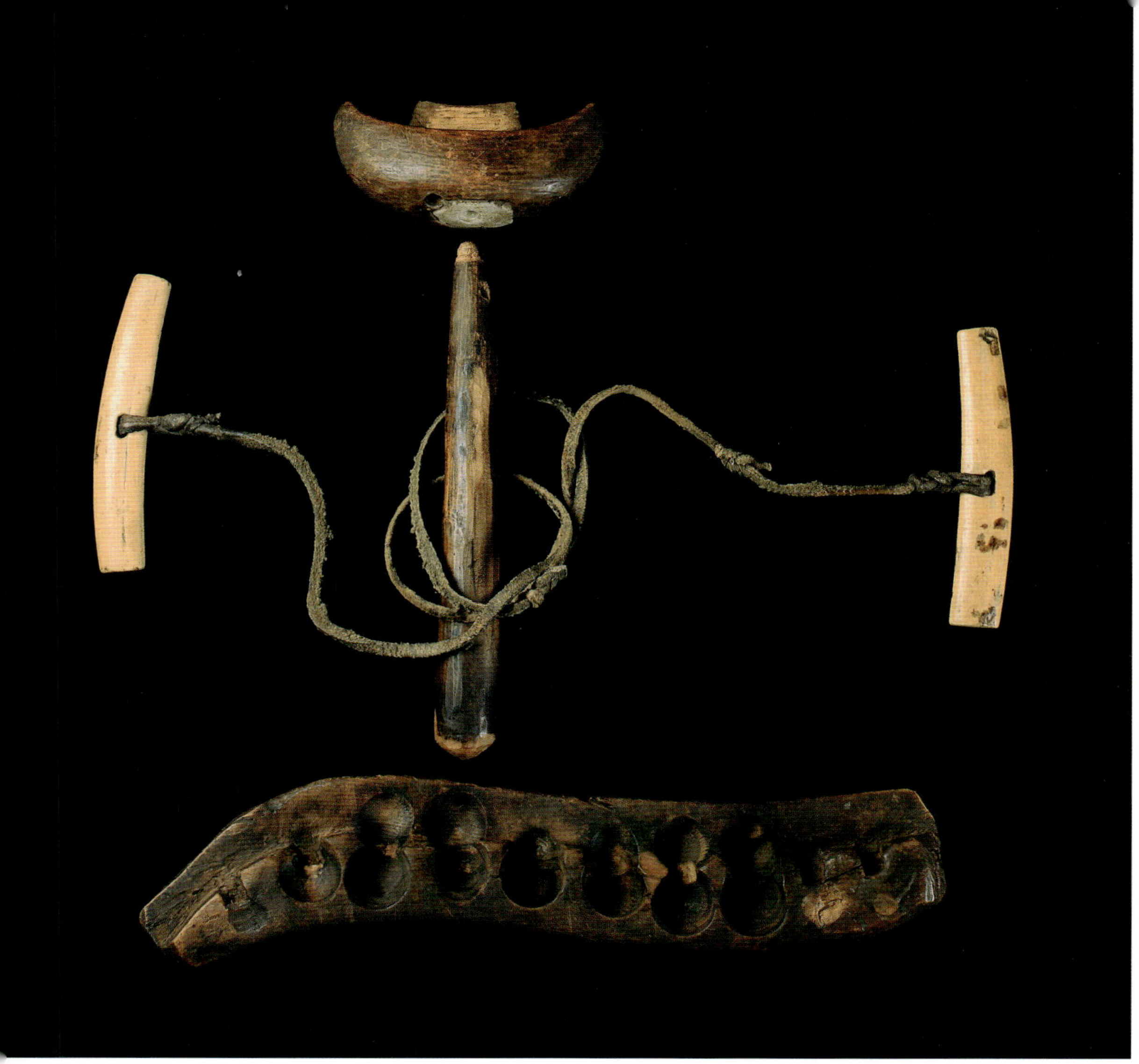

7.20 Complete fire-making outfit, including fire board, mouthpiece, and fire drill turned by a sealskin thong. IVA4558.

7.21 When demonstrating the use of the fire drill, Paul noted: "You might be repulsed by the idea of holding it with your teeth, but in my opinion, our Provider has not brought it to us with bad intentions. Back when it was used, it was regarded as clean and was used by many individuals. . . . Looking at it in its present condition, we wouldn't want to hold it with our teeth because it appears grimy and looks as if it might start a serious illness, but it was not viewed that way in the past.

"One would wind this [line] to this [drill]—in its time this was flexible, but now it is hard. One held this with one's teeth, like this. And since the sparks caused by the friction spray from [the drill's base], this part is called anarcuun. When that happened, they'd say anartuq [it has defecated]." IVA4558.

like this, too. She and my mother, since they were sisters, shared the tool. This tool is good for salmonberries."

Catherine took the pestle in hand and continued:

Women always shared a tool like this. The one we used was made of driftwood. . . . One day my stepmother said, "Would you get my *passin*." She was sitting down with a huge bowl in front of her. I looked and saw fish roe inside the bowl. Then she quickly crushed them with the *passin*. . . . She said she was going to make *mak'aq* [fish-roe *akutaq*]. After she crushed the roe, she began to use her hand to whip it, adding seal oil and water sparingly. There were some very soft berries on the side to put in later. As she whipped the contents, they started to double in size. Then when she was done, she asked me to pour the berries into the bowl. The *akutaq* was called *amnginaq*. It's very delicious.

178 THE RETURN GIFT

Now Wassilie took a turn, recalling a woman who put her *passin* to an unusual but effective use:

Women used to go on berry-picking trips in skin boats. *Angyirlureng* [going in an *angyaq* (skin boat)] was the word they used for that, and they'd solely depend on the boat owner out there. While the women from Akulirarmiut were going up the Iinrayaq River, they saw a bearded seal way up on the beach. The tide had gone down while the seal was sleeping there. They discussed how to kill the seal, and one of them said, "We would have that up there for food while we are out here; how can we kill it?" Then one said that she had brought her heavy *passin* with her. . . . She began to go up toward the animal while the others followed from behind. As she crept toward the sleeping seal and reached it, she aimed and struck it with her *passin*. The seal began to quiver, and she again struck its head and killed it. The women caught a seal using a *passin* as a weapon. They ended up staying out for many days with enough meat and seal oil.

Kenrgessuutet / Fire Starters

We ended our day in the museum dramatically with the investigation of two fire-making outfits (fig. 7.20) from the Kuskokwim and tundra areas, each including a fire board (*kumartessuun*, "Allekak"), mouthpiece (*neg'utaq*, "Nerrutak"), and fire drill (*ussukataq*, "Osugatak").[19] The drill was turned by a sealskin thong with handles (*nucugcuutek*, "Nutjun") rather than a bow like those used to the north. Wassilie began with enthusiasm:

These were the ones I had hoped to see . . . used to make fires in the dwellings and *qasgit*. They include *neg'utat* [mouthpieces] and *ussukatat* [rotating sticks used as fire drills]. . . . Two people were required to operate it. One person would pull this *nucugcuutek* [line] back and forth after winding it around the stick, which the other person controls. In those days, seal-hide twine was for the *nucugcuutek*. . . . There is a *kumartessuun* [fire board, from *kumarte-*, "to light a fire, ignite"] with a socket into which the stick fits, and the board has an indentation, the *anarcuun* [literally, "device to release *anaq* (feces)"] next to it. The intense heat generated by friction would cause sparks to ignite tinder here. And beginning from this flame, the *qasgit* and *enet* would get fire for heat, cooking, and light.

These devices were used by our ancestors to make fire before matches were introduced. This *neg'utaq* was held with the mouth. . . . A person could use one to make fire even if he was alone in the wilderness. Those used in the wilderness were smaller . . . like this. . . . The end part of that piece would be the *asupet* [skin-stretching tool]. This one was used for a long time. And these two weren't used. . . .

My late dear father had one that looked almost like this. . . . This [string] was threaded through the hole found on this *nucuutaak*. . . . His *neg'utaq* was made out of *mimernaq* [tree stump], and it was inlaid with beautiful stones. And the part where you bite on was nicely made. When starting a fire out in the wilderness, he'd bite it here and apply pressure. He did a back-and-forth motion with this line to make fire. . . .

Here is a collection of *kenngessuutet* [fire starters, from *ken-*

nge-, "to start to burn"], and they have all their components.

Putting the *neg'utaq* to his mouth, Wassilie added, "*Neg'utaq* would be slightly wider with handles like this. This is where a person would bite it to hold it, and perhaps he would insert his tongue here. My, he must have had a very slender tongue. . . . My false teeth won't work too well for this."

Paul added linguistic detail, noting that on Nelson Island the terms were the same except for the drill, which was called *nucugcuun*. He also suggested that we demonstrate how the piece was used (fig. 7.21), noting: "One person can use this by holding this in one's teeth. You can see teeth marks here. . . . If we show you how it was used and put it into the video camera, a young person will see it later and know how to use this kind of device." Annie concluded, "You've just demonstrated it correctly."

We looked briefly at parts of fire-making outfits from the Yukon, used in the same way as the Kuskokwim fire drills but called by different names, including drill (*ussukataq*, "Udsukadak"), mouthpiece (*uqumyak* (quartz), "Okommisak," "K'neiak"), and line (*nucugcuutek*, "Arullausett").[20] A group of mouthpieces excited more interest.[21] Some were pieces of stone or mammoth bone meant to be held in the hand or inserted into a wood base and held in the mouth, while others included both wooden base (sometimes carved in the shape of an animal) with stone inserts to hold the drill in place. Jacobsen commented that "serpentine" inserts were used widely on Nelson Island, and Paul added what he knew:

Some of these look like *uqumyiit* [quartz, so called because of its light color, resembling *uquq* (seal fat)]. This one has the same shade as the ones they called *teggalqupiat* [literally, "genuine stones," from *teggalquq*, "stone"]. These five rocks are different from the ones that are found in my area. This is not a rock but a kind of ivory they called *quugiinraq* [mastodon]; it comes from a large animal that lived in our area long ago. People still find mastodon bones when they look for them.

Annie agreed with all that the men had said, then asked Paul to hand her the mammoth-bone mouthpiece insert (fig. 7.22)[22]:

They said that this was the bone of a *quugaaq* [legendary creature said to live underground, sometimes identified with the mammoth or mastodon]. . . . Up above Cauyarnaq, there's a big bluff. . . . It was said that was the place where a *quugaaq* surfaced. . . . And coming up at that time, it evidently dropped its bones in that area. And Ap'allraq collected bones there, including the shortest segment of the rib bones, . . . but it was big. And also he got some of the rocks, which were evidently the *iqlerpiit* [molar teeth] of the *quugaaq*.

As we examined the stones, the conversation turned to their use as medicine. Wassilie commented: "The *angalkut* used to give their *yuungcarat* stones as *iinrut* [amulets, medicines]. They also gave them figures of *tuullget* [common loons] . . . and different objects as *iinruq* . . . wrapped in seal gut to keep them concealed. Little rocks like this were used as medicine,

7.22 Two wooden mouthpieces from Cape Vancouver and two mouthpiece inserts to hold the drill in place, one of mammoth bone and the other stone. IVA4900, IVA4921, IVA4008, IVA4912.

too. It was regarded as a powerful *iinruq*." Paul added that he knew about the use of stones as medicine. His ancestors reasoned that since nothing could enter a rock, disease could not enter a person's body likewise made impermeable by a stone amulet:

The *angalkuq* used it to help people with weak hearts. They would rub the rock on the person's heart to help that person get better. When a family heard of sickness in another family, the grandmother would take her sharpening stone and rub her grandchild's body with it. This process helped to cover the child with protection from the sickness. Our ancestors used the rock for many purposes. When our ancestors didn't have medical doctors and clergy to turn to, they used these kinds of rocks for healing. Since rock is hard, nothing can enter it. And since they knew the strength of rocks, they'd use it to keep sickness away from their youth by putting it around their necks.

EIGHTH DAY Personal Adornment and Human Figures

The day began at 7 A.M. with phone calls from home. Dora called to tell Catherine that her sister, Rosanne Sipry, had passed away. She had already heard the news from Andy, whose wife had told him the night before. When Annie called her daughter Nellie, she learned that a friend from Manokotak had died, and she sat down in the lobby and cried openly. Wassilie called home too and, after a five-minute conversation halfway around the world, was so flustered that when he tried to go back to his room, he went the wrong way on the stairs. Even with all the emotion and excitement, we were noticeably slower after the sauna we'd enjoyed the night before.

Nuyiurutet / Combs

We began our day in the museum quietly with Annie commenting on four hair combs (fig. 8.1, fig. 8.2) from Cape

8.1 *Nuyiurutet (hair combs) from Cape Vancouver and the Kuskokwim. Those with wider-spaced teeth were used for combing hair, while those with longer teeth were used to remove lice. Annie noted, "Long ago, after the young women washed their hair with urine and combed it carefully, they would take bowls of food to the qasgi, and the sweet aroma of the cleansing agent from their hair would fill the qasgi." Clockwise from the top: IVA4782, IVA4784, IVA4778, IVA4785.*

8.2 Nushagak comb, which Jacobsen said was a "showpiece" used both to comb hair and to clean caribou pelts used for clothing: "The comb can be carried on the belt, therefore the ring at the upper end. The handle is ornamented with a seal decorated with circles." IVA4774.

Vancouver and the Kuskokwim,[1] two made of caribou antler and the third of caribou or moose hooves: "These are *nuyiurutet*. . . . You could still use this to comb your hair. This is also the kind they called *nuyiurutpiayaar* [genuine comb?]." Taking one of the combs and fixing it into her thick black hair, she added, chuckling, "We also used to see these hair pieces they called *nuyitet* to put on your hair. . . . How's that? Does it look nice? Where are the men?"

Catherine recalled that in the past, combs were more than decoration: "My stepsister and I also used these to remove lice and lice eggs from our hair. They called these *nerescissuutet* [literally, "devices for removing *neresta* (louse)"]. These with wider-spaced teeth were used for combing hair, and these [with longer teeth] were used to remove lice." Catherine then described how her stepmother had made her wash her hair and body in urine to remove the lice. Not a docile child, she objected, but her stepmother had pointed to the stone "people" on the mountain above Tununak, saying that if she didn't wash, she would become infested with lice, and they would take her up in flight and place her with those figures. Catherine was scared and allowed herself to be washed. Later, however, she climbed to the mountain only to find that the human figures were no more than stone piles: "I was confused and annoyed, and realized that they had lied to me, saying that they were people. When I went down, I said to my stepmother, 'Those up there aren't people. They are just piles of rocks.' She responded, 'You are so daring. Every time we caution you, you always go out to see if it's true.'"

Catherine then described how a woman who was an orphan had asked her to look for lice in her hair: "When I looked at her head, I noticed lumps on both sides. I started looking, and each time I handed her a louse, she'd eat it. Then as I started to part the hard lump to check underneath, oh my gosh, I couldn't believe what I saw. I was so terrified. There were so many lice there that their movement looked like boiling water. Apparently she was infested with lice." After another story about a boy similarly infested, she returned to the poor orphan:

One time I was with people staying up all night talking about something. When I listened . . . I realized they were talking about [the orphan]. That was the time I saw shameless cruelty being practiced. I watched the other women grab her and remove all of her clothes until she was naked. The poor woman was crying. She was actually an older woman at the time, and I felt very sorry for her. When the other women let her go, they were laughing at her. When they were done with her, another person and I helped her put her clothes back on.

Following Catherine's personal accounts, Paul brought us back to the fine points of linguistic variation. Noting that he had also seen *ilairyaraq* (the process of removing knots from the hair) as he was growing up, he pointed out that Nelson Islanders used the word *tegunret* (tangles) for the hair that came off, while others referred to them as *ilaillret* (literally, "those that are removed").

Lice were something all the elders had directly experienced, and Wassilie added what he remembered:

In the upper regions, people called lice *ungiliit* because *neresta* was used as a name for people. Back when I was little, I noticed that orphans had more lice on them . . . since they didn't have parents to provide for them. The combs with wider teeth were also called *tegurrliurutet* [tangle removers, from *tegute-*, "to be tightly tangled"]. And these with longer teeth were used to remove lice.

In those days, people hung their parkas outside in the cold to freeze the lice. Then . . . they'd beat the parkas so the dead lice would fall off. The lice would freeze to death out in the cold, but their nits used to hatch.

They also shaved off the hair of boys who had lice. When our mother was alive, we were usually free of lice. Then after she died we started to have lice on us. About the time "black" soap was introduced in the Kuskokwim area, I was aware of my surroundings. The soap was effective on dirt and grime. When people bathed with that soap, they would become squeaky clean and their lice were removed. They called it *miilapiat* [genuine *miilat* (soap)].

Paul recalled using the same black soap, and Catherine described having Buhach (ground pyrethrum flowers, a natural insecticide) sprinkled on her body to remove lice. Both Catherine and Wassilie remembered the early BIA teachers in Tununak and Nunapitchuk introducing soap-making to the communities: "They made soap by cooking ash. They'd boil the mixture, then put it in a cloth bag and hang it and collect the liquid that dripped. Then they'd add the mixture to the washing. . . . If too much was added, it made your hands break out when you used it. That kind of detergent could remove stains and dirt that was difficult to come off." Tiny combs had opened a window to a great deal more than well-groomed hair.[2]

Cungarpiit wall' Mengkuut / Labrets

Until now we had examined large items, the weapons and tools that made daily life possible. Jacobsen had also collected a multitude of tiny objects of ivory, stone, and bone, which the museum stored in a single metal container with twelve narrow compartments stacked one on top of the other. The cabinet in its entirety was known as Drawer D, and its hundreds of objects were simultaneously a researcher's blessing and curse. Although their variety and abundance were exciting, our limited time in Berlin made the task of exploring the cabinet's contents daunting. True to form, the elders plunged in.

First we looked at a box of men's labrets, including four from the Yukon,[3] seventeen from Cape Vancouver and the Kuskokwim,[4] and six from Cape Vancouver and Nunivak Island.[5] The labrets were made to be worn in holes in the right and left corners of a man's lower lip. The exceptions were two ancient and peculiarly formed labrets from Cape Vancouver, which Jacobsen suggested were made to be worn in the middle of the lower lip, although adding that Nelson Islanders could tell him nothing about them (fig. 8.3). Most were plain and made from a variety of materials, including marble, serpentine, quartz, animal teeth, mammoth ivory, and wood. Wassilie and Paul were particularly impressed by several jade labrets collected north of St. Michael, noting that they were probably "really expensive."

Jacobsen wrote that two of the labrets from Cape Vancouver were in the form of upturned boats, a specialty of that area.[6] Five of the labrets from Nunivak and the opposite mainland depicted the tails of white whales (fig. 8.4) and, according to Jacobsen, the desire for white whale blubber, which was regarded as a delicacy. Jacobsen noted that the names for labrets meant "tail-like," and indeed "Tokssorarrut" and "Tuksorarrut=Kakopit" may designate *teqsuqaq* (adipose fin of a fish), while "Palloktutt" may be *papsalquq* (fish tail).

Labrets worn on each side of the lower lip immediately identified a figure as male. Examining a doll with bead labrets (fig. 8.5), Wassilie later explained: "Men wore *cungarpiit* [labrets]. It's a man. It has labrets. . . . Some men wore labrets all the time. . . . Men didn't pierce their nose septums and wear *cigviit* [nose beads]. . . . If a woman was pierced on the chin, the decorations there would be called *caqiqsiik*."

Paul noted simply that men's labrets were also called *mengkuk* (dual) on Nelson Island and *tuutat* on the Yukon. He then gave a detailed account of their origin:

It might be okay if I tell you the reason they started using these as decorations. . . .

Ilu'urqelriik [two related men] [from Nunivak Island] were lost on the ocean. Since they had been adrift, they had not seen land for a long time. The phrase in Yup'ik *imarpiim arulatlinikek* was one of the ways commonly used to describe people lost out on the ocean, meaning "two who were in constant motion with the ocean currents."

One of them saw a group of men carrying their kayaks up a slope. The one who saw them as actual people was just an ordinary person himself. Although that man saw actual humans, his companion did not join them, but proceeded to go up a short distance away from the group of men. The younger man wondered why his companion had chosen not to approach the other men since they had not seen people for so long. Finally the older man said, "Do you think those are real people?" The younger man answered, "I believe they are people because that's what I'm seeing." Then

8.3 Jacobsen suggested that these two unusual labrets from Cape Vancouver were made to be worn in the middle of the lower lip. IVA5053, IVA5054.

8.4 The four labrets in the center depict the tails of white whales in diving position with only flukes exposed, while one on each side is in the form of an upturned boat, a specialty of the Cape Vancouver area on Nelson Island. The two ivory labrets in the lower right are also from Cape Vancouver. Clockwise from the top: IVA5040, IVA5046, IVA5047, IVA5048, IVA5038, IVA5039, IVA5045, IVA5042.

the older man said that they were walruses. He added that they would not harm them and that he might go mingle with them if he wanted to. . . .

When they joined them, they saw that all the men had labrets on their chins. The younger ones had labrets that were just beginning to come out, but the older men had labrets that were sticking out here on their chins [fig. 8.6]. The men stayed with them. After they announced their hunger, they'd all go in a group to a hill covered with salmonberries. Once they were there on the hill, they'd start eating berries. What they were actually eating were *taavtaat* [clams], *aliruat* [razor clams], and other kinds of clams. While they ate, the two men would see the clams as berries. The men they were staying with were gentle and kind and made wonderful hosts.

Sometimes they'd go to a different place to eat, and there they'd find *tan'gerpiit* [curlewberries] growing on the land. . . . When the other men ate the curlewberries, they told the two not to eat. . . .

Apparently they told them not to eat curlewberries when they were eating little pebbles. . . . Since what they were eating was not appropriate food for humans, they told them not to eat them. The walrus viewed the little pebbles as curlewberries. Finally they came up on shore on the south side of Nunivak Island. When they came up on land, the older man told the younger one that if they came to the village in their kayaks, the people there would not be able to see them. He told him that they had to leave their kayaks on the lowest bluffs before they approached the village.

They carried their kayaks to the lowest part of the land close to the shoreline and left them there. They walked toward a village, but the people there couldn't detect their presence. Then the older man said that to become visible to the people, they had to roll in the *qanitaq* [refuse pile] first. They found the *qanitaq* and rolled on it. They stood up and, after brushing their bodies, walked up closer to the people, who were able to see them.

Later on they saw that their kayaks were on top of the highest part of the bluffs on the southern coast of Nunivak. The walrus habitually tend to enjoy climbing up on higher ice floes to rest. People who discovered the abandoned kayaks on the highest parts of the bluffs understood more why walrus enjoyed being on high ice floes when they come out of the water. In the eyes of the walrus, the high bluffs on the coastal shore appeared low enough for them to easily climb.

Then after the two men told of their experience out on the ocean, people realized that the labrets they saw on the men out there were the actual tusks on the walruses that helped them to survive, and they started to wear labrets on their chins to remind them of being walruses. These *mengkuut* here were created, and men started to wear them on their chins. . . . I actually saw several men from Nunivak wearing *mengkuut,* but I never saw men from Nelson Island using them. Perhaps men on the mainland wore them at one time, but I was not aware of their use.

The next day, when a box of a half dozen heavy stone labrets was set down on the table, Paul picked out a large, flat serpentine plug from Cape Vancouver[7] and held it up to the corner of his lower lip. It purportedly depicted an umiak, or large skin boat, an indication that its owner possessed such a boat. Reminded again of the walrus people and their labrets, Paul sat back and told us a *quli'ir* about five brothers and their younger sister. When the brothers hunted, they always stopped at the mouth of the river below their settlement to give a food offering to the fox who had a den by the riverbank. One day when they returned from hunting, their sister failed to greet them. When they entered their house, they noticed her *akin* (wooden headrest) lay sideways on the floor, a sign that she had been pulled from her bed against her will. Having no idea where she had been taken, the brothers went to the fox's den, where they offered food and pleaded with the fox to guide them to their sister:

Then shortly after they prayed, a beautiful woman with a gorgeous bronze-skinned face came slowly out of the den. The fox had transformed into a human and *yuurulluki* [revealed herself to the brothers]. When she came out she said, "A young man from the other side of the ocean came and took your sister away."

The woman then advised the brothers to make a wooden walrus with a hole on the top and room enough for two people. She told them to put it in the water, pat its side, saying "Take me to the other side of the ocean where our sister is located." The brothers followed her instructions, and the eldest entered the wooden walrus, which immediately transformed into an actual walrus and swam away downriver out into the ocean.

Reaching the other side, the brother left the walrus and entered the first house he encountered. Its occupants—a grandmother and grandchild—helped him disguise himself in the grandmother's parka and go with the grandchild to the *qasgi,* where the young man saw his sister being tormented by a cruel *nukalpiaq,* whom the brother quickly killed. The man then picked up his sister and returned to the grandmother's house, where she advised him that a second, stronger adversary would challenge him the next day. During the night she instructed him, and before he left she gave him a little bow and arrow to strike his enemy.

The next morning a messenger came for the brother, and when he went out, he saw his enemy sitting in a boat, with a *ussugcin* (device that creates erosion) in his hand. As the man in the boat made a striking motion toward the ground with the *ussugcin,* the riverbank below the house began to erode, and the water got closer and closer. After several tries, as the man lifted his arm up, the brother shot his enemy in the armpit and he died. After thanking the grandmother, the brother and sister entered the walrus and returned home.

8.5 The bead labrets and upturned mouth identify this human figure as male. IVA4197.

8.6 Paul holding a labret, depicting a whale's tail, in the corner of his lower lip.

Caqiqsiik / Women's Labrets

We looked briefly at a group of *caqiqsiik*, sickle-shaped ivory lip ornaments worn by women in the center of the lower lip (fig. 8.7).[8] Some were plain, while others had decorative bead attachments. Jacobsen had collected them all on the north shore of the Kuskokwim as he headed upriver toward Bethel and described them simply as lip ornaments worn by young girls. He recorded that one girl became so frightened when he asked to buy her ornament that she bit off the head of the plug[9] to be able to give it to him more quickly. Annie balanced a pair on her chin for us to admire (fig. 8.8), but the group made no further comment.

As'utet Aqlitet-llu / Earring Hooks and Earrings

The group spent time admiring more than two dozen pairs of ivory *as'utet* (earring hooks, which go through the ear) from all over the region (fig. 8.9).[10] Most had holes for the attachment of bead pendants and neck chains, and Jacobsen wrote that many were used by young girls. Annie modeled a pair of large, rectangular bone hooks with pyrite fastened to the hollowed-out front face (fig. 8.10).[11] She also pointed out the blue *pipigaat* (Russian trade beads) set into several of the hooks, which Jacobsen noted were considered particularly valuable. This reminded her of Kukugyarpak, a famous traveler who had journeyed north to St. Lawrence Island and returned to the Yukon years later:

I'll just mention a little bit about the time Kukugyarpak was lost out on the ocean. . . . The place called Ukiivak was located somewhere around the Yukon River. When he entered through Ukiivak,

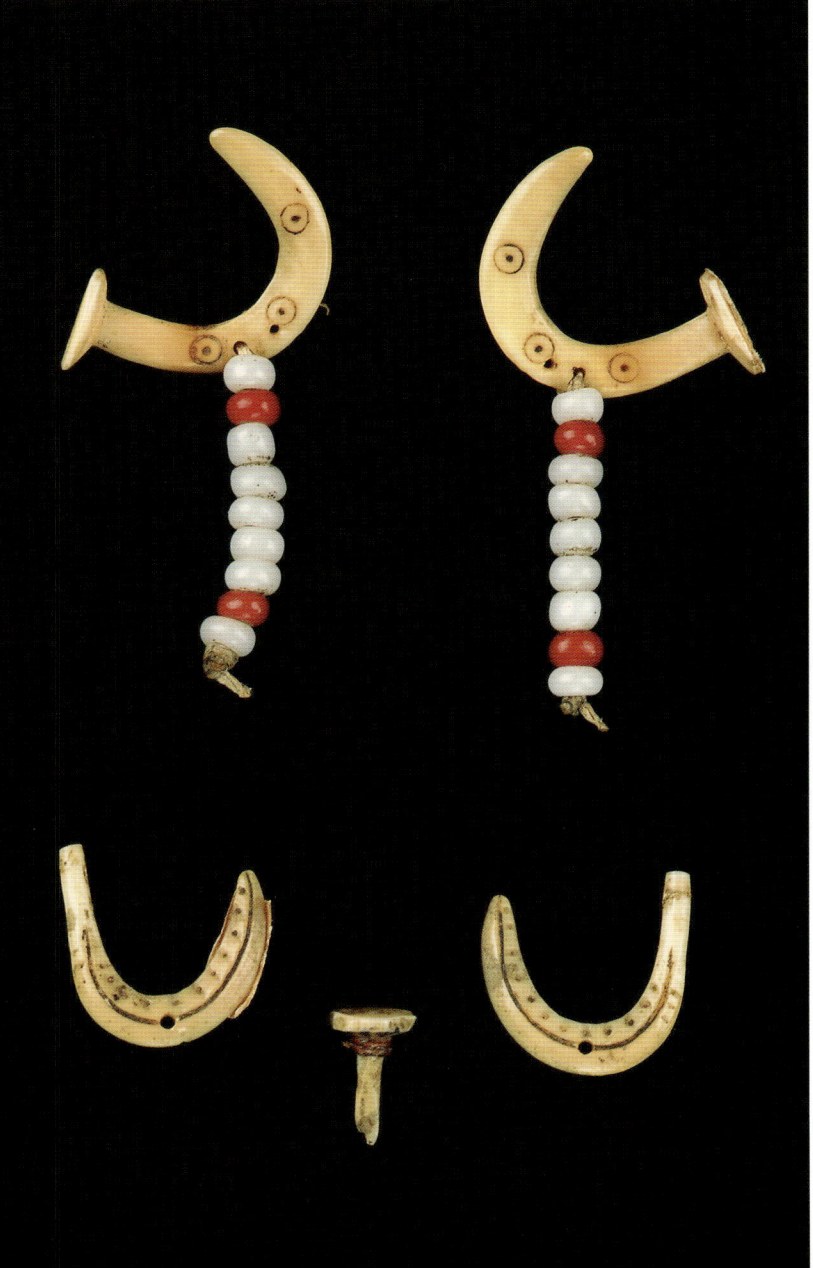

8.7 Two pairs of sickle-shaped ivory lip ornaments, one plain and the other decorated with strands of beads. Jacobsen wrote: "Young girls make three holes into the lower lip—in the middle and to the right and left. Into these small holes are placed nails of bone so that the nail head touches the gums. The bone nails that extend outward from the right and left holes are usually curved, whereas the center plug is straight. The labrets extend out a few millimeters; one or more strings of beads, reaching to the chin, are hung thereon." IVA5109a, b, c; IVA5100a, b.

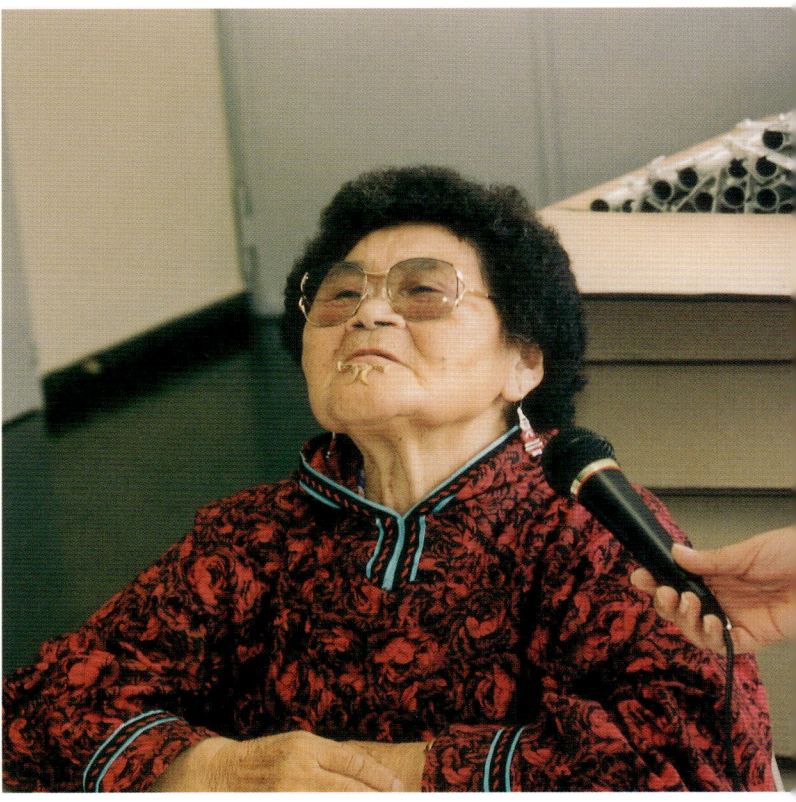

8.8 Annie balancing a pair of caqiqsiik (women's sickle-shaped labrets) just below her lower lip.

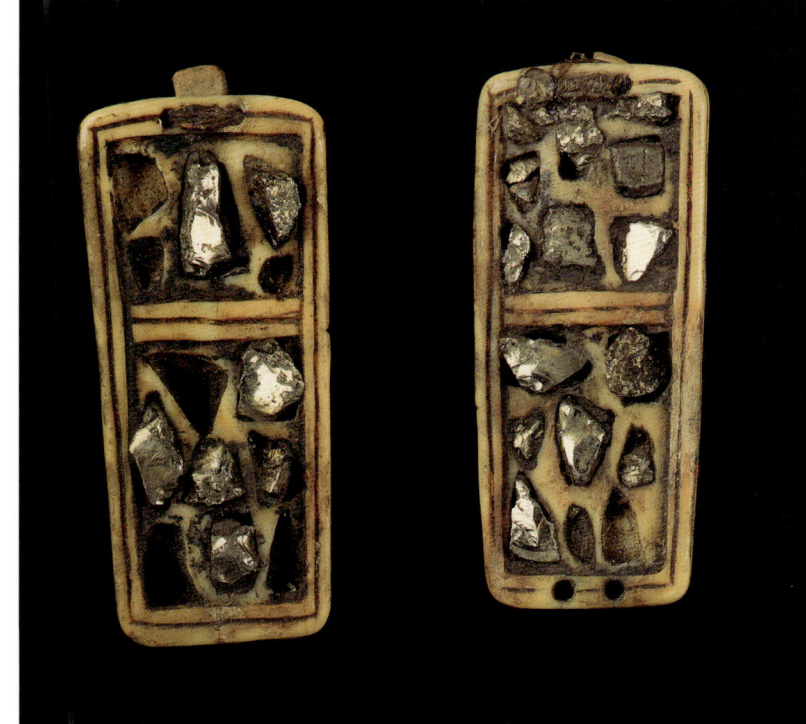

8.9 *Aç'uret* (earring hooks) from all over the region. Clockwise from the top: IVA5082, IVA5079, IVA5063, IVA3624, IVA5076, IVA5071.

8.10 Large bone hooks with pyrite fastened to the hollowed-out front face by means of adhesive. Jacobsen described these and five similar pairs from Cape Vancouver as particularly beautiful and as valuable as diamonds, worn by only the wives of men of high position. Catherine recalled seeing raw pyrite on Nelson Island when she was a child. IVA5073a, b.

traveling [magically] underneath the land, flickering objects were falling like rain all around him. As they fell, he'd reach down and take some of them. They were objects beaming with light. When he suddenly came out to our land, the light was still shining on them. Apparently they were *pipigaat,* like these here. Some of the ore he saw at that time were so beautiful and as long as little puppy feces. But since they were heavy, he only took a few home.

Later in the week, we would see a half dozen pairs of *aqlitet* (earrings) with ivory hooks and bead pendants from the mouth of the Kuskokwim.[12] Jacobsen wrote that one pair with shell and bead pendants (fig. 8.11) pointed toward trade,[13] because mussel shells were usually found only on the west coast of Nelson Island and the nephrite might have come from Kotzebue Sound. Annie unsuccessfully tried to put the hooks through her own ears, then held up another pair from the lower Kusko- kwim with a connecting necklace.[14] Jacobsen wrote that some people always wore earrings with neck chains, while others wore bead pendants, and he wondered whether this indicated that the girl was married.

8.11 Two pairs of aqlitet (earrings), one with a connecting necklace and the other with shell and bead pendants, which Jacobsen wrote pointed toward trade. Annie commented: "These earrings are connected with a few strings of beads with mink teeth strung between them.... It's so good to see this pair, especially since I had a pair like this when I was a girl. They called these earrings made to be worn by girls nakacuguarraat [tiny pretend bladders]." IVA5092, IVA5093a, b.

8.12 Catherine modeling a pair of earrings connected with a strand of beads. IVA5090.

Catherine modeled a second pair of earrings from the lower Kuskokwim (fig. 8.12),[15] and Annie held up a third pair from the lower Kuskokwim[16] with a button fastened to its tip: "These are nicely done, too, with strands of beads between the earrings, *agluirun* [literally, "device for an *agluquq* (jaw)"]. These were called *agluirutet*" (fig. 8.13).

Iinrut, Uyat-llu / Amulets and Human Figures

After lunch we looked at a group of antler and ivory dolls (fig. 8.14)—four from the lower Yukon,[17] five from Cape Vancouver,[18] and five from the Kuskokwim[19]—all of which Jacobsen said were intended as toys for children (fig. 8.15). Many were ornamented with necklaces and labrets, and some had bead or metal eyes. Two were described as shamanic devices, and Jacobsen noted that dolls were often made as amulets for young girls (fig. 8.16).[20] The last and largest ivory figure from Nushagak was tied around with caribou sinew and had labret holes in its lower lip (fig. 8.17).[21] Jacobsen wrote that a shaman could have made it to represent a "protecting spirit." Paul picked up where Jacobsen left off:

Some were probably *iinrut* [amulets] and some were probably *inuguat* [toy dolls, from Iñupiaq *inuk,* "person"]. As I look at these, I know some are play dolls and some aren't. The play dolls had clothing and were flexible enough to be set in a sitting position.... When children played, they did not keep their dolls in a standing position but sat them down, too. This dressed figure is not a toy doll because it is inflexible and its garment has no sleeves. It could be an *iinruq.*

8.17 For Wassilie, this unassuming piece was the most impressive—a simple wooden storage device from the Kuskokwim to protect earrings that were not in use, as the ivory hooks on earring backs easily broke. He recalled: "This piece of wood was tied on both ends; an ivory piece was placed here and was made into an earring hook. Once the earring hook's front and sides were done, it was placed in this vice and decorated. Gosh, people back in those days were so resourceful. These fasteners are made out of sinew thread." IVA5091.

Paul thought that most of the figures Jacobsen had collected were *iinrut*.

Wassilie then spoke about the use of *uyat* (human figurines, literally, "necks") as *iinrut* in the Kuskokwim area:

These are what we called *uyat*. The parkas and bodies of the *uyat* were made from bird-neck skins. People in the upper regions of the Kuskokwim River put figurines they called *yugat* [dolls, from *yuk* "human being"] out in the wilderness. But the figures they called *uya* . . . were used as *iinrut*. I have heard that these figurines made whistling sounds. When a person heard a whistling sound, he'd know that it was the sound of an *uya*.

Apparently, at Caunermiut a person had an *uya* the same size as an *irniaruaq* [toy doll, literally, "pretend child"]. It was kept in a house fully dressed and equipped with a bowl and dipper. In the fall time, a person would fill the *uya*'s bowl and dipper. Ikamratkuk, a family provider from Caunermiut, put a bit of food in the *uya*'s bowl. The disappearance of the food and water predicted that the people there were going to catch a lot of caribou in the coming season. One of those times, the *uya* started making whistling sounds. Then one day when it whistled continuously, they moved it to the cache and kept it there. Since our own perceptions are not the same as theirs, the *uya* always had a parka on it. Villages always had *uyat*, and they were like *iinrut* for the community. They also used the *uyat* to predict whether they would have lots of game throughout the coming year.

At the end of the week, we would see two such large, clothed wooden dolls—one a woman with nose beads and the other a smiling male figure with bead labrets (fig. 8.18). Jacobsen said they were called "Inerak or Inrok=Numnayorte=Yuoak meaning 'the woman whose spirit protects the house'" (probably *iinruq enem nayurtii yua*, "medicine doll for the house"). He wrote that in the past, such images were hung or placed at the house entrance to provide protection for both the dwelling and its occupants and viewed the figures as evidence of ancestor worship: "At least it is believed that deceased shamans helped their living relatives." Wassilie reiterated what he had said earlier: "Some *uyat* hanging in houses made noises. . . . Some people in the upper Kuskokwim area put their *uyat* outside in the wilderness, but some kept them in their house in the back or set them on the end of the *nakirqatak* [sidewall]."

Later that week, we also looked at two small ivory faces from Cape Vancouver.[22] Paul noted that one was that of a man, judging from the labrets placed on each side of its chin, and mentioned again that labrets were used by those on Nunivak to remind them of the walrus people their ancestors had encountered. Jacobsen had said that the tiny masks might have been toys for children or decoration. Paul was certain they had a special use: "These weren't just made for no reason but were used for some purpose. . . . Perhaps these faces were on *uyat*, or perhaps this was the face on an *iinruq*. Objects like these were used to bring well-being and good health."

Along with the dolls, Paul and Wassilie identified a number of other ivory carvings as possible *iinrut*, including two tiny owls, a seal, and a belt decoration from the Kuskokwim (fig. 8.19). Jacobsen had also collected three small bone human figures (fig. 8.20) from Cape Vancouver, but he did not know their use and suggested that they might be either amulets or toys.[23] Wassilie viewed them, like the larger figures, as *iinrut*.

Catherine then spoke about *iinrut* in use today. She said that she used to think all *iinrut* came from *angalkut*, but after listening to Wassilie and Paul, she now viewed the crucifix she wore around her neck as a kind of *iinruq*. She then told the story of two boys at the mission school who had stolen something. That night, as they slept, a presence appeared in their dormitory,

8.14 Antler and ivory dolls identified by the elders as iinrut (amulets) as opposed to play dolls, which had clothing and were flexible enough to set in a sitting position. Clockwise from the top: IVA4510, IVA4039, IVA4525, IVA4538, IVA4531, IVA4532.

8.15 Ivory doll from Cape Vancouver identified by the elders as an iinruq (amulet) as opposed to a play doll, as Jacobsen suggested. IVA4531.

8.16 Ivory iinruq from Cape Vancouver. IVA4525.

8.17 Ivory iinruq from Nushagak tied around with caribou sinew. IVA5320.

Two large, clothed wooden dolls, one a woman with nose beads from Russian Mission and the other a smiling male figure from the lower Yukon with bead labrets. IVA4197, IVA4198.

8.19 Paul and Wassilie identified these small ivory carvings as iinrut, including two tiny owls, a seal, and a belt decoration. Describing the last, Paul said: "This piece with human face designs on both ends—one has red eyes, and one has black eyes. . . . Back in those days, people had objects they called iinrut, which they kept for protection. I'm quite certain this was an iinruq." IVA4761, IVA4760, IVA4768, IVA4718.

8.20 A small bone figure, which Wassilie identified as an iinruq, adding: "The yuungcarat [ones under a shaman's care] always kept their iinrut covered. The iinrut protected the yuungcarat from harm. [My oldest brother] Qunun'aq's iinruq depicting a common loon was always kept in a case and protected by our parents." IVA4534.

8.22 Close-up of two tiny ivory carvings. IVA4756, IVA5460.

sitting at the feet of all the children. The next morning, one of the boys was found dead, while the other—the one wearing a cross—was spared from death. Catherine concluded: "We who are Catholics have to wear this cross all the time. It is our protection." Paul took up the comparison with gusto:

Today we have priests who are granted the power to help people. And back before Christianity was brought to our people, we had our own appointed healers already recognized by the Creator. But when missionaries arrived, they came with their own theology.... When they first came, they should have said, "You have been granted life by God with a belief system adapted to your own culture. Continue to live as you have done, following your faith in your customs and heritage...." We would have continued our culture, maintaining our traditions.

Catherine then told of one of her relatives who maintained both a belief in God and in the power of *iinrut*:

She told me that she couldn't abandon the use of *iinrut*. She said that when she first became aware, people practiced those traditions. Then she added that . . . she had strong faith in God's laws. She mentioned that an *angalkuq* had helped her into health, too, when she became sick. The *angalkuq* told her that her womb was not well . . . and doctored her and replaced her womb with a spotted seal's womb. The *angalkuq* said, "As long as you live, don't eat a blackfish's tail." She followed the instructions of the *angalkuq* and didn't eat blackfish tail after that.

Jacobsen had also collected more than three dozen small ivory and bone carvings in the shape of fish, seals, walrus, bears, wolves, caribou, birds, and creatures of indeterminant nature from all over the region (fig. 8.21, fig. 8.22).[24] He gave no Yup'ik names for any of the carvings and wrote that, as with human figures, most were made as toys for children. Commenting on three pieces from Fort Alexander,[25] he said that "such carvings are made as a pastime in winter, and in summer when the ships arrived, they are traded for some little thing." We took our time examining the figures, and Annie began to tell the origin story of life-size human figures that Jacobsen saw along the coast near Togiak, which can be seen in that area to this day.

Across from Togiak River is a river called Ingricuaq, which flows right in front of the cannery. On the north side of Ingricuaq are two mountain peaks . . . called Ingricuak. The small house of the two grandchildren is still visible at the end of one of the peaks. The grandmother and her two grandsons lived there.

The two boys had a little skin boat. Their grandmother allowed them to play with their boat only when the tide was low. One day after the boys had gone out, their grandmother began to hear a faint yelling sound. When she went to investigate, they were in the middle of the river, furiously trying to get back to land. One of the boys was pushing with an *asaurun* [pole, oar], and one was trying to paddle with an *anguarun* [paddle]. She yelled out instructions to them, then rushed back into the house. She

8.21 Ivory and bone carvings in a variety of forms, which Jacobsen took to be children's toys, made as a pastime in winter. From left to right: IVA4744, IVA4749, IVA5456, IVA5460, IVA4734, IVA5375, IVA4841, IVA4756.

grabbed her fox-fur piece, wrapped it around her shoulders, and went out. . . . She started running along the shore, crying and singing to her grandchildren.

> You two down there
> You two down there
> To the big mountain
> Let the wind blow you up to it
> Down there
> You two down there
> You two down there
> To Nunivngayaq
> Let the wind blow you up to it
> Down there

As the strong tide was coming in, the current was shifting and their boat was flowing fast with the current. Their grandmother ran, following the curves of the river. . . .

As she continued to sing, their voices became harder to hear. As she watched them, they disappeared behind the islands down below their house. Then at their southernmost base, their grandmother abruptly sat down, still wearing her red-fox fur piece draped down her back. They say that rock used to be shaped exactly like a human. The upper back of the humanlike rock figure was covered with red rock flowing like a shawl, and the figure had a lifelike head with a face. The rock figure was located at the point of Ungalaqliq. . . .

The two grandsons apparently were pulled by the current up to Nunaalukaq Bay. I've heard that there was a rock that looked exactly like a skin boat with two human figures in it. One figure at the front appeared to be pushing away from the shore with an *asaurun,* and another figure at the back appeared to be pushing with an *anguarun.* . . .

Then the same year as the Great Death [1918 influenza epidemic], two hunters heard noise coming from those two rock figures. The two rock figures were merrily laughing and whistling. And during the same year, Unkuugiiq also lifted her chest up and turned around, as if to look at something, . . . turning toward her old village, Tarunguaq. During the same time, Ugli was found bending over her bowl. All of the rock figures changed positions just before the Great Death worldwide epidemic. I've heard that Unkuugiiq was taken by someone not too long ago . . . but apparently it broke through the bottom of the ship and sank.[26]

NINTH DAY Women's Sewing Tools and Belts and Men's Hats

Mingqusviutat / Needle Cases

We began our day with a box of finely decorated needle cases (fig. 9.1), including fourteen from the lower Yukon[1] and thirteen from between Cape Vancouver and Nushagak.[2] Jacobsen identified twelve more from the Yukon as "Ojamit=Minkusivit," which he translated as "hanging needle box."[3] A number were made from the hollow wing bones of swans, with wooden plugs resembling the heads and tails of animals. Some had elaborate engravings, including one (fig. 9.2) showing a five-masted ship and a giant riding a kayak. These were made to be stored in sewing bags, whereas cases from the Yukon were also often carved from ivory in the shape of an arrow point and attached to the belt with a pulled-through leather strap into which the needles were placed (fig. 9.3). The ends of these straps were decorated with tiny bird bones, animal teeth, and once-valued items, such as broken labrets. Jacobsen commented on one Kuskokwim piece that such cases were often the gift of a groom to his bride.[4] Annie immediately tackled this diversity:

We women are always searching for containers for our needles, and here are many needle cases, . . . but they were not made identically. Some were made to look like land animals and some like sea mammals. They are beautifully crafted. I like this cute one here. Although they were meant to be needle cases, some wore them as necklaces [fig. 9.4]. . . .

In those days they made holders for needles from quills by stopping up the tip openings. *Anguarutnguat* [three-cornered skin-sewing needles] were kept in a separate case, while *mingqutpiat* [genuine needles] were kept in another. They knew exactly which case of needles to pick for various sewing projects.

They made sure the cases closed tightly. This is a miniature animal carving with its mouth wide open. This one is very beautiful. It is something a woman would cherish owning because it is so lovely. And it is decorated with circles within circles and dots. Its lid is made out of a miniature carved head with such beautiful little eyes.

I've heard that the *amllit* [monster fish] are never seen without spots when they surface suddenly from the depths of lakes [see

9.1 Three ivory needle cases, carved in the shape of fish and sea mammals. From top to bottom: IVA5028, IVA3994, IVA5345.

9.2 Ivory needle cases with wooden plugs. The top case shows a five-masted ship and a giant riding a kayak. From top to bottom: IVA3813, IVA3986, IVA3809.

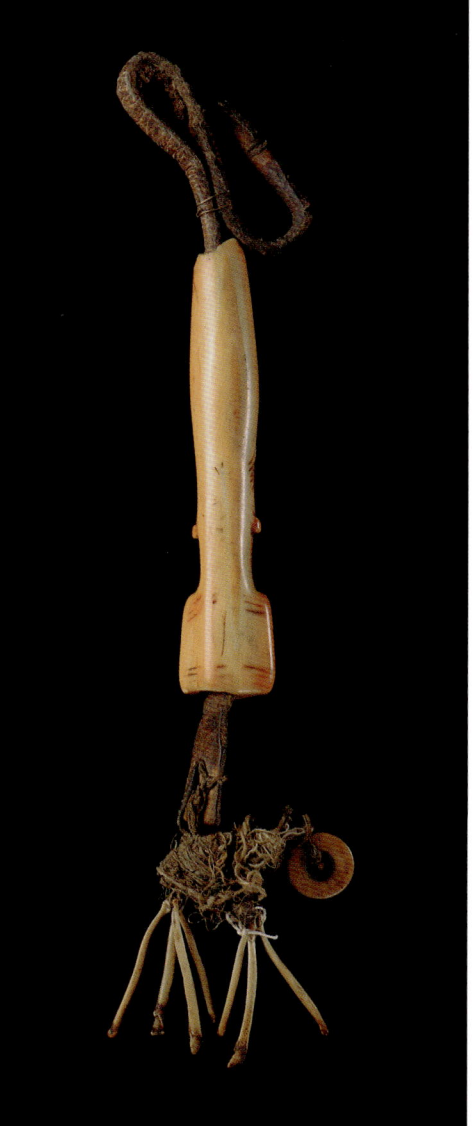

9.3 Hanging needle case carved in the shape of an arrow point and made to attach to the belt with a pulled-through sealskin strap into which the needles were placed. Attachments include animal teeth, broken labrets, and other valued objects, perhaps viewed as iinrut (amulets). IVA5490.

9.4 Picking up one of the needle cases that Jacobsen said was meant to hang from one's belt, Annie pretended to hang it around her neck, saying: "This one has a hole where a line was strung through. These are its miniature gunwales. This needle case has a walrus-head design on its front. The holes on both ends were covered with something at one time, but the covers are gone now. People back in those days engraved their own designs on their things. This has an arrow design on it. Perhaps the owner of this piece was related to [the warrior] Apanuugpak. Perhaps this needle case belonged to Apanuugpak's wife."

9.5 Ivory needle case finely engraved with circle-and-dot designs (detail from fig. 9.14). IV/53

9.6 Bag fasteners from Cape Vancouver and the Kuskokwim. IV/4986, IVA4980.

Third Day]. The spots on them were as large as the opening of a kayak. The designs on some of these objects we're looking at probably depict them. I'm suddenly reminded of some of the stories I heard when I see designs like these. (fig. 9.5)

Nunguyutet, Tekret, Mingqutet-llu / Bag Fasteners, Thimbles, and Needles

As Jacobsen traveled down the coast from St. Michael, he must have purchased the ivory and bone sewing-bag fasteners of every woman he met. By the end of his journey, he had accumulated dozens, including fifteen from the Yukon, twenty-six between Cape Vancouver and the Kuskokwim, and twenty-two from the Kuskokwim to Nushagak (fig. 9.6, fig. 9.7, fig. 9.8). Four from the Yukon (fig. 9.9) were made from the penis bones of otters or other pelt animals.[6] Jacobsen wrote that a strap would be attached to a sewing bag at one end with a fastener at the other. To store the bag, it would be rolled up and wound around with the strap, then secured with the fastener. In some cases, the "sewing-bag pendants" were sewn directly to the bag and a strap wound around the fastener to close it. Many were beautifully decorated with line and circle designs (fig. 9.10), and some were carved in the shape of fish, birds, and other animals (fig. 9.11).

Jacobsen collected fewer thimbles, although still a healthy sample, including fifteen from the coast south of Cape Vancouver (fig. 9.12, fig. 9.13), two from the Kuskokwim, and one from the Yukon.[7] All were made of either ivory or bone and were used for all kinds of skin sewing. Jacobsen noted that they were most often found along the coast between the Yukon and Kuskokwim Rivers and that they resembled the shape of European thimbles, which may have served as their models.

Marie summed up the information that our group provided, noting that names for bag fasteners included *nunguyutet* (bag or garment fasteners), *kuukicaat* or *puukicaat* (buttons, both from Russian *pugovitsa*), and on Nelson Island *iqugmiutaat* or *kakiyutet* (from *kaki-*, "to take a stitch"). Wassilie identified the four bone fasteners as otter penis bones.[8] He also gave the name for thimbles as *tekret* (literally, "pointer fingers"),

9.7 Bag fasteners with a variety of circle-and-dot designs. IVA4977, IVA4973, IVA5325.

9.8 Bag fasteners from the Kuskokwim to Nushagak, except the last fastener, which is from the Yukon. IVA5334, IVA5327, IVA5338, IVA3832.

9.9 Bag fasteners, the top one made from an otter's penis bone. IVA3838, IVA5326, IVA5339.

3.□ Bag fastener with a striking circle-and-dot design. IVA4985.

3.□ Bag fasteners carved as sea mammals, from the Kuskokwim to Nushagak. IVA5322, IVA34□

3.□ Ivory thimbles. IVA5019, IVA5017.

3.□ Ivory and bone tekret (thimbles) from Cape Vancouver. IVA3910, IVA3911, IVA3914, IVA13□ IVA3909.

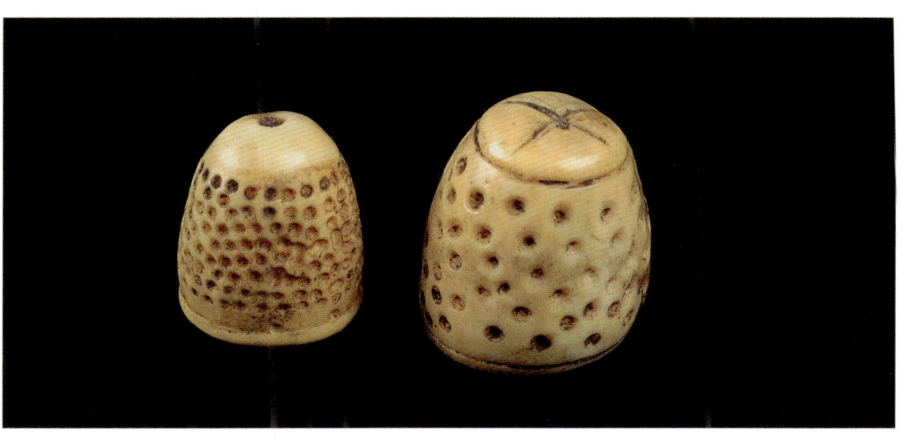

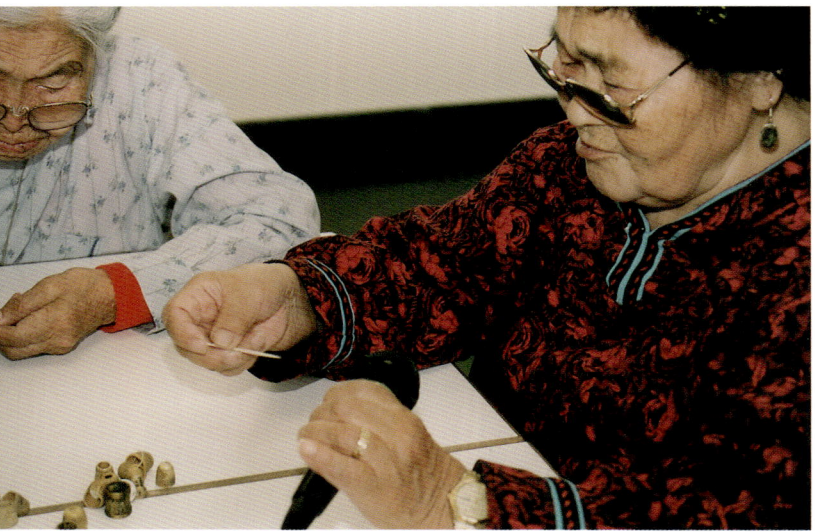

9.14 Ivory thimble, needle case, and bone needle. IVA5006, IVA5347, IVA3777.

9.15 Annie using a bone needle to sew an imaginary seam.

noting that some people call them *akngirnailitat* (literally, "something that prevents pain") and that on Nunivak they call them *keniutet.* Annie added what she remembered:

These *tekret* are nice. . . . At present we use metal thimbles. . . . A needle wouldn't slip when a woman sewed using them. They come in different sizes since our fingers aren't all the same. . . .

When a young man started to court a young woman, he made her these things. . . . I was reminded of this when I was looking at the *iqugmiutaat.* He'd make her bag fasteners and thimbles and give them to her in private or when he happened to run into her outside. That was the custom of the people.

When a young man was captivated by a young woman, he'd give her carefully made bag fasteners and story knives. At times a young man will fail in wooing a young woman . . . as if he had lost his catch. We all have experienced almost catching an animal or a fish escaping when we thought we caught it. They say this is not so different from actual courting and losing the one pursued. At times the young woman changes her mind, . . . goes back to him, accepts the things he made for her, and marries him.

One last group of sewing implements remained—five bone needles and a container for sinew thread, all from the lower Yukon (fig. 9.14).[9] The needles were for skin-sewing in places where European goods had not come. The term for needle that Jacobsen recorded is probably a variation on *kapun* (from *kape-,* "to poke in"), translated today as "hypodermic needle," but our group used the term *mingqun* (from *mingqe-,* "to sew"). Annie took one in hand and pulled it toward her, sewing an imaginary seam (fig. 9.15):

These needles go with the cases. . . . This is a needle made out of ivory that looks like it would work well in mending grass. . . . You'd push the threaded needle through the material and pull it out on the other side and repeat the process. I'd use this for weaving grass baskets.

This needle would be good to use on material that is not easily torn. These needles are extremely sharp. A young girl's lessons in sewing begin with sewing unravelled seams or old, torn parkas. Some girls discovered that they enjoyed sewing early in life, and some didn't.

Wassilie then described needle-making in the tundra region: "People down on the coast made needles out of ivory. But in the Akula area, people made needles out of the fibula from a crane's lower leg, for use on thick leather. They took them out in a raw state. They were very sharp because a crane's skeletal parts are very strong. A cooked one would not be the same, so they made the needles without cooking them first. We called these kinds of needles *kakuutet.*"

Once again, Paul took these tools as evidence that God had given Yup'ik people the ability to create the things they needed to survive before Euro-Americans arrived. He also identified one so-called sewing needle (fig. 9.16) as a net-making device: "I don't see this one as a needle. Back at my home, we have fish we call *quarruuget* or *cukilget* [sticklebacks or needlefish]. My grandmother had a needle that was exactly the same size as this

9.16 Paul identified this tool as a needle used to knit nets to catch needlefish, rather than to sew skins or cloth. IVA3772.

were stronger than the rounded kind we called *mingqutpiat* [genuine *mingqun* (needle)]. When [you are] sewing thick skins, they penetrate without much effort, but when you use a regular needle, it is hard to push it through. . . . We used rounded needles when we sewed cloth because they did not cause it to fray. When I first became aware, I saw women using needles like that. Sewing machines were a rare item. . . .

Tegglit [beads] were sewn on things with a tiny *quagulek*. The regular needles were used to thread beads when they made necklaces. That was how those needles were used.

Once again, Annie wished she could take one home. Paul closed with a third term for skin-sewing needles: "The kind she called *quagulek*, back home we call them *ciilat* [three-cornered needles]. *Ciilat* and not *seal-at*." Everyone laughed.

Naqugutet / Women's Belts

We now spread six elaborate caribou-mandible belts on the table. One was from Andreafski, two from between the lower Yukon and Cape Vancouver (fig. 9.17), and three from between the Kuskokwim and Nushagak (fig. 9.18, fig. 9.19).[11] Jacobson said that all were women's belts made of a wide strip of seal leather on which one to three rows of "reindeer teeth" were sewn as "trophies of the hunt." The belt fasteners did not sit at the belt ends but one-third from the end, held in place by a leather loop attached a third of the way along the opposite side. Ivory hooks were occasionally used as fasteners, especially on the lower Yukon. All kinds of valued items hung from the different belts, including beads, cartridge shells, beluga teeth, and metal watch parts. Marie held one highly decorated belt in the air and shook it gently so that we might record its tinkling sound. She and Annie then took turns holding them gently around their waists and presenting them in an imaginary dance.

Laying the belts back on the table, Annie was the first to speak:

Here lie different belts, and some are very long and some are short. Their fringes are all made from small animal teeth, and they look very beautiful. And these caribou teeth are sewn onto leather that has a very thick backing made out of sealskin that is commonly

[...] that she used to knit a device to catch needlefish. [...] was knitting with was gathered here, and the end of the twine was tied to this one. As she sat and knitted and as the [...] shorter, she'd pull it here to lengthen the thread." [...] agreed with Paul, adding that needlefish dip nets were bag and deep, and their sides had larger mesh than the bottom.

These were not the only needles in the collection. On Tuesday, Annie's attention had been drawn to two iron skin-sewing needles from the Kuskokwim made from filed-down nails[10]:

These needles were used on thick skins. They were called *quagulget* [three-cornered needles, from *quaguk*, "sharp edge"], and some called them *anguarutnguat* [imitation *anguarun* (paddle)]. These

9.17 Woman's belt from the coastal tundra below the Yukon decorated with double rows of white beads instead of caribou incisors, separated by rows of black and blue beads. A row of beluga teeth—as valued on the coast as caribou teeth were upriver—hang from its lower edge. IVA4504.

9.18 Massive woman's belt from the Kuskokwim, containing more than three hundred and fifty sets of caribou incisors in three rows, as well as large brass buttons sewn at the end of each row. IVA5441.

9.19 Caribou-mandible belt with a single row of caribou incisors decorated with teeth and bullet shells. IVA5439.

used for boot soles. These belts are very nice, as well as wide. They are beautifully decorated.

These look like *pat'luunat* [cartridge shells] dangling from these strings, mixed with teeth. . . .

At present, we never see women wearing belts. In the old days, belts were very important. In those days *caagnitellriit* [people restricted from certain activities due to puberty, childbirth, miscarriage, or death] were required to wear belts at all times. Women wore belts all the time [to keep their personal debris, like dust, from falling or spreading out to the boys or men].

Women wore these types of belts, but I've never heard people talking about men wearing them. When my mother stopped using her belt, she put it away up at Cauyarmiut, but her cousin started to tease her and said, "You evidently wore a belt decorated with human teeth." My mother got annoyed at her and said that her belt was decorated with caribou teeth. Her cousin said, "You are so impoverished." She didn't know how caribou teeth looked. My mother just laughed.

Paul then spoke at length about the hard work and skill such belts represented:

The process of acquiring materials for these finished items was not an easy task. When other people saw women wearing belts like these, they automatically knew that their husbands were excellent hunters. When women wore belts like these during the big dance festivals, the ones who looked at them would feel awe and applaud their husbands' proficiency at hunting. In those days, since people knew that men clothed their women, they would automatically recognize what type of man a woman had married. . . .

These cartridge shells were for gunpowder . . . and were attached to the belt at the place where the *kenervik* [primer] goes.

These teeth came from many caribou. Evidently, someone caught more than one hundred caribou and provided teeth for his wife's belt. . . .

These are the ones that were mentioned in stories.

Wassilie spoke last, commenting on how heavy each belt was and adding detail concerning their construction:

When they collected teeth for belts, they took teeth from the front jaws only. The women wore their belts when they danced and also when they took their men's meals to the *qasgi*. The wife and daughter of a *nukalpiaq* would wear belts like this. Fathers hunted caribou to collect teeth like these for their daughters' belts, too. . . . Our late sister had a belt like this. . . . And like those across there, the belt had *cipnermiutaat* [ends dangling down in the front] with copper decorations, one on each side. *Cipnermiutaat* aren't identical. That one down there also has fasteners made of ivory . . . with anchor designs on it.

Belts were self-fulfilling prophecies—if a woman wore one, she protected her male relatives from her harmful debris, allowing them to be good hunters; and as good hunters, they were able to bring home the animals needed to make her an elaborate belt.

Nagtuqat / Belt Fasteners

The last boxes from Drawer D contained close to one hundred tiny belt fasteners and belt pendants like those Wassilie remembered seeing on his sister's belt.[12] Carved from ivory, bone, and animal teeth in an array of sizes and shapes, they included miniature seals, whales, walrus, wolves, bears, otters, birds, fish, caribou and animal heads. Especially along the lower Yukon, fasteners were also sometimes carved in geometric forms, many etched with circles, dots, and lines. Jacobsen wrote that these fasteners and pendants were used exclusively on belts worn by women and young girls.

Belt pendants also had holes bored through for attachment. Commenting on a pendant from Cape Vancouver,[13] Jacobsen wrote that such pieces hung close to each other on the belt's lower edge and served as decoration: "Often these pendants are carved by young men for their brides and by men for their wives. One finds all kinds of figures among them, those that should bring luck. Also hanging are all kinds of carvings that formerly served other uses, such as broken earrings, needle case pendants, etc. The collective name for such accumulated attachments is "Akkowlongaujit" [aqevlungauyiit, from aqevla- "to dangle"]." He concluded: "Such belts are regarded as special and are often hung on the grave of the deceased."

Altogether, Jacobsen collected sixty-two nagtuqat (belt fasteners from nagte-, "to get snagged")[14] and thirty belt pendants from all over the region. Everyone pored over the box, picking pieces out to examine (fig. 9.20, fig. 9.21, fig. 9.22, fig. 9.23, fig. 9.24). One unusual hand-shaped ivory fastener from Cape Vancouver (fig. 9.25) prompted Paul to describe how a hunter out on the ocean would spot a *citaak* (coffin) on the ice with a hand coming up on its side:

A hunter would aim and spear the hand through the hole in the center. When the spear goes through, the object falls into the water with a rustling sound. The hunter would feel the line being pulled by something caught down in the water. Shortly after, an object would go up resembling a bearded seal and dive back into the water. It would come up and down in the water five times, and each time it came up it would look more like a bearded seal. On the fifth time, it would come up as a complete bearded seal.

Marie asked if they were dangerous, and Paul continued:

When a hunter saw one and didn't know what it was and how to behave around it, he would be frightened. But since the young men had already heard about what they were, they would know what to do if they saw one while hunting. But if a hunter saw one in human form, it would be sitting on the ice with the bottom part of its seal-gut garment flowing out. A hunter would aim and spear it on the hem of its garment. Once hit, the person would fall into the water. And just like the coffin, it would come up and down in the water five times, turning into a bearded seal. I've just recounted what I heard.

As we concluded our study of belts, the conservator, Frau Gesell, brought in a cart of Yup'ik masks that she had just inspected after their return to Berlin. She carried a mask over

9.20 Belt fastener and pendant from the Kuskokwim. IVA4935, IVA4857.

9.21 Belt fastener from the Kuskokwim. IVA4926.

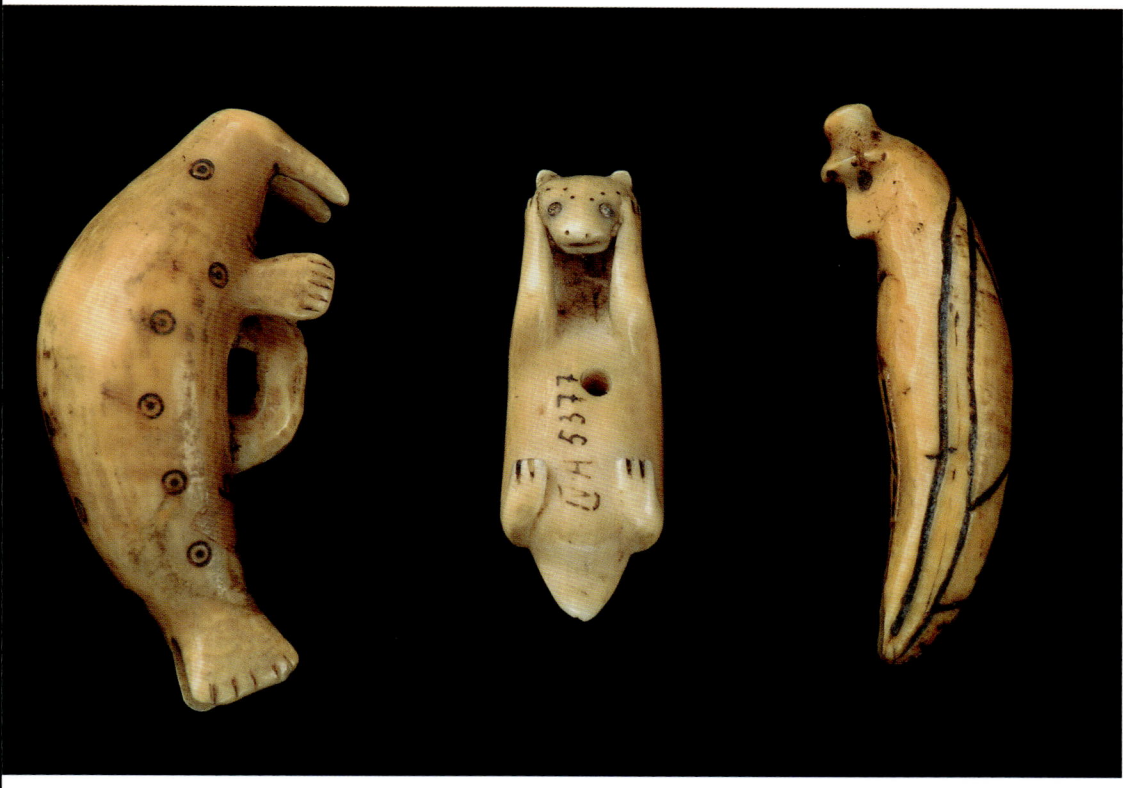

9.22 Belt fasteners from the Kuskokwim. IVA4950, IVA4940.

9.23 Belt fastener from between the Kuskokwim and Nushagak. Jacobsen wrote that most fasteners had holes through which a leather thong could be strung to attach them to the belt. IVA5348.

9.24 Two belt fasteners and a belt pendant in animal form, from between the Kuskokwim and Nushagak. IVA4937, IVA5377, IVA4733.

9.25 Unusual hand-shaped ivory belt fastener from Cape Vancouver. IVA4492.

ice. Further, the form of the hat is more triangular." He later added that Kuskokwim hats had fewer bone ornaments but were also often painted white.

Everyone handled the hats and visors with enthusiasm, trying them on and posing for photos (fig. 9.27). When we settled down to work, Paul was the first to speak:

Nelson Island people call this a bentwood hat. And some would say that so and so is wearing a hat that has an *elqiaq* [visor]. A hunter put this on when he hunted seals perched on the ice. They were painted with *urasqaq* [white clay] back in those days so that a hunter wearing it would blend with the ice. Some called them *ugtarcuutet* [devices to get seals on ice floes, from *ugtaq*, "seal on an ice floe"]. Although they wore hats when it was wet and the water was splashing on them, the main purpose of wearing them was to get close to a seal when they hunted on the ice.

Paul noted that the plainer *elqiat* were worn by men as everyday hats to keep the sun's glare out of their eyes when they paddled in their kayaks.[18] When *angalkut* performed rituals, however, they wore more elaborate headpieces to enhance their powers (fig. 9.28).[19] Jacobsen agreed that "the shamans use the prettiest hunting hats" and that hats decorated with walrus carvings and seagull beaks "could have belonged to a medicine man, as these are their symbols." He described an elaborate visor from the lower Yukon (fig. 9.29) as follows:

to comfortable, speaking enthusiastically in German. Everything had returned unscathed, and her pleasure in pointing this out was spoken in smiles and gestures everyone could understand.

Cayut Elqiat-llu / Bentwood Hats and Visors

Small ivory objects worn by women gave way to large wooden ones worn by men as we turned our attention to a group of bentwood hunting hats and visors. Several were beautifully decorated with ivory and feather attachments (fig. 9.26).[16] Commenting on a relatively plain hat from Togiak[17] painted with a thin layer of white clay, he wrote: "On the Togiak River, where the men are outstanding hunters, the kayak, as well as the harpoons and the lance staff, are painted white; this allows the hunters to get close to the sea animals between the floating

9.26 Describing this hat from the lower Kuskokwim, Jacobsen wrote: *"Wooden hunting hat, [made from one piece of wood] bent and brought together in the back with a piece of reindeer antler sewn on with roots. A leather strip hangs from the back of the hat, [decorated] at the end with bone carvings and three bone beads. Hunters from the Yukon River to the western Aleutians wear this kind of hat to protect the head from moisture and, more important, the eyes from ice and snow reflections. The hat is fastened to the head with a strong leather thong. The two reindeer-antler strips on the right and left show at the front an eagle's head." IVA5475.*

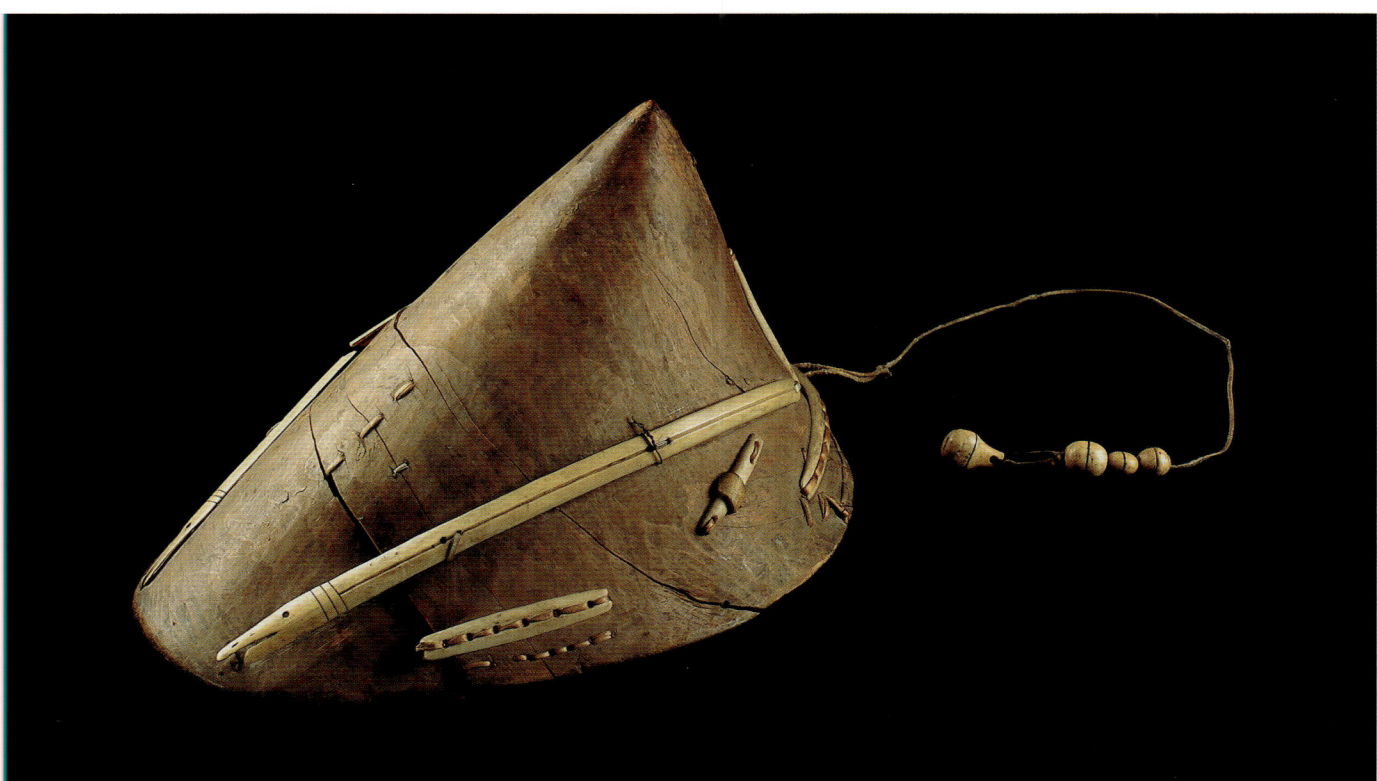

9.27   Andy, Wassilie, and Paul modeling bentwood hunting hats and visors.

9.28   Hunting visor decorated with the tail feathers of male old-squaw ducks, enhancing the birdlike appearance of the hunter. IVA4189.

The hat is partly decoration and partly an eye protection against the sun. After the long, dark winter the eye is more sensitive toward light in the spring. The hat is decorated on the shade [with] two carved walrus heads. Farther to the right and left there is a seagull head carved out of walrus ivory—the shaman's messenger. At each ear [is] a decorated bone, and at the back [is] a feather decoration.

Jacobsen underscored the hat's functions—eye protection and decoration. In contrast, Paul's emphasis on the importance of a hunter donning such a hat during seal hunting was a brief but telling reference to the hat's power to transform the hunter into a seabird in the eyes of the seals he sought. In the well-known story of the boy who lived with the seals, the skilled hunter placed such a hat on his head and disappeared behind an ice floe, emerging on the other side as a murrelet whose soporific breath mesmerized the seals, allowing the hunter to take them. In the water, these closed-crowned visors do indeed give the paddler a much more birdlike appearance, and a distant paddler so equipped looks very much like a bird on a drift log. Such hats are also effective sound collectors, amplifying a hunter's perception of sound in the same way as cupping your hands behind your ears and making it easier for a scattered group of paddlers to remain in voice contact.[20]

Catherine then described seeing Nelson Island hunters wearing similar hats, performing a ritual at the ocean's edge:

I saw these for the first time at Up'nerkillermiut. I think there were four kayaks. When I saw hats like this one, I observed the men before they went down onto the ocean. . . . It was a very windy day, and there were large waves. The white caps all over the ocean made it look so bright. . . . The four men put on their seal-gut rain parkas and their fish-skin mittens. Then each drew the string around his hood and the strings around his wrists . . . and put the skirt of his rain parka around the kayak coaming and drew and securely

9.29 Elaborately decorated hunting hat, possibly worn by an angalkuq to enhance his powers. Wassilie noted: "Its ivory decorations are called cauyat. And these are allgiinraat [male old-squaw duck feathers] . . . used by angalkut to use in their work. They come from ducks that could fly very fast.

"Obviously a man from the coast owned this since it is decorated with walrus designs. When shamans performed rituals wearing these hats, they did it to help the hunters who would be going out to hunt on the ocean in the coming season. These carved walrus were what they wanted . . . to be available to the hunters when they hunted. These look like seagull beaks since seagulls are also ocean creatures." IVA4191.

in the spring. Finally they put on their helmets like these.

The four men were already in their kayaks, and they pushed off in unison, propelling themselves forward using double-bladed paddles. They would go forward, then the waves would drag them back. I do not know what they were up to. Then one of them rolled his kayak, and when it righted nothing had changed and the person was still wearing his helmet. After they rolled their kayaks several more times, they rushed back in unison.

Paul remarked with feeling:

I'm sure they were doing something very significant. I've heard that it is a *mengniarcuun* [song for this particular event, from *menge-*, "to sing a song with drumming preliminary to dancing"] that was always performed by Aternermiut beginning from the olden times. They were probably performing that event at that time. "Aa-aa-aa-aa. Those two waves down below, they are about to break down." Then over from the side someone called out, "Even though they are giving you back talk, go ahead and face them." Then all the drummers would hit their drums in unison and start the beat to the *mengniarcuun*.

Catherine had also observed men wearing bentwood hats performing in the *qasgi*:

As Arnaqulluk and I were playing, we heard people singing from somewhere. When we realized that the singing was coming from the *qasgi*, we ran to it and looked in. Men were sitting on both sides of the room, facing each other. I didn't see any drummers nor did I hear any drums at that time. The men were sitting down, naked to their waists and wearing these hats. They would move and lean to one side in unison and straighten up . . . and then sway to the other side again. I learned the song they were singing at that time.

> *Iyaar iyaar agi-ii-ii-yaa*
> *Iyaar iyaar agi-ii-ii-yaa*
> *Agi-ii-yaa kia-inga-yaa*
> *Iyaar iyaar-aa agi-yai*

I heard the song once that time, and I never forgot it. They also sang it during winter in Nightmute. . . . The song had verses to it, but I have forgotten the words.

Wassilie remarked that male old-squaw ducks, the tail feathers of which men used to decorate their hats, also had a song: "Old-squaw ducks sing like this, *Aarraaraangi*." Paul concluded: "I've heard that when *angalkut* used hats during their rituals, they called their hats *ciayat*. I suspect that was the kind of hat they used with feather decorations on it."[21]

Igauget / Eyeshades

Bentwood hats were not the only means a hunter had to protect his eyes from the sun's glare. We briefly examined a group of six painted wooden eyeshades (fig. 9.30).[22] Paul commented simply, "Before commercially made sunglasses were introduced to our people, they used *igauget* [eyeshades, snow goggles] to keep the sun's rays out of their eyes. These kept people from getting snow blindness in the spring."

Trying one on for size, Wassilie (fig. 9.31) followed Catherine's lead and contributed a song:

> *Igaugek are you taken aback by a ptarmigan*
> *Had you always been startled by a ptarmigan*
> *A ptarmigan has shocked me*
> *A ptarmigan has terrified me*
> *A ptarmigan abruptly landed next to me*
> *And captured all my spirit*
> *Igaugek are you taken aback by a ptarmigan*
> *Had you always been startled by a ptarmigan*

9.30 Hunters used wooden eyeshades such as these both to protect their eyes from snow blindness in the spring and to increase their distance vision by focusing the light. IVA4559.

9.31 Wassilie holding up a pair of eyeshades.

Paul sang another teasing song, and everyone laughed: "You don't have *igauget. Kaviuk, kaviuk, kaviuk* [the sound a ptarmigan makes]."

Nacat, Maqissuutet-llu /
Hats and Things for the Fire Bath

We took a lunch break, singing hymns as we walked down the sidewalk and through the doors of Frei University's nearby student cafeteria. Returning an hour later, we began examining another kind of hat. Along with wooden hunting hats, Jacobsen had brought back four bird-skin hats worn by men as protection from the heat during fire baths.[23] Paul said that the larger hats might be called *nacarpiat* (literally, "genuine hats"). He observed that two were made from the skins of red-throated loons (fig. 9.32). A third was dark owl skin. The last was *tulukaruk* (raven), which Wassilie called *akmaliarall'er* (the one across there), offering as explanation a familiar story:

It's the other name for raven. . . . "Hey you across there, old woman *akmaliarall'er*, where are you going?" "I'm looking for some fat," replied the one across there. "Aa-a. Then when you return home, pass me." "Urru," he replied.

This reminded Marie of the story of owl and raven, and she asked her uncle to tell it, which he did in abbreviated form:

The mother owl was cooing her babies. When the old raven came, he told her to sing to her babies like this, "When your father comes home, you will eat five *kuculut[?]*." But she cooed to her cute little babies with cute long beaks. She noticed that her babies started to look down. Then the old raven sang again, "When your father comes home, you will eat five *kuculut*." Since they remained looking down, she looked closer and noticed that their little beaks, which had been straight, had suddenly curved downward. When the raven said they would be eating five *kuculut*, their beaks suddenly changed shape and became curved. . . . When the raven left, she avenged them by making a curse, saying that the raven would soon be eating old dead dog meat and garbage. Today the raven eats those foods.

Chuckling, Wassilie concluded, "She sang to him, 'You go peck, peck, pecking feces.'"

Earlier in the week, we had looked at other *maqisuutet* (tools for the fire bath)—two respirators from the Yukon, used by sweat bathers to filter out smoke and hot air (fig. 9.33).[24] Both Paul and Wassilie had examined the pieces with great interest. Wassilie spoke first: "Apparently these pieces are *qanermiat* [things held in the *qaneq* (mouth)]. They aren't like the ones I used to see. . . . They are bound with spruce wood. And in the middle is braided line to keep the wood from spilling out. A person would bite into this wooden attachment." Paul said there was little to add but did note that he had seen an elderly man who kept a *qanermiaq* in his mouth when he went out in cold weather to keep from breathing in cold air. He also observed that the string holding the piece together looked like it was made of braided strands of *kelugkat* grass.

Jacobsen also described how men washed with urine and snow after their bath, then dried themselves with bundles of grass like one we had seen earlier in the week.[25] Wassilie remembered their use and how they were made:

These are the tops of a delicious plant that grows on the ocean shore. After the plant is dried, they are split into strands with a *talun* [shredder]. If these were still good, one would attach a handle to the bundle to use as cloth for wiping things. At the end of the wooden piece would be a little loop. After one used this to wipe something, it would be hung on the wall. The split fiber was usually strong, but since this has gotten old, it's brittle. My late father's

9.32 Examining this loon-skin hat and smoke respirator for the fire bath, Paul said: "Men wore these nacat [hats] during their fire baths. These don't appear to have been worn. . . . I've seen only one man with a hat made out of raven skin. He also used the hat when he hunted in the wilderness." IVA4192, IVA4194.

brother had a sponge like this to wipe things. They look like hair. Perhaps these are the roots of negaasget [a kind of edible plant].

Paul listened to Wassilie, then added that people used them to wipe things when towels weren't around:

When men used these in fire baths, they'd wipe their bodies over and over. They'd squeeze these to get rid of the water, and they'd wipe their bodies again until they were dry. They also used split grass to make sponges like these. . . . They'd squeeze them only to get rid of the water because they could break if they were wrung. These are perriutet [towels] for wiping water.

Yuraryaraq / Feather or Fur Hood

The last pieces of headgear we viewed were the most remarkable. Jacobsen described the first as a man's eagle-skin hood from between the Kuskokwim and Nushagak Rivers (fig. 9.34).[26] Wassilie greeted it with recognition:

Back in those days, women made some parkas without hoods. They'd sew a thicker skin collar around the neck opening so it would not tear so easily. Parkas had no hoods. This piece called yuraryaraq [hood, literally, "way of checking outside," from yurar-, "to come up and out of an opening"] was pulled on over the head after a person put on a hoodless parka. . . . People never go without the hoods during the cold winter weather.

This is made from a huge bird. . . . The bird's beak is here at the back of the hood. Big birds like these were called metervik [bald eagle] back in those days. Long ago, two giant eagles lived in the Yukon River area. They called them qiirayulirpiik [big peregrine falcons]. Those giant eagles sang, "Qii-qii-qii."

As Andy pulled the "four-star hood" over his head (fig. 9.35), Wassilie commented on the healing effects of such an action. Like the use of stone amulets, the hood created a boundary, preventing disease from entering one's body.

Our young man here is putting on the yuraryaraq. Now, since I've suddenly remembered what people used to say back in those days,

9.33 Paul holding up a respirator from the Yukon, used by sweat bathers to filter out smoke and hot air. IVA4194.

when he took it off, I said, "Mingugturtuten [you are covering your body with protection]. You will be strong and unyielding." Back in those days, a grandfather would put something of his on his grandson and say, "You are being covered with protection. You will be strong and unyielding. Sickness will not touch you."

Commenting on another squirrel-skin yuraryaraq collected between the Kuskokwim and Nushagak Rivers,[27] Jacobsen wrote that "the head cover shows an animal in fur mosaic." Although Wassilie had never seen a hood like this in use, he added that he had heard that people sometimes wore them alone without a parka. This particular yuraryaraq, he noted, was worn by an adult and would cover the person's shoulders.

Two more squirrel-skin hoods from the same area evoked Annie's admiration[28]:

9.34 Eagle-skin *yuraryaraq* (hood) for use with a hoodless parka. IVA5464.

9.35 As Andy donned the "four-star hood," Wassilie recalled the healing effects associated with putting on and taking off such a garment, acts that covered the wearer with protection from illness.

As an old woman, I'm seeing a *yuraryaraq* for the first time. This squirrel-skin *yuraryaraq* is an adult-size one. This hood is trimmed with caribou skin, and the rest is made of squirrel skin, tails and all. These squirrel skins were from a summer catch. Squirrels with bright spots like these were called *usrapakiiqertellriit*. These pieces were sewn in to lay out the skins. And in the front, since this part of the skin is thin, it was strengthened with backing under the chin, such as a caribou *qaliluk* [old, well-worn caribou parka] would be. And on the sides are the [skin pieces] called *uminguak* [pretend arrow-point designs (dual)]. The workmanship of people back then was very precise.[29]

Uivqurrat / **Round Fur Caps**

We turned to two *uivqurrat* (men's circular skin caps with beaded decorative bands, from *uive-*, "to circle") from Nunivak[30] and three more from Nushagak,[31] each made from a combination of furs, including squirrel, muskrat, caribou, and wolverine. The next day, we also looked at two round sealskin pieces decorated with glass beads from between Cape Vancouver and the Kuskokwim.[32] Jacobsen had described them as decorations for basket covers, a use he had never observed and therefore found questionable. Our group concurred, identifying them as tops for *uivqurrat*.

Drawing particular interest was a piece from the Kuskokwim, which Andy jokingly referred to as "Yup'ik earmuffs."[33] Jacobsen wrote: "Head ring made of leather mosaic with embroidered ear flaps and worn by men to hold the hair smooth; the ear flaps protect the ears against frost. The fur side lies against the ears. The bands are tied under the chin." Trying it on, Annie added what she knew:

This is made with decorations so fine. This part, *maqii* [from *maqaq*, "warmth"] . . . that looks like caribou ears . . . would cover the ears to keep them warm. Since it's turned this way, this side is decorated nicely for people to see. The caribou beard hair does not fade . . . even though it got old. This white part is called *nerukar*. It's sealskin that was bleached by cold winter weather and decorated with beads. The *tungunqucuk* [dark fur trim] is made of caribou skin. . . . When a child puts it on, he'd tie it in front.

The day was ending, and the flow of artifacts in and out of collections had stopped. This was also the end of Paul and Andy's work in Berlin, as both needed to return to Alaska. To mark their departure, that evening we would all be guests at Peter Bolz's home. We walked in his garden and visited his wife and two young children, both of whom impressed Paul as they chattered away in both German and English. That morning, we had discussed what we might bring as gifts to the family and had decided to buy the grass basket Annie had brought to sell at the museum. After the meal, Paul and Andy presented it to Peter and his family on behalf of our Yup'ik delegation.

TENTH DAY Ceremonial Regalia

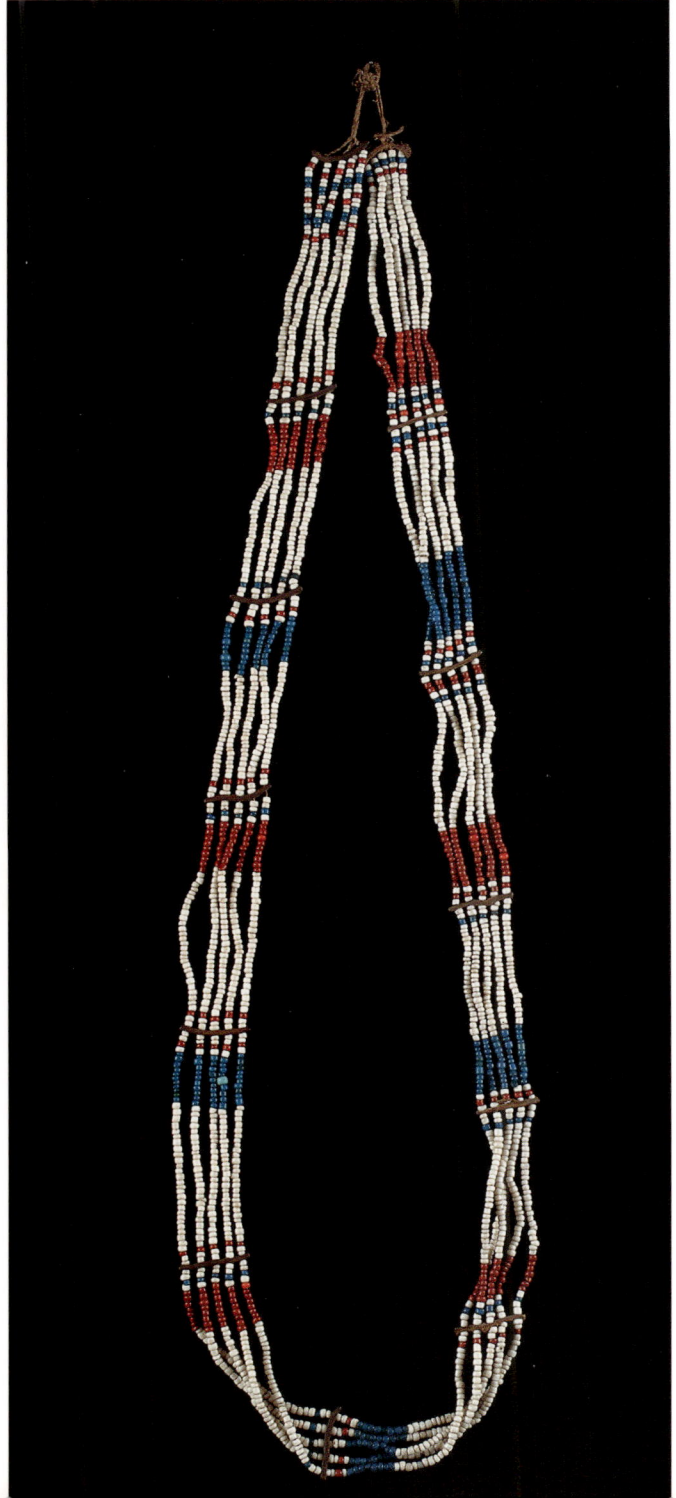

We said goodbye to two of our companions after breakfast, and for the last time Andy and Paul went down the steep staircase at Pension Dahlem, then out to a cab waiting to take them to the airport. A half-hour later, the rest of us took another cab to the museum. This was the last day of an eventful week, and little was said during the ride. When we reached our familiar tables, however, the mood shifted to expectation. What we had come to examine helped lighten our spirits—an array of objects highly prized.

Uyamiit / Necklaces

A variety of bead necklaces lay before us, including a child's necklace from the Kuskokwim (fig. 10.1).[1] Marie identified them collectively as *uyamiit*, and Wassilie began to speak:

Back in those days, the *uyamiit* [necklaces] I saw were not worn very much but were mainly hanging in homes. Girls and young women wore necklaces like these. And also during the Messenger Feast and dances, the *apallirturta* [dance director] wore one like this coming down from his neck and flowing down below his armpit. He would borrow a necklace from one of the women. When dancers wore necklaces, they were appealing to watch as they danced.

Annie, who had worn necklaces like these when she was young, said that the small white beads were *qaterliaraat*.

Wassilie noted the separators, called *iqatat*, included in each necklace: "They counted the beads as they threaded them and added a piece of skin for support between the strands of beads." Some of the necklaces also had ivory bars as separators.[2] Earlier in the week, the men had recognized a small, seal-shaped bone carving from Bushagak, which Jacobsen said was used to separate strings of beads.[3] Paul had noted that *kakauyat* (parka hood tassels) made of *cungauyaraat* (beads) were also strung with pieces of bone to keep them separate.

10.1 Child's uyamik (necklace) from the Kuskokwim, worn on special occasions. IVAE. CO.

Catherine remembered gathering old beads from graves to make new necklaces:

Over at Tununak one day, I was asked to dig for old things with some people up on top of this mountain and in the area below the village. I realized that there were enormous amounts of beads buried underground in the burial sites. Perhaps the beads came from old necklaces like these, or did people pour beads in those areas at times? After we took them home, some women strung them into necklaces after they washed them. I still make necklaces since I have so many grandchildren. . . . I used to see necklaces like these, some

10.2 Young girl's beaded hair ornament from the Kuskokwim, worn on the top of the head with the long pieces on each side pulled forward to the front. IVA5799.

10.3 Nushagak ornament made of beads, box covers, and pieces of an old lamp, worn by a woman over her parka and around her neck during dances. IVA5390.

10.4 Holding up the Nushagak ornament, Catherine commented: "I'm looking at manumiit, my goodness. I'd stand in front of her, wishing I could have one.... These were given to older girls. I used to hold one and put my hands on it, wishing I could own one like it. I left Tununak long before I ever wore one."

very long. Dancers put long necklaces on and wound them around their necks several times when they wore them. I've also seen men wearing these when they direct songs. The necklaces hung from their necks and dangled below their armpits.

Next we looked at a woman's beaded neck ornament from the upper Nushagak.[4] Annie spoke: "The front area of the piece looks very decorative, and if worn by someone, it would lie flat on her chest below her chin.... These black beads with white beads in the middle are all *tegglipiat* [real beads]. This looks like an adult-size piece."

Annie admired a simple strand of bone beads from Nushagak,[5] like those common before glass beads replaced them, saying simply, "If worn by someone, they would look beautiful from a distance." Wassilie suggested that a group of ivory pieces with old-squaw feathers on them from Nushagak,[6] which Jacobsen wrote were used by women when dancing, could have been part of a *nasqurrun* (dance headdress). Earlier that week, we had looked at a bundle of feathers from Nushagak that both Paul and Wassilie identified as *allgiinraat* (tail feathers of male old-squaw ducks), used as adornment in a variety of ways.[7] Paul explained: "Old-squaw duck feathers were used for centuries on many things. Women used them on their *taruyamaarutet* [dance fans]. [Wassilie] also mentioned that they were used on *apallirtuutet* [dance wands]. People back in those days used these as *qirussit* [decorations] on dance paraphernalia."

A young girl's beaded hair ornament from the Kuskokwim (fig. 10.2) drew Annie's particular admiration, and she asked Catherine to stand and model it.[8] At first she interpreted it as *kakauyat*, the decorations hung from the backs of parka hoods. Looking at Jacobsen's record, Marie later pointed out that it was indeed a hair piece worn on the top of the head with the long pieces on each side pulled forward to the front.

Jacobsen described another rare ornament from the Nushagak (fig. 10.3), made for women to wear over their fur coats and around their necks during dances.[9] Both Annie and Catherine greeted it with enthusiasm (fig. 10.4). Annie spoke first:

We are so happy to see these objects that are placed in front of us. Objects like these were made when new things were being introduced to the people. *Manumik* [brooch, pin, from *manu-*, "front side"] is the word given on the paper. These two identically made brooches were designed to hang opposite each other in the front lapel of a person's garment. These are *kakikaraat* [pins] ... made of metal and ... have a piece of *nerun* [dried esophagus] sewn on.

Aaggaqtaat / Gloves

We turned to four pairs of fancy gloves. The first was a pair of men's tanned caribou-skin dancing gloves from the lower Yukon (fig. 10.5).[10] Annie spoke enthusiastically, "We called these gloves made with decorations *aaggaqtaat*.... And fake nails were put on the gloves.... Some called them *aaggsiik*. Beads were stitched on pieces of dried esophagus on the backs of the gloves." Wassilie said that in the Akula region, they called such gloves *aigsaat* or *yuaralget*, while on the Yukon they called them *aasgaat*.

Annie noted that the back of the gloves was painted with *uiteraq* (red ocher), and she spoke with feeling about its significance.

Uiteraq was a very important item to have at all times.

It is known that *uiteraq* is very shy and unpretentious. When a person painted something with red ocher, she turned her back away from others and concealed her work. And when someone came into the house as she was applying red ocher to something, she'd put away her work quickly so that it would not be seen. When a person painted something with red ocher with others watching her, the color came out weak. But when someone applied red ocher to something without observers, the color would come out sharp and distinctly red, because it did not feel intimidated. It is said that *uiteraq* is bashful.

We briefly examined another pair of thumbless embroidered-leather dance gloves from the Togiak River, decorated with cormorant feathers and a smaller pair of thumbless *aliimatet* (mittens) from the Yukon.[11] Jacobsen viewed the small size of the second pair as reflecting the small size of the female dancer who wore them, and he wrote that the mittens lacked thumbs so the dancer could hold a stick while dancing. A third pair of thumbless mittens (fig. 10.6) from the Togiak River excited Annie's interest and evoked a different explanation for the small size and lack of a thumb[12]:

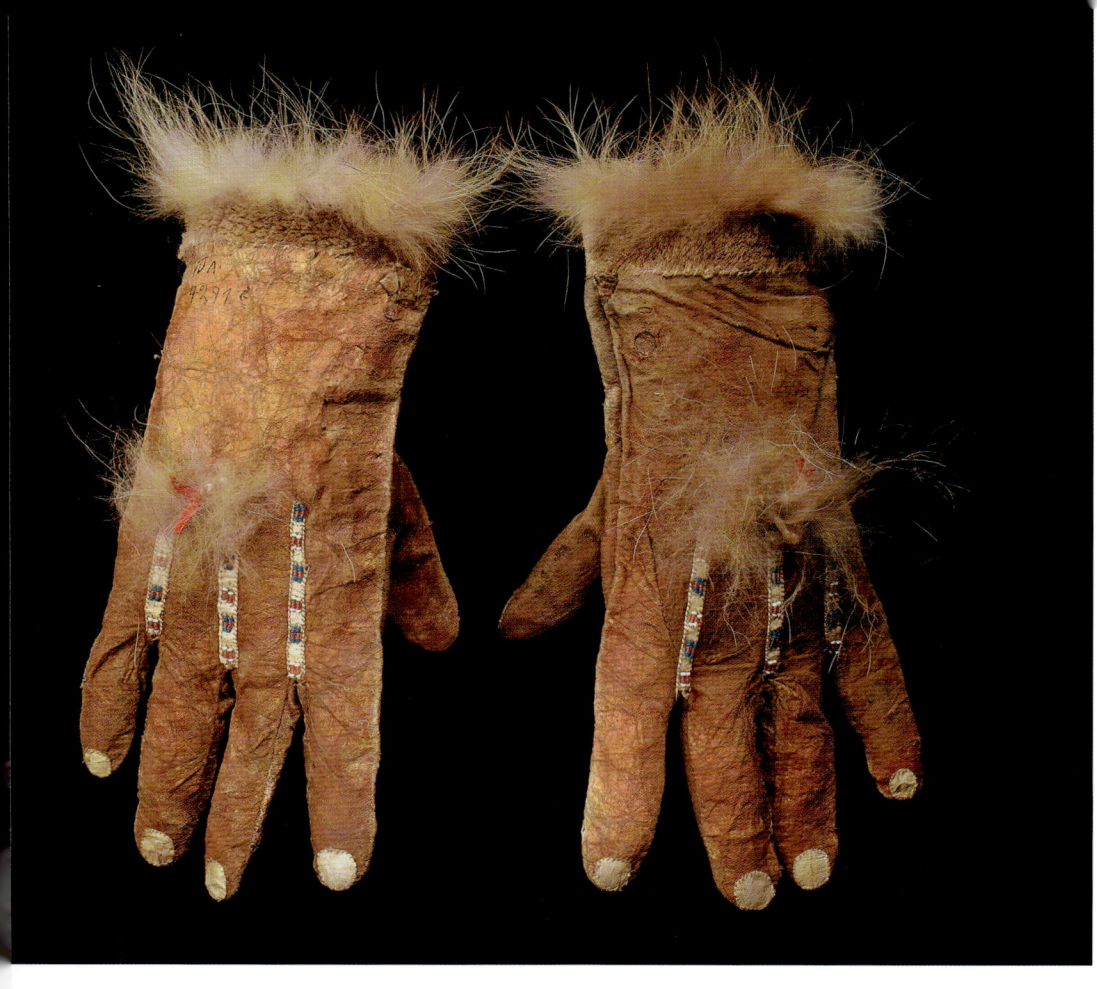

10.5 Pair of men's tanned caribou-skin dancing gloves from the lower Yukon, embroidered with seal throat-skin "fingernails" and beads. IVA4291.

10.6 Thumbless mittens worn by a girl following her first menstruation, when her activity was restricted and her body covered to separate her from those around her, as protection for both her and them. IVA5484.

These mittens are complete, but they have no thumb. They are decorated with pieces of *nerun* [dried esophagus]. The fur trim is made from some kind of bird. And here are the *kepcetaaq* [dyed leather] designs. Since my mother used to say this, I understand these mittens to be for one purpose. She said that when a girl reached puberty, they required her to use mittens with a hole at the thumb. This was back when people observed abstinence laws, *eyagyarat*. . . . During this time people say, "Since these young girls don't observe the *eyagyarat*, they have caused our world to be contaminated. In times to come, along with pollution, people in it will also become corrupt. I wonder what people will do when *Ellam Yua* turns its back on them?" These are mittens an *aglenrrar* [girl who has recently menstruated for the first time and is subject to various restrictions] used when she handled fish and food. . . .

Back in those days, a young girl at puberty wore these kinds of mittens with no thumbs when she did chores in the house. She did not handle things with her bare hands.

Catherine had also seen mittens like these in use. Like Annie she related the disappearance of this past practice to problems in the world today:

The one I saw wore one of a pair of mittens. When a young girl menstruated for the first time, she sat for five days . . . next to the entryway with a twined grass mat hanging to separate her from the others. . . . The girl I observed menstruated in the summer. She did not go out to urinate during the daytime . . . and stayed in isolation for five days. . . . Before she went out to urinate, she put on the mitten, belt, and hood over her head. During that time when people talked about respect for the land, they would say that the world will become polluted. At this time now, what they prophesied has come true. Our earth is polluted today, and its people are corrupt. People are still talking about worse times to come.

10.7 Dance headdress from the Togiak River, made from a band of bleached esophagus rimmed with fur and caribou throat hair on the upper edge. IVA5424.

Nasqurrutet / Dance Headdresses

Now six dance headdresses lay before us on the table (fig. 10.7).[13] Jacobsen noted that this type was most often used on the Togiak River, but this seems unlikely, as other collections and photographs show them in use both on the coast and along the Kuskokwim River. Each consisted of a band decorated with cormorant feathers, *iglak* (bleached esophagus), quill work, and beads, with a rim of caribou throat hair on the upper edge. Jacobsen wrote that they were usually worn by women, although men might sometimes use them. Wassilie elaborated: "Several of these headdresses were worn by men when they conducted music during the dances. These were all dance accouterments. Women always wore headdresses when they danced. The one with porcupine skin is probably a woman's headdress."

Annie held out one headdress, showing how the caribou hair would stand aloft when used in a dance. She commented that women's headdresses usually had *cukluuk* (dangling bead ornaments attached to each side of the forehead) and continued: "These are very old headdresses, and their caribou throat hair has been crushed from being stored. These big ones were probably worn by men. . . . But this fancy headdress was worn by a woman." She then returned to the porcupine quill design work:

I hunted porcupine as a girl. When I caught one, I'd pluck the quills before I went home. When I brought my catch home, our father would scrape the skin to remove the scent of the carcass. After it was cleaned, it was prepared for a meal. As a girl, when I hunted I would take one of my younger brothers with me. You don't have to be a male to catch a porcupine. Since the porcupines moved slowly, I'd club them and kill them. Porcupine meat is very delicious.

Marie asked Annie if porcupines were dangerous, and Annie answered that their quills could be. She had been stuck once and had had to have her hand operated on, and she was told never to hunt porcupine again. Catherine remembered seeing a dog who had been "quilled" and feared them as a result: "Oh please, a human should not ever be struck by a porcupine." This reminded Annie of a story about a porcupine:

One day as the porcupine was wandering along a river, he saw many, many rosehips across the river. To the porcupine, rosehips are very appetizing and delightful to the eye. The porcupine tried to go across to the rosehips, but he couldn't. As he started to cry, he closed his eyes and sang:

*Across there, there,
My Turr'un [cousin] across there
rubbing, rubbing, rubbing*

At the end of the song he opened his eyes and saw a mink swimming along down in the river. The porcupine said, "Hey, you old mink, with a tail that can be used as a ladle, perhaps you could take me to my food across there." Mink answered and said, "I'll come right back and take you across after I take care of something upriver. Wait for me!" Porcupine waited and waited for the mink, but the mink disappeared and was not seen again.

Poor old porcupine closed his eyes and started to cry again, for he was very hungry by now.

*Across there, there,
My Turr'un across there
rubbing, rubbing, rubbing*

When he opened his eyes again, he saw an otter swimming along. The porcupine got excited and said, "Hey! Old otter with a tail that can be used as an *aquun* [wooden frame inserted into squirrel skins to stretch them], perhaps you could quickly take me to the rosehips across there so I can eat." The otter quickly responded, "Oh my, I should take care of something upriver first. I'll be right back. Wait for me." Convinced by the otter, the poor old porcupine waited for him to come back. He waited, but the otter never returned. Overwhelmed with sorrow, he started to cry. (His visitors probably weren't happy because he was calling them names.)

*Across there, there,
My Turr'un across there
rubbing, rubbing, rubbing*

He opened his eyes again and saw a beaver swimming along. Porcupine yelled at him, "Hey, beaver! One with a tail that can be used as a small cutting board, perhaps you could take me across to my food." (That porcupine sure blurts things out without thinking.) The beaver said, "Okay, you come down and lie belly-down on my back." The porcupine quickly waddled down and flopped himself on the beaver's back. Then the beaver said, "As I take you across, stay on my back and don't move."

As the beaver took him across, the porcupine moved and fell into the water. The porcupine started to thrash and wallop trying to stay afloat and managed to swim to the shore. In the meantime, the beaver got disoriented and started to swim back downriver. As the beaver headed downriver, porcupine heard him calling. The beaver said, "Poor old porcupine, the spot where you laid on my back, let it be lean and have no fat." Porcupine quickly answered and yelled, "Yes, the spots where we touched each other will indeed have no fat." As soon as the beaver swam around a bend and disappeared, porcupine ran to the rosebushes and started

10.8 Nacarrluk (literally, "bad hat") from the Kuskokwim. IVA5086.

eating. Today . . . beavers indeed have no fat on their backs, and just as the beaver predicted, porcupines have no fat on their bellies. May [the story] go forward in a straight and continuous path.

Camatat, Nacarrluut-llu / Beaded Dance Hats

In discussing hats and hoods, Marie asked her uncle to describe the *camatat* (beaded dance headdresses) used in the tundra area:

The *camatat* I saw were shiny and covered with beads, and they had fringes all the way around. The part that was called the *camataq* was a bit wide, made of copper, which was quite valuable back in those days. Aguralria [Nastasia Keene] and our late sister Yuuguaria . . . each had a *camataq* with a shiny piece of metal across the middle. There were strings of beads on the sides and hanging over the forehead. The *cuklut* [beaded fringes dangling across the forehead] were short, and as one went back from the forehead, strings of beads increased in length. A dancer wore the *camataq* during *Itruka'ar* [ceremonial dancing with masks]. When they exhibit the *nacarrluut* [dance hats], you will also see them.

No sooner had Wassilie mentioned *nacarrluut* (literally, "bad hats") than we had an opportunity to see one Jacobsen had collected on the Kuskokwim (fig. 10.8).[14] He wrote: "Cap [with] beads strung on twisted animal-sinew thread. It is the hat of a famous shaman-woman who wandered from the Kuskokwim to the Yukon." Jacobsen made the questionable assumption that the woman must have come from Prince William Sound, since at the time such beaded headdresses with long pendants on the back were worn by women and girls living only in that area. In fact, Wassilie had seen *nacarrluut* used along the Kuskokwim when he was young. The day before, he had said that very few people had *camatat* and *nacarrluut* in those days. Wassilie had mentioned that a much-loved eldest daughter might own a *nacarrluk,* and Paul had captured everyone's attention with his description of a *uilingiataq* (from *ui,* "husband," literally, "one without a husband"):

A girl was termed a *uilingiataq* when her father refused to give her away until the mightiest young hunter asked to marry her. Young men who didn't view themselves as notable hunters didn't even bother to ask. A young man who thought of himself as a *nukalpiaq* would feel brave enough to ask to marry her. . . . Under those circumstances, a young girl would begin to be recognized as a *uilingiataq*. In Yup'ik lore, we've heard stories about some unfortunate young men who vanished after attempting to marry a *uilingiataq.*

There's an ancient story about a *uilingiataq* who would marry only a man who could capture all of her human attributes. Evidently she welcomed all of the young suitors, but she would begin the process of transforming herself into many forms. . . . Then one time a young orphan, a *tutgara'urluq* [poor grandchild], took her and held on to her, even though she transformed into many frightening creatures. Previously several notable young men, *nukalpiat,* had tried to capture her, but they would release her when they became frightened of her other forms. But that impoverished young orphan boy held her, even though she began to growl and changed into different animals. Then as he was holding on, she suddenly became herself and stood up with a sigh and said, "You have captured all of my attributes; now you can have me for a wife."

We took time to look at a beautiful beaded headdress from the village of Katmai south of Nushagak (fig. 10.9). Although not from our area, it evoked strong memories, and Marie suggested that its makers may have been Aglurmiut. Catherine was the only one small enough to wear it, and she gladly placed it on her head and began to dance. Annie then described the beads from which it was made:

I've seen beaded dance hats called *nacarrluut,* but this is the first time I've seen this kind of hat . . . with such big beads.

Long ago I heard people talking about how they gathered *nengyuaryuut* [dentalia?] from a place near Ugaassat. They would tie boot-sole grass together and throw it into the water in the lake so they would catch the *nengyuaryuut,* which they used as ornaments. The *nengyuaryuut* would quickly swarm over the grass. After they took the grass out from the water, they'd kill them. Their little ribs are a hollow cord like a tube. They'd remove the ribs and cut them into assorted lengths, some short and some long. . . . Then they set the cut pieces outside to bleach in the sun. . . . I heard that they were easy to cut when they were fresh, but when they dried and bleached, they became hard to cut with an *uluaq.* They would become beautiful beads . . . and they made them into beautiful necklaces and earrings back in those days. . . .

Girls used to wear *nacarrluut.* They were adorned like this and had *agluirutet* [earrings connected with strands of beads hanging under the jaw like a necklace]. . . . This *nacarrluk* is nicely adorned.

Kay'urrutet / Armbands

Continuing with ceremonial regalia, we now looked at four pairs of armbands worn for dances, two from the Yukon (fig. 10.10) and two from the tundra area.[15] Jacobsen gave the name "Kassoarotit=Naijan=Gaksoutit" (*kay'urrutet nayangarcuutet,* "armbands for dancing") for one Yukon pair and wrote that another pair possibly imitated the shoulder insignia or epaulets seen on Russian and American overcoats.[16] Annie had never seen such bands in use but recognized the paired strips of *nerun* (dried esophagus) from which they were made. She noted that the esophagus was soaked in water and freeze-dried outside, similar to fish skin. Their widths varied since they came from different-size bearded seals.

Catherine had not seen *kay'urrutet* (armbands) like these while she was growing up on Nelson Island, but when she moved to the Yukon, she saw people being presented in their "first dance." Each wore a wolverine-skin band on the left arm and a wolf-skin band on the right, a practice that continues today. Wassilie remembered another use: "I'd say that these were worn by male *apallirturtet* [dance directors] . . . when they called out the *apallut* [lyrics to the dance songs]. If I was to be the *apallirturta,* I'd put these bands around my upper arms [biceps]."

Wassilie added that during *Kevgiryaraq* [Messenger Feast], when many people gathered in the *qasgi,* the men who were

10.9 Elaborate beaded headdress from the village of Katmai south of Nushagak, made with large glass beads that hung over the ears and down the back. IVA6382.

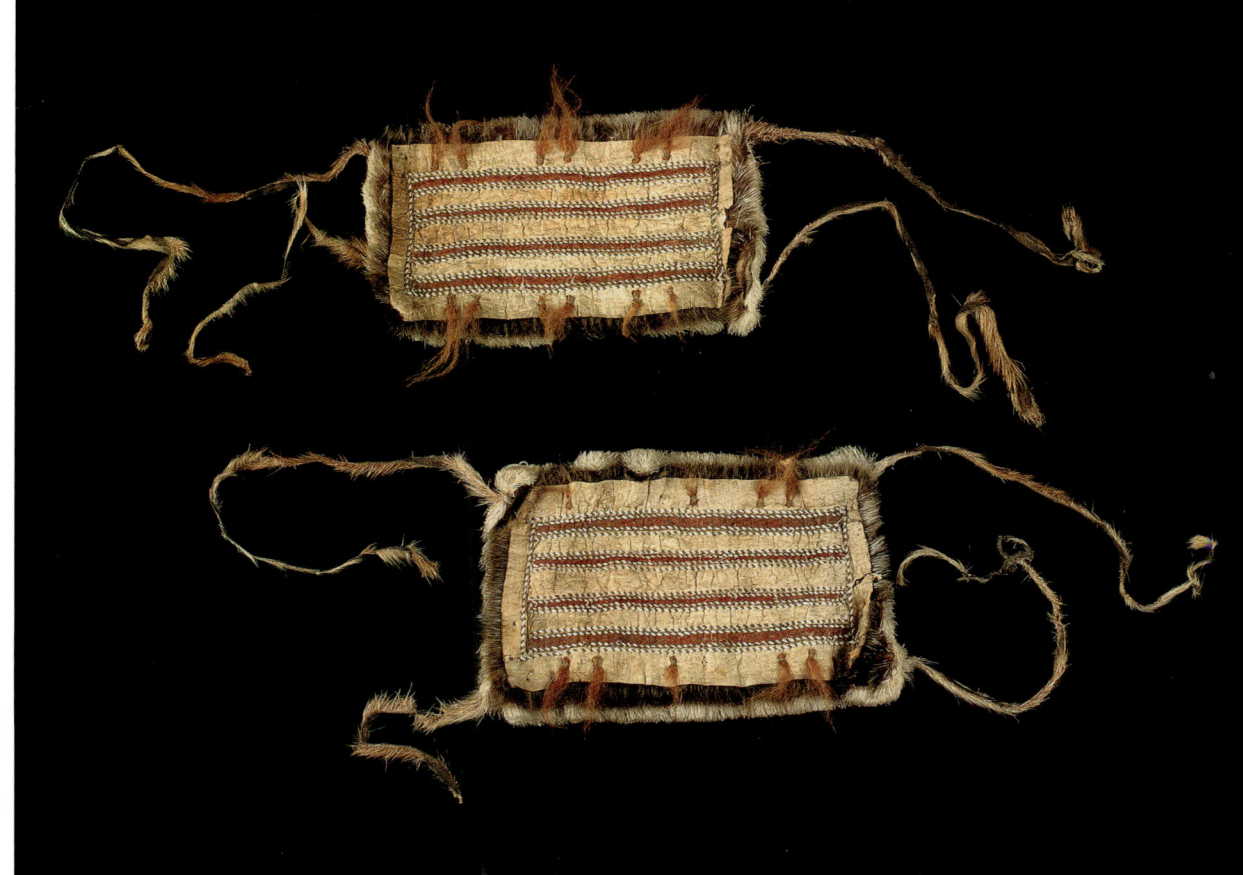

10.10 Kay'urrutet (armbands) worn for dancing on the Yukon, made from rectangular strips of dried esophagus, decorated with kavirqu' (fancy stitches) and beads, with wolf fur on the sides and tassels dangling down. IVA6287a, b.

designated to direct the songs wore armbands made of different furs. He then took up a pair and tied them on over his shirt, noting that when men wore kay'urrutet during dances, they were bare chested. Jokingly he added that since he was "less gifted with words," he would be selected as an apallirta (conductor), while his companion Paul, being gifted with words, would be chosen as an agniurta (one calling out the words to a song).

Agayat / Hanging Wooden Figures

After lunch we considered a wealth of carved wooden figures. Jacobsen identified a piece from Fort Alexander (fig. 10.11) merely as a white-painted bird perched on a wooden mountain, brought to the qasgi for a particular dance. Wassilie immediately recognized it as an anipaq (snowy owl): "Snowy owls usually sit on trees and high areas. They are usually perched on hills, being white searching for their prey. Snowy owls could catch big animals, too. They could kill a jackrabbit in a second. This was probably owned by an angalkuq." Catherine also had a story to tell about a wooden owl her husband made:

Since we use snowy owl feathers on dance fans, I turned to my late husband and said, "Gee whiz, you haven't caught a snowy owl in a long time." Then my husband made a snowy owl. He cut the wood in three pieces, and as he threaded the pieces onto a string and pulled, the object started to go up. When he dropped the string it dropped and came apart. Then, as he pulled the string again, the pieces came together and the object formed again.

That one time at a dance, they had a snowy owl like this. . . . It was left hanging . . . inside a ellanguaq [literally, "model universe," made of wooden hoops and sinew hung with down and

10.11 Snowy owl perched on a hilltop. Jacobsen labeled this unusual figure a "shaman's mask," noting that many such objects were found in qasgit. The owl was often associated with angalkut, in part because of its extraordinary vision. IVA5429.

10.12 Figure of a bowhead whale, hung from the inside of the qasgi during a celebration. IVA4465.

10.13 Model of a ship Jacobsen said terrorized the people of the Yukon in ancient times. IVA4195.

feathers]. It fell. After it dropped, it went back up again. . . . I saw a snowy owl used like that one time, . . . the kind that comes apart when it falls.

Wassilie then described the *ellanguaq* he had observed:

The *qasgi* ceiling was covered with feathers, including snowy owl feathers. The *ellanguaq* would come down and go up again above the *apallirturtet*. Over in Nushagak, perhaps they had these kinds of *atqatat* [figures hanging down from the inside of the *ellanguaq*]. The *atqataq* was made as a human figurine. . . . Shortly after the

ellanguaq presentation, the weather used to get very cold.

Jacobsen identified a second figure as a Yukon dance hat in the shape of a white whale (fig. 10.12), which he compared to the totem animals of the "Chilkat Indians," from whom he mistakenly assumed the Yupiit had learned to use such "hats" and dance masks. Annie spoke up, correcting his interpretation: "I'm intrigued by this figure of a bowhead whale. . . . Its eyes are here, and this is its blowhole. When they blow the water out, it sprays straight upward. The *teraat* [blowhole] is very delicious, but they are quite chewy. . . . Its mouth looks

220 THE RETURN GIFT

dangerous because it is so large that a person can disappear in it."

Wassilie related the whale to the previous hanging figure: "This bowhead whale figure surely . . . adorned the inside of a qasgi, representing an important event. . . . Objects like these were used by angalkut to enhance their powers. . . . They'd bring them out for people to see."

Jacobsen also acquired a model ship from the Yukon (fig. 10.13), for which he supplied detailed information. Used in dances, it told the story of two monsters in the shape of women who lived along the lower Yukon and possessed a "devil's animal" that was half monster and half fish, which they used to roam the river, killing and eating everything that came near, including people. Jacobsen suggested that this referred to the first Russians to sail upriver. The story goes on to say that a famous angalkuq brought the ship aground, splitting it in two (thus the mended break in the boat model). Its name is "Arnak=Karak=Tjukwagoak=Angisok=Taimani Pirsarillerik," translated by Jacobsen as "Women old their animal boat big everything many people killed" (arnarkaraak cuukvaguaq angis uag tamaani pitsarillerik, literally, "the two women's pike image that killed many people"). The people of St. Michael told Jacobsen that the ship represented a vessel that once sailed the Yukon, half-ship and half-monster (perhaps the toothy pike referred to in the Yup'ik designation), with the rear equipped as a lookout. Jacobsen suggested that it could have been the Russian vessel Ladie, which terrorized the inhabitants (especially the women) for a long time until a famous angalkuq used his powers to break it in two. The model ship was used in dances to commemorate this event.

Wassilie began: "This is a qayaruaq [model kayak] with two women figures on it. The back side looks like a kayak. There's a huge mouth with all tuluryak [canine teeth] on it. I believe an angalkuq also used this in his work. It probably represented the essence of his power." Annie continued: "Perhaps it is a representation of a fish . . . with its mouth filled with canine teeth. And yet its tail looks like a kayak. A bird's head is looking up in the front. Perhaps the mighty bird was emerging from down under. And there are two women figures on the top sitting back-to-back without any paddles. Perhaps this is the way these two traveled around."

Wassilie related the piece to a Kuskokwim story:

The figure was probably the masterpiece that one of the angalkut used to prevail over the others. Its mouth is flat like a pike's mouth. . . . Perhaps this represents Anelrayuli [literally, "the one really good at going downstream"], Qarcaq's power source. . . .

Qarcaq, the angalkuq, sent his power source Anelrayuli, the pike, to capture [the angalkuq] Neq'ayaraq. . . . It swam downriver. In the meantime, Itrayuli [literally, "the one going upriver"], the power source of Neq'ayaraq, was swimming upriver. Anelrayuli was much bigger than Itrayuli. The two other shamans assisting Neq'ayaraq in the ritual would make motions in the air to reduce the size of their opponent's power source. As they continued the process, Anelrayuli got smaller and smaller. When Itrayuli, the sculpin, reached Anelrayuli, the pike, it bit it and flattened its mouth.

Catherine suggested the figure's relation to a Yukon story: "If that came from the Yukon, I've heard about it, too. An angalkuq told people not to go near the lake around Ingril'er. . . . Since some people tend to defy rules, one of the women went there and picked berries. . . . As she was picking, a huge pike came up and swallowed her. She disappeared and was never seen again."

Iinrut / House Protectors

Jacobsen labeled another wooden figure from the Yukon a "house protector in which a well-intentioned spirit dwells."[17] In the form of a beaver, it was hung at the entrance or laid down nearby to protect the house. He supplied the name "Inrok=Paloktakrok=nom na Yorte, the spirit=in beaver

10.14 Wooden figure from the lower Yukon, which Jacobsen described as an "idol" made by shamans, into which a spirit was introduced to protect a child. He noted that the slit in the figure's back was to "lock in the spirit of the lightning" and marked it as a protective spirit. Such slits are widespread on wooden figures and masks, but neither living elders nor the records of other collectors have explained their meanings. IVA3670.

form=who protects the house" (probably *iinruq paluqtaruaq enem nayurtii*, "imitation beaver amulet for the house"). The third figure from the lower Yukon (fig. 10.14) was the most intriguing. Jacobsen called it "Slaowikmiu=Tonnerak, or child protector," which translates *Ellam Yua tuunraq*, "the spirit of the Person of the Universe," and wrote that it was an "idol" made by shamans, into which a spirit was introduced by magic to protect the children. This type of "idol," he wrote, was placed in a specially prepared sack and kept safe in the house or behind the door when children were very young. He noted that the deep slit in the figure's back was intended to "lock in the spirit of the lightning" and marked it as a protective spirit.

Later that day, we examined two larger wooden figures (fig. 10.15) from the lower Yukon with similar features.[18] Both were also designated "Slaowikmiu=Tonnerak," translated by Jacobsen as both "thunder devil" and "lightning spirit," and they were also said to have been hung in the entranceways of houses as protective figures for children: "Among rich people the children are entrusted into the care of a shaman, meaning that he is responsible for keeping the children healthy. This is the reason for making such figures; then he forces the spirits under his power to go into the mask, which will then protect the children during his absence." The toothy cavity on the back of each figure again was said to signify that the "lightning spirit," among others, was in each figure to help protect the child. One was also named "Inrok=Palok=Aderok=Nomnajorte" or "spirit in beaver form guarding the house."[19] These were valued items and not something people were willing to part with. Jacobsen candidly wrote: "I obtained this figure in a house whose inhabitants had gone on a reindeer hunt; the protective god was left behind. This gave me the opportunity to obtain the seemingly unattainable figure, something I had tried for months."[20]

Yugat / Human Figures

Now we looked at two enormous wooden figurines. As with the protective house figures, the elders had little to say about these pieces clearly associated with shamanism and, more specifically, burials. Jacobsen, on the other hand, waxed eloquent, although the veracity of the details he divulged is unclear.

10.15 Wooden figure from the lower Yukon, also said to have been hung in the entranceway of a house as a protective figure for a child. The toothy cavity on its back was said to signify the protective "lightning spirit" within the figure. IVA4196.

10.16 Figure from the Yukon standing three feet high and designated "Innerok=Numnajorte=Yuoak," which Jacobsen translated "the spirit in the human form which watches the house" (*iinruq enem nayurtii yuguaq*, "human figure of the house's helping spirit"). IVA4202.

10.17 Qelutviaq (stringed musical instrument) collected from the middle Yukon but in use throughout southwestern Alaska in the 1880s. IVA 425.

Jacobsen identified the first figure as the grave marker he collected during his fall journey down the Yukon.[21] The second was a tall, thick, armless figure from the Yukon (fig. 10.16) standing three feet high. Jacobsen wrote that such figures protected the house against misfortune, mainly illness, and he compared them to "idols" found among the Goldi and Gilyak peoples on the Amur River. Although he said the figure was a woman, its upturned mouth indicates a man. Jacobsen noted that he had seen several such figures in grave houses but none in use, making it likely that this was collected from a burial.

Qelutviaq / Stringed Musical Instrument

We turned briefly to an unusual musical instrument (fig. 10.17) that Jacobsen had acquired from the Yup'ik and Ingalik borderland along the middle Yukon. It resembled a mountain dulci-

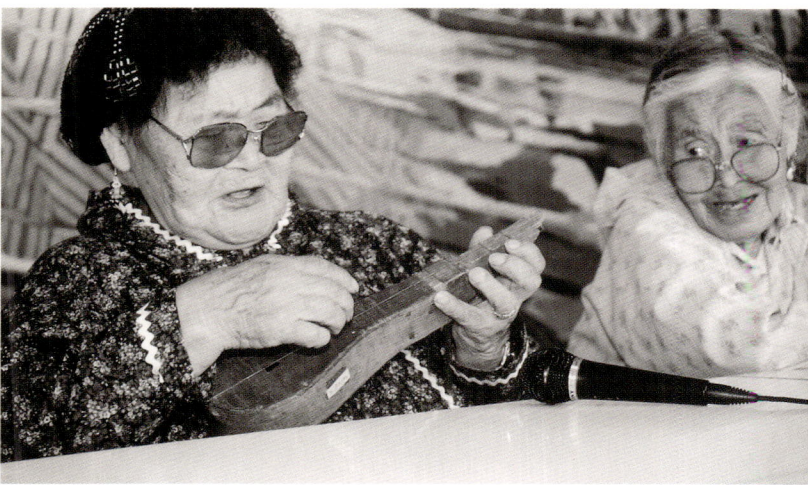

10.18 Annie playing the "Yup'ik guitar."

mer with metal strings, and Jacobsen wrote that it was probably a copy of the European guitar: "Nowhere have the Eskimos a stringed musical instrument of their own creation. . . . Since I later saw it farther downriver . . . it cannot be regarded as the only example."

Annie recognized it as a *qelutviaq* (stringed instrument, from *qelun*, "string under tension") and demonstrated its use (fig. 10.18):

When I was little, people had little musical instruments like these. They would attach a piece of wood on an empty tobacco can, then put four *negavgutet* [spruce roots] on it for strings. *Negavgutet* were found in the ground and were quite strong and durable. . . . The strings on this instrument created melodious sounds. Even old men used the instrument to create music. You would do this and make pleasing musical sounds. Since people use guitars now, I've heard my peers say, "If they were here today, the people who played little homemade instruments would be very good at playing the modern-day guitars. They sure created nice music with those old instruments. . . ." People sang traditional Yup'ik songs and not songs composed by Westerners.

Apqara'arcuun, Paplut-llu / Shaman Drum and Drum Handles

We turned next to three wooden drum handles. The first was from the Kuskokwim in the shape of a salmon.[22] Wassilie identified it immediately as the *paplu* (handle) for a shaman drum:

This handle does not look like those that go on regular drums. It's quite long. This looks like the size handle that would be held by *angalkut* when they went into meditative songs scrutinizing events. *Angalkut* used drums that were called *apqara'arcuutet* [literally, "devices for asking," from *apqara*-, "to ask about something"].

Jacobsen described the second fish-shaped handle from Nushagak (fig. 10.19), with two perforated hands and an open belly studded with caribou teeth, as a shaman's drum.[23] Catherine demonstrated how to hold the handle with the drum frame (fastened on the top of the fish's head) close to and covering her face, and Wassilie described its use:

This was the handle of an *apqara'arcuun* [shaman drum]. The front part is shaped like a mouth with teeth . . . and a huge hand figure. . . . Such drums were small, and I've seen them, too. They held them [in front of their faces] and struck their drumsticks toward them.

Another Nushagak handle (fig. 10.20) was also fish shaped, with pieces of the drum frame on its neck.[24]

Finally we came to three *cauyat* (drums), all from the Yukon. One was small and, according to Jacobsen, used by the shaman to cure the sick. Originally it had a painted drum skin, but only the rim remained. The second (fig. 10.21), with a painted drum skin, was much larger and used to accompany dances as well as shamanic rituals.[25] Jacobsen wrote: "The drummer sits on the floor or on benches along the house walls. While speaking predictions or singing offensive songs, the shamans can transplant the words by whispering to the drum skin so that only the one to whom the matter is addressed can hear." Wassilie described how *angalkut* had special songs they sang *apqara'arluteng* (asking for things) when they communicated with their *avneq* (literally, "other half," from *avek*, "half"). As the *avneq* spoke in song, the *angalkuq* was able to understand what was said. Wassilie then held a third small drum (fig. 10.22) with a salmon-shaped handle, and Catherine described a personal experience:

The person I saw beating the drum toward herself . . . had a drum with a short handle, and each day she sat and drummed and sang, covering her face with the drum. Her drum was small, but it was a genuine drum. . . . Her mother told us not to go near her, but her mother would sit next to her as she drummed. The woman's skin had some kind of festering cuts. . . . When I came in from playing, she would still be sitting at the same spot and singing. And the rest of the people in the house didn't complain about her singing and allowed her to do that. When she and her mother stayed with us for a short time, she did that. Perhaps she was an *angalkuq* because she drummed and sang every day. . . .

The little boy I saw at that time being trained by an *angalkuq* . . . was very lively and nimble. And since we knew that he was being trained to be an *angalkuq*, we were afraid of him.

Catherine then described how once she and a friend had been alone in a house when the boy had entered and asked

10.19 Fish-shaped drum handle with thumbless hands as fins. An *apqara'arcuun* (shaman drum) like this was held in front of one's face and struck from beneath. IVA5428.

10.20 Another fish-shaped drum handle from Nushagak. Jacobsen said that a shaman might have used the small stick fastened to the handle, as their drumsticks were much shorter than regular ones. IVA4549.

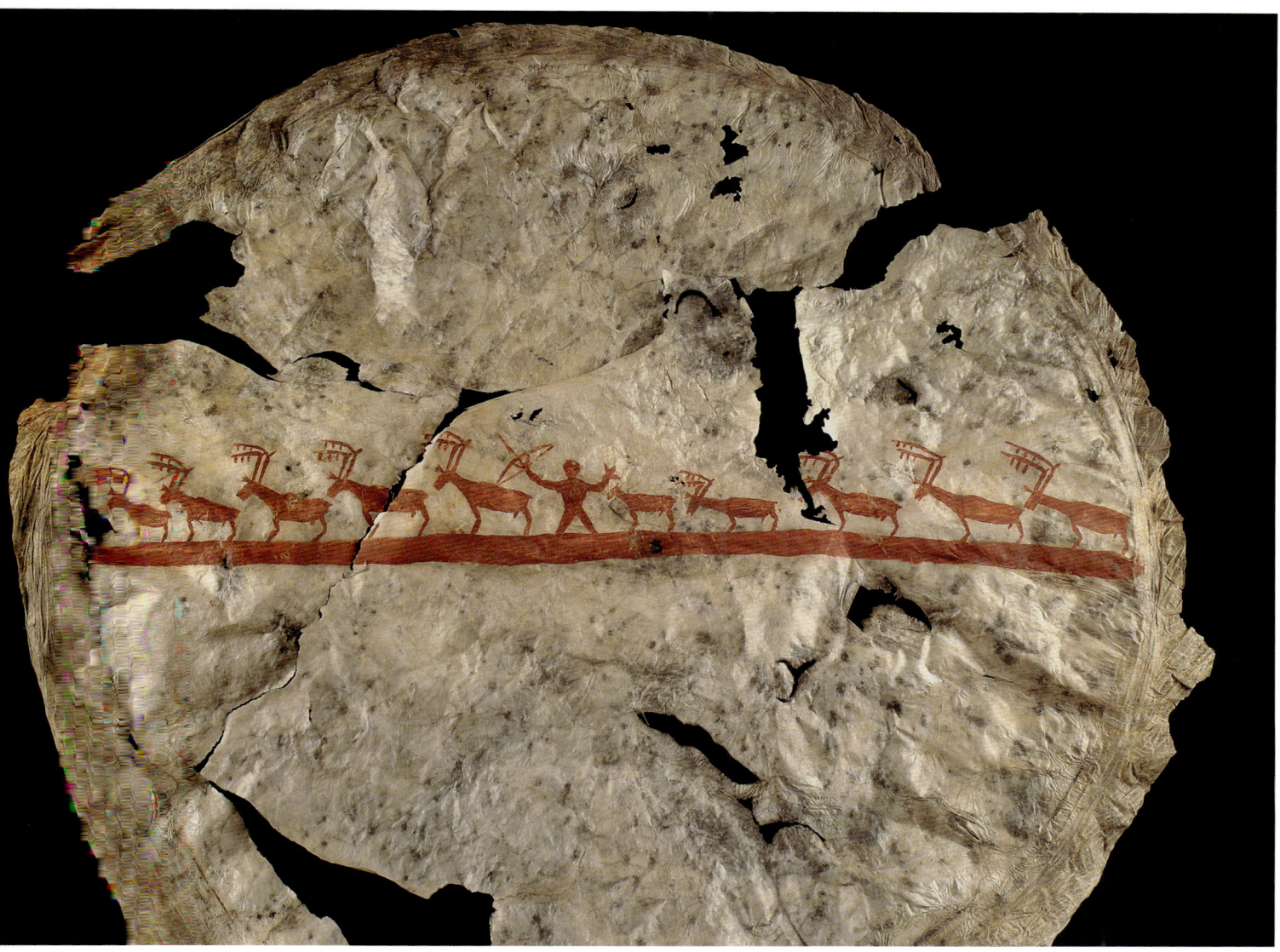

10.21 Painted drum skin depicting a hunter surrounded by many caribou. IVA3095.

them if they wanted to hear his *avneq* as it came up from underground. He proceeded to cover his head with a seal-gut garment and to mumble something to summon it while rustling the garment. Then the girls heard someone's voice coming up from the ground, but muffled and low, and they ran from the house in terror: "His *avneq* was coming up to meet him as he was singing and mumbling words." Later the boy's grandfather stopped his training when he began mumbling and snickering to himself and acting strangely.

Finally Catherine took up the small *apqara'arcuun* and sang (fig. 10.23) while Annie, still seated, began the motions of a dance.

> Let me bring you out to the place of ciitaarayulit
> Let me bring you out to the place of thrushes
> Let me bring you into the land of swallows
>
> Ayaaya iyaara yiingirri-ii-ii
>
> My life spirit
> Let me bring you out
> To the ocean down there
> Let me bring you out
> To look for seals

> Ayaaya iyaara yiingirri-ii-ii
>
> My life spirit
> Let me take you
> To the land back there
> Let me take you
> To the place where plants and berries grow
>
> Ayaaya iyaara yiingirri-ii-ii

"*Kaa-ak!*" [There you go!] Wassilie exclaimed, and everyone laughed. Then he picked up the drum and began to sing an *apqara'arcuun* that Marie's grandmother used to sing:

> Snowflakes have fallen
> Snowflakes have fallen
> Envelop yourself on his snowshoes
>
> Ayarrii ayarrii iirriyaa aarraa
>
> Dear old man of the north has stood up
> Wrap yourself on his snowshoes

10.22 Small shaman drum with a salmon-shaped handle. IVA6990.

10.23 Catherine holding the small shaman drum and singing a song. IVA6990.

Ayarrii ayarrii iirriyaa aarrai

Dear old man of the east has stood up
Swath yourself on his snowshoes

Ayarrii ayarrii iirriyaa aa-aa-rraa

When Wassilie was done, we put away the drums and headed home.

ELEVENTH DAY Dancing with Masks

We began our last week with new group members seated around our familiar tables. The day after Andy and Paul's departure, Esther Ilutsik from Dillingham and Henry Alikayak from Manokotak arrived in Berlin, hungry for information about objects from the Nushagak area. Both their enthusiasm and the fresh supply of dried fish and *akutaq* they brought bolstered us. Esther's laughter was infectious, and Henry, a self-described "elder in training," provided Wassilie the male companionship he needed to make our group complete.

Among the most important objects we had yet to see were the several hundred dance masks that Jacobsen had collected during his spring sled trip down the coast from St. Michael to Bristol Bay. Marie and I approached these creations with knowledge gained working on the Yup'ik mask exhibit *Agayuliyararput* (Our Way of Making Prayer).[1] Originally the word *agayu* had meant "dancing with masks to request an abundance of things to come in the future." With the coming of Christian missionaries, however, the word came to mean "prayer." Paul had been central to the exhibit-making process, and in his taped interview the night before he left Berlin, he talked at length about the "mistake" that had been made when Christian missionaries had "brushed away" traditional dancing with masks:

Though we are of different races . . . in the beginning God created us with traditions we were to live by. But some tribal groups evidently lost our traditions when an error was made.

The church I go to is Catholic, and I'm a devout member. But our priests . . . [recently] mentioned their regret, saying that by putting their religion on us they had brushed away our way of life. And upon understanding what had happened to our people, I have an immense feeling of loss to this day. Their testimony made me realize the priests had literally brushed away our way of making prayer. They said they should have just baptized us . . . and said, "Our way of life was granted to you by God. Continue to live in your truth; however, if you want to change something in your life, do so."

I just mentioned this, thinking it might help you understand the masks our people used in prayer and supplication . . . before the arrival of priests and white people. . . . In those days, people didn't use the word *Agayun* [God], but they'd say *Ellam Yua*. In their daily lives, they were keenly aware of the presence of *Ellam Yua* and behaved accordingly with respect. . . . Now we realize that they were referring to *Agayun*, and yet in those days people didn't know that priests existed.

I want to mention the use of masks in prayer. Nowadays white people use the method of passing resolutions to achieve certain goals. After you make the resolutions to ask for something, you wait with anticipation that what you asked for will come to pass. Our ancestors used masks, calling it *agayuliyaraq* [way of making prayer], as resolutions to petition God for things they needed.

The *Agayuliyararput* exhibit had taught us many things about masks: the role of the *angalkut* in creating them, the stories associated with them, and the dances in which they were publicly presented. Perhaps most important, it had allowed many Yup'ik people to re-own masks—once condemned as signs of heathen superstition and idolatry—as legitimate forms of making prayer. It was in this context that I laid the first three masks on the table, and Annie spoke of her brief encounters with masks:

Once I saw a person dancing down in the middle of the floor wearing a mask. I remember seeing what looked like bird feathers on the mask. My paternal aunt was dancing at that time with that masked dancer kneeling and facing her. When my aunt danced, she looked radiant. She had a headdress and dance fans . . . and a beautiful *qaspeq* on, too. She was wearing long, beautiful white caribou-skin boots with striking long strips coming down the fronts and dangling tassels on the sides. I was fascinated by the mask that man wore.

And after that, I saw two masked dancers when a dance gathering was held in Qissayaarmiut. I saw those dancers for a brief time and didn't see any after that.

Catherine also described her encounter with masks:

I saw masks like these belonging to the *angalkut* only once in my life. When I saw them, there were many men with masks. . . . They

11.1 *Kuskokwim mask said to depict the sun. IVA5167.*

were practicing in the evening. While we sat in the *qasgi*, a person came in and slowly walked in a complete circle around the floor. Shortly after, another person came in wearing a red fox mask, and as he walked slowly in a circle, he was vocalizing fox sounds. When he left, another person walked in wearing a white fox mask. He, too, walked a complete circle on the floor, making white fox sounds, and also went out. Then after he left, the drummers began to beat the drums.

I didn't attend when they danced the next day because the priest told me not to go. These kinds of masks belonged to the *angalkut*. When the first priests came and saw masks being used, they didn't approve.

Kegginaqut / **Masks**

We turned now to a range of masks, all of which Wassilie and Annie acknowledged as the work of *angalkut*, but about many they had nothing to say (see Appendix).² First was a "spirit mask" from the lower Yukon. The second was a dish-shaped mask from Cape Vancouver that Jacobsen said had been used by young people in a fall dance to portray their longing for feast invitations: "Therefore, the mask is in the shape of a bowl. The face within the bowl could represent any spirit." Next was a white-painted mask with huge nose from the Yukon, which Jacobsen called "Tunrak=Kinakok=Nunat=Paiemut," translated as "devil's face of the country Paiemut" (*tuunraq kegginaquq nunat Paimiut*, "mask of a helping spirit from Paimiut"), said to inflict grief on the inhabitants. Annie noted that the mask once had labrets, and so represented a man, and that it was probably made after white people arrived because it had twine on it.³

The next mask from the Kuskokwim (fig. 11.1) was given as a "dance mask of the type often found on the Yukon, probably depicting the sun." Holding the mask up to his face, Wassilie said simply: "This mask was worn by an *angalkuq*. When they worked with their *tuunraq* [spirit guide], they would wear a mask like this . . . that was not adorned. An *angalkuq* probably wore the mask when he worked on his patient." Marie tried on a wolf mask (*kegluneq kegginaquq*) from the lower Yukon with a human face in its right eye, identifying it as a spirit in wolf form.⁴ She commented that *ircenrraat* [extraordinary persons] might appear as wolves and that some powerful *angalkut* possessed the wolf as their *tuunraq*.

The elders were reluctant to comment about these objects of which they had limited personal experience. Jacobsen, however, showed no such compunctions and wrote lengthy descriptions of many masks. He often recorded a mask's Yup'ik name as well as an abbreviated, sometimes confusing, but nonetheless suggestive explanation of its particular features and the story it embodied. In his very first letter to Bastian after his arrival in St. Michael, Jacobsen had described these remarkable creations: "One needs 'boxes' for the masks from the upper Yukon River, especially the special shaman masks. Often a mask for each special task is made, such as masks to produce weather, masks to entice salmon into the river, masks to bring animals into the land, etc. Ordinary dance masks are burned immediately after use, and then remade the next year."⁵

Perhaps most telling of the scholarly context in which Jacobsen worked was his attempt to trace the origins of Yup'ik masks and their relationship to the masking traditions of other northern peoples. For example, commenting on a St. Michael mask (fig. 11.2), he wrote:

Mask representing a spirit . . . that shows a resemblance to those at the seacoast and the prairie. Among the coastal Indians, it represents a god (spirit) who causes people to drown. The Kwakiutl call him Sonnekin. I could not ascertain more detailed information about him. Judging by the name, he is a sand spirit (probably the monster causing earthquakes and making riverbanks crumble).⁶ Among the Yukon, masks are made to represent such spirits. The use of masks seems to have come downstream to the Eskimos since one finds these characteristic masks most frequently at the upper range of this river and the neighboring Kuskokwim River. Toward the north and south, these masks gradually disappear. In earlier times, the masks were used only by Aleuts, who no doubt had found them among the Yakutat (Tlingit). The shamanism of both peoples has many similarities.

Jacobsen wrote that another dance mask from the lower Yukon represented a spirit that haunted a village, adding, "One of the greatest deities of the southern Indian tribes is exactly like this" (fig. 11.3). Noting the black rings around the eyes of yet another mask, Jacobsen wrote: "It is remarkable that this mask has black rings around the eyes like glasses. In the Bella-Coola legends, this is a sign of divine descent (see the legend of the [mink?] who wandered to the sun)."⁷

Nepcetaq / Mask that Sticks to the Face

Everyone was fascinated by a huge mask with a tooth-filled mouth (fig. 11.4), and Wassilie said it was certainly owned by an *angalkuq*. Jacobsen wrote that another enormous plaque mask from the lower Yukon (fig. 11.5) was used by a shaman to save the people from starvation: "He put on the mask, in which the spirit "Kouonek" lived. [The spirit] had to lure the animals [caribou and walrus] on the mask. This mask was also worn for bigger dance occasions, to remind people of the gifts received from the spirit through the shaman."⁸ Wassilie added to Jacobsen's description: "I've heard stories about shaman masks like these. This mask has no straps or anything. This was called a *nepcetaq* [literally, "something that sticks"]. The person would bow down over the mask on the floor in performance, and when he stood up again, the mask would adhere to his face."

Jacobsen also recognized that the plaque masks contemporary elders designate as *nepcetat* had special status as particularly powerful shamans' masks.⁹ Concerning another plaque mask from the lower Yukon, he wrote: "Shaman mask used for holy rituals and sometimes for fortune telling. . . . When the shaman calls for fish and animals by magic, he makes [the animals] look through the holes." He said of another "Tungtun-

11.2 Dance mask from St. Michael. IVA4460.

11.3 Jacobsen said this lower Yukon mask represented a cannibalistic "mountain demon," adding: "This seems to be crafted after a legend that exists with the southern Indians. [It is] the spirit 'Bek-Bek-(Knallanit?)' or as he is called in the Kwakiutl language 'Pah-Pah-Knallamisiva.'" IVA4404.

11.4 Mask with a tooth-filled mouth that opens and shuts when worn by a dancer. Jacobsen wrote that the mask was worn by the messenger sent to invite guests to a feast: "The mask indicates 'Come to the festival, there are many good things to eat!'" IVA5143.

...ook=Kinakok, meaning reindeer face" (*tuntuguaq kegginaquq,* "imitation caribou mask") from Russian Mission (fig. 11.6): "Shaman mask representing the reindeer spirit.... The shamans often used such masks to lure animals ... while those representing humans in the form of fish or animals are probably not used by shamans." Other plaque masks included a "shaman mask" from the lower Yukon (fig. 11.7), which Jacobsen designated "Asiwokrak=Pitsitasekok" (*asveruaq pitsaquq,* "pretend walrus acting intentionally"?) and said represented a spirit shown in walrus form used when walrus did not come to Norton Sound.[10]

Qununit / Legendary Seal Creature

Although we let many masks pass without comment, others loosened our tongues. Immediately following the "Konanek" mask was a second large shaman mask with five-fingered hands with holes in their centers attached to either side (fig. 11.8).[11] Jacobsen wrote that the shaman used the mask in the spring to "charm" the wild animals. The extended arms and feet signified the shaman's power, reaching over the entire world, while an "assisting spirit" sat on his forehead along with models of a reindeer and white whale, indicating that through the shaman's power, the time of the animals' return drew near. As with other masks, Jacobsen suggested its relation to masks of the "southern Indians"—that is, the Bella Coola and Bella Bella—but provided no evidence to support his claim.

Everyone had something to say about the mask. Marie began by mentioning the creature *qununiq* that Paul had talked about the week before when we had seen a small hand-shaped ivory belt fastener—a human figure that would fall into the sea, reemerging five times until it transformed into a bearded seal (see Day Nine). Instead of a human figure, a hunter might see a coffin on the ice with a pierced hand on its side. If the hunter struck the hole on the hand's palm with his spear, the figure would fall into the water, popping in and out like the carving as it turned into a seal. Marie asked if anyone else had heard stories about it, and Annie spoke up:

I've heard about *qununit,* but I've heard that the lower part of its body was a seal, while the upper part ... was a woman with long hair.

The late Ap'aller told a story about a man who caught a bearded seal while hunting. The man said that although he had found the circumstances of his hunt strange, he had killed the bearded seal. The shoulder blades of these creatures usually have a hole. Since it was the man's first catch of the season, it was cut up and cooked and brought to the men in the *qasgi.* One of the men who had received a portion of the shoulder blade lifted the bone saying, "We have eaten human flesh, not a bearded seal." He noticed the hole in the middle of the seal's *keggasek* [shoulder blade]....

One time my late cousin Aassinaaruyuq told me that he heard someone yelling from down below Enpakuq. When he turned around to look, he saw something swimming with a human face. It was yelling and would lift its arms into the air sometimes. When

11.5 Wassilie demonstrating a *nepcetaq* (that which sticks to the face) from the lower Yukon, with four holes on the plaque representing the passages that animals follow to repopulate the earth. IVA4430.

it raised its arms, he would see light through the palms of its hands. After it did that, it disappeared into the water. As he watched, the figure would come up, and each time it would be farther away until it disappeared. One of the women in the village told him, "You have seen a *qununiq.*" It evidently appeared to that individual.

Finally Wassilie added what he knew:

I've heard of *qununit,* too. . . . A hunter paddling in his kayak out on the ocean might see a person sitting on the ice but not its face. A *qununiq* would wear a *qaspeq* with its skirt spread out on the ice. The hunter would approach the figure and thrust his spear through the hem of its *qaspeq.* The figure would then fall into the water and swim off, pulling the line, and pop in and out of the water as a human figure. As it came up for the fifth time, it would be . . . a very fat, healthy bearded seal.

I've also heard that *qununit* call out with *oo*-ing sounds out on the ocean. After hearing such sounds, a hunter would see a person walking in the water, submerged to its waist. As it moved, it would call out. That *qununiq* would be wearing a seal-gut garment. I've never heard of anyone hunting the ones they saw swimming. Hunters still hear such calls out in the ocean. They aren't actual humans but that kind of creature.

11.7 "Imitation caribou mask" used to insure an abundance of caribou in the coming season. The plaque may represent the heavens, with caribou models looking through sky holes to the earth they will soon repopulate. IVA4410.

11.? "Imitation walrus mask," with the downturned mouth characteristic of representations of sea mammals. Jacobsen wrote: "On the forehead are two auks (diving birds), the messengers of spring and the breakup of the ice that indicate the arrival of the walruses. The shaman wears the mask in March and April when the hunters go on the hunt." IVA4431.

11.8 Mask with outstretched feet and arms signifying the shaman's power. Above the forehead sits a tuunraq (helping spirit) identified through special "totems," caribou (land animal) and white whale (sea mammal): "This means that the time is coming when game will soon come back through the power of the shamans." IVA4422.

Tuullget / **Common Loons**

We turned to a mask from between Cape Vancouver and the Kuskokwim (fig. 11.9, fig. 11.10), which Jacobsen said depicted the face of a shaman's helping spirit in the form of the edible "sea parrot" or dovekie (small short-billed auk) that comes each summer with the herring run. Jacobsen noted that he could not obtain the name or other information on the piece because the advancing season forced him to travel quickly. Annie made up for this deficiency by reclassifying it as a *tuullek* (common loon), followed with her version of a story told all across the Arctic to this day. In the story, a grandson living with his grandmother had two pet loons with whom he always shared his food. When he was old enough to hunt and started providing for his grandmother, he continued to feed his pets. Then one night he awoke to find his eyes filled with something, making it impossible for him to see. Unable to hunt the next day, he went to the lake behind his house and told his pets of his ailment. One said, "You are about to go through a condition your grandmother has cast upon you." On hearing this, the boy was very sad.

After this, the grandmother began feeding him very little food and giving him foul-smelling water. Then one day she took him caribou hunting. Following her lead, he shot his arrow and thought he heard the sound it made when it struck an animal. The grandmother, however, insisted he had missed. Returning home, the boy told his pets about his failure and apologized that he could no longer bring them food. The birds, however, told him that he had in fact succeeded and that the grandmother was lying, and they told the boy to return to them that night. Annie continued:

When he got to the edge of the lake, the birds came to him. They began to nurse him like humans. One of them said, "Oh my, how sad. It was your grandmother who . . . blinded your eyes, filling them with a mixture of old food and ashes while you were asleep." Then after they told him that, they took him by the arms and dove into the water. They swam here and there and around, holding their owner. When he finally came up into the air and opened his eyes, he noticed a flicker of light. Then one of the loons said, "How's that? Can you see anything?" When he said that he could see a little bit of light, they dove into the water with him again. And this time they swam around and around in a circle inside the lake. When he came up out of the water and opened his eyes, he could see again. Everything around him was very bright and sharp.

The boy returned to his grandmother's house, where he could now see the fresh caribou meat in the corner, which she had planned to keep for herself. He angrily grabbed his grandmother's hair and dragged her to the dumping place, where he submerged her head in human waste until she was dead. Leaving her, he returned to the loons, explaining to them that he had killed his grandmother because she could no longer be trusted. The loons supported his action. Annie concluded: "Like swans, loons are very powerful. Someone in the past carved this loon mask to honor the power of the loon. This is a loon's head. How amazing! I'll say that much about that story."

Annie then described how she had heard loons howling when she stayed up in Kangcilek in the spring and summer: "That was a place where they would raise their young. . . . Our late dear father used to say, 'Listen to the mighty loon calling.'" She had also heard that loons didn't fly when people were around unless something bad was about to happen to that person or their family. It was also a bad sign when loons cried out, falling back in the water with their wings outstretched and revealing their white breasts.

Catherine agreed that loons do not fly when people are present and that if a loon cries and flies over a village, one of its residents will soon die. Wassilie mentioned loons taking flight in windy weather:

They also run on water flapping their outstretched wings, which is called *putukuyuarluteng* [from *putukumyuar-*, "to tiptoe"]. *Tunutellget* [arctic loons] also behave in that way when their viewer is not well. When they come in contact with someone who isn't well, they walk on water, *takulluggluteng* [a bad omen to the viewer]. *Tuullget* [common loons] usually howl when they call. They submerge their bodies in the water when people are present; all you see is their neck and head. Common loons behave in many different ways. *Putukuyuarluteng* [running on water with outstretched wings], *nevaarluteng* [falling on their backs] . . . when their viewer or one of his/her relatives or child is soon to die. These birds, which don't walk on land, behave in different ways and fly very little when people are present.

Finally Henry spoke: "I've also heard stories that they rescued people in need out on the ocean by leading them home after transforming themselves into human form."

Ircenrraruaq Kegginaquq / **Ircenrraq Mask**

Jacobsen wrote that the next mask we looked at (fig. 11.11) represented a "mountain spirit" living by the Yukon River, called "Ersinekat=Kinakut" (*ircenrraruaq kegginaquq*, "mask of an *ircenrraq* [an extraordinary person who can appear in either animal or human form]").[12] Although Henry had never seen masks in use, he had heard of *ircenrraat* and spoke up:

I heard that they were amazing . . . and able to transform into many forms. I've also heard that their capabilities were infinite. They could reveal anything to humans. Their power was unbounded. They were capable of doing what a person was incapable of doing. I have not encountered them, but I was amazed seeing the place where others reported having seen them. A person could be brought into the realm of the *ircenrraat* and see something that humans in our world could not see.

Annie had also heard of *ircenrraat*: "I've heard that *caagnitellriit* [people restricted from certain activities] were told not to roam in mountains. *Ircenrraat* would recognize a person going through that process and throw rocks at them . . . and the places where the rocks landed on the person's body would become diseased later in life."

109, 110 Jacobsen wrote that this mask depicts the face of a shaman's helping spirit. The chevron forehead is common on Kuskokwim and Nushagak masks and may represent the visor that ocean hunters wore as practical protection and to appear more bird-like to the seals.

Catherine was the only one among us who had personally experienced *ircenrraat*, having seen one in human form outside her village. She said it had a dark face and dark legs and an enlarged head. Her companions told her to roll downhill toward her village, which she did, and it disappeared. Another time, she heard the *ircenrraat* stomping, making a thundering sound. She and her cousin had been playing with their dolls on a hill behind the village when they heard a noise and looked up to find a weasel moving swiftly back and forth. Terrified, they hurriedly gathered up their dolls and ran home. After they arrived, they heard a thundering sound three times: "They called it *tukararluteng* [kicking with both feet from a lying position like a baby]." After that, Catherine's cousin began to have

235 ELEVENTH DAY DANCING WITH MASKS

seizures and was sick for a while, but eventually recovered.

Wassilie added what he knew about *ircenrraat*, which was a great deal:

Ircenrraat revealed themselves to people in human form. They looked exactly like us. Hunters sometimes met *ircenrraat* out in the wilderness. One time, two hunters weren't seeing any animals as they hunted. As they were roaming the land, they met an *ircenrraq*. They all stopped to share a meal. The humans took out their *akutaq* to share with their visitor. The *ircenrraq* looked at the bowl for a while and said, "I won't eat this *akutaq*." The human asked him why he refused to eat it. Then the *ircenrraq* reached into the bowl, pinched the *akutaq* in the middle, and lifted the whole mixture into the air. And when he released it, the *akutaq* fell back into the bowl with a big smack.

Back in those days, people chewed caribou fat and then mixed it with oil in a bowl to make *akutaq* . . . trying not to mix their saliva with it. The *ircenrraq* taught the hunters the method humans now use in making *akutaq*. He told them to start melting the caribou fat over the fire instead of chewing it. He didn't eat any of the *akutaq* the humans offered. The *ircenrraq* who interacted with those hunters looked exactly like a human. Since the two hunters hadn't caught anything, when they were done eating and were ready to part, the *ircenrraq* told them that over the hill there was some meat that he had left. He said that he had taken only the skin. When the hunters left, they saw a caribou standing erect without its fur. It wasn't lying down. When they reached it, they made a slight motion and the caribou fell to its side.

There are many stories about *ircenrraat* and their encounters with humans. They appear to people as humans. They also choose individuals they want to bring into their world. . . .

I've heard people talk about the powerful *angalkuq* from Kangiracuar. Up [the Johnson] River in the area behind Naparyarraq on the same side where Atmauthluak is located, there are bluffs. As you go along the bluffs, you come to the area where the bluffs turn in, forming a big bay. The *ircenrraat* that live there are called Kangiquyugpagmiut [people of the big bay] and were fond of bringing people into their realm. . . .

One time, those *ircenrraat* took a young boy and his hunting companion into their place. Once there, they asked the boys where they were from. The boys told them that they were from Kangiracuar, the village where the powerful *angalkuq* lived. Then the elders in the *qasgi* began to talk among themselves. When the discussion ended, one of the elders said, "Aullutarr'u, don't mess with that boy! Send him back to his village right now." Some of the men didn't agree right away, but when everyone agreed, the boys were taken to the exit. . . . They saw three exits. Before they were sent out, an old man sitting next to the exit said, "Remember the *angalkuq* down in Kangiracuar, this boy's grandfather, always presented a mask during *Itruka'ar*, and when he comes here, he takes

11.11 Mask depicting an ircenrraq, an extraordinary person appearing in either animal or human form. IVA4428.

whatever he wants and leaves. And even if you want to keep it for ourselves, he takes it. . . ." He told them to push the boys out through the way that would bring them back to the world as we know it. Then immediately after being pushed out through the middle entrance, one boy was back in our world. And when they started to push the other boy into the lower entrance, he stepped on the *elltek* [where one places one's hands at the entranceway] and sprang out through the middle door, following his partner. They both went out to our world.

When people from the tundra area traveled downriver past Kangiacuar, they always stopped to make food offerings to the powerful *ellgelkuq* at his grave. After these food offerings, people would get nice food by catching seals that sometimes swam up their river.

11.12 *Walrus mask (asveruaq kegginaquq) from the Yukon that Jacobsen reported did much evil: "Every year it falls down onto the riverbanks, flushing away a lot of sand and causing avalanches." He noted incorrectly that the river people had never seen walrus and imagined them as monsters. In fact, they were well aware of coastal animals, and if Jacobsen's description of the piece is correct, the mask may represent the legendary tusked quugaarpak, often said to cause banks to erode as it emerged from its underground lair. IVA4406.*

Tegumiat wall' Taruyamaarutet / Dance Fans

We turned from large masks worn by men to smaller faces and designs carved on paired women's dance fans. These handheld

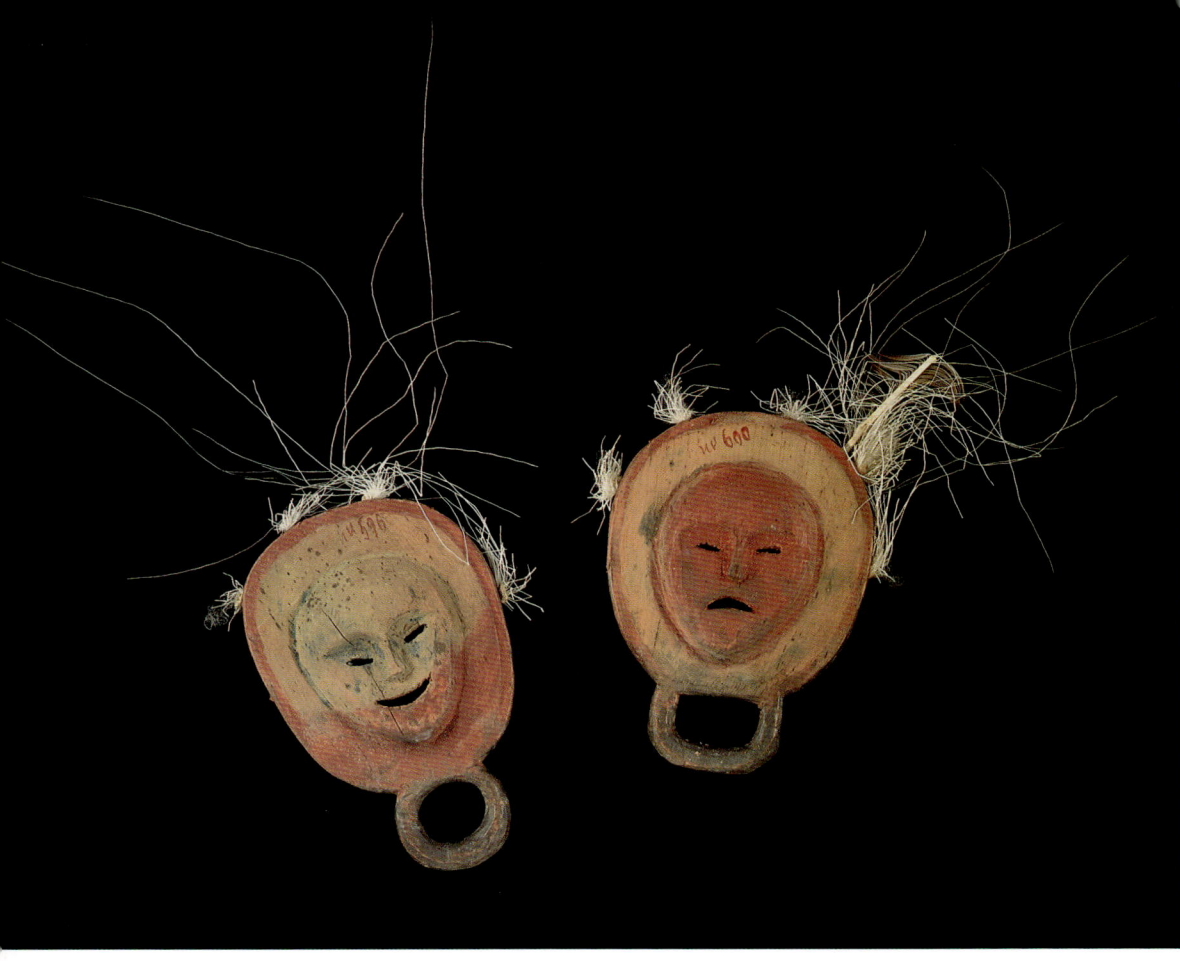

11.13 Pair of women's dance fans from between Cape Vancouver and the Kuskokwim, originally rimmed with caribou hair and feathers. As was often the case, the fans are opposites, one with a woman's downturned mouth and the other the smiling face of a man. IVA5199a, b.

ornaments, sometimes called "finger masks" in English, are known as *tegumiat* (literally, "things held in the hand," from *tegu-*, "to take in the hand") or, south of Hooper Bay, *taruyamaarutet* (an untranslatable word derived from *taru*, "human spirit"). Jacobsen had collected dance fans from all over the region (fig. 11.12, fig. 11.13, fig. 11.14).[13] Like the masks, many had feathers and wisps of caribou hair still attached and were painted with white, red, black, and blue pigments. As to their use, Jacobsen wrote: "The [woman] dancer, standing at one place, moves herself as she continuously bends her knees as to do a curtsey, and gesticulates once with the right and then with the left hand, and so keeps the rattle in motion."[14]

Some displayed geometric designs, while others had carved faces depicting seals, walrus, birds, salmon (fig. 11.15, fig. 11.16), or creatures with crooked or toothy mouths like those on larger masks. Often, paired finger masks presented opposites of each other, such as a smiling face on one and a frowning face on the other, and different sides of the same dance fan could also display different faces. Esther demonstrated how women held the fans, by placing their index and middle fingers through two holes at the base of each fan (fig. 11.17). Two of the pairs were hollow and filled with stones to make a kind of rattle, and Jacobsen described them as related to the rattles used by "southern Indians."[15] In fact, men also held simple willow-root or wood fans while they danced, to which the stiff feathers of snowy owls were attached, though Jacobsen collected only one such pair.

Unlike Jacobsen, everyone in our group was a dancer and had direct experience with dance fans. They quickly divided the array of fans into three groups—one each from the Yukon, Kuskokwim, and Bristol Bay areas. Catherine was the first to comment:

The dance fans in the Yukon River area all had handles made of wood . . . carved into little face masks. The two masks over there—one has a face with its mouth downturned and the other has a face with its mouth turned up. My family—my daughters, my granddaughters, and I—have identical designs consisting of the moon and the sun. Families used their own family designs on their dance fans. Designs that different families used are bear, fox, mink, and wolf. Those were the main animal designs used on women's dance fans. . . .

Some dance fans had three male mallard tail-feather attachments. And if snowy owl feathers weren't available, swan wing feathers were used on fans. . . . A girl dancing for the first time is expected to have new clothing and new dance fans when presented to the audience.

Catherine commented that such carved fans are rare today, and women often use dance fans with coiled grass handles decorated with caribou beard hair. She also noted that the designs on a woman's fan came from her husband and the men in her family rather than from the woman's side. She gave an example of a woman who had dance fan handles shaped like a bear's face. The woman's father was an accomplished bear hunter, able to kill them without either gun or bow. Instead he would tease the bear until it got angry and when it turned around, thrust wood into its anus.

Wassilie said that the dance fans he had seen in the Kuskokwim area were like those decorated with a ring and cross (fig. 11.18) or other geometric design: "Caribou beard hair and old-squaw duck tail feathers were attached to fans . . . and they were painted with red ocher. Dance fans I saw weren't made like these [with animal faces], but the Kuskokwim people before that time had dance fans like these. One of a pair of dance fans would represent a man and the other a woman."

Wassilie then spoke of the events in which he had seen dance fans used, launching into a description of dancing that the more dramatic but rarely seen masks had failed to elicit:

People danced with fans like these during *Itruka'aryaraq* [masked dances], an event also known as *Agayuyaraq*. . . . I used to drum with others sitting around the back wall of the *qasgi*. There was a platform around the back and side walls. At times, when the drummers did not have a singer, one of the elders would call me to come forward to join them while I stood by the front wall among the audience.

You knew Aguralria. Her late father used to call, "*Uqsungiaraq*, come and drum." I would feel intimidated and say, "I might crack the drumhead if I drum too hard." He'd respond, "It's okay if you break it as long as you are singing." I was just a boy at the time. I used to drum during *Itruka'ar*. There'd be many people in the *qasgi*. People came from Nanvarnarrlak, Nunacuaq, Paingaq, and sometimes we'd have guests from Naparyarraq. I would drum in front of our many guests from those villages, trying not to make any mistakes when I sang.

A designated person would set the pitch for the song, *mengluni* [singing while drumming softly]. . . . They also had *apallirturtet* [dance directors, literally, "ones who made the *apalluq* (verse)"]. One sat on one side of the drummers and the other on the opposite side. They would take off their parkas and garments beneath . . . because it would get very hot in the crowded *qasgi*. When the singers and dancers proceeded with the song, the song director on one side called out the words . . . and the singers sang them out.

11.14 Describing this pair of women's dance fans from the Yukon, Jacobsen wrote: "This kind of ornament is usually decorated with feathers. The faces . . . show exactly the faces . . . on the masks: seagull with human face, walrus, mountain spirit, etc. As I did not have the opportunity to witness a dance ceremony among the Yukon and tundra people, I know very little about masks. Since few women dance with masks, it is possible that [the ornaments] are either a substitute for masks or are held [in memory] of the deceased." IVA4369a, b.

12.15   One of a pair of dance fans.

12.16   Jacobsen reported that the faces on these lower Yukon paired dance fans may depict "the king of salmon." As in other dance fans, the spirit faces peer out from feather frames representing holes in the sky world." VA4372.

12.17   Esther holding a pair of dance fans. IVA5209.

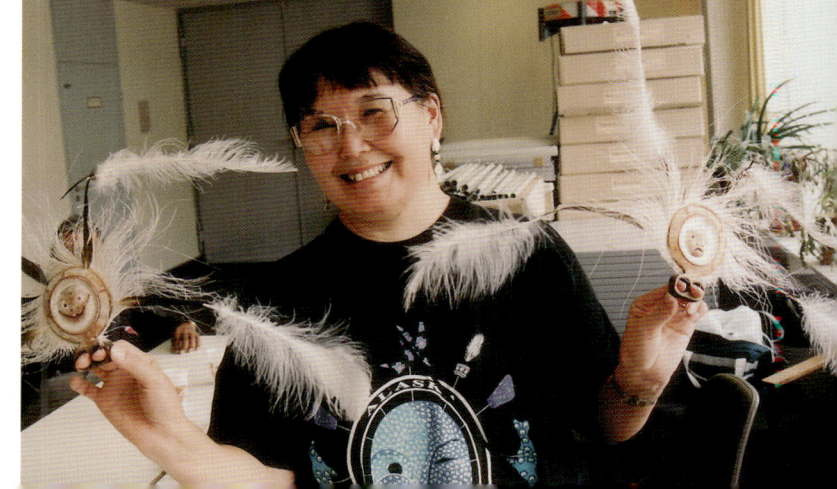

241   ELEVENTH DAY DANCING WITH MASKS

11.18 Kuskokwim dance fans decorated with ring and cross, like those Wassilie saw in use when he was young. The central hole recalls numerous ritual acts, such as pouring water in the ice hole before the bladders are sent away at the close of the Bladder Festival. IVA5204.

And the *agniurta* [one on the opposite side] would begin moving like this to the rhythm and call out the words to the song. As he called out the words, the singers would sing using the words he called out. As the words flowed out of the singers, he described them with his motions. They would sing as described.

The *apallirturta* called out the words to the song, directing the singers. When the song came to the *apalluq* [verse], the *apallirturta* called out the words to the *apalluq* before the singers sang out. And the dancer down there would move with the rhythm, illustrating the story with body and arm movements. . . .

The *agniurta* would call out all the words to the *agneq* [chorus]. . . . The two men sitting on opposite sides directed the songs. Their job was to make sure that the singers sang with the rhythm of the song, just as the song directors do in church choirs today. . . .

Meng'uralria is the one who sings the chorus quietly and slowly three times in the beginning. . . . Only the chorus was sung quietly, accompanied with a soft drumbeat, and the main dancer would gently move hands and bounce knees slowly with the drumbeat, *ayakata'arluni*. . . .

The dancer made soft movements as the singer sang softly. At times, two dancers were presented during *Itruka'ar,* and other times just one. Sometimes a male cousin would be pulled down to the floor by his *nuliacungaq* [female cross-cousin]. As she danced and came to the *cauyaquciara* [added motions accompanied by drumming], she motioned to her *uicungaq* [male cross-cousin] to come down. Captured by her movements and the drumbeat and singers, he would suddenly remove his garments and don a little face mask. He would go down to dance by his *nuliacungaq*. At this time, the drummers and singers would get more adamant. When her *uicungaq* joined her, she would dance with more vigor.

The singers sing the first *apalluq*. Then the *akuliik* [middle part of two] follows it with the chorus. Then the second *apalluq* is sung. If [Henry] was the *apallirturta,* he would call out and say, "There are no more *apallut.* It's time to dance!" At this time, the drumbeat would get faster and louder, and the singers would sing with more vigor.

Everyone nodded in agreement to this vivid description of dance dynamics—quiet to loud, slow to fast, subdued to exuberant.

Tulukaruguaq / **Pretend Raven**

After looking at fans, we returned to masks. Several passed by unremarked before we encountered a "Tullukarokoak= Ginakok" (*tulukaruguaq kegginaquq,* "pretend raven mask") from the lower Yukon (fig. 11.19).[16] A simple piece without ornamentation, it brought to mind the creator bird about whom so many stories are told to this day. Annie began at once with a *quliraq* about raven bringing daylight.

Long ago, there was a community that never saw daylight . . . so it was always dark. A raven lived with the people there, and everyone called him *Tulukarugaurluq* [poor, dear raven]. *Tulukarugaurluq* lived and ate with them.

Then one day one of the old men in the *qasgi* said, "*Alingnaqvaa* [My goodness!], we have been living in darkness and not been able to see things in their actual form for so long. There is no daylight to illuminate the area around us." Then he added, "Is that how this village is always going to be?" Then another old man said, "*Alingnaqvaa,* if we ask *Tulukarugaurluq* to search for daylight, perhaps he will bring it to us."

When *Tulukarugaurluq* said that he was willing to look for daylight, everyone helped provision him for his journey. Soon after, he left. Everyone in the village waited in anticipation for daylight to come.

Before *Tulukarugaurluq* left the *qasgi,* he said, "Perhaps soon daylight will come your way." He had requested a pair of new snowshoes and a long staff. When he left the village, he walked toward *calaraq* [the east]. He headed toward *keluvaraq* [another word for "east"]. It was from there he returned, holding a bladder with light in it. He returned wearing snowshoes across the middle of the sky. When he reached the center, he stopped and thrust his long staff there and said, "People in the coming generations will always be able to see my staff here in the middle of my snowshoe tracks." After he said that, he popped the bladder . . . and light came to the world and to the people he had once lived with.

People in the village were tremendously grateful to *Tulukarugaurluq*. Perhaps he was the ancestor of our people. They praised him for granting daylight to the people he lived with at that time.

In the earlier years, his snowshoe tracks were more distinct. People in those days knew exactly where he left his staff up there, and they used to say that the three stars represented his staff.

This is where I end this story as I tell it to you.

Vasilie then added what he remembered:

The story she just told is a song that Anirtuun's father taught to Ayagkaq. Back in those days, the trail that *Tulukaruk* made, wearing his snowshoes as he crossed the sky, was more distinct. People used to call them *tanglurallret* [the Milky Way, literally, "those made with snowshoes"]. It was said that he traveled across the sky, *ellam cavara aturluku* [following the universe]. From our vantage point back home, he traveled toward the north. But we don't know the way he returned. Or perhaps it was the trail he made when he

11.19 Mask depicting the creator bird, Raven. IVA4415.

returned after getting the light. When he reached the middle of the sky, he popped the bladder filled with light. I only know this part of the song that went with the story:

> I hope I give them light
> From this bladder
> By popping it
> Searching for light for the future generations.

Ayagkaq used to tell the story by singing . . . this beautiful song.

Henry commented that the Milky Way that stretches across the sky indeed looks like a trail: "When I see the Milky Way, I too have said that raven's trail was visible in the sky."

Uiluruyak / Meadow Jumping Mouse

Another evocative mask was one that Jacobsen designated "Yualle-Resak" (fig. 11.20) and said represented a fish or crab.[17] The explanation is simple enough, and in fact crabs are known as *yuale'rsaq* on Norton Sound. In trying to sound out Jacobsen's sometimes indecipherable orthography, however, Marie pronounced the mask's name *uiluruyak* (mouse), and Annie immediately took up the challenge. She mentioned that she had seen meadow mice near her home. When she was young, however, people regarded them as mysterious and believed that if they entered a house, it was a bad sign. Moreover, when a hunter found a *uiluruyak* caught in his trap, he always buried it on the spot rather than taking it home, allowing the mouse to be buried in his stead. Annie concluded: "I suppose the fear grew out of past experiences. The presence of these animals had resulted in harm to people they came to."

The meadow mouse reminded Annie of another story concerning how one's attitude toward a situation affects the outcome.

> One time I also heard about *egatek* [two cooking pots] talking to each other. . . . As a person was entering a house, he heard two people talking inside. One of them said, "I don't know what we are going to do now. If someone heard us talking back and forth, I'm sure they would be afraid. If they regard us as a bad omen, their prediction will come true, and we will bring bad luck to them." When he opened the entrance flap, he saw two cooking pots tipping this way and that way. They had been talking to each other.

11.20 Crab mask. As Jacobsen pointed out, "since nearly all animals are represented through masks, the crab could not be left out." IVA4453.

Then they gathered and talked, hoping that the bad omen would not come true but that good would prevail. They also hoped that seals would be plentiful in the coming season, with healthy young to increase their numbers. "They have spoken, and we hope the event brings good to our people."

After that incident, people said that the cooking pots were merely thinking about food that would be cooked in them in the future. The following spring, seals were plentiful in the ocean as predicted by the people, and young seals were numerous. After the encounter with the talking cooking pots, whenever the people believed that the positive would result, then it would come true. On the other hand, when they believed that the outcome would be negative, then that prediction would come true. . . . The people in that community were grateful to those pots rather than being afraid of them. They maintained their belief that the pots were speaking about the food to be cooked in them in the future. They lived as before, and nothing bad happened to them.

Wassilie confirmed what Annie had said—that in the past when people saw a *uiluruyak*, they regarded it as a bad omen. Their interpretation had missed the mark regarding the crab mask, but had been rich nonetheless.

Angenqacuutet / Warriors

Jacobsen collected only one dance mask from the Nushagak region (fig. 11.21), where he reported such masks had "gone out of fashion."[18] Jacobsen said it was made by the "Aglemutten" of the Iliamna district, a group well known for its warlike character. Annie spoke first, explaining how these legendary warriors came to ruin.[19]

I've only heard about the Aglurmiut in warrior stories. They were quite arrogant people in wartime and were abusive to women. During war, women were never harmed because they *kelgatuata* [invited wrathful vengeance]. But in spite of that, Aglurmiut included women in their killings. . . .

'Ve heard that the women's *kelgaat* [vengeance] was long during that time. . . . When those men began abusing and killing women, they became weak and unsuccessful in their pursuit of animals. . . . Those who harm women invite unluckiness in their pursuit of animals. That happened to the Aglurmiut.

Annie then described an incident when two women went out to pick berries and were attacked by warriors. When one of them stood up, she was struck by so many arrows that her body remained suspended in the air. Annie had also heard that the passion for killing humans was much stronger than for killing animals. Finally she told one of many versions of how warfare came to an end:

I've heard a story about Aglurmiut toward the end of wars. When Aglurmiut began participating in *kaataryaraq* [a hand game], they didn't want to fight anymore. When I was very little, I saw people taking part in *kaataryaraq* in the *qasgi*. Women were allowed to play, too. Two pieces of wood were used, one with a mark in the middle and another plain one that was considered its female mate. Two men would play the game and sing, facing each other on the floor. Ten pieces of wood were used as *tegutet* [stakes or antes]. The opponent on one side would be the one pointing. Some people were quite clumsy in the match and some were sharp. The good player would keep winning the stakes and would win all the stakes from his opponent, *meqluku* [from *meqe-*, "to lose hair, fur, feathers"]. When the opponent began to lose his pieces, he got agitated. It was after the introduction of that game that the wars ended. People became friendly to each other.

Later in the trip, Annie taught Marie the game in which one person sang out and hid the two wooden pieces (a plain "female" and a "male" with two encircling rings across its middle) behind her back, while her partner tried to guess which hand held the *ui* (husband). We all smiled as Annie playfully defended her bits of wood against Marie's challenges (fig. 11.22, fig. 11.23, fig. 11.24).

Henry was also familiar with the history of the Aglurmiut and shared what he remembered:

I've heard that before Aglurmiut were almost wiped out, the survivors tied their bodies to logs and drifted down from Iguk toward the Alaska Peninsula. . . . I imagine there were only a few survivors who decided to escape in that manner. The mask we were looking at apparently was made by one of the survivors of the Aglurmiut . . . living in the Iliamna area and also down toward the Aleutian Islands.

Finally, Wassilie shared what he had heard when he worked as a young man in a Dillingham cannery: "When we weren't working, the elders from Dillingham and Aleknagik got together and talked about these events. They said that Aglurmiut were killed off with only a few survivors. When white people came into the area, the Kuskokwim people stopped waging wars."

The next day, we would look at another carved depiction of warfare—an ivory battle scene between Kuskokwim and northern Eskimos (fig. 11.25) from Fort Alexander, consisting of three men in kayaks. Wassilie began: "I assume that these were made to remind people of the time of warfare. They were used for decoration." Again, the scene brought to mind Apanuugpak and his companions. Henry recalled: "They mentioned three warriors that went down Iiyuussiiq River. . . . If this depicts Apanuugpak, these are the other two with him. People talked about three kayaks in the story. And as they came downriver, they killed an enemy warrior named Aqlillugpak."

Annie remembered Apanuugpak as well as other warriors, including Tunuqerpalek, Kukumyaq, and the brothers Sungnak and Cuqaar. She said regretfully, "If I had been observant when I was younger, I would have a lot of stories to tell." Saying that he, too, had forgotten many of the names, Wassilie recalled some of the old war stories:

I've heard that Apanuugpak and his comrades were from the Kuskokwim area. . . . During the time of war, they killed many people along the trail they were taking toward Bristol Bay. And Qaguyaurluq, too, ran on the beach alongside the enemy village, leaving his footprints so the people would see how far he could

stride, attesting to his agility. . . . Double-bladed paddles were a little bit longer than the distance between one's outstretched arms. When the enemy warriors in that village measured his tracks the next morning, that was the length of Qaguyaurluq's stride when he ran. He was the fastest runner in the group.

Then Wassilie retold the story that Paul had recounted the last week, of the warriors Apanuugpak, Iruvertuq, and the young men Qanerciigalnguq, Paluqtaaralek, and Quarruuk, who were surrounded by enemy warriors below Eqtarmiut. Qanerciigalnguq kept following Apanuugpak from behind, and they could hear women laughing up in the village, saying, "Look at the poor guys from the Kuskokwim, they look like baby birds following their mother."

Apanuugpak would wet his mouth with salt water from the side. Pillugta would say, "*Turrull'*, why are you drinking salt water? What is the matter?" Apanuugpak's mouth was drying up. Then finally he said, "I'm worried about these young men who are with us. I don't want them to get hurt." Then Qanerciigalnguq said to his uncle, "You've always said that I was slow to respond when I was a boy. Now, in my youth, we are about to be slow to respond together . . ."

Then one of the men from Eqtarmiut came down and paddled around Apanuugpak and his warriors. He would turn upside down with his legs in the air holding onto his paddle, pretending to dodge arrows. The bold warrior paddled around Apanuugpak and his warriors while the other warriors from Eqtarmiut encircled them.

Then one time, as he flung himself upside down, his hands landed outside of the cockpit coaming stanchions and slipped. . . . He had rubbed oil on his kayak before he came down from the village determined to kill the enemy. He fell, and his kayak capsized. As soon as he fell into the water, one of Apanuugpak's warriors called, "*Quaq, quaq.*" He quickly took his spear and harpooned him. The spear helped to keep the dead man afloat in the water. Apanuugpak quickly paddled toward him and grabbed his *paangcun* [paddle]. He went back and gave the paddle to Paluqtaaralek, who took it and pretended to paddle in the air, saying, "It's like I'm already paddling up the Kuskokwim."

Apanuugpak and his warriors stayed together. The enemy warriors surrounded them. Some of the kayaks were afloat close together, and some were far apart. Pillugta would call Apanuugpak, "*Turrull'*, I thought the enemy was afraid of your voice. When are you going to let it out?" Then he finally said, "If you were in command, what would you do to bring these young people out

11.21 The single mask Jacobsen collected from the Nushagak region, a relatively plain piece with red-painted face, caribou-teeth mouth, and fur eyebrows and mustache. IVA6371.

11.22, 11.23, 11.24 Annie and Marie facing each other and playing a game in which one person hides wooden pieces behind her back while the other tries to guess which hand holds the *ui* (husband), the piece with encircling bands. The introduction of this game was said to have coincided with the end of bow-and-arrow warfare.

11.25 Ivory battle scene between Kuskokwim and northern Eskimos. According to Jacobsen, one warrior already had two arrows through his kayak ring: "He escapes equipped with a double rudder (sign of a northern Eskimo). He picks up a wooden club for his protection. When he looks back at his pursuers, he is hit by an arrow in his eye. . . . The battle scene seems to be a spontaneous act of revenge." IVA5697.

of harm's way?" Then Pillugta said, "See the open gaps between the kayaks? Perhaps we could help our young men escape through them." Apanuugpak said, "No. See the kayaks afloat closer together? They are manned by young warriors who are afraid to be out by themselves." He told him that they would help their young warriors escape through there. . . .

Apanuugpak and his men were waiting, holding their paddles in position, and now Paluqtaaralek had a paddle in his hands. It was at that time he finally called out his victory song. . . . He sang out, letting out his mighty voice. Then the enemy warriors on the outskirts yelled, "Ii-ii-ii. So, Apanuugpak is with them. No wonder they waited a long time before doing anything. And look at his kayak with the huge mouth in front to show his power and ferocity."

Then Paluqtaaralek sprang forward toward the kayaks in groups. Apanuugpak grabbed the stern of his kayak and pulled it back and said, "Paluqtaaralek, what are you doing? Watch your companions here. . . ." He looked and noticed that the others were making paddling motions in the air. And even though they were not moving, the enemy warriors ahead started . . . making room for Apanuugpak and his men to escape. They quickly paddled toward the opening. Since the enemy warriors had paddled too far to the side, they were not able to close in the opening fast enough. . . . When Apanuugpak's men paddled toward the ocean, the only thing the enemy warriors could see was water spraying out from behind their kayaks. They sped down toward the open ocean and escaped. In those days, men were taught not to follow warriors that sped out into the ocean.

Wassilie's story built on Paul's, adding details and omitting others. Annie commented: "Warrior stories like these come out a little different in each village."

While Wassilie had been talking, Annie had been thinking. She returned to the story of Apanuugpak's pursuit of the warrior Aqlillugpak, which Henry had originally suggested that the ivory figures might represent. Annie described how Aqlillugpak was taken unawares while salmon fishing with his wife as the tide was coming into the mouth of the Iiyuussiiq River. Then she sang the *anqaraun* (warrior song) that went with the story.

*Aqlillugpak is yelling
and trying to get away
Don't say
Iiyuussiiq is filling up with water*

Wassilie also remembered the story of Aqlillugpak's attempted flight, and he chuckled when he recalled how annoyed the enemy warriors were when they discovered that Aqlillugpak's spear had only crane quills for stabilizers. Stories of encounters between enemy warriors in Bristol Bay are still very much alive in memory one hundred years after Jacobsen purchased the ivory replica of events like those recalled.

Inglupgayuk / The Half-faced One

Next we examined a half-face mask, "Ingelukpiat=Kinakut," or *inglupgayuk kegginaquq* (fig. 11.26), that Jacobsen had collected from the Yukon. He described it as a "memorial death mask" that the dancer used to impersonate the spirit of the dead: "At these memorial festivals in the Yukon area, women wear masks that show one-half of a human face to begin a dance. In each hand the dancer carries a staff on whose end a feather is attached. They believe that by this dance, they are seen and inspired by the departed and often report how the dead person fares in the other world."[20]

While working on the mask exhibit, Jack Angaiak of Newtok had told me, "In half-face masks, the missing part of the face was called *tuquneq* [part that is deceased]. And they said the other half was a human face." This supports Jacobsen's statement regarding another half-faced mask, that a dancer wearing such a half-mask would report from the land of the dead how the deceased was faring, how often he or she thought of living relatives, and how many caribou and fish he or she sent to them during the past year.[21] People believed that the spirit of the dead was really before them.

In Berlin, Annie spoke up once again, having heard about *Inglupgayuk* (from *inglu*, "other one of a pair") in a *quliraq* about Qelkaraurluq's journey, possibly to the land of the dead:

When he came upon a house, he entered it . . . and found many women of all sizes sitting in the room. . . . As he looked around, he saw a half-faced woman sitting across in the corner. She was half a woman. Then he began to sample the *akutat* set by each woman, beginning from the left side of the room. The women were busy with their work and talking, not paying attention to him. He tasted some *akutaq* from each bowl as he went around the room, but he didn't like them. When he reached the corner where *Inglupgayuk* was sitting, he found a bowl filled with *akutaq* behind her. He took the bowl and tasted some *akutaq*. As he chewed, he realized that it had bearberries in it. It was delicious. This time he had another mouthful of the *akutaq*, then he slipped behind *Inglupgayuk*'s bowl.

Then soon one of the women in the room announced, "It is time to eat lunch." As they were getting ready, one of the women took down a bowl filled with dried fish pieces. When the bowls were ready, the first woman on the left side took her bowl of *akutaq* down. Then she exclaimed, "Oh, look at the little fingerprints in my *akutaq*! Who ate from my *akutaq*?" The woman next to her got curious and took down her *akutaq*. She also found little fingerprints in her *akutaq*. Then everyone got excited and began taking down their bowls, and each found that someone had tasted their *akutaq*, too. The first woman sitting on the left side of the entrance said, "The person who finds this child will keep him." Then *Inglupgayuk* said, "*Uugguuk* [Oh wow!]. Let me see." When she took down her bowl of *akutaq*, she found two sets of little fingerprints. . . .

Then the women began to search the room. When *Inglupgayuk* looked under the grass mat in the corner behind her, she found a little child. "*Uugguuk*. I found him." Everyone began to argue and tried to claim the child, but since *Inglupgayuk* had found him, she claimed him with gratitude. All those women tried to take him, but *Inglupgayuk* took him and said, "*Uugguuk*. I'm going to raise him." That's the story I've heard about *Inglupgayuk*. I'm sure there's another version to this story.

Wassilie had commented earlier on another half-faced mask from the Yukon, which Jacobsen also described as a memorial or death mask and Wassilie labeled *inglupgayuk*.[22] Then he began tossing the song others sang to a person named Ciguarpak to scorn his effort, *kingullugtelliniat* (literally, "they shun or ridicule him after he performs a task"). Wassilie continued:

When Ciguarpak realized that the others were making fun of him,

11.26 Jacobsen reported that half-faced masks, such as the one Annie modeled, were used by women during "memorial festivals" to impersonate the spirit of the dead and report from their world. This mask is also illustrated on page 36. IVA4386.

he came into the *qasgi* wearing a tiny *inglupgayuk* mask and singing:

Let Keliskacungaq
push him in the sled
wearing a half mask

When they sang the song, ridiculing him, he wore a tiny half-mask and danced in the middle of the floor, moving his neck back and forth.

The day was done, and we went home full of stories.

TWELFTH DAY Toys and Clothing

Naanguat, Uivcetaat-llu / **Toys and Spinners**

Nearing the end of our work in Berlin, we shifted our focus from masks with serious intent to toys used to pass the time. The first was a kind of twirler from St. Michael (fig. 12.1), made from a wooden rod with a string attached.[1] According to Jacobsen, it was thrown in the air by children "like a forest devil" and used for superstitious purposes in ancient times. Wassilie recognized the toy and said it was called *elevlugtaq* on the Kuskokwim and *elevlevaaq* in Bristol Bay.

Next was a *ellaraq* (wooden spinner) from the Kuskokwim (fig. 12.2), also a child's toy.[2] Wassilie recognized it as well: "In fall right after freeze-up, . . . string was attached here, and when it was pulled, this would take off with a ringing sound. It would spin for a long time on newly frozen ice. . . . It has a piece with a slit that made the sound, but it seems to be missing. . . . They made little grooves on it that made sounds as it spun."

Caukia / **Turn to Me**

A high point of our day was a tiny wooden top *(uivcetaaq)* from the Kuskokwim (fig. 12.3), a child's toy that could be either pulled with a string or spun by hand.[3] Wassilie picked it up and delightedly showed us how it worked: "When you play *caukia*, you spin the *uivcetaaq* inside a bentwood bowl with an *allungak* [bottom part]. And as it spins, you'd say, '*Kitaki wani caukia, caukia, caukia* [Okay now, turn to me, turn to me, turn to me!].' All the players would say, '*Caukia, caukia, caukia.*' Oh, it faced my partner here."

We later found similar German-made wooden tops at a shop, which we brought back to our hotel, where the game went on.

Aavcaat / **Darts**

We turned now to a pair of darts from Eratlewik near Golovin Bay (also shown in fig. 12.3).[4] Although not from our area, they resembled a familiar toy, and Wassilie spoke with gusto:

People played darts in the *qasgi*, sitting across from each other on the floor. A square wooden or thick paper board was used as a target with a dark spot painted in the center, surrounded by a circu-

12.1 Wooden twirler and wooden spinner, both children's toys. IVA3103, IVA5015.

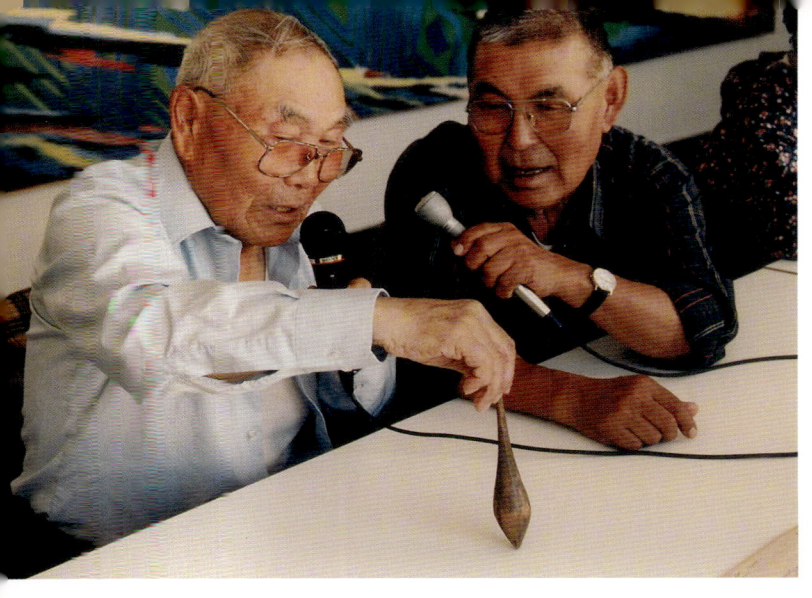

12.2 Wassilie trying out an ellaraq (wooden spinner), which could be either pulled with a string or spun by hand. IVA5015.

12.3 Wooden top from the Kuskokwim and a pair of cigar-shaped wooden darts, each with a metal point at one end, and one with a trimmed feather at the other. IVA2665, IVA3270, IVA3269.

lar line. . . . There were four players altogether, two on each team. Each team had four stakes. When a person hit the spot in the middle with the dart, he'd win two sticks. And if the dart hit the area within the circle, the person would get one stake.

Aavcaaryaraq [a dart game] was played like that. At times, people played this game to acquire wood for fire bathing. The losing team was obligated to bring firewood for the bath. When daylight became longer in the spring, people started playing this game.

Angqat / Balls

We turned our attention to a round grass rattle from the Yukon (fig. 12.4), also said to have been a child's toy.[5] Wassilie identified it as an angqaq (ball), and as he described its use, he stood and pretended to throw it across the room to Catherine:

I used to see people playing a game with a ball: patkartaaryaraq [slap ball, from pateg-, "to slap"]. Women were partners playing against the men. This man [Henry] would be my partner and would stand over there. And if I was to start the game, these women would be in the center trying to take the ball away from us. And if I threw the ball and he hit it from his position, these two women would try to take it. As they tried to take the ball, I'd hit it again back to my partner. As he hit it to me again, I would hit it back to him. And if one of us miscalculated our aim, one of the women would grab the ball . . . and begin throwing it to her partner. We'd hit the ball with our hands, slapping it.

Examining a set of a half dozen stone balls from St. Michael,[6] Wassilie continued: "People used these kal'utarcuutet [round pucks] to play kal'utaryaraq [a hockey-like game] . . . during early freeze-up. There was a line on one side that was a goal. The team would push and hit the puck, trying to take it across to the goal line, while the opposing team tried to retrieve it. They used a wooden stick to push it across and a rounded piece

12.4 *Grass ball, decorated with red thread and filled with little stones, along with dark-colored stone balls from St. Michael and four light-colored clay balls from the lower Yukon. IVA4235, IVA4228, IVA4227.*

of wood as a puck." Catherine, too, remembered the game, but said that the balls they used weren't stone but homemade balls with weight in them. Jacobsen had never seen the balls used, but said that they were the playthings of young girls on ice or sand, perhaps similar to our marbles.

The last set of four clay balls from the lower Yukon drew no comment.[7] Jacobsen wrote that they were also used by young girls, often playing in groups of five: "The balls were thrown into the air just like the jugglers [do] and caught until the playing child completed a song. When the playing child lost a ball, she lost the game, and the next one in the game followed. The playing children used hardly more than two or three balls because the song is very long. The same game is also often played on Norton Sound."

Yaaruin / Story Knives

The balls and twirlers were not the first toys we had seen during our visit. The week before, we had examined an ivory *yaaruin* (story knife) from the Kuskokwim (fig. 12.5), an instrument for sketching out stories in the mud or snow.[8] Paul had explained it in contemporary terms as a "cartoon-*arcuutellraq*":

I regard this as our ancestors' cartoon maker. This instrument was used by young, curious minds to explore their imaginations. The young ones used this to illustrate their thoughts, beginning from the time they first remembered things, to their peers like the way children are entertained by cartoon characters on TV. It was mostly the young who used this instrument and a few adults.

Today when children watch cartoons on TV in the morning, their attention is captured by the story unfolding in front of their eyes. As they are doing this, they are preparing their minds for conceptual thinking. This tool was used to illustrate stories like the way cartoons are made today.

Marie asked if only girls used story knives, and Paul said yes. "So girls were the only ones who watched cartoons?" she queried. "I guess so," he chuckled.

Annie took up the story knife and described how she had used one to learn how clothes and boots were made:

As girls back in those days, we couldn't be without this *yaaruin*. Our story knives were not all made out of ivory like this, but some were made out of hardwood. The handles were usually nicely dec-

125 Story knives used for sketching stories in mud or snow. IVA3169, IVA5005.

126 Ivory story knives in different shapes and sizes, the top two from the Yukon and the one on the bottom from Cape Vancouver. IVA3783, IVA5003, IVA3803.

created like this. I had one like this that was once owned by my late older sister . . . made from ivory with the handle fixed so my hands fit right into it. . . .

Today I don't see any of our young ones using story knives like these. But I've seen young girls using metal butter knives illustrating stories on the mud.

When I was a girl, I didn't sew or make crafts, but . . . I was always helping my mother with chores. And sometimes when I began to play, she'd tell me, "Look. You should do chores instead of playing. If you don't learn now, you will run into barriers later on in life." But I would always use a *yaaruin* like this to illustrate houses and the activities that go on inside. I also illustrated parkas, since I always examined parkas that were hanging outside houses and airing out. I would also use a *yaaruin* to illustrate . . . boot designs and borders. This is the only instrument I used to learn about putting together clothing. Anyone can use a *yaaruin* to learn about clothing construction.

Turning to Catherine, Annie concluded: "Since we are women, would you add more about this?" Catherine continued:

When I was a girl, we also used story knives. Our Ap'ayagaq's [little grandfather's] eldest daughter had a huge ivory *yaaruin* like this. We younger ones didn't have ivory ones. But when she wasn't looking, my younger sister and I would grab it and use it on new-fallen snow. . . . When she found out, she'd run over and snatch it away from us. My *yaaruin* was made of driftwood. I used to wish I had an ivory *yaaruin* like my sister. She always kept it under her pillow.

The *yaaruin* that each had owned reflected their different histories. As an adopted child, Catherine had never had an ivory *yaaruin*. Annie, however, inherited one from her older sister: "You know, back in those days, when a girl had her first menses, they did something called *ugayiqurluki* [from *ugayar-*, "to strip one's clothing or belongings"]. Girls who had their first menstruation gave their things away to other younger girls. When her *yaaruin* was given to me, I was very happy. But I don't know what happened to it."

Earlier we had examined a box of twenty story knives (fig. 12.6) from the Yukon and one from Cape Vancouver.[9] Jacobsen gave two names to each, "Jerruin" (*yaaruin*) and "Atitueititt" (*ateknguitet*), and he said that they were used not only by young girls, but also by women for pleating the soles of boots, by men when telling stories, and for scraping snow from boots when entering a house. They had been made in different sizes and from different materials, including ivory, caribou antler, and wood. Those of antler were called *cirunqaaraat*, while those of wood were *equaq* (literally, "pretend wood"). Annie briefly reflected: "Back in those days, when a *nukalpiaq* married a young woman, he'd provide her with a *yaaruin* and ivory earring posts." Paul had handled them as Annie spoke, observing: "These were made *carumigcetaak* [for a left-handed person]. And this was *tallirpigcetaq* [for a right-handed person]."

Inuguat / Playing Dolls

Next we looked at a group of children's dolls. Spread before us were wooden human figures in a range of sizes, and most were clothed.[10] Like the ivory and bone figurines we had looked at the week before, Marie noted that some were probably dolls that young girls played with—known variously as *inuguat* (from Iñupiaq *inuk*, "person," plus *-(ng)uaq*, "imitation"), *irniaruaq* (pretend child), *yugat*, or *sugat* (from *yuk* or *suk*, both words for person)—which may also have been used as *iinrut* (amulets).

Jacobsen identified all four of the largest wooden dolls as children's toys. The first, from Nushagak, represented a young girl "Arneak=Kotzingoat" (*irniaq irniaruaq*, "child doll"), wearing a squirrel-skin parka with cotton trousers and decorated boots, a bead necklace and earrings, and hair covered by a scarf.[11] Annie noted that the doll was so old that its parka was

12.7 Clothed doll from the Kuskokwim, like those sewn on parkas between the shoulders of young girls, possibly to imitate the babies they would someday carry. Jacobsen wrote: "The doll constantly beats against the back when the girl runs. This indicates that the doll not only seems to protect houses but individuals. . . . I saw such dolls with several young girls between twelve and sixteen." IVA5311.

12.8 Doll's wooden torso with bone eyes and mouth from the lower Yukon. Often only the upper torso of a doll was made out of hard material, and clothes could be easily slipped on and off its armless body. IVA4199.

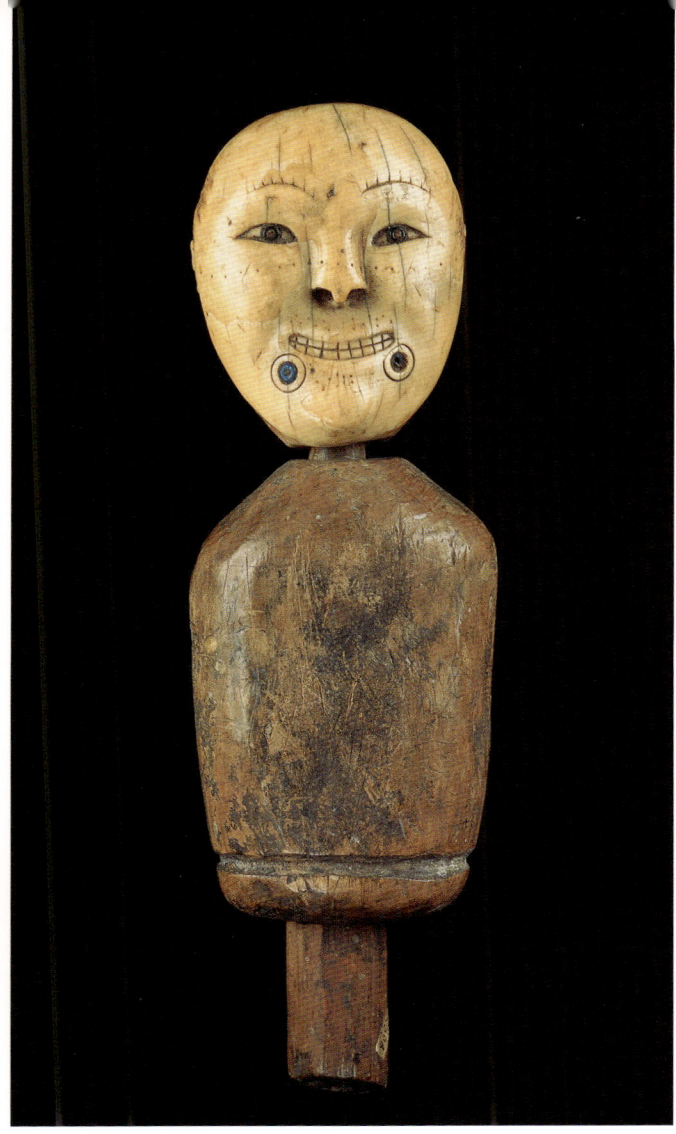

12.9 Doll torso from the lower Yukon, which Wassilie suggested was used as an iinruq (amulet). IVA4512.

full of holes made by *parut* (fur insects): "It has boots made of sealskin with bead decorations [over the top of the foot] called *itgutek*. . . . It also has gloves made of dark fur. It has a wooden face with eyes made of bone with dark spots as pupils. And its mouth is made of *uqumyak* [quartz]. This doll is well made." Annie turned the doll over, noting that it had a *kakauyaq* (parka hood decoration) but that the bugs had eaten that, too.

Jacobsen labeled two more clothed figures from the Kuskokwim "child doll" (fig. 12.7) and noted that such dolls were often "worn" by young girls, who sewed them to the backs of their parkas. Both had nose beads, and the first also had a tattooed chin. Annie commented that squirrel-belly skins had been sewn together to make the second doll's parka, decorated with fringes called *uategiit* and trim on both sleeves between the shoulder and elbow called *tusrutek*.

Last we looked at a doll's wooden torso from the lower Yukon (fig. 12.8), which Jacobsen designated "Jungoak" (*yugaq* or *inuguaq*). Although Jacobsen had been told it was a toy, he suspected otherwise, as he had seen such figures on graves on the lower Yukon and in the tundra villages. Wassilie agreed with

him, and he commented on this piece as well as two other dolls (fig. 12.9) from the Yukon[13]:

Those two aren't dolls to play with, but they are *uyak*. *Uyat* were used like *iinrut*. I have seen memorial figures like these on burials without any clothing. . . .

But these other figurines are *inuguat* [playing dolls] because they are adorned with clothing and such. And this little one could be an *iinruq* doll, or it could be an *uya*. Some *uyat* were small. And these that are decorated and adorned are *inuguat*. On burials, human figures like these were visible as *alailutet* [objects placed on burials]. They would be surrounded by other objects. *Alailutet* were memorials to the deceased.

The group of toy dolls adorned with clothing and bead jewelry included thirteen *yugat* from the Yukon (fig. 12.10), six *inuguat* from between the Kuskokwim and Nushagak (fig. 12.11), two from Nushagak, and one from Nunivak (fig. 12.12).[14] Jacobsen also listed "Erneak" or "Arneak" (*irniaq*, "offspring, child") and "Kotzongoak" or "Kotsungoak" as names for Kuskokwim and Nushagak dolls. Three Yukon dolls (fig. 12.13) were

12.10 Toy doll from the Yukon. IVA4514.

dressed in Russian women's costumes,[15] which Jacobsen said was considered very fine, and one unclothed doll was made of tree bark.[16] A number had rings carved at the base of their wooden torsos so that pants and feet with skin boots could be attached.

Jacobsen wrote that any of these "toys" could also serve as amulets if "consecrated" by a shaman, and he mentioned again in regard to one small wooden doll that it might be sewn between the shoulders of a young girl's parka to protect her from harm: "This is practiced particularly along the coast from Cape Vancouver to Cape Avinoff. On the Yukon I saw many such figurines, particularly at the graves, where they were probably left behind by the deceased." He later wrote:

For the newborn child, the shaman carves a wood idol which is placed for safekeeping in a specially made sealskin sack along with other amulets. This idol is called "Slaowikmiu-Tomerak" [*Ellam Yua tuunraq*, "spirit of the Person of the Universe"], ruler of the lightning, and has the shape of a person. The back, from the seat of the head, is split and presents a large mouth with protruding teeth. The Eskimo will never sell such an idol. The shaman creates a small human figure out of a walrus tooth, which serves the young as an amulet.

In the tundra area between the Yukon and Kuskowkim, as well as on the seacoast between them, I often saw young girls with a wooden doll about one and one-half feet long. This was sewn tightly, with face outward, onto the sealskin jacket. It was always an unusual sight when the young girls, as often was the case, would take flight at my sudden appearance in the villages, and the wooden doll on the back of the girls' jackets would flop up and down. I never saw older women carry such an idol, and it seems that this custom was connected with the girls' marriageability.[17]

Commenting on the use of children's dolls as *iinrut*, Annie remarked: "I have not seen *iinrut*. There weren't that many people living in Cauyarnaq, where I grew up.... But my parents used to talk about people keeping little human figurines as *iinrut*. My aunt's daughter used to have a little human figurine as an *iinruq*, but her mother used to keep it all the time."

Even the use of "playing dolls" was carefully regulated. Earlier, Paul had described the rules surrounding toy dolls:

People used to say that it was time to bring out play dolls when people first heard a red-throated loon's call in the spring. It was common knowledge that red-throated loons arrived in the spring when it wasn't going to be cold anymore. A red-throated loon's arrival was a definite sign of summer. I've just added this to what the two women mentioned about the custom of toy dolls and when they were brought out at the end of winter after they had been put away.

Annie now described her experiences playing with dolls when she was young:

As a girl, I used to love to play with my *sugaruaq*.... We've always called them *sugat,* but when my mother made me dolls, she used to say that she was making me *inuguat*. Her *ilungaq* [female cross-cousin] used to tease her saying, "Gee, the mother of Kenerkalge keeps calling these *inuguat*. Could it be that she is a *sugaq* herself?" Well, that's a word she used because she was originally from the Kuskokwim area. As they talked about these, they'd start laughing and joking. We could not do without *sugat*.

Among these *inuguat* are some *irniaruat,* too.... That one with an ivory face is made very nicely.... And those newer ones were made with well-finished parkas and boots. This one has a parka with the fur inside and its boots are made of furless leather. The soles seem to be sewn with stitches called *inuguarcetuat*. They weren't sewn on as they would be normally.

These cute *inuguat* are dressed with clothing made of fabric....

12.11 *Inuguaq (toy doll) from between the Kuskokwim and Nushagak Rivers. IVA5317.*

12.12 Nunivak doll. IVA7243.

12.13 Yukon doll dressed in a Russian woman's costume. IVA4508.

When I was a girl, I used to see this cloth, which they called either *ellutmuayaaq* or *tiiguayaaq* [striped cloth, calico]. . . . And these cute *sugat* are quite well made, too. . . . The parka on that one appears to be made of weasel skin. And this other one has on a leather garment with the fur inside. That one is wearing a beautiful *qaliq* parka [with fancy front and back plates].

Although strong on rocks and bones, Jacobsen's collection was pitifully lacking in clothing. Many dolls, however, were beautifully attired, and Jacobsen wrote that girls learned early how to cut and sew clothing for their dolls, which were dressed as nicely as their human counterparts.[18] Annie was happy to use the dolls and their tiny parkas as an excuse to speak about parka construction:

Parkas made out of caribou fawn skins were called *qaliluut*. . . . I saw a woman cut out a parka pattern from a caribou skin. She would make a cut out in the middle of the skin. Then she would cut another opening following a pattern, and then another one on the other side equally distant from the middle. Then the *uminguak* [arrow-point designs] were sewn in those openings called *pakinrek*. When the two caribou fawn skins were sewn together into a parka, the designs called *qulitak* were sewn on. . . . My *qulitak* were made with *cauyaruarraak* [two drum designs], which is my family crest.

Others had crests they called *cetumquruarraak* [design of hooves or claws]. People had their own family crests. When caribou parkas became old, they [also] called them *qaliluut*. A parka made in this style was called an *atkupiaq* [genuine parka]. The *uminguak* on the parka were sewn in below the shoulder areas on the upper chest. This *qaliitaq* parka did not have *uminguak* on the back; *qulitak* were also sewn on the upper back. . . . Two wolverine tails were placed here on the back, sewn on quite close together.

Women finished young caribou fawn parkas decoratively in those days. . . . Both men and women could have caribou parkas. . . . The *uminguak* were always sewn on men's parkas. Men's parkas didn't have *qulitaq* designs on them but other designs specific to men.

Everyone enjoyed looking at the dolls, and we admired them for a long time. Annie was particularly moved and, as happened so often during the preceding days, she took a doll in her hands and began to tell a story:

This cute little *inuguaq*—sometimes when I see them, they remind me of the story about a girl.

Long ago there lived a grandmother and her orphaned grandchild *maurgara'urluqellriik* [literally, "grandchild related ones"]. The poor grandmother's orphaned granddaughter was quite modest. Whenever the poor girl tried to join the other girls outside, they rejected her and refused to play with her. At times the girl's grandmother felt sorry for her poor grandchild and cried. The girl would come back into the house after attempting to play with other girls and tell her grandmother that the others refused to look at her. Her grandmother would become upset and wondered why the other girls were so cruel.

As the poor grandchild played by herself, she could see the other girls having fun together. She sat alone telling stories to herself using her story knife. She couldn't join the other girls as they played because they ran away whenever she approached them.

As years passed, the girl grew up. One day she walked up to join the girls playing with their toy dolls. When they ran away, she found a little doll adorned with fine clothing and jewelry where they had played. The doll's face was made with care and looked adorable.

She picked up the beautiful little *inuguaq* and ran home. When she came into the house with the doll, her grandmother said, "Oh, I'm very, very thankful. Now you will never say how the other girls ignore you and refuse to play with you ever again. Now, go out and stand in front of our porch where the girls can see you and start singing a song. And when you sing, place this doll on the palm of your hand with your arm stretched out. While you sing, it will definitely stand up and dance."

The grandchild went out. She stood in front of the porch, put the doll on her palm, extended her arm toward the girls playing, and started to sing:

Yugaanaqaa yugaanaqaa [my doll]
Yugana yugana yugaanaqaa-a-a-a
What is this, what is this
that I have found
Yugana yugana yugaanaqaa-a-a-a

The girls heard her song and looked toward her, and they all screamed with excitement, "Aa-aa-aa. Dear grandchild, what is that in your hand? Please let us join you so we all can look at it. Wait. We're coming." While the girls were running toward her as she sang, she began to ascend toward the sky. The girls ran toward her excitedly, but by the time they reached the porch front, the grandchild was already too high, and they couldn't see the dancing doll in her hand. The little doll was dancing vigorously on the palm of the grandchild's hand.

Yugaanaqaa yugaanaqaa
Yugana yugana yugaanaqaa-aa-aa
What is this, what is this
that I have found
Yugana yugana yugnaqaa-aa-aa

The grandchild and the doll continued to ascend toward the east where the sun rises each morning. While the girls were calling, the grandchild went toward the dawning light and disappeared. The girls on the ground kept calling her to come back, but after a long time they finally stopped and went home.

Before the grandmother released her grandchild she said this to her, "The others have rejected you and refused to look at you. From now on, people in the whole world will always look at you . . . until the end of our universe."

The girls went home. The next day, they went out and saw a new star above the dawning light before sunrise. It was a huge star. The grandchild had moved to the spot where people would see her every morning at daybreak. And just as the grandmother had promised, people would always look at her when they went out every morning. The star was impressive to look at. We all have seen the star when we go out at dawn to examine the sky. The star we see is the grandchild.

Commenting on Annie's story, Wassilie added detail about the morning star (called *ulugturalria*, "one that twinkles"), into which the child had been transformed. He noted that in the morning before sunrise, the star can be seen flickering. People say this is because the granddaughter is constantly changing her parka. When she wears her beautiful red-fox parka, the star flickers red, and when she wears her other parka, it flickers white. Wassilie also noted that in the past, people were taught to pay attention to that star: "The star is the insignia of our world and weather. We were told that it would give off vapor if the whole world was about to experience *ellarrluk* [upheaval or food shortage]. The vapor would arch toward the north, the direction the prevailing winds would be going when *ellarrluk* occurred." When this happened, travel would be impossible in the bays and ocean where the coastal people hunted.

Wassilie later added more about *ellarrluk* (times of famine and food shortage due to prolonged bad weather).

When *ellarrluk* was going to occur . . . people would begin seeing that vapor at nightfall. The *angalkut* . . . would travel to that star. After they went there, they would say . . . that the smoke was coming from the cooking, which the person in that star was constantly doing for she had so much food.

Then one day an *angalkuq* from Paingaq went to check on her. When he got to the star, he looked in through the skylight and saw an old woman . . . busy cooking, and her pot was boiling. As it boiled, he'd see human bones popping in and out of the broth. . . . Soon she looked up toward the skylight, and he noticed that her poor eyes kept closing. The old woman was very skinny. . . . She said to take a good look at her, that she was experiencing what people on earth were about to go through that coming winter, which was going to be long.

Wassilie closed with a long description of the second *ellarrluk*. Just before it occurred, one man in Paingaq instructed his sons to make a pit near his cache and fill it with fish slime, scales, and tails, which he covered in the fall: "When *ella yagtellrani* [earth extended its arms], it was the contents of that pit that kept them from starving." Everyone else in the village, as well as the people of nearby Qecugivigmiut, died, except for a child named Kavialek (from *kaviaq*, "red fox"), who saved himself by hunting mice. Later he killed a muskrat but almost died from overeating after his long period of fasting. Then he remembered his father's words and saved himself by digging a hole along the pond in the moss until the bottom section of the moss, called *qayuyuaq* (pretend broth or pretend blood?), began to

surface. He took a tiny pinch and swallowed it, then pulled up his garment and lay belly down at that spot, facing the sunrise. As soon as he lay down, he blacked out. He awoke to the voices of two people talking. When he lifted his head he saw two foxes walking away, turning their heads to look at him and then continuing on. Later in the spring, he traveled downriver and joined the Paingaq family, who had also survived. He told them about his experiences, including the foxes he had heard conversing, and he said that his name, Kavialek, was truly a name that fit him perfectly.

Finally we looked at close to a dozen miniature household items from the Yukon, all made as practice pieces and used for playing with dolls (fig. 12.14).[19] The first was a tiny wooden *qantaq* (bowl), which Jacobsen wrote was put in front of a toy doll for eating.[20] Wassilie recognized it immediately: "It is a little bentwood bowl with an *allungak* [fitted bottom]. It resembles the huge ones we used to see. But this went with doll figurines." Annie continued:

This is a pretend bowl for a figurine family, a *tumnaruaq* [pretend *tumnaq* (large oval bowl)]. It looks like the ones we used for making *akutaq*. It would be the biggest bowl in the toy family possessions. My doll family used to have toy bowls, and some were made out of tree bark. You can easily tell what this is. Since people in those days were skilled, they made tiny bentwood toy bowls like this.

The other miniatures were all made of grass. Moving through them one by one, Catherine noted that one was a mattress, another a *mallegtarpak* (large grass bag), another a *curuq* (mat for bedding), and the last two small mats. There were also two small baskets made of tundra grass and leather, another basket

12.14 Miniature household items, made as practice pieces and used for playing with dolls. Clockwise from the upper left: grass mat, wooden bowl, willow-bark basket, storage container, bedding mat, grass bag, grass boot, and grass basket. IVA4285, IVA3669, IVA4493, IVA5520, IVA4279, IVA4492, IVA5407, IVA4490.

12.15 Model paitallek (two-person kayak) with a mouth-shaped bow. IVA4285

of grass and willow bark, and a tiny *kellarvik* or storage container.[21] Annie added what she remembered:

These are doll families' possessions. . . . This [IVA4279] is a bedding mat, which we girls loved to play with . . . for our doll families back in those days. The bedding was made out of *uyat* [bird-neck skins]. We always had doll families back in those days and really treasured them. . . . This bag was made with *mallegtat* [close twined stitches]. This toy *akluinqun* [clothing bag] was also stitched with *mallegtat*. My, people back in those days were so skilled . . .

This is another cute toy *akluinqun*. They probably filled it with things. These two sets of doll families were the most desirable in those days. . . . My companion will talk more about these. Perhaps she also owned toy doll families as I did.

Indeed, Catherine had also played with *inuguat*:

My past life just flashed before me. Multiple families used to dwell in one house back in those days. These [IVA4285, IVA4279] are made of *ivrat* [tall cotton grass]. And the others are definitely *taperrnat* [coarse seashore grass]. And they called ones with tops like this *kangcirat* [tarpaulins, sled sheets]. They were placed behind their toy houses. And *mallegtarpak* was the name for this toy bag [IVA4292]. And this narrow toy bag was called *mallegtayagaq*. These took a long time to make. I think these were used as door flaps. Doorways had covers like these. They would be longer if they were *kangcirat*.

Qayaruaq / Model Kayak

We played with the dolls for quite a while and then turned to a wooden kayak model (fig. 12.15) from north of the Copper River, which Jacobsen said was like those used for traveling or trading rather than for hunting. Wassilie described it as a replica of the real thing:

This is a kayak made for a warrior, with a bow shaped like a mouth. They called this type of kayak a *paitaalek* [two-person kayak, from Russian *baidárka* or from Yup'ik *pai-*, "opening of a kayak"]. . . . It has no "tail" since it's from a different area. The front has no *ukinqucuk* [tote hole] but is shaped like a mouth, even though it didn't belong to [the famous warrior] Apanuugpak. . . .

I've heard that he had a kayak with a bow shaped like a mouth when he sang his song of accomplishment in front of Eqtarmiut. This probably resembled kayaks used by famous warriors. These kinds of kayaks were large and could hold a lot in the front and back, and two people could ride in them.

Earlier in our trip, we had examined several ivory models—a carving of a seal hunter and a model of a walrus hunt, both from Nushagak (fig. 12.16).[22] Paul had interpreted both as commemorative rather than merely decorative or recreational:

In those days, when artists created their crafts, they invariably revealed their psyche to the public. This creation that includes a carving of a seal reveals the hunter's awesome experience as he hunted on the ocean. The spear used to kill these animals was also placed on [the model]. The paddle was added since the hunter used it to journey to distant places.

After a hunter experienced an extraordinary event or hardship, he actualized his experiences in art, like a warrior does after victorious feats out in the field by composing songs called *anqarautet*. When people escaped a certain life-threatening incident or an unusual event, they usually created an object or song to portray their story.

This figure's head is covered with, a bentwood hat that hunters wore on the ocean . . . when they encountered large waves. They also put them on . . . when hunting seals perched on the ice.

This walrus figurine tells of the hunter's extraordinary experience when he speared it near its nose, killing it. . . . Walruses are huge animals, but the hunters pursued them using their skills. That is why we are seeing many objects made out of walrus ivory. When they acquired walrus tusks, they made them into items they used in daily life.

We looked briefly at several more ivory models from Fort Alexander, including a hunting scene and a group of travelers on a dogsled, but the group had nothing to add.[23]

Qasgiruaq / Model Qasgi

Everyone had something to say when we examined a model *qasgi* (fig. 12.17)—consisting of a house frame, six human

12.16 Model of a walrus hunt, which Paul said was made to commemorate a successful hunt. IVA5700.

12.17 Ivory figures from Fort Alexander including, from left to right, a dancer, a drummer wearing a "bird mating cap," a "sea monster" carrying a white whale in its mouth, and a man holding a hand rattle. These models were produced in winter and sold to the sailors in the summer when the American ships arrived. IVA5698.

262   THE RETURN GIFT

figures, and a "sea monster" carrying the figure of a white whale in its mouth, meant to hang from the *qasgi* ceiling. According to Jacobsen, one figure sang, another beat a drum and wore a peculiar "bird mating cap," a third danced, and a fourth held a hand rattle like those used in Bristol Bay.²⁴ The fifth figure wore feathers in his hair instead of head rings like the others, and the sixth also held rattles and seemed to dance. Jacobsen explained the hanging figure, saying that "since the Eskimo like to exaggerate, it often happens that a hunter insists having seen one or the other sea monster and makes one for the next catching feast and hangs it in the "Kassigit" or dance house."

Marie began the discussion, suggesting that someone made a model of an event he witnessed. Annie agreed: "People somewhere danced one time like this. They probably used this fish as a talisman. In dancing, they honored everything they received." She then noted the *nacarpiaq* (fancy bird-skin hat) that one of the figures was wearing was like those we had looked at the week before (see Day 9). She had heard that in the past, *nukalpiat* wore *nacarpiat*, and this brought to mind a story not about dancing but about starvation. She spoke at length, moved by what she was viewing through this ivory window to the past to share knowledge that would impact her people's future:

There is a story about a mighty *nukalpiaq*. It happened recently. This *nukalpiaq* lived during the time of the second *ellarrluk*.

Back when store-bought food was not available, people experienced real hunger during food shortages. Presently, *ellarrluk* does occur, but since we can buy food from the stores, we don't experience starvation like they did in the past.

People talked about a *nukalpiaq*, perhaps his name was Qengarrlugtuaq. . . . He lived in Angvanermiut, up the Togiak River. His village was right above Mequutmiut. Many people lived in his village. When the second *ellarrluk* occurred, Qengarrlugtuaq, who was a mighty *nukalpiaq* at that time, couldn't catch animals anymore, *elarlugluku*, as they called it. During *ellarrluk*, men who were recognized *nukalpiat* usually lost their skill in hunting. A man's proficiency in hunting changes during *ellarrluk*. Men who had not been proficient in hunting usually gained proficiency in pursuit of animals during *ellarrluk*.

Since his family no longer had food to bring him, Qengarrlugtuaq started waiting in the porch for the women when they brought food to their men in the *qasgi*. He'd grab a bit of food from the bowls as the women walked by him. After he did that several times, the men in the *qasgi* decided to do something about his conduct. At that time, he also started searching for food in other people's houses.

One night, pretending to be a dog, he entered a house where a couple was sleeping. When he reached for something, the husband struck him with a double-bladed paddle. As he hit him, the paddle broke in half. When he yelped, pretending to sound like a dog, the sound was far from being a dog sound. He ran out on all fours, still pretending to be a dog.

The next morning, the husband went out and saw that it had snowed wet snow during the night. As he examined the ground, he saw footprints leading toward the *qasgi*. The person had left his boots in the porch and had run toward the *qasgi* on bare feet.

He went to the *qasgi*. When he inquired, the men told him that Qengarrlugtuaq had left the *qasgi* during the night. Then the men in the *qasgi* met and decided to send Qengarrlugtuaq to Utngugnarmiut, a village located downriver from where they were. The two neighboring villages were quite populated at that time.

When the men in the *qasgi* told him that the shellfish were starting to be plentiful in Utngugnarmiut, he left on foot. There, he soon became the talk of the town again. The once stout and healthy *nukalpiaq* was now very skinny.

In [Utngugnarmiut], people started to tell him that people down in Tarunguarmiut were starting to eat shellfish from the beach. When he heard that, he left, but just when he passed Ekviggaak, . . . the poor man couldn't move anymore and sat down. When the *nukalpiaq* left Utngugnarmiut, he was wearing a parka referred to as *uulungiiq* . . . made out of squirrel-skin bellies. The parkas were adorned with trimming and appropriate designs specific to that style. The *tusrulluuk* designs on the shoulder areas of the parka were very bright, with very distinct dark fur borders. He was wearing a perfectly made *nacarpiaq*, too. . . . His tassels flew and danced with the wind as he moved. Of course, as a great hunter, his parka would not have flimsy tassels. As he sat and saw people below going by, he would wave his hand for them to come, but they would just ignore him and go on their way.

Then as Angalgaq, a young woman, was going by, he waved at her to come. When she came, he asked her to help him get to Tarunguarmiut. He told her that he would marry her when *ellarrluk* was over if she helped him. Not because she wanted to be his wife someday but because she felt such pity toward him, she tried to help him get to Tarunguarmiut, but he didn't make it. His legs gave out as she tried to help him, *qeluarcilutek*. When people suffer from starvation, their legs start having severe muscle cramps they called *qeluarciluteng*.

When she couldn't help him anymore, she left him and Qengarrlugtuaq died there. As she was trying to help him, other people just walked by and didn't even stop to help. His body was left there, and no one came to do a proper burial. People in that area didn't show pity for that man at all at that time.

I've added this story I heard so others could hear it, too. *Ellarrluk* will show no mercy to anyone. When the stomach begins to shrink from hunger, the pain that occurs is intense. The suffering during that time was more painful than any other sickness. That is why we were always told not to make a mess and throw food particles on the ground where people would walk on them. That has been a law our people followed from the ancient past. We were told not to walk on spawned fish on the beach. If people do that, *Ellam Yua* will punish them. Even if a tiny particle of food is dropped on the floor and stepped on, it will know and say, "My goodness! May this person's stomach be empty someday." It is true that a tiny piece of food is able to think and feel. That is why we have that law, and that law needs to be passed on to our children.

Since I came here to work, I have learned more, and now I want to encourage our people to learn about our ancestral ways. It will be good if our people keep their ways rather than losing them. I'd like to see an awakening instead of ignorance.

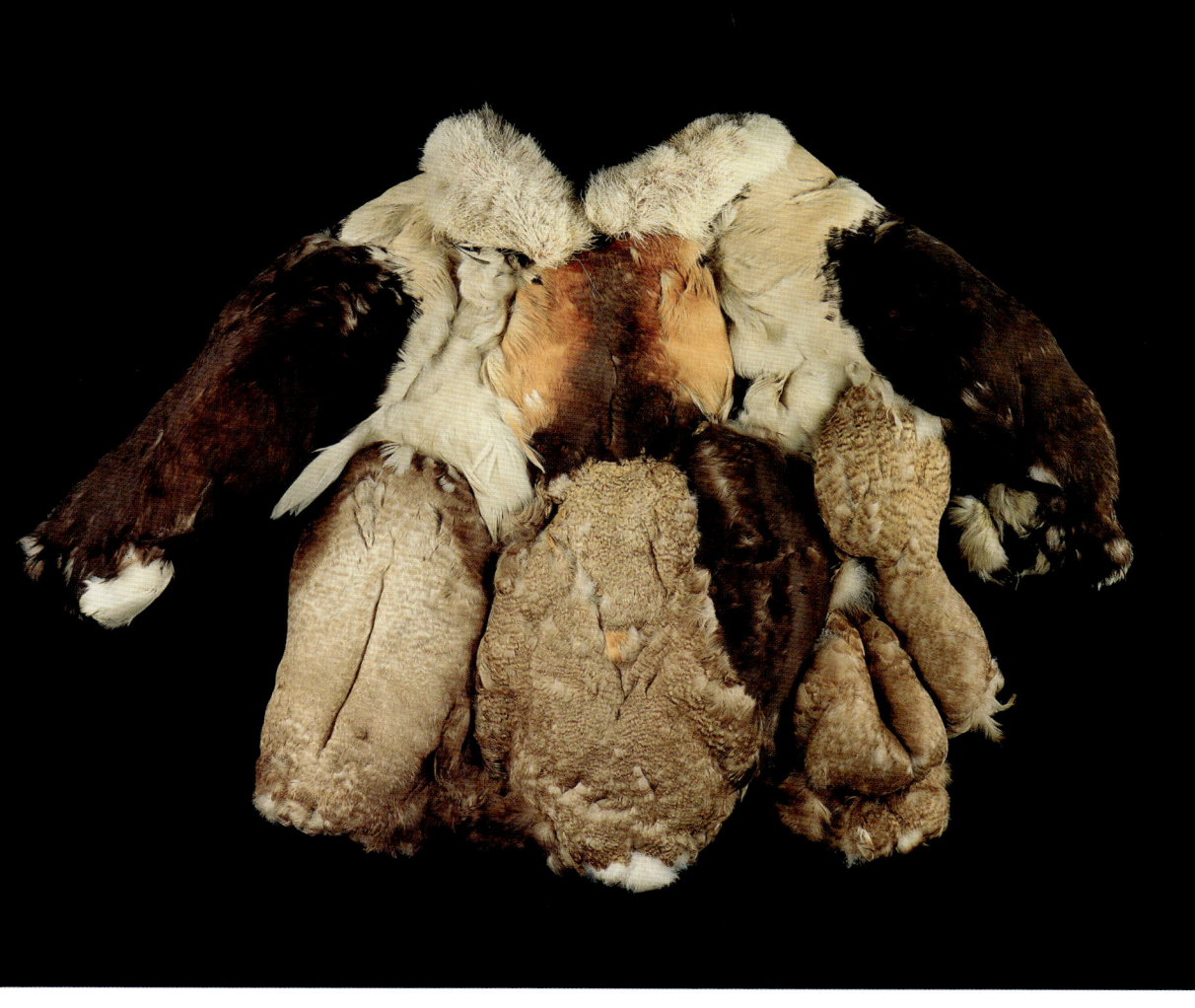

12.18 Child's bird-skin parka from Togiak. IVA5418, IVA5419.

Yaqulek Atkuk / Bird-skin Parka

The last things we would examine at the museum were the dozen pieces of clothing that Jacobsen brought home. First was a child-size *atkuk* (parka) from the Togiak area, made from the skins of what Jacobsen described as "diving birds," and meant to be worn with an ermine-skin cap (fig. 12.18).[25] Annie agreed with Jacobsen that the cap was made from the red phase of an animal caught in the summer rather than the white fur of a winter catch.

Jacobsen wrote that bird skins were the main "undergarment" among most Eskimos from Alaska to Greenland and that in winter they were worn with the feathers toward the body, while in summer they were reversed. Annie described the variety of bird skins used to make the parka:

This is a parka for a small person. The *tusailitak* [two shoulder bands] look like eider duck skins. And this *cacarqerra* [front piece] is made of loon skin. Perhaps it is two red-throated loons. . . .

The ruff is made of caribou fur. . . . This back part is made of female common eider skins. This *pequara* [upper back part] could be grebe or old-squaw duck. . . . I bet these are warm.

When I was a little girl, my mother used to skin birds and soften the whole skins and make them into boots. She also made whole red-throated loon skins into parkas. They had very durable skins. I never saw adults wearing bird-skin parkas in my area, but I saw coastal people wearing cormorant parkas. . . . Even elderly men and women wore cormorant parkas . . . that looked beautiful and shiny. On the back of the parkas were two square spots . . . called *milqeruak* [from *milqar-*, "to throw at?"] . . . with little tassels hanging at the bottom. . . .

When we first moved to the coast, we saw people wearing beautiful cormorant parkas. We were envious, but the skins for the parkas weren't easy to come by. I used to wish I had one because they were shiny and beautiful to see. In'uli [Henry] over there probably used to see old women wearing cormorant parkas. Many coastal people wore them.

Wassilie had eagerly waited his turn to contribute:

When I first became aware, many Kuskokwim people wore bird parkas. These skins came from ocean birds . . . and look like eider duck skins. . . . Bird skins were sewn into parkas. The old-squaw duck skins, since they were thinner, were made into women's parkas. Loon skins, which were tougher, were made into boys' parkas. My mother made my older brother, Unguvalria, loon-skin parkas. When he wore his loon-skin parka in the winter, he used to run to the top of a snowbank, fall on his back, and slide down. The loon-skin parkas make one glide very easily in the snow. But since I was less active, my mother made me a parka out of old-squaw ducks. They are very warm. Adults used female old-squaw duck skins for parkas. They used the whole bird skin to make parkas. . . .

Swan-skin parkas lasted longer. Their feathers were plucked first, leaving the down on the skin. A woman could wear a single swan parka for many years with the down inside. When men wore swan parkas, the feathers were always on the outside. Women also wore parkas made of old-squaw ducks and female common eiders . . . with the feathers inside.

12.19 Ermine-skin cap from Nushagak, front and side views. Jacobsen wrote that ermine skins, particularly those trapped in summer, were mainly used for children's head coverings and that often the stuffed animal head sat on top of the child's cap, complete with bead eyes and nose rings. IVA 5373.

One time we were moving. It was in autumn. It was raining hard, and I fell asleep as we were going. When I woke up, we were inside a house. It was dark inside, but I was sitting in front of an old woman who was softening the skins of my parka. When I looked closer at her, I saw that she was wearing a parka with designs in the front. Her parka was white. When daylight came, I saw that she had on a ptarmigan-skin parka. Oh dear me! Parkas worn by old people had no hoods, but we younger folks had parkas with hoods. They also made parkas out of crane skins with the feathers out for the boys. When they were worn in the rain, water merely rolled down the feathers and did not penetrate them. . . . Many people had bird parkas back in those days.

People didn't hold a lot of possessions, but children of great hunters wore parkas made of caribou and squirrel skins. . . . Young people also wore mink parkas.

The mother of that late Russian Orthodox priest, Paul Tinker, made him a crane-skin parka. When he wore it in the rain, water would just roll down his parka. . . . Some people thought he was cute and would follow him and pluck off some of the feathers.

Catherine had equally strong memories of bird-skin parkas and hunting for seabirds along the Nelson Island coast:

When I was small, people made parkas out of skins they acquired. I had parkas made with different bird skins. People used whatever was available to make parkas. On the cliffs below Up'nerkillermiut, Arnaquluk and I went with Avegyaq's father when he hunted cormorants. . . . There were so many birds on the cliff, they looked like a swarm of mosquitoes. . . . Evidently they gather in great numbers in that area. Avegyaq's father was shooting cormorants for his wife's parka. . . . Many fell into the water, and he packed them on his back when we went home.

One time I skinned some swans, then during the fall I made a parka for my second daughter. After she played outside, she would say that this parka was very lightweight. When we were in Qalulleq one time when I was young, Marpak caught enough young seagulls to make me a parka with the feathers inside.

Kankiik, Tangluk-llu / Ice Skates and Snowshoes

Next came a realistic pair of wooden *qilangak* (tufted puffins) painted black with wide beaks and tufts of fur attached to each side of their heads. In the museum they were shelved with the ceremonial objects. Each had a rusty iron blade at its base, and Catherine wondered if perhaps they were a special kind of knife. The pair was from Togiak (fig. 12.20),[26] and Annie recognized them at once:

Evidently, these are *kankiik* [pair of ice skates, from Russian *kon'ki*] . . . that boys used to have fun on newly formed ice. These boy's skates have bird figures in the front. The owner would know by the designs if they were stolen by someone. The blades are made of metal . . . after white people arrived.

I've heard a story about a man from Togiak. When a wolverine escaped from him, he put on his skates and started after it. When he caught up with the animal, he clubbed it to death. I've heard that he was very fast when he was a young man and animals always presented themselves to him. They started calling him Cuuyiiq after he became an older man. He has many grandchildren in Togiak now.

Everyone was equally engaged by a pair of *tangluk* (snowshoes) from the mouth of the Yukon (fig. 12.21).[27] In fact, Jacobsen had worn them during his winter in Alaska. His written description was comparative in focus:

Snowshoes similar to the ones worn by the Malemiuts in Norton Sound. Toward the west, with the inhabitants of Cape Prince of Wales, the snowshoes are pointed toward the front and the weaving consists of wide sealskin strips, loosely woven. The ones in Kotzebue Sound are wider and more rounded in shape. On the upper Yukon, they reach a considerable size. In America one does not know the longer wooden skis; therefore unlike in Europe and Siberia there are no artisans [producers] of such skis. Snowshoeing (like this) requires a certain skill. The fastening of the shoe is rather simple. The foot rests between the two wooden crosspieces.

Wassilie added what he knew from personal experience:

These snowshoes are complete and ready to put on. They have straps for the feet and mesh on the front and back. I had a pair of snowshoes I wore for a long time. Our dear father made us snowshoes. We used to hunt foxes wearing these during the cold winter months when deep snow was difficult to travel on and during *aniulluk* [soft, melting snow]. You could run in these quite easily. . . . One time when I was hunting while wearing these, I shot a fox and wounded it. It ran away, and I ran after it. When I caught up with it, I stepped on it and killed it. I ran after it in my snowshoes.

This is the *tutneq* [wooden crosspiece, literally, "place for one's foot," from *tut'e-*, "to step on"]. The *elngut* [birch trees] were used for snowshoes. The wood was cut and shaped into the right thickness, and when men took a fire bath, the pieces were made pliable in the steam to bend into shape. Then a pair that was already bent was tied together where the ends meet, then the process of setting the permanent shape with steam was done during several fire baths. When the wood was set and the snowshoe was in shape, the *tutneq* was put in. And this is the *nuluq* [webbing]. This is a crosspiece, and if one steps on something protruding from the snow, it would prevent the wearer from falling forward.

12.20 Kankiik (ice skates) carved in the shape of puffins and, according to Annie, "used by boys to have fun on newly formed ice." IVA5389.

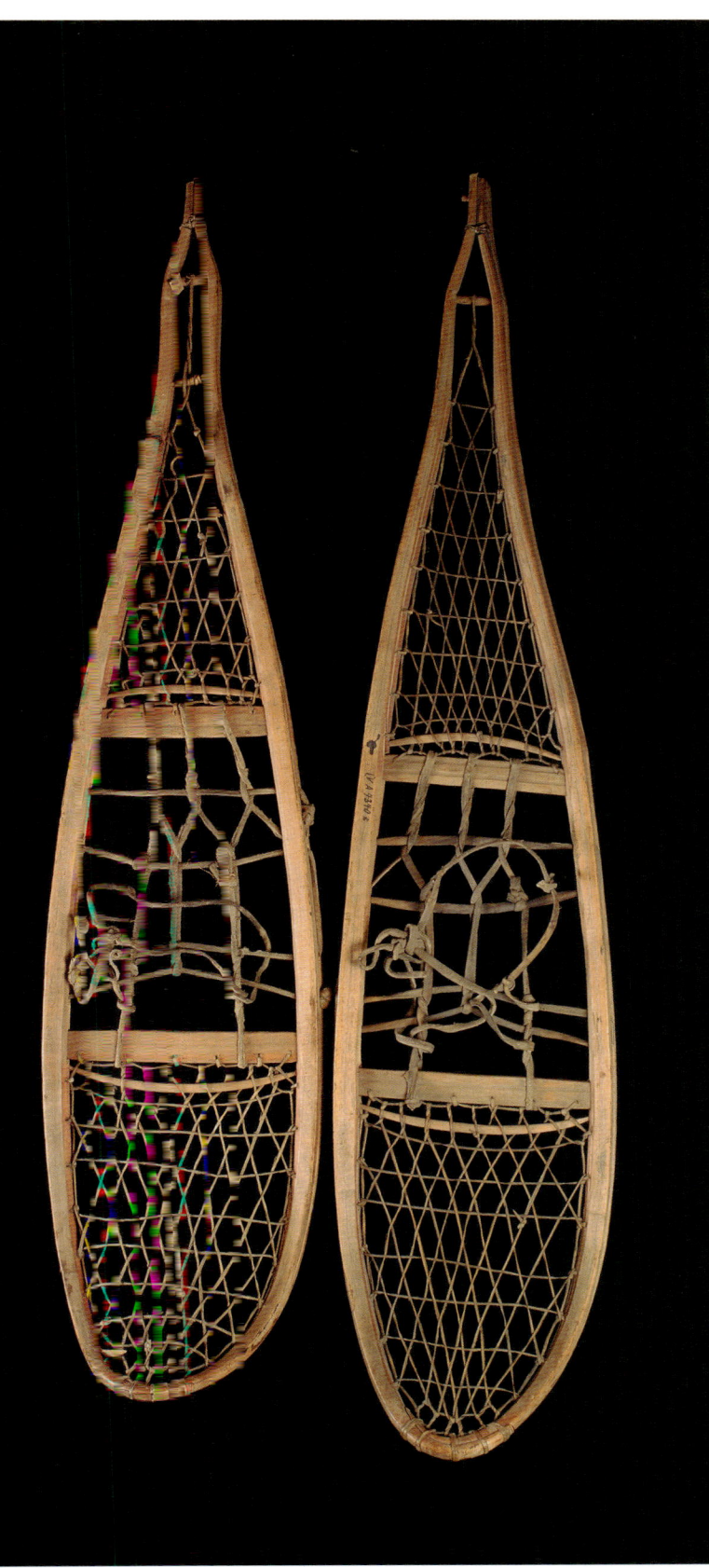

12.21 Snowshoes Jacobsen wore during his winter in Alaska. IVA4340.

Both Annie and Catherine had also had snowshoes and agreed with what Wassilie had to say.

Next, we looked at a pair of *nat'rak* (wooden slippers) from Nushagak made to be tied over the boot to prevent slipping on the ice and as insulation when standing for long periods.[28] "The first sandals," Henry quipped.

Arilluut / Fish-skin Mittens

Next we turned to four pairs of mittens.[29] Jacobsen noted that all were made of salmon skin and were used while kayaking and sled driving. Particularly toward springtime when the snow started to melt, they protected well against moisture. In winter they were lined with braided grass liners. Annie began:

These are all well-made *arilluut* [fish-skin mittens] . . . sewn with regular, straight stitches. They are truly made in the traditional style, lined with twined grass inserts. These were probably used in traveling, also in cold weather. I've heard that fish skin was the only material that was windproof and capable of keeping cold air out. . . . I'm reminded of my late husband's grandmother and her younger sister, Uulia, because as a girl I used to watch them making things like these. . . . I've finally made a connection to my past here on the other side of the ocean. While we are making the connection, we should begin singing and dancing the songs of the past.

Catherine took up the suggestion. "How does the melody go again?" she asked, and she began to sing the chorus of a very old song.

Your arilluk is coming toward us
Your arilluk *is coming toward us*
Take it
This aliir
Yii-ii-ii-rrii

Alliqsiit / Twined Grass Liners for Skin Boots

Mittens were not the only things lined with grass, and we again marveled at its insulating properties when we examined eight pairs of *alliqsiit* (grass boot-liners) from the Yukon and three pairs from the Kuskokwim and Togiak Rivers (fig. 12.22).[30] Jacobsen noted that such "grass stockings" were used by both men and women, especially with waterproof fish-skin boots, which, like fish-skin mittens, provided little insulation. Skin boots, he wrote, were not an option "because throughout the winter such great rivers along the shores continuously throw water upon the ice, and the traveling Eskimo must walk through such water to reach the shore, and with reindeer-leather boots would have to perish." The ingenuity of using this simple material to craft something so essential impressed the descendants of their makers. All had used grass socks and immediately recognized their importance. Annie began:

Up Togiak River, we called these *alliqsiit* [grass liners]. . . . I've become an old woman and still haven't learned to make these. But when I was a girl, I watched women twining them. Men used them as liners in their hunting boots. These are twined with *mallegtat* [closely twined stitches]. And this [other] pair of socks is called *tupi-*

12.22 Pair of grass boot liners used with waterproof fish-skin boots, which provided little insulation. IVA5387.

12.23 Pair of ivrucik (fish-skin boots) from Nushagak that Mr. Clark had given Jacobsen as a present. IVA5481.

Catherine added detail:

They dried the cotton grass before they used it for twining. When the grass was twined, it was soft and easy to work with. My, someone sure was skilled in making these *mallegtat* stitches. . . . When my stepmother was teaching me how to twine, I was thinking, "Gosh, I wonder when I'm going to be done with this one?" She taught me to twine socks starting from the soles. The front part of the sock was made a little wider. And when I got to the toe part, . . . she showed me how to decrease the stitches. You'd repeat the same stitches, going back and forth. And when you get to the part that will cover the ankles, you twine until you reach the appropriate length. . . . I finally finished a pair of socks like these. But I've never made a pair with *mallegtat* stitches. They look difficult to twine.

Annie added detail on the different methods used to twine grass socks:

The socks twined in a spiral manner were called *alliqsiit*. The area that would cover the toes was twined by going back and forth. The upper part of the sock, which would cover the ankles, was twined with stitches going upward in a spiral manner until it was the right height. And for the socks they called *qugcuutet*, they began twining the grass, and when it was a certain length, they'd fold it to the part you would pull on when you put on the sock. And they twined the sides of the socks going back and forth, and then they joined the two sides.

Annie followed with a short anecdote, recalling the time she

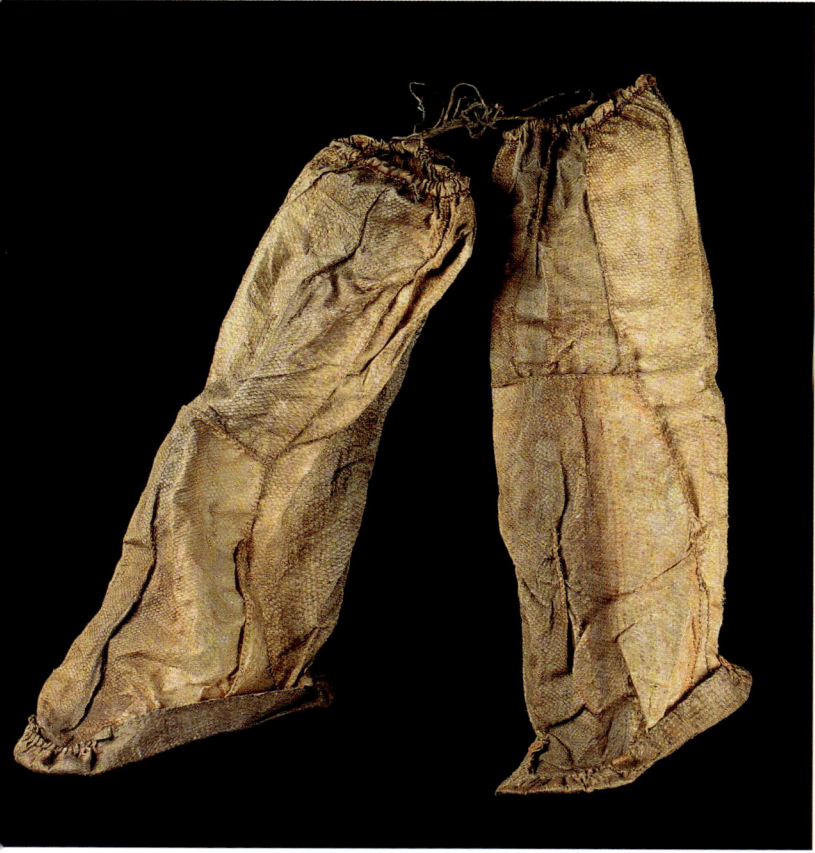

piarumalriik [literally, "those two that are genuinely twined," from *tupig-*, "to twine"]. . . .

These are made out of cotton grass. I used to go with women gathering it. We'd bring a bundle of grass into the house, then cut off the bottom parts and put them into a bowl. When we got enough, we'd store them in seal oil, and people would eat them with great enjoyment.

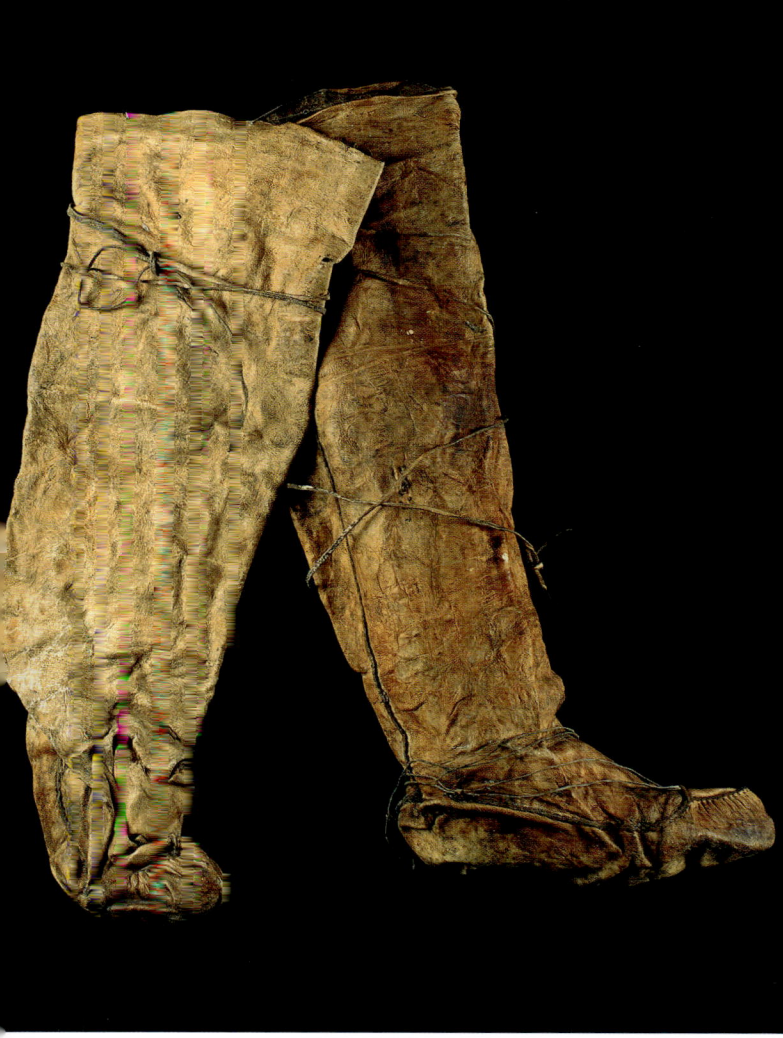

12.24 Caribou-skin wading boots from Nushagak, another present from M. Clark. VA5482.

was in the Tacoma hospital for tuberculosis treatment. There an old woman received twining grass from home and made two pairs of socks like the ones we were looking at: "Gosh, as she was weaving a pair, someone would claim them before they were done. In no time, her grass was all gone. People really wanted to buy these kinds of socks." Catherine also described how bore grass was used as insulation: "Twined socks this size were large enough to be stuffed . . . with *piineq* [dried grass used for insoles] in cold winter weather." Annie concluded, "When a person put on a nice pair of skin boots, these were used to line the boot."

Ivrucik / Waterproof Skin Boots

Having looked at grass socks, our next piece of clothing was a pair of fish-skin boots (fig. 12.23) from Nushagak.[31] Again, Annie was the first to speak:

Pay, you could look at these for a long time. Look at these *kelugquaraat* [fancy stitches]; these skin boots were always sewn with a piece of skin placed between the two edges to create a seam, *aufun*. These types of boots were sewn with tight stitches so they would be waterproof. These would be worn in the winter with twined grass liners. The boots' soles were made of *iqalluk* [dog salmon]. When I was a girl, I had boots like these. The boot lace was pulled through these *putulrik* [two loops] and then tied. When the boots were damp, the lace was always kept loose.

The fish skins were scraped clean of meat and membrane before they were sewn. The scraped meat, when eaten, tasted very good. We heard that if a girl ate scraped meat from fish skin, she would marry an unsuccessful hunter. Those people told us not to eat certain foods that were delicious. Perhaps they wanted to keep them for themselves.

These are *ivrucik* [waterproof skin boots, from *iver-*, "to step into water"] . . . sewn very nicely.

Wassilie continued, noting that fish-skin *ivrucik* were known as *amiriik* [from *amiq*, "skin"] and used in dry, cold winter weather, while *ivrautet* [caribou-skin wading boots, from *iver-*, "to step into water"] were used in wet spring weather. These wet-weather boots had soles made of the same material and were sewn so tightly that they couldn't leak. Wassilie noted that the *amiriik* were so old that the drawstrings at the boot tops were leather thongs. They were lined with grass in the bottom and worn with grass socks by both men and women. Wassilie recalled that his father also used gunnysacks to wrap his feet before socks became available.

Wassilie then described fish-skin boots in detail:

These were called *iqertiik* [two things made of fish skin, pair of fish-skin boots]. The whole boot was made of fish skin. The back parts of the boots were made of young king-salmon skin. The front parts were made of dog-salmon skins. The bottom parts were sewn with an *uminguaq* [arrow-point design], and a piece of leather was put in between two edges of fish skin to make a seam and sewn tightly together to make it waterproof. . . . Wading boots made of salmon skins were used in the spring thaw. Later on, *ivrucit* were worn when men started to paddle in their kayaks.

They are soft when they are new . . . because the skin was freeze-dried. They soaked and washed the fish skins in a urine bucket to remove the excess meat . . . and then they were taken out, hung, and *qerrecqertelluki* [freeze-dried]. The leftover parts were put in bags for later use or consumption during food shortage.

We now had a chance to examine a pair of caribou-skin wading boots from Nushagak (fig. 12.24).[32] Annie recognized them immediately:

They also called them *melqurrilnguut*. These boots were big, . . . but when they were wet and were dried without any kind of stuffing, they shrank . . . and got damaged. If they had been dried stuffed with grass, they would have kept their shape.

These were worn instead of *amiriit*. And, also, when men hunted in the mountains, if they didn't wear these, they wore the ones called *kamegciqat* [short boots]. The upper parts of those boots were made of canvas with skin soles. . . .

The soles were sewn on with stitches called *ellipiarat*. People from the upper regions used stitches they called *inuguarcetuat* when the soles were sewn on. . . . These have *putulrik* [loops], two on each side of the boot, sewn on where the sole is attached. When boots were tied this way, the foot didn't move around too much in the boot.

These also have drawstrings right below the knees to keep the boots from sliding down. And the long boots had strings attached to the waistband to keep them up.

Wassilie commented from his experience: "This pair was worn in the cold winter weather. Beluga skins were used for boot soles like this. The skin was tough and lasted for a long time. These were made for a man."

Wassilie noted that if the caribou-skin boots had been *ivrucik*, they would be dark from the oil that had been applied to them for waterproofing. He went on to describe the *ivrucit* he had used:

I used *ivrucit* all the time with strings attached to my waistband to keep the boots from sliding down. They were sewn carefully with *asuirun* [an extra piece of leather sewn onto seams for reinforcement], and the stitches were very fine. After I used them in the springtime I'd take them off, stuff them with grass, rub oil on them, and hang them up. We stopped using *amiriit* when we started using our kayaks in the spring. Factory-made shoes were around, but we preferred not to wear them but wore our *ivrucit* all the time. Your late grandmother made me a pair one time, and I wore them for a very long time. . . . They were extremely waterproof. Boots never become tough and hard when they are rubbed with oil all the time. But when I was in my kayak, I'd put a piece of gunnysack between my rear and the boots because if I didn't do that, my pants would become oily, and soon the oil would become rancid.

Catherine then spoke about the preparation of skins: "When skins were prepared for *ivrucit*, the fur was removed from the skin by applying ash and scraping the fur off. The regular method of removing fur from skin was not used. These were carefully cared for." Wassilie added:

Caribou skins were made into *ivrucit* after the fur was removed. . . . To remove the fur, the skins were put in water to soften. Then the bitter part of the alder bark was removed and added to the water. After the water got dark, the skin was put in to give it color. The dyeing process helped keep the skin from shrinking. After the skin was dyed, it was stretched out to dry.

A piece of wood with a wide front was used to prepare sealskin for waterproof boots. Ash was applied first, and the wood was used to scrape off the fur. Annie recalled: "When my aunt was preparing a skin to make *ivrucik* for her eldest son, she had a difficult time trying to remove fur from the skin. . . . She said she was going to let her husband finish the scraping. . . . When we went in, . . . the spotted-seal skin was pulled on the thin paddle to keep it in place while he scraped off the fur. . . . A few days later, I saw the skin drying outside."

Looking at these waterproof boots brought Wassilie memories of their use, and our day closed with a long account in which *amiriik* played an important part. Wassilie described when the villagers of Nunapicuar invited the villagers of Nunacuaq to a Messenger Feast, during which people gathered for three days, returning home on the fourth. The messenger that Nunapicuar sent to invite their guests had the fastest dog team in the village, and he continued to carry messages back and forth between the two villages until the guests' arrival. As soon as they came, they went to the *qasgi*, where two guests—a man and woman—performed the *tekiqata'ar* (arrival dance). Wassilie described how the male dancer came in wearing a white *qaspeq* with its hood pulled up, gloves, and a belt and danced fully clothed. When they were done, two more dancers from the invited village came forward to do another dance, *ciuqilutek* (literally, the "first two"), including the presentation of gifts.

When this part of the arrival ceremony was complete, the guests were served food. Just as they began to eat, their hosts began to sing a *nernerrlugcetaarun* (ridicule song, from *nere-*, "to eat," plus *-nerrlugte-*, "to have trouble doing"). Sometimes such "songs of indigestion" caused their guests great anxiety. In this case, the hosts sang out "People of Nunacuaq, come in sweet accord, we welcome you with hugs and kisses," and their guests laughed and sighed with relief. The guests presented the dances the first evening. The next day, people requested that the foot races begin, and Wassilie recalled what followed:

The young married men who were just starting families prepared to run against their teasing cousins. That time, there was a lot of snow on the ground. When the race was being prepared, a man would leave the *qasgi*. He would come back in holding *amiriik* that were already lined with grass. When he came in, he would stand in the middle and look at all the young men around the room. Then he would choose one young man, have him sit, remove his boots, and replace them with new boots. Another man would do the same. After all the young men were dressed, a man on the side would turn to them and say, "As you run on this race, proceed without any worries. We have just released the old life. It will not be remembered again. Run with all your might." Then the young men went out . . . wearing *qasperet* and holding staffs. They were also wearing belts around their waists.

They all started the race together from the upper part of the village. They started running through the lake behind Nunapicuar. They ran toward the mouth of Kasigluk River. They were gone. Soon some of the runners came back, and some were holding *qasperet*. They had picked up *qasperet* that the other racers had abandoned. The remaining runners were gone for a long time. Soon someone spotted a person down below the village. Everyone watched. Another person appeared. When the third one appeared, he ran and started to catch up with the other two up ahead. He passed the second runner. The person who appeared first reached the village before that person overtook him.

When the runners were getting close to the village, everyone gathered outside and began to yell and scream. That was the end of that part of the festival.

Our day at the museum had ended as well.

THIRTEENTH DAY Heavenly and Ceremonial Cycles

HOLDING THEM IN OUR HANDS

After weeks packed with surprises, only a few objects remained unseen, so on Wednesday morning we took time to reexamine a handful of items and photograph them in use. The atmosphere was relaxed, and Henry and Esther, who had not been with us to see these objects on their first appearance, provided an appreciative audience.

Wassilie began by taking up things we had seen on Day 6: a caribou-antler *ekiarqin* (wedge) from the Yukon[1] and a piece of wood with a knot on each end, marked by worms, which Jacobsen had picked up along the banks of the Yukon. He showed us how the wood could be held as a *kaugtuutacuar* (small club)[2] and used to pound the wedge. He continued talking about wood, demonstrating how he would carry it: "If I find an *unrapigaq* [small, thin log], I'd grab the bottom part of the tree under my arm and take it home."

Wassilie then demonstrated using a crooked knife (fig. 13.1) and a stone skin scraper with a wooden handle (fig. 13.2). Henry hefted the enormous ax we'd seen on Day 7, and Wassilie noted how a piece of wood was wedged between the blade and the handle to tighten the blade.[3] Both Henry and Wassilie used the wooden shovel[4] to clear the museum hallway of imaginary snow, and Henry demonstrated the use of a digging tool.[5] We looked once more at the beautifully carved seal-shaped box out of which Annie pretended to take snuff.[6] And Henry donned a bentwood hat, first taking up a paddle and then showing how a harpoon was held and thrown (fig. 13.3).

As we moved through these special pieces, stories began to flow. Wassilie found the king-salmon net[7] especially thought-provoking and began to tell the history of the giant Uayaran, a tale as two people, who had used such a net in the Nunacuaq River. Like Wassilie he was a trapper, and he could travel from the tundra area to check traps he had set on Nelson Island, returning in a single day. Uayaran wore boots like those we had seen the day before:

As he walked, his feet would begin to slide in his boot when his grass lining got worn and crumbled. Then over at the tip of Akuli-rarmiut, he'd climb on the high ground . . . where the bluffs begin to come down, the place they called Kinkinret. It was there he'd climb to the top and change the grass in his boots. The place where he changed his grass is now grown with *taperrnat* [coarse seashore grass].

Uayaran could run as fast as a wolf, and during warfare the enemy never bothered him because he was a dangerous man.

13.1   Wassilie using a crooked knife. IVA4158.

13.2   Wassilie demonstrating the use of a stone-bladed skin scraper. IVA5443.

13.3 Henry wearing a bentwood hat and showing how to hold and throw a harpoon. IVA5474, IVA5245.

Once, however, the enemy attacked and killed his brother, a cripple, and Uayaran followed from behind as they fled, killing all but one, whom he left alive to tell the story. Eventually Uayaran's two wives began to fear that their husband would kill them when he didn't have enough to eat:

They started to plot to kill him . . . using an *everquun* [prying tool] made out of caribou antler. One day they took his little hammer he used for splitting straight-grained wood. Normally, when he came home from being out, he took a fire bath and got very sleepy afterward. Then when he fell asleep, one of them held him while the other used those tools to poke him violently in his ear. . . . When his ear was poked, his giant body sprang in a stretched position and died.

Cill'aq / Circular Calendar

With our work drawing to an end, we looked at two last unusual pieces. The first was a wooden disk with six holes on the rim corresponding to the days of the week (fig. 13.4). Wassilie began: "This is called a *cill'aq* [circular calendar with a pointer that is moved to point to the days of the week, from Russian *chisló*]. This is Monday, Tuesday, Wednesday, Thursday, Friday, Saturday, and this [hole in the center] is Sunday. This is an *ernercuun* [calendar]." Marie asked whether such calendars were used before people started to observe Sunday, and Wassilie said no: "After people were baptized in the Russian Orthodox church, they started using these. Sunday used to fall in the middle. Then on Monday you'd move to the hole up above. From here you would come down to the hole below it, going down again to Sunday. . . . When the hole in the middle was filled, that day was very important and people respected it. My parents had one like this that was very nice and painted with red ocher." Marie asked Wassilie how people identified the days before they started observing Sunday, and he answered: "There were no words for days of the week. They calculated days by watching the moon's cycle."

Annie had also seen wooden calendars:

We're amazed by this piece . . . we used to call a *nitiliq* [from Rus-

sian *nedélya*, literally, "week"]. My mother had one like this, without decorations. They've said that these were sacred even though they were just made of wood. A person always washed his hands before moving the day reminder. My dear mother had a longish wooden piece like this. And down in the middle was a rounded thing, and it was decorated with the design of a cross. Each day the day reminder was moved. Saturday was located next to the design of the cross. When the day reminder was in the middle of the cross it was Sunday, and the hole on the top was Monday. . . . I'd hear people say that Sunday was going to arrive. And when the day was good, they'd say, "Sunday is a good day."

A second calendar disk from Fort Alexander drew no comment, although everyone recognized it as a *cill'aq* and handled it with interest.[8] Made to hang on the wall, it showed an entire year. January was at the top, and holes marking days had been carved down a straight line to the center. Moving clockwise, there was a line with twenty-eight holes for February and so on all the way around. The most important church days were marked with a plus sign. Although the inhabitants of Fort Alexander were identified as Russian Orthodox and were served by two Russian missionaries, in Jacobsen's opinion they were no more than "baptized heathen." Their possession of calendars, however, was evidence that Russian influence had, indeed, been felt.

Ellam Qaralii / Designs of the Sky

The morning had gone fast, and things we viewed for a second time were treated like old friends. In the afternoon, the object-filled carts were returned to storage, and we sat and talked. Marie asked her uncle about his childhood, and he described with emotion what happened after his mother's death. His father made forty wooden pegs, and starting from the day she died, he put one peg in a hole each day until he completed his required *eyagyaraq* (period of abstinence). During that time, Wassilie's father stayed home and never hunted. He abstained from using bladed tools and avoided eating certain foods, including raw meat and fish. After forty days, when he was again permitted to work with the ground, he buried his wife (whose body had remained outside securely covered with a bearskin) and moved with his family to another camp. Wassilie remarked that Yup'ik people of the Russian Orthodox faith still observe these *eyagyarat*.

Marie then asked her uncle to describe how people measured day and timed their activities before calendars were introduced. He said that people paid close attention to the moon and stars, particularly in March, a time when much bad weather occurred. Wassilie recalled:

From my observations, I have learned that the moon could forecast what the weather is going to be like in the coming days. As the moon fills up, the weather would continue to be nice, and as it wanes, bad weather would become more prevalent. But when it first appears lying down on its back, that is not a good sign. . . . People up in the Akula region always said that when the moon appeared lying down on its back, it had bad weather stored in its belly. On the other hand, people from the coast say that when the moon appeared lying down like that, its belly was filled with animals and fish to be caught by people in days to come.

Wassilie then described how people understood the cycles of the moon and stars. For example, people carefully observed the three stars, *sagquralriit*, just before sunrise during November and December to determine changes in the weather:

The *sagquralriit* would show people when the birds would be migrating north and when the salmon would be migrating upriver in June. . . . If the birds and fish were to come at their usual time, those stars would be visible during the early morning in November. . . . And if the weather was going to fluctuate from warm to cold in the spring, prolonging the winter season, the *sagquralriit* would start disappearing just at daybreak in December. . . . They say that those *sagquralriit* are the timekeepers for the seasons. And in my observation, they are quite accurate.

Henry then asked Wassilie to name the moons, which he did, noting that the names people had given them were also quite accurate: "The moon up there now, *Amirairun* [shedding of velvet, September] is about to end. The following new moon will be called *Qerrlurcarturvik* [time of using *qerrlurcaq* (ice-fishing hook), October]. Following these are *Cauyarvik* [time of drumming, November], *Uivik* [time of going around, December], *Iralull'er* [the bad month, January], *Kanruyauciq* [base frost, February], *Kepnerciq* [cutting time, March], *Tengmiirviguaq* [geese come, April], *Maniit Anutiit* [coming of eggs, May], *Kaugun* [hitting (of fish), June], *Ingun* [molting (of birds), July], *Tengun* [flight (of birds), August], *Amirairun* again. That's it." Wassilie noted that the coastal people had fewer names for the moons: "The birds get to the coast earlier than they do on the mainland. When the birds come to their area, they called that moon *Tengmiirviguaq*." Then, chuckling, he again explained *iraluiraucaraq* (the way people argued over the name for the new moon):

If we were competing over the moons, you would sit over there, a little way from me. . . . Soon we'd be arguing. I'd say, "*Amirairun* is just about to end now. *Qerrlurcarturvik* is about to begin." What about you? What would you call it?

Henry (a coastal resident) said that in his area, *Cauyarvik* would be about to begin. Wassilie continued: "Your moon is a shorter cycle. And I'd disagree and say, 'Oh no, *Qerrlurcarvik* is just about to begin.'"

Getting into the spirit, Henry responded, "The moon that is just about to arrive is not *Qerrlurcarturvik*. It will be *Cauyarvik*."

"The moon that is about to begin is *Qerrlurcarturvik*," Wassilie answered. "I would say which moon it will be, and I'm getting angry. Now we are in a heated argument. . . . I take my little hammer and throw it at him and yell, 'The new moon coming is *Qerrlurcarturvik!*' We then start throwing the hammer at each other in anger." Henry concluded: "Perhaps others would come forward and begin arguing on his side, and others would do the same for me. We would start fighting, arguing about the name for the new moon that is just appearing. That was how *iraluiraucaraq* was performed. Then one of them

Wooden *cill'aq* (circular calendar), with holes on the rim corresponding to the days of the week. The calendar was purchased in 1911 from the Herrnhuter Moravian Mission, which had a station in Bethel beginning in 1885. The accession card that lies underneath gave it general Alaska provenance and interpreted it as an obvious copy of a European pocket watch. IVA8297.

would say, 'You should hunt and subsist so you would not depend on the moons.'"

Still thinking about the sky, I asked Wassilie if people paid attention to the sun in the same way. In answer, he described how people observed the rising and setting sun to determine the weather. He also talked about the winter solstice, when the sun "sat down" on the horizon:

I've just talked about where the sun comes up and goes down at the shortest days of the year. At that time, the sun would rise in the same place and set a little distance from where it rose. That is the time when they say the sun is sitting down for a little bit, *aqumgaqerluni*. Then it would begin to go and gain a few minutes each time. It went faster and faster each day. . . . When the sun rose and traveled swiftly, people considered it a good sign, as that meant it was going in the direction of warmer weather.

Annie said that in her area, the sun briefly "sat down" in the Arulaqurvik area. At that time, people paid attention to the two stars, a large one above a small one, that only appeared over the horizon during the winter.

Those old ones said that when those two stars came out over the dawning light . . . it alerted people that winter was at its midway point. . . . After the appearance of the two stars, the daylight increases faster each day. And soon after that, the two stars disappear. . . . People used those stars as a signal for change. . . . When they first came out and snow began to fall, they said that the snow had come down to fill in the spot where the sun had sat briefly. The stars normally go up higher and higher and disappear into the night sky.

Annie then spoke briefly about how people watched other stars as clues for changes in time, including the *sagquralriit, kaviaraat* (Ursa Minor or the Pleiades, literally, "little foxes"), *tunturyuk* (Ursa Major, from *tuntu-*, "caribou"), and *taluyat* (literally, "fish traps"): "When [the stars known as] *taluyat* were seen open, it was a sign that a lot of fish were going to swim into them. . . . Since those old ones were keenly aware of everything, they mentioned the designs of the sky and the interpretations of their activities."[9]

"DIFFERENT CEREMONIES TOOK PLACE FROM FALL TO SPRING"

After we talked about the sun, moon, and stars, Marie asked Wassilie if people used them to determine when to observe the special events that took place in villages.[10] This ceremonial cycle had been referred to often during our weeks together, but it was only now at the end of our stay that Wassilie, Annie, and Catherine spoke about it freely and at length. Because these events were performed a little differently in each area, everyone listened with interest to what the others had to say.

Wassilie began by describing *Qaariitaaq*, the first fall ceremony celebrated in the tundra area. He noted that it was held for three nights right after freeze-up. The house-to-house visiting of *Qaariitaaq* was followed on the fourth day by *Qaarpagyaraq* and on the fifth day by *Elciyaraq*, during which women delivered bowls of food to men in the *qasgi*. As each entered, she would call out the name of the man who was to receive it. This presentation of special foods to men in the *qasgi* was followed by *Aaniryaraq*, during which two men referred to as *aanak* (mothers) would visit house-to-house followed by another person referred to as their *qimugta* (dog). Each "mother" sat on a grass mat and was given a bowl of food. After offering a pinch of food to the spirits, each would take a bit of *akutaq* and throw it over their shoulders in the direction of their "dog." If the *akutaq* landed in his open mouth, it was regarded as a good sign. If one of the "mothers" and the "dog" were teasing cousins, the "mother" might hit the "dog" lightly as he ate, and the "dog" would imitate a yelp of pain.

In the tundra area, the next major ceremony was *Nakaciuryaraq*, during which the bladders of both caribou and bearded seals were "sent off" through a hole in the ice to return the following season. Although he had never witnessed the event in a village involving many people, Wassilie had observed both his father and older brother "sending off bladders." The men slept very little during the time the inflated bladders were in the *qasgi*, and constantly offered the bladders water. They also filled *tumnak* (two big wooden bowls) with food, to aid the bladders on their journey. After a certain number of days, men gathered wild celery and made it into a bundle referred to as the *kangaciqaq*. Then they carried the bladders and *kangaciqaq* to an ice hole and pushed them through. Wassilie recalled it as a spectacular event.

After *Nakaciuryaraq*, toward the end of November, people might send out *kevgak* (two couriers) to another village to invite them to *Kevgiryaraq* (a Messenger Feast), during which "first-time dancers" would be presented and gifts exchanged between host and guest. The feast itself would not take place until after the winter solstice.

Finally, as the days got longer at the end of February or early March, a village would invite several villages to celebrate *Itruka'ar*, also known as *Agayuyaraq*, during which masked dances were performed and first-time dancers presented.

Annie had witnessed the same cycle of ceremonies in her area, and she described what she had seen. As a child, she had participated in *Qaariitaaq* and related ceremonies during freeze-up in October. On three successive nights, she and the other children were taken to the *qasgi*, where the men painted their faces with white clay. Then, after chewing charcoal, the men painted black designs over the clay, which, Annie noted, were never the same. The men then spoke to the children about the rules they were expected to follow during the house-to-house visiting lest they *aciiruciiqniluta* (go into the other dimension). They were especially advised never to go in front of their leader.

The children would call out *"Empaa!"* three times in front of each family dwelling before their leader brought them inside, where the household head gave them a variety of foods. After they had visited all the houses, they were taken back to the *qasgi*, where the food they had gathered was distributed to the men, the children taking home the leftovers.

Annie described the same ceremonial sequence on the coast as Wassilie had described for the tundra villages, with *Qaariitaaq* followed by *Qaarpak*, then *Elciyaraq*, and then *Aaniryaraq*. She noted that during *Aaniryaraq*, the "mothers" might sit on a caribou skin by the entrance of each house while they fed their "dog." She also noted the gratitude of the *tariit* (soul spirits) of their deceased relatives for the foods and gifts they received during the ceremony. The presence of the spirits of the dead during *Aaniryaraq* also required that people refrain from traveling away from the village at night while the house-to-house visiting was under way.

Annie then retold the story of her uncle who, as a young boy, had waited by the graves and observed the grateful dead returning from the feast, including the unhappy daughter of the *tukalpiaq* and his stingy wife. "When he returned," Annie said, "he also cautioned people about this. He told them not to give animal or fish heads to the deceased when they offered food to them in a ceremony." She continued:

My uncle recognized the people who had died. He saw them exactly as they were when they were alive and saw that they were very grateful for the gifts they had received. Our people have always known that the spirits of our deceased relatives are fed and clothed through gift giving and food and water offerings. They do receive gift offered to them exactly as they were.... While the two "mothers" go around in the village, their deceased relatives would move about in the village at that time.

Annie then described the celebration *Petugtaq* that in her area followed *Aaniryaraq*. Men would prepare *petugtat* (models of requested items) and hang them from a stick, which someone would take house-to-house. Each woman would take one of the models and prepare the requested item. Often men requested foods that they had been longing for, and Annie commented that those who enjoyed good food took this opportunity quite seriously. Requests for sexual favors were also sometimes made, and Annie gave an example:

A young man from another village had moved to a certain village and married the daughter of a couple there.... I normally don't tell stories I feel embarrassed about. I usually skip them.

Anyway, [during *Petugtaq*] one of the women pointed to one of the *petugtat* and said that it was from a man asking for a sexual partner. So one of the women selected it. After doing so, she prepared some food with care. While the men were waiting in the *qasgi*, she came in holding a dish filled with *akutaq* topped with some seeds.

She entered and stood in the middle of the room and said, "This bowl is for the man who asked for a sexual partner. He should come take this bowl now and visit me tonight as requested." Then she placed the bowl on the floor and left.

Then men in the *qasgi* began to talk, and one of them said, "Gosh! Someone sure is naughty and conspicuous." Then after a short while the [woman's] son-in-law came down from the back of the room with his things fully packed and walked out of the *qasgi*.

Then one of the men said, "Perhaps it was he who requested a partner." The dish sat in the middle of the floor, and no one came down to claim it.

The son-in-law was not seen in that village after that. He apparently went back to his village, divorcing his wife, because it was his mother-in-law who took his *petugtaq*.

Annie noted that *Nakaciuryaraq* was celebrated after *Petugtaq*. Once when she was small, she had seen bladders hanging in the *qasgi*, some of which moved as the men talked. She had also noted one lone porcupine bladder hanging in the corner. Apparently porcupine bladders were hung separately because they were considered bad-tempered and tended to kick other animal bladders that were near them. Annie observed: "It is known that other animals, including bears, feared porcupines, who shoot with their quills when they get angry."

Nakaciuryaraq was followed by *Kevgiryaraq*. At that time, the host village would send two greeters called *paiqak* (from *pairte-*, "to meet or encounter") to escort the *curukat* (guests, literally, "attackers"] from the invited village. When the guests arrived, designated *agyut* (gift exchange partners) would receive new clothes in the *qasgi*, and Annie mentioned how she envied both her older brother and youngest sibling, who received new garments from their *agyut* during the feast.

Moved by Annie's account, Wassilie gave a detailed description of the Messenger Feast, adding to what he had shared the day before. He told how villagers met during November to plan the upcoming *Kevgiryaraq*. After they reached a decision, they sent couriers to carry the invitation to the designated village.

Wassilie had been such a courier, carrying the invitation from Nunapicuar to Nunacuaq. When he and his companion arrived, they went straight to the *qasgi* and sat on the inside of the entryway. After a brief moment of silence, someone said, "What's up. Are they the *kevgak*?" The young men nodded, and everyone in there yelled, "*Kevga-a-a-ak* (Couriers are here)!" Wassilie noted that he was a little scared by the dramatic reception, as he was young and timid. After that, an old man brought a bowl of delicious food to welcome them, which they shared. The two then left the *qasgi* while the men enjoyed a fire bath. Smiling, Wassilie recalled what followed:

When we reentered the *qasgi*, they told us to sit anywhere. The men moistened the heads of their drums with water and got them ready for dancing. The drums were big. They sang the songs that were composed for the upcoming dance festival. Women began to come in and young girls, too. I noticed that some were very pretty. Then I thought to myself, "When I'm old enough to marry, I'm going to try and marry a girl from this village." When I saw this particular girl down there, I promised to remember what she looked like. She became my wife later on in life.

The next day Wassilie and his companion were given messages to take home. After the initial invitation had been accepted, a second pair of messengers carried special gift requests to the invited village. Mentioning the name of his child, a man would hang on a long stick an object representing

an item he wanted to acquire from a family in the other village. When the couriers went back to the invited village the second time, they would bring these requests, known as *petugtat* (literally, "things tied on"), as in the intravillage *Petugtaryaraq* Annie had described. Selected children would then become *agyut* (gift exchange partners) of children in the host village. The couriers would then go back to their village with *petugtat* for the people involved in the gift exchange. Each family would then prepare gifts for their child's *agyuk* in the opposite village. Wassilie noted that the gifts exchanged during *Petugtaryaraq* were minimal, while during *Kevgiryaraq,* people demonstrated their ability to provide by sharing valuable things.

Catherine then described what she had experienced, including both *Qaariitaaq* and *Petugtaryaraq,* during which she requested and received a pair of earring hooks. She had also witnessed *Nakaciuryaraq* as a young girl. At that time, she saw many inflated seal bladders hanging in the back of the *qasgi,* and she noted that in the coastal area, only sea-mammal bladders and not those of land animals were used in the ceremony. She recalled gathering wild celery and taking it into the *qasgi.* Later she witnessed the ceremony's dramatic ending, during which the bladders were returned to the sea:

The porch was filled with women waiting to bring small bowls of *akutaq* into the *qasgi.* We were asked to stand along the wall of the porch. Then someone said, "They will begin running out with their inflated seal bladders along with wild celery plants with their tips on fire. When they drop pieces of the plants on the floor, grab them. And when you go out, pick up all of the plant parts they dropped on the ground, too." We waited. I was impatient as usual.

Then after the bowls were brought inside, suddenly one of the men ran out holding burning plants. We were all screaming in the porch as he ran out. Once the men were all out there, one of the women apparently followed them as they proceeded. She later told a story about it. She said that when they came to a hole in the ice and the deflated bladders tied to a piece of wood were pushed into the hole, they immediately disappeared. How amazing.

Back home, the women smudged their bodies with the smoke of tundra plants every day until the plants they had gathered were gone.

Catherine had also participated in masked dances:

When I first moved to the Yukon River area, I never went to the dance celebrations. But I took part in the celebration when masks were presented. . . . When a song started . . . we dancers didn't all come down to the dance floor. The designated dancers for a certain song would come down and dance, *nayangarluteng.* My dancing partner was always my husband's brother's wife. Whenever her husband began to sing, we'd come down and dance. The songs sung at this particular celebration were *apallulget* [songs with verses].

13.5   Eagle-feather dance stick from the Yukon. IVA4365.

Wassilie described the power of *nayangaryaraq* [dancing accompanied by songs] in the past:

Long, long ago, the *nayangaryaraq* was different. During the *ellarrluk* [period of protracted bad weather], people were starving. And in one of the villages in the Yukon River area, a woman carried her grandchild down the village singing a song and stopping at each food cache . . . and letting her grandchild look into the doorway and smell the food. . . . When her grandchild started crying from hunger she sang a song and carried him down the village, stopping at each food cache.

As they went from cache to cache, the child would stop crying and begin to burp. When he burped, she would smell the scent of food. He would no longer be hungry and would fall asleep.

Wassilie noted that in times of food shortage, people in Nanvarnarrlak sang that particular *cauyara'arcuun* (drum song, from *cauyaq*, "drum") in a ceremony attended by people from surrounding villages. During the ceremony, fish-trap ribs were tied together and used when such songs were chanted. Conversely, if people sang such songs when they had enough to eat, they would no longer be satisfied with food and begin eating large amounts. Wassilie recalled how this happened to a man named Qayista. After he sang a *cauyara'arcuun*, his descendants were able to eat and eat and never get satisfied. Eating wolf meat was also said to cause a person to eat large amounts without getting full.

Our conversation might have ended here, but we had one last piece to examine—an eagle-feather dance stick from the Yukon area (fig. 13.5, fig. 13.6).[11] Catherine had witnessed the use of such wands during the presentation of gifts during the Messenger Feast and described what she had seen:

In Nightmute, I first saw people getting together and dancing, *cu...karlueng*. At that time, since it was my first visit to the *qasgi*, I remember clearly what happened. As children, that was the only time we were allowed to go to the *qasgi*.

I saw men drumming and singing . . . and moving to the rhythm. When a singer said, "May he bring it forward, . . ." a person would bring the thing mentioned in the song into the *qasgi*. If

13.6 Wassilie moving the dance stick to the rhythm of a song.

the requested item was too big, like a sled, it was brought in through the skylight up there. . . .

The Messenger Feast was very important to people . . . and many gifts were presented. . . . If a request song was sung, a member would bring in the requested item.

Standing up and holding his coat over his head, Wassilie (fig. 13.7) vividly described *anerquciaryaraq*, the process of bringing in gifts while loudly yelling and calling attention to one's prowess:

When the singers began to sing the request song for the gift presenter, the presenter sometimes did a performance *anerquciaraluni*. He would describe his hunting feats and how he had successfully acquired the gifts he was about to present. He would stand before the audience and swing his arms and yell, "My arms!" And moving to the rhythm, he would describe his hunts and the animals he had caught. At this performance, men lifted up their arms to show their strength and stamina.

And they performed *aqumutet* [sitting dances] by pulling the wall benches down and creating a space in the back of the room

13.7 Wassilie using his coat to demonstrate the process of bringing in gifts during the Messenger Feast.

13.8 Catherine singing and summoning Wassilie to come forward.

where there was no traffic.... The drummers would stand and drum, singing and bouncing to the beat. The directors down below would also get excited. They would all be bouncing vigorously to the drumbeat....

One of the directors would yell, "Would he bring the gifts forward...." He would call out the requested item and mention the person's name to bring it forward. The other director would also be calling. That was how it was done.

Catherine said that when she first saw a man *anerquciaralria*, she was scared because he was yelling so loud. She then sat holding the microphone (fig. 13.8), summoning Wassilie to come forward with a song:

Oh how happy I feel looking at these
Oh how joyous I feel seeing these
They are delightful to see but my eyes are getting blurry
Looking at all these canned goods which can roll and spill
I wish I could take them and burp and burp loudly

Chuckling, she added, "Then one of the dance directors would say, 'Would Uqsungiar bring them forward.'" As Wassilie and Henry waved their gifts over their heads, Catherine sang out:

Would Uqsungiar bring them forward
Would he bring in his coat and these here
Oh so many canned goods here that can roll and spill
I wish I could take them and burp and burp loudly.

Catherine concluded: "He has now performed *anerquciaraluni*."

At the end of the day, we had time to pull twenty Nushagak pieces for Esther and Henry to admire. I went back into collections to examine the contents of Drawer D one last time, trying to burn them into my mind. After our work, Esther and Marie went shopping for gifts to bring home to their families, and I cooked rabbit soup following Marie's recipe. We had a cheerful meal followed by a game of *caukia*, ending a good day.

FOURTEENTH DAY AND RETURN TO ALASKA

Our last day in Germany was not a work day but a time to celebrate. Friday morning, we arrived at the museum at our usual hour to prepare for a midmorning press conference planned by the museum. Reporters, photographers, and various museum officials arrived at ten and stayed for more than an hour. Instead of viewing objects, we were being viewed, and the group took it as a compliment. Annie told a story, Henry modeled masks, and Catherine and Marie danced in front of a map of Alaska. When we were done and the reporters were gone, Herr Wedel—originally so apprehensive of the elders' work in his collections—wanted his picture taken with them.

At noon, we all enjoyed a surprise luncheon prepared by the staff of the museum's Native American department (fig. 14.1), including smoked fish, breads, sparkling juice, potato salad, and plum cake (a specialty of the fall season). Wassilie offered a prayer before we ate, and Annie had us join hands and pray at meal's end.

After lunch, Marie and Esther took the elders back for a final visit to the Brandenburg Gate flea market to buy more wristwatches and souvenirs for family back home, and I spent the afternoon in collections. We met back at the hotel for soup and afterward turned on the television to enjoy our sixty seconds of fame, featuring Henry in the raven-skin hat. The rest of the evening we spent packing and making phone calls. Everyone was excited about going home.

Our farewells began at breakfast Saturday morning, with the proprietor of our pension wishing us a warm good-bye. After that, Esther and Henry left for their flight back to Alaska, and Marie left for one to Copenhagen, where she planned to meet up with her sons—both accomplished singers—who were traveling there. Wassilie, Catherine, and Annie finished packing while I shuttled our gear down the creaky stairs and out to the curb. We changed our money at the airport, and twenty-four hours later we were safely home.

14.1 Farewell luncheon on our last day at the museum.

VISUAL REPATRIATION

When we left Anchorage, some of us had known each other only by name, but after a few days in Berlin, we were living together as an extended family, and our patterns of working together at the Berlin Ethnological Museum became second nature.

On our first day in Berlin, I remember teasing Wassilie, calling him my *uicungaq* (teasing cousin, literally, "dear little husband"). This endearment had often worked to break the ice. Instead of laughing, Wassilie looked at me seriously and said, "No, you are my daughter." He said this in part because, since we had met, I had served him like a daughter. In the days that followed, he changed his mind. He and the other elders sometimes called me their mother because, along with Marie, I cooked and cared for them in a faraway foreign country. Catherine confided how scared she was when I went out of sight, and I realized the depth of their dependence.

I was humbled one morning near the end of his stay when Paul, the acknowledged leader of our group, said that we had been chosen by God to do this work. Although we had fun on our trip, this was very serious business.

WORK IN COLLECTIONS

When we began our work in collections, we discovered that although Yup'ik and Iñupiaq collections were mixed, most objects were stored separately by type (e.g., net sinkers, spear points). Fortunately they had not been divided by Alaska region (Yukon, Kuskokwim, Bristol Bay), which would have made our diverse group's task much more difficult. When presented with a group of bows, for example, the elders commented in turn on those from their area, being careful to mention the differences from the other bows. The separation between men's and women's things that I had anticipated did not take place. Annie and Catherine knew almost as much about the use of bows and arrows as Wassilie and Paul. Conversely, Paul and Wassilie spoke eloquently about the making of sinew, technically "women's work."

Group dynamics followed Yup'ik protocols. We had a number of English-speaking visitors during our stay, but we did our best work when discussions were carried out in Yup'ik. The balance between men and women was also critical. Because of his full-time teaching job in St. Marys, Andy originally planned to return home after the first week. It soon became clear, however, that the other men would not feel comfortable without him. He was the only man among them who spoke fluent English and, as their roommate, provided an irreplaceable measure of security. Because of the value Andy placed on this work, he agreed to stay another week. Had he not done so, the whole trip might have fallen apart.

Elders rested their authority to speak in collections on personal experience, which also limited what they had to say. When examining a seal-gut bag, Catherine remarked: "Since I don't know the names of some of the parts of these objects, I've only mentioned this part that I know about." Wassilie commented: "Since my parents had wooden bowls when I first became aware, I'm only mentioning what I saw and not adding other information."

Formal Yup'ik etiquette dictated our roles as speakers and listeners. As the eldest man, Wassilie spoke first, followed by Paul as the recognized expert orator, with, as Andy liked to say, "a mind like a computer." When Paul knew more about an object than Wassilie, he would still listen to Wassilie before giving a full explanation. When we looked at something that both men were familiar with, Paul would often tell Wassilie to talk first. That "talk" took a range of forms, including names, personal experiences, actions, stories, and songs.

The detailed vocabulary associated with the collected objects was a major point of interest. When looking at a box of harpoon points, elders sorted them by named type. Arrows and arrowheads also had a multitude of specific names. The comment "*Ayuqut* [They are the same]" let us move quickly through boxes of objects of a type we had already discussed.

Regional differences in design and designation were points of great interest. When presented with a box mixing Yup'ik and Iñupiaq ivory spear points, the elders picked out ones from their area to comment on, ignoring those of their northern neighbors. Things from Unalakleet, although technically the hard work of Yup'ik speakers, were dismissed as Iñupiaq and not investigated.

Elders made old things familiar in their comments, emphasizing similarity between past and present rather than difference. Paul designated an ivory story knife a "cartoon maker." Catherine called a bladder water bottle a "Yup'ik thermos." And when looking at ivory pieces, Andy compared them to gas hose connectors.

Jacobsen's diverse collection also evoked a wide range of personal experiences, as when Wassilie took up a young boy's bow, like one he used as a child, and related the *inerquutet* (rules) from his area about what could and could not be placed in it. Looking at the large wooden snow shovel, Paul recalled that a young man would shovel for four years before he would "graduate" (become a good hunter). Again and again, I heard the traditional rules for living I had recorded in *Boundaries and Passages*,[1] but in this context they were organized dramatically around real objects and activities rather than didactically around ideas of what it meant to be a "real person."

The elders continually used objects to make points in an ongoing conversation among themselves. This was never more striking than when we looked at the model dance house. Its delicately-carved ivory figures and unusual costumes drew no comment, but Andy and Paul both gave long explanations of the tiny drum model, stating that the drum holds the elders and all that is good, but that half of the Yup'ik people today are outside this drum. I was listening to a political statement about what it meant to be Yup'ik in the modern world.

The handling of objects was savored as a personal experience that would be talked about for years to come. The elders noticed everything—an ivory story knife carved for a "lefty," a restored ax with the blade put on backward. Commenting on the inlay of a wooden box, Wassilie exclaimed, "The workmanship on this object is quite amazing." They also repeatedly expressed thanks, not only for the opportunity to see these old things but to the men and women who had created them. Holding a large slate-bladed *uluaq* in her hands,[2] Annie said, "How thankful I am that those people were given the ability to survive with implements like these." When we were done examining objects each day, Paul advised us to rub the dust onto our bodies as protection from harm, instead of washing our hands.

Observations often were animated. Elders demonstrated chopping with axes, shooting arrows, digging for mouse food, shoveling snow, mixing *akutaq,* and making fire with the bow drill. Among the most dramatic explanations was Annie's preparation of snuff tobacco. Assembling tools from different parts of the collection, she first pretended to cut, pound, and strain the tobacco; mix it with ash; and then sniff it into one nostril, sneezing and wiping the water from her eyes when she was done. Her presentation was so realistic that the group later questioned whether today's young people should be shown the video lest they want to revive the custom.

When we looked at the eagle-feather dance wand, Wassilie told Catherine to sing the "asking song," then showed his muscles and danced to the beat. In fact, every day I had the overwhelming feeling of attending a dance festival. Unlike the mask exhibit, *Agayuliyararput,* for which exploring collections had paved the way for a major series of events, this work in collections *was* the event, not mere preparation. A book might be the result, but the action was here and now.

Just as the objects evoked names, remembrances, and dramatic displays, they also conjured a multitude of stories. The numerous bows and arrows started an avalanche of war stories that continued through lunches and long evenings at the hotel. A cutting board reminded Annie of the story of the woman who turned into a bear by dressing in bearskin with a board behind her back to take revenge on her unfaithful husband, Picartuli. Looking at spearheads, Andy asked Paul to describe the detailed division of a seal after the hunt.

Planning our trip to Berlin, I had envisioned it as a time and place where many forgotten facts about old objects would come to light. Elders did indeed provide invaluable information, but rarely communicated in a straightforward manner. For example, examining an enormous king-salmon net, Paul described the person who traveled under the water with a pair of king salmon, choosing which net to enter based on the care the fishermen gave them in previous years. He then related this story to the current fishing crisis in the region, blaming the decline on wasteful practices by both Native and non-Native fishermen.

I had heard this story before, but never with this precise meaning. Like Annie's account of the creature *paalraayak,* the tale's meaning was not fixed but emerged in that particular telling. Although interesting, the net was not the focus but valuable insofar as it allowed elders to recall and share with each other stories and their relation to particular contemporary situations.

As each made plain, rules guided a young person's actions in the past, and we ignore these rules today at our peril. They want the younger generation to hear their stories and gain awareness of their history to avoid very real dangers in the world today.

15.1 Annie holding up a caribou-tooth belt to record the sounds made by teeth tinkling against empty bullet shells.

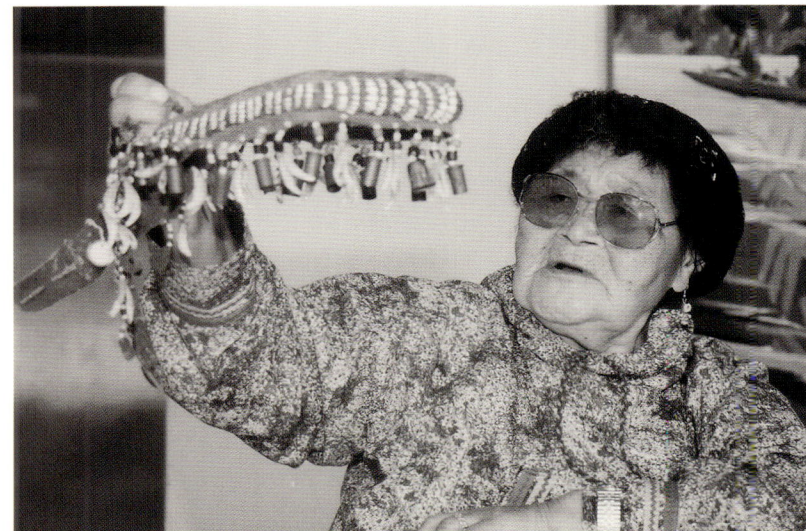

Along with stories, Jacobsen's collection evoked many songs. A loonskin hat for the sweat bath brought out a song about a loon, complete with its call. Holding two squirrel skins, Annie told a story about squirrel and ptarmigan singing a slow-style *ingula* song. Wassilie sang the arrow song of the famous warrior Apanuugpak while we looked at slate blades. In fact, objects made of slate were particularly poignant, as they had gone out of use before these elders were born.

We even recorded the sounds of the objects, holding up a caribou-tooth belt to record the teeth tinkling against empty bullet shells (fig. 15.1) or shaking a pair of thumbless dance mittens to hear the wooden dangles. Marie's response to one song was, "That's a good one; we'll have to bring it back." Just as objects evoked songs and stories, we sometimes treated those songs and sounds as objects to take home.

Last but not least, we laughed. When we looked at a large wooden bowl, Paul joked that it was Apanuugpak's home-brew pot but not to record that on tape because it wasn't true. When we looked at a double bowl with a handle,[3] Paul said it was a bowl for twins, and Wassilie added that one side was for pee and one for poop. This Yup'ik ribaldry brought on peals of laughter, both in the privacy of collections and at home in our hotel. When we were in public, however, Wassilie was constantly putting his finger to his lips in a futile attempt to hush us giggling women. Catherine agreed that we should not laugh in the presence of strangers, as they might think we were laughing at them.

OUTSIDE THE MUSEUM'S WALLS

Exploring Berlin wearing a mix of modern Yup'ik and Western clothing—*qasperet* for women, shirts and pants along with the ubiquitous baseball cap for men—our group drew considerable interest. We answered queries by saying that we were from Alaska, and doors opened wide. Everywhere we went, people helped us make purchases and tried to point us in the right direction.

Just as Berliners took note of us, their Yup'ik guests were taking stock of them. Fresh off the airplane after twenty-four hours without sleep, the elders immediately spotted differences. Vasilie looked around in surprise and announced, "No caps!" Annie was also all eyes: "No long hair." Paul later remarked, "Since their diet has always been the same, their physical build appears to be uniform and regular. I didn't see any fat people there at all." Catherine noted that even though we hadn't always understood what people said to us, they had been kind, and it had been nice to hear them speaking in English sometimes. Vasilie was impressed by the orderliness of the German people: "Though this place is very populated, I haven't heard a disturbing noise anywhere. These people seem to live according to God's plan. They are very clean and neat. . . . That's how I've seen this place since I came here. There are many cars on the streets, but it gets very quiet . . . when everybody retires for the night."

Although struck by differences, they sought the familiar. "When in Germany, do as the Yupiit do" was our motto. Halfway around the world, the elders found many familiar things—berries and plants they knew from Alaska growing in the Berlin Botanical Gardens, lakes full of ducks and swans, boats on the rivers and planes in the sky. Although they had brought some Native food, they also discovered German dishes strikingly similar to Yup'ik delicacies, including smoked fish in a downtown department store and fried herring at an all-day fair. The Germans even had a delicious berry dessert that the elders judged almost as good as Yup'ik *qerpertaq* (fish-egg and cranberry *akutaq*).

The elders were disappointed that they could not locate a bingo hall or a drum to use for dancing, but news that there was a German equivalent to the Yup'ik steam bath created great excitement. We did, indeed, try out one of the private saunas a cab ride away from our hotel. Paul was shocked when he saw me handing the attendant 200 Mark for our entrance fee: he viewed steam baths as gifts money could not buy. The elders were even more surprised by the easy mingling of naked men and women inside. Draped in multiple towels and discreetly looking at our toes, our men and women took turns inside the steam room and went home with stories to tell.

Most evenings, we rested in our hotel rooms after dinner. Weekends, however, we explored the city and surrounding countryside, including the River Havel (fig. 15.2), the zoo, the Brandenburg Gate (fig. 15.3), and nearby Sanssouci Palace, home of Frederick the Great and dubbed by the elders "the king's big house." Among the elders' favorite spots was the Berlin Botanical Gardens, which we visited twice (fig. 15.4). Catherine later recalled, "When we went to the botanical garden, I began to grieve for our ancestors. I was imagining the Garden of Paradise. If they hadn't committed the first sin, we'd be living in a beautiful place. I felt great joy in the garden."

Perhaps the most memorable exchange outside the walls of the museum took place spontaneously when we attended a medieval fair and Saturday market near our hotel (fig. 15.5, fig. 15.6). For an hour, we walked from booth to booth, sampling foods and watching the costumed performers who roamed the crowds. Paul was particularly impressed with this display of traditional activities and later commented: "Since [the Germans] are still living according to their own culture, certain days are set aside to carry out their cultural ways, including constructing tools using fire. They also wore traditional clothing as they baked bread using firewood. People were still practicing the old ways even though they were rich."

Tired and thirsty, we settled at a tea stall at the far end of the fairgrounds. Everyone who passed by stared at us, trying to figure out our nationality. As we rested, a troubadour dressed in bells and bright colors approached, playing a lute and singing in Italian. When he finished, he bowed in our direction and motioned for us to do the same.

This was the moment the group had been waiting for.

15.2, 15.3, 15.4 Snapshots of weekend travels around Berlin, including a boat ride on the River Havel, a visit to the Brandenburg Gate, and an encounter with an organ grinder outside the botanical gardens.

15.5, 15.6 Our afternoon at the medieval fair.

All had expected our visit to Berlin to include a public dance performance, as drumming and dancing are among the most expressive aspects of contemporary Yup'ik culture and are performed publicly both locally and abroad. At the troubadour's request, Paul and Andy began to sing and beat the table in time, as the women rose to their feet and began to dance. They stopped after one verse, however, and waited. The troubadour responded with a second song, this time in French, and we answered with another verse. We repeated the sequence several times, gathering a tightly packed crowd around us.

When we finally stopped, the booth owner brought us tea and cakes, and we stayed in our comfortable spot for the rest of the afternoon, alternately eating and dancing each time the troubadour came our way. The event captured the core of our experience in Berlin. Paul and the others had not come to Germany to see sights, but to be seen and, through their acts and words, tell the world what it means to be Yup'ik. They expected that this was something people would want to know and so

were surprised when the museum did not suggest such a performance. The afternoon at the fair left everyone satisfied that they had succeeded in presenting and making themselves understood in this new global context.

THE SIGNIFICANCE OF COLLECTIONS

We had looked at many rare things at the Berlin Ethnological Museum: thumbless mittens worn by a young girl during her first menstruation, an eagle-feather hood, a painted bladder, and ice skates carved in the shape of puffins. Yet I think the elders were not as impressed by what they saw as by what they heard from our hosts and from each other. Along with sharing what they knew, all eagerly listened to their companions, learning as well as teaching. In the middle of our trip, Andy had said that he was reminded of what his father had taught him—that when you die, you are still learning.

Although apprehensive about traveling so far from home,

Catherine noted that she had participated because of the young people back home: "When they ask me to speak to students in the school, I willingly go. My hope is that they might learn about how the Yupiit lived in the old days and not be tempted to use the bad things that are available in our villages today.... If our ancestors' things ... were used to educate our young people they will begin to stimulate their minds." Annie was moved by Catherine's words and added: "My dear friend just talked, and we are on the same path.... I wish for the best for today's young people ... who I always view as my children, who have passed away.... And back in Alaska, every young person who sees me calls me Mom.... It seems like when they do that, my ground gets elevated."

Vasilie was also thankful for the objects he had seen: "Back home, we don't see such things anymore." He expressed his appreciation for Jacobsen, who came to such a harsh environment so far from home to collect, and to the museum for the good care they were giving these things. He was impressed by the meticulous organization of objects and glad that they would be there for his children's children to observe: "Gosh, I'm so grateful for what he did. If he hadn't collected them, they would have disappeared long ago. Not one of the items would be visible now if our counterparts, the white people, hadn't collected them." Most of all, he expressed gratitude to his fellow group members for all they had taught him. He had not realized how much there was to learn from these old things, and he was thankful that he had been chosen to come. Later he added that he would like to do this kind of work again, although he hoped he would not have to travel so far.

Marie was impressed by how many old things we had seen—things that until now she had only heard about in stories. She was also happy to have learned more about her family: "I've learned about my grandparents and how they lived.... By looking at the objects, I've realized that they were very skilled and imaginative craftsmen, and I've been filled with appreciation." Marie added that many in her generation are in the same situation:

Our traditions were totally severed when the schools and churches were introduced. In the past, I was resentful that outsiders looked down on our culture and worked to wipe it out.... And I'd tell myself that our ways were probably discontinued because they were indeed sinful.

I always tried to understand what happened to our people.... I didn't think our Creator placed us in this world with bad traditions. In the village where I grew up, there was no dancing, and when I asked questions about past festivals, they'd only say that they were sinful.... As we looked at this very old collection, I seemed to understand deeper into my past.

Marie mentioned the many *qulirat* she had heard, all told in their complete form from beginning to end. Like the objects, these had been missing from her childhood, and she was grateful to hear them.

Although Henry had been with us only a week, he had much to say. Like the others, he had been apprehensive about coming, wondering why he needed to travel to such a faraway place to see a few old things: "But my stay here has been a total reverse of my thinking.... I found that there were many, many objects here that were once used by our ancestors ... kept in a very good place.... And these people that have welcomed us display themselves so nicely and show their kindheartedness, even though I can't understand their language."

The final words were Catherine's, thanking Marie and me for leading them on this trip: "Since this place is so far away from home, I get very frightened when one of you is gone ... that you might have an accident. Thank you very much for working so hard to keep me safe."

Andy and Paul had also reflected on our trip on the evening before their departure. Andy, the teacher, spoke of his desire that what we had learned would be brought home for the benefit of the younger generation: "Our work seems to have opened up times ahead and filled it with information.... With this work, our roots and culture will come closer to us." Yet pride was mixed with regret. He concluded, "Evidently our ancestors lived a clean life. Their life was very good. Seeing their work, I envy them."

A determined leader as well as an eloquent orator, Paul's words were perhaps the most pointed and far-reaching, moving beyond the walls of the museum. Doing his first fieldwork in a non-English-speaking country, he had been observing the German people and was impressed: "Here in Germany, I see that people truly live according to their traditions. I see that they have kept their ways."

He contrasted their cultural integrity to the situation back home in Alaska:

When I think about our home, I feel sad realizing that we Yupiit are not holding on to our traditional ways. And through my observation of this land and its people, I've realized that by not holding on to our traditions, our people have become confused about their own identity....

Even though I've heard about the vast ocean, I had not pictured it in my mind before. And since I came here, by looking at the time difference, I now believe that we indeed have reached the other side of the ocean. When night comes to our families back home, it would be morning here. Our places are so far apart.

Though we live far apart, we've realized that people here have held onto their culture.... God indeed created many tribes with their own traditional ways and beliefs, which were to be practiced until the end of time.

Finally, Paul spoke about how our work in the museum might help to remedy this situation:

When we were looking at the objects that were once used by our ancestors, I began to realize that they were persevering and hardworking people.... Though they didn't have excellent tools, their workmanship was so fine. The fact that they had taken care of themselves could be seen by their work. Western-made material was totally absent from their work. Gosh, our ancestors took charge of their lives....

Since we have no understanding, we've abandoned our cultural ways. But those of us who came here have been granted more understanding regarding our people. . . .

My vision is this. Many of us seem to have been in the dark for many years. And now, stories and information about our roots have emerged from this unknown, faraway place across the ocean. Now that the knowledge is out, I hope our work together will be written and presented to our people. . . .

If our people begin to see these things and begin to understand the culture of our ancestors, they might begin to believe and gain pride in their own identity. I envision our people gaining more faith in themselves by seeing the objects or seeing their pictures or reading about them in books. . . . My hope is that our work will bring our people closer to their own culture.

Much more important than any specific information that objects evoke, Paul sees collections as tools capable of teaching self-reliance and pride to young people who have grown up as second-class citizens in an English-only world. Knowledge is power, and it is Paul's strong hope that young people use this long-hidden knowledge as ammunition in their battle to take control of their land and lives.

MUSEUMS: PART OF GOD'S PLAN

Since our return, these elders have been honored in different ways. Catherine's family gave her a surprise birthday feast on her return to Anchorage. Wassilie has publicly described his experiences, stating how looking at these old things has increased his understanding of his own people. Togiak threw a villagewide potluck for Annie, after which she talked and shared the pictures she had taken with her disposable camera. In October 1997, she was flown into Anchorage to receive the Alaska Federation of Natives' "Elder of the Year" award, including a beautiful wristwatch, which she joked she would keep on German time.

Paul is often invited to speak at gatherings, and twice during September 1998 he publicly described his experiences in the Berlin Ethnological Museum. First he spoke to a group of more than one hundred Yup'ik elders and students seated on bleachers in the Kasigluk High School during an elders conference organized by the Calista Elders Council. There he, Wassilie, Marie, and I made short presentations about our work in Germany. We sat behind a long table, on which were spread two dozen old things (including stone tools, painted wood bowls, and gut-skin garments) borrowed from the Anchorage Museum of History and Art to demonstrate our talk. Paul spoke at length:

When we went into the places they call museums in New York and Germany and saw our ancestors' objects, I always thought about the things I heard people talk about when I was young. . . . So at this time, using these old things as examples, let us work together and begin pulling forward the culture of our ancestors so it can be included in the school curriculum. Though we seem to have forgotten our past, when we hear others speaking, we remember it. . . .

I'm obliged to tell you these things because of the contents of this table, which are here to teach our ancestors' way of life. . . .

It was also God's plan that our ancestral objects be revealed to us through an unknown, faraway place. In God's eyes, it was inevitable that we allow our tribal ways to disappear. Our old things surfaced in a place totally unanticipated by us. . . .

And our discovery has brought us a broader understanding of who we are. Since these old things can be used to give us a wider view of our heritage, we are seeing a few of them here on this table. . . .

I just mentioned what I saw in the museum in Germany. It is true that old things from every tribe in the world are housed there. A building of several stories is filled with artifacts from every tribal group. Throughout, it is as if God is talking to everyone, saying, "You all are getting too displaced. Find your identity through these things."

We also saw many objects in New York [at the National Museum of the American Indian in April 1997], but I couldn't leave the adze and an ax for a long time. . . . Realizing that they had been used by someone long before metal and nails were introduced, . . . I kept looking at them in astonishment. The ax had an ivory blade with a wooden handle glimmering . . . from constant sweat and oil from the hand that held it. The adze had a stone blade, too, and its handle was also well worn. It was those two objects that I kept going back to look at in awe.

Paul's second presentation was made to a gathering of more than three hundred museum professionals at the annual meeting of the Western Museums Association in Anchorage. Marie stood by his side, translating for the non-Native audience. He opened by giving his name in both English and Yup'ik and offered what he said was a traditional prayer by singing the blessing song, *Tarvarnauramken,* which we had sung together before we began our work in Berlin. Then he spoke:

Now to the story I wanted to mention. At times a person might dig quite deep into the ground before finding an artifact, and they knew that it was quite old because of the depth of the land. The person knew the object had been dropped at the site before the land covered it.

Long ago, a Yup'ik person who predicted the future of his people went into a long chant with a drum, and afterward he spoke about his vision. Using his leg as an example, he said that when the land had grown on his grave and the soil was as deep as his leg, his descendants would begin to use goods that were shimmering. And now our belongings do shine. He obviously knew the future we were going to.

That is why I truly believe that we were not supposed to lose our culture that God granted to us long ago, when there were no white people in our area. And as I observe it, since God knew that our priests were going to brush away our culture, God evidently had our ancestral objects collected so that they would be revealed to us through a place totally unexpected, through Germany, a place underneath our home. That is how I look at the situation today. If we had kept the objects while our priests were brushing our culture away, we would have lost them and allowed the land to cover them by now. But since God had planned that they be revealed to us through an unexpected place, they are now being revealed down in Germany. When we went to Germany, we saw this truth. . . .

As I consider our Yup'ik culture, I'm hopeful that we can continue to strengthen our knowledge through the objects that are housed in museums. If we used those objects as our statutes, we will gain knowledge and our cultural identity will get stronger.

The objects in museums, our ancestral objects, are not insignificant. If we live using them as our strength, we will get closer to the ways of our ancestors. And when we are gone, our grandchildren will be able to continue to live according to the knowledge they have gained.

FIELDWORK TURNED ON ITS HEAD: YUP'IK CULTURALISM IN A GERMAN MUSEUM

The phrase "fieldwork turned on its head" refers to our project's reversal of the traditional fieldwork paradigm in cultural anthropology. Whereas anthropologists are known to travel to distant lands to study the resident Natives, in this case Native elders traveled to one home of anthropology—the Berlin Ethnological Museum—to do their own fieldwork, coming to their own conclusions about the value of the ethnographic collections they explored. Archaeologists and material culture specialists within anthropology have always done research in museum storerooms, and Franz Boas, Alfred Kroeber, and George Byron Gordon are but a few anthropologists who had indigenous people working in their collections.[4] The thrust of their work has been to increase non-Natives' knowledge and understanding of Native peoples, but in this case it is the Natives who seek to understand both collections and the collecting process so that they can use them for their own ends.

Our "reverse fieldwork" was full of ironies. Adolf Bastian and his Support Committee underwrote Johan Adrian Jacobsen's collecting work as part of nineteenth-century German national identity formation, and today this same collection contributes directly to an emergent Yup'ik identity.[5] Masks that the Yupiit viewed as prayers rather than property became owned objects in a European museum. These and other things that were originally part of lived dramas became, in Bastian's hands, static indicators of culture or custom. By the late twentieth century, the objects that Jacobsen had appropriated were being "reappropriated," reemerging as central in an ongoing dialogue concerning Yup'ik distinctiveness.

The Yup'ik men and women who traveled to Berlin examined Jacobsen's collection to understand their unique "culture." In fact, this much-debated concept had roots in the German Counter-Enlightenment, when objects were likewise used to understand "cultures." Both Bastian and Boas were grounded in the German anthropological tradition extending back to the Boos, and the concept of culture that Boas brought with him into American ethnology is a direct descendant of Bastian's *Völkergedanken*, Johann Gottfried Herder's *Volksgeist*, and Wilhelm von Humboldt's *Nationalcharakter*. Whereas the philosophers of the French Enlightenment wrote of the essential sameness of human beings as rational actors and the steady progress of civilization, Bastian and Boas saw the common bond of humanity expressed in the diversity of distinct "cultures," which they sought to document through empirical research. Both focused on the individuality and diversity of phenomena as opposed to their similarity and universality, to actual history as opposed to generalities[6]—and the Yup'ik elders did the same. Both these founding fathers of ethnology would, I think, have appreciated what the elders had to say.

Just as collecting was Bastian's means toward the ends of understanding humanity, examining collections was the elders' means toward the goal of understanding Yup'ik culture. For Bastian, Jacobsen's collection was a sign of the Yup'ik place in human history, while for contemporary Yupiit, the collection is a sign of heritage. Both were driven by a sense of mission—Bastian to know, to understand, to preserve a dying past, and the elders to teach, to inspire their younger generation, to create a future in which Yup'ik distinctiveness continues to have a place.

Our work in Berlin is an example of how, as Marshall Sahlins reminds us, "even as the world becomes more integrated globally, it continues to differentiate locally, the second in some measure stimulated by the first." This process of differentiation is what many before me have termed "culturalism," that is, the process of self-conscious, deliberate use of identity, culture, and heritage in the struggle for recognition of a distinctive way of life. Far more than nostalgic ruminations on "the good old days," it is an active effort to apprehend a changed world in familiar terms.[7]

Thirty years ago, I never heard the word "culture" used in southwestern Alaska. Today it is ubiquitous. Conscious culture is the trademark of the new millennium in Alaska as elsewhere, requiring effort to preserve and reproduce past practices and defend them against assimilative pressures. For those who traveled to Berlin, as for indigenous leaders elsewhere, "culture is not only a heritage, it is a project," a demand for specific forms of modernity that are only possible if the next generation shares their view of the world, that is, their culture.[8]

Our work in museums clearly represents "a permutation of older forms and relationships made appropriate to novel situations," displaying, as Sahlins says so well, not the invention but the inventiveness of tradition.[9] Elders presented information in group settings as was traditional, based on their own personal experiences: "I tell what I know." Like good "afterologists" (Sahlins's term for postmodern, postcolonial, poststructuralist thinkers), they made no claims to completeness or to imparting the one true faith.[10] Their sense of their own culture was neither essentialist nor bounded, and the emphasis was not on presenting a unified, homogeneous, systematic view (as in some instances of cultural revival and renewal). A number of authors exploring issues of identity emphasize peoples' stabilizing rhetoric, their attempts to forge "unity out of diversity."[11] This, for the Yupiit, is not the issue. They are not among those indigenous people who talk about their culture in "the bounded, reified, essentialized, and timeless fashion that most [anthropologists] do now reject."[12]

Although both Catherine and Paul spoke some English, they never used it during our work together. This strategic use of the Yup'ik language as a symbol of Yup'ik identity achieved an unmistakable "profit of distinction" in encounters both within and beyond the museum.[13] Whatever the limits on practical communication, the power of their presence and their assertions of distinctive elder status were in part due to their opacity.

The elders' oratory was simultaneously "authentic" and "innovative," reproducing "with a difference."[14] Their contemporary narrative references to the past were active efforts to shape the future—a future in which they believe Yup'ik distinctiveness should be recognized and valued. They came to Germany not because they wanted to reclaim objects, but because they wanted to be heard. As important as it was to communicate among themselves in collections, they sought to communicate about Yup'ik culture nationally and internationally in an effort to gain respect and understanding for their way of life. They viewed themselves as teachers communicating to non-Natives something about who Yup'ik people really are, whether or not it was something listeners expected to hear.[15] Donning masks and dance headdresses, they appeared to reporters as exotic Eskimos during our final press conference, but they viewed themselves as a "Yup'ik delegation" representing their people.

These public encounters, in turn, reflect back on the elders' image of themselves, sometimes changing them in the process. Beth Conklin notes that as people "see themselves reflected in new ways—in the eyes of sympathetic outsiders, as well as on video screens—some have begun to envision and project new self-images."[16] Photographers, journalists, museum staff, as well as anthropologists do not merely represent Yup'ik people in what they report, picture, and display but contribute to new Yup'ik self-images and representations. The elders observed with satisfaction their pictures in both German newspapers and on television, projected for an international audience. Their listeners are changing, their reach is extending, and the impact on their sense of what they are about will last long after their visit to Berlin. In formal presentations both during and after our trip, they have used traditional dress, speech, and even song to advocate for recognition of the special status and rights of Yup'ik people. Like many other contemporary Alaska Natives, their extended contacts have contributed to their awareness of the political value of their "culture" in relations with the non-Native world.[17]

Keith Basso has described how places become the "durable symbols of distant events, and indispensable tools for remembering and imagining them."[18] In a similar way, the objects our group of elders examined at the Berlin museum grounded everything they said, enabling them to publicly describe and discuss practices long hidden from view. Museums and the collections they housed likewise grounded ethnology in Jacobsen's time. By the mid–twentieth century, however, material culture studies fell from grace as social anthropology looked to other sources to illuminate the human condition. Beginning in the 1980s, the pendulum began to swing back as issues of representation came to the fore in anthropological debates. Museums were criticized for interpretive approaches that froze indigenous people in time and space.[19] Native cultures, many noted, were dynamic and changing, and to represent them fairly, Native people must be involved in the exhibit-making process.

In fact, the idea of "collaboration" has become almost as commonplace as the idea of "culture" in anthropological museums in the United States and Europe, many of which include Native consultants.[20] These collaborative efforts, usually structured as a partnership between professional curators and nonprofessional Native "advisors," have had varying degrees of success in addressing issues of representation. Although power relations often remain unequal, the process is characterized by coalition building and dialogue in new and important ways.

Along with collaboration in the exhibit-making process, collaboration also increasingly characterizes research in museum collections. This can happen in several ways. Many museum curators in charge of collections from particular parts of the world are actively engaged in bringing together collections and indigenous people as part of their curatorial mandate.[21] The growth of culturalism worldwide, as well as legislation such as the Native American Graves Protection and Repatriation Act of 1990, underlie some of these efforts.[22]

Like Boas before them, individual researchers familiar with an area or object type may also invite Native men and women to work with them in collections, both to answer their questions and to engage questions of their own.[23] Most recently, and perhaps most promising, are self-initiated visits by intergenerational teams of Native researchers, with or without an anthropologist in tow. As political authority (and funds) become available to them, more and more indigenous groups are sending teams comparable to our "Yup'ik delegation" into museums to rediscover their past, "not merely to mark their identity but to seize their destiny."[24]

Yup'ik elders' work in the Berlin museum is an example of what I have described elsewhere as "visual repatriation."[25] As in Yup'ik elders' comments on masks and mask-making in preparation for the *Agayuliyararput* exhibit, their primary concern was not to reclaim museum objects but to re-own the knowledge and experiences that the objects embodied. As with the mask exhibit, instead of resentment at what has been lost and taken from them, they expressed profound gratitude toward both the collectors and the museums for preserving them. By not seeking to reclaim their ancestors' handiwork, they indirectly reject the "objectifying logic" that establishes ownership at the cost of reinterpreting cultural things in the terms of those who collected them.[26] While repatriation and struggles

For the physical control of objects remain contentious issues, Yup'ik elders' work in collections provides an example of the profound benefits of Native access to collections for everyone involved.

Although a number of indigenous people have made short visits to the Berlin Ethnological Museum's world-famous ethnographic collections, ours was the first to carry out a systematic study of an entire collection. Staff members were initially both concerned for the safety of their collections and wary of Native efforts to reclaim them. They were, however, willing to allow the visit, and their respect for these indigenous researchers grew as the days went by. Our work space in the large, well-lit hallway allowed passing staff members to watch the elders' animated interactions with collections, ask questions, and share in their excitement. Moreover, elders' expressions of thanks reassured them that it was not the objects that elders coveted, but the opportunity to use them both to teach and to learn. Not one object was broken or damaged during our stay. Instead, each was enriched with myriad bits of information, stories, and songs.

Boarding the plane to Berlin, exhausted by efforts to get passports for elders with multiple names and dates of birth, I vowed that I would never again try to take elders to objects. A week later, I knew absolutely that it was worth the effort. Ironically, though fragile objects such as grass socks and gut-skin parkas will endure in museum collections, elders will not. As more and more Native men and women come into museums, we have an opportunity to understand collections in ways that Jacobsen and his contemporaries never imagined. More important, in the hands of community leaders throughout southwestern Alaska, this knowledge of the past is already being used to shape the future.

APPENDIX Additional Masks

Jacobsen collected seventy-nine masks that the elders viewed but did not comment on. The accession numbers and translated information recorded for these masks are given below:

IVA4402. "Mask representing a porcupine. Yukon. Idlaukutsenkok=Kinakok, porcupine face [*ilaanquciq kegginaquq*, "porcupine mask"]."

IVA4403. "Dance mask portraying a wolf? On top of the head it shows the face of the spirit having the likeness of a human. Lower Yukon."

IVA4404. "Bad demon living in the mountains and pursuing the hunters to devour them. It also plagues the people by breaking everything. See [IVA]4403. Lower Yukon. Thunrak [*tuunraq*] or spirit." [Fienup-Riordan 1996, 67]

IVA4405. "Represents a spirit that brings tragedy to humans, especially haunting one village. Lower Yukon. Thunrak [*tuunraq*, "helping spirit"]."

IVA4406. "Mask representing a village spirit. Lower Yukon. Thunrak [*tuunraq*] meaning spirit."

IVA4407. "Dance mask used for winter ceremonies during which the dancer becomes a spirit, similar to carnival for the Western culture. Lower Yukon. Thunrak=Kinakok [*tuunraq kegginaquq*, "spirit mask"]."

IVA4408. "Evil demon devouring people whose mouth is always smudged with blood; he lives in the mountains and follows the hunters. The devil wears a Totak [*tuutaq*] or lip ornament on the right corner of the mouth. Yukon. Thunrak [*tuunraq*]." [Fienup-Riordan 1996, 67]

IVA4403. "Mask of an evil demon living in the mountains who eats people, with a crooked nose and distorted mouth smudged with drops of blood. Yukon. Thunrak=ghost [*tuunraq*, "helping spirit"]."

IVA4410. "Mask representing the spirit of the walrus. This spirit makes riverbanks fall or mountains slide. The people of this region . . . only know about the walrus from hearsay, because there are no walruses at the mouth of the Yukon. Lower Yukon. Ersikwok or Arsiwokoak=Kinakok [*asveruaq kegginaquq*, "pretend walrus mask"]."

IVA4408–IVA4409. "Two dance masks . . . used in winter . . . showing the so-called dog salmon. Once the common silver swims in fresh water for a long time, it starves and its jaws deform, which makes them look like hooks. The Europeans called it dog salmon because of its sharp teeth. This mask shows the salmon in a stage of dying. Yukon. Makloksunuak=Kinakok, meaning the dog-salmon face [*kegginaquq*, "mask"]." [Fienup-Riordan 1996, 220]

IVA4412. "Men's dance mask representing a demon or spirit. . . . It is possible that this mask represents an ancestor since the mask shows the face of an ordinary human. Demons are usually depicted with an abhorrent face. Lower Yukon. Thunrak-Kinakok [*tuunraq kegginaquq*], meaning devil or spirit face."

IVA4416. "Mask depicting jellyfish, which often get stranded on the beach in fall . . . recognized by a cross running through the middle of their body. Yukon. Iggarnekrak=Kinakok [?*kegginaquq*, "mask"]." [Fienup-Riordan 1996, 63]

IVA4417. "Dance mask said to be the protective spirit of children, the lightning (therefore probably the cut-open face). The protective god of the children was called Slaowkmiu [*Ellam yua?*, "the Person of the Universe"], i.e., heaven, which they believe to be in the shape of this spirit or lightning. The back of the god is always cut open. Lower Yukon."

IVA4421. "Mask depicting a spirit living in the depths of the fresh water . . . still seen once in a while. Lower Yukon. Kookoak=Kinakok [*kegginaquq*, "mask"]."

IVA4423. "Mask representing a seal . . . but showing no similarity to a seal. But a spirit is allowed to have all kinds of faces and here as anywhere else: no rule without exception. Lower Yukon. Najekkok [*nayiruaq*, "pretend ringed seal"]."

IVA4424. "Mask exhibiting an evil spirit; almost the entire face is mouth, filled with teeth, and within the mouth there is a face. Lower Yukon."

IVA4425. "Dance mask painted blue. This color is rarely used for masks depicting a human face but more for masks showing animals and fish. Lower Yukon."

IVA4426. "Mask representing a mountain spirit who was very feared on the Yukon . . . shown with a round mouth with hair growing out of it. Lower Yukon. Ersinekat=Kinakut [*ircenrraq kegginaquq*, "mask of an extraordinary person"], meaning the fearful face."

IVA4427. "Mask representing a very feared mountain spirit living on the lower Yukon and doing a lot of harm to the people. Lower

Ivory plug to close the hole in a seal float. IVA4526

Yukon. Ersinekat=Kinakut? [*ircenrraq kegginaquq*, "mask of an extraordinary person"]."

IV A 4429. "Mask with two faces, one on the other. Lower Yukon."

IV A 4432. Large shaman mask used . . . to lure the salmon with magic to the Yukon River. This explains the four salmon [beside four holes] on the left and right side of the face that seem to look out of the mask. The mask supposedly shows the spirit of the salmon kin. Russian Mission."

IV A 4435. "Two dance masks symbolizing the sun (similar to the Bella-Coola and Kwakiutl, who claim their descent partly from the sun). The meaning was not fully explained due to my quick collecting and a bad interpreter. It could have to do with the return of the sun and the party as the Kwikpagemiuts hold a big celebration at the end of January and the beginning of February. Lower Yukon. Marsakoak [?]."

IV A 4436. "Dance mask symbolizing the spirit of halibut or similar fish. Lower Yukon. Nette=Kenarok=Kinakok [?*kegginaquq*, "mask"]."

IV A 4439. "Dance mask with movable mouth. Lower Yukon."

IV A 4441. "Dance mask with a movable lower jaw and strip of polar-bear skin. Lower Yukon. Kinakok [*kegginaquq*] meaning mask."

IV A 4442. "Mask, showing the face of a goddess or the wife of a renowned spirit. . . . The stripes on the chin are tattoo marks, always used among the northern Eskimo. Yukon. Thunrak=Arneit =Kinakut, Devil wife's face [*tuunraq ?arnaq kegginaquq*, "female helping spirit mask"]."

IV A 4443. "Mask said to depict the face of an inhabitant of Kotzebue Sound. It calls attention to the lip ornament, but it is difficult to say whether this is a caricature of a deceased Malemiut or the spirit of a deceased medicine man from this area, whose help should be [told] by a living descendant (having lived on the Yukon River). It is well known that shamans had spirits which belonged to deceased relatives. Lower Yukon. Malleme'unguak=Kinakok [?*mallemiuguak kegginaquq*, "pretend Malemiut mask"]."

IV A 4444. "Wife of a famous spirit . . . recognizable by the tattooed lines stretching from the corner of the mouth to the chin. Yukon. Thunrak=Argneit=Kinakut, meaning devil spirit's wife [*tuunraq arnaq kegginaquq*, "spirit woman mask"]."

IV A 4446. "Mask representing the spirit of the marten king. Lower Yukon. Imearmut=tak=roak [*imarmiutaguaq*, "pretend mink"]."

IV A 4448. "Mask symbolizing the wife of an evil spirit. The collective name is Thunerak=Arne or thunrak=Aggne Kinakut, meaning the devil's wife mask [*tuunraq arnaq kegginaquq*, "female helping spirit mask"]."

IV A 4449. "Mask showing a demon. Lower Yukon. Thunrak=Kinakok [*tuunraq kegginaquq*, "helping spirit mask"] meaning devil's face."

IV A 4450. "Dance mask symbolizing the fish otter. It probably represents the animal's spirit, . . . who takes on the animal's form. At the same time it is seen as the king of animals under whose special protection he is placed. Lower Yukon. Snikaroak=Kinakok [*senkaruaq kegginaquq*, "pretend land otter mask"]."

IV A 4452. "Mask symbolizing a big seal . . . [with] a face that indicates a spirit in seal form and not the actual seal. Lower Yukon. Maklak or Makklak [*maklak*, "bearded seal"]."

IV A 4454. "Mask representing the face of a Russian, done with a sense of humor typical for Eskimos. . . . The mask was made at a place where the Russians had a mission station for half a century, and where one finds that Christianity and shamanism peacefully coexisted. The representatives of each of these religions profited from one another. Russian Mission. Kassaroak=Kinakok [*kass'aruaq kegginaquq*, "pretend white person mask"] meaning the cossack's face."

IV A 4456. "Mask symbolizing a demon or spirit . . . with red mouth and many teeth. Yukon."

IV A 4457. "Mask representing a demon or mountain spirit. Lower Yukon."

IV A 4458. "Dance mask in form of a female face that shows tattoo marks in bluish vertical stripes on the chin . . . and a cut wound across the face. This person probably represents the wife of an evil spirit or the face of a long-dead medicine woman, and her descendants use her as a patron saint for curing. St. Michael. Thunrak=Nuleka [*tuunraq nulira*] meaning devil's wife."

IV A 4459. "Mask of legendary person. . . . The Eskimos portray all spirits with extraordinary teeth while humans are often shown with their lip ornament only. St. Michael. Angut=Kanekpalk, young man [*angun*, "man"]."

IV A 4462. "Mask depicting an Eskimo living at the [Russian] Mission in the olden days . . . and held in derision. Russian Mission. Hao=Angesak=Yum=Ajolotsia=Tamani [?], meaning Hoh=old one, everything is bad with her."

IV A 5148. "Shaman mask depicting a sea otter that is swallowing a fish. On its back, the otter carries the face of the shaman spirit (or the spirit of its true shape, who likes to assume the otter form). Cape Vancouver to Cape Avinoff. Anorallerek or Anurallerek [*arrnaruaq*, "pretend sea otter"]."

IV A 5149. "Mask with two faces and beads in its nose, kept in the house as a good-luck charm. Cape Vancouver. Arnarok [*arnaq*], woman."

IV A 5150. "Dance mask depicting an owl. Kuskokwim." [Fienup-Riordan 1996, 207]

IV A 5151. "Shaman's dance mask whose face is the spirit helper. The messenger of the medicine man takes the form of a diver [loon?] when the shaman sends it to reconnoiter. (It could also be the king of the diver serving the shaman.) Cape Vancouver." [Fienup-Riordan 1996, 69]

IV A 5152. "Small mask or child's mask, without attachment straps, likely left behind by a shaman as a cure. Resembles those masks used on the Yukon. It either represents a reindeer or a seagull. Kuskokwim. Kinakutt [*kegginaquq*] meaning face mask." [Fienup-Riordan 1996, 84]

IV A 5154. "Mask, the same as [IV A]5168 and [IV A]5165, belonging to a shaman and showing the king of the wolves. Kuskokwim. Kegelimoak [*keglunuaq*, "pretend wolf"]."

IV A 5155. "Mask depicting a human face with ears of a wolf. The whole could show a wolf. Kuskokwim River, Cape Vancouver."

IV A 5156. "Mask in the form of a human face with bird beak, wings, and legs. Kuskokwim."

IV A 5157. "Small owl-head dance mask. The Eskimos fear these animals. Kuskokwim." [Fienup-Riordan 1996, 63]

IV A 5158. "Small mask similar to shaman's masks with a walrus face, a reindeer on the right, and a seal on the left. Kuskokwim. Kinakutt [*kegginaquq*, "mask"]." [Fienup-Riordan 1996, 84]

IV A 5159. "Child's mask . . . similar to a shaman's mask [*nepcetaq*] found on the Yukon, the laughing gull (the shaman's messenger); only in this case the face color is slightly different. . . . The feathers and the holes are equal to [IV A]4455. Kuskokwim. Mekjeltingarorok [*mikelnguruaq*, "pretend child"]."

IV A 5160. "Miniature mask showing an evil spirit, which according to a Yukon legend pursues people to devour them. Its small, crooked mouth indicates its lust for human flesh and blood. Kuskokwim." [Fienup-Riordan 1996, 219]

IV A501. "Small dance mask (children's mask?) that probably depicts the king of whales . . . painted white in former times. Kuskokwim."

IV A502. "Dance mask depicting an evil spirit; a mouth studded with teeth . . . runs across the nose from one ear to the other. Kuskokwim."

IV A505. "Shaman's dance mask? depicting a wolf's head. Lower Kuskokwim. Kegelungoak [*keglunuaq*, "pretend wolf"]."

IV A506. "Mask with movable mouth and small, monkeylike face. . . . Similar masks were used by messengers who invited people to the party and symbolized that the guest should bring a healthy appetite, therefore the movable mouth. Kuskokwim."

IV A508. "Mask with a big face and mouth . . . representing a wolf. Kuskokwim. Kegelunoak [*keglunuaq*, "pretend wolf"]."

IV A571. "Mask representing a seagull . . . well suited as a shaman's messenger [and] used particularly to locate the sea animals. Cape Vancouver." [Fienup-Riordan 1996, 159]

IV A573. "Little dance mask depicting a fox? Kuskokwim."

IV A574. "Dance mask representing a woman's face. Kuskokwim."

IV A575. "Mask representing a spirit that protects children on the Yukon, and is thus thought of as a child's god. A mouth fitted with teeth runs the length of the mask. Kuskokwim."

IV A582. "Mask with four lampposts. Young people use a similar mask when the time between the festivals seems too long. They place the masks on bowls or upon another utensil belonging to the festival and dance with it. Cape Vancouver." [Fienup-Riordan 1996, 222]

IV A5183. "Mask representing a woman with pierced nose and holes in the lower lip as is the custom in the area. Kuskokwim."

IV A5184. "Dance mask representing a spirit or demon with half-closed eyes. Kuskokwim."

IV A5185. "Dance mask with pierced nostrils and three holes in the lower lip, which indicate a woman. Kuskokwim. Nulika=Kinakok, woman's face [?*nulira kegginaquq*, "wife mask"]."

IV A5187. "Mask representing the king of seals or its spirit. Kuskokwim."

IV A5188. "Mask with upper part representing a person with earrings like those the Ingalik put on their masks and the lower part an animal head. Upper Kuskokwim."

IV A5189. "Red-painted dance mask . . . that appears to be a caricature that may once have had a movable mouth. Kuskokwim."

IV A5191. "Peculiar face mask, likely to portray a monster. The mask seems to have been white . . . [and] is covered with reindeer hair. Kuskokwim. Kinakutt [*kegginaquq*], meaning mask."

IV A5192. "Small mask portrays the face of the king of seals. Kuskokwim."

IV A5195. "Mask portraying a duck or diving bird . . . probably without religious meaning. Kuskokwim."

IV A5196. "Mask with movable mouth. Kuskokwim."

IV A7187. "Little dance mask in the shape of a walrus. Kuskokwim."

IV A7188. "Little wooden dance mask. Kuskokwim."

IV A7189. "Children's dance mask. Kuskokwim."

IV A7236. "Dance mask, man with two labrets. Yukon."

IV A7238. "Dance mask, fish. Yukon."

NOTES

Notes include three kinds of information.

First are references to published literature cited by author, publication date, and page number, with complete publication information contained in the References.

Second are references to archival sources such as correspondence, journals, reports, and unpublished manuscripts, which are cited by place where the correspondence originated, author's name to recipient's name, correspondence date, and location of the document—in either the Ethnologisches Museum Berlin (EMB) or the Museum für Völkerkunde Hamburg Archive (HA).

Third, notes for *The Return Gift* contain parenthetical information useful to the specialist, including museum accession numbers (preceded by the abbreviation IVA—IV for North America and A for the Arctic and Northwest Coast) of all objects the elders examined, the area from which Jacobsen collected the objects—Yukon, Kuskokwim, Cape Vancouver (Nelson Island), and Nushagak—and the names, capitalized and in quotation marks, that Jacobsen recorded for the objects. During our work, elders often examined objects in groups. For example, when we looked at small barbed harpoon points, all twenty-seven points Jacobsen had collected were spread out for comment, and one endnote records accession numbers for each. As elders worked through the collection (and readers through this book), they encountered every Yup'ik object in Jacobsen's collection. The several dozen objects that drew no comment are also listed in endnotes to provide a complete list of the collection.

Finally, endnotes immediately following the introduction of an object type include cross references to E. W. Nelson's description of similar objects collected from the same area during the four years prior to Jacobsen's arrival.

PREFACE

1. Thode-Arora 1989, 52.
2. Bolz and Sanner 1999, 40–42; Höpfner 1995.
3. Bolz and Sanner 1999, 40–42; Höpfner 1995.

Nushagak ornament made of beads, box covers, and pieces of an old lamp, worn by a woman over her parka and around her neck during dances. IVA 6390.

4. Cole 1985, 324; Corey 1987, 33; Ray 1987, 33; Westphal-Hellbusch 1973.
5. Bolz and Sanner 1999, 45–49; Höpfner 1995. The Native American department received a total of 9,000 objects, including most of its missing South American items. An accurate account of which objects went where following the war is not possible. Pieces have returned from unexpected places, while others have not come back at all. Some objects that were moved out of the museum for safekeeping were destroyed, while others that were left in the museum basement survived. Where the objects went can often be determined only by their return route, as few records have survived.
6. Dissellhoff 1935, 1936; Fienup-Riordan 1996, 216–26; Hipszer 1971.
7. Fienup-Riordan 1996, 23–30.
8. Godelier 1999, 15, in Smith 2002, 60; Mauss [1925] 1967.
9. Fienup-Riordan 1983.
10. Jacobsen [1884] 1977.
11. Nelson 1899, 44–50.
12. For insights into the ways in which Yup'ik protocols affected our work in collections, see the last chapter, "Visual Repatriation."
13. Ames 1992; Kahn 2000, 72.
14. Sahlins 1999, 407.
15. Cruikshank 1998, 163.
16. Clifford 1988; Clifford and Marcus 1986; Conklin 1997; Cruikshank 1998; Sahlins 1995, 2000.
17. Myers 1994, 679.
18. Cruikshank 1998, 140, 162.
19. Sahlins 1995, 14, 71.

THE GIFT

1. Jacobsen 1931; [1884] 1977, 216, 217. "If one is accustomed to the outdoors and from childhood has experienced wind and weather, these adventures are not injurious to one's health . . . ; my European home lies about twenty English miles north of Fort Saint Michael in latitude and the weather is much the same" (Jacobsen [1884] 1977, 117).
2. Jacobsen 1931; [1884] 1977, 216–18.
3. Cole 1985, 59; Jacobsen 1931; [1884] 1977, 220.
4. Jacobsen 1931; [1884] 1977, 221.
5. Jacobsen [1884] 1977, 221–22.

6. Jacobsen 1931; [1884] 1977, 222–23; "A Sailor's Life," no date, Hamburg Archives (HA).

7. Hamburg, Hagenbeck to Jacobsen, November 9, 1880, HA; Hamburg, Hagenbeck to Jacobsen, January 16, 1881, HA; Berlin, Bastian to Jacobsen, January 20, 1881, Ethnologisches Museum Berlin (EMB); Haberland 1987, 337; Jacobsen [1884] 1977, 223; Taylor 1981. Although Jacobsen described the trip to Labrador and his subsequent work for Bastian in both *The White Frontier* (1931) and an earlier manuscript, "A Sailor's Life" (no date, page 4), in the Hamburg Archives, neither directly discuss the Eskimos' death.

8. Berlin, Bastian to Jacobsen, October 23, 1880, HA; Berlin, Bauer to Jacobsen, November 13, 1880, HA; Berlin, Bauer to Bastian, March 27, 1881, EMB; Berlin, Bastian to Jacobsen, March 1881, HA.

9. Jacobsen, "A Sailor's Life," no date, 33, HA.

10. Berlin, Bastian to unnamed man, written in Russian, November 1884, EMB; Bastian, circular, February 15, 1900, EMB; Cole 1985, 56.

11. Location unknown, Bastian, letter draft, 1881, EMB; Jacobsen [1884] 1977, ix.

12. Berlin, Bastian, letter, 1881, EMB; Bolz and Sanner 1999, 29–31; Cole 1985, 58.

13. Berlin, Bastian, letter, 1881, EMB; Cole 1985, 48, 57.

14. Berlin, Bastian, Report to the General Administration of the Royal Museum, April 1, 1884, EMB; Berlin, Bastian, undated letter, EMB.

15. Berlin, Bastian to Jacobsen, March 1881, HA; Darmstadt, Le Coq to Bastian, May 16, 1881, EMB; Darmstadt, Le Coq to Bastian, May 22, 1881, EMB.

16. Darmstadt, Le Coq to Bastian, May 28, 1881, EMB; Bad Soden, Emil Hecker to Bastian, June 3, 1881, EMB; Darmstadt, Le Coq to Hecker, June 10, 1881, EMB.

17. Berlin, Richter to Bastian, July 26, 1881, EMB. The Support Committee remained active until 1925. During that time, it provided funds for dozens of expeditions, the first three by Jacobsen. The museum staff asked the committee's assistance only when an expedition or purchase would be approved by the general administration and the advisory board, but no funds were available in advance (Westphal-Hellbusch 1973, 65–68).

18. Berlin, Bastian, Report to the General Administration of the Royal Museum, April 1, 1884, EMB; Hamburg, Jacobsen to Bastian, July 15, 1881, EMB; Jacobsen, "A Sailor's Life," no date, 4, HA; Jacobsen 1883, 525.

19. Place and group names have been standardized throughout this discussion to avoid the confusions that Jacobsen's multiple creative variations would engender.

20. Toronto, Consulate of the German Empire to Jacobsen, August 24, 1881, HA; San Francisco, Jacobsen to Bastian, August 28, 1881, EMB; Berlin, Bastian to Jacobsen, September 9, 1881, HA; Jacobsen [1884] 1977, 3, 43. In Alaska, letters were also sent with him from post to post, introducing him as a "man of science" (Kodiak, Ivan Petroff to Major Wm. Governour Morris, July 13, 1883, HA) and "a gentleman collecting for the German government" (Kasilof, Mr. Kendall to Mr. Cutting, January 7, 1883, HA); Berlin, Bastian to Jacobsen, December 1, 1881, HA; Berlin, Richter to the Hudson's Bay Company's Victoria office, March 3, 1882, EMB.

21. Location unknown, Jacobsen to Bastian, 1881, EMB; Masset, Queen Charlotte Islands, Alexander Mackenzie to Jacobsen, October 3, 1882, HA; Port Essington, Jacobsen to Bastian, September 18, 1881, EMB; Jacobsen [1884] 1977, 1, 3, 12.

22. Port Essington, Jacobsen to Richter, September 18, 1881, EMB; location unknown, Jacobsen to Bastian, 1882, EMB; Skidgate, Jacobsen to Bastian, October 4, 1881, EMB. The purchase of duplicates characterized Jacobsen's Alaska collecting as well. The Royal Museum later traded many duplicates to other museums, and as a result Jacobsen material is spread worldwide.

23. Port Essington, Jacobsen to Bastian, September 18, 1881, EMB; Skidgate, Jacobsen to Bastian, October 4, 1881, EMB; Jacobsen [1884] 1977, x, 35, 40, 48.

24. San Francisco, Jacobsen to Bastian, May 27, 1882, EMB; Jacobsen [1884] 1977, 22–24, 27–28, 32.

25. St. Michael, Jacobsen to Bastian, January 20, 1882, EMB; Jacobsen [1884] 1977, 33, 38.

26. Jacobsen [1884] 1977, 50, 53.

27. Port Essington, Jacobsen to Hagenbeck, September 18, 1881, HA.

28. Berlin, Ethnological Department of the Royal Museum, draft letter, January 9, 1885, EMB; Cole 1985, 64; Jacobsen [1884] 1977, 9.

29. Fort Rupert, Jacobsen to Bastian, May 5, 1882, EMB.

30. Victoria, Jacobsen to Hagenbeck, November 3, 1881, HA.

31. Berlin, Richter to Jacobsen, January 18, 1882, HA; Hamburg, Hagenbeck to Jacobsen, November 26, 1882, HA; Victoria, William Charles, Hudson's Bay Company, to Bastian, December 13, 1882, EMB.

32. Jacobsen met one trader from Alaska who boasted that fifteen years before, one could load a whole schooner full of collectibles for $100.

33. Berlin, Bastian to Jacobsen, December 8, 1881, HA; location unknown, Jacobsen to Bastian, January 20, 1882, EMB; Victoria, Jacobsen to Bastian, January 24, 1882, EMB.

34. Victoria, Jacobsen to Bastian, January 24, 1882, EMB; San Francisco, Jacobsen to Bastian, February 7, 1882, EMB.

35. Hamburg, Hagenbeck to Jacobsen, December 2, 1881, HA; Berlin, Bastian to Jacobsen, January 3, 1882, HA; Hamburg, Hagenbeck to Jacobsen, January 5, 1882, HA; Berlin, Richter to Jacobsen, January 18, 1882, HA; Hamburg, Hagenbeck to Jacobsen, 1882, HA.

36. Victoria, Jacobsen to Hagenbeck, November 3, 1881, HA; Hamburg, Hagenbeck to Jacobsen, telegram care of Gutte and Frank, March 17, 1882, HA; Hamburg, Hagenbeck to Jacobsen, March 17, 1882, HA; Hamburg, Hagenbeck to Bastian, March 23, 1882, HA. In his letter to Bastian, Hagenbeck directly referred to the unhappy parallel between these tragic losses: "These misfortunes vividly remind me of the sad fate of the Eskimos and have brought me to the resolve to give up the import of alien tribes in the future."

37. Berlin, Bastian to Jacobsen, February (1?), 1882, HA; Berlin, Bastian to Jacobsen, March 1882, HA.

38. Victoria, Jacobsen to Bastian, April 30, 1882, EMB; San Francisco, Jacobsen to Bastian, May 27, 1882, EMB.

39. San Francisco, Jacobsen to Bastian, June 1, 1882, EMB.

40. Unalaska, Jacobsen to Bastian, July 17, 1882, EMB; Jacobsen [1884] 1977, 80, 82–83.

41. St. Michael, Jacobsen to Bastian, August 1, 1882, EMB.

42. St. Michael, Jacobsen to Bastian, July 30, 1882, EMB.

43. St. Michael, Edward Nelson, December 26, 1878, National Museum of Natural History, Smithsonian Institution. This letter indicates that Nelson had a collecting allowance of $500 as well as $250 for rations. (William Fitzhugh, personal communication, 2001.)

44. Jacobsen [1884] 1977, 86, 87.

45. St. Michael, Jacobsen to Bastian, August 18, 1882, EMB.

46. Jacobsen, journal, August 13, 1882, HA; Jacobsen [1884] 1977, 9, 91, 96, 103.

Jacobsen, journal, August 16, 1882, HA; journal, August 25, 1882, HA; Jacobsen [1884] 1977, 98, 100.

Jacobsen, journal, September 2, 1882, HA; Jacobsen [1884] 1977, 107.

Jacobsen, journal, September 7, 1882, HA; Jacobsen [1884] 1977, 105.

Jacobsen [1884] 1977, 109, 112.

Jacobsen, journal, September 8, 1882, HA; Jacobsen [1884] 1977, 111.

Jacobsen, journal, September 10, 1882, HA; Jacobsen [1884] 1977, 116, 117, 119.

St. Michael, Jacobsen to Bastian, August 18, 1882, EMB; Jacobsen [1884] 1977, 113.

Jacobsen, journal, September 16, 1882, HA; journal, December 16, 1882, HA; Jacobsen [1884] 1977, 91.

Jacobsen [1884] 1977, 114–16.

St. Michael, Jacobsen to Bastian, March 15, 1883, EMB; Jacobsen [1884] 1977, 118.

St. Michael, Jacobsen to Bastian, March 15, 1883, EMB; Jacobsen [1884] 1977, 146.

Jacobsen, journal, October 31, 1882, HA; journal, November 22, 1882, HA; journal, November 26, 1882, HA—Jacobsen observed a shaman healing ceremony; see also Jacobsen [1884] 1977, 135, 149; Nelson 1899, 363ff.

Jacobsen [1884] 1977; Nelson 1899.

Jacobsen, journal, November 17, 1882, HA; journal, November 18, 1882, HA; journal, December 2, 1882, HA; journal, December 5, 1882, HA; journal, January 14, 1883, HA. Jacobsen's complaints contrast remarks by some other non-Native travelers in the region. For example, the voluminous journal accounts that Moravian missionary John Henry Kilbuck wrote, beginning in 1885, about his travels on the lower Bering Sea coast rarely express such annoyance (Fienup-Riordan 1988). This may in part reflect their different objectives—saving souls rather than acquiring artifacts, and seeking to give service rather than expecting to receive it.

Jacobsen, journal, February 12, 1883, HA; Jacobsen [1884] 1977, 156, 158, 190.

The use of needles and other sharp tools by relatives of the deceased was proscribed lest they interfere with the deceased's journey to the land of the dead.

Jacobsen [1884] 1977, 141, 143, 164.

Jacobsen, journal, October 20, 1882, HA; Jacobsen [1884] 1977, 123–24.

Jacobsen, journal, December 24, 1882, HA.

St. Michael, Jacobsen to Bastian, March 15, 1883; Jacobsen, journal, January 30, January 31, and February 3, 1883, HA. Jacobsen ([1884] 1977, 156, 159) reiterates these complaints. Woolfe shared Jacobsen's frustrations, and in a letter to Jacobsen from "No Place, Alaska" (December 25, 1882, HA) complained that the locals had "played hell with our things during our absence. Eaten bacon, *my* crackers, and actually traded off my 2 bags flour. . . . I am so *disgusted* with the damn crowd."

Jacobsen, journal, February 5, 1883, HA; Jacobsen [1884] 1977, 159.

Jacobsen, journal, February 9, 1883, HA; Jacobsen [1884] 1977, 162.

Jacobsen, journal, December 1, 1882, and January 25, 1883, HA; St. Michael, Jacobsen to Bastian, March 15, 1883, EMB.

Berlin, Bastian to Jacobsen, September 15, 1883, HA; Jacobsen [1884] 1977, 167; Jacobsen 1931; Jacobsen, "Lecture: Travels in Alaska before the Discovery of Gold," no date, handwritten manuscript, 39 pages, HA.

71. St. Michael, Jacobsen to Bastian, March 15, 1883, EMB.

72. Kuskokwim River, Jacobsen to Bastian, April 17, 1883, EMB; Jacobsen [1884] 1977, 167–68.

73. Jacobsen, journal, March 20, 1883, HA; Nushagak, Jacobsen to Bastian, May 1883, EMB; Jacobsen [1884] 1977, 171, 175.

74. Jacobsen, journal, March 20 and 22, 1883, HA; Jacobsen [1884] 1977, 170.

75. Jacobsen, journal, April 2 and 3, 1883, HA; Jacobsen [1884] 1977, 174.

76. Jacobsen, journal, April 3 and 5, 1883, HA; Jacobsen [1884] 1977, 175; see also Fienup-Riordan 1994, 220–24.

77. Jacobsen, journal, April 6 and 7, 1883, HA.

78. Jacobsen, journal, April 9, 10, and 12, 1883, HA. Jacobsen's published accounts ([1884] 1977, 179; 1924–25b, 72) make no reference to this incident.

79. Jacobsen, journal, April 15, 1883, HA; Jacobsen [1884] 1977, 179; Jacobsen 1924–25b, 74.

80. Jacobsen, journal, April 15 and 17, 1883, HA; Jacobsen [1884] 1977, 180, 181.

81. Jacobsen, journal, April 23 and 24, 1883, HA; Jacobsen [1884] 1977, 181, 185.

82. Jacobsen, journal, April 27, 1883, HA; Jacobsen [1884] 1977, 185.

83. Nushagak, Jacobsen to Bastian, May, 1883, EMB; Jacobsen, journal, May 1, 1883, HA.

84. Nushagak, Jacobsen to Bastian, May 1883, EMB; Nushagak, Jacobsen to Bastian, undated letter in one of the boxes sent from Nushagak, EMB.

85. Nushagak, Jacobsen to Bastian, undated letter, EMB; Jacobsen, journal, May 19 and 29, 1883, HA; journal, June 6, 1883, HA; Jacobsen [1884] 1977, 188, 190.

86. St. Paul, Jacobsen to Bastian, July 11, 1883, EMB; Jacobsen, journal, May 5 and 20, 1883, HA. Compare Jacobsen's outburst with his mild published description (Jacobsen [1884] 1977, 195).

87. Jacobsen, journal, June 27 and July 7, 1883, HA; St. Paul, Jacobsen to Bastian, July 11, 1883, EMB; Jacobsen [1884] 1977, 226.

88. St. Paul, Jacobsen to Bastian, July 11, 1883, EMB; San Francisco, Jacobsen to Bastian, October 8, 1883, EMB; Jacobsen, journal, July 27 and 28, 1883, HA; Jacobsen [1884] 1977, 201, 204.

89. Jacobsen, journal, August 18 and 28, 1883, HA; Berlin, Bastian to Jacobsen, September 15, 1883, HA.

90. San Francisco, Jacobsen to Bastian, October 8, 1883, EMB; St. Louis, Jacobsen to Bastian, October 25, 1883, EMB; Jacobsen [1884] 1977, 213.

91. Nushagak, Jacobsen to Bastian, May 1883, EMB; St. Paul, Jacobsen to Bastian, July 11, 1883, EMB; Jacobsen, journal, October 27–29, 1883, HA.

92. Berlin, Bastian to the manager of the Alaska Commercial Company in Sitka, August 8, 1883, EMB; Berlin, Richter to Bastian, August 17, 1883, EMB; Hamburg, Hagenbeck to Jacobsen, September 6, 1883, HA; Berlin, Richter to Jacobsen, September 11, 1883, HA; Berlin, Bastian to Jacobsen, October 29, 1883, HA; Berlin, hectographed copy of unaddressed, unsigned letter, December 1, 1883, EMB.

93. Berlin, Bastian to Jacobsen, October 29, 1883, HA; Berlin, Bastian to Jacobsen, telegram c/o Hagenbeck in Hamburg, November 22, 1883, HA; Berlin, Richter to Jacobsen, December 17, 1883, HA.

94. Berlin, Bastian to the General Administration of the Royal Museum, December 1, 1883, EMB; Berlin, hectographed copy of un-

addressed, unsigned letter, December 1, 1883, EMB; Bastian, et al., 1883; Berlin, Bastian to the General Administration of the Royal Museum, March 24, 1884, EMB; Berlin, Bastian to O. T. Mason, April 11, 1889, EMB. Reviews of Bastian's book on the Northwest Coast collection also generally praise Jacobsen's collecting efforts, the selfless work of the Support Committee, and Bastian's expeditious publication of the material, reiterating Bastian's admonitions to hurry and collect before it is too late.

95. Berlin, Bastian to unnamed man, undated draft letter, EMB; Berlin, Bastian to Le Coq, December 1893?, EMB; Pasadena, California, von den Steinen to Weisbach, April 18, 1898, EMB. Although the Support Committee was generally praised, only Richter (the committee's chairman) was formally decorated by the Prussian government for services to the museum, receiving the Order of the Red Eagle. This caused Bastian some embarrassment, as Le Coq had hinted to Dotti, who contributed the most toward Jacobsen's trip, that he would receive a decoration. Bastian pled unsuccessfully on Dotti's behalf, noting that he avoided Le Coq in the street for shame (Berlin, Bastian to the General Administration of the Royal Museum, December 11, 1884, EMB; Berlin, Ministerium der geistlichen, Unterrichts- und Medicinal-Angelegenheiten [Ministry of Religious, Educational, and Medical Affairs], October 9, 1885, EMB; Berlin, Le Coq to Bastian, July 18, 1891, EMB; Berlin, Bastian, report to the General Administration of the Royal Museum, July 30, 1891, EMB; Berlin, Ministry of Education and Health to the General Administration of the Royal Museum, October 21, 1891, EMB).

96. Bolz 1996; Woldt 1884 (March 21). Other articles in this issue of Scientific Correspondence deal with the death of a geographer in Gotha, the liquefaction of hydrogen, observation of a white rainbow, and research on the physical properties of small planets.

97. Berlin, Jacobsen to Hedwig Klopfer, March 30, 1884, HA; Berlin, Ministerium der geistlichen, Unterrrichts- und Medicinal-Angelegenheiten to the General Administration of the Royal Museum, December 10, 1884, EMB; Cole 1985, 66; Jacobsen [1884] 1977, 213.

98. Breslau, Andreas Arzruni to Bastian, November 16, 1883, EMB; Breslau, Arzruni to Bastian, November 26, 1883, EMB; Dresden, A. B. Meyer, director of the Anthropological-Ethnological Museum, to Jacobsen, December 11, 1883, HA; Berlin, Jacobsen to Hofrath, December 19, 1883, EMB; Arzruni 1883a, 1883b; Jacobsen 1891a, 314–17.

99. Berlin, Bastian to Hermann Costenoble, February 1884?, EMB; Berlin, Bastian to an unknown person, letter draft, no date, EMB.

100. Leipzig, Max Spohr to Jacobsen, February 2, 1884, EMB; Jena, Hermann Costenoble to Jacobsen, February 2, 1884, HA; Leipzig, Spohr to Bastian, March 4, 1884, EMB; Berlin, Bastian to Spohr, no date, EMB.

101. Berlin, Jacobsen to Klopfer, January 3 and 14, 1884, HA.

102. Berlin, Jacobsen to Klopfer, January 18, 1884, HA; Berlin, Jacobsen to Klopfer, February 18, 23, and 27, 1884, HA; Berlin, Letter of Agreement signed by Woldt and Jacobsen, March 4, 1884, EMB; Leipzig, Spohr to Bastian, March 17, 1884, EMB; Berlin, Jacobsen to Bastian, May 16, 1884, EMB.

103. Berlin, Woldt to Bastian, January 27, 1884, EMB; Berlin, Jacobsen to Klopfer, March 9, 1884, HA; Leipzig, Spohr to Bastian, March 17, 1884, EMB; Berlin, Jacobsen to Klopfer, April 19, 1884, HA; Berlin, L. von der Vecht to Jacobsen, May 10, 1884, HA; Berlin, Woldt to Jacobsen, June 14, 1884, HA.

104. Berlin, Woldt to Jacobsen, July 24, 1884, HA; Leipzig, Spohr to Bastian, January 5, 1885, EMB; Berlin, Woldt to Jacobsen, September 8, 1885, HA; Leipzig, Spohr to Jacobsen, March 15, 1886, HA; Leipzig, Spohr to Jacobsen, August 12, 1886, HA; St. Michael, Neumann to Jacobsen, August 25, 1886, HA; Leipzig, Spohr to Jacobsen, May 3, 1887, HA. Although Jacobsen later made efforts to publish translations of his work in England and Norway, nothing came of them.

105. Jacobsen [1884] 1977.

106. A few objects still bear the original cardboard labels.

107. Jacobsen [1884] 1977, 170.

108. Berlin, Bastian to Powell, July 20, 1881, EMB; Masset, Queen Charlotte Islands, Mackenzie to Jacobsen, October 3, 1882, EMB.

109. Franz Boas, unidentified journal, November 1887, 368, edited by Dr. N. Kiepert, EMB; Jacobsen 1891c, 386; Thode-Arora 1989, 52. In an 1886 letter to his colleague Felix von Luschan, Boas wrote from Vancouver Island: "Heaven forgive the sins committed by earlier collectors. The masks, when their stories are not simultaneously collected here, will remain for the most part forever incomprehensible" (Bolz and Sanner 1999, 183; Kasten 1992, 82).

110. Düsseldorf, Bauer to Jacobsen, March 27, 1881, HA.

111. Haberland 1987, 370.

112. Dresden, Meyer to Jacobsen, December 11, 1883, HA.

113. Hamburg, Henny to Jacobsen, July 27, 1885?, HA.

114. St. Michael, Neumann to Jacobsen, November 29, 1882, HA; St. Michael, Neumann to Jacobsen, January 3, 1883, HA; San Francisco, Maria Langrehr to Jacobsen, October 25, 1883, HA; San Francisco, Langrehr to Jacobsen, October 25, 1883, HA.

115. Berlin, Jacobsen to Klopfer, December 9, 1883, HA.

116. Dresden, Klopfer to Jacobsen, December 10, 1883, HA; Berlin, Jacobsen to Klopfer, December 20, 1883, HA; Berlin, Jacobsen to Klopfer, February 17, 1884, HA.

117. Dresden, Klopfer to Jacobsen, December 10, 1883, HA; Berlin, Jacobsen to Klopfer, December 21, 1883, HA. A year later he "reassured" Hedwig that he remained true: "When I am traveling I have lots of other things to think of besides courting womenfolk, I only do that when I have nothing better to do because I can never be without occupation" (Nikolaevesk, Jacobsen to Klopfer, October 3, 1884, HA).

118. Dresden, Klopfer to Jacobsen, December 22, 1883, HA; Hamburg, Jacobsen to Klopfer, December 28, 1883, HA; Berlin, Jacobsen to Klopfer, March 25, 1884, HA; Jacobsen [1884] 1977.

119. Berlin, Jacobsen to Klopfer, December 15, 20, and 28, 1883, HA; Hamburg, Hagenbeck to Jacobsen, December 20, 1883, HA.

120. Hamburg, Hagenbeck to Jacobsen, September 6, 1883, HA; Hamburg, Hagenbeck to Jacobsen, November 28, 1883, HA; Hamburg, Hagenbeck to Jacobsen, December 20, 1883, HA; Berlin, Bastian to the Support Committee, February 18, 1884, EMB.

121. San Francisco, Woolfe to Jacobsen, December 11, 1883, HA; San Francisco, Woolfe to Jacobsen, January 29, 1884, HA; Point Hope, Woolfe to Jacobsen, July 24, 1884, HA.

122. San Francisco, Max Heilbronner, Alaska Commercial Company, to Jacobsen, February 14, 1884, HA; Berlin, Jacobsen to Klopfer, February 17, 18, and 23, 1884, HA; Berlin, Jacobsen to Klopfer, March 30, 1884, HA; Berlin, Jacobsen to Klopfer, April 8, 1884, HA.

123. Berlin, Jacobsen to Klopfer, April 19 and 22, 1884, HA; Westphal-Hellbusch 1973, 13.

124. Berlin, Richter to Bastian, May 6, 1884, EMB; Berlin, minutes of meeting of the Support Committee, May 12, 1884, EMB; Berlin, Jacobsen to Klopfer, May 12, 1884, HA; Alert Bay, Fillip Jacobsen to Johan Adrian Jacobsen, in Norwegian, August 14, 1884, HA; Haberland 1989, 337.

25. Berlin, Bastian to Jacobsen, July 10, 1884, HA; Lake Baikal, Jacobsen to Klopfer, August 15, 1884, HA.

26. Berlin, Bastian to Jacobsen, July 10, 1884, HA; Nikolaevsk, Jacobsen to Bastian, October 3, 1884, HA; Berlin, Krause to Jacobsen, April 1885, HA.

27. Kazan, Jacobsen to Bastian, June 20, 1884, EMB.

28. Berlin, Bastian to Jacobsen, December 12, 1884, EMB; Yokohama, Jacobsen to Klopfer, May 8, 1885, HA; Jacobsen 1931.

29. Biisk, Jacobsen to Bastian, July 17, 1884, EMB; Tomsk, Jacobsen to Bastian, July 27, 1884, EMB; Nikolaevsk, Jacobsen to Bastian, October 4, 1884, EMB; Nikolaevsk, Jacobsen to Bastian, January 31, 1885, EMB.

30. Victoria, Jacobsen to Klopfer, July 22, 1885, HA; Cole 1985, 67; Haberland 1989, 338–40.

31. Hamburg, Hagenbeck to Jacobsen, July 2, 1885, HA.

32. Haberland 1987, 343, 345–46, 353.

33. Dresden, Jacobsen to Bastian, October 21, 1885, EMB; Breslau, Jacobsen to Bastian, February 21, 1886, EMB; location unknown, Jacobsen to Hedwig, June 8, 1886, HA; location unknown, Jacobsen to Hedwig, July 18, 1886, HA; Cole 1985, 71; Haberland 1987, 356, 361, 368.

34. Location unknown, Jacobsen to Hedwig, July 1, 1886, HA; Cole 1985, 71; Haberland 1987, 361, 368, 370.

35. Leipzig, Jacobsen to Bastian, October 13, 1885, EMB; Hamburg, Jacobsen to Bastian, June 2, 1886, EMB; Berlin, Bastian to Jacobsen, June 8, 1886, HA; Gerhard 1992.

36. Köln (Cologne), Jacobsen to Hedwig, June 10, 1886, HA; Elberfeld, Jacobsen to Hedwig, July 3, 1886, HA; Elberfeld, Jacobsen to Bastian, July 8, 1886, EMB.

37. In a letter to Bastian (July 27, 1897, EMB), Karl von den Steinen would later write: "I visited the west coast of Vancouver from Victoria, was a guest of Fillip Jacobsen in Clayoquot. . . . [He] has been collecting for years, actually at Boas' stimulation, who fortunately has been unable to pay up to now, so that Jacobsen felt free to let me choose at will. I think I obtained a valuable completion of the Berlin material. . . . F. Jacobsen is very intelligent, devoted to the cause whole-heartedly and will hopefully be used more, but he did not know himself what he possessed." Hamburg, Henny to Hedwig and Adrian, July 27, 1886, HA; Dresden, I.O.U. between Jacobsen and Emil Hugo Klopfer, October 1886, HA; Dresden, Jacobsen to Bastian, November 5, 1886, EMB; Filip Jacobsen 1891.

38. Christiania (Oslo), Jacobsen to Hedwig, May 23, 1886, HA; Berlin, Bastian to Jacobsen, November 1886?, HA; Hamburg, Hagenbeck to Jacobsen, March 22, 1887, HA; San Francisco, Frank to Jacobsen, April 23, 1887, HA; Limburg, J. Menges to Jacobsen, January 11, 1891, HA.

39. Berlin, Bastian to Jacobsen, April 28, 1887, HA; Berlin, Jacobsen to Hedwig, September 5, 1887, HA.

140. Dresden, Hedwig to Jacobsen, September 5, 1887, HA; Dresden, Hedwig to Jacobsen, September 12, 1887, HA.

141. Singapore, Jacobsen to Hedwig, November 11, 1887, HA.

142. Location unknown, Jacobsen to Hedwig, 1887–1888, HA; Jacobsen, "A Sailor's Life," no date, handwritten manuscript, HA; Janssen 1931.

143. Berlin, Bastian to Jacobsen, November 1, 1888, HA; Berlin, *Globus* to Jacobsen, November 23, 1888, HA; Berlin, Westermann to Jacobsen, November 27, 1888, HA.

144. Berlin, Bastian to Jacobsen, February 19, 1889, HA; Berlin, Jacobsen to Hedwig, March 1, 1889, HA; Berlin, Jacobsen to Hedwig, March 9, 1889, HA.

145. Berlin, Jacobsen to Hedwig, April 26, 1889, HA; Dresden, Jacobsen to Hedwig, July 8, 1889, HA.

146. Aachen, James Dodd to Jacobsen, August 4, 1889, HA; Stockholm, Jacobsen to Hedwig, October 19, 1889, HA; Berlin, reference letter for Jacobsen from Virchow, Dr. Ulrich Jahn, and Schonlaus, October 1, 1890, HA; Heidelberg, Dr. Richard Andree, editor of *Globus*, to Jacobsen, December 14, 1890, HA; Limburg, J. Menges to Jacobsen, January 11, 1891, HA; Janssen 1931.

147. Köln (Cologne), Directorial Board of the Exhibit Park, Kaisergarten, to Jacobsen, contract, April 1891, HA; Marburg, Karl von den Steinen to Jacobsen, May 28, 1891, HA; Janssen 1931.

148. Berlin, Jacobsen to Mr. Bull, National Ethnographiske Forening, March 1892, HA.

149. Bergen, Bull to Jacobsen, May 5, 1892, HA; Trondheim, Jacobsen to Hedwig, September 1, 1892; Odalen, Jacobsen to Hedwig, September 19, 1892, HA; Bergen, Jacobsen to Hedwig, October 10, 1892, HA.

150. Jacobsen 1883.

151. Berlin, Woldt to Jacobsen, December 31, 1885, HA; Halle, Otto Genest to Jacobsen, May 13, 1886, HA; Halle, Genest to Jacobsen, September 3, 1886, HA; Halle, Genest to Bastian, September 26, 1886, HA; Leipzig, Spohr to Jacobsen, October 12, 1886, HA; Halle, Genest to Jacobsen, May 16, 1887, HA; Genest 1887a, 1887b, 1887c, 1887d, 1890.

152. Jacobsen 1889; 1890a; 1890b; 1890c; 1890d; 1890e; 1890f; 1891a; 1891b; 1891c; 1891d; 1891e; 1891f; 1891g; 1891h; 1892a; 1892b; 1892c; 1894a; 1894b; 1896.

153. Drawer: Korrigierte und abgedruckte Manuskripte ethnographischen Inhalts ("Corrected and Published Manuscripts of Ethnographic Content"), envelope inscribed in Jacobsen's hand: Plane zum Artickeln, Skitzen ("Plans for Articles, Drafts"), HA; Marburg, von den Steinen to Jacobsen, February 1, 1890, HA; Marburg, von den Steinen to Jacobsen, February 9, 1890, HA.

154. Corrected and Published Manuscripts of Ethnographic Content, Jacobsen collection, HA; Jacobsen 1891a.

155. Hamburg, Hagenbeck to Jacobsen, June 24, 1892, HA; Hamburg, Jacobsen to Hedwig, March 2, 1893, HA; Price List of Ethnographic Collections Exhibited at Carl Hagenbeck's Zoological Arena, 1893, HA; Cole 1985, 131; Haberland 1987, 368–69.

156. Hamburg, Hagenbeck to Jacobsen, March 6, 1894, HA; Berlin, Weisbach to Jacobsen, March 9, 1895, EMB; Janssen 1931.

157. Dresden, Hedwig to Jacobsen, July 17, 1895, HA.

158. Dresden, Henny to Jacobsen, December 29, 1897, HA; Jacobsen correspondence, binder for 1896–1899, HA.

159. Berlin, Jacobsen to Klopfer, March 25, 1884, HA; Köln, Jacobsen to Hedwig, June 15, 1886, HA; Trondheim, Jacobsen to Hedwig, September 1, 1892, HA; Tromsö, Jacobsen's father to Jacobsen, November 11, 1900, HA.

160. Flensdorf, Willy to Adrian and Hedwig, January 5, 1913, HA; Cole 1985, 324; Haberland 1988b; Janssen 1931.

161. Stellingen, Hedwig to Jacobsen, October 4, 1915, HA; Hamburg, Jacobsen to Inspektion der Fliegertruppen, September 1917, HA.

162. England, Red Cross to Jacobsen, December 12, 1914, HA; Russian Front, Willy to Adrian, July 31, 1915, HA; Berlin, Professor Heck, Berlin Zoo, to Jacobsen, July 3, 1923, HA; Jacobsen, "Deutsche Jagd- und Forschungsreisen ins nördliche Eismeer" ("German Hunting and Research Trips to the Northern Polar Sea"), 1925, handwritten manuscript, 19 pages, HA; Jacobsen, "Lecture: Travel in Alaska before the Discovery of Gold," no date, handwritten manuscript, headings of

pictures to be shown added in red ink, 39 pages, HA; Janssen 1931; Thode-Arora 1989, 49–52, 174.

163. Jacobsen correspondence, 1914, HA; Chicago, Field Museum to Jacobsen, July 18, 1921, HA; New York, American Museum of Natural History to Jacobsen, July 21, 1921, HA.

164. Hamburg, Janssen to Verlag Enblin und Laiblin, February 1, 1939, HA; Hamburg, Janssen to Jacobsen, February 21, 1939, HA.

165. Berlin, the Prussian State to Jacobsen, pension certificates, 1926, 1929, and 1932, HA.

166. Certificate of Residence, Mrs. A. Jacobsen Hedw. nee Klopfer, HA; Hamburg, Hagenbeck to Jacobsen, November 21, 1937, HA; Risö, Jacobsen to Hedwig, July 12, 1946, EMB; Cole 1985, 324; Hamburger Fremdenblatt, November 28, 1933; Kahler 1968, 48–56; Niemeyer 1966, 1974.

167. The Museum of Ethnology Hamburg requested a box of Haida objects, the Christchurch Museum desired pieces, and the Municipal Museum of Hildesheim wanted to exchange Batak collections for objects from Jacobsen's Alaska collection, to name but a few. Berlin, order from Bastian, May 8, 1883, EMB; Christchurch Museum, Australia, to Royal Museum, 1887, EMB; Florence, Professor Giglioli to Bastian, 1887, EMB; Hildesheim Municipal Museum to Royal Museum, 1888, EMB; Berlin, Bastian to the General Administration of the Royal Museum, July 30, 1891, EMB; Berlin, *Springer's Kunsthandbuch für das Deutsche Reich* ("Springer's Handbook of Art in the German Empire"), draft entry on the Support Committee, July 28, 1894, EMB.

168. Berlin, E. Henkelmann to Bastian, May 18, 1884, EMB; Naumburg, Georg Sanftleben to Bastian, June 8, 1884, EMB; Segeberg, Richard Stolle to Bastian, July 13, 1884, EMB; Washington, D.C., Spencer F. Baird to Bastian, January 13, 1885; Christiania (Oslo), Rink to Jacobsen, 1880s and 1890s, HA; Haberland 1987.

169. Berlin, Bastian to Jacobsen, November 13, 1886, HA.

170. Cole 1985, 288.

171. Cole 1985, 310.

172. Chicago, Boas to Bastian, May 8, 1893, EMB; Cole 1985, 107.

THE GIFT-GIVERS

1. Jacobsen [1884] 1977; 1891d.
2. Jacobsen [1884] 1977, 110.
3. Jacobsen 1891d, 595.
4. Oswalt 1990, 51.
5. Jacobsen 1891d, 598.
6. Jacobsen 1891d, 636.
7. Jacobsen 1891d, 595.
8. Jacobson, 1984, 190.
9. Lenz 1986, 4, 5.

THE RETURN GIFT

1. For details on Yup'ik etiquette, see "Visual Repatriation," at the end of this section.
2. For a detailed biography of Paul John, see Shield and Fienup-Riordan 2003.

FIRST DAY

1. "Narrekojak" or "Osarak" IVA5230; see also Nelson 1899, 135–37.
2. IVA2846, IVA4864, IVA4866, IVA4867, IVA7220; see also Nelson 1899, 140–43.
3. "Kreuitak" IVA5392; see also Nelson 1899, 140–45.

4. Three from Cape Vancouver ("Totapit" IVA4522, IVA4526, IVA4530), three from the Kuskokwim ("Toutapit" IVA4960, IVA4961, IVA4962), and the rest from Nushagak ("Totapit," "Totapak" IVA5359, IVA5361–IVA5366).

5. IVA4526.

6. "Arnarok" IVA4561, IVA4562.

7. "Totapit?" IVA4521, IVA3241. We also looked at a Nushagak harpoon float ("Kloktak" IVA5518) that Jacobsen identified as a bladder. Paul disagreed, concluding that it was the *kap'egtelquq* ("narrow part"?) of an adult beluga's stomach: "Since the people of Qinaq hunted and killed many belugas, they were referred to as *arrluknginat* [literally, "merely killer whales," from *arrluk*, "killer whale," which also hunted belugas]. When I lived among those people, I watched them inflating these . . . beluga stomachs, which resemble fish stomachs."

8. "Ketsekotak" IVA4696; see also Nelson 1899, 73–74.

9. "Marrawik," meaning "that from which one drinks" IVA4691, IVA4692, IVA4694, IVA5400, IVA5434, IVA7002.

10. "Katsekotak" IVA5370.

11. "Assakok" IVA5235; see also Nelson 1899, 134–37.

12. "Unnerak" IVA4585, IVA4586, IVA4587.

13. "Narrekojak" IVA4575. Later we looked at another *nagiiquyaq* ("Narrekojak?" IVA5231) from Fort Alexander, similar to the first but longer and with eagle-feather attachments.

14. IVA7222.

15. "Narrekojak?" IVA171a, b; see also Nelson 1899, 135–37.

16. "Essaktok," "Pai=iktut=Swogit in complete condition" IVA4590.

17. IVA4805.

18. IVA7171; "Angerojak" IVA5244.

19. "Anguarut" IVA5597; see also Nelson 1899, 223–26.

20. IVA5245.

21. "Anguarut" IVA4345.

22. "Bastiit or Baotitt?" IVA4589.

23. "Eksiksok" IVA5243; see also Nelson 1899, 222–23.

24. "Eksiksok?" IVA4574.

25. "Nikt-Siutak," "Niktsik," "Mitzerrisutuk" IVA4344.

26. Two from the Kuskokwim ("Ner=esit" IVA7005, IVA4795) and one from the Yukon (IVA7279).

27. "Nikt=Sintok" or "Netsik" IVA4038, IVA3638.

28. "Neksit" "Nekuk" "Niktsuitok" IVA3631, IVA3628.

29. "Mitzerrisutuk" "Neksik" IVA4035, IVA4048.

30. See also Nelson 1899, 147–49.

31. The group included two from Cape Prince of Wales ("Kokararak" "Kokarat" IVA5877, IVA5895), eight from Norton Sound ("Kokararak" "Kokkarat" IVA2999–IVA3005, IVA6062), seven from the Yukon ("Kokkak, big harpoon," "Kokarat or Kokkarat, bigger harpoon," "Kokararak, biggest harpoon" IVA3919–IVA3924, IVA3979), three from the Kuskokwim ("Kokak" "Kokaran" IVA4808, IVA4810, IVA4812), one from Cook Inlet (IVA6633), and one of unknown provenance (IVA3009).

32. One from the Yukon ("Kokkak" IVA3918), two from above the Kuskokwim ("Kokak" "Kokaran" IVA4807, IVA4792; about manner of fastening on shaft, see IVA4591), and three from between the Kuskokwim and Nushagak ("Kokkak," "Kokak" IVA5402, IVA5403, IVA3257).

33. "Kagiret," "Kappokkaum?" "Kokkokat?" IVA3954, IVA3955; "Noknem=Nowusem" IVA3959, IVA7272, IVA7273.

34. IVA3954.

35. The group included eight from Norton Sound ("Kokkak?"

"Toutak" IVA2983–IVA2985; "Sawokpak," "Sawok," "Resiun" IVA3697, IVA3696, IVA3699, IVA3670; "Resiun," "Kokkiak" "Ukirisun" IVA3701), one from Cape Prince of Wales ("Narok" IVA6685), three from Port Clarence ("Kokkiak" IVA3251, IVA5879, IVA5880), one from East Cape (IVA6686), three from the Yukon ("Sawok" IVA3703–IVA3704; "Nanarkpit," "Piteksirat," "Resiun," "Ukiresiun" IVA3705, Jacobsen adding that he could not find out which was the most correct name), two from Prince William Sound ("Eikutt" IVA6246, IVA6298), one from north of the Copper River (IVA6357), and one from the Aleutians ("Peeicktutt" IVA182).

2. "Kjaok" IVA3598, IVA3600; see also Nelson 1899, 147–52.

3. "Toutak?" IVA4624; see also Nelson 1899, 147–49.

4. One each from the Yukon ("Sawok" IVA3963), Cape Vancouver ("Piktut=Sawogit" IVA4626), the Kuskokwim ("Kokak" IVA4623), and Fort Alexander ("Sawogik" IVA4627); see also Nelson 1899, 147–49.

5. "Sawogik" IVA5248.

6. "Aikatett or Aikattet" IVA4232; see also Nelson 1899, 129–30.

7. "Kajrlorotit" IVA3649, IVA3650; see also Nelson 1899, 218–22.

8. IVA4056.

9. IVA4169; see also Nelson 1899, 219.

10. "Ilnuero" IVA4788.

11. No one commented on a set of four greenstone amulets (IVA4471) from the lower Yukon, which Jacobsen labeled "Issignak, i.e. nephrite" and "Hojamik, amulet." We also looked at a stone figure from the lower Yukon ("Kjinok=Yugak" IVA3690), which Jacobsen said was used by the shamans, who maintained that spirits lived in such dolls and protected the owners.

15. Five from the Yukon ("Akuwselkutiit" IVA4108, IVA4109, IVA4112–IVA4114), two from Cape Vancouver ("Akagojelkutit" IVA4540, IVA4746), and twelve from between Nelson Island and Nunivak ("Akagojelkoutiit," "Akagieltun" IVA4875, IVA4872, IVA4873, IVA4877–IVA4881, IVA4885, IVA4887, IVA4888, IVA4897); see also Nelson 1899, 218–22.

17. "Elkold" or "Tungita" IVA4697–IVA4710, IVA4813, IVA4814, IVA3956; see also Nelson 1899, 142–43.

18. Two are from between Cape Vancouver and the Kuskokwim (IVA4825, IVA4711) and the rest are from the Kuskokwim and Nushagak (IVA4750, IVA4725, IVA7208, IVA7505).

19. "Kappon" IVA5136, IVA5137.

20. "Onmit" IVA5142.

21. IVA6334.

22. IVA5893.

SECOND DAY

1. "Nemidlik=Orolak" IVA4360; see also Nelson 1899, 155–57.

2. "Nemidlik=Orolak" IVA4359.

3. "Orollewok" IVA4588.

4. "Oroak," "Orloak" IVA4356.

5. "Orollewok" IVA5246, "Nemidlik=Orloak" IVA6976.

6. IVA6976.

7. See also Nelson 1899, 110–12.

8. Later that week, Annie and Paul identified a piece of reindeer antler, which Jacobsen had taken for an incomplete arrowhead ("Ilusue" IVA3939), as an *ikgun* (small lever or prying tool, from *ig-*, "to lift by lever action") for sewing leather and mending kayak holes. Paul explained the process he had seen: "The skin seam on one side was picked up with this and pulled, then the needle was pierced through and the process was repeated on the other side. It was used to pull the skin before the needle was poked through. . . . When *ikavsiarutet* [cross-stitching] on the top edge and upper and back parts on kayak covers were undone, this kind of tool was used to pull out the thread. The stitches around the kayak hole were pulled with this kind of a tool . . . that had multiple uses."

9. "Satko" IVA5930.

10. "Orolowak," "Ketwiak" IVA6364.

11. See also Fienup-Riordan 1990, 146–66; Nelson 1899, 327–30.

12. IVA7177; see also Nelson 1899, 159–61.

13. "Kutfik" IVA4320, IVA4321; see also Nelson 1899, 159–60. Later we looked at two blunt wooden bird arrow tips ("Akkitnut" IVA4998, IVA4999) from Cape Vancouver.

14. Catherine noted that *augtuaraat* (red phalaropes, from *auk*, "blood," because of their red bellies) used to be plentiful in the Yukon area: "Then we found out that one of the boys had played with an *augtuaraar* he caught. As a result, they disappeared totally from the area." Paul noted that there were also few phalaropes today around Nelson Island.

15. IVA5222.

16. "Nursat" IVA4314.

17. "Nursat" IVA6974a.

18. "Kutfik" IVA6974b.

19. "Omiligit," "Kjinginat" IVA6974c, IVA6974f.

20. "Pititsirak" IVA5236, IVA5238; see also Nelson 1899, 157–59.

21. IVA4578, IVA4579, IVA4580, IVA5237, IVA5239, IVA5240, IVA5241, IVA5242.

22. "Kjingit?" IVA5404.

23. "Osarak" IVA138g, IVA138b; see also Nelson 1899, 157–59.

24. "Omiligit" (Y), "Kjingiligit" (BB), IVA138d, IVA138f.

25. IVA138.

26. "Narrekjak" IVA138c, IVA138a.

27. "Kjinginat" IVA4322, IVA4323, IVA4325, IVA4326, IVA4327.

28. "Omiligit" IVA4328, IVA4329, IVA4331, IVA4336.

THIRD DAY

1. "Iggun" IVA4593 used with IVA4573, IVA4575–IVA4577, IVA4591; "Norkak or Noreak" IVA4306, IVA4307; "Iggun" IVA5232; IVA5233 used with IVA5230; see also Nelson 1899, 152–55.

2. As we finished looking at throwing boards, we were momentarily distracted by elevator doors opening and a bustle of activity. The collection manager, Herr Wedell, emerged from the hallway, wheeling crates toward the storage area. The crates contained the masks Jacobsen had collected from the Kuskokwim and Yukon Rivers that had been on exhibit in Alaska the year before, just now returning from New York where the mask exhibit had subsequently traveled. Herr Wedell was justifiably apprehensive about the fragile pieces, but all returned in good condition.

3. "Okei Stakson" IVA5353; see also Nelson 1899, 73.

4. "Neujat" IVA4350; see also Nelson 1899, 151–52.

5. "Neujakpak," "Norseakpak," "Neuerek" IVA6368.

6. "Neujeret," "Nujeret" IVA3957, IVA3958, IVA7278; see also Nelson 1899, 194–96.

7. IVA3938.

8. "Kagiret," "Kapokkaum," "Kokkokat" IVA3940, IVA3941, IVA3944, IVA3945, IVA3947, IVA3950, IVA3956.

9. IVA3944.

10. "Neujeret" IVA3949; see also Nelson 1899, 149–52.

11. "Eruingok" IVA3658, IVA4210; see also Nelson 1899, 163.

12. "Nallkit sautitt," one (IVA4642) from the Kuskokwim and the

other (IVA3643) from the Yukon; "Eerongoarewik" IVA4959; IVA5406.

13. "Koron Kjimat" IVA4121–IVA4123; see also Nelson 1899, 164.
14. "Kapselautlok" IVA4656; see also Nelson 1899, 163–66.
15. "Pijokkaun" IVA4654.
16. "Capselautlok," "Kapselautlok," "Kapseliarun" IVA4653, IVA4656, IVA4660, IVA4661, IVA4669.
17. "Soppiut" IVA3752, IVA3762, IVA3781, IVA4955, IVA4956, IVA4958, IVA7219.
18. "Soppiut" IVA4957.
19. "Dassitak" IVA4554; see also Nelson 1899, 211–12.
20. "Atmak=Sutitt," probably *atmagcuutet*, IVA4185, IVA4186.
21. "Neget=Makausuet=Sititt" IVA4224; see also Nelson 1899, 122–26.
22. "Makkiksett" IVA4997.
23. "Makkiksett" IVA5426.
24. See also Nelson 1899, 183–85.
25. "Kanaiaan," "Knneruetik" IVA4341, IVA4343, IVA4216; "Kannoeronn" IVA4563; see also Nelson 1899, 174–75.
26. "Kannoeriann" IVA4564.
27. "Kauneruetik" IVA4061.
28. Twenty-three from the Yukon ("Kitzak," "Etsetzuak=Sukwakt=Sutiit" IVA3840–IVA3846, IVA3848, IVA3849, IVA3851, IVA3852, IVA3856, IVA3858–IVA3863, IVA3865–IVA3869), sixteen from the Kuskokwim ("Eksak," "Karlotsett" IVA4633, IVA5125, IVA5131–IVA5135, IVA5378–IVA5386), and one *manaq* (fish lure) from Cape Vancouver ("Manak," "Mannet" IVA5128); see also Nelson 1899, 173–83.
29. "Eksak" IVA5379.
30. "Kitsakt or Kitzak" IVA3884.
31. IVA3887.
32. IVA3870–IVA3880, IVA3882; see also Nelson 1899, 173–83.
33. IVA4072, IVA4073, IVA4075, IVA4078, IVA4247; see also Nelson 1899, 185–90.
34. IVA4077.
35. IVA4059, IVA4062–IVA4071.
36. "Tarsan=Paksun=Atlik" IVA4288; see also Nelson 1899, 185–90.
37. IVA4293; "Peekatluk=Atlik" IVA4290, IVA5094.
38. Net sinkers made of stone (IVA4092), reindeer antler (IVA1993, IVA4081, IVA4082, IVA4086, IVA4087, IVA4091, IVA6991), and mammoth bone (IVA1871, IVA1872, IVA4079, IVA4080, IVA4083, IVA4084, IVA4088, IVA4089, IVA4090, IVA6992).
39. "Koesetzuak" IVA4286, IVA4289.
40. "Killautitt" IVA3619, IVA3715–IVA3718, IVA3722, IVA3723, IVA3724, IVA3891, IVA3892.
41. "Inneroutitt," "Immerojutak" IVA4673–IVA4678, IVA7249; see also Nelson 1899, 191–93.
42. "Ugimak?" IVA4018.
43. "Junneroutitt" IVA4055, IVA4093–IVA4096, IVA4099–IVA4104, IVA4107, IVA7248; see also Nelson 1899, 190–91.
44. "Naknem=Nowiseum" IVA4672.
45. "Kauk=Tudak=Neknen" IVA5435.

FOURTH DAY

1. "Ekmiutak," "Ettmiutak"; see also Nelson 1899, 278–80.
2. IVA4666, IVA3154.
3. "Agometzoak or Agometgoak" IVA4636; see also Nelson 1899, 273–75.
4. They made no comment on a tin pipe bowl found in the ground during house construction at Fort Alexander ("Kuninek" IVA5447). Jacobsen wrote that the piece was unusual, because in the south almost no one smoked.
5. "Kwentak," "Tjiluttuingok" IVA4204; see also Nelson 1899, 93–98.
6. IVA3663.
7. "Eksetz Wiewik," "Ekwiutatt" IVA3661, IVA3662, IVA3663, IVA3664, IVA3673; "Tjiluttitungok" IVA3666, IVA3674, IVA3675; see also Nelson 1899, 93–100.
8. See Fienup-Riordan 1994, 86.
9. "Eketz Wiewick," "Ekwintatt" IVA3677.
10. "Metziwik?" IVA3902; see also Nelson 1899, 70–72.
11. "Kaltasiungak," probably from *qaltaq*, "pail or bucket"; IVA4254.
12. "Kaltosiungak" IVA4246.
13. "Truek?" (perhaps *qurrun*) IVA4249.
14. IVA4253; see also Nelson 1899, 70–72.
15. IVA4246; see also Nelson 1899, 70–72.
16. IVA4243; see also Nelson 1899, 70–73.
17. "Metziwik" IVA4217.
18. "Eckkock or Esoch" IVA4475, IVA4479, IVA4484, IVA4485, IVA4487; see also Nelson 1899, 201–2.
19. "Gatsisun" IVA4180.

FIFTH DAY

1. "Klullerokkek" IVA4275, IVA4294, IVA217; see also Nelson 1899, 43–44.
2. "Klullerokkek" IVA4275, IVA217.
3. IVA391, IVA7071.
4. IVA216; see also Nelson 1899, 104–6.
5. "Kaksiwit" IVA5627.
6. "Ersarumerok" IVA5472.
7. "Willerutitt?" IVA4295.
8. Bags from the lower Yukon ("Kakkiwitt," "Kalsiwit" IVA4299, IVA4300, IVA4302, IVA4503, IVA4498, IVA6014, IVA6015), Kuskokwim ("Kakkiuwit" IVA5416), and Bristol Bay ("Kalangak" IVA6377).
9. This bag (IVA6988) originally came to Berlin in 1884 from vice-consul Jakutsk Priklowki and was placed in the museum's Asian department. Jacobsen was able to identify it as Alaskan and wrote a description on the original accession record (Bolz and Sanner 1999, 197).
10. "Kakkiwit?" IVA4503.
11. "Willerutitt" IVA5471.
12. For the complete story of the boy who went to live with the seals, as told by Paul John, see Fienup-Riordan 2000, 58–81.
13. Kuskokwim bag ("Kwintettsuak" IVA5414), Nushagak bags ("Ersarumerak?" IVA7186, IVA5543), and Yukon bag ("Willerutitt?" IVA4385).
14. "Ullufak" IVA5488 (probably *ul'utvak*, "newborn seal").
15. "Konersiwisiugak" IVA5517.
16. "Konersiwisiugak" IVA5515.
17. "Kakiwit" IVA4499.
18. IVA4284; see also Nelson 1899, 166–67.
19. "Konersiwisingak?" IVA5388; see also Nelson 1899, 84–85.
20. "Issret" IVA4255 (probably *issratet*); see also Nelson 1899, 202–5.
21. "Klarowit" IVA5525.
22. Another ten grass storage bags—"Ilakstat" from the Yukon, "Issrett or Isrann" from the coast, "Klarowit" from the Kuskokwim,

IVA4256–IVA4259, IVA4494, IVA4495, IVA5478, IVA5522–IVA5524—that Jacobsen had collected drew no comment.

2. Yukon bags ("Kakiwit=Amerit" IVA4260, IVA4276, IVA4391) and Kuskokwim bag ("Ullan?" IVA4468).

3. IVA4264.

4. Paul identified another small grass bag from the Yukon (IVA4261), which Jacobsen said young girls had woven for practice and to keep toys in, as a little *qemaggvik*.

5. "Aklomat," "Akoinat," "Aggomat" IVA4229, IVA4230, IVA4233, IVA4434, IVA4485, IVA5521, IVA7266.

SIXTH DAY

1. "Iggukarsok" IVA4153.

2. "Okhtitsun," "Kapotarkakartlak" IVA4163–IVA4167; see also Nelson 1899, 81–85.

3. IVA4165, IVA4166.

4. "Kolkiksak" IVA5433, IVA2885.

5. "Krilet" IVA3732–IVA3738, IVA3741–IVA3743, IVA3745–IVA3748, IVA3763–IVA3765.

6. IVA6003, IVA6004; see also Nelson 1899, 205–9.

7. "Pirilatt" IVA3996–IVA4001.

8. "Kabgiet" (*cavget*) and *umit*, IVA5261.

9. "Daleutit," "Daleutitt," "Dalutitt" IVA4794, IVA4796–IVA4803; see also Nelson 1899, 106–8.

10. "Tautik," "Tallutik" IVA3725–IVA3731, IVA3749, IVA3751, IVA3754, IVA3755, IVA3759, IVA4193, IVA7260, IVA7261; see also Nelson 1899, 57–58.

11. Three more awls ("Dalutitt" IVA3639, IVA5341, IVA5343) from the Yukon and Nushagak regions drew no comment.

12. "Kalliutit" IVA2783.

13. Seven from the Yukon ("Paloksinerat=Kuutit" IVA3708–IVA3714) and six from the Kuskokwim and Nushagak ("Ipiksaun" IVA4781, IVA4783, IVA5396, IVA5405, IVA5408, IVA7233), plus several teeth (IVA3707); see also Nelson 1899, 89–90.

14. "Palok sinerat=Kuutit" IVA3707.

15. IVA3439, IVA3463, IVA3469, IVA4117.

16. IVA6023.

17. IVA4044.

18. IVA4736, IVA4773.

19. "Ommikak" IVA5449, IVA5450.

20. "Ignak" IVA4377; see also Nelson 1899, 91–92.

21. "Hopokotit" IVA4022–IVA4031, IVA4116, IVA5430; see also Nelson 1899, 88.

22. IVA4028.

23. "Aban=Kjalek=Akruk" IVA4263; see also Nelson 1899, 79–80.

24. "Hargotett" IVA4136–IVA4138; see also Nelson 1899, 79–80.

25. Lower Yukon scrapers (IVA3385–IVA3391, IVA3393, IVA3395–IVA3397, IVA3399–IVA3404, IVA3406, IVA3408–IVA3410, IVA3412, IVA3413, IVA3416, IVA3417) and Kuskokwim and Nushagak scrapers (IVA4864, IVA4870, IVA4871, IVA4889, IVA5305, IVA5306, IVA5442–IVA5444, IVA7189); see also Nelson 1899, 112–16.

26. IVA3399.

27. IVA5444.

28. "Dail'tkon" IVA5442.

29. Ten from the Yukon ("Kjimak=Ulluak or Kjimat=Ulloak" IVA3465, IVA3466, IVA3468, IVA3470, IVA3472–IVA3477) and twelve from Cape Vancouver and the Kuskokwim ("Ulloet," "Ulloak" IVA4687, IVA4689, IVA4690, IVA5274–IVA5276, IVA5278, IVA5281, IVA5283, IVA5295, IVA6275, IVA8095); see also Nelson 1899, 108–9.

30. "Ulluat" IVA3903 from the Yukon, "Ulloak" IVA4688 from Nelson Island, and "Ulloak" IVA4695 from the Kuskokwim.

31. "Kapiatsun" IVA4680; see also Nelson 1899, 171–72.

32. "Sawikak," "Sawik-kak," "Igluktulik" IVA3505, IVA3506, IVA3514, IVA3818; see also Nelson 1899, 85–86.

33. This function may account for the name Jacobsen recorded: "Igluktulik" or "house defender."

34. "Kappan" IVA4160.

35. "Mil'tkarrat," "Mitlek" IVA4151, IVA4152, IVA4158, IVA4159, IVA4161.

36. "Killiutak" IVA5016.

37. "Pitknoat (knife)," "Kassrearusutitt (horn knife attached)" IVA4004a, b; also IVA3786, IVA4003, IVA4006, IVA4178.

38. IVA4953.

39. "Kakkinneron" IVA5431.

40. IVA5349.

41. All boxes were in case 27, right side. The first box (shelf 3, right box) included one stone knife blade ("Sawik" IVA4906), two stone *uluaq* blades ("Ulloet" IVA4683, IVA4684), and one stone ax blade (IVA3347) from Cape Vancouver; six stone *ellumerrutet* (skin scrapers; "Plomeron or Plomeroutitt" IVA4890, IVA4893–IVA4896, IVA5451) from Cape Vancouver and Nushagak; and thirty-six stone *calugcissuutet* (skin scrapers; "Kjalugotit," "Kjalugotitt," "Kaulok," "Orro=on" IVA3418–IVA3421, IVA3424–IVA3431, IVA3433–IVA3436, IVA3440–IVA3444, IVA3446–IVA3448, IVA3450–IVA3461) from the Yukon, each originally either tied to a wooden handle or wrapped with skins for use; see also Nelson 1899, 108–9, 112–16, 171–72. The second box (shelf 9, right box) held four large stone blades, including a stone ax blade ("Kjimat=Sakkiun" IVA3351) from Cape Vancouver, a stone tool that had once been used as a *kepun* (adze) and later as a scraper ("Kapootit?" "Plomeroutitt?" IVA5298) from the Kuskokwim, and two more stone ax blades ("Osoksin"? IVA5299, IVA5300) from Nushagak.

42. IVA335.

43. The third box (shelf 8, center box) included one blade ("Ojamik," "Sawikak," "Kappotitt" IVA3583) from the lower Yukon and eleven ("Sawik," "Milkak" IVA4902, IVA4903, IVA4909, IVA4911, IVA5284, IVA5285, IVA5291–IVA5294, IVA5297) from Cape Vancouver and the Kuskokwim; see also Nelson 1899, 85–86. The fourth box (shelf 8, left box) included one stone blade for a *caviggaq* ("Sawikak" IVA3449) from the Yukon used as a scraper after it was broken, one stone *uluaq* blade ("Omikak=Ulloak" IVA5286) from the Kuskokwim, and two stone blades for a *mellgar* ("Millkak or Milkak," "Omikak=Milkak" IVA4907, IVA5290) from the Kuskokwim and Nushagak. The fifth box (shelf 10, middle box) contained thirteen stone ax blades ("Kjimat=Sakkiun" IVA3352, IVA3353, IVA3357, IVA3361, IVA3363, IVA3364, IVA3366, IVA3372, IVA3374, IVA3375, IVA3377, IVA3432, IVA3437) from the lower Yukon. The last heavy box (shelf 9, left box) held seventeen more stone ax blades ("Kjimat=Sakkiun as ax," "Kleikut," "Kjalugotit as scraper" IVA3343–IVA3346, IVA3349, IVA3350, IVA3354, IVA3356, IVA3358, IVA3360, IVA3362, IVA3365, IVA3367, IVA3368, IVA3370, IVA3371, IVA3422) from the Yukon.

44. IVA3370, IVA3422.

45. The sixth box (shelf 8, middle box) included eighty-three "fish and skin" knives from the Yukon ("Ullon," "Ulloak," "Ullokak," "Ullo" IVA3478–IVA3503, IVA3523–IVA3531, IVA3533–IVA3565,

IVA3567–IVA3580, IVA3604), six woodworking blades from the Yukon ("Sawikak," Sawikok," "Sawogak," "Igluktulik (house defender)" IVA3504, IVA3507–IVA3509, IVA3511, IVA3520), three *uluat* blades ("Ulloet," "Ulloak" IVA4682, IVA4684, IVA4685) and two *caviggaq* blades ("Sawik" IVA4905, IVA4908) from between Cape Vancouver and the Kuskokwim, and six *uluat* blades from between the Kuskokwim and Nushagak ("Ulloak," "Omikak Ulloak" IVA5272, IVA5282, IVA5287–IVA5289, IVA5296).

46. IVA3479; "Kjimak Ulloak" IVA3580.

SEVENTH DAY

1. IVA4265, IVA4266, IVA4267; see also Nelson 1899, 202–5.
2. Left-handed mat IVA4267; right-handed mat IVA4265.
3. IVA4266.
4. "Kowarotitt" IVA4226; see also Nelson 1899, 63–65.
5. Yukon lamps (IVA4473, IVA4474, IVA4476, IVA4478, IVA4480, IVA4482, IVA4483, IVA7265) and Nushagak lamp ("Knokak" IVA5369).
6. Mortars ("Akujutik" IVA3668, IVA3706), pestle ("Passin" IVA4996), sieves (IVA4786, "Kattaun" IVA3689, IVA3692), and pipe ("Sop=Sluet" IVA4169); see also Nelson 1899, 271–76.
7. "Heidtlak" IVA3083, IVA4207; see also Nelson 1899, 326–27.
8. "Kallun," "Kaleutak" (*qalutaq*) IVA3769, IVA3780, IVA4551, IVA4552; see also Nelson 1899, 67–70.
9. "Oelok" (probably from *uiluq*) IVA4775–IVA4777, IVA4779; "Wieluk" IVA4780, IVA4806, IVA7228.
10. IVA5454, IVA5455.
11. "Kallauretitt" IVA3639, IVA3691, IVA3694, IVA4115 from the Yukon, and "Kalorin" IVA4555, IV4556 from the Kuskokwim and Nushagak; see also Nelson 1899, 65–67.
12. "Konn" IVA3694.
13. "Oielujak" IVA5367, IVA5368. Later we looked at three more freshwater clamshells from the tundra area ("Wieluk" IVA3888–IVA3890), also used as soup spoons and known by the same name: *uilut*.
14. IVA6358.
15. "Siklak" IVA4183, IVA4184; see also Nelson 1899, 75.
16. "Pekoutak" IVA4342; see also Nelson 1899, 78–79.
17. IVA5256; see also Nelson 1899, 79.
18. "Koksut" IVA5427; see Nelson 1899, 73.
19. IVA4557, IVA4558; see also Nelson 1899, 75–77.
20. "Udsukadat" IVA4015, IVA4203, IVA4209, IVA4212, IVA4213.
21. Seven (IVA4008–IVA4014) from the Yukon, thirteen ("Nerutatt" IVA4899–IVA4901, IVA4912–IVA4921) from Cape Vancouver, and one (IVA7232) from the Kuskokwim.
22. IVA4008.

EIGHTH DAY

1. "Neujeorot" "Nujeorot" IVA4774, IVA4778, IVA4782, IVA4784; see also Nelson 1899, 57–58.
2. The day before, we had looked at a tool fragment ("Jerruin" IVA3792; see also Nelson 1899, 108) from the Yukon that Jacobsen said was used to pleat doll boots. It also featured a toothed end for combing the hair of reindeer skins used in making doll clothes. Paul recognized it as part of a *nuyiurun* (hair comb), but could say no more about it.
3. "Tontak" IVA3905–IVA3908.
4. "Tontak," "Palloktutt" IVA5033–IVA5037, IVA5045–IVA5048, IVA5050–IVA5052, IVA5055–IVA5057, IVA7229, IVA7230.
5. "Tuksorarrut=Kakopit" IVA5038–IVA5043; see also Nelson 1899, 44–50.
6. "Tokssorarrut" IVA5045, IVA5046.
7. "Toksorarrut" IVA5049.
8. "Sakeksek" for side pieces, "Okkaklekak" for middle piece, IVA5099, IVA5100, IVA5106–IVA5115.
9. IVA5109.
10. "Assiutitt," "Assiutik" IVA3620–IVA3624, IVA3626, IVA5058, IVA5061, IVA5063–IVA5074, IVA5076, IVA5079, IVA5081, IVA5083–IVA5085, IVA5088, IVA5619.
11. "Kowelakset or Kogeloksett" IVA5073.
12. "Assiutitt" or "Assiutik" (K), "Thuntek" (Y) IVA5078, IVA5088, IVA5089, IVA5093, IVA5095, IVA5096; see also Nelson 1899, 52–57.
13. IVA5093.
14. "Aglaurutitt" IVA5092.
15. "Aglaurutitt" IVA5090.
16. IVA5087.
17. "Yugoak," "Yugak," "Jugatt" (*yugaq*, "doll") IVA4039, IVA4040, IVA4510, IVA4528.
18. "Innuet" (*inuguat*) IVA4525, IVA4531, IVA4532, IVA4536, IVA4538.
19. IVA4759, IVA7196–IVA7199; see also Nelson 1899, 42–45, 379, 494–97.
20. IVA4525, IVA4535.
21. "Innugoak" (*inuguaq*) IVA5320.
22. "Kinakok" (*kegginaquq*, "mask") IVA4513, IVA4904.
23. IVA4533, IVA4534, IVA4537.
24. Most were from either the Kuskokwim (IVA6997–IVA6999, IVA7201–IVA7204, IVA7206, IVA7207, IVA7212) or the area between the Kuskokwim and Nushagak (IVA4713, IVA4715, IVA4716, IVA4717, IVA4719, IVA4720, IVA4722, IVA4724, IVA4732, IVA4734, IVA4735, IVA4749, IVA4762, IVA4815, IVA4833, IVA4841, IVA4844). Four were from Cape Vancouver (IVA4751, IVA4756, IVA4828, IVA4845) and six from Fort Alexander (IVA5373, IVA5375, IVA5376, IVA5456, IVA5457, IVA5460).
25. IVA5456, IVA5457, IVA5460.
26. Later in the week, the group identified two wooden figures from the Kuskokwim (IVA4790, IVA4791) as shaman's *iinruk*, but said no more about them.

NINTH DAY

1. "Minkusiwit" IVA3806, IVA3808–IVA3819, IVA7258.
2. "Minkotmutitt," "Minkatsiutitt," "Minkontauten" IVA5021–IVA5029, IVA5031, IVA5032, IVA5345, IVA5347; see also Nelson 1899, 103–4.
3. IVA3807, IVA3983–IVA3988, IVA3990, IVA3992–IVA3995.
4. IVA5022.
5. Fasteners from the Yukon ("Minkusiwit," "Krifitt" IVA3821, IVA3822, IVA3824, IVA3826–IVA3833, IVA3835–IVA3837, IVA3981), Cape Vancouver and the Kuskokwim ("Krrfit" IVA4823, IVA4966–IVA4971, IVA4973, IVA4975–IVA4977, IVA4979–IVA4983, IVA4985, IVA4986, IVA4988–IVA4995), and the Kuskokwim to Nushagak ("Krrfit," "Ekkogemiutak" IVA4714, IVA4747, IVA4811, IVA4972, IVA4984, IVA5321–IVA5332, IVA5334–IVA5339, IVA5346, IVA7214–IVA7216); see also Nelson 1899, 104–6.
6. "Krefitt" IVA3838, IVA5772a, b, c.
7. Thimbles from Cape Vancouver ("Aknerreneitit," "Aknerreneilit" IVA3771, IVA3774, IVA3776, IVA3909–IVA3915, IVA5006, IVA5008, IVA5017–IVA5019), the Kuskokwim ("Aknerrenelit" IVA5009, IVA5010), and the Yukon (IVA7256); see also Nelson 1899, 109–10.
8. IVA3838, IVA5772a, b, c.

9. "Kaputat=Komsissiutitt" IVA3772, IVA3773, IVA3775, IVA3777, IVA5062; see also Nelson 1899, 106–7; IVA3657.

10. "Minkutitt" IVA4642a, b.

11. Belts from Andreafski (IVA7102), the lower Yukon and Cape Vancouver ("Nakogutitt" IVA4504, IVA4206), and between the Kuskokwim and Nushagak ("Nakkogutitt" IVA5439–IVA5441); see also Nelson 1899, 59.

12. See also Nelson 1899, 59–62.

13. IVA4850.

14. Seven from the lower Yukon ("Naggiwik" IVA3894–IVA3900), one between the Yukon and Cape Vancouver ("Naksallkult" IVA4949), seventeen between Cape Vancouver to the Kuskokwim ("Naksallkult" IVA4541, IVA4542, IVA4547, IVA4737, IVA4738, IVA4753, IVA4758, IVA4825, IVA4835, IVA4839, IVA4842, IVA4923, IVA4943, IVA4950, IVA4952–IVA4954), twenty-five from the Kuskokwim ("Naksallkult" IVA4544, IVA4545, IVA4757, IVA4924–IVA4941, IVA4951, IVA7001, IVA7210, IVA7211), eleven between the Kuskokwim and Nushagak ("Naksallkott," "Naksallult" "Naksalkult" IVA4721, IVA4726–IVA4729, IVA4769, IVA4830, IVA4846, IVA5348, IVA5352, IVA5374), and one from Nushagak (IVA5377).

15. Ten ("Akowlongaujit," "Akowlangaujit") between Cape Vancouver and the Kuskokwim (IVA4754, IVA4817, IVA4820, IVA4822, IVA4826, IVA4831, IVA4847, IVA4849, IVA4850, IVA4858), six from the Kuskokwim (IVA4851–IVA4856), ten between the Kuskokwim and Nushagak (IVA4723, IVA4724, IVA4730, IVA4733, IVA4740–IVA4742, IVA4767, IVA4818, IVA4819), and four between Cape Vancouver and Nushagak (IVA4824, IVA4827, IVA4840, IVA4848); see also Nelson 1899, 62.

16. Four were from the Yukon ("Ilkeak," "Ilkeat" IVA4187, IVA4189–IVA4191), two from between Cape Vancouver and the Kuskokwim ("Ilkatt" IVA4565, IVA4566), two from the Kuskokwim ("Iltkiak" IVA5475, IVA7235), and one from Togiak ("Il'tkiak" IVA5474); see also Nelson 1899, 167–69.

17. IVA5474.

18. IVA4187, IVA4566.

19. IVA4191, IVA4189.

20. Skip Snaith, letter to the author, 1997. See Fienup-Riordan 1990, 58–81) for Paul John's version of the story of the boy who went to live with the seals.

21. No comment was made on six ivory hat decorations ("Kaggelit," "Iket" IVA3632, IVA4857, IVA4861, IVA4862, IVA6012, IVA7003). See hunting hat IVA4190, described in note 16 of this chapter, for similar attachments.

22. Three from the Yukon ("Iggant" IVA4133, IVA4134, IVA7264), two from the Kuskokwim ("Illtket," "Iggaak" IVA4559, IVA4568), and one from Fort Alexander ("Iggaovvik" IVA4560); see also Nelson 1899, 69–71.

23. One from St. Michael ("Nissak" IVA6018), one from the Yukon ("Nissak" IVA4192), and two from Togiak ("Nisakpak" IVA5410, IVA5457); see also Nelson 1899, 288.

24. "Ikmeak" IVA4194, IVA6016; see also Nelson 1899, 287–88.

25. "Krentit" (IVA4193) from the Yukon.

26. "Jorariarett" IVA5464; see also Nelson 1899, 32–33.

27. IVA5465.

28. "Jorarirett," "Jorariarett" IVA5466, IVA5473.

29. A last small squirrel-skin hoodlike cap ("Jorariarett?" IVA5415) from Nushagak, which Jacobsen said might have been used by a young boy, as well as a moose-skin hood ("Nasakpak or Jorariarett" IVA5412) collected between the Kuskokwim and Nushagak, drew no comment.

30. "Wiffkok" IVA4497, IVA4500.

31. "Nesan," "Nesak" IVA5409, IVA5411, IVA5417.

32. "Allingan" IVA5020.

33. "Nelt'kun" IVA5397; see also Nelson 1899, 37–38.

TENTH DAY

1. "Ojamik" IVA5800.

2. Jacobsen collected eight ivory bead spacers (IVA5116–IVA5123), which he said were called "Senerotitt=Atanneritt" on the Kuskokwim, "Kaleluktett" on the Yukon, and "Tunusoromiutak" at Nushagak.

3. IVA4770; see also Nelson 1899, 52–57.

4. "Ojamik" IVA5391.

5. "Ojamet" IVA5371.

6. IVA5333.

7. IVA5333.

8. "Tunusurumiut" IVA5799.

9. "Nanomik" IVA5390.

10. "Assegatt" IVA4291.

11. "Torrejorarotitt" IVA5483; "Allemak" IVA4501.

12. "Tarojorarrotit," "Tarojoatitt" IVA5484.

13. Two from the Togiak River ("Neskotitt" IVA5424, IVA5468), two from between the Kuskokwim and Nushagak ("Neskotitt" IVA5462, IVA5469), and two from Nushagak ("Naskonn" IVA5470, IVA7183); see also Nelson 1899, 417–18.

14. "Angakut=Nisarat" IVA5086.

15. "Kjuarotik" IVA4502, IVA4287a, b; "Kajuarotik" IVA3107, IVA3126; see also Nelson 1899, 418–20.

16. IVA4287, IVA307.

17. IVA3667.

18. IVA4196, IVA4464.

19. IVA4464.

20. IVA4196.

21. IVA4200; see page 12 above; see also Nelson 1899, 317.

22. "Paptlo," "Paptlok" IVA4548; see also Nelson 1899, 350–52.

23. "Paplok" IVA5428.

24. "Paplok" IVA4549. A small, drum-shaped rattle from the Kuskokwim (IVA5194), consisting of a wooden ring filled with stones and covered in gut, drew no comment.

25. "Kjaojak" IVA3095, IVA4395, IVA6990.

ELEVENTH DAY

1. See Fienup-Riordan 1996; Meade and Fienup-Riordan 1996.

2. See also Nelson 1899, 393–412.

3. IVA4440, "Kinakut" IVA5193, IVA4414.

4. "Krillunukuak=Kinakok" IVA4451.

5. St. Michael, Jacobsen to Bastian, August 1, 1882, EMB.

6. "Tannak=sitak" (*tuunraq kegginaquq?*) IVA4460.

7. "Thunnerak=Kinakok" IVA4437, IVA4404, IVA4444.

8. "Momajuleroak" IVA5143, "Konanek" IVA4430.

9. Fienup-Riordan 1996, 77–84.

10. "Kinakok" IVA4433, IVA4410, IVA4431.

11. "Angakok=Kinakok" IVA4422; see also Fienup-Riordan 1994, 82–83.

12. See also Fienup-Riordan 1994, 63–76.

13. Nine pairs from the lower Yukon ("Tigomiet" IVA4369, IVA4371, IVA4373, IVA4375, IVA4381, IVA4383, IVA4419, IVA7241, IVA7242), seven pairs between Cape Vancouver and the Kuskokwim ("Tarrajararotit" IVA5197, IVA5199, IVA5203, IVA5209, IVA5211, IVA5212, IVA7193), five pairs from the Kuskokwim (IVA7190–IVA7192,

IVA7194, IVA7195), and ten pairs between the Kuskokwim and Nushagak ("Tarrajararotitt" IVA5204, IVA5207, IVA5208, IVA5213, IVA5215–IVA5219, IVA5437); see also Nelson 1899, 412–15.

14. Fienup-Riordan 1996, 156–58; Jacobson 1891d, 636.
15. IVA5199, IVA5212.
16. See also Nelson 1899, 425–27, 452–67.
17. Jacobsen collected another Yukon mask ("Yuolle=Resak" IVA4388), which he said represented either a fish or a crab.
18. "Kinakok" IVA6371.
19. See also Nelson 1899, 327–30.
20. Jacobsen 1891d, 636; see also Fienup-Riordan 1996, 241.
21. IVA4390.
22. IVA4387.

TWELFTH DAY

1. "Kalluroroaram" IVA3103; see also Nelson 1899, 341.
2. "Tinngait" IVA5015.
3. "Tinngait" IVA2665; see also Nelson 1899, 333, 340–41.
4. "Jurroktan" IVA3269, IVA3270; see also Nelson 1899, 333–34.
5. IVA4235; see also Nelson 1899, 335–37.
6. "Iuglugiak" or "Juglitak" IVA4228.
7. IVA4227.
8. "Jarroit" IVA5005; see also Nelson 1899, 345–46.
9. Twenty from the Yukon (IVA3169, IVA3782–IVA3785, IVA3787–IVA3789, IVA3794–IVA3799, IVA3802–IVA3804, IVA3809, IVA3860, IVA5003) and one from Cape Vancouver (IVA5003).
10. See also Nelson 1899, 342–45.
11. IVA5310.
12. "Arneak=Kotsimgoak" IVA5309, "Arneak=Kotzungoat" IVA5311.
13. "Innuct" IVA4512, IVA7244.
14. Dolls from the Yukon ("Jugatt," "Jugak" or "Innuet" IVA4505–IVA4509, IVA4514–IVA4516, IVA4518, IVA4519, IVA7242, IVA7245, IVA7246), from between the Kuskokwim and Nushagak ("Innugoak," "Innugaet," "Innungoet" IVA4787, IVA5315–IVA5319), from Nushagak (IVA7179, IVA7180), and from Nunivak (IVA7243).
15. IVA4505, IVA4508, IVA4519.
16. IVA4524.
17. IVA4509; Jacobsen 1891d, 637.
18. Jacobsen 1891d, 639.
19. See also Nelson 1899, 345.
20. "Kautag" IVA3669.
21. IVA4279, IVA4285 (both made of tall cotton grass), IVA4490, IVA4491, IVA4492, IVA4493, IVA5407, "Klarowitt" IVA5520 (rest made of coarse seashore grass).
22. IVA5699, IVA5700; see also Nelson 1899, 347.
23. IVA5702, IVA5696.
24. Jacobsen also referred to this dance ornament (IVA6370) in his description of the unnumbered Nushagak dance house (see page 120 above).
25. "Atkutt" IVA5419; "Natsat" IVA5418. We also looked at two other girl's caps from Nushagak ("Samatak" IVA6378, IVA6398); see also Nelson 1899, 33–34.
26. "Kjikoleureisiut" IVA5389.
27. "Dageluk" IVA4340; see also Nelson 1899, 212–14.
28. "Natterak" IVA5393; see also Nelson 1899, 215–16.
29. One from the Yukon ("Arrituk" IVA4467) and three from Nushagak ("Arekluk," "Alimakara=Angoar=Soutitt, i.e., glove for men for rowing" IVA5479, IVA5480, IVA5519); see also Nelson 1899, 38–40.
30. Socks from the Yukon ("Aklikset," "Akliksett" IVA4277, IVA4278, IVA4280–IVA4282, IVA4292, IVA4394, IVA6972) and Kuskokwim and Togiak Rivers ("Atleksett" IVA5387, IVA5420, IVA5425); see also Nelson 1899, 43.
31. "Amerik" (*amirak*) IVA5481; see also Nelson 1899, 40–43.
32. "Atjekak" IVA5482.

THIRTEENTH DAY

1. "Hopokotit" (*qupun*) IVA4022.
2. "Aban=Kjalek=Akruk" IVA4263.
3. IVA5256.
4. IVA4342.
5. IVA4183.
6. IVA3677.
7. IVA4288.
8. "Sisslak" IVA5399.
9. See also Nelson 1899, 234–35, 449.
10. See also Fienup-Riordan 1994, 251–370; Nelson 1899, 357–93.
11. Earlier we had seen an *apallirtuun* (dance wand) ("Apatlar=Asiun" or "Apatlar=Tusiun" IVA4237) from the Yukon, which Jacobsen described as a speaker's staff held in the hand during festivals, about which the elders did not comment.

VISUAL REPATRIATION

1. Fienup-Riordan 1994.
2. Wooden box inlay, IVA3939; *uluaq*, IVA4687.
3. IVA4217.
4. Drooker 1995; Fowler 1995; Wood and Shelton 1996.
5. The role of museums in nation building has been widely discussed (see Appadurai and Breckenridge 1992; Bennett 1995; Handler 1988; Kaplan 1994; Karp et al. 1992; Steiner 1995; White 1997).
6. Bunzl 1996, 17–78; Sahlins 2000, 163–65.
7. Sahlins 1995, 13–14; Sahlins 2000, 170, 192; Turner 1992.
8. Sahlins 2000, 200.
9. Sahlins 1999, 408–9.
10. Sahlins 1999, 404.
11. Gellner 1987, 10, 1983; Hiwasaki 1998.
12. Brumann 2000.
13. Bourdieu 1984.
14. Babcock 1993, 239.
15. Conklin 1997, 724.
16. Conklin 1997, 719.
17. Turner 1992, 301.
18. Basso 1996, 7.
19. Ames 1990, 1992; Bennett 1988; Clifford 1988, 1991, 1997; Hooper-Greenhill 1992; Kahn 1995, 2000; Karp and Lavine 1991; Karp, Kreamer, and Lavine 1992; Lumley 1988; Mitchell 1989; Price 1989; Price and Price 1992; Stocking 1985; Torgovnick 1990; Vergo 1989; Walsh 1992.
20. Ames 1992; Baizerman 1994; Day 1994; Dubin 1999; Dustan 1999; Fienup-Riordan 1996, 2000; Fuller 1992; Hedlund 1994; Jacknis 1990; Kahn 2000; Laforet 1993; Salvador 1994.
21. Crowell et al. 2001; King 2001; Loring 2001.
22. Kahn 2000, 57; Krech 1994, 3.
23. Driscoll-Engelstad 1995, 1996; Issenmen 1985, 1990, 1991, 1997; Kaplan 2001; Kingston 1999.
24. Sahlins 2000, 163.
25. Fienup-Riordan 1996, 23–30.
26. Handler 1985, 194.

GLOSSARY

Notes: italics are in the standard Yup'ik orthography (see Jacobson 1984). Words ending in the letter *q* are singular, the end letter *t* indicates a plural word, and the end letter *k* is dual. Abbreviations in parentheses indicate place of origin: (Y) = Yukon; (K) = Kuskokwim; (NI) = Nelson Island; (N) = Nunivak; (BB) = Bristol Bay. Object names recorded by Jacobsen have been capitalized and placed in quotation marks, as they appear in Jacobsen's original German accession records.

aaggaqtaat gloves (from *aaggaq,* "hand"); also *aaggsiik, aasgaat, aigsaat, aliiman, arilluuk, yuaralget*

aaggsiik/aaggsiit glove/gloves; also *aaggaqtaat, aasgaat, aigsaat, aliiman, yuaralget*

aangruyak/aangruyiit weapon/weapons to dispatch an animal hit by a harpoon; also "Angerojak," "Unnerak"; see also *asaaquq*

Aaniraq ceremony during which two men referred to as *aanak* ("mothers," dual) visited house-to-house followed by another man referred to as their *qimugta* (dog); spirits of the deceased were present to receive food and gifts; follows three nights of *Qaariitaaq*

aasgaat (Y) gloves; also "Assegatt," *aaggaqtaat, aaggsiik, aigsaat, yuaralget*

aavcaat darts; also "Jurroktan"

agayaniat cormorant-feather flight stabilizers on arrow shafts; see also *culut, nakrun*

Agayun God

Agayuyaraq way of making prayer, dancing with masks requesting abundance in the coming season, held in late February or early March (from *agayu,* "mask, prayer"); also *Itruka'ar*

agiyautaq tool used to cut soil to cover the *qasgi* or to cut snow

agleerta girl who has recently menstruated for the first time and is subject to various restrictions

agluirun/agluirutet earrings connected with strands of beads hanging under the jaw like a necklace (literally, "device for an *agluquq* [jaw]"); also "Aglaurutitt," *aqlin, as'un, nakacuguarraak*

agneq chorus of a dance song

agnirta dance director who calls out the *agneq* (chorus) of a dance song; see also *apallirturta*

aguumaq/aguumat (NI) storage bag/bags or basket/baskets; also "Aggomat," "Akkomat," "Akoinat," *issran, kalngak, kellarvik, qatengvik, qungasvik, ugalguun*

agyuk/agyut gift exchange partner/partners from the opposite village during the Messenger Feast

aiggatet seal-scratcher, used to imitate the sound of a seal working at its breathing hole, to lure it to the hunter (from *aiggaq,* "hand, seal flipper"); also "Aikatett," "Aikattet," *cetugyugun*

aigsaat (K) gloves; also *aaggaqtaat, aaggsiik, aasgaat, aliiman, arilluuk, yuaralget*

aivagun wood splitter, wedge; also *ekiarqin, equgcuun, qupurrun*

akagyailkutet spear guards, ivory or bone spear-holder attachments to kayaks, used to prevent weapons from falling overboard (from *akag-,* "to roll"); also "Akagieltuṇ," "Akagojelkoutiit," "Akagojelkutit," "Akuwselkutiit"

ak'allat things of the past, artifacts (literally, "old things")

akin wooden headrest, log on the outer edge of floor bedding

akitnaq/akitnat arrow/arrows with blunt-tipped point/points; also "Akkitnut," "Kutfik"; see also *akulmiqurcetaaq, cingigturat, meq'ercetaaq, pingayupegcetaat, pitegcaun, umilek, urugnaq*

aklanquq curved bone from the front appendage of a seal

aklegaq/aklegat seal-hunting harpoon/harpoons with bladder float; see also *asaaquq, nagiiquyaq, nanerpak, tegun*

aklicaraq/aklicarat small peg/pegs at the end of a throwing board joint/joints at the end of a spear used to attach the point

akluinqun clothing bag

akmagartaa willow-bark lashing?

akmaliarall'er raven (from *akemna,* "the one across there"); also *tulukaruk*

akngirnailitaq/akngirnailitat thimble/thimbles (from *akngirte-,* to get hurt, literally, "something that prevents pain"); also "Aknerreneilit," "Aknerreneitit," "Aknerrenelit," *keniutet, tekeq, tekrun*

akulmiqurcetaaq two-pointed bird-hunting arrow; see also *akitnaq, cingigturat, meq'ercetaaq, pingayupegcetaat, pitegcaun, umilek, urugnaq*

akunriuresqevkenaki telling them to control their consumption (of water)

akutaq "Eskimo ice cream," literally, "a mixture," including berries, seal oil, shortening, sugar, and, in some areas, boned fish

alailutet objects placed on burials as memorials to the deceased

alerquun/alerquutet instruction/instructions

algarcaraq/algarcarat ivory buckle/buckles or connecting link/links on harpoon lines (literally, "keeper")

aliiman/aliimatet glove/gloves, mitten/mittens; also "Allemak," "Allemek"; see also *arilluk*

allegpak/allegpiit willow-bark fishing net/nets; also "Peekatluk=Atlik"; see also *taryaqvagcuun*

allek/allget inner fibrous layer of young willow bark that can be twisted into rope or twine for net making (from *alleg-*, "to tear")

allgiar/allgiaraat old-squaw duck/ducks

allgiinraat male old-squaw duck feathers (from *allgiar*, "old-squaw duck")

alliit mitten palms

alliqsak/alliqsiit woven grass liners for skin boots, grass socks woven in a spiral manner; also "Aklikset," "Akliksett," "Atleksett"; see also *qugcuun*

allungak bottom part of a bowl or bucket

alngat (Y) decorations, marks; also "Allingan," *qaralit*

aluqatkaq/aluqatkat dried beaver scent gland/glands, castor/castors; also *ic'ukcat*

aluuyacuar little wooden bowl; see also *alvik, ilutuliar, qantaq*

alvik large food container; see also *aluuyacuar, ilutuliar, qantaq*

amaaret (Y) willow roots; willow-root strapping around wooden slats on a fish trap; also *uqviinraq*

amiik entranceway

amikuk/amikuut extraordinary underground creature/creatures, usually depicted as changeable and difficult to capture

amirak/amiriik/amiriit waterproof fish-skin boot/boots used in cold, dry weather (from *amiq*, skin, hide); also "Amerik," *ivruciq*

amlliq/amllit monster fish/fishes with large spots, which surface from the depths of lakes (from *amllir-*, "to step over")

amnginaq fish-roe *akutaq* with salmonberries

amrayak backpack (from *amaq*, "load carried on the back")

amuvik kayak stem

anarcuun indentation on the fire board (literally, "device to release *anaq* [feces]")

angalkuq/angalkut shaman/shamans

angassacuaraat (NI) small ladles (from *angassaq*, "ladle"); see also *arulamirun, ipuun, qalutaq, qassuutaq*

angiikvak common eider; also *metrar*

angqaq/angqat ball/balls

anguarun single-bladed paddle; also "Anguarut," *asaurun*

anguarutnguat three-cornered skin-sewing needles (literally, "imitation paddle," from *anguarun*, "paddle"); see also *ciilaq, kakuutet, kapun, mingqun, quagulek*

angyapiaq large skin boat (literally, "genuine boat")

angyaq skin boat other than a kayak or canoe

anipaq snowy owl

anqaraun/anqarautet warrior song/songs

apallirturta/apallirturtet dance director/directors, conductor/conductors who call out the lyrics to the *apallut* (verses) of a song; see also *agniurta*

apallirtuun/apallirtuuet dance stick/sticks or wand/wands (literally, "device used in calling out the lyrics to the *apalluq* [verse] of a dance song"); also "Apatlar=Asiun," "Apatlar=Tusiun"

apalluq/apallut verse/verses of a song

apallulget songs with verses

apqara'arcuun/apqara'arcuutet shaman drum/drums (from *apqara-*, "to ask about something," literally, "device for asking")

aqevlequtat/aqevlungauyiit dangling ornaments (from *aqevla-*, "to dangle or hang down"); also "Akkowlongaujit," "Akowlangaujit"

aqlin/aqlitet earring/earrings, earring decoration attached to an *as'un* (hook); also "Assiutik," "Assiutitt," "Thuntek," *agluirun, nakacuguarraak*

aqumutet sitting-down dances

aquun wooden frame inserted into squirrel skins for stretching and drying

araq punk or willow ash

arilluk/arilluut fish-skin mitten/mittens; also "Alimakara=AngoarSoutitt," "Arekluk," "Arrituk"; see also *aaggaqtaat, aaggsiik, aasgaat, aigsaat, aliiman, yuaralget*

arr'inaq/arr'inat/arr'inarkiurat seal-skin hunting bag/bags; also "Ullufak"

arulamirun long-handled ladle (literally, "device to move things around" [in a cooking pot]); see also *angassaq, ipuun, qalutaq, qassuutaq*

arviiq sharpening stone found in the Platinum area; see also *ellin, teggalqupiaq, uqu'urniq*

asaaquq/asaaqut harpoon/harpoons used to kill seals on and around ice floes; also "Asiakok," "Assakok," "Essaktok," "Pai=iktut=Swogit"; see also *aangruyak, aklegaq, nagiiquyaq, nanerpak, tegun*

asaurun pole, paddle, oar; also *anguarun*

assipek skin-stretching and scraping tool; also *tuluruaq*

asuirun/asuirutii extra piece/pieces of leather sewn onto a seam for reinforcement

as'un/as'utet earring hook/hooks that go through the ear; also "Assiutik," "Assiutitt," "Kowelakset," "Kogeloksett"; see also *agluirun, aqlin, nakacuguarraak*

atanrautaq sinew binding on a toggling harpoon

atauciqerrnat arrows with points that detach in the quarry; also "Kjinginat"

ateknguitet story knives; also "Atitueititt"; see also *cirunqaaraat, equaq, yaaruin*

atkuk parka; also "Atkutt"

atkupiaq women's fancy parka with a band across the chest area and eight tassles hanging front and back (literally, "genuine parka")

atmagcuun/atmagcuutet carrying device/devices, yoke/yokes; also "Atmak=Sutitt," *tassiitaq*

atqataq/atqatat human figure/figures hanging down inside the *ellanguaq* (hoop used during special dances)

avisgaq black paint or pigment

avneq shaman's "other half" (from *avek*, "half")

ayallaq/ayallat cutting board/boards; also "Heidtlak"

ayaperyaraq/ayaperyarat cockpit coaming stanchion/stanchions, central deck stiffener/stiffeners on which one braces one's hands when getting in and out of a kayak; also "Thunnerasut"

ayaruq walking stick, staff, cane

ayimtat skins that have been rendered pliant (from *ayimte-*, "to break or sever")

caagnitellria/caagnitellriit person/people restricted from certain activities due to puberty, childbirth, miscarriage, or death; for example, girls menstruating for the first time, women suffering from miscarriage or who have lost their husbands, eldest daughters of mothers who died, men who have lost their wives, husbands of women suffering from miscarriage

cacarqerra front piece of a parka

cagnirqun/cagnirqutet cross lashing holding the sinew backing onto the body of the bow (literally, "device for tightening," from *cagni-*, "to be tight, taut") *calugcissuun/calugcissuutet* skin scraper/scrapers (from *calugte-*, "to tan a skin by scraping," literally, "device for scraping"); also "Kauloc," "Kjalgotik," "Kjalugotit," "Kjalugotitt," "Kleikut," *elumerun, urumerun*

caniitaq/camatat decorative dance cap/caps, beaded dance headdress/headdresses with a copper band across the top

canengalnguut bullets with lines on the top resembling grass roots (from *canek*, "grass"); also *kaapcelaat*

canek/canget grass/grasses in general

caniryak/caniryiik extra point/points midway down an arrow shaft

caqiqsak/caqiqsiik sickle-shaped labret/labrets worn on the chin by women, side labret/labrets; also "Okkaklekak," "Sakeksek"

carigluk debris, dust, grass

carrqaq baby seal that has lost its newborn skin (from *carrir-*, "to clean or clear off")

caturnilria one who is turning the kayak skin?

caukia a top-spinning game that uses the word *caukia* (turn to me) in its chant: *kitaki wani caukia, caukia, caukia* (okay now, turn to me, turn to me, turn to me)

cauyaq/cauyat drum/drums; also "Kjaojak"

cauyaqucira added motions accompanied by drumming

cauyara'aruun drum song (from *cauyaq*, "drum")

cauyaruaraak two drum designs on a parka; a family crest

caveq/cavget toggling harpoon point/points that turn sideways under an animal's skin, holding it fast (from *caveg-*, "to work"); also "Kalogiet," "Kja'ok," "Paiiktut=Sawogit" (NI), "Resiun," "Sawogik," "Sawogit" (BB), "Sawok," "Sawokpak" (Y), "Tontak?" "Toutak?" "Usinaresiun," "Usinarisun"; see also *kakgar, umi*

cavigaq/caviggaat cutting knife/knives; also "Igluktulik," "Kapiattun," "Kappotitt," "Kjimat=Sakkiun," "Ojamik," "Sawik," "Sawisak," "Sawik-kak," "Sawikok," "Sawogak"

cavituucaraq a game to acquire firewood for a fire bath (from *cavtu-*, "to pull something")

cengaq/cengat kayak bow or keel protector/protectors; also "Eajalootit"

ce'ntar/cetrautaq etched design, mark (from *ceter-*, "to mark, to engrave")

ce'ntarcuun tool to make designs on ivory (from *ceter-*, "to mark, to engrave")

ceugtaq/ceugnat implement/implements to go after fish swimming close to the surface; also *neqsuutet*

cetugun seal scratcher (from *cetuk*, "claw, nail," literally, "device for clawing or scratching"); also *aiggatet*

ceturquq caribou-nail scraper; also *keligcuun*

ceturqurucaraak parka design of hooves or claws; a family crest

ceturaq kayak front area

ciayaq/ciayat bentwood hat/hats decorated with feathers; see also *elciaq, uytarcuutet*

cigvik/cigviit nose bead/beads, bead/beads worn on a short string placed through a hole in the septum of the nose

cigyaq/cigyiit split strip/strips of spruce wood used as slat/slats in a wooden fish trap

ciiqciiat (NI) three-cornered needle/needles; also *anguarutnguat, kazuutet, kapun, mingqun, quagulek*

ciklaq/ciklat/ciklauraat (NI) root digger/diggers, root pick/picks, pickax/pickaxes (from *ciklaur-*, "to chop or hack loose"); also "Kimat=Sakkiun," "Siklak"

cikuirun/cikuliurutet ice chisel/chisels; also *tugeq*

cilkiayaraq the process of harsh daily training that men underwent to become good providers and people with insight and wisdom

cill'aq circular calendar with a pointer that is moved to point to the days of the week (from Russian *chisló*); also "Sisslak"; see also *ernercuun, nitiliq*

cingigturat arrows with barbed ivory points; also "Kjinginat," *urugnaq*; see also *akitnaq, akulmiqurcetaaq, atauciqerrnat, meq'ercetaaq, pingayupegcetaat, pitegcaun, umilek*

cingilegiit arrow points

cipnermiutaat ends dangling down in front of a woman's *naqugun* (belt)

cirla substance with the power to harm

cirliqsuutem kangiqliik third step on a barbed harpoon point (literally, "two closer to the *kangia* [top end] of the *cirliqsuun* [thing that makes one suffer]")

cirliqsuutem qullia second step on a barbed harpoon point (literally, "one above the *cirliqsuun* [thing that makes one suffer]")

cirliqsuun first step on a *kukgar*, barbed harpoon point (literally, "thing that makes one suffer"; from *cirliqe-*, "to have a hard time")

cirunqaaraat antler story knives (from *ciruneq*, "antler"); see also *ateknguitet, equaq, yaaruin*

cirunqatak old antler

ciulilriit those making the front of the kayak skin

ciuqilutek dances during the Messenger Feast (literally, "the first two")

cukluuk/cukluut dangling bead ornament/ornaments attached to each side of the forehead

culut feather flight stabilizers on arrows and spears; see also *nakrutet*

cungagaq alder-bark dye applied to reduce shrinkage (from *cungag-*, "to be greenish in color")

cungagartaq dyed leather piece used to decorate sewn items (from *cungag-*, "to be greenish in color")

cungarpak/cungarpiik/cungarpiit labret/labrets; see also *mengkuk, tuutaq*

cungavseq/cungauyar/cungauyaraat bead/beads; see also *pipigaq, teggliq*

curmak/curmiit tobacco bag/bags to keep tobacco leaves moist

Curukaq feast wherein one village goes over to another to dance and exchange gifts or challenges; also *Kevgiryaraq*

curukat guests (literally, "attackers") invited to the *Curukaq*

curuq mat for bedding, mattress

egan/egatek cooking pot/pots (dual)

eglu/eglut underlayer/underlayers of backbone muscle or ligament split to make sinew; see also *eglupik, uliutet, yualuq*

eglupik/eglupiit genuine sinew/sinews made from *eglu* (underlayer of backbone muscle); see also *eglu, uliutet, yualuq*

egun/egutet (K) throwing board/boards, spear thrower/throwers; also "Iggun," *nuqaq*

ekiarqin/ekiarqitet wood splitter/splitters, wedge/wedges; also *aivagun, equgcuun, qupun*

ekillugnarqellria arrow point that could cause bad injury to the flesh; also "Kjingiligit," "Omiligit"

elavurcautet flat part of a seal's stomach (from *elave-*, "to come down close to the ground")

Elciyaraq one-night ceremony in which all men receive bowls filled with food in the *qasgi*; follows *Qaariitaaq* and *Qaarpagyaraq*

elevlevaaq (BB)/*elevlugtaq* (K) wooden top spun with a string; also "Kalluroroaram" *ella yagtellrani* "earth extended its arms," implying bad weather

ellam ayanra aturluku following *ella* (the universe)

ellam iqua narqerraarluku living long enough to smell the tail-end of life, living to an old age

ellam qaralii designs of the sky

Ellam Yua the Person of the Universe; God

ellangualissuun device to make *ellanguaq* (circle-and-dot) designs; also *kassugaliilissuun*

ellanguaq/ellanguat circle-and-dot design/designs (literally, "model or pretend universe"); also, hoop/hoops around masks, hoop/hoops decorated with fur and feathers hanging in the *qasgi* and moved up and down during special dances; see also *kassuugaliiret*, *iinguat*

ellaraq wooden spinner or spindle used as a toy; also "Tinngait"

ellarrluk time of famine and food shortage due to prolonged bad weather

ellin/ellitet sharpening stone/stones; also "Slinn"; see also *arviiq*, *teggalqupiaq*, *uqu'urniq*

ellipiarat type of stitching used on boot soles

ellumerrun/ellumerrutet (BB) skin scraper/scrapers; also "Plomeron," "Plomeroutitt," *calugcissuun*, *urumerun*

ellutmuayaaq striped cloth, calico; also *tiiguayaaq*

elqiaq/elqiat bentwood visor/visors, hunting hat/hats; also "Ilkatt," "Ilkeak," "Ilkeat," "Ilket," "Il'tkiak," *ciayaq*, *ugtarcuutet*

Elriq/Elriyaraq ceremony honoring the soul spirits of the dead, referred to in the literature as the Great Feast for the Dead

ena/enet sod house/houses; also *nepiaq*

equaq wooden story knife (from *equk*, "wood"); see also *cirunqaaraat*, *yaaruin*

equgcuun/equgcuutet wood splitter/splitters, wedge/wedges; also *aivagun*, *ekiarqin*, *qupun*

equgcuutnguarraq man's bag for woodworking tools (from *equg-*, "wood")

ernercuun calendar; see also *cill'aq*, *nitiliq*

everquun/everquutet tool/tools for prying or unraveling; also "Kadliutit"

eviutet loosely woven grass mats placed between the planks and sod to insulate houses (from *evek*, "grass"); also *qerqulluut*

eyagyaraq/eyagyarat traditional abstinence practice/practices associated with pregnancy, birth, miscarriage, puberty, and death

ic'ukcat dried male beaver castors; also *aluqatkaq*

igaugek/igauget eyeshade/eyeshades, snow goggles; also "Iggaak," "Iggant," "Iggaovvik," "Illtket"

iglak freeze-dried esophagus; also *nerun*

iinguat circle-and-dot designs (literally, "pretend eyes"); see also *ellanguat*, *kassugaliiret*

iinruq/iinrut amulet/amulets, contemporary word for medicine; also "Hojamik," "Ilnnero," "Innerok," "Inrok," "Issignak," "Kjinok=Yugak"

iitaq/iitat tall cotton grass (*Eriophorum angustifolium*)

ikaraliitet grass kayak mats; see also *tupigat*

ikavsiaq/ikavsiarutet cross-stitching (from *ikani*, "across there")

ikavsiarutkanek completed sinew thread

ikgun leather-sewing tool, small lever or prying tool (from *ikug-*, "to lift by lever action")

iluliraq funnel for a fish trap

ilungaq/ilungapak female cross-cousin of a female, by extension a woman's female friend

iluraq cross-cousin, teasing cousin, specifically male cross-cousin of a male, by extension a man's male friend

ilutuliar large bowl or container (from *ilutu-*, "to be deep"); also *alvik*, *qantaq*; see also *aluuyacuar*

imairitek dipper for removing fragments of ice from water (from *imaite-*, "to be empty"); also *qenuirun*

imaq/imat bullet/bullets, ammunition

imarkaq lead (metal) (from *imaq*, "bullet, ammunition")

imarnin/imarnitet seal-gut rain parka/parkas, raincoat/coats

imarpalget muzzle-loading guns; also *itukellriit*

imgun/imgutaq coiled sealskin line on a seal-hunting harpoon (from *imeg-*, "to roll up"); also *kinguliraq*, *usaaq*

imin/imitet bullet mold/molds; see also *puulissuun*

imruyutaq/imruyutaat netting shuttle/shuttles or string holder/holders; also "Immerojutak," "Inneroutitt," *qilagcuun*

inerquun/inerquutet prohibition/prohibitions, rule/rules

Inglupgayuk the half-faced one, legendary being with half a face

ingula dance performed by women to *ingulautet* (slow, old-style songs)

ingulaun/ingulautet slow old-style song/songs

inuguaq/inuguat toy doll/dolls, human figure/figures (from Iñupiaq *inuk*, "person," plus +(*ng*)uaq, "imitation"); also "Innuct," "Innuet," "Innugaet," "Innugoak," "Innungoet," "Jungoak," *irniaruaq*, *sugaq*, *yugaq*

inuguarcetuat special kind of stitching used on boot soles

ipuun/ipuutet ladle/ladles (from *ipug-*, "to ladle"); see also *angassaq*, *arulamirun*, *qalutaq*, *qassuutaq*

ipuutet wooden snare attachments; also *meluurutet*

iqataq/iqatat separators, leather pieces strung between beads on necklaces; also "Kaleluktett" (Y), "Senerotitt=Atanneritt" (K), "Tunusoromiutak" (BB)

iqertak/iqertiit thing/things made of fish skin

iqmiutak/iqmiutaat tobacco box/boxes (from *iqmik*, "chewing tobacco"); also "Ekmiutak," "Ekwiutat," "Ettmiutak"

iqugmiutaq/iqugmiutaat (NI) bag fastener/fasteners (from *iquk*, "end"); also "Ekkogemiutak," *kakinquka'ar*, *nunguyun*; see also *kuukicaaq*, *puukicaaq*

iqukeggun/iqukeggutet engraving tool/tools with beaver incisor-tooth points; also "Ipiksaun," "Palok sinerat=Kuutit," "Paloksinerat=Kuutit"

iraluiraucaraq arguing over the name for the new moon (from *iraluq*, "moon, month")

ircaqinraq caribou bladder bag (from *ircaquq*, "heart")

ircenrraq/ircenrraat extraordinary person/persons who may appear in either animal or human form, often called "little people"

irnerrlugtalria hunter receiving the rib portion of a seal; literally, "the one with the *irnerrluk* (seal gut)"

irniaq offspring, child; also "Arneak," "Erneak"

irniaruaq/irniaruat toy doll/dolls (literally, "fake or pretend child"); also *inuguaq*, *sugaq*, *yugaq*

irunguaq rifle or arrow support (from *iruq*, "leg," literally, "pretend leg"); also "Eerongoarewik," "Eruingok"

issraka'ar small bag; see also *aguumaq*, *issran*, *kalngak*, *kellarvik*, *qemaggvik*, *qungasvik*, *ungalguun*

issran/issratet twined grass bag/bags; also "Isrann," "Issret," "Issrett"; see also *aguumaq*, *issraka'ar*, *kalngak*, *kellarvik*, *qemaggvik*, *qungasvik*, *ugalguun*

itercaraq attachment to a harpoon shaft

it'galqinraq/it'galqinrat black decorative strip/strips from dried swan-foot leather used as a base for *kelurqut* (decorative stitching) on sewn articles (from *it'gaq*, "foot")

itgiek bead decorations (over the top of the foot of a boot)

Itruza'ar/Iruka'aryaraq ceremonial dancing with masks; held in late February or early March; also *Agayuyaraq*

ituzallrait muzzle-loading guns; also *imarpalget*

ivrencun/ivrautet caribou-skin wading boot/boots used in wet weather (from *iver-*, "to step into water"); also "Atjekak"

ivruciq/ivrucit waterproof skin boot/boots (from *iver-*, "to step into water") also *amirak*

kaapelcat bullets, caps; also *canegngalnguut*

kaapelautek primer box; also "Capselautlok," "Kapselautlok," "Kapselerun," *kenivik*

kaaaryara a hand game

kakeryaq/kakauyat parka hood tassle/tassles, decoration/decorations hung from the back of a parka hood

kakeggluqueyaat nose septum decoration? (from *kakeggluk*, "snot, nasal mucus")

kakiiaraat pins

kakiauka'er/kakiyutet bag fastener/bag fasteners (from *kaki-*, "to take a stitch"); also *iqugmiutaq*, *nunguyun*; see also *kuukicaaq*, *puakicaa*

kakizeun/kakinqutet woodworking tool/tools, blade/blades (from *kakite-*, "to prick or pierce, poke with a sharp pin"); also "Kakkineron," "Kakkinneron," "Kassrearusutitt," "Pitknoat," *kakisvik*

kakisvik piece of a sewing bag through which needles are pierced (from *kaki-*, "to take a stitch, to pierce a needle into and back out the same side"); also "Kaksiwit," *kakinqun*

kakivik/kakiviit needle case/cases, sewing bag/bags (from *kaki-*, "to take a stitch"); also "Kakiwit," "Kakkiuwit," "Kakkiwit?" "Kakkiwit," "Kalsiwit," "Kalangak," "Kalsiwit"

kakuutet needles made from the front part of a crane's foot; see also *anguarutnruat*, *ciilaq*, *kapun*, *mingqun*, *quagulek*

kalngak storage bag; see also *aguumaq*, *issraka'ar*, *issran*, *kellarvik*, *qemaggvik*, *qungasvik*, *ugalguun*

ka'utacuute round pucks; also "Iglukiak," "Juglitak"

ka'utaryaraq a hockeylike game

kameqeqak/kamegciqat short lightweight boots

kanga'tjaq bundle of wild celery used during *Nakaciuryaraq* (Bladder Festival)

kangcireq/kangcirat tarpaulin/tarpaulins, sled sheet/sheets, grass mats/mats to line the wall of a house

kangkupaguac (K) paddle handle grip; also *qaquaq*

kankiic ice skates (dual) (from Russian *kon'ki*); also "Kjikoleureisiut"

kap'issuun implement for piercing patients during doctoring, poker (from *kape-*, "to pierce or poke in"); also "Kappan," "Kappon," *kapit*, *kaputalgaar*, *kaputaq*, *qiivuusaaq*, *ukicissun*

kapun/keputet needle/needles or spear point/points (from *kape-*, "to pierce or poke in"); also "Kapotitt," "Kappan," "Kappon," "Kapotat=Komissiutitt"; see also *anguarutnguat*, *ciilaq*, *kakuutet*, *mingqun*, *quagulek*

kaputaar/kaputalqaar small *kaputaq* (drill)

kaputaq/kaputet poker/pokers, drill/drills (from *kape-*, "to pierce or poke in"); also "Kapotarkakartlak," "Kappan," "Kokkiksak," *kap'issuun*, *kaputalqaar*, *qiivuusaaq*, *ukicissuun*

kassaq/kass'at white person/people (from Russian *kazák*, cossack)

kassugalissuun implement to make circle-and-dot designs (literally, "device for going around"); also *ellangualissuun*

kassugaliiret circle-and-dot designs (from *kassug-*, "to go around, to encompass"); also *ellanguaq*, *iinguat*

kataagun snuff strainer, sieve (from *katag-*, "to fall out"); also "Kattaun"

kaugtuutacuar small hammer or club (from *kaugtur-*, "to strike with an object"); also "Aban=Kjalek=Akruk"

kaugtuutaq/kaugtuutat club/clubs, fish striker/strikers, hammer/hammers (from *kaugtur-*, "to strike with an object"); also "Kargotett," "Kauk=Tudak=Neknen"; see also *qenngitaq*

kaullriqerluku removing the ash from the oil-lamp wick

kaviaraat the Pleiades or Ursa Minor (literally, "little foxes")

kaviragtaq red material (from *kavirliq*, "red")

kay'urrutet armbands used by men directing the dance songs; also "Kajuarotik," "Kjuarotik"

keggalrun literally, "device to rub or smooth out"

kegginailitaq blade covering for a *mellgar* (crooked knife)

kegginaquq/kegginaqut mask/masks (from *kegginaq*, "face," literally, "thing that is like a face"); also "Kinakok," "Kinakut," "Kinakutt"

kelevyat fringes (from *kelve-*, "to cut into strips")

keligcuun scraper (from *kelig-*, "to scrape"); also *cetumquq*

kelipacuk/kelipacuut excess material scraped from the inside of fish skins, considered a delicacy (from *kelig-*, "to scrape")

keliutaq/kelipacuutaq scraper (from *kelig-*, "to scrape"); also "Killiutak"

kellarvik storage bag or container; also "Klarowit," "Klarowitt," "Kllullerokkek"; see also *aguumaq*, *issraka'ar*, *issran*, *kalngak*, *qemaggvik*, *qungasvik*, *ugalguun*

kelugkat coarse grass used for weaving mats and baskets

kelurquq/kelurqut/kelurquaraat special stitching with caribou throat hair and sinew on thin strips of dyed skin or dried bird-foot leather on fancy parkas and other items (from *keluk*, "stitch")

kenervik primer for gunpowder

keniutet (N) thimbles; also *akngirnailitaq*, *tekeq*, *tekrun*

kenivik primer box; also *kaapcelautlek*

kenngessuutet fire starters (from *kennge-*, "to start to burn"); see also *kumartessuun*, *neg'utaq*, *nucugcuutek*, *ussukataq*

kenret flames, matches

kenurraq/kenurrat lamp/lamps; also "Knokak"

kepcetaaq/kepcetaat dyed leather piece/pieces used to decorate sewn items

kepelmurluku cutting a skin into sections all the way around instead of opening it in the stomach

kepirtat line attachers (from *kepe-*, "to cut off")

kepun/keputet adze/adzes, ax/axes; also "Kapootit?" "Kjimat=Sakkiun," "Okoksin"

Kevgiryaraq the Messenger Feast, named for the *kevgak* (two messengers) sent to invite the guest village to the festival, during which first-time dancers are presented and gifts exchanged; also *Curukaq*

kingulilriit those making the back of the kayak skin

kinguliralget arrows with *kingulirat* (lines) behind the tip

kinguliraq/kingulirat line/lines for a harpoon (from *kingu-*, "back part, area behind"); also *imgun*, *usaaq*

kis'un/kis'utet weight/weights for fishhook, bottom lead line sinker/sinkers on nets; also "Kitet," "Kitett," "Kitsakt," "Kittet," "Kitzak"

kukgar/kukgarat barbed harpoon point/points; also "Kohkae," "Kokak," "Kokaran," "Kokararak," "Kokarat," "Kokkak," "Kokkarat," "Kokkiak"; see also "Nanarkpit," "Narok," "Peeicktutt," "Peiktutt," "Piteksirat," "Toukak," *cavek*, *kukgaracuar*, *umi*

kukgaracuar/kukgaracuaraat/kukgarapiayagaat small barbed harpoon point/points

kukgarpak/kukgarpiit large barbed harpoon point/points (from *kukgar*, "barbed harpoon point")

kumartessuun fire board with indentation for a drill stick (from *kumarte-*, "to light a fire"); also "Allekak"; see also *kenngessuutet, neg'utaq, nucugcuutek, ussukataq*

kumarun/kumarutet/kumarulluut dried-moss lamp wick/wicks; also "Kowarotitt"; see also *uruq*

kumgaq/kumgat incised design/designs carved into wood or ivory (from *kumeg-*, "to scratch")

kuukicaaq/kuukicaat button/buttons (from Russian *púgovitsa*); also "Krefitt," "Krifitt," "Krrfit," *puukicaaq*; see also *nunguyun*

kuusqutet rigid, upright grass baskets; also *naparcilluk*

kuvyacuar small-mesh gill net; also "Koesetzuak"

kuvyakuiner bottom mesh of an ice dipper

kuyagtaraa third portion of a catch, including the animal's lower part, from *kuyak*, "hip"

llumarraq cloth

lugluquссaaq/lugluquссaat net float/floats, buoy/buoys; also *pugtaqutaq*

luuskaat spoons (from Russian *lózhka*); see also *qaaluuciaq, qalussnguarraat, qassuukar/qassuuciarraq, yuurqaarcuun, uiluq*

mak'aq fish-roe *akutaq* with salmonberries

makikcaq/makikcat ground-squirrel snare/snares; also "Makkiksett"; see also *puukaqercetaat*

makugtalriit literally, "those who live through hardship, hard work, endurance"

mallegtaq/mallegtat closely twined, flexible grass bag/bags, closely woven stitch/stitches (from *malleg-*, "to be close together")

mallegtarpak large, closely woven, flexible grass bag

mallegtayaqaq narrow bag

mamcat flat part of a seal's stomach (from *mamcarte-*, "to be flat")

manaq (NI) fishing lure with hook; also "Eksak," "Etsetzuak=Sukwakt=Sutitt," "Karlotsett," "Kitzak," "Manak," "Mannet"

manaqutaq (NI) fishing hook, line, and pole; also "Menakutak," "Nerallenlok"

manigcissuun tool for decorating or smoothing clay pots (from *manig-*, "to be smooth"); also "Gatsisun"

manumik/manumiit brooch/brooches, pin/pins (from *manu-*, "front side"); also "Nanomik"

maqissuun/maqissuutet men's fire-bath hat/hats

mellgar/mellgaraat crooked knife/knives; also "Milkak," "Millkak," "Mil'tkarrat," "Mitlek," "Omikak=Milkak"

melqurrilnguut caribou-skin wading boots; see also *ivrarcuun*

melugcuun tube or device for taking *meluskaq* (snuff tobacco); also "Sop=Sluett," *meluurun*

meluskaq snuff tobacco (from *melug-*, "to suck in")

meluskarvik/meluskarviit container/containers for snuff tobacco, snuff box/boxes; also "Agometgoak," "Agometzoak"

meluskautek/meuskautaak open snuff container from which one could sniff *meluskaq* (snuff tobacco), from *melug-*, "to suck in")

meluurun tube for taking *meluskaq* (snuff tobacco); also *melugcuun*

meluurutet wooden attachments to snares; also *ipuutet*

mengkuk/mengkuut (NI) men's labret/labrets; also *cungarpak, tuutaq*

meq'ercetaaq/meq'ercetaat arrow/arrows with a point that detaches in the flesh, arrow point/points that detaches in the flesh (from *meqe-*, "to shed"); see also *akitnaq, akulmiqurcetaaq, cingigturat, pingayupegcetaat, pitegcaun, umilek urugnaq*

Merr'aq Feast for the Dead (from *meq*, "water," which the thirsty dead desire)

mertarcuun water bucket (literally, "device for carrying water")

metrar common eider; also *angiikvak*

mer'un/mer'utet dipper/dippers; also *qalun*

miilapiat genuine *miilat* ("soap")

miilissuun mortar for making snuff tobacco (from *miili-*, "to grind")

milqeruak two square spots on the back of a parka (from *milqar-*, "to throw at"?)

mimernaq/mimernat tree stump/stumps, root portion/portions of a driftwood tree trunk

mingqepiarumalriit regular stitches (from *mingqe-*, "to sew")

mingqun/mingqutet needle/needles (from *mingqe-*, "to sew"); also "Minkutitt"; see also *anguarutrguat, ciilaq, kakuutet, kapun, quagulek*

mingqusviutaq/mingqusviutat needle case/cases; also "Minkatsiutitt," "Minkontauten," "Minkotmutitt," "Minkusiwit," "Ojamit=Minkusivit," *kakivik*

mingqutpiat genuine needles (from *mingqun*, "needle")

miryaruak white fur designs on a fancy parka (literally, "two representing *miryaq* [vomit]")

munalriit those who are dexterous, with skillful hands

naanguat/naanguapiat toys

nacaq/nacat hat/hats, parka hood/hoods, cap/caps; also "Natsat," "Nesak," "Nesan," "Nissak," "Samatak"

nacarpiaq/nacarpiat fancy hat/hats (literally, "genuine hat"); also "Nasakpak," "Nisakpak"

nacarrluk/nacarrluut dance hat/hats (literally, "bad hat"); also "Angakut=Nisarat"

nacitet split-wood flooring

nagiiquyacuar small seal-hunting spear

nagiiquyaq/nagiiquyat (K) seal-hunting spear/spears, harpoon/harpoons thrown with an *egun* (spear thrower); also "Nagikojak," "Narrekojak," *nanerpak*; see also *aklegaq, asaaquq, tegun*

nagtuqaq/nagtuqat belt fasteners (from *nagte-*, "to get snagged"); also "Naggiwik," "Naksalkult," "Naksallkott," "Naksallkult," "Naksallult"

Nakaciuryaraq Bladder Festival, in which bladders of caribou and seal are sent on a journey under the ice to return the following season; held in late fall (literally, "way of doing something with *nakacut* [bladders]")

nakacuguarraak/nakacuguarraat girls' earrings; see also *agluirun, aqlin, as'un*

nakirqatak side wall

nakrun/nakrutet fletching, flight-stabilizing feathers on arrows; also *agayiinraat, culut*

nanerpak/nanerpiit (Y) seal-hunting harpoon/harpoons used with spear throwers; also *nagiiquyaq*; see also *aklegaq, asaaquq, tegun*

nanilraq/nanilrat wooden stand/stands for a seal-oil lamp (from *naniq*, "lamp")

naniq lamp

naparcilluk/naparcilluut (NI) rigid, upright grass bag/bags (from *napa-*, "to stand upright"); also *kuusqutet*

napatii support, something that helps one stay alive

naqugun/naqugutet belt/belts; also "Nakkogutitt," "Nakogutitt"

narussuli skilled harpooner

nasqurrun/nasqurrutet dance headdress/headdresses (from *nasquq*, "head"); also "Naskonn," "Neskotitt"

natrak slip-on soles to keep one from slipping on ice, boot soles (dual); also "Natterak"

nangaryaraq dancing accompanied by songs

necepiaq snare that springs into the air when it catches something

negeq/negat rabbit snare/snares; also "Neget=Makausuet=Sititt"; see also *ipuutet*

negaqeggun/negaqeggutet net gauge/gauges, used during net-making to make mesh uniform (from *negaq*, "single mesh of a fishnet"); also "Junneroutitt," *qilakeggutet*

negevgutet spruce roots, used as strings on *qelutviaq* (a musical instrument)

negcigpak large gaff or boat hook; see also *negcik*, *negcikcuar*

negcik gaff, boat hook; also "Neksik," "Neksit," "Nekuk," "Ner=esit," "Netsik," "Niktsik"; see also *negcigpak*, *negcikcuar*, *tallirpacuar*

negcikcuar small gaff or boat hook; also "Eksiksok," "Mitzerrisutak," "Mitzerrisutuk," "Nikt-sintok," "Nikt-Suitak," "Niktsuitok"; see also *negcigpak*, *negcik*

neg'utaq/neg'utat fire starter mouthpiece/mouthpieces; also "Kamiak," "Eneiak," "Nerrutak," "Nerutatt," "Okommisak"; see also *kenngessuutet*, *kumartessuun*, *nucugcuutek*, *ussukataq*

nenaarun very strong, thin strip of wood used as strapping

nengeq/nengiit portion/portions or share/shares of a catch

nengerrassaagartuq going to receive a share of the catch

nengvauyuut dentalia?

nepetaq/nepcetat shaman mask/masks (literally, "something that sticks," from *nepete-*, "to stick, cling, or adhere")

nepiq family dwelling, sod house; also *ena*

neqsunneqsuutet fish spear point/points; also "Kagiret," "Kapokkaum," "Kappokkaum?" "Kokkokat?" "Naknem=Nowisem," "Noknem-Nowusem," *cetugnat*

nerescissuun/nerescissuutet comb/combs (literally, "device for removing *neresta* [louse]"); also *nuyiurun*, *tegurrliurutet*

neresta louse; also *ungiliit*

nerenrlugcetaaurun ridicule song, song of indigestion (from *nere-*, "to eat," plus +*nerrlugte-*, "to have trouble doing")

nerruar skin head ring with earflaps; also "Nelt'kun"

neruq/nerutet bleached esophagus (from *nere-*, "to eat"); man's large wooden bowl/bowls (literally, "device for eating"); also *iglak*

nillarun wooden stretcher for harpoon line

nissek quill attachments for squirrel snares

nitiik calendar (from Russian *nedélya*, literally, "week"); also *cill'aq*, *ercaun*

nucugcuun (NI) fire drill; also *ussukataq*; see also *kenngessuutet*, *kumartessuun*, *neg'utaq*

nucugcuutek/nucuutaak line or strap pulled back and forth after winding around the drill stick; also "Arullausett," "Nutjun"; see also *kenngessuutet*, *kumartessuun*, *neg'utaq*, *ussukataq*

nuigciret point/points for bird or rabbit spear; also "Neujeret"

nukalpiaq/nukalpikcat great hunter/hunters and provider/providers

nuliacungaq female cross-cousin of a male (literally, "sweet little wife")

nulucnulut webbing on snowshoes, bottom mesh on a *qenuirun* (ice dipper)

nunguun/nunguyutet bag or clothing fastener/fasteners (from *nungute-*, "to fasten a button or other garment fastener"); also *iqemiutaq*; see also *kakinquka'ar*, *kuukicaaq*, *puukicaaq*

nuqucinuat (NI) spear thrower/throwers, throwing board/boards; also "Narcak," "Narrekjak," "Norkak," "Noreak," *egun*

nutegcuun device for shooting (from *nuteg-*, "to shoot a firearm")

nuulek thing with a point; also *nangqulek*

nuusaaq three-pointed bird spear; also "Nausett," "Nosak," "Nousett," "Nursat"

nuusaarpak/nuusaarpiit large three-pronged fish or bird spear/spears; also "Neuerek," "Neujakpak," "Neujat," "Neujeret," "Norseakpak," "Nujeret," "Nursakpit"

nuussiq cutting knife

nuyitet hair pieces (from *nuyaq*, "hair")

nuyiurun/nuyuurun/nuyiurutet comb/combs (from *nuyaq*, "hair"); also "Jerruin," "Neujeorot," "Neujoron," "Nujeorot," *nerescissuun*, *tegurrliurutet*

paalraayak/paalraayiit extraordinary underground creature/creatures encountered in the mountains

paangrun kayak paddle with a blade at each end

paiqak two greeters, meeters during *Kevgiryaraq* (from *pairte-*, "to meet or encounter")

paitaalek two-person kayak (from Russian *baidarka*, or from *pai-*, "opening of a kayak")

pakinrek parka openings

pall'illrit stitches around the opening of a kayak

pall'itak where one places one's hands at the entranceway of the qasgi to push oneself up

paplu/paplut drum handle/handles; also "Paplok," "Paptlo," "Paptlok"

passiissuun pestle for grinding snuff tobacco (from *passi-*, "to crush"); see also *passin*

passin pestle (from *passite-*, "to press by putting pressure"); see also *passiissuun*

pasvaagun/pasvaagutet stopper/stoppers or plug/plugs for a water container or seal poke

patkartaaryaraq slap ball (from *pateg-*, "to slap")

pat'luunat cartridge shells

pekutaq snow shovel (from *peke-*, "to make a movement that attracts notice"); also "Pekoutak," *qanikciurun*

pequara upper back part of a parka

perriun/perriutet material for wiping things, sponge/sponges, towel/towels; also "Krentit," "Kreuti"

pertaq bentwood rim (from *perte-*, "to bend"), bentwood thing

Petugtaq/Petugtaryaraq intravillage feast during which men and women exchange small gifts (from *petug-*, "to tie")

petugtat models of requested items (literally, "things tied on")

piineq loose grass used to line boots and grass socks for warmth

piirraq/piirrayagaq/piirrayagaat (NI) three-stranded braided line made from grass, sinew, or tree bark; also "Peekatluk=Atlik"; see also *qip'aq*, *yualu qip'aq*

pingayupegcetaaq/pingayupegcetaat three-pronged arrow/arrows (from *pingayun*, "three"); also "Nursat"; see also *akitnaq*, *akulmiqurcetaaq*, *cingigturat*, *meq'ercetaaq*, *pitegcaun*, *umilek*, *urugnaq*

pipigaq/pipigaat Russian trade bead/beads (from *pipik*, "real or genuine thing"); see also *cungavseq*, *teggliq*

pirlaaq/pirlaat sled-runner sheathing; also "Pirelatt"

pitaryaraq the process of distributing a seal to a group of hunters after a hunt

pitegciraq/pitegcirat lance/lances, large arrow/arrows or spear/spears; also "Kjingit?"

pitegcirarpiit arrows with huge points; see also *pitegcaun*

pitegcaun/pitegcautet arrow/arrows; also "Osarak," "Piktsautit," "Pititsirak"; see also *akitnaq, akulmiqurcetaaq, atauciqerrnat, cingigturat, meq'ercetaaq, pingayupegcetaat, pitegcirarpiit, qerrut, umilek, urugnaq*

pugtaqutaq/pugtaqutat gill-net float/floats, buoy/buoys; also "Pok= Takkiutak," "Poktareutitt," *lugluqussaaq*

pugyaraq hole at the end of the tunnel entrance where a person comes up into the semi-subterranean *qasgi* (from *puge-*, "to emerge from a hole")

pukirraq white fur from a caribou fawn

pupsugcetaat snowshoes with pointed fronts (from *pupsug-*, "to pinch"); see also *tangluk*

putulirissuutet peg hole punchers

putulrik two loops on a boot

puukaqercetaat touch and spring snares for ground squirrels; see also *makikcaq*

puukicaaq/puukicaat button/buttons (from Russian *púgovitsa*); also *kuukicaaq*; see also *iqugmiutaq, kakinquka'ar, nunguyun*

puuli/puuliit bullet/bullets

puulissuun/puulissuutet bullet mold/molds (from *puuli*, "bullet"); also "Koron Kjimat"; see also *imin*

puya tundra-moss *akutaq*

puyurkarvik gunpowder holder (from *puyurkaq*, "gunpowder"); also "Pijokkaun," "Soppiut"

puyurkirissuun gunpowder measure

qaaluuciaq/qaaluuciat spoon/spoons; also *luuskaat, qalussnguarraat, qassuukar, uiluq, yuurqaarcuun*

Qaariitaaq ceremony in the fall after freeze-up when children with painted faces visit house-to-house receiving food and water

Qaarpak/Qaarpaagyaraq one-night ceremony following *Qaariitaaq* in which participants wear fake noses and visit house-to-house

qacurqin/qacurqissuutet shaman song/songs to ridicule another shaman

qaglak upper part of a bowl or bucket, everything except the bottom piece, hat rim

qaglayaaq bowl with a *qaglak* (upper part)

qaliluk/qaliluut old, well-worn caribou parka/parkas; parka/parkas made out of caribou fawn skin, which are also very soft

qaliq/qalit front and back plate/plates on a woman's fancy parka; see *qemirrlugun*

qall'iluku topstitching (from *qalli-*, "to be on the top, surface")

qaltaq bucket, pail; also "Kaltasiungak," "Kaltosiungak," "Metziwik?"

qalun/qaluurin/qaluuritet dipper/dippers (from *qalu-*, "to dip, to bail a boat"); also "Kallauretet," "Kalorin," *mer'un*

qalussnguarraat spoons; also *luuskaat, qaaluuciaq, qassuukar, uiluq, yuurqaarcuun*

qalutaq ladle; also "Kaleutak," "Kallun," *angassaq, arulamirun, ipuun, qassuutaq*

qamigautek kayak sled carried on the kayak's stern while traveling on the ocean

qanermiaq/qanermiat fire-bath smoke respirator/respirators, wood-chip ball/balls held in the mouth during fire baths (literally, "things held in the mouth," from *qaneq*, "mouth"); also "Ikmeak"

qaneryaraq saying, way to say something

qaniit wooden roofing planks

qanikciurun (NI) snow shovel (from *qanikcaq*, "snow on the ground"); also *pekutaq*

qaniqussuaq a shamanistic rite to protect a person from illness

qanitaq/qanitat refuse pile/piles, dumping place/places, midden/middens

qanruyun/qanruyutet teaching/teachings, word/words to live by

qantaq/qantat bowl/bowls; also "Eckkock or Esoch," "Kautag," *aluuyacuar, alvik, ilutuliar*

qapiarcuun seal-skinning knife; also "Kapiatsun"

qapiaryaraq the process of skinning a seal by pulling the skin back over the body rather than splitting it

qaquaq/qaquat (NI) paddle handle grip/grips; also *kangkupaguaq*

qaquaqnginaq paddle with a grip (*qaquaq*) that is one piece with the handle

qaralit (NI) decorations, marks; also *alngat*

qasgi/qasgit communal men's house/houses; also "Casigit," "Kassagim," "Kasschim," "Kassegim," "Kassigit"

qasgiruaq model *qasgi*

qaspeq/qasperet cotton dress/dresses, parka cover/covers

qasrulek/qasrulget birch-bark bucket/buckets (literally, "one with *qasruq* [birch bark]")

qassuuciat small ladles

qassuukar/qassuuciarraq/qassuuciarraat spoon/spoons; also *luuskaat, qaaluuciaq, qalussnguarraat, uiluq, yuurqaarcuun*

qassuutaq/qassuutat large ladle/ladles; see also *angassaq, arulamirun, ipuun, qalutaq*

qaterliaraat small white beads

qat'gaqyui ribs and intestine portion of a catch (from *qat'gaq*, "chest"); also *irnerrlugtalria*

qatviat leather

qavyak/qavya walrus-skin line

qayaruaq model *qayaq* (kayak)

qeciqutaq inflated walrus-bladder water container or net float; also "Katsekotak," "Ketsekotak," "Neggasuk Agligakrak" (painted bladder)

qecugat woven things (from *qecug-*, "to pull out"); also "Ilakstat"

qel'ketalria one who treasures and takes good care of possessions so they last for a long time

qeltairissuun implement for removing scales

qelun bowstring (from *qelu-*, "to pull, to tighten")

qelutviaq stringed musical instrument (from *qelun*, "string under tension")

qeluyarak (NI) two notched ends of a bow (literally, "the way the *qelun* (bowstring) is pulled"); also *teruk*

qemaggvik/qemaggviit container/containers for something precious (from *qemage-*, "to put something away in a container or bag"); also "Eketz Wiewick," "Eksetz Wiewik," "Ekwintatt," "Ekwiutatt," "Kwentak," "Tjiluttitungok," "Tjiluttuingok"; see also *aguumaq, issraka'ar, issran, kalngak, kellarvik, qungasvik, ugalguun*

qemiq sinker and float line for a gill net

qemirrlugun/qemirrlugutet smaller plate/plates below the large front and back plates on a woman's fancy parka (from *qemirrluk*, "spine"); see also *qaliq*

qengartaq/gengartat (NI) central ridge/ridges on a paddle blade; also *quaguk*

qenngitaq (NI) fish striker (from *qennguq*, "head cartilage," where fish is struck); see also *kaugtuutaq*

qenuirun/qenuirutek ice dipper/dippers (dual); also "Kanaiaan," "Kanneruetik," "Kannoeriann," "Kannoeronn," "Kauneruetik," "Knneruetik," *imairitek*

qerpertaq whitefish roe and cranberry *akutaq*

qerqutuut loosely woven grass mats to insulate houses; also *eviutet*

qerrlucaq/qerrlurcat ice-fishing hook/hooks

qerruaq/qerruinat harpoon float/floats; also "Kloktak," "Kreuitak"

qerruqerrut arrow/arrows used during warfare; also *pitegcautet*

qerruun float inflation nozzle

qiguaq blue paint, vivianite

qiq inner layer of seal intestine separated from outer layer

qivuitaq drill (from *qiive-*, "to quiver, tremble"); also *kaputalgaar, kaputaq, kap'issuun, ukicissuun*

qia cry

qilagcuun/qilagcuutet netting shuttle/shuttles (from *qilag-*, "to knit or make net"); also "Killautitt," "Ugimak?" *imruyutaq*

qilkegcutet net gauges (from *qilag-*, "to knit or make net"); also "Ugimak?" *negaqeggun*

qilirtet pieces of ivory inlay; also "Kritlet"

qipaq two-stranded braided sinew line or thread; see also *piirraq, qua, qip'aq*

qirussiq/qirussit design/designs, decoration/decorations, decorative appendage/appendages

cisan/cisratet arrow-point or harpoon-blade sheath/sheaths or coverings, coverings

qiugaarulleq "water sky," that is, the reflection of open ocean water seen in the sky as a dark blue line

quaguk/quaguut central ridge/ridges on a paddle blade; also *engitaq*

quagulek/quagulget three-cornered skin-sewing needle/needles (from *kag'k*, "sharp edge"); see also *anguarutnguat, ciilat, kakuutet, apu, mingqun*

qugcuun/qugcuutet grass sock/socks, boot liner/liners; see also *liqsk*

qugrurtet flight stabilizers made from swan quills (from *qugyuk*, "whistling swan")

qel'yaraq the way of giving objects different names out of respect for deceased humans with similar names

quliraq/qulirat traditional tale/tales, legend/legends

qulitek designs on women's parkas

qulqet raised platforms or shelves

qunacuun shredder for making thread from animal muscle or for splitting tree fiber; also *talun*

qungasvik/qungasviit storage bag/bags or container/containers; also "Ersarumerak?" "Ersarumerok," "Konersiwisingak?" "Konersiwisiugak," "Konersiwisugak," "Kuninek," "Kwintettsuak"; see also *aguuyaq, esran, kellarvik, qemaggvik, ugalguutet*

qunanek/qunanunit legendary creature/creatures that appear human and transform into seals; also "Kouonek," "Konainek"

qupuqurrun (NI) wood splitter/splitters, wedge/wedges; also "Hapoootit," *aivagun, ekiarqin, equgcuun*

qupuruyli powerful woman of the sea

qurrulluk/qurrulluut urine bucket/buckets or container/containers; also "Metziwik," "Truek?"

qugeq/qugaarpak legendary tusked creature that causes riverbanks to erode as it emerges from its underground lair, sometimes identified with the mammoth or mastodon

qugirrac mastodon ivory

sagqurriit three stars seen just before sunrise in November and December

sugaq/sugaruaq/sugaruat/suguaq miniature toy doll/dolls (from *suk*, "person"); see also "Suukquak," *inuguaq, irniaruaq, yugaq*

sugarviutaq bag for miniature doll figurines

taiq inner layer of seal gut removed before processing

tallirpacuar/tallirpacuaraat small, short-handled gaff/gaffs (from *talliq*, "arm," literally, "small, big arm"); see also *negcik, negcikcuar*

talun/talutet shredder/shredders for making thread from animal muscles, splitting tree fiber, or combing grass; also "Daleutit," "Daleutitt," "Dalutitt," "Tallutik," "Talutik," *qunavun*

taluyacuar/taluyaruat small fish trap/traps

taluyaq/taluyat fish trap/traps; also, a constellation of stars

taluyarpiit large fish traps

tamuanat spawning fish hung to dry

tangluk/tanglut snowshoes (dual)/snowshoes; also "Dageluk," *pupsugcetaat*

tanglurallret the Milky Way (literally, "those made with snowshoes")

tapengyaarayaagaq binding at the butt end of an arrow

taperrnaq/taperrnat coarse seashore grass (*Elymus mollis*)

tapraq/taprartaq skin line

taruyamaarutet dance fans (an untranslatable word derived from *taru*, "soul spirit"); also "Tarojoatitt," "Tarojorarrotit," "Tarrajararotit," "Tarrajararotitt," "Torrejoraroritt," *tegumiak*

taryaqvagcuun king-salmon gill net (from *taryaqvak*, "king salmon"); also "Tarsan=Paksun=Atlik," *allegpak*

tassiitaq breastplate for a backpack, carrying yoke; also "Dassitak," *atmagcuun*

teggalqupiaq/teggalqupiat small stone/stones used for sharpening (literally, "real stone," from *teggalquq*, "stone"); see also *arviiq, ellin, uqu'urniq*

teggera'ar/tegg'eraq hardwood (from *tegge-*, "to be hard or firm")

tegglipiat real *tegglit* ("beads")

teggliq/tegglit bead/beads; also *cungavseq, pipigaq*

tegumiak/tegumiat (Y) dance fans (dual), finger masks (literally "two things held in the hand," from *tegu-*, "to take in the hand"); also "Tigomiet," *taruyamaarutet*

tegun/tegutet large harpoon/harpoons used without a throwing board; see also *aklegaq, asaaquq, nagiiquyaq, nanerpak*

tegurrliurutet combs with wide teeth, tangle removers (from *tegute-*, "to be tightly tangled"); also *nerescissuun, nuyiurun*

tegutet stakes or antes

tekeq/tekret thimble/thimbles (literally, "index finger"); also *akngirnailitaq, keniutet*

tekiqata'ar arrival dance at the Messenger Feast

tengayut caribou throat hairs

teru butt end, notch at the end of an arrow shaft

teruk two notched ends of a bow used to tighten the string; also *qeluyarak*

tevtara'araat decorative design/pattern on sewn items (from *tevte-*, "to drape over something")

tiiguayaaq striped or calico cloth; also *ellutmuayaaq*

tugeq ice chisel; also *cikuliurun*

tugrutii/tugrutait ice pick/picks? shaft/shafts

tukarta twine, rope (from *tukar-*, "to kick with both feet")

tulukaruk raven

tuluq piece of walrus ivory

tuluruaq skin-stretching and scraping tool (from *tuluq*, "ivory," literally, "likeness of ivory"); also "Dail'tkon," *assipek*

tuluryaaq/tuluryak animal's canine tooth/teeth

tumnacuar/tumnacuaraat small oval wooden bowl/bowls

tumnaq/tumnat large oval wooden bowl/bowls

tungunqucuk added strip of dark skin or fur (from *tungu-*, "to be black") on a parka or other sewn object

tunturyuk Ursa Major (from *tuntu-*, "caribou")

tupigaq/tupigat twined thing/things, grass mat/mats (from *tupig-*, "to weave"); also "Kakiwit=Amerit," "Ullan?"; see also *ikaraliitet*

tupipiarumalriik grass socks (literally, "those two that are genuinely woven," from *tupig-*, "to weave"); also *alliqsaq, qugcuun*

tuqmik bucket

tusailitak two shoulder bands of a parka

tusrulluuk parka designs

tusrutek decorative trim on parka sleeves between shoulder and elbow

tutneq wooden crosspiece for one's feet on snowshoes (literally, "place for one's foot," from *tut'e-*, "to step on")

tuunraq/tuunrat helping spirit/spirits, animals or extraordinary beings that help the *angalkuq* (shaman) and represent the essence of his or her power; also "Thunrak," "Tonnerak"

tuutaq/tuutat labret/labrets; also "Toksorarrut," "Tokssorarrut," "Tontak," "Totak," "Toutak," "Tuksorarrut=Kakopit"; see also *cungarpak, mengkuk*

tuvqertat set of twenty loche fish

tuvraq hunter on sea ice, someone on whom one can depend

ucuilleq front lateral fin (from *ucuk*, "genitalia")

ugalguun/ugalguutaq/ugalguutet little storage containers made of skin or cloth; also "Willerutitt," see also *aguumaq, issran, issraka'ar, kalngak, kellarvik, qemaggvik, qungasvik*

ugayiqurluki giving one's things away on first menses (from *ugayar-*, "to strip away one's clothing or belongings")

ugtarcuutet bentwood hunting hats (from *ugtaq*, "seal on an ice floe," literally, "devices to get seals on ice floes"); see also *ciayaq, elqiaq*

uicungaq teasing cousin, male cross-cousin of a female (literally, "dear little husband")

uilingiataq one who refuses to have a husband (from *ui-*, "husband")

uiluq/uilut spoon/spoons, clamshell/shells; also "Oeluk," "Wieluk," *luuskaat, qaaluuciaq, qalussnguarraat, qassuukar, yuurqaarcuun*

uiluuyaaq clamshell spoon (from *uiluq*, "clam, clamshell, spoon"); also "Oielujak"

uiteraq red ocher

uivcetaaq wooden top; also "Tinngait"

uivqurraq/uivqurrat circular skin cap/caps with beaded decorative band (from *uive-*, "to circle"); also "Wiffkok"

ukicissuun/ukicissuutet drill/drills, awl/awls, or other hole-making device/devices (from *uki-*, "to get a hole"); also "Iggiukarsok," "Okkitisun," *kaputaq, kaputalgaar, kap'issuun, qiivuusaaq*

ukilqaar/ukilqaaraat open-weave grass bag/bags (from *ukineq*, "hole"); also "Ilakstat," "Klarowit"; see also *issran*

ukinqucuk tote hole in a kayak

uliutet top layer of backbone muscles split to make sinew (from *ulik*, "cover, blanket"); see also *eglu, yualuq*

uluaq/uluat semilunar woman's knife/knives (from *ulu*, "tongue"); also "Kjimak=Ulloak," "Kjimak=Ulluak," "Kjimat=Ulloak," "Omikak=Ulloak," "Ullo," "Ulloak," "Ulloet," "Ullokak," "Ullon," "Ulluat"

ulugturalria morning star, one that twinkles

ulukaq/ulukat slate or other stone formerly used as a blade on women's knives and as *umit* (stone points); also "Ommikak"

ul'utvak newborn seal

umi/umit stone arrow or harpoon point/points; also "Omi," "Omilik," "Ommit"; see also *cavek, kukgar, puturcuutnguluki*

umilek/umilget arrow/arrows with *umit* (stone points); also "Kjingiligit," "Kjinginat," "Omiligit"; see also *pitegcaun*

uminguaq/uminguak/uminguat pretend arrow-point (V-shaped) design/designs sewn below the shoulders on men's parkas

unarciaq/unarciat prepared piece/pieces of straight-grained wood used to make things such as fish traps

unarciiyurcuutet tools used to work on wood

unguquutaq/unguquutat plug/plugs to close holes on a sealskin float; also "Totapak," "Totapit," "Toutapit"

unrapigaq small, thin log

uqisaqsuun blubber carrier (from *uquq*, "oil, seal oil"); also "Okei Stakson"

uqumyak/uqumyiit quartz, so called because of its light color, resembling *uquq*, seal fat

uqu'urniq/uqu'urnit stone/stones used to sharpen knives and blades (from *uquq*, "oil"); see also *arviiq, ellin, teggalqupiaq*

uqviinraq willow root; also *amaaret*

urasqaq white clay, white clay paint

urciq loop or hole at the end of a line

urluveq/urluvret bow/bows; also "Ketwiak," "Nemidlik-Orloak," "Nemidlik=Orolak" (Y), "Orloak" (Y), "Orlowak" (K), "Oroak," "Orolak" (Y), "Orolowak," "Orrollewok" (K), "Satko," "Urloak"

urugnaq/urugnat arrow/arrows with barbed ivory point/points; also *cingigturat*; see also *akitnaq, akulmiqurcetaaq, meq'erctaaq, pingayupegcetaat, pitegcaun, umilek*

urumerun/urumerutet skin scraper/scrapers; also "Orro=on," *calugcissuun, ellumerrun*

uruq/urut tundra moss (*Sphagnam sp.*); see also *kumarun*

usaaq/usaat leather line/lines made out of sealskin; also "Ussett," *imgun, kinguliraq*

usrapakiiqertellriit squirrels with bright spots (in summer)

ussugcin device that creates erosion

ussukataq/ussukatat rotating stick/sticks used as a fire drill; also "Osugatak," "Udsukadak," "Udsukadat"; see also *kenngesssuutet, kumartessuun, neg'utaq, nucugcuutek*

utngugartaq trigger string for a squirrel snare

uulunqiiq/uulungiit decorative fringe/fringes; squirrel-skin belly/bellies

uurcaryaraq announcing one has caught a bearded seal by returning to the village holding one's gaff aloft

uya/uyak/uyat human figure/figures (literally, "neck," from the bird-neck-skin parkas some wore); see also *yugaq*

uyamik/uyamiit necklace/necklaces; also "Ojamet," "Ojamik"

yaaruin story knife; also "Jarroit," "Jerruin," *ateknguitet, cirunqaaraat, equaq*

yagneq length of one's arms fully extended

yualu qip'aq (K) twisted sinew twine; see also *piirrayagaq*

yualuq/yualut sinew/sinews, ligament/ligaments, muscle/muscles, thread/threads; see also *eglu, uliutet*

yuaralget gloves; also *aaggsiik, aaggaqtaat, aasgaat, aigsaat*

yugaq/yugat (Y) doll/dolls, human figure/figures (from *yuk*, "person, human being"); also "Jugak," "Jugatt," "Jungoak," "Yugak," "Yugoak," *inuguaq, irniaruaq, sugaq, uya*

yuk/yuit person/persons

Yup'ik/Yupiit native people of southwestern Alaska (from *yuk*, "person," plus +*pik*, "real or genuine"; literally, "real person/people")

yuaryaraq feather or fur hood for use with a hoodless parka (literally, "way of checking outside," from *yurar-*, "to come up and out of an opening"); also "Jorariarett," "Jorarirett"

yuungcaraq/yuungcarat one/ones who were ministered to and given life by a shaman, contemporary word for patient

yuurqaarcuun spoon (from *yuurqaaq*, "broth or plain soup"); see also *luuskaat, qaaluuciaq, qalussnguarraat, qassuukar, uiluq*

yuuyaraq Yup'ik way of life, way of living

REFERENCES

Ames, Michael. 1990. "Cultural Empowerment and Museums: Opening up Anthropology Through Collaboration." In *New Research in Museum Studies. Vol.1, Objects of Knowledge,* edited by Susan Pearce. London: Athlone, 158–73.

———. 1992. *Cannibal Tours and Glass Boxes: The Anthropology of Museums.* Vancouver: University of British Columbia Press.

———. 1994. "The Politics of Difference: Other Voices in a Not Yet Post-Colonial World." *Museum Anthropology* 18 (3):9–17.

Appadurai, Arjun, and Carol A. Breckenridge. 1992. "Museums Are Good to Think: Heritage on View in India." In *Museums and Communities: The Politics of Public Culture,* edited by Ivan Karp, Christine Mullen Kreamer, and Steven D. Lavine. Washington, D.C.: Smithsonian Institution Press, 34–55.

Aszruni, Andreas. 1883a. "Nephrit [Nephrite]." *Verhandlungen der Berliner Gesellschaft für Anthropologie, Ethnologie und Urgeschichte* 15:1–12.

———. 1883b. "Neue Beobachtungen am Nephrit und Jadeit [New Observations on Nephrite and Jadeite]." *Zeitschrift für Ethnologie* (Berlin) 15:177–204.

Babcock, Barbara. 1993. "At Home, No Women Are Storytellers." In *Feminist Messages: Coding in Women's Folk Culture,* edited by Joan N. Radner. Urbana: University of Illinois Press, 221–48.

Bazerman, Suzanne. 1994. "Representation and the Small Museum: Korean Arts in Celebration of Life Events at the Goldstein Gallery." *Museum Anthropology* 18 (3):44–47.

Basso, Keith H. 1996. *Wisdom Sits in Places: Landscape and Language Among the Western Apache.* Albuquerque: University of New Mexico Press.

Bastian, Adolf. 1884. "Erwerbungen der Ethnographischen Abtheilung des Berliner kgl. Museums von der Nordwestküste Nordamerikas" [Acquisitions of the Ethnographic Department in the Berlin Royal Museum from North America's Northwest Coast]. *Globus* 45:8–11, 24–29.

Bastian, Adolf, ed. 1883. *Amerika's Nordwest-Küste. Neueste Ergebnisse ethnologischer Reisen. Aus den Sammlungen der Königlichen Museen zu Berlin* [America's Northwest Coast. The Latest Results of Ethnological Travels. From the Collections of the Royal Museums in Berlin]. Berlin: A. Asher and Co.

Bennett, Tony. 1988. "Museums and 'The People.'" In *The Museum Time-Machine: Putting Cultures on Display,* edited by Robert Lumley. London and New York: Routledge.

Bennett, Tony, ed. 1995. *The Birth of the Museum: History, Theory, Politics.* London and New York: Routledge.

Boas, Franz. 1895. "The Social Organization and Secret Societies of the Kwakiutl Indians." *Report of the United States National Museum.* Washington, D.C.: U.S. Government Printing Office, 311–737.

Bolz, Peter. 1996. "Johan Adrian Jacobsen: Collector for the Royal Ethnological Museum in Berlin." Paper presented at opening symposium for Yup'ik mask exhibit *Agayuliyararput* (Our Way of Making Prayer). Anchorage, Alaska.

Bolz, Peter, and Hans-Ulrich Sanner. 1999. *Native American Art: The Collections of the Ethnological Museum Berlin.* Berlin: Staatliche Museen zu Berlin-Preussischer Kulturbesitz; Seattle: University of Washington Press.

Bourdieu, Pierre. 1984. *Distinction: A Social Critique of Judgement and Taste,* translated by Richard Nice. Cambridge, Mass.: Harvard University Press.

Brumann, C. 2000. "Writing for Culture: Why a Successful Concept Should Not Be Discarded." *Current Anthropology* 40, supplement. Quoted in Marshall Sahlins, "Two or Three Things that I Know About Culture," *The Journal of the Royal Anthropological Institute* 5 (3):399–421 (1999).

Bunzl, Matti. 1996. "From *Volkgeist* and *Nationalcharakter* to an Anthropological Concept of Culture." In *Volkgeist as Method and Ethic: Essays on Boasian Anthropology and the German Anthropological Tradition,* edited by George W. Stocking Jr. Madison: University of Wisconsin Press, 17–78.

Clifford, James. 1988. *The Predicament of Culture: Twentieth-Century Ethnography, Literature and Art.* Cambridge, Mass.: Harvard University Press.

———. 1991. "Four Northwest Coast Museums: Travel Reflections." In *Exhibiting Cultures: The Poetics and Politics of Museum Display,* edited by Ivan Karp and Steven D. Lavine. Washington, D.C.: Smithsonian Institution Press, 212–54.

Painted drum damaged during World War II and recently restored. Compare with photographs of the same drum on exhibition before the war (p. 34) and after the war, before restoration. IVA3095.

———. 1997. *Routes: Travel and Translation in the Late Twentieth Century.* Cambridge, Mass.: Harvard University Press.

Clifford, James, and George E. Marcus, eds. 1986. *Writing Culture: The Poetics and Politics of Ethnography.* Berkeley: University of California Press.

Cole, Douglas. 1985. *Captured Heritage: The Scramble for Northwest Coast Artifacts.* Seattle: University of Washington Press.

Conklin, Beth. 1997. "Body Paint, Feathers, and VCRs: Aesthetics and Authenticity in Amazonian Activism." *American Ethnologist* 24 (4):711–37.

Corey, Peter, ed. 1987. *Faces, Voices, and Dreams: A Celebration of the Centennial of the Sheldon Jackson Museum, Sitka, Alaska, 1888–1988.* Sitka: Alaska State Museum.

Crowell, Aron L., Amy F. Steffian, and Gordon L. Pullar, eds. 2001. *Looking Both Ways: Heritage and Identity of the Alutiiq People.* Fairbanks: University of Alaska Press.

Cruikshank, Julie. 1998. *The Social Life of Stories: Narrative and Knowledge in the Yukon Territory.* Lincoln: University of Nebraska Press.

Day, Jane. 1994. "Aztec: The World of Montezuma, an Exhibition with Multiple Voices." *Museum Anthropology* 18 (3):26–31.

Dissellhoff, H.-Dietrich. 1935. "Bemerkungen zu einigen Eskimomasken der Sammlung Jacobsen des Berliner Museums für Völkerkunde [Observations on Some of the Eskimo Masks in the Jacobsen Collection of the Berlin Ethnological Museum]." *Baessler-Archiv* 18:130–37.

———. 1936. "Bemerkungen zu Fingermasken der Beringmeer-Eskimos [Observations on Finger Masks of the Bering Sea Eskimos]." *Baessler-Archiv* 19:181–87.

Driscoll-Engelstad, Bernadette. 1995. "Silent Echoes: The Displacement and Reappearance of Copper Inuit Clothing." Paper presented at the 94th Annual Meeting of the American Anthropological Association, November 1995, Washington, D.C.

———. 1996. "Beyond Anonymity: The Emergence of Textile Artists in the Canadian Arctic." *Museum Anthropology* 20 (3):26–38.

Drooker, Penelope B. 1995. "Asking Old Museum Collections New Questions: Protohistoric Fort, Ancient Social Organization, and Interregional Interaction." *Museum Anthropology* 19 (3):3–16.

Dubin, Steven. 1999. *Displays of Power: Memory and Amnesia in the American Museum.* New York: New York University.

Dustan, Carol. 1999. "Fostering Symbiosis: A Collaborative Exhibit at the California State University Sacramento Museum of Anthropology." *Museum Anthropology* 22 (3):52–58.

Fienup-Riordan, Ann. 1983. *The Nelson Island Eskimo.* Anchorage: Alaska Pacific University Press.

———. 1984. "Regional Groups on the Yukon-Kuskokwim Delta." In *The Central Yupik Eskimos,* edited by Ernest Burch Jr. *Études/Inuit/Studies* 8, supplement:63–93.

———. 1986a. "The Real People: The Concept of Personhood Among the Yup'ik Eskimos of Western Alaska." *Études/Inuit/Studies* 10 (1–2):261–70.

———. 1986b. *When Our Bad Season Comes: A Cultural Account of Subsistence Harvesting and Harvest Disruption on the Yukon Delta.* Monograph Series 1. Aurora: Alaska Anthropological Association.

———. 1988. *The Yup'ik Eskimos as Described in the Travel Journals and Ethnographic Accounts of John and Edith Kilbuck, 1885–1900.* Kingston, Ont.: The Limestone Press.

———. 1990a. "The Bird and the Bladder: The Cosmology of Central Yup'ik Seal Hunting." In *Hunting, Sexes, and Symbolism,* edited by Ann Fienup-Riordan. *Études/Inuit/Studies* 14 (1–2):23–38.

———. 1990b. *Eskimo Essays: Yup'ik Lives and How We See Them.* New Brunswick, N.J.: Rutgers University Press.

———. 1990c. "Eskimo Iconography and Symbolism: An Introduction." In *Hunting, Sexes, and Symbolism,* edited by Ann Fienup-Riordan. *Études/Inuit/Studies* 14 (1–2):7–12.

———. 1991. *The Real People and the Children of Thunder: The Yup'ik Encounter with Moravian Missionaries John and Edith Kilbuck.* Norman: University of Oklahoma Press.

———. 1992. "Culture Change and Identity Among Alaska Natives: Retaining Control." *Alaska Native Policy Papers.* Anchorage: Institute of Social and Economic Research, University of Alaska Anchorage.

———. 1994. *Boundaries and Passages: Rule and Ritual in Yup'ik Eskimo Oral Tradition.* Norman: University of Oklahoma Press.

———. 1996. *The Living Tradition of Yup'ik Masks: Agayuliyararput (Our Way of Making Prayer).* Seattle: University of Washington Press.

———. 1997. "Present Yup'ik Recollections of Past Shamans." In *Shamanism/Christianization/Possession,* edited by Bernard Saladin d'Anglure and Francois Therien. *Études/Inuit/Studies* 21 (1–2):229–44.

———. 2000. *Hunting Tradition in a Changing World: Yup'ik Lives in Alaska Today.* New Brunswick, N.J.: Rutgers University Press.

Fienup-Riordan, Ann, ed. 1999. *Where the Echo Began, and Other Oral Traditions from Southwestern Alaska Recorded by Hans Himmelheber.* Fairbanks: University of Alaska Press.

Fitzhugh, William W., and Susan A. Kaplan. 1982. *Inua: Spirit World of the Bering Sea Eskimo.* Washington, D.C.: Smithsonian Institution Press.

Fowler, Catherine S. 1995. "Digging in Museums: Symposium Comments." *Museum Anthropology* 19 (3):72–75.

Fuller, Nancy J. 1992. "The Museum as a Vehicle for Community Empowerment: The Ak-Chin Indian Community Ecomuseum Project." In *Museums and Communities: The Politics of Public Culture,* edited by Ivan Karp, Christine Mullen Kreamer, and Steven D. Lavine. Washington, D.C.: Smithsonian Institution Press, 327–65.

Gellner, Ernest. 1987. *Culture, Identity, and Politics.* Cambridge: Cambridge University Press.

Genest, Otto. 1887a. "Die Burjaten [The Buriats]." *Globus* 52 (1):11–16.

———. 1887b. "Kapitän Jakobsen's Besuch bei den Koreanern [Captain Jakobsen's Visit Among the Koreans]." *Globus* 52 (4):58–61; 52 (5):71–75.

———. 1887c. "Kapitän Jacobsen's Reisen im Gebiete der Giljaken und auf der Insel Sachalin [Captain Jacobsen's Travels in the Territory of the Gilyaks and on the Island of Sakhalin]." *Globus* 52 (24):378–82; 53 (1):9–14 (1888); 53 (2):25–31 (1888).

———. 1887d. "Kapitän Jakobsen's Reisen im Lande der Golden [Captain Jakobsen's Travels in the Country of the Goldis]." *Globus* 52 (10):152–56; 52 (11):171–74; 52 (13):205–8; 52 (14):220–23.

———. 1890. "Ein Besuch in einem Kirgisenaul [A Visit to a Kirgiz Camp]." *Globus* 57 (4):57–60.

Gerhard, Thomas. 1992. "Die Sammlung der Nordwestküsten-Indianer im Kölner Rautenstrauch-Joest-Museum: Ihre Entstehungs und Verkaufsgeschichte [The Collection of Northwest Coast Indians in the Rautenstrauch-Joest Museum, Cologne: History of Its Origin and Sale]." Master's thesis, Rheinische Friedrich-Wilhelms Universitat, Bonn.

Godelier, Maurice. 1999. *The Enigma of the Gift.* Chicago: University of Chicago Press.

Haberland, Wolfgang. 1987. "Nine Bella Coolas in Germany." In *Indians and Europe*, edited by Christian Feest. Aachen: Rader, 337–74.

———. 1988a. "Adrian Jacobsen on Pine Ridge Reservation, 1910." *European Review of Native American Studies* 2 (1):11–15.

———. 1988b. "'Diese Indianer sind falsch': Neun Bella Coola im Deutschen Reich 1885–1886 ['These Indians Are False': Nine Bella Coolas in the German Empire 1885–1886]." *Archiv für Völkerkunde* 41.

———. 1989. "Remarks on the "Jacobsen Collections" from the Northwest Coast." In *Culturas de la Costa Noroeste de America*, edited by Jose Luis Peset. Madrid: Turner Libros, 185–93.

Handler, Richard. 1985. "On Having a Culture: Nationalism and the Preservation of Quebec's Patrimoine." In *Objects and Others: Essays on Museums and Material Culture*, edited by George W. Stocking Jr. Madison: University of Wisconsin Press, 192–217.

———. 1988. *Nationalism and the Politics of Culture in Quebec.* Madison: University of Wisconsin Press.

Hedlund, Ann Lane. 1994. "Speaking for or about Others? Evolving Ethnological Perspectives." *Museum Anthropology* 18 (3):32–43.

Hipszer, Hermine. 1971. "Les Masques de Chamans du Musée Ethnographique de Berlin [Shaman Masks in the Berlin Museum of Ethnography]." *Baessler-Archiv* 19:421–50.

Hiwasaki, Lisa. 1998. "Presenting Unity, Performing Diversity: Sto:lo Identity Negotiations in Venues of Cultural Representation." Paper presented at the Eighth International Conference on Hunting and Gathering Societies. October 27, Osaka.

Hooper-Greenhill, Eilean. 1992. *Museums and the Shaping of Knowledge.* London and New York: Routledge.

Höpfner, Gerd. 1995. "Die Rückführung der 'Leningrad-Sammlung' des Museums für Völkerkunde [Return of the 'Leningrad Collection' of the Museum of Ethnography]." In *Jahrbuch Preussischer Kulturbesitz*. Vol. 29. Berlin: Gebr. Mann Verlag.

Isserman, Betty. 1985. "Inuit Clothing: Construction and Motifs." *Études/Inuit/Studies* 9 (2):101–19.

———. 1990. "Inuit and Museums: Allied to Preserve Arctic Patrimony." Paper presented at the Eighth Inuit Studies Conference. Quebec.

———. 1991. "Inuit Power and Museums." *Information North: The Arctic Institute of North America* 17 (3):1–7.

———. 1997. *Sinews of Survival: The Living Legacy of Inuit Clothing.* Vancouver: University of British Columbia Press.

Jacknis, Ira. 1990. "Authenticity and the Mungo Martin House, Victoria, B.C.: Visual and Verbal Sources." *Arctic Anthropology* 27 (2):1–12.

Jacobsen, Johan Adrian. Papers. Letters and journals. Jacobsen Archives, Museum für Völkerkunde, Hamburg.

———. 1883. "Reise nach der Nordwestküste von Amerika [Journey to the Northwest Coast of America]." *Zeitschrift für Ethnologie* (Berlin) 9:525–31.

———. 1884. *Capitain Jacobsen's Reise an der Nordwestküste Amerikas, 1881–1883 [Captain Jacobsen's Journey to the Northwest Coast of America, 1881–1883].* Edited by Adrian Woldt. Leipzig: Max Spohr.

———. [1884] 1977. *Alaskan Voyage 1881–1883: An Expedition to the Northwest Coast of America.* Abridged translation by Erna Gunther, from the German text edited by Adrian Woldt. Chicago: University of Chicago Press.

———. 1889. "A. Jacobsen's und H. Kuhn's Reise in Niederländisch-Indien [A. Jacobsen's and H. Kuhn's Voyage in the Dutch Indies]." *Globus* 55 (11):161–68; 55 (12):182–86; 55 (13):200–204; 55 (14):213–17; 55 (15):225–29; 55 (16):244–48; 55 (17):261–65; 55 (18):279–80; 55 (19):299–302.

———. 1890a. "Bella-Coola-Sagen [Bella Coola Legends]." *Das Ausland* 63 (18):352–54.

———. 1890b. "Eigentümliche Kultusgegenstande im Museum für deutsche Volkstrachten [Curious Cult Objects in the Museum of German Folk Costumes]." *Das Ausland* 63 (42):825–26.

———. 1890c. "Geheimbünde der Küstenbewohner Nord-Amerikas [Secret Societies of the Coastal Dwellers of North America]." *Das Ausland* 63 (14):267–69; 63 (15):290–93.

———. 1890d. "Nordwestamerikanische Sagen [Northwestern American Legends]." *Das Ausland* 63 (22):421–25; 63 (50):981–86.

———. 1890e. "Reisen im ostindischen Archipel [Travels in the East Indian Archipelago]." *Petermanns Mitteilungen* 4:1103–5.

———. 1890f. "Steine als Amulette bei Wilden und Civilisierten Völkern [Stones as Amulets Among Savage and Civilized Peoples]." *Das Ausland* 63 (27):534–36.

———. 1891a. "Amerikanische und Sibirische Nephritgeräte [American and Siberian Nephrite Tools]." *Globus* 59 (20):314–17.

———. 1891b. "Bilderschrift der Eskimos [Pictographic Writing of the Eskimos]." *Das Ausland* 64 (1):1–4.

———. 1891c. "Geheimbünde der Küstenbewohner Nordwest-America's [Secret Societies of the Coastal Inhabitants of Northwest America]." *Zeitschrift für Ethnologie* (Berlin) 23:383–95.

———. 1891d. "Leben und Treiben der Eskimo [Life and Ways of the Eskimos]." *Das Ausland* 64 (30):593–98; 64 (32):636–39; 64 (33):656–58.

———. 1891e. "Nordwestamerikanische-polynesische Analogien [Northwest American-Polynesian Analogies]." *Globus* 59 (11):161–63.

———. 1891f. "Nordwestamerikanische Totempfeiler [Northwest American Totem Poles]." *Globus* 60 (16):253–55.

———. 1891g. "Pfeilspitzen der Eskimos in Alaska [Arrowheads of the Alaskan Eskimos]." *Das Ausland* 64 (17):336–39.

———. 1891h. "Der Seehundfang im Beringsmeer [Seal Hunting in the Bering Sea]." *Das Ausland* 64 (8):150–52.

———. 1892a. "Der Kosiyut-Bund der Bella-Coola-Indianer [The Kosiyut Society of the Bella Coola Indians]." *Das Ausland* 65 (28):437–41.

———. 1892b. "Rezension von Berghaus' Physikalischem Atlas, Abt. VII: Atlas der Völkerkunde [Review of Berghaus' Physical Atlas, Part VII: Ethnographic Atlas]." *Das Ausland* 65 (15):239–40.

———. 1892c. "Die Sintflutsage bei den Haida-Indianern (Königin Charlotte-Insel) [The Myth of the Great Flood of the Haida Indians (Queen Charlotte Islands)]." *Das Ausland* 65 (11):170–72; 65 (12):184–88.

———. 1894a. "Die Stammessage der Tongasindianer (Süd-Alaska) [The Tribal Legend of the Tongas Indians (South Alaska)]." *Globus* 65 (24):390–93.

———. 1894b. "Der Zweite Typus der Geheimbünde bei den Nordwest-Americanern [The Second Type of Secret Society among the Northwest Americans]." *Zeitschrift für Ethnologie* (Berlin) 26:104–15.

———. 1896. *Reise in die Inselwelt des Bandameeres (Voyage to the Islands of the Banda Sea).* Edited by Paul Roland. Berlin: Mitscher and Rostell.

———. 1924–1925a. "Fortsetzung der Lebensbeschreibung Jacobsens vom Buche *Captain Jacobsens Reise an der Nordwestküste Amerikas*, undatiertes handschriftliches Manuskript [Continuation of Jacobsen's Biography from the Book *Captain Jacobsen's Journey to the Northwest Coast of America,* undated handwritten manuscript]." Hamburg Archives.

———. ca. 1924–1925b. *Unter den Alaska-Eskimos: Erlebnisse und Forschungen [Among the Alaska Eskimos: Experiences and Investigations].* Berlin: Ullstein. Unpublished translation by Richard Bland in Ann Fienup-Riordan's collection, Anchorage.

———. 1931. *Die weisse Grenze: Abenteuer eines alten Seebaren rund um den Polarkreis [The White Frontier: Adventures of an Old Sailor All Around the Arctic Circle].* Leipzig: F. A. Brockhaus.

Jacobsen, Philipp [Fillip]. 1891. "Reiseberichte aus unbekannten Teilen Britisch-Columbiens [Accounts of Travels from Unknown Parts of British Columbia]." *Das Ausland* 64 (47):921–28.

Jacobson, Steven A. 1984. *Yup'ik Eskimo Dictionary.* Fairbanks: Alaska Native Language Center, University of Alaska.

Janssen, Albrecht. 1931. "Das Leben des Capitäns Adrian Jacobsen [The Life of Captain Adrian Jacobsen]." In *Die weisse Grenze [The White Frontier],* by Johan Adrian Jacobsen. Leipzig: F. A. Brockhaus, 149–59.

Kahler, Hans. 1968. "Adrian Jacobsen." In *Festschrift zur Stellinger Heimatwoche [Festival Paper of the Stellingen Hometown Week].* Stellingen: Arbeitsgemeinschaft "Stellinger Heimatfest" [Stellingen Homefest Work Community], 48–56.

Kahn, Miriam. 1995. "Heterotopic Dissonance in the Museum Representation of Pacific Island Cultures." *American Anthropologist* 97 (2):324–38.

———. 2000. "Not Really Pacific Voices: Politics of Representation in Collaborative Museum Exhibits." *Museum Anthropology* 24 (1):57–74.

Kaplan, Flora, ed. 1994. *Museums and the Making of Ourselves: The Role of Objects in National Identity.* London: Leicester University Press.

Kaplan, Susan. 2001. Personal communication (comments on manuscript) with author, June 29.

Karp, Ivan, Christine Mullen Kreamer, and Steven D. Lavine. 1992. *Museums and Communities: The Politics of Public Culture.* Washington, D.C.: Smithsonian Institution Press.

Karp, Ivan, and Steven D. Lavine. 1991. *Exhibiting Cultures: The Poetics and Politics of Museum Display.* Washington, D.C.: Smithsonian Institution Press.

Kasten, Erich. 1992. "Masken, Mythen und Indianer: Franz Boas' Ethnographie und Museumsmethode [Masks, Myths, and Indians: Franz Boas' Ethnography and Museological Method]." In *Franz Boas: Ethnologe, Anthropologe, Sprachwissenschaftler; ein Wegbereiter der modernen Wissenschaft vom Menschen [Franz Boas: Ethnologist, Anthropologist, Linguist: A Trailblazer of Modern Human Science],* by Michael Dürr et al. Berlin: Staatsbibliothek [State Library] zu Berlin, 79–102.

King, Jonathan C. H. 2001. "Exhibitions." *Native American Studies* 15 (1):51–58.

Kingston, Deanna. 2003. "Remembering Our Namesakes." In *Screening Culture: Constructing Image and Identity,* edited by Heather Norris Nicholson. Lanham, Md.: Lexington Books, 113–25.

Koepping, Klaus Peter. 1983. *Adolf Bastian and the Psychic Unity of Mankind: The Foundations of Anthropology in Nineteenth Century Germany.* St. Lucia, Qld: University of Queensland Press.

Krause, Aurel. [1885] 1956. *The Tlinget Indians: Results of a Trip to the Northwest Coast of America and Bering Straits* [originally published in German]. Translated by Erna Gunther. American Ethnological Society Monograph 26. Seattle: University of Washington Press.

Krause, Eduard. 1884. "Capitän Jacobsen: Ethnologische Gegenstände aus seiner im Alaska-Territorium zusammengebrachten Sammlung [Captain Jacobsen: Ethnological Objects from His Collection Made in the Territory of Alaska]." *Zeitschrift für Ethnologie* (Berlin) 16:221–24.

Krech, Shepard III. 1994. "Museums, Voices, Representations." *Museum Anthropology* 18 (3).

Krieger, K., and G. Koch, eds. 1973. *100 Jahre Museum für Völkerkunde [One Hundred Years of the Berlin Ethnological Museum].* Baessler-Archiv, n.s. 21.

Laforet, Andrea. 1993. "Time and the Grand Hall of the Canadian Museum of Civilization." *Museum Anthropology* 17 (1):22–32.

Lenz, Mary. 1986. "Alaska Native Teens are Nation's Highest Risk Suicide Group." *Tundra Drums* (Bethel, Alaska), March 6, 4–5.

Loring, Stephen. 2001. "Repatriation and Community Anthropology: The Smithsonian Institution's Arctic Studies Center." In *The Future of the Past: Archaeologists, Native Americans, and Repatriation,* edited by Tamara Bray. New York: Garland Publishing.

Lumley, Robert. 1988. *The Museum Time Machine.* London and New York: Routledge.

Mauss, Marcel. [1925] 1967. *The Gift: Forms and Functions of Exchange in Archaic Societies.* Translated by Ian Cunnison. New York: W. W. Norton and Co.

Meade, Marie, and Ann Fienup-Riordan. 1996. *Agayuliyararput, Kegginaqut, Kangiit-llu: Our Way of Making Prayer, Yup'ik Masks and the Stories They Tell.* Seattle: University of Washington Press.

Mitchell, Timothy. 1989. "The World as Exhibition." *Comparative Studies in Society and History* 31 (2):217–36.

Myers, Fred. 1994. "Culture-Making: Performing Aboriginality at the Asia Society Gallery." *American Ethnologist* 21 (4):679–99.

Nelson, Edward William. [1899] 1983. "The Eskimo about Bering Strait." *Bureau of American Ethnology Annual Report for 1896–1897,* Vol. 18, Pt. I. Reprint, Washington, D.C.: Smithsonian Institution Press.

Niemeyer, Günter. 1966. "'Sind diese Riesenhunde bissig?' fragte der Seehundjäger Ukubak ["Do Those Huge Dogs Bite?" Asks Seal-hunter Ukubak]." *Hamburger Abendblatt,* February 26–27.

———. 1974. "Hagenbecks 'Menschenfänger': Stellinger Strassenname erinnert an den Forscher mit Kapitänspatent [Hagenbeck's "Manhunter": Stellingen Streetname Reminds of the Researcher with a Captain's Commission]." *Hamburger Abendblatt,* January 17.

Oswalt, Wendell. 1990. *Bashful No Longer: An Alaskan Eskimo Ethnohistory, 1778–1988.* Norman: University of Oklahoma Press.

Price, Richard, and Sally Price. 1992. *Equatoria.* London and New York: Routledge.

Price, Sally. 1989. *Primitive Art in Civilized Places.* Chicago: University of Chicago Press.

Ray, Dorothy Jean. 1987. "Eskimo Artifacts: Collectors, Collections, and Museums." In *Faces, Voices, and Dreams: A Celebration of the Centennial of the Sheldon Jackson Museum, Sitka, Alaska, 1888–1988,* edited by Peter Corey. Sitka: Alaska State Museum, 29–43.

Sahlins, Marshall. 1995. *How "Natives" Think, about Captain Cook, for Example.* Chicago: University of Chicago Press.

———. 1999. "Two or Three Things that I Know About Culture." *The Journal of the Royal Anthropological Institute* 5 (3):399–421.

———. 2000. "'Sentimental Pessimism' and Ethnographic Experience; or, Why Culture Is Not a Disappearing 'Object.'" In *Biographies of Scientific Objects,* edited by Lorraine Daston. Chicago: University of Chicago Press.

Salvador, Mari Lynn. 1994. "'The Kuna Way': Museums, Exhibitions, and the Politics of Representation of Kuna Art." *Museum Anthropology* 18 (3):48–52.

Shield, Sophie, and Ann Fienup-Riordan. 2003. *Qulirat, Qanemcit-llu Kinguvarcimalriit (Stories for Future Generations): The Oratory of Yup'ik Eskimo Elder Paul John.* Seattle: University of Washington Press.

Smith, David M. 2002. "The Flesh and the Word: Stories and Other Gifts of the Animals in Chipewyan Cosmology." *Anthropology and Humanism* 27 (1):60–79.

Smith, Skip. 1997. Letter to the author.

Steiner, Christopher B. 1995. "Museums and the Politics of Nationalism." *Museum Anthropology* 19 (2).

Stocking, George W. Jr. 1985. "Essays on Museums and Material Culture." In *Objects and Others: Essays on Museums and Material Culture,* edited by George W. Stocking Jr.. Madison: University of Wisconsin Press, 3–14.

Taylor, J. Garth. 1981. "An Eskimo Abroad, 1880: His Diary and Death." *Canadian Geographic* (Ottawa) 101 (5):38–43.

Thode-Arora, Hilke. 1989. *Für fünfzig Pfennig um die Welt: Die Hagenbeckschen Völkerschauen [Around the World for 50 Pfennig: Hagenbeck's Ethnographic Shows].* Frankfurt am Main, Germany: Campus Verlag.

Torgovnick, Marianna. 1990. *Gone Primitive: Savage Intellects, Modern Lives.* Chicago: University of Chicago Press.

Turner, Terrance. 1991. "'We Are Parrots,' 'Twins Are Birds': Play of Tropes as Operational Structure." In *Beyond Metaphor: The Theory of Tropes in Anthropology,* edited by James W. Fernandez. Stanford, Calif.: Stanford University Press, 121–58.

———. 1992. "Representing, Resisting, Rethinking: Historical Transformations of Kayapo and Anthropological Consciousness." In *Colonial Situations,* edited by George W. Stocking Jr.. Madison: University of Wisconsin Press, 285–313.

Vergo, Peter, ed. 1989. *The New Museology.* London: Reaktion Books.

Walsh, Kevin. 1992. *The Representation of the Past: Museums and Heritage in the Post-Modern World.* London and New York: Routledge.

Westphal-Hellbusch, Sigrid. 1973. "Zur Geschichte des Museums [About the History of the Museum]." In *100 Jahre Museum für Völkerkunde Berlin [One Hundred Years of the Berlin Ethnological Museum],* edited by K. Krieger and G. Koch. *Baessler-Archiv* 21:1–99.

White, Geoffrey. 1997. "Introduction: Public History and National Narrative." *Museum Anthropology* 21 (1):3–7.

Woldt, Adrian. 1884. "A. Woldt's Wissenschaftliche Correspondez No. 64. II Jahrgang [A. Woldt's Scientific Correspondence, Vol. 2, No. 64]." Berlin.

Wood, Deborah, and Catherine N. Shelton. 1996. "New Data from Old Collections: The 1949 Stirling Collection from Panama in the National Museum of Natural History." *Museum Anthropology* 20 (1):3–20.

INDEX

Aaniryaraq, 274, 275
Abstinence: practices, 73, 131, 272–73; rules, 130, 275
Accession records, 64, 149, 151, 273
Admiralensky, Alaska, 19
Adoption, 43
Adze, 12, 154, 286; blades, 161
"Aformogists," 287
Agayuliyararput (Our Way of Making Prayer) (mask exhibit), 49, 119–20, 227, 281, 288
Agayuyaraq. See Itruka'ar
Aglemiut ("Aglemutten"), 78, 79, 90, 138, 217; in warrior stories, 245–48
Aimo, 2
Akiak, Alaska, 42
Akula (tundra) area, 47, 213, 273
Akula miut, Alaska, 179, 271
Akulmiut (tundra region, people), 49, 138, 255
Akutnik, Alaska, 41, 48
Akutaq (food mixture): eating, 227, 236, 249, 283; making, 166–67, 173, 177–79, 260, 281; use in ritual, 274–76
Alamneek, Alaska, 19
Alaska, 12, 21, 22, 24–27, 29, 32, 40, 48; collections from, 20, 51; collecting in, 6, 9; pluralism in, 287; Jacobsen's work in, 9–19, 23; southwestern, 9; statehood, 42
Alaska Commercial Company (AC Company), 5, 16, 18–20, 25, 28; agents, 8, 9, 16, 23, 119; posts, 10
Alaska Federation of Natives, 48, 49, 286
Alaska Native Claims Settlement Act (ANCSA), 42, 43
Alaska Natives, 41; as disadvantaged, 42
Alaska Peninsula, 19, 140, 245
Alcohol, 42, 43; introduction of, 124
Alder bark dye, 270; red, 137
Aleknagik, Alaska, 49, 245
Alert Bay, British Columbia, 7
Aleutian Islands, 54, 205
Aleut masks, 229
Alowak, Henry (Qilu), 49; reaction to collections, 285, 287

Altai, 26
Aluskaq (trader), 172
America, 25–27, 29
American Museum of Natural History, New York, 31
America's Northwest Coast: The Latest Results of Ethnological Travels. See Royal Museum of Ethnology
Amikuut, 95, 116
Amlliq, 122–23, 195, 197
Ammunition, 99. See also Guns
"Among the Cannibals of Vancouver," 22
Amulet (*iinrut*): as desirable collectible, 15, 35; dolls, 188–89, 254–56; as protection, 55, 56, 69–71, 73, 85, 109, 121–22, 179–80, 192, 196, 209; contemporary, 189–90; house protection, 221–22; hunting, 71; white whale, 71
Amur River, 26, 223
Ancestors, 155, 159, 161; worship of, 189
Anchorage, Alaska, 49, 286
Anchorage Museum of History and Art, 286
Andreafski, Alaska, 10, 11, 16, 19, 144, 201; trader, 58
Andrew, Frank, 37
Angaiak, Jack, 248
Angalkut, 41, 154, 173, 179–80, 189; curing by, 172. See also Shaman
Angvanermiut, Alaska, 263
Angyaq, 40. See also Skin boat
Animal designs, 76, 159, 275; carvings, 203; teeth, 183, 195–96, 203
Animals, 125, 197; as nonhuman persons, 41, 111–12, 115; rebirth of, 41; speaking Yup'ik, 133. See also Relationships: between humans and animals
Ankasagemut, Alaska, 12
Anthropology, 9, 15, 27; collections, 16; fieldwork, 287; salvage, 5, 20. See also Ethnography; Ethnology
Antler, 62, 89; caribou, 66; dolls, 188, 190; prong, 154. See also Caribou-antler; Reindeer: antler
Anvik, Alaska, 10
Apaches, 19

Apanuugpak (warrior), 81, 84, 87–89, 124, 134, 164, 196, 245–48, 261, 282
Ap'ayagaq, 55. See Tuqluun
Apruka'ar, Alaska, 68, 84
Aqlillugpak (warrior), 245, 248
Archaeological site, 11, 107
Arctic, 40; "Arktis," 51
Arctic cod, 107
Arizona, 9, 19
Armbands, 217, 219
Arolik River, Alaska, 18
Arrow parts, 80–81, 99; feather fletching, 60, 80, 81, 83, 85; flight stabilizers, 59, 86, 93; sinew binding, 80, 87. See also Arrows; Arrow points
Arrow points, 67, 82–83; barbed ivory, 82–83, 86; bone, 80–81; caribou-antler, 86; covers, 87; designs, 258–59, 269; detachable, 84; ivory-pointed, 84; schist, 86; stone, 82, 83
Arrows, 11, 12, 18, 47, 74–76, 83–89, 93, 132, 161, 185; bird-hunting, 81–82; boy's, 81; construction of, 80; design, 196; imitation, 12; length, 80–81; slate-bladed, 87; three-pronged, 80, 82; "thrust," 81; two-pronged bird, 82; types, 79, 80–82, 83, 87
Artifacts: fake, 12; prices of, 19. See also Bows
Arulaqurvik area, Alaska, 274
Arviirmiut (Platinum), Alaska, 153
"Aryan" migrations, 21
Arzruni, Andreas, 21
Ash, 118–19, 183, 270
Asia, 6, 21; Jacobsen's travel through, 26, 29, 31, 33
Asking songs, 224–26. See also Dance
Assigyugpak, Alaska, 94
Association of Village Council Presidents, 48–49
Assur, 30
Astruc, Father Rene, 155
Aternermiut, Alaska, 124, 207
Athapascan people, 40
Atmauthluak, Alaska, 236
Auks (diving birds), 233–34
Ausland, Das, 29–30
Australia, 6
Avneq, 224–25
Awl, 113, 151
Ax, 13, 132, 177, 271, 286; blade, 161; stone, 12
Ayikatarmiut, Alaska, 129
Aztecs, 30

Eagle-skin yuraryaraq (hood) for use with a hoodless parka. IVA5464.

Backbone muscles, 54, 152. *See also* Sinew
Backpack, 101
Bag fasteners, 138, 140, 141, 197–200; bone, 197; ivory, 138, 197
Bags: bird-foot-leather, 144; caribou-bladder, 141; clothing, 161; for dolls, 137; gut-skin, 141; salmon-skin, 137–38; storage, 121, 138, 144–46; travel, 143
Baidarka/baidarki (skin boat), 10, 19. *See also* Skin boat
Baikal, Lake, Russia, 26
Baird, Spencer F., 19, 33
Balls, game of, 251–52
Barbed points, 52–53, 67, 82, 86; for fish-spear, 67; for harpoon, 65, 71, 93; large, 67. *See also* Harpoons; Points
Barter. *See* Trade
Basso, Keith, 288
Bastian, Adolf, 8, 13–14, 21; and Berlin collection, 4–10, 12–16, 18–22, 24–30, 229; support of Jacobsen, 33, 287
Bauer, Mr., 4, 24
Beads, 10, 18, 58, 138, 144, 201, 213, 217; on belts, 19, 201; bone, 205, 213; embroideries, 19; glass, 107, 210, 213, 218; from graves, 11, 19, 212; on hats, 11, 19, 216–19; as jewelry, 18; labret, 191; nose, 124, 189; ornaments, 212, 215; pendants, 186; as separators, 211; on squirrel skin, 103; white, 211
Bear, 39, 75; carvings, 11–12, 193, 203, 238; hunting, 87, 238; intestines, 141
Bearded seal: bladders, 56, 274; in human form, 203. *See also* Seal
Beaver, 216, 221; castors, 173–74; population, 173; tooth tool, 153
Bella Bella, 8; masks, 231. *See also* Kwakiutl
Bella Coola, 27; collection, 30, 33; legends, 29, 229; masks, 231, 292
Belt(s), 201–5, 215, 270; caribou-mandible, 141, 201–5, 281–82; decorations, 154, 189; fastener, 201, 203–5, 231; in graves, 19; man's, 162; magical, 82, 84; sounds made by, 281–82; woman's, 18, 115, 141, 201–3
Beluga whale: design, 72; hunting, 39, 53, 58, 64, 67–68, 73, 114; sinew, 54, 76, 125, 270; skin, 125, 270; stomach, 57; teeth, 201. *See also* White whale
Bentwood: container, 124, 129; dipper, 171, 172; hats, 205–7, 261, 272; rim, 127. *See also* Wood
Bergen, Norway, 29
Bering Sea, 16, 29, 39; coast of, 3, 9, 18, 40, 41, 48; major species of, 3
Bering Strait, 9, 39
Berlin, Alice, 47
Berlin Anthropological Society, 20, 21
Berlin Botanical Gardens, 283
Berlin Ethnological Museum [Ethnologisches Museum Berlin (EMB)], 35, 280, 286–88; method of working in, 51–52; oldest Yup'ik pieces, 85; significance of trip to, 121; storage area, 51. *See also* Bastian, Adolf
Berlin, Germany, 8, 16, 20, 22, 24–31, 35, 40, 41, 85; elders travel to, 43, 49. *See also* Völkerschau
Berlin museum. *See* Berlin Ethnological Museum; Royal Museum of Ethnology
Berlin, Wassilie (Uqsungiar): personal history, 47, 83–84, 93, 154, 165, 272–73, 275; reaction to collections, 285, 287
Berries, 145, 184; harvesting, 57, 127, 179; picked, 221. *See also* individual species
Bethel, Alaska, 18, 41–42, 48–49, 186
Bidarka, 10. *See* Baidarka
Birch: bark, 11, 127, 160; trees, 266
Bird, 96; arrow, 79; bones, 195; carvings, 193; feathers on mask, 227; leg bone, 167; skins, 118, 154, 261; spears, 90, 92. *See also* Arrows; Feather
Birds, 75, 197; arrival of, 273; carving of, 203; designs, 238; good hunters, 108; hunting, 78, 81, 96; legendary, 12, 32; molting, 80; muscles, 54; ocean, 264; parka made from skins of, 264. *See also* individual species
Birth, 95, 202
Bismarck, Chancellor Otto von, 6
Blackberries, 144, 166; color, 137; gathering, 58
Blackfish, 39, 65; bags for, 145; eating restrictions, 193; frozen, 152; story, 115; skins, 136–38, 141; traps, 105–7, 115
Black: paint, 116, 131; pigment, 63, 99
"Black" soap, 183
Bladder Festival (Nakaciuryaraq), 13, 20, 41, 130, 242
Bladders, 275; with light, 243–44; pretend, 188
Blade, 73, 154; copper, 66; covering for, 68, 159; double-edged, 163; metal, 64, 132, 157, 161; slate, 157, 161–62
Blankenship, Mr., 6
Bleichröder, Gerson von, 6
Blood, 60, 158
Blubber carrier, 94–95
Blue, Annie (Cungauyar): personal history, 47–48, 131, 254; reaction to collections, 281–87
Blueberries, 39; color, 137
Blue paint, 86
Boarding schools, 42
Boas, Franz, 23–24, 27, 35, 287, 288
Boat, 183; construction of, 152; hook, 64; large frame, 55; seams, 167; skin covers, 73, 78. *See also* Angyak; Baidarka: Gaff; Skin boat
Body measurements, 81, 91, 113–14
Bolz, Peter, 51, 106, 210
Bone, 69, 183; arrow points, 80, 81; bag fasteners, 197–98; bird, 167, 195; caribou, 66; carvings, 8, 10, 12, 193, 203; cleaning of, 161; collecting of, 8, 10; containers, 101, 195; decoy, 109; discarded, 173; figure, 189, 192; fish, 96; gauge, 114; harpoon points, 108; hooks, 63, 186; knives, 159; nail, 155, 186; objects, 9, 10, 21, 148; ornaments, 205–6, 203, 213; penis, 78, 197–98; pipe, 167; seal, 94; sewing tools, 121–22, 195, 197, 200; sinkers, 107, 109, 111; snuff tube, 168; swan, 195; whale, 149. *See also* Mammoth
Boots: caribou-skin, 227; construction, 151, 156–57, 254; for dolls, 257; fish-skin, 135, 137, 267–69; gifts, 13, 15; grass insulation, 217; short, 269; skin, 137, 169, 269–70; soles, 76, 201
Bow-and-arrow warfare. *See* Warfare
Bowl, 40; bark, 260; bentwood, 160, 250; bottom part of, 148, 160; care of, 131; child's, 131–32; for a doll, 189; making, 127–28, 148–49, 160; man's, 131–32; mask, 228; metal, 132; seal-oil, 132; toy, 260; upper part of, 130, 148; woman's, 131; wooden, 79, 127–33, 177–78, 274
Bowl-making tool, 148–49
Bows, 18, 160; children's, 78–79; designs on, 77; measuring length of, 75; Nushagak, 77; sinew binding, 77, 87; strings for, 74–76, 83, 87
Boy who lived with seals (story), 141, 171, 206. *See also* Seal
Box: fish-shaped, 124; gear, 124, 125; seal-shaped, 123, 271
Brandenburg Gate, Berlin, 283
Breastplate, 101–2
Bremen, 8; Geographical Society, 6
Bristol Bay, Alaska, 8, 19, 41, 47–49, 120, 138, 170, 248, 250, 263
Bristol Bay Native Corporation, 42
British Columbia, 30; Boas' travel in, 27; Jacobsen's travel in, 6, 8, 16, 23, 26, 28, 31–32
Brooch (pin), 213
Brussels, Belgium, 4
Bucket, 130, 160, 173; upside-down, 171; water, 11, 97, 119, 126, 128, 172
Buhach (insecticide), 183
Bull, Mr., 29
Bullets, 121; making, 99
Bullet shells as decoration, 202
Burbot (Loche), 39, 106, 115
Bureau of Indian Affairs (BIA): ANCSA Office, 49; schools, 42
Burials, 222, 255, 263, 273; in caves, 19; sites, 11, 212. *See also* Human remains
Buryats, Russia, 26
Butcher: big game, 162; caribou, 162
Buttons, brass, 202

Caagnitellriit, 94–95
Calendar, 272–73
Calico, 258
Calista Corporation, 42
Calista Elders Council, 48, 286
Canada, 8; Arctic coast, 39; collections from, 51. *See also* British Columbia
Caniliaq, Alaska, 65
Canoe, birch-bark, 11, 153. *See also* Boat
Cap: ermine-skin, 264–65; men's circular skin, 210; skin, 40. *See also* Hats
Cape Avinoff, Alaska, 60, 256
Cape Prince of Wales, Alaska, 125, 266
Cape Prince of Wales Peninsula, Alaska, 16
Cape Romanzof, Alaska, 39
Cape Vancouver, Nelson Island: collections from, 56, 68–69, 71, 148, 150, 153, 158, 161, 167, 180–85, 187–90, 195–96, 201, 203, 210, 228, 234, 238, 253, 254, 256. *See also* Nelson Island
Captain Jacobsen's Journey to the Northwest Cost of America, 1881–1883, 22
Caribou: antler, 66–67, 97, 151–52, 167, 182, 254, 272; beard hair, 210, 215, 238; black-painted, 132; bladder, 141, 274; body parts, 154, 182, 210; bone, 66; carving, 161, 193, 203; fat, 236; figures, 75, 131–32, 233; furs, 129, 182, 210; hair, 45, 238; hunting, 39, 74, 79, 86–87, 101, 162, 189; mask, 231, 233; meat, 88; models, 231, 233; parka, 79, 88, 155, 210, 259; pictures of, 75; sharing, 92, 93; sinew, 54, 76, 107, 150–51, 188, 190; skin, 129–30, 141, 155–56, 213–14, 258, 270; stories of, 115, 236; teeth, 201, 223. *See also*

326 INDEX

Caribou-antler; Caribou-skin; Reindeer
Caribou-antler: gauge, 114; hammer, 155; handle, 155; ice dipper, 106; nails, 155; point, 97; powder measure, 101; prongs, 79; sinker, 111, 113; wedge, 271
Caribou-skin boots, 227, 269–70
Cartridge shells, 201
Carvings, 8–9
Catch, distribution of, 92, 94, 125. *See also* Gifts; Sharing
Catholic, 193; mission, 41
Caulking, 167
Caunermut, Alaska, 189
Caurarnaq, Alaska, 179, 202, 257
Central America, 21
Central Yup'ik: grammar, 49; language, 42–43. *See also* Yup'ik
Ceremonial cycle, 40, 41, 274–78; and regalia, 35, 51, 211–19
Charles, William, 6
Chefornak, Alaska, 48
Children: abuse of, 42; protector of, 221–22; rearing of, 128; restrictions accompanying birth, 202; toys, 188, 250–61; training, 78
Chilkat Indians, 220
Chilkoot, Alaska, 8
China Poot Bay, Alaska, 19
Christianity, 7, 193. *See also* Missionaries
Chum (dog) salmon, 39, 92. *See also* Salmon
Ciikayaaraq, 175–76
Circle-and-dot design. *See* Design
Ciulistet Research Group, 49
Civilization, corrupting effects of, 18
Clams, 145, 173, 184
Clan property, 8, 33–35
Clark, Mr., 119, 170, 268
Clay balls, 252; pots, 133–34
Clearing a path, 41, 126, 175
Cloth, 138, 141; lining, 144; striped, 258
Clothing, 19, 25, 264–70; cotton, 52; dolls', 254–59; women's, 98. *See also* Boots; Gloves; Hats; Mittens; Parka
Club, 271
Coastal population decline, 41–42
Coffin, 203; with pierced hand, 231
Coho (silver) salmon, 39
Cole, Douglas, 35
Collaboration: in exhibit-making, 288
Collecting, 18, 35; prices, 6–10, 15; "vacuum cleaner" approach to, 6
Collections, 8; from Alaska, Canada, Greenland, as evidence of antiquity, 21; of masks, 10; as sign of heritage, 287; significance of, 284–89; of stone and bone, 10; Yup'ik work in, 280–82
Cologne (Köln), Germany, 4, 29
Coltsfoot leaves, 118
Combs, 181–83
Commercial fishing and trapping, 41–42, 48
Common eider, 65, 264. *See also* Eider duck
Common loon: mask, 234–35; story of, 234. *See also* Loon
Communal men's house, 40. *See also* Qasgi
Conkin, Beth, 288
Containers: baleen, 117; bentwood, 124, 129; bone, 65; gunpowder, 100–101; gut-skin, 141; ivory,

101; large food, 128; round wood, 124; seal-oil, 131; snuff, 116–19; storage, 121–27, 141; for precious things, 144; urine, 127–28; walrus-shaped, 101; water, 56–58. *See also* Bags; Bowl; Grass
Cooking, 157, 169; pots, 244–45
Cook Inlet, Alaska, 16, 18–19, 64
Copenhagen, Denmark, 3–4
Copper, 217; blade, 66
Copper River, Alaska, 19, 73, 261
Cormorant: feathers, 60, 83, 213, 215; feathers as fletching, 80, 85; head, 100; hunted, 265–66; parkas, 264
Costenoble, Hermann, 21
Cotton grass, 146, 268; roots, 171; tall, 145, 164, 261. *See also* Grass
Courier, 275
Cousin, 128. *See also* Cross-cousin; Teasing
Coverings: kayak-skin, 76, 167; skin, 85. *See also* Canoe; Kayak
Crab mask, 244
Cranberries, 39; mixture, 170
Crane: feather stabilizers, 89; skin parkas, 265. *See* Sandhill crane
Crooked knife, 80, 97, 152, 159, 271
Cross-cousin, 143; female, 104, 132; male, 87. *See also* Cousin; Teasing
Cross lashing, 74–77
Crowberries, 39
Crow Village, Alaska, 40
Crucifix as amulet, 189–93
"Culturalism," 287
Cumberland, Baffin Island, 4
Cuqaar (warrior), 245
Curing, 173; painted drum skin, 224
Curios, 15, 18, 25; American, 20; purchase of, 14, 19
"Curiosities," 8, 33
Cutting board, 136, 169, 216
Cycling: ceremonial, 41; seasonal, 42

Dakkitkjaremut, Alaska, 12
Dall, William H., 20
Dance: animal, 104–5; arrival, 270; celebration, 120; in contemporary Yup'ik culture, 284; director, 211, 217, 219, 239, 242, 278; drum, 275–78; dynamics, 242; fans, 213, 219, 227, 237–42; festivals, 43, 78, 166, 202; headdress, 213, 215–19; masks, 16, 27, 41, 217, 220, 227, 239, 274–76; ornament, 212; paraphernalia, 27, 119, 213, 215, 277; purpose of, 119–20; in *qasgi*, 242, 270, 275; songs, 217, 219, 276–78; traditional, 48; woman's old-style, 105. *See also Agayuliyararput* (Our Way of Making Prayer); *Itruka'ar*
Dance-house model, 35; ivory, 119–20. *See also* Dancer; *Qasgi*
Dancer: first time, 238, 274; woman, 238; with necklace, 211, 213
Darmstadt, Germany, 4
Darts, 16, 84, 250–51
Dead, 41, 275; gifts to, 130, 275; land of, 25, 130, 249; memory of, 239; spirit of, 248–49. *See also* Feast for the Dead
Death, 95; restrictions accompanying, 202. *See also* Disease; Sickness

Decorations, ivory, 116; nose septum, 103, 128. *See also* Beads; Jewelry; Personal adornment
Decoys, 97; fish, 108–9; ivory, 109
Dentalia beads, 217
Designs, 58, 63, 78–79, 87, 135, 138, 160, 169; animal, 75; black, 60, 274; caribou, 131; circle-and-dot, 99, 116, 123, 140, 148, 150, 167, 177, 195, 197–99, 203; of claws, 259; engraved, 150, 196; facial, 172; family, 117, 125; incised, 63, 90, 121, 131, 161, 172; Kuskokwim, 75; mink and land otter, 132; ownership of, 124; painted, 81; as prayers, 125; pretend arrow-point, 210; pretend vomit, 129; raven's foot, 159; walrus-head, 196
Design-making tool, 148
Devils, 8; animal belonging to, 221
Digging tool, 271
Dillingham, Alaska, 42, 49; cannery, 245; University of Alaska, 49
Diomede Islands, Alaska, 9
Dip net, 137, 201; herring, 113. *See also* Nets
Dipper, 169–73; bentwood, 171–72; for a doll, 189; ice, 106–7; water, 11, 127–28
Dirt, as protective barrier, 176, 281
Disease, 17, 176, 180; protection from, 209–10. *See also* Great Death; Influenza; Sickness; Smallpox
Dog: imitation, 274–75; Jacobsen's sled, 12, 14, 15, 18, 32; kennel, 130; skull, 65; sled, 3–4, 109; story, 115
Dog (chum) salmon skin, 269
Dolls, 35, 235; antler and ivory, 188–90; as amulets, 255; boots, 257; decorations for, 103; female, 189; (ground) squirrel, 103; male, 189; parkas, 257–58; rules surrounding, 257; toy, 188–94, 254–61; worn by girls, 254–55, 256
Dotti, Johann Baptist, 6
Drawer D, 183, 203, 278
Drebert, Rev. Ferdinand (Makneq), 48. *See also* Moravian
Dresden, Germany, 23, 27, 28, 30, 31; Museum of Anthropology and Ethnology, 24; zoological garden, 4
Drift net, 109; salmon, 111. *See also* Nets
Driftwood, 39, 57, 121, 154, 178, 253; bending, 107; root portion, 109, 113. *See also* Wood
Drills, 99, 148; nephrite, 148
Drinking, rules for, 171
Drum, 4, 35, 119–21; dance, 275–78; designs, 79, 127, 131, 258; handles, 223–26; song, 277; symbol of a festival, 127; use in *qasgi*, 239
Ducks, 39. *See also* individual species
Dwelling, 167. *See also* Sleeping places; Sod
Dye, alder-bark, 137

Eagle-feather: dance stick, 277; hood, 209–10, 284
Eagles, 8; giant, 209; head, 177, 205
Earmuffs, 210
Earrings, 186, 217; broken, 203; with connecting necklace, 187–88; for dolls, 103; storage device, 189
East Asia, 21
Eating restrictions, 136, 193, 269, 272. *See also* Food
Egg hunting, 122
Egypt, 30

Eider duck skins, 154. *See also* Common eider
Eisbär (ship), 4, 6
Ekviggaak, Alaska, 263
Elciyaraq, 130, 274, 275
Elders: knowledge of English, 47–49; personal histories, 47–49; reaction to collections, 235, 284–85
Eldorado, 39
Ell'allaller, 123
Ellam Yua, 215, 227, 263. *See* Person of the Universe
Elriq, 105
Elriyaraq, 97
Emmonak, Alaska, 48
Engelumiut, Alaska, 84
Engert, W., 31
England, 28
Engraving, 195; tool, 99, 148, 152; beaver-tooth, 152–53
Eqtarmiut, Alaska, 87, 88; warriors, 89, 247, 261
Ermine skins, 264–65
Erosion, 173, 237; device that creates, 185
Eskimettes, 13, 24
Eskimo, 13, 16, 18, 25, 40–41; begging, 15; beliefs, 39; graves, 11; living conditions of, 14; objects collected from, 4; pictographic writing, 29, 30; potatoes, 174; "Stone Age," 12; tribes, 21; villages, 9; Völkerschau, 4
Eskimo about Bering Strait (Nelson), 94
Esophagus: bearded seal, 217; bleached, 215; dried, 144, 213, 215, 217, 219
Ethnic exhibition, 3, 25, 29, 30; scholarly reaction to, 27. *See also* Völkerschau
Ethnography, 29. *See also* Anthropology
Ethnologisches Hülfscomite (Ethnological Support Committee). *See* Support Committee
Ethnology, 20; American, 287; diffusionist, 21; history of, 5; twentieth-century, 14. *See also* Anthropology
Euro-Americans, 40–41, 200
Europe, 9; imitation of, 273
Exchange Feast, 130. *See also* Messenger Feast
Exhibit-making, 227
Explorers, 18
Extraordinary persons, 179, 229, 231–33. *See also Ircenrraat*
Eyarralek (warrior), 89
Eyes, 122; bead, 188; metal, 188; protection for, 206–8

Falcon, peregrine, 209
Family: design, 63, 238, 258–59; relations, 40, 42, 43. *See also* Relationships
Far East, 26
Fasteners. *See* Bag fasteners
Feast for the Dead, 13, 41; Great, 41, 105. *See also* Dead
Feather, 103, 161, 195, 238; cormorant, 60, 80, 83, 213, 215; crane, 89; decoration, 206, 220; eagle, 209–10, 277, 284; fletching, 60, 80, 81, 83; flight stabilizers, 59, 86, 93; mallard tail, 238; on mask, 227; old-squaw, 206–7, 213, 239; raven, 103; seagull, 103; snowy owl, 238; swan, 238
Festivals, 170, 270; songs for, 275
Fiber splitter, 111
Field Museum, Chicago, 30, 31

Fieldwork: in anthropology, 287; long-distance, 23; nineteenth-century, 14
Figures: hanging, 219–21, 263; rock, 194; sea monster, 263. *See also* Grave; Human figure
Finger masks, 238. *See also* Dance fans
Finns, in Alaska, 10, 26
Firearms, nineteenth-century, 100. *See also* Guns; Rifles
Fire bath, 40, 80, 97, 107, 128, 133, 175, 176–77; equipment for, 208–9; hats for, 143; wood, 176–77, 251, 266
Fire: board, 178, 179; drill, 178, 179; pit, 40; uses of, 179; starter, 179–80
Firewood: gathered, 145; process of acquiring, 176–77, 251
First catch, 231; celebration, 78
Fish, 8, 39, 121, 197; adipose fin, 183; bones, 96; camp, 84, 102; carvings, 193, 203; counting catch, 115; cutting, 161; decoys, 108, 109; dried, 65, 131; eggs, 129, 171, 173; head, 130, 275; monster, 122, 123, 195, 197; parts to avoid, 131; representation of, 221; skin, 135–37; striker, 114; tail, 150, 183; traps, 64, 105–6, 115; treatment of, 96. *See also* Fish-skin; individual species
Fishhooks, 121, 124; box, 122; caribou antler, 107; walrus-ivory, 107
Fishing, 40; equipment, 97, 107–9, 114–15, 121, 122, 124; line, 107; pole, 107
Fish-skin: bags, 135, 137, 141; boots, 135, 137, 267–69; freeze-dried, 136; mittens, 135, 206, 266; preparation of, 136, 269
Fish spears: barbed points, 66, 67; points, 97; three-pronged, 90
Fish traps: making, 114–15, 154; ribs, 277
Fletching, 83; types, 81; feather, 60
Flight-stabilizing feathers, 59, 60, 80, 83, 86
Floats, 54–56, 60, 111; bladder, 52–54; loon throats, 109, 111; nozzle, 54; plugs, 54; walrus-bladder, 54; wooden, 113
Flounder, 39
Folk shows. *See* Ethnic exhibitions; Völkerschauen
Food cache, underground, 128
Food: care of, 263; distribution of, 274–75; famine, 65; offering, 185, 189, 237, 274; preparation and serving, 123, 134; preparation of special, 274; prohibitions, 136; restrictions, 269, 272; shortage, 259. *See also* Eating restrictions
Foot races, 270
Fort Alexander, Alaska, 18, 19, 68, 101, 154, 161, 170, 193, 219, 245, 261–62, 272
Fort Edmonton, British Columbia, 8
Fort Garry, Canada, 8
Fort Kenai, Alaska, 19
Fort (Prince) Rupert, British Columbia, 6
Fort York, Canada, 8
Fox, 39; designs, 238; in human form, 185; hunt, 266; mask, 228. *See also* Red-fox
Frame boat, 55
Frank, Mr., 28
Frederick the Great, 283
Freeze-dried skin, 269
Frei University, Dahlem, 208
Friedrich, Crown Prince, 21
Funnel, 105

Furs, 210
Fur trade, 41
Future, prediction of, 172–73, 244–45, 286

Gaff, 62, 63–64, 93
Games, 16, 84, 148, 188, 250–61; ending warfare, 245
Gauges, 113–14
Gear box, 124; wooden, 125
Geese, 39; fletching, 83; hunting, 81
Genest, Otto, 29, 30
German-Nordic Society, 33
Germans, in Alaska, 10
Germany, 5, 26, 28, 31; and anthropological tradition, 287; colonial expansion, 4; national identity, 287; unification, 4
Gesell, Frau (conservator), 203
Geyser Lake, Alaska, 14
Gifts, 1, 41, 165; courting, 200; declined, 14; exchange, 274, 275–76; presentation, 13, 37, 166, 254, 270, 275–78; return, 45; to women, 203
Gilyak(s), 26, 223
Girls: learning to sew, 258; "wearing" dolls, 254–55, 256
Glass beads, 107, 210, 213, 218. *See also* Beads
Globus (journal), 21, 29
Gloves, 13, 135; dancing, 213–14
God, 173, 176, 200, 227, 286; belief in, 193
Gold, 41; miners, 9. *See also* Nome, Alaska
Goldberger, M. L., 6
Goldi, 26, 223
Golovnin Bay, Alaska, 12, 13, 16, 250
Good provider, 41, 87. *See also Nukalpiaq*
Gordon, George Byron, 287
Grandchild: poor, 217; transformed into a star, 259
Grass, 134, 137; backpacks, 57; bags, 56, 144–46; ball, 252; baskets, 57, 105, 144, 146, 200, 210; bedding, 144; boot-liners, 267–69; boot insulation, 217; braided, 208; clean, 151; coarse seashore, 144, 164, 261, 271; dance fans, 238; harvesting, 57, 164; insoles, 217, 269; as insulation, 269; kayak mats, 144, 164; liners, 267; mats, 164–66, 215; miniatures, 260–61; rattle, 251; respirator, 40; roots, 121; split, 209; storage baskets, 147; story of discontented, 166; terminology of, 164; towels, 40, 208–9; use of, 164. *See also* individual species
Gratitude, 84, 93, 125, 143, 245, 281; of elders, 285, 288–89
Grave: figures, 255, 256; goods, 11, 35, 203; houses, 223; monument, 11, 17–18, 223; robbing, 15; yards, 7
Graves, 4, 16, 18, 19
Great Death, 194. *See also* Death; Influenza
Great hunter (*nukalpiaq*), 97, 159, 162. *See also Nukalpiaq*
Great Feast for the Dead, 41, 105
Great Society, The, 42
Greenland, 8, 39, 264; collections from, 51; Eskimo families from, 3, 4
Greens, 145; edible, 39
Greenstone, 13, 161; knives, 16; pipe, 15. *See also* Nephrite
Ground squirrels, 94; dens, 102, 103; hunting, 104;

parkas from, 103, 143; skins, 103; snares, 102–3
Gunpowder container, 100–101
Guns, 8, 98; front-loading, 121; introduction of, 12; muzzle-loading, 79, 99; primer box for, 100–101. See also Firearms; Rifles
Gunther, Erna, 7, 22, 23
Gut skin: bag, 141; parka, 13; sieve, 168. See also Seal

Haberdeck, Carl, 3–6, 8–9, 20, 22, 24–31, 33
Haberdeck (Unalitschok) River, Alaska, 14
Haida, 6, 8, 19
Hair: care of, 181–82; as decoration, 121; human, 13; ornament, 212
Hair seal. See Seal
Half-face mask, 248–49
Halibut, 39
Halle, Germany, 29
Hamburg, Germany, 3, 5, 6, 20, 27–29, 33; dialect, 25
Hamburg Ethnological Museum, 33
Hamburg-Stellingen, Germany, 33
Hamburg Zoo, 32
Hammer, 155, 273; caribou-antler, 155
Handle, caribou-antler, 159; fish-shaped, 223–24
Hand rattle, 263. See also Rattles
Hands: huge, 164; pierced, 203–4, 224, 231, 233; thumbless, 224
Hanging figure. See Figures
Hardwood, 62, 76, 155, 160, 252. See also Wood
Hare, 39; snowshoe, 102; tundra, 102
Harpoons, 9, 23, 53, 74, 90, 271–72; child's, 60; floats, 54, 72; head, 68, 113; line, 68, 72; large animal, 58–60, 68; points, 64–68, 71, 93, 108; seal-hunting, 52–55, 60, 66, 82–84, 86, 113; shafts, 60; throwing and retrieving, 64, 66–67, 90, 271. See also Barbed points; Toggling harpoons
Harvesting activity, 42, 43
Hats, 18, 60; bentwood, 205–7, 261, 272; bird-skin, 208, 263; for fire bath, 208–9; functions of, 206; loon-skin, 209; raven-skin, 209, 279. See also Cap; Dance
Havel River, Germany, 50, 283
Headdress. See Dance
Heads, 185
Heads. See Human skulls
Healing, 121, 122, 180; ceremonies, 13. See also Medicines
Health care, 42
Hebron, Labrador, 4
Heller, Emil, 6
Helping spirit, 222, 228–29, 231, 233, 234
Herder, Johann Gottfried, 287
Herring, 39; fishing, 25
Hide, 137; squirrel-belly, 138
Hole-punchers, 149–50
Holes, piercing, 161
Hood: as protection from illness, 209–10; types of, 209–10, 284
Hook, 64, 109; bone, 63, 186; caribou-antler, 62, 63; ivory, 187, 189
Hooper Bay (Naparyaar), Alaska, 65
Hootch v. Alaska State Operated Schools. See Molly Hootch decision
Hope Island, British Columbia, 7

Hopi, 19
Horn, 155; blade, 156
Hospital, 42
Hotel Bauer, Berlin, 30
House. See Dwelling; Qasgi; Sleeping places; Sod houses
Household miniature items, 260–61
House protectors, 221–23
Hudson's Bay Company, 6, 8
Hülfscomite für Vermehrung der Ethnologischen Sammlungen der Königlichen Museen (Committee to Support the Expansion of the Ethnological Collections of the Royal Museums). See Support Committee
Human figure, 188–94, 220, 222–23, 254–61; in houses, 189; life-size, 193–94; as male, 185. See also Mouth
Human: remains, 7, 11; skull, 7, 15, 16, 32; society, 41. See also Burials; Human figure
Humboldt, Wilhelm von, 287
Humpback whale, 76, 124
Hunter: birdlike appearance of, 206; skillful, 130. See also Nukalpiaq
Hunt, George, 23
Hunting, 58; caribou, 162; equipment, 55; geese, 81; hats, 205–7; marine mammals, 85; partnerships, 43; by women, 78, 93

Ice: chisels, 161; dipper, 106–7; hunting on, 60, 205; jam, 126; needle, 69; skates, 266, 284
Iceland, 25
Identity, issues of, 288
Idols, 4, 9, 13, 26, 35, 221–23, 256
Iguk, Alaska, 245
Iinrayaq River, Alaska, 179
Iiyuussiiq River, Alaska, 87, 88, 245, 248
Ikogmiut (Russian Mission), Alaska, 41
Iliamna district, Alaska, 96, 245
Iliamna, Lake, Alaska, 19
Illness. See Disease; Sickness
Ilutsik, Esther (Arnaq), 49
Incised designs, 63, 90, 121, 131, 161, 172. See also Designs
India, 28
"Indian Archipelago." See Indonesia
Indians, 10, 11, 14, 15, 18, 25, 35; authentic "red," 31; "hostile," 15, 32; as "local Jews," 6, 8; stereotypic, 27; "unreliable," 12
Indonesia, 27, 28, 31
Infant mortality, 42
Inflation nozzle, 55
Influenza, 40; epidemic, 41; 1918 epidemic, 194. See also Disease; Great Death
Ingalik, 15, 16; collection, 11, 134; objects, 12, 21; people, 32; territory, 10
Ingeritla (Ingril'er), Alaska, 16
Ingniktok, Alaska, 13
Ingricuaq River, Alaska, 183
Inlay, 179; ivory, 117, 118, 148
Intergroup relations, 40
Inuit (people), 3, 4, 16, 40; Labrador, 5, 9; linguistic continuity, 39
Inupiaq, 188; hospitality, 14; language, 39; objects, 64; points, 66; tools, 150
Ircaqurrluk (shaman), 97, 98
Ircenrraat, 95, 116, 234, 236

Iron, 67; blade, 156, 159; knife, 162
Iruvertuq (warrior), 88, 247
Isaac (guide), 14, 15
Itruka'ar (Agayuyaraq), 119, 144, 217, 236, 274.
Ivory, 55, 100, 117, 150, 183, 197, 203, 252–53; arrow point, 82, 83, 84, 86; bag fastener, 138, 197; carvings, 189, 192, 193; cases, 195–97; containers, 101; dance-house model, 119; decorations, 207; decoy, 109; dolls, 188, 190; faces, 189; figures, 262; fishhook, 107; funnel, 56; gauge, 114; harpoon-line attacher, 72; hooks, 187, 189, 201; inlay, 117, 118, 148; likeness, 157; lip ornament, 186; mastodon, 179, 183; models, 261–62; objects, 148; pestle, 167, 168; pieces, 72, 132; points, 82, 85, 86; powder measure, 101; plugs, 56; shuttle, 113; socket pieces, 60; tobacco box, 116. See also Walrus

Jacobsen, Harald (son), 28, 31, 32
Jacobsen, Hedwig (daughter-in-law), 33
Jacobsen, Henny (sister-in-law), 24, 31
Jacobsen, Hjalmar (son), 31, 32
Jacobsen, Johan Adrian, accession records, 22–24; in Alaska, 6, 8, 9–19, 24, 33; attitude toward Natives, 6–7, 19; bringing Bella Coola to Europe, 27; career as hat maker, 27–28; childhood 3; collection for Royal Museum, 19, 20, 25, 28, 33, 64; collections of, 4, 10, 12, 13, 16, 19, 20, 27; command of German, 3, 24, 30; death, 33; description of southwestern Alaska, 39; drawings, 35; to East Asia, 33; education of, 3, 4, 26; elders' view of, 285; end of collecting, 28; engagement, 24–25; as ethnographer, 14, 30; family of, 23, 25–32; good trading, 15; grave-robbing by, 15; illustrated talks on Alaska, 31; inconsistent records, 23; to Indonesia in 1887, 27–28, 33; interpretation of masks, 229, 231; journals, 12–15, 18–24; lack of formal education, 30, 33; letters, 13, 21, 24; major expeditions, 33; as man of action, 4, 14, 19, 24, 33; map of trip, 7, 11; in North America, 33; on Northwest Coast, 6–9; Northwest Coast collections, 20, 27; payment of, 20, 22, 24–26, 28–29, 32, 33; personal papers, 24, 31; publications of, 3, 4, 7, 12–16, 18, 21, 25, 28, 30, 32, 33, 39; racist leanings, 33; restaurant business, 31; return to Germany, 19; scholarly aspirations, 29–30; as scientific traveler, 22, 33; shortcomings, 20; social class, 24; stealing artifacts, 18, 32, 222, 223; third expedition, 14; travel book, 21, 25; trip to Siberia, 25–27, 33; upbringing, 14, 32; visit to Smithsonian, 19–20; womanizing, 24, 25, 31; work in the museum, 24–29; work outside the museum, 30
Jacobsen, Johan Fillip (brother), 25–28, 30, 31
Jacobsen, Johan Martin (brother), 3, 25
Jacobsen, Paul (son), 28, 30–32
Jacobsenweg (street), Hamburg, 33
Jacobsen, Wilhelm (son), 31, 32
Jacobshaven, Greenland, 4
Jadeite, 21
Jade labret, 183. See also Labret; Nephrite
Janssen, Albrecht, 32
Japan, 26–28
Jena, Germany, 21

Jesuit priests, 48
Jewelry, 18. *See also* Brooch; Earrings; Labret; Necklace; Personal adornment
John, Paul (Kangrilnguq), 68, 210–11; personal history, 48; reaction to collections, 285–87
Johnson, President Lyndon B., 42
Johnson River, Alaska, 236
Jukkak, Nelson Island, 16

Kachemak Bay, Alaska, 19
Kaisergarten, 29
Kajaluigemuitten (Kayalivik), Alaska, 49
Kajatolik, Alaska, 15
Ka-krome, Alaska, 11–12
Kalmucks, 26
Kamkoff, Mr., 16, 23
Kanakanak, Alaska, 49
Kangcilek, Alaska, 234
Kangerenarremiut, Alaska, 18
Kangiracuar, Alaska, 236–37
Kangirracungarpak Point, Alaska, 122
Kangrilnguq. *See* John, Paul
Kasigluk, Alaska, 47, 106; High School, 286; River, 270
Kaskinak, Alaska, 19
Kass'at, arrival of, 47, 48
Kassigit, 14. *See also* Qasgi
Katmai, Alaska, 217, 218
Kaviaq, Alaska, 48
Kawiarsak (Qawiaraq), Alaska, 12
Kayak, 3, 12, 82; bow or keel protector, 69–71; capsizing, 54, 89; child's first, 60; coaming, 69–70, 206; construction of, 76, 78, 134, 152–53; cover, 69, 73, 76, 152; deck stiffener, 70; equipment, 60–67, 69–71; float board, 60; frame, 78, 85, 153; hunting with, 53–57, 63–64, 83, 93, 111; landing of, 184; mats, 164–66; model, 221, 261; with mouth, 248; painted white, 205; pathway for, 126; repair, 85, 152; ritual, 206–7; rolled, 207; skin, 67, 73; with skin rope, 71; sled, 54, 63, 109; stem, 78; tote hole, 118; traveling, 40, 56–57, 87–88, 143; women's, 94
Kayalivik, Alaska, 16
Kazan, Russia, 26
Keene, Nastasia (Aguralria), 217
Kevgiryaraq. *See* Messenger Feast
Kialiq River, Alaska, 93
Kiimaaq River, Alaska, 47, 48
Killer whale, 124–25, 154. *See also* Whale
King eider (duck), 39
King Island, Alaska, 16; collection, 78, 149; people of, 9
King (chinook) salmon, 39, 97, 110, 157; heads, 114; in human form, 111; net, 110, 114, 271, 281; skin, 269. *See also* Salmon
Kinkinret, Alaska, 271
Kirgiz Steppe, Russia, 26
Klingelhöfer, 29
Klopfer, Emil Hugo, 28
Klopfer, Hedwig, 21–22, 24, 26–32; death, 33
Knives, 10, 15, 18, 97; blade, 157, 162; bone, 159; carving, 153; to cut fish, 157; fish and skin, 161; men's, 157–59, 161; sharpening, 152–53; to skin animals, 157; stone, 12; women's, 125, 153, 157–59, 161
Knots, 81

Knowledge: re-owning of, 288; sharing of, 47, 49; used to shape future, 284–89
Kodiak Island, Alaska, 16, 19, 20
Königliches Museum für Völkerkunde, Berlin. *See* Royal Museum of Ethnology
Korea, 26
Koserowski, Alaska, 11
Koskimo, British Columbia, 7; natives of, 8–9
Koslewak [Kusilvak] (Black River), Alaska, 16
Kotlik, Alaska, 10, 16
Kotzebue Sound, Alaska, 9, 14, 16, 187, 266; mask of inhabitant, 292
Krause, Arthur, 6, 8
Krause, Aurel, 6, 8; Northwest Coast traveler, 27
Krause, Eduard, 26
Krefeld, Germany, 4
Kroeber, Alfred, 287
Kuhn, H., 28, 29
Kuiggluk, Alaska, 101
Kuigpagmiut [Kuigpakmutten, Kwikpageuit, Kwigpagmiut, Kwigpagmiut], Alaska, 11, 22. *See also* Yukon River
Kukugyarpak (traveler), 186–87
Kukumyaq (warrior), 245
Kulukak (Quluqaq), Alaska. *See* Quluqaq
Kusilvak (Black River). *See* Koslewak
Kuskokwim area, 189, 234, 238; Bay, 74; collections from, 54, 60, 62, 68, 71, 75, 83, 90, 100–102, 107, 109, 111, 113, 116–17, 138, 141, 143, 145–47, 150, 154–55, 159, 167, 170, 177, 179, 183, 186, 188, 195, 197, 198, 201–4, 210–13, 216, 217, 223, 229, 242, 250, 252, 254–57; man, 124; mask, 35; people, 88, 264; story, 115, 221; warriors, 79
Kuskokwim River, 9, 16, 18, 19, 40, 47, 49, 55, 89, 118, 137, 186, 209, 215, 217, 247, 267; lower, 94, 188; middle, 41; mouth of, 81
Kwakiutl, 8, 26, 27, 35; legend, 230; masks, 229, 292. *See* Bella Bella
Kwigillingok, Alaska, 37
Kwiguk, Alaska, 48
Kwik-pak (Yukon River), 16. *See also* Yukon River
Kwikpakmiut (Kwigpagmiut). *See* Kuigpagmiut; Yukon River

Labrador, 4, 39; Inuit, 5, 9; tea, 118. *See also* Inuit
Labret, 9, 15, 16, 25, 55, 58, 125, 188, 229; bead, 191; broken, 195, 196; jade, 183; men's, 183–85; nose, 189; shape of, 183–85; side, 124; stone, 185; women's, 186
Ladie (ship), 221
Ladle, 169–73; long-handled, 127
Lamppost, 69, 134, 166, 167
Lamps, 41, 120; clay, 134, 166–67; dried-moss wick, 134, 166–67; kerosene, 167; oil, 166; seal-oil, 134, 167; soot, 167
Lances, 18, 83, 93
Land animals, 157, 195; skins, 155; throat skins, 138
Land of the dead, 249. *See also* Dead; Feast for the Dead
Länder- und Völkerkunde (Geography and Ethnology) exhibition, 29
Langrehr, Maria, 24
Lapland, 4, 8
Lapps, 31
Larch, 75, 155
Lead, 99
Learn by observing, 140

Leather, 137, 143; bindings, 155; bird-foot, 135, 144; dyed, 138, 141; freeze-dried, 141; rope, 55
Le Coq, August von, 5, 6
Le Coq Island, Alaska, 14
Left-handed, 164; tools, 254
Le Havre, France, 4
Legendary creature, 179; seal-persons, 231–33
Legends, 122, 166, 173, 185, 243–44. *See also* Story; Storytelling
Leipzig, 21, 29
Lena River, 26
Lice, 12; removing, 181–83
"Life and Ways of the Eskimos" (Jacobsen), 30, 39
Lightning spirit, 221–22, 256
Line, 54, 65, 83, 85, 91; attachers, 71; bark, 113; coiled sealskin, 52; for spears, 143; walrus-skin, 55, 143; willow-bark, 102, 111
Lip ornaments, 15, 120; ivory, 186. *See also* Labret
Loche. *See* Burbot
"Longheads," 26, 27
Loon, 159; arctic, 111, 143, 234; behavior of, 234; common, 122, 143, 179, 192; in human form, 234; red-throated, 109, 208, 257; skins, 118, 154, 159–60, 208. *See also* Common loon
Loon-skin: bag, 118, 143–44; parkas, 264
Lorenz, Mr., 15, 16
Lorenzen, Hans Lorenz, 12, 31
Lower 48, 42
Lower Yukon, 15, 16, 173, 188; collections from, 62, 64, 109, 111, 137, 138, 141, 148, 149, 151, 153, 155, 159, 166, 191, 195, 200, 201–3, 213, 222, 228–29, 243, 252, 255; visor, 205

Macassar, 28
Mackenzie, Alexander, 6, 23
Makneq. *See* Drebert, Rev. Ferdinand
Malemut ("Malemiut"), 17, 18, 266
Mallard tail-feathers, 238
Mammoth, 12; bones, 15, 25, 111, 114, 179, 180; ivory, 179, 183
Mamterilleq, Alaska, 18
Manokotak, Alaska, 49, 181
Marble, 183
Marburg, Germany, 29
Marine mammals. *See* Sea mammals
Mark (unit of German currency), 20–22, 24, 26
Marks ownership, 175
Marriage, 144; arranged, 47; sign of, 187. *See also* Relationships
Marsh marigold, 39
Mask exhibit. *See* Agayuliyararput
Masks, 7–9, 11, 17, 19, 23, 30, 35, 222, 228–37; collection of, 10; dancing with, 16, 41, 239, 274, 276; disposal of, 229; exhibit of, 49, 227, 281, 288; fish and animal, 121; names of, 12; to produce good weather, 229; return to Berlin, 203–5; tiny, 189; use in prayer, 227
Mask that sticks to the face, 229–33
Mask types: Aleut, 229; Bella Coola, 292; child's, 292; crab, 244; dance, 291; demon, 291; diving bird, 292, 293; dog salmon, 291; evil demon, 291; "female helping spirit," 292; fish, 293; with four lampposts, 293; fox, 293; half-face, 248–49; halibut, 292; "helping spirit," 291; jellyfish, 291; Kotzebue Sound, 292; Kwakiutl, 292; land otter, 292; of legendary person, 292; man with two labrets, 293; with movable

mouth, 293; mink, 292; memorial, 249; mountain spirit, 291; owl, 292; Person of the Universe, 291; porcupine, 291, 293; "pretend Malemiut," 292; protective spirit of children, 292; reindeer, 292; ringed seal, 291; seagull, 292, 293; seal, 292, 293; sea otter, 292; shaman, 292; spirit, 291; spirit of salmon kin, 292; spirit or demon, 293; spirit or lightning, 291; "spirit woman mask," 292; sun, 69, 229, 292; with two faces, 292; village spirit, 291; walrus, 292–93; whale, 293; "white person," 292; "life," 293; wolf, 291–93; woman, 292, 293
Masset, British Columbia (Queen Charlotte Islands), 6; arrival of missionaries in, 7
Mastodon, 111, 179. See also Mammoth
Matches, 10, 101
Material culture studies, 288
Mats: grass, 164–66, 215; kayak, 144, 164–65; sleeping, 164, 165
Mauner, Wilhelm, 6
Mauss, Marcel, 1, 45
McKay, Charles L., 18
Mead, Marie (Arnaq): personal history, 49; reaction to collections, 285, 287
Meadow mice, 244
Meat: butchering, 157; distribution, 125
Medicines, 15, 173. See also Healing
Medievalfair, Dahlem, 283
Memorial, 12; feast, 165; festivals, 248–49; figures, 249; mask, 249
Mending, 124, 128. See also Sewing
Menges, J., 28–30
Men of science, 28–29, 33
Men's items, 74, 131; knives, 157–59, 161; labrets, 183–85; tools, 169
Menstruation: first, 47, 95, 131, 254; rules surrounding, 214. See also Women
Mequtmiut, Alaska, 122, 263
Messenger Feast (Kevgiryaraq), 41, 47, 78, 104, 165, 211, 217, 270, 274–78
Metal, 73, 213; points, 86; scarcity of, 160
Mexico, 21
Meyer, A. B., 24
Midden, 84
Middle Kuskokwim, 41
Middle Yukon: collections from, 74–75, 77, 133, 137, 138, 223
Migratory birds, 39. See also individual species
Milky Way, 243–44
Mines, 9, 41
Mink: designs, 132, 238; hunting, 39, 141; pelts, 130, 141; story, 132, 216; teeth, 141, 188; traps, 106
Miscarriage: restrictions accompanying, 202. See also Women
Missionaries, 7, 41, 272; arrival of, 193, 227; Russian, 18. See also Christianity; God
Mittens, 135, 206, 266; thumbless, 213–15, 284
"Mit Pagen, Boot und Schlitten durch Sibirien und Ostasien" (Jacobsen manuscript), 31
Miyaoka, Osahito, 49
Models, 4; as commemoration, 261
Model universe, 117, 219
Mohave, 19
Molly Hootch decision, 42
Moon, 273; arguing over, 155, 273–74; cycle of, 272–73; names for, 273
Moore, Catherine (Akiuk): personal history, 48;

151–52, 182, 224, 235, 254; reaction to collections, 285
Moose, 39; hooves, 182; hunting, 157
Moravian Children's Home, Alaska, 47
Moravian mission, 41, 48
Morning star, 259
Mortars, 167–69. See also Pestles
Mosquitoes, 12
Moss: dried, 167; as caulking, 167
Mountain Village, Alaska, 49
Mouse food, 171
Mouth: caribou-teeth, 247; downturned, 56, 233, 238; upturned, 185, 223
Mouthpiece, 148, 178, 179, 180
Mummy, 15, 16, 19; mummies, 120
Murrelet, 206
Museum für Deutsche Volkstrachten und Erzeugnisse des Hausgewerkes (Museum of German Folk Costume and Products of Domestic Craft), 28, 30
Museum Island exhibit, 20
Museums, 4–5; elders view of, 235, 285; part of God's plan, 286
Muskrat, furs, 210; hunting, 39, 75, 79–80; tanned, 169
Mussels, 145

Nails, 201; of antler, bone, seal teeth, 155; wooden, 149
Nakaciuryaraq (Bladder Festival), 274–76
Name avoidance, 90
Namesakes, 41, 97; of deceased, 130
Nanvarnarrlak, Alaska, 239, 277
Napakiak, Alaska, 83
Naparyarraq, Alaska, 65, 236, 239
Napaskiak, Alaska, 81, 83
Nationalcharakter (Wilhelm von Humboldt), 287
National Ethnografiske Forening (National Ethnographic Association), 29
National Museum of the American Indian, 49, 177, 286
Nationalzeitung (newspaper), 22
Native American, 41
Native American Graves Protection and Repatriation Act (1990), 288
Native: informants, 23; as "natural people", 5, 20; population decline, 41; researchers, 288; unreliable, 14; on verge of extinction, 5, 8
Navajo, 19
Naval Medical Museum, Washington, D.C., 20
Necklace, 188, 195, 211–17; doll, 103; making, 201. See also Jewelry; Personal Adornment
Needlefish (stickleback), 39, 105, 113, 177, 200
Needles, case, 121–22, 140, 196–97, 203; bone, 121–22, 200; iron, 149; making, 200; skinsewing, 69, 78, 137–38, 195, 200–201; stonepoint, 73; three-cornered, 201; for trade, 18
Nelson, Edward William ("Mr. Nielson"), 8, 9, 12–15, 18, 23, 24, 27, 33, 70, 166; collection of, 10; Eskimo about Bering Strait (book), 94
Nelson Island (Qaluyaat), Alaska, 16–18, 39, 41, 47–49, 67, 84, 118, 124, 125, 127, 131, 143, 154, 173, 187, 271; collections from, 60, 62, 68, 101, 106, 174, 179, 184, 197, 205–6; people, 88, 170, 182, 185. See also Cape Vancouver
Neolithic sites, 21
Nepcetaq, 229–33

Nephrite (jade), 15, 24, 66, 154, 187; amulets, 35; tools, 21, 29, 148. See also Greenstone
Nerevkartuli, Alaska, 118
Net-making tools, 113, 114, 200. See also Gauges
Nets: dip, 113, 137, 201; to catch seals, 114; drift, 109, 111; floats for, 108, 109; king salmon, 110, 114, 271, 281; retrieving, 64; small-mesh, 112; sinkers for, 111
Neumann, Henry, 9, 16, 22, 24
New Museum. See Royal Museum of Ethnology
New York, 6, 20, 31, 49, 286
New York Herald, 9
New Zealand, 21
Nightmute, Alaska, 48, 105, 207, 277
Ninilchik, Alaska, 19
Nome, Alaska, 31, 41
Nonhuman persons, 183–85. See also Animals
Non-Native: influence, 47; people, arrival of, 245; travelers, 23
Nordenskjold group, 16
North America, 5, 30
Northern Alaska, 39
Northern Eskimos, 248
Northern pike. See Pike
Northwest Coast: collections, 9, 19–23, 27, 29, 35; Jacobsen on, 6–8; secret societies, 29–31
Norton Sound, Alaska, 9, 12, 14, 97, 149, 152, 231, 244, 252, 266
Norway, 29–31, 33
Nose beads, 183, 189, 191, 255
Nose rings, 266
Novaia Zemlia, 31
Nukalpiaq, 87, 97, 128, 159, 162, 169, 174, 202, 217, 254, 275; cruel, 185; Nukalpiat (plural), 263; training of, 176. See also Good provider
Nuklukayet, Alaska, 11
Nulato, Alaska, 10, 15
Nunaalukaq Bay, Alaska, 194
Nunacuaq, Alaska, 144, 239, 270, 275
Nunacuaq River, Alaska, 271
Nunalcanahuk, Alaska, 12
Nunapicuar, Alaska, 270, 275
Nunapitchuk, Alaska, 49, 119, 165, 183
Nunivak Island, Alaska, 39, 184; collections from, 16, 19, 52, 58, 183, 185, 189, 198, 210, 255, 257; people, 170, 185
Nunivngayaq, Alaska, 194
Nushagak, Alaska: collections from, 53, 54, 56, 58, 75, 77, 79, 83, 85, 90, 103, 113, 138, 141, 143, 144, 147, 155, 167, 188, 190, 195, 197, 198, 201, 204, 210–12, 217–18, 220, 223, 224, 254, 255, 257, 267, 269, 278; region, 173, 177, 227, 245, 247
Nushagak River, Alaska, 16, 18, 39, 43, 143, 209. See Yukon, Kuskokwim, and Nushagak Rivers

Oar, 193
Ocean hunting, 206–7; people lost during, 183; story of, 91
Oglala-Sioux, 31
Old-squaw (duck), 39; feathers of, 206, 207, 213, 239; parka, 264; songs of, 207
Open water, reflection of, 65
Oral instruction, 42. See also Rules for living
Origin story, 193
Ornaments, 141, 213. See also Jewelry; Personal adornment
Orphan, 48, 83, 158, 217; treatment of, 182

Otter: carving of, 122, 203; land, 78, 94, 95, 122, 132; penis bones, 78, 197, 198; sea, 41, 54; story, 216
Owl: figures, 189, 191; great horned, 133; mask, 8; skin, 208; snowy, 219, 238

Paalraayak, 94, 116
Pacific coast of Alaska, 39
Pacific Northwest, 10
Pack, 101
Paddle, 193; double-bladed, 81, 207, 247, 263; in hunting, 68; needle, 201; Noshagak, 62; Togiak, 60–62, 63
Paimiut, Alaska, 40, 228
Paingaq, Alaska, 239, 260
Paint: black, 131; red, 127; red ocher, 83, 131; white clay, 60
Painted bladder, 284; faces, 167
Paiyaq (Wassilie Berlin's father), 93
Paluqtaaralek (warrior), 247
Pangalgalria (warrior), 87, 88
Paris, France, 4
Parka: bird-skin, 264–66; care, 182; construction, 156, 258–59; designs, 128, 143, 211, 255; doll, 189, 254, 255; fox, 194; gut-skin, 13; hoodless, 209, 210; loon-skin, 111; man's, 104; squirrel, 103, 143; squirrel-skin belly, 263; woman's, 98, 104, 135
Pastolik, Alaska, 12, 16
Patagonians, 4, 9
Pathways, clearing, 41, 126, 175
Paukan, Andy: personal history, 48–49; reaction to collections, 285, 287; return to Alaska, 210–11
Pension Dahlem, Dahlem, 50, 211
Percussion caps, 10
Personal adornment, 181–94. *See also* Jewelry
Personal experience, knowledge based on, 280–81, 287
Person of the Universe, 76, 164, 215, 227, 256, 263
Pestles, 169, 177–79. *See also* Mortars
Petersen, Charles ("Carl Pettersen," "Karel Pettersen"), 19, 58, 144
Petka (Creole interpreter), 10, 12
Petugtaq celebration, 41, 275–76
Phalaropes: northern, 81; red, 81
Philippines, 28
Pickaxes, 161
Pike: catching, 39, 97, 106–9, 114; story, 221
Pillugta (warrior), 247
Pingokpagemut, Alaska, 18
Pink (humpback) salmon, 39
Pintail duck, 39
Pipe, 15, 16; bone, 167
Plants, edible, 63, 209
Platinum (Arvirrmiut), Alaska, 153
Plugs, 55–56. *See also* Floats
Point Hope, Alaska, 25
Points: caribou-antler, 97; detachable, 58, 86; with steps, 66. *See also* Arrow points; Barbed points; Ivory; Stone; Toggling harpoons
Poke. *See* Seal skin
Pokers, 148, 159. *See also* Drills
Polar Sea, 28, 32
Polynesia, 6
Porcupine: bladder, 275; hunted, 215–16; mask, 291; quill design, 215; quills, 138; skin, 215
Port Clarence, Alaska, 12
Port Simpson, British Columbia, 7
Pottery, 133
Powder, gun, 10, 101. *See also* Guns
Power source, 126, 221. *See also* Shaman
Prague, Czechoslovakia, 4
Prayer, 227, 279. *See also Agayuliyararput* (Our Way of Making Prayer); Masks
Prediction of future, 189
Prescriptions, 177. *See also* Rules for living
Pretend eyes, 99. *See also* Designs: circle-and-dot
Primer box. *See* Guns
"Primitive," 72; peoples, 33. *See also* Native: as "natural people"
Prince Rupert, British Columbia, 6
Princess Louise (ship's name), 85
Prince William Sound, Alaska, 19, 39, 120, 217
Prohibitions, 131–32, 177; food, 136. *See also* Rules for living
Protective spirit, 188–89, 221–22
Proverb, 18, 25
Prying tools, 152, 154, 272
Ptarmigan, dancing story, 104–5; skin parka, 266; song, 207–8. *See also* Snares
Puberty, restrictions accompanying, 202, 214–15
Pueblo (people), 19
Pumice, 127
Punk, 167
Purification, 51, 276
Putukuilnguq (warrior), 81, 82, 84
Pyrethrum ground flowers. *See* Buhach
Pyrite, 186

Qaariitaaq, 130, 167, 274–76
Qaarpagyaraq, 274–75
Qacungatarli (Uyamigaaq), 172
Qaguyaurluq (warrior), 245
Qalulleq, Alaska, 266
Qaluyaat (Nelson Island), Alaska, 124. *See also* Cape Vancouver, Nelson Island
Qanagaarniarun (great hunter), 175. *See also Nukalpiaq*
Qanerciigalnguq (warrior), 247
Qanruyun, 169. *See also* Rules for living
Qasgi, 13, 18, 88, 166; construction, 164; instructions in, 41; lamp, 167; men performing in, 207; model, 35, 119, 261–62; skylight, 132; social position in, 40; women in, 128, 130–32, 181
Qecugivigmiut, Alaska, 260
Qengarrlugtuaq (great hunter), 263. *See also Nukalpiaq*
Qilagtaq, 79
Qinaq, Alaska, 49, 133
Qinaruuq, Alaska, 48
Qissayaarmiut, Alaska, 27, 227
Qissunaq, Alaska, 49
Quarruuk (warrior), 247
Quartz, 152, 179, 183, 255
Quatsino Inlet, British Columbia, 26
Queen Charlotte Islands, British Columbia, 6, 7
Quills, 195; feather, 161; raven-wing, 103; sandhill crane for stabilizers, 248; vanes, 103. *See also* Porcupine
Quinhagak, Alaska, 84, 86, 155
Quluqaq (Kulukak), Alaska, 49
Qunikok, Alaska, 14
Qupurruyuli (seal person), 126
Quugaarpak. *See* Erosion

Rabbit, 102, 155. *See also* Hare
Rasboinsky, Alaska, 12
Rattles, 7, 120, 238, 251, 263
Raus, Professor, 20
Raven, 8, 208; the Creator bird, 243–44; mask, 243–44; wing feathers, 103
Red-fox: fur piece, 194; in human form, 260; mask, 228
Red ocher (*uiteraq*), 71, 81, 86, 116, 144, 169, 239, 272; bashfulness of, 213; designs, 125. *See also* Paint
Red (sockeye) salmon, 39
Reed, Irene, 49
Refuse, making people visible, 184
Regional groups, 40; variation in, 127
Reindeer: antler, 167, 170–71, 205; herding, 42; pelts, 182; skin bedding, 165
Relationships: brother and sister, 185; courting, 200; cousin, 176–77, 242, 270, 274; grandmother and grandchild, 259; grandmother and grandson, 234; group, 40; host and guest, 40, 41, 111, 270, 274–75; human and animal, 43, 111, 115, 125, 132, 183; human and nonhuman, 41; human, animal, and spirit world, 41; between hungry hunters, 65; of hunter and hunted, 206; husband and wife, 41, 97, 131, 162–63, 176, 195, 202, 272; living and dead, 41, 130; men and women, 202, 217, 251; parent and child, 217; sister, 178
Relatives, distant, 79
Religious customs, 26
Representation, issues of, 288
Request song, 277–78. *See also* Messenger Feast
Respirators, 208–10. *See also* Fire bath
Restricted ones, 94–95
Revenge, 185, 248
Richter, Isidor, 6, 9, 18, 20, 28
Richter Lake, Alaska, 14
Ridicule, songs of, 172, 249, 270
Rifles: front-loading, 100; support, 99, 132. *See also* Guns
Ringed seal. *See* Seal
Rink, Hinrich, 33
Risø, Norway (island), 2, 3, 29
Ritual, 173; distributions, 42, 94; hunting, 206–7
Rocks, 87; bluish, 163; classification of, 153; thrown at people, 234. *See also* Stone
Roof planks, 164
Root picks, 174
Roots, 205; split, 106, 107
Royal Museum of Ethnology: collecting by, 6, 16, 19–21, 35; collecting for, 5, 9–11, 24, 28, 33; purchasing Eskimo objects, 4, 21; new building, 5, 25, 26, 27; salaries, 26, 29. *See also* Bastian, Adolf; Berlin Ethnological Museum
Rules for living, 41, 95, 132, 281
Russia, 26, 27
Russia: clothing of, 256, 258; influence, 272; loan words, 272; mission, 10, 41, 191–2, 292; Orthodox church, 47, 272; Orthodox priests, 41; trade beads, 124, 141, 186–87; trade network, 19, 40–41, 98. *See also* Bethel, Alaska;

Visionaries
Russians, arrival of, 40, 221

Sacred property, 8, 33–35
Sagali (Kuskokwim man), 124
Sabine Marshall, 287
St. Lawrence Island, Alaska, 186
St. Louis, Missouri, 19
St. Marys, Alaska, 48, 280
St. Marys Catholic Mission, Alaska, 42
St. Michael, Alaska, 9, 10, 12, 15, 22, 24, 25, 32, 42, 67–73, 154, 172, 183, 197, 221, 227, 229, 250–51; as Jacobsen's base camp, 16
Sakhalin, 26; whaling station on, 28
Salwa, 236
Salmon: aged heads, 173; commercial fishery, 39–41; designs, 238; drying, 114; figure, 241; harpoons, 66, 97; nets, 108–9, 110–13; skin, 136–38, 141, 269; story, 111. See also individual species; Nets
Salmonberries, 39, 57, 96, 178, 184
Sandhill crane, 39; bone needle, 200; quills for stabilizers, 248. See also Crane
San Francisco, California, 6, 8, 9, 10, 18, 19, 24
Sans Souci Palace, 283
Schankwirtschaft (public house), 31
Schanzelin, Mr., 15
Schantz, Fritz von, 22, 28
Schist: point, 86; harpoon points, 66–68; scrapers, 156, 161
Schoepf, Adolf, 4, 23
Schools, 48
Science, 4, 14, 22, 30; collecting for, 16; "ungrateful men of," 28
Scoter (duck), common, 159
Scotsmen, 10
Scraper, intestine, 141; skin, 136, 154–57, 159–61; slate-bladed, 155; Yukon, 156
Sculpin, 221
Sea anemones, 145
Sea animals. See Seal; Sea mammals
Seabirds, 13, 39; hunting, 83; ocean, 264
Seagull: beaks, 207; carved head, 101, 206; decorations, 205; parka, 266; wing feather quills, 103
Seal, 138, 141, 143; bearded, 56, 63, 65, 92–94, 114, 151, 175, 179; bladders, 13, 56, 276; blubber, 93, 122, 169; bone, 94; breathing hole, 68; carvings, 111–12, 116, 193, 203, 211; decoration, 182, 192; design, 150, 238; distribution of, 94; female, 56; figure, 189; gut, 13, 122, 141, 167, 168, 179; hair, 57, 63, 114, 157, 158; hunting, 29, 52–54, 55, 83, 87, 90–93, 97, 113–14, 135, 157, 205–6; hunting by women, 179; on ice, 205; oil, 97, 128, 134, 149, 159, 166, 167, 178, 179; person, 126, 231–33; poke, 57, 131, 158; ringed, 143; scratcher, 68–69; skinning, 157–58, 162; skin of unborn, 142–43; song, 119; spotted, 57, 114, 143, 158; story, 93, 141, 171, 206; throat skins, 138; usefulness of, 39–40
Seal-gut: bag, 140; garment, 145; parka, 57, 84, 206
Seal harpoon. See Harpoons
Seal hunter, carving of, 261
Seal intestine, 167; dyed, 137; preparation of, 141. See also Seal: gut
Seal oil: containers, 131–33; extraction of, 159; as food, 128, 166–67, 178–79; food stored in, 268;

mixed with moss as caulking, 167; processing of, 173
Seal skin: belt backing, 201; bleached, 210; line, 52, 55, 43, 71, 179; poke, 48, 54, 57, 131, 158; preparation of, 158–59, 270; thong, 178–79; uses, 136, 138, 142–43, 149, 155
Sea mammals, 39–40; hunting, 52–53, 65, 85, 91, 95, 205; shape, 71, 122, 195, 198, 233; uses, 37, 173
Seasonal camps, 33, 40; spring, 16. See also Winter: villages
Secret society. See Northwest Coast
Seldovia, Alaska, 19
"Serpentine," 179, 183, 185
Seward Peninsula, Alaska, 14, 64
Sewing: bags, 138–43, 197; boots, 157, 257, 269; caribou-foot skin, 138; clothing, 253; fancy, 169; fish skins, 136, 267; kit, 141; learning, 200, 252–53, 258; by men, 143; with sinew, 76; tools, 195–201; walrus-throat skin, 138. See also Stitches
Sexual assault, 42, 275
Shaft straightener, 99
Shaktolik, Alaska, 14
Shaman: care of, 73, 85, 188, 192, 256; coat, 26; deceased, 189; drum, 223–26; as healers, 193; helping spirit, 235; Jacobsen and, 10–13; journey, 259–60; masks, 206, 227–37; messenger of, 206; power source, 126, 221; powerful, 236–37; rituals, 207, 224; story, 97, 221; training, 224–25; use of visors, 205; woman as, 217. See also Angalkut (shamans)
Shamanism, 222
Shame, 93
Sharing, 43; catch, 92, 94, 124, 125, 143; knowledge, 49
Sheefish, 39
Sheldon Jackson Museum, Sitka, 49
Shellfish, 263
Shells, 8; clam, 173; dentalia, 217; mussel, 84; pendants, 187–88
Ship model, 220–21
Shovel, 174–77, 271
Show business, 30
Shredders, 111, 150–52, 208
Shuttles: ivory, 113; net-making, 112–13; wood, 113
Siberia, 6, 21, 26, 29
Sickness, 154; immunity to, 176; protection from, 180, 209–10. See also Death; Disease
Sieves, 167; gut-skin, 168
Sinew, 53, 87, 102, 135, 144; binding, 77, 80, 86; genuine, 76; line, 67, 107, 113; making, 76, 151–52; thread, 150, 200, 217; twine, 52, 76, 110
Singapore, 28
Singing: while drumming, 239, 242; in English, 68
Singrak, Alaska, 12, 14
Sinkers: bone, 107, 109, 111; caribou-antler, 111, 113; and float line, 112
Sitka, Alaska, 8, 20
Sitting dances, 277–78. See also Dance
Skidgate Inlet, British Columbia, 6
Skin: animal, 155, 159; bearded-seal, 55; beluga, 125, 270; bird, 137–38, 141, 154, 208, 261, 264–65; blackfish, 137–38, 141; boots, 137, 169, 227, 267–70; cap, 40, 210, 264, 265; caribou, 129, 130, 138, 141, 155–56, 227, 258, 270; cari-

bou-ear, 140; caribou-fawn, 140; caribou-foot, 138; cleaners, 12; cormorant, 141; dog salmon, 135; dyed, 135, 138, 141; eagle, 209–10; ermine, 264, 265; fish, 135–37, 141, 206, 266–69; freeze-dried, 138, 269; hair-seal, 136; line, 64, 92; loon, 111, 118, 143–44, 154, 159, 160, 208, 209, 264–66; mink, 140; owl, 208; porcupine, 215; preparation, 157, 159, 270; ptarmigan, 266; raven, 209, 279; reindeer, 165; rope, 52, 55, 71, 143; salmon, 137, 138, 141, 269; scraper, 155–57, 161, 271; sewing, 76, 197, 200, 201; spotted-seal, 136; squirrel, 103, 209–10, 263; stretching, 179; tanning, 155–56, 173; thread, 189; throat, 138, 141, 143. See also Fish skins; Seal skin; Sewing; Skin boat; Thread
Skin boat: construction of, 76, 78, 85, 155, 159, 167; early travel by, 9, 10, 12, 19, 40, 65, 179, 193; in Europe, 4; image of, 185, 194. See also Angyak; Baidarka; Boat
Skis, 266
Skulls. See Human skulls
Skylight, 128. See also Qasgi
Sky world, 241
Slate, 60, 73, 153, 154; blade, 64, 157, 161, 162
Slate-bladed: arrow, 87; knife, 157, 158; scraper, 155
Sled, 3, 14, 146; making, 152, 153, 160; runner, 109; travel 18, 175
Sledge Island, Alaska, 9, 16
Sled-runner sheathing, 149
Sleeping places, 165. See also Mats; Qasgi
Slippers, 267
Smallpox epidemic of 1838–39, 40
Smelt, 39, 109
Smithsonian Institution, Washington, D.C. (Smitzsonia), 8, 9, 18, 33
Snares, 102–3. See also Ground squirrel
Snowshoes, 153, 266–67; binding, 152; construction, 127, 152; collectible, 4; in story, 127–29, 243
Snow: drifts, 129; goggles, 4, 12, 18, 207–8; scraper, 254; shelter, 175; melting, 266
Snuff: box, 23, 167; containers, 116–19; snorting, 169; tube, 117, 168, 169
Snuff tobacco, 167–69; accouterments, 168; Annie's preparation of, 281; traded, 167. See also Tobacco
Soap-making, 183
Soapstone, 99
Social control, 41
"Social Organization and Secret Societies of the Kwakiutl Indians" (Boas), 23
Society of Anthropology, Ethnology, and Prehistory, 29
Socket piece, 52, 53, 59
Sod: covering, 164; houses, 16, 40, 132, 165, 167
Songs, 207; child's, 252; with drumming preliminary to dancing, 207; evoked by collections, 282; of indigestion, 270; about loons, 143; old, 267; power of, 194, 259; shaman, 172; old-style, 88, 105; traditional Yup'ik, 223; with verses, 276. See also Warriors, songs of
Soonroodna, Alaska, 19
South America, 6, 21
South Dakota, 31
Southwestern Alaska, 41, 42; coastal landscape, 39; cultural reformation, 43; non-Native

Southwestern Alaska *(continued)*
  population, 10; weather, 39
Spears: bird, 96–97; caribou-antler point, 97; fish, 96–97, 107–8; guards, 71–72; points, 10, 73, 89, 93; rabbit, 97; seal-hunting, 83, 84, 92; and throwing boards, 90–91
Spear thrower, 66, 90; compared to guns, 91. *See also* Throwing board
Spinner, 250, 251
Spirit, 275; of Person of the Universe, 222; of the dead, 249, 275; protective, 188, 189, 221–22; in walrus form, 231
Spitsbergen, Norway, 3, 31
Spohr, Max, 21, 29
Sponges, 151
Spoons, 169–73; reindeer-antler, 170–71; clamshell, 173; painted wooden, 171; similar to Korean spoons, 170
Spotted seal. *See* Seal
Spruce roots, 128, 223; binding, 81
Squirrel: furs, 210; hunting, 104, 143; parka, 143, 265. *See also* Ground squirrel
Stars: as signal for change, 274; grandchild who became, 259
Starvation, 260, 277; story of, 263
Stealing, 14, 18
Steam bath, 16, 19. *See also* Fire bath
Steinen, Karl von den, 29, 30
Stellingen, Germany, 30, 33
Stellingen Animal Park (also Stellingen zoo), 30, 31, 33
Stickleback. *See* Needlefish
Stitches: caribou throat hair, 135, 137, 140, 144; closely woven, 145, 261, 267–68; cross, 78, 137, 141; fancy, 219, 269; genuine woven, 145; regular, straight, 137, 141, 267; top, 78, 137. *See also* Sewing
Stone, 153, 180, 183; amulets, 29, 180, 209; arrow point, 82, 83, 87; axes, 10, 12, 18, 21; balls, 251–52; blades, 72, 73, 159, 161–63; bullet mold, 99; figure, 194; items, 9, 21, 148; knives, 12, 159, 161; labret, 185; lance point, 12, 73; people, 18, 182; points, 60, 67, 72, 73, 84, 86, 148–49, 154; sinkers, 111; tools, 67, 72, 148, 161; tool to smooth clay, 134. *See also* Rocks; Stones; Whetstone
Stone Age, 8, 12, 21, 135; civilization, 67, 148; Eskimos, 12; to Iron Age, 159
Stones, 157; collecting of, 10; genuine, 179; as medicine, 179–80; sharpening, 153, 180; as weapons, 173. *See also* Whetstone
Storm surge, 15
Story, 124, 162, 172; of Apanuugpak, 245, 247–48; Apanuugpak's companion, 164; betrayal and revenge, 97–99; blind boy and loons, 234; boy who lived with seals, 141, 171, 206; journey to land of the dead, 249; hunting, 91–93, 94; orphan girl and her doll, 259; owl and raven, 208; porcupine, 216–17; raven, 208; raven brings daylight, 243–44; starvation, 263; two cooking pots, 244–45; walrus people, 183; woman who would not marry, 217; for Yup'ik culture, 286
Story knife, 117, 148, 252–55, 259; as gift, 200; renamed, 281
Storytelling, 31, 35, 280–82, 285–86, 289; as lessons for youth, 281

Straw-hat business, 28
Stretching frame, 68, 216
String: braided, 133; instrument, 223. *See also* Sewing; Thread
Subarctic environment, richness of, 39
"Subsistence digging," 148
Subsistence harvesting, 42
Suicide, 42
Sumatra, 28
Sun: observations of, 274; mask, 69, 229, 292
Support Committee, 5–6, 8–10, 20, 22, 24–26, 29, 33, 287; purchase of Jacobsen's collections, 26
Surabaya, 28
Swallow, 137
Swan: feathers, 238; feet, 138, 144; parkas, 264, 266; quill fletching, 81; skin, 137; whistling, 39, 81; wing bones, 195
Sweat bath, 41. *See also* Fire bath
Sweden, 29
Swedes in Alaska, 10
Switzerland, 29

Taboos, disregard for, 14
Tacoma, Washington, 48, 269
Takkjelt-Pileramiut, Alaska, 11
Talliquq, Alaska, 48. *See also* Fort Alexander
Tanana, Alaska, 15
Tanana River, Alaska, 10
Tanning: skins, 155, 173; process, 155–56. *See also* Skin
Tarpaulin, 164
Tarunguaq, Alaska, 194
Tarunguarmiut, Alaska, 122, 263
Tarvarnauramken, Alaska, 51
Tattoo(s), 18, 56, 120, 255
Tea, 94, 118
Teachings, 131. *See also* rules for living
Teamwork, 64
Teasing: animals, 238; between cousins, 202, 257, 274; between elders, 161, 208, 280; as lesson, 87
Teeth: animal, 183, 195, 196, 203; canine, 141, 154, 221, 222; beaver, 152–53; beluga, 201; caribou, 201–3, 223, 247, 281, 282; as decoration, 202; mink, 141, 188; seal, 155; walrus, 154, 256
Thimble, 138, 143, 197, 199–200; metal, 200. *See also* Sewing
Thread, 76, 138; from animal muscle, 150, 151; from beluga, caribou, whale, 151; braided, 113; length, 78; sinew, 83; skin, 152. *See also* Sinew
Throat skin, freeze-dried, 138
Throwing board, 52–53, 59, 60, 86, 90–94, 96; grips, 90; measuring, 92. *See also* Spear thrower
Throwing harpoon, 90
Thunder devil, 222
Tiurnen (schooner), 9
Tlingit ("Tlinkit"), 8, 27; masks, 229
Tobacco: bag, 118; begging for, 14; boxes, 38, 116, 124; leaf, 167; pouch, 138, 147; processed, 167; shredded, 168; song about, 119; as thanks, 94; trading, 10, 14, 15, 18, 41. *See also* Snuff tobacco
Toggling harpoons, 59, 60, 67, 91, 92; points, 64–65, 67, 71. *See also* Harpoons; Barbed points
Togiak, Alaska, 18, 32, 48, 79, 122, 154, 264, 286; cannery, 122; collections from, 61, 63, 148, 266
Togiak River, Alaska, 47, 103, 104, 118, 133, 143, 173,

193, 205, 213, 215, 263, 267
Toksook Bay, Alaska, 48
Tomcod, 39
Tools, 148–63; bowl-making, 148–49; design-making, 148; left-handed, 154; prying or unraveling, 73; skin-stretching, 179; stone-bladed, 161
Toothy cavity, relationship to lightning spirit, 222
Toothy mouth, 230, 256
Top, 250, 251
Totem poles, 7, 23, 26, 30
Toutak, 16. *See also* Labret
Toys, 189, 250–61; for children, 193
Trade, 55, 148–49, 176, 187–88, 261; goods, 10, 18, 19, 41, 134; coast and inland people, 9, 60, 134, 136; difficulties, 14, 15; along the Kuskokwim, 55; non-Native, 193, 262; poor, 18; posts, 10, 42; route, 7; for tobacco, 118; Yupiit and Ingalik, 127
Traders, 12, 18, 19, 28; Alaska Commercial Company, 10, 15
Tradition, inventiveness of, 287
Traditional tale, 99. *See also* Story
Trans-Alaska Pipeline, 42
Trapping, 40. *See also* Fur trade
Traps: metal leg-hold, 103; wire, 106. *See also* Fish traps; Snares
Travel book, 21, 25. *See also* Jacobsen, Johan Adrian
Traveling magically, 187
Tree, 160; bark, 256, 260; burls, 155; spruce, 160; stumps, 160, 179. *See also* Driftwood; individual species; Wood
Tribal court, 48
Tribes of America and Asia, 9
Tromsø, Norway, 3
Trondheim, Norway, 3
Trout, 39, 107, 173
Tsimshian (people), 7, 8, 19, 27
Tuberculosis, 42, 48; treatment, 269
Tufted puffins, 266
Tundra: moss, 166; villages, 255. *See also* Akulmiut
Tununak, Alaska, 18, 42, 48, 55, 107, 172, 182, 183, 212, 213; trader, 172. *See also* Nelson Island
Tunuqerpalek (warrior), 245
Tuqluun (kinship term), 55. *See also* Ap'ayagaq
Turkestan, 21
Twine, 71, 86
Tyonek, Alaska, 19
Tyrol, Austria and Italy, 29

Uayaran (giant), 271
Ugaassat, Alaska, 217
Ukiivak, Alaska, 186
Uluat. See Knives, women's
Umiak (skin boat), 3. *See also* Skin boat
Umkumiut, Alaska, 18, 48
Umlaff, Mrs., 30
Umlauff, Johann Freidreich Gustav, 29
Unalakleet, Alaska, 15, 154, 281
Unalaska, Alaska, 9
Unalitschok. *See* Hagenbeck River
Underwater homes (*qasgit*), 40; world, 141
Ungalaqliq, Alaska, 194
United States, 8, 28
University of Alaska Anchorage, 49
University of Alaska Fairbanks, 49

"Unter den Alaska-Eskimos: Erlebnisse und Forschungen" (Jacobsen), 31
Up'nerkillermiut, Nelson Island, 125, 131, 154, 206, 208
Upper Yukon River, 41, 266
Uqsumiar. *See* Berlin, Wassilie
Urine, 36, 157; baby boy's, 131; buckets, 133, 136, 172; as cleanser, 40, 181; container, 127–28; washing with, 208, 269
Urluvepak (warrior), 81
Ursa Major, 274
Ursa Minor, 274
Utngunamiut, Alaska, 263

Valparaiso, Chile, 3
Vancouver Island, British Columbia, 7, 27, 35
Vengeance, 245
Victoria, British Columbia, 6, 7, 8, 26, 27
Village, 40, 42–43
Violent crime, 42
Virchow, Prof. Rudolf, 21, 27, 28
Vision, 169; extraordinary, 219; restriction of, 48
Visiting, house-to-house, 274–75
Visor, 205, 235
"VISTA" (Volunteers in Service to America), 42
Visual repatriation, 280–89
Vocabulary, 170; regional variations, 170, 174, 179, 182–83, 201, 254, 257, 280
Volga River, 26
Völkergedanken (Adolf Bastian), 287
Völkerschau (folk show), 4, 8, 9, 26, 27, 31
Völkerschauen (folk shows or ethnic exhibitions), *See also* Ethnic exhibitions
Volksgeist (Johann Gottfried Herder), 287
Voss, Dr., 28

Wage employment, 42
Walton, Mr., 15
Walking stick, 62–64, 97, 162
Walrus: bladder water container, 54, 56–58; carvings, 56, 117, 161, 193, 203, 206; decorations, 205; designs, 207, 238; in human form, 183–85, 189; hunting, 39, 53, 261; ivory, 59, 66, 67, 96, 114, 154, 206, 261; mask, 233, 237; newborn, 143; skin, 55; throat skin, 143; tooth, 154; tooth amulet, 236; tusk, 76, 131, 161, 177
Wansee, Germany 50
Warfare, 245–48, 261, 271; beginning of, 84; bow-and-arrow, 67, 76–81, 85, 99; end of, 245; knife, 159; negative effects of, 80–81; song, 89; strategy, 99, 128–29. *See also* Warriors
War on Poverty, 42
Warriors, 99; songs of, 87–89, 245–48, 261. *See also* Warfare
Wasky, Frank (Uaski) (trader), 141
Watch parts, 201
Water: buckets, 11, 97, 119, 126, 127–28, 172; walrus-bladder container, 56–58

Waterfowl, 79, 109; quill vanes, 86. *See also* individual species
Waterproof: with oil, 270; seams, 167; skin boots, 269–70
Wealth, redistribution of, 41
Weasel, 235; skin parka, 258
Weather, 65; prediction, 259–60, 273–74
Wedell, Horst, 51–52, 54, 75, 83, 87, 161, 279
Wedge, 154–55
Weight, 87
Weisbach, Valentin, 6
Werdau, Germany, 24
Western material, imitation of, 217, 223
Western Museum Association, 286
Wetlands, 39
Whale, 114; bone, 114; bowhead, 41, 76, 125, 220–21; carving of, 203; commercial hunting of, 9; sinew, 76. *See also* individual species
Wheat grass, 57, 105, 146. *See also* Grass
Whetstone, 152, 153; in healing, 154. *See also* Stone
White clay, 61, 63, 205, 274. *See also* Paint
Whitefish, 39, 106–7, 112–14, 170, 173; eggs, 171
White Frontier (Jacobsen), 3, 22, 32
White paint as disguise, 205
White people (*Kass'at*), 79, 118, 177; after arrival of, 266; first, 149
White whale, 71, 220, 231; figures, 233, 263; models, 231. *See also* Beluga whale; Whale
Wild celery (*tarvaq*), 39, 51, 274; gathering, 276
Wild parsnip, 39
Willow: ash, 167; bark, 110–12; root, 63, 106, 113, 115, 158; tree, 166; twine, 102, 113
Winter: solstice, 274; villages, 33, 40, 41. *See also* Seasonal camps
Wirchow, 28. *See* Virchow
Woldt, Adrian, 21, 22, 25, 29, 30
Wolf: carvings, 193, 203; designs, 238; fur, 219; mask, 229; meat, 277; skin, 156; skin band, 217
Wolverine, 266; furs, 210; skin, 65, 144, 156; skin band, 217
Woman, 189; ideal, 169; of the sea, 125
Women: debris of, 202; tools of men and, 143; figures, 221; hunting by, 78, 93, 94, 215; parkas, 264; tools, 63, 169, 177; work, 143, 164. *See also* Knives, women's
Wood, 99, 183, 271; bending of, 160, 205, 250, 266; bowls, 79, 127, 131, 274; carvings, 8; chisels, 152; drilling, 160; figures, 18, 222; fire bath, 176; floats, 113; gear box, 125; hard, 62, 76, 155, 160, 252; kinds of, 160; nails, 201; preferences for, 8; sheath, 68; shuttles, 113; small, thin, 65, 271; split, 65, 160; spoons, 171; spruce binding, 208; straight-grained, 80, 106, 127, 155, 160; stretcher, 68; thin-grained, 75; working with, 127, 151, 266. *See also* Driftwood; Fire bath; Firewood; individual species; Tree
Woodworking tools, 147, 153–54, 159–61; small hammer, 106; splitters, 106, 147, 154–55;

wedge, 154–55
Woolfe, Henry D., 9, 10, 14, 15, 23, 25
Work: significance of, 177; woman's, 164
"World of Polar Animals" (manuscript), 32
World's Columbian Exposition, 30, 35
World War I, 31–33
World War II, 33

Yakutat (people). *See* Tlingit
Yaqui (people), 19
Yoke, carrying, 101
Young girls: amulets for, 188; ornaments worn by, 186
Young people: awareness of history, 286; teaching of, 176
Yukon, Kuskokwim, and Nushagak Rivers, 9, 39, 41
Yukon-Kuskokwim delta, 41; map of, 17
Yukon Kuskokwim Health Corporation, 48
Yukon (Kuigpak) River, Alaska, 8, 9, 11, 14, 15, 16, 20, 32, 40, 41, 43, 47, 48, 53, 65, 186, 209, 248, 267, 276, 277; collections from, 60, 63, 64, 67, 68, 69, 75, 83, 86, 87, 90, 93, 97, 99, 101, 105–8, 113, 124, 127, 128, 131, 132, 136, 138, 141, 143–47, 155, 159, 161, 165, 167, 169, 170, 171, 179, 183, 197, 198, 208, 217, 221, 228–31, 237, 238–39, 249, 251, 253, 254, 256, 258, 260, 266, 271; prospecting party, 10; story, 221. *See also* Lower Yukon; Middle Yukon; Upper Yukon
Yuma (people), 19
Yupiit (n., plural), 134; complex cultural tradition, 40; as impoverished, 42; population, 41; superstitions of, 25; traditional character, 41; traveling among, 16; turn-of-the-century, 39–42
Yup'ik (adj.): attitude toward objects, 33–35; collection of artifacts, 9; culturalism, 286, 287; distinctiveness, 288; guitar, 223; heartland, 33; homeland, 9; identity, 286–88; and Ingalik borderland, 223; language, 288; masks, 18, 21, 51; material culture, 10; patrimony, 35; people today, 281; population, 40, 42; protocols, 47, 280; territory, 40; traditions, 193, 227, 263, 285–86; view of the world, 177, 281. *See also* Central Yup'ik
Yup'ik delegation, 46, 47–50; arrival in Berlin, 49; gift from, 210; gratitude of, 285; group dynamics of, 280–82; outside Museum, 282–84; reflections on collections, 284–87; self-images, 288; work in collections, 280–82, 284

Zeitschrift für Ethnologie (Journal for Ethnology), 29
Zoological Arena and World's Museum, 30
Zoological Garden, Dresden, 4, 27, 28, 31
Zuni (people), 19
Zwickau, Germany, 24

ABOUT THE AUTHORS

ANN FIENUP-RIORDAN (right) is the author of numerous books on the Native peoples of Alaska, including *The Living Tradition of Yup'ik Masks*, *Freeze Frame: Alaska Eskimos in the Movies*, and *Eskimo Essays: Yup'ik Lives and How We See Them*. She has been honored with special awards by the Alaska Federation of Natives, the Alaska Historical Society, and the Alaska Humanities Forum. She lives in Anchorage.

MARIE MEADE (left) is a Yup'ik Eskimo raised in Nunapitchuk, Alaska. In addition to translating *Yup'ik Elders at the Ethnologisches Museum Berlin*, she collaborated with Ann Fienup-Riordan on *Ciuliamta Akluit / Things of Our Ancestors* and *Agayuliyararput / Our Way of Making Prayer*. She has worked as a translator and Yup'ik language expert, and presently teaches classes in Yup'ik language and culture at the University of Alaska, Anchorage.

Photograph by Katherine Fogden. Smithsonian Institution, National Museum of the American Indian.